"The *packaging* of ... *oa...* *s come up*
with something ... **vered editions**
collect papers fro... ...ive of The Stationery Office into verbatim narratives, so, for
instance, in UFOs in the House of Lords *we get a hilarious recreation, directly from*
Hansard, of a nutty debate that took place in 1979 ... This is inspired publishing, not
only archivally valuable but capable of bringing the past back to life without the usual
filter of academic or biographer." **Guardian**

"The Irish Uprising *is a little treasure of a book and anyone with an interest in Irish*
history will really enjoy it. Its structure is extremely unusual as it is compiled from historic
official reports published by the British government from 1914 to 1920 ... For anyone
studying this period of history The Irish Uprising *is a must as the correspondence and*
accounts within it are extremely illuminating and the subtle nuances of meaning can be
teased out of the terms and phrasing to be more revelatory than the actual words
themselves." **Irish Press, Belfast**

"Voyeurs of all ages will enjoy the original text of the Denning report on Profumo. It
is infinitely superior to the film version of the scandal, containing such gems as: 'One
night I was invited to a dinner party at the home of a very, very rich man. After I arrived,
I discovered it was rather an unusual dinner party. All the guests had taken off their
clothes ... The most intriguing person was a man with a black mask over his face. At first
I thought this was a party gimmick. But the truth was that this man is so well known and
holds such a responsible position that he did not want to be associated with anything
improper.'" **Times Higher Education Supplement**

"Very good to read ... insight into important things ... inexorably moving ... If
you want to read about the Titanic, you won't read a better thing ... a revelation."
Open Book, BBC Radio 4

"Congratulations to The Stationery Office for unearthing and reissuing such an
enjoyable vignette" [on Wilfrid Blunt's Egyptian Garden] **The Spectator**

uncovered editions
www.uncovered-editions.co.uk

Series editor: Tim Coates
Managing editor: Michele Staple

Other titles in the series

Other compendium titles in the *uncovered editions* series

Forthcoming titles

uncovered editions

THE
WORLD WAR II
COLLECTION

∞⊶⧉⊷∞

WAR 1939:
DEALING WITH ADOLF HITLER

D DAY TO VE DAY: GENERAL EISENHOWER'S REPORT
1944–45

THE JUDGMENT OF NUREMBERG
1946

London: The Stationery Office

© The Stationery Office 2001

All rights reserved. No part of this publication may be reproduced, stored in
a retrieval system, or transmitted in any form or by any means, electronic,
mechanical, photocopying, recording or otherwise, without the permission
of the publisher.

Applications for reproduction should be made in writing to
The Stationery Office Limited, St Crispins, Duke Street, Norwich NR3 1PD.

ISBN 0 11 702463 5

War 1939: Dealing with Adolf Hitler was first published by HMSO as
Cmd. 6115 (1939) and Cmd. 6106 (1939).
© Crown copyright
Also available separately, ISBN 0117024112, © The Stationery Office 1999

D Day to VE Day: General Eisenhower's Report was first published by HMSO as *Report of the
Supreme Commander to the Combined Chiefs of Staff on the Operations
in Europe of the Allied Expeditionary Force* (1946).
© Crown copyright
Also available separately, ISBN 0117024511, © The Stationery Office 2000

The Judgment of Nuremberg, 1946 was first published by HMSO as Cmd. 6964 (1946).
© Crown copyright
Also available separately, ISBN 0117024066, © The Stationery Office 1999

A CIP catalogue record for this book is available from the British Library.

Cover photograph © Hulton Getty.
Maps on pages 6 and 394 produced by Sandra Lockwood of Artworks Design, Norwich.

Typeset by J&L Composition Ltd, Filey, North Yorkshire.
Printed in the United Kingdom by The Stationery Office, London.
TJ4394 C30 8/01

CONTENTS

About the series

Uncovered editions are historic official papers which have not previously been available in a popular form.
The series has been created directly from the archive of The Stationery Office in London, and the books have been chosen for the quality of their story-telling. Some subjects are familiar, but others are less well known.
Each is a moment in history.

About the series editor, Tim Coates

Tim Coates studied at University College, Oxford and at the University of Stirling. After working in the theatre for a number of years, he took up book-selling and became managing director, firstly of Sherratt and Hughes bookshops, and then of Waterstone's. He is known for his support for foreign literature, particularly from the Czech Republic. The idea for *uncovered editions* came while searching through the bookshelves of his late father-in-law, Air Commodore Patrick Cave OBE. He is married to Bridget Cave, has two sons, and lives in London.

Tim Coates welcomes views and ideas on the *uncovered editions* series. He can be e-mailed at tim.coates@theso.co.uk

WAR 1939:
DEALING WITH
ADOLF HITLER

∞⊂⊃∞

CONTENTS

United Kingdom

Prime Minister	Mr Neville Chamberlain
Secretary of State for Foreign Affairs	Viscount Halifax
Secretary of State for Foreign Affairs in 1914	Sir Edward Grey
Secretary of State for Foreign Affairs in 1935	Sir Samuel Hoare
Leader of His Majesty's Opposition	Mr C. R. Attlee
Polish Ambassador	Count Edward Raczyński
German Ambassador	Herr von Dirksen
German Chargé d'Affaires	Dr Kordt

France

President of the Council	M. Daladier

Poland

Polish Statesman	(The late) Marshal Pilsudski
Polish Statesman and Inspector-General of Polish Army	Marshal Smigly-Rydz
Minister for Foreign Affairs	M. Josef Beck
Vice-Minister for Foreign Affairs	M. Arciszewski
British Ambassador	Sir H. Kennard
British Chargé d'Affaires	Mr Norton

Danzig

League of Nations High Commissioner	M. Burckhardt
Polish Commissioner-General	M. Chodacki
Nazi Gauleiter	Herr Forster
President of Senate	Herr Greiser
State Counsellor dealing with Foreign Relations	Dr Boettcher
British Consul-General	Mr G. Shepherd
Acting British Consul-General (from 10th July)	Mr F. M. Shepherd

Germany

Prime Minister of Prussia	Field-Marshal Göring
Nazi leader and Deputy to the Führer	Herr Hess
Minister for Propaganda	Dr Goebbels
Minister for Foreign Affairs	Herr von Ribbentrop
State Secretary at Ministry for Foreign Affairs	Baron von Weizsäcker
Under-Secretary at Ministry for Foreign Affairs	Dr Keppler
Official Interpreter at Ministry for Foreign Affairs	Dr Schmidt
Former Minister for Foreign Affairs	Freiherr von Neurath

Germany (continued)

British Ambassador	Sir Nevile Henderson
Polish Ambassador	M. Josef Lipski

Soviet Union

Leading Statesman	M. Stalin
Prime Minister and Minister for Foreign Affairs	M. Molotov

Czecho-Slovakia

Former President	Dr Beneš
President (after the Munich Agreement)	Dr Hacha

Italy

Duce	Signor Mussolini
British Ambassador	Sir P. Loraine

Holy See

British Minister	Mr Osborne

Belgium

British Ambassador	Sir R. Clive

Netherlands

British Minister	Sir N. Bland

Lithuania

British Chargé d'Affaires	Mr Preston

The expansion of Germany, 1935–9

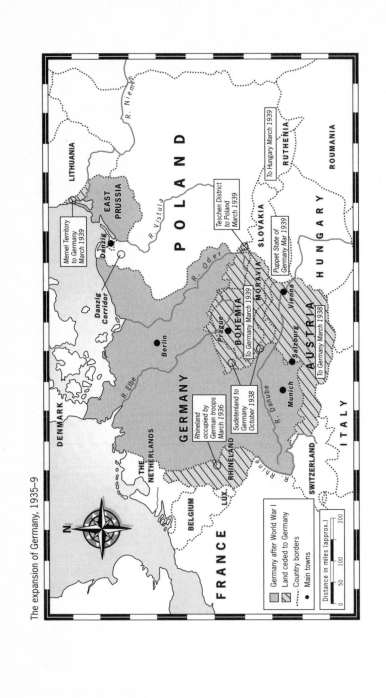

Legend:
- Germany after World War I
- Land ceded to Germany
- Country borders
- Main towns

Distance in miles (approx.)
0   50   100   200

Map labels:
FRANCE
DENMARK
THE NETHERLANDS
BELGIUM
LUX.
SWITZERLAND
ITALY
GERMANY
POLAND
LITHUANIA
EAST PRUSSIA
BOHEMIA
MORAVIA
SLOVAKIA
RUTHENIA
ROUMANIA
HUNGARY
AUSTRIA
RHINELAND

Towns:
Berlin
Prague
Vienna
Salzburg
Munich
Danzig

Rivers:
R. Niemen
R. Vistula
R. Oder
R. Elbe
R. Danube
R. Rhine

Annotations:
Memel Territory to Germany March 1939
Danzig Corridor
Teschen District to Poland March 1939
To Hungary March 1939
Puppet State of Germany Mar 1939
To Germany March 1939
To Germany March 1938
Rhineland occupied by German troops March 1936
Sudetenland to Germany October 1938

The Treaty of Versailles, signed at the end of the First World War, brought an uneasy peace to Germany. A large area of the Rhineland was given over to the Allies, and a new Poland cut off East Prussia from Germany in order to provide the Poles with 'a corridor to the sea'. When Hitler came to power in 1933, his intention was to re-establish Germany geographically as well as politically and militarily. Thus he began to rearm and rebuild her fleet, and in 1936, in contravention of the Versailles Treaty, Germany reoccupied and refortified the Rhineland. This was followed in 1938 by the invasion of Austria, giving Hitler a useful platform from which he could direct operations against Czechoslovakia. His next move was to annex Sudetenland to this Greater Germany.

Britain and France were in too weak a position to respond at the time, and the Munich Agreement, signed in September 1938, was perceived as a capitulation to Hitler. Its most useful purpose for Britain was to give her time to rearm. In the meantime, Hitler continued his drive for expansion, occupying Prague and the rest of Czechoslovakia in March 1939. He then turned his attention to Poland, demanding that Danzig should be incorporated within the German Reich, and that the land across the Polish corridor should be ceded to Germany for communication with East Prussia.

This book describes the policies of both Hitler and the British Government during the months that followed. The first part gives an account of events leading up to the outbreak of war by Sir Nevile Henderson, the British ambassador in Germany. The second part contains documents concerning German-Polish relations up to September 1939.

PART I

⚬∞⚭∞⚬

FINAL REPORT BY SIR NEVILE HENDERSON ON THE CIRCUMSTANCES LEADING TO THE TERMINATION OF HIS MISSION TO BERLIN

20 SEPTEMBER 1939

Presented by the Secretary of State for Foreign Affairs to Parliament by Command of His Majesty

London, 20 September 1939

My Lord,

Events moved with such rapidity during the last fortnight of my mission to Berlin that it proved impossible at the time to give any consecutive account of them. If I have the honour to do so now, while the facts are still fresh in my memory, it is with the hope that such an account may be both of immediate interest to your Lordship and serve a purpose from the point of view of historical accuracy.

Nevertheless, it is not these last-minute manœuvres which have the real importance, except in so far as they confirm the principles and demonstrate the methods and technique of Herr Hitler and of Nazism. A brief description of the background to August 1939 is consequently indispensable, if the events of the last few weeks are to be visualised in their proper perspective.

Herr Hitler and National Socialism are the products of the defeat of a great nation in war and its reaction against the confusion and distress which followed that defeat. National Socialism itself is a revolution and a conception of national philosophy. Contrary to democracy which implies the subordination of the State to the service of its citizens, Nazism prescribes the subordination of its citizens to the service of the State, an all embracing Moloch, and to the individual who rules that State.

So long as National Socialism remained an article for internal consumption, the outside world, according to its individual predilection, might criticise or sympathise or merely watch with anxiety. The government of Germany was the affair of the German people. It was not until the theory of German nationalism was extended beyond Germany's own frontiers that the Nazi philosophy exceeded the limits compatible with peace.

It would be idle to deny the great achievements of the man who restored to the German nation its self-respect and its disciplined orderliness. The tyrannical methods which were employed within Germany itself to obtain this result were detestable, but were Germany's own concern. Many of Herr Hitler's social reforms, in spite of their complete disregard of personal liberty of thought, word or deed, were on highly advanced democratic lines. The "Strength through Joy" movement, the care for the physical fitness of the nation, and, above all, the organisation of the labour camps, an idea which Herr Hitler once told me that he had borrowed from Bulgaria, are typical examples of a benevolent dictatorship. Nor can the appeal of Nazism with its slogans so attractive to a not over-discerning youth be ignored. Much of its legislation in this respect will survive in a newer and better world, in which Germany's amazing power of organisation and the great contributions which she has made in the past to the sciences, music, literature and the higher aims of civilisation and humanity will again play a leading part.

Nor was the unity of Great Germany in itself an ignoble ideal. It had long been the dream of some of the highest-minded of German thinkers, and it must be remembered that even in 1914 Germany was still immature as a political concept. In spite of the potential political danger for its weaker neighbours of a national philosophy which could so easily be distorted and extended beyond its due and legitimate frontiers, the unity of Great Germany was a reality which had to be faced, no less than that other reality, the paramount economic importance of Germany in Eastern, Central and South-Eastern Europe. It was not the incorporation of Austria and the Sudeten Germans in the Reich which so much shocked public opinion in the world as the unscrupulous and hateful methods which Herr Hitler employed to precipitate an incorporation which would probably have peacefully come in due course of its own volition and in accordance with the established principle of self-determination.

Yet even those methods might have been endured in a world which had experienced 1914–1918 and which sought peace as an end in itself, if Herr Hitler had been willing to accord to others the rights which he claimed for Germany. Revolutions are like avalanches, which once set in motion cannot stop till they crash to destruction at the appointed end of their career. History alone will determine whether Herr Hitler could have diverted Nazism into normal channels, whether he was the victim of the movement which he had initiated, or whether it was his own megalomania which drove it beyond the limits which civilisation was prepared to tolerate.

Be that as it may, the true background to the events of August 1939 was the occupation of Prague on the 15th March of this year, the callous destruction thereby of the hard and newly-won liberty of a free and independent people and Herr Hitler's deliberate violation by this act of the Munich Agreement which he had signed not quite six months before. In 1939, as in 1914, the origin of war with Germany has been due to the deliberate tearing up by the latter of a scrap of paper. To the iniquities of a system which employed the barbarism of the middle ages in its persecution of the Jews, which subjected Roman Catholic priests and Protestant pastors alike to the inhumanities of the concentration camp for obedience to their religious faith, and which crushed out, in a fashion unparalleled in history, all individual liberty within the State itself, was added the violation not only of international agreements freely negotiated, but also of that principle of self-determination which Herr Hitler had invoked with such insistence so long as it suited his own purpose to do so. Up to last March the German ship of State had flown the German national flag, and in spite of the "sickening technique" of Nazism it was difficult not to concede to Germany the right both to control her own destiny and to benefit from those principles which were accorded to others. On the 15th March, by the ruthless suppression of the freedom of the Czechs, its captain hoisted the skull and crossbones of the pirate, cynically discarded his own theory of racial purity and appeared under his true colours as an unprincipled menace to European peace and liberty.

Two of the less attractive characteristics of the German are his inability either to see any side of a question except his own, or to understand the meaning of moderation. It would have been understandable to argue that a hostile Bohemia in the centre of Germany was an untenable proposition. But Herr Hitler could see no mean [middle position] between rendering the Czechs innocuous as a potential enemy and destroying their liberty as an independent people. There is some surprising reason to believe that Herr Hitler himself was disagreeably and literally astonished at the reaction in Britain and the world generally, which was provoked by the occupation of Prague and his breach of faith with Mr Chamberlain. But while he may have realised his tactical mistake, it did not deter him from prosecuting his further designs.

As I had reported to your Lordship, at the beginning of the year Germany's immediate objectives, apart from the complete political and economic domination of Czecho-Slovakia and the eventual restoration of German colonies, were Danzig and Memel. Herr Hitler felt that it would not add much to the general execration of his aggression and ill-faith in March if he settled these two problems simultaneously with Prague. The Democracies were, he thought, so averse to war that they would accept any *fait accompli*. They would be less disturbed if everything was done at once. Thereafter, the agitation would, he anticipated, gradually subside until, after consolidating his gains, he was once more in a position to strike again.

With this plan in view the Lithuanian Government was at once brow-beaten into surrendering Memel. The same method was employed at Warsaw, but the Poles were made of sterner stuff. Negotiations had been proceeding ever since Munich for a settlement of the Danzig and the Corridor question. After Prague Herr Hitler decided that they must be abruptly concluded, and Herr von Ribbentrop peremptorily dictated to the Polish Ambassador the terms which Herr Hitler would be pleased to impose on the Polish Government. The reply of the latter was given on the 26th March and constituted a refusal to accept a Dictate, while expressing readiness to continue free and equal discussion. Alarmed at the threatening attitude adopted by the German Government in consequence of this refusal, the Polish Government mobilised part of its forces (the German army was already largely mobilised), and the British guarantee to Poland was given on the 31st March.

The Ides of March [15th March] constituted in fact the parting of the ways and were directly responsible for everything which happened thereafter. Thenceforward no small nation in Europe could feel itself secure from some new adaptation of Nazi racial superiority and jungle law. The Polish guarantee was followed by unilateral guarantees on Britain's part to Greece and Roumania as well as by an attempt on the part of the British and French Governments to induce the USSR to join in a peace front against aggression, ill-faith and oppression. The Nazi Government, for its part and with considerable success in Germany, represented this attempt as a renewal of the alleged pre-war British policy of encirclement. As a war-cry for the German people it was exceedingly effective up to the signature of the Russo-German non-aggression pact on the 23rd August. The rest of Nazi propaganda was on two entirely contradictory lines either of which was destined, according to the development of the situation, to serve Herr Hitler's purpose. The first spread the persistent report that Britain would never go to war for the sake of Danzig. It was calculated to undermine the confidence of the Poles and to shake the faith of the smaller Powers, as well as of the United States of America, in the determination of Britain to resist any further German aggression. The second represented Britain as resolved to make war at the first opportunity on Germany in any case and in order to crush her before she became a too formidable political and economic rival. Both were fallacies but the Germans are a credulous race and, since the first has failed, it is the latter argumentation which forms the basis of Germany's present war propaganda.

Up to the beginning of August, though the clouds were black and the peace front negotiations dragged on interminably, the situation remained serious but not immediately dangerous. Instead, however, of there being any sign of a relaxation of tension at Danzig the position there had gradually become more and more strained. From the end of March till the end of August all personal contact between Warsaw and Berlin was suspended. The remilitarisation of the Free City [of Danzig], alleged by the Germans to be purely defensive, but no less adaptable for offensive purposes, had proceeded apace, and other measures had been taken indicative of a German intention to effect a sudden coup there. The Poles for their part, in view of the great increase in arms smuggling, had been obliged to strengthen their customs inspectors by a number of frontier guards. They had also taken certain economic counter-measures of a nature to prejudice the trade of the Free City.

What was, however, even more ominous were the extensive preparations which were being made by the Germans for the twenty-fifth celebration of the battle of Tannenberg on the 27th August, and a German warship was scheduled to visit Danzig at the same time and ostensibly for the same purpose. Early in July I drew your Lordship's attention to the menace involved by these equivocal preparations, which corresponded so closely to Hitler's usual technique of preparing for all eventualities, under cover of a plausible excuse.

The first mutterings of the storm were heard on the 4th August. At four posts on the Danzig–East Prussian frontier, the Polish Customs Inspectors were informed that they would not be permitted henceforward to carry out their duties. Alarmed at the gradual sapping of Polish rights and interests in the Free City, the Polish Commissioner General there was at once instructed to deliver a note to the Danzig Senate, warning the latter that the Polish Government would react in the strongest manner if the work of the inspectors was interfered with. The Senate subsequently denied that it had issued any instructions to the effect alleged but the German Government replied to what it described as the Polish ultimatum by a verbal note, which was handed by the State Secretary to the Polish Chargé d'Affaires at Berlin on the 9th August. The Polish Government was therein warned that any further demand addressed to the Free City in the nature of an ultimatum or containing threats of reprisals, would at once lead to an aggravation of Polish-German relations, the responsibility for which would fall on the Polish Government. The latter retorted on the following day by a similar verbal note, denying the judicial right of Germany to intervene in the affairs between Poland and the Free City, and warning in its turn the German Government that "any future intervention by the latter to the detriment of Polish rights and interests at Danzig would be considered as an act of aggression."

I have little doubt but that the latter phrase served more than anything else to produce that final brainstorm in Herr Hitler's mind on which the peace of the world depended, and upon which it always must have depended so long as the fate not only of Germany but also of Europe, rested in the hands of a single irresponsible individual.

The tragedy of any dictator is that as he goes on, his entourage steadily and inexorably deteriorates. For lack of freedom of utterance he loses the services of the best men. All opposition becomes intolerable to him. All those, therefore, who are bold enough to express opinions contrary to his views are shed one by one, and he is in the end surrounded by mere yes-men, whose flattery and counsels are alone endurable to him. In my report on the events of 1938 I drew your Lordship's special attention to the far reaching and unfortunate results of the Blomberg marriage.★ I am more than ever convinced of the major disaster which that—in itself—minor incident involved, owing to the consequent elimination from Herr Hitler's entourage of the more moderate and independent of his advisers, such as Field Marshal von Blomberg himself, Baron von Neurath, Generals Fritsch, Beck, etc. After February of last year Herr Hitler became more and more shut off from external influences and a law unto himself.

People are apt, in my opinion, to exaggerate the malign influence of Herr von Ribbentrop, Dr Goebbels, Herr Himmler and the rest. It was probably consistently sinister, not because of its suggestiveness (since Herr Hitler alone decided policy), nor because it merely applauded and encouraged, but because, if Herr Hitler appeared to hesitate, the extremists of the party at once proceeded to fabricate situations calculated to drive Herr Hitler into courses which even he at times shrank from risking. The simplest method of doing this was through the medium of a controlled press. Thus what happened in September last year, was repeated in March this year, and again in August. Dr Goebbels' propaganda machine was the ready tool of these extremists, who were afraid lest Herr Hitler should move too slowly in the prosecution of his own ultimate designs.

The 1938 stories of Czech atrocities against its German minority, were rehashed up almost verbatim in regard to the Poles. Some foundation there must necessarily have been for a proportion of these allegations in view of the state of excitable tension which existed between the two peoples. Excess of zeal on the part of individuals and minor officials there undoubtedly was—but the tales of ill-treatment, expropriation and murder were multiplied a hundredfold. How far Herr Hitler himself believed in the truth of these tales must be a matter for conjecture. Germans are prone in any case to convince themselves very readily of anything which they wish to believe. Certainly he behaved as if he did believe, and, even if one may give him the benefit of the doubt, these reports served to inflame his resentment to the pitch which he or his extremists desired.

Until the 8th August the campaign against the Poles had been relegated to the more discreet pages of the German press. Up to that date, public enemy No. 1 had been Great Britain and the alleged policy of encirclement. From that date, however, the stories of Polish atrocities began to take the leading place, and by the 17th August the campaign was in full swing.

Herr Hitler is a master of turning events to suit his own purpose, and the so-called ultimatum to the Danzig Senate of the 4th August and the subsequent foreign press comments on a Danzig "climb down" gave him the

---

★ The marriage of Hitler's field marshal to a convicted prostitute in January 1938 caused a public scandal, and led to Blomberg's resignation.

opportunity which he was seeking. The Polish note of the 4th August provided an excuse for the German *note verbale* of the 9th August, which provoked in its turn the Polish reply of the 10th August. In the midst of these exchanges M. Burckhardt, High Commissioner of the League of Nations for Danzig, flew to Berchtesgaden [Hitler's mountain retreat, near Salzburg] in a last effort to place the position at Danzig on a more satisfactory footing. He saw Herr Hitler on the 11th August, while Count Ciano and Herr von Ribbentrop were meeting at Salzburg.

Intransigent as he appears to have been at his interview with M. Burckhardt, there is little doubt in my mind that Herr Hitler would have been far more so had he at the time been in possession of the text of the final paragraph of the Polish reply of 10th August, which had only been communicated to the Ministry for Foreign Affairs at Berlin on that day. He was aware of it, however, when Count Ciano visited him at Berchtesgaden immediately after M. Burckhardt's departure, and it undoubtedly rendered unavailing the Italian Foreign Minister's laudable intention of pouring oil on the troubled waters. Once again, as in 1938, the inexorable fatality of the Greek tragedy was in evidence, and the coincidence of the Polish note of the 10th August with the Ciano visit was a striking example of it. Count Ciano returned to Italy and a day or so later the Italian Ambassador at Berlin was hurriedly summoned to Rome.

Herr Hitler's carefully calculated patience was, in fact, exhausted, and on the 18th August I telegraphed to your Lordship that I had come to the definite conclusion that, if peace was to be preserved, the present situation could not be allowed to continue and that the only alternative to war must be some immediate and mediatory action. In this connection I repeated a suggestion which I had made some time previously, namely, that a personal letter should be addressed by the Prime Minister to Herr Hitler and be delivered by some emissary from London. Two days later I again telegraphed to the same effect, and stated my conviction that Herr Hitler had now finally decided upon some form of immediate action which would force the issue. I drew attention at the same time to the increased German military strength which had been assembled in East Prussia under cover of the Tannenberg anniversary and expressed my apprehension lest that celebration might prove the starting point for the action which Herr Hitler contemplated. I have little doubt but that such was Herr Hitler's original and premeditated intention.

On the 21st August information reached me that the long expected but carefully concealed German military concentrations were already in progress, and that instructions had been given to complete them by the 24th August. A report which reached me at that time actually mentioned the 25th August as the date fixed for the German advance into Poland.

I shall return to this point later, but I must here refer to the bombshell which was exploded late in the evening of the 21st August by the announcement that negotiations had been concluded for the signature of a

Russo-German non-aggression pact and that Herr von Ribbentrop would fly to Moscow on the 23rd to sign it.

The secret, which on the German side had been known to not more than a few persons, had been well kept. It had been realised that German counter-negotiations had been proceeding throughout the summer, but it was hoped that they had been abandoned after the actual arrival at Moscow of the French and British military missions. Comment on the subject is, however, outside the scope of this report, except in so far as it concerns the effect of this announcement on the German public. The first impression in Berlin was one of immense relief, partly at the removal of the dreaded Russian air menace, but more particularly because, in the minds of a public which had been led to believe by Goebbels propaganda that the British negotiations with the USSR were really encirclement with a view to a preventive war, the conclusion of a Russo-German non-aggression pact meant that peace was assured, since Britain would not, it was told, fight for Danzig or Poland without Russian aid. Once more the faith of the German people in the ability of Herr Hitler to obtain his objective without war was reaffirmed. Its satisfaction was, however, short-lived and the deception considerable when it was realised that Britain's word to Poland did not depend on Russian support. Those who had fought the war of Nazism against communism were furthermore puzzled by this complete *volte-face*. The Nazi theory of racial purity had been discarded in March and in August a second of its basic principles was thus equally relegated to the scrap-heap. To most Germans the old hereditary enemy is Russia, nor was their confidence in the sincerity of her good intentions towards Germany greatly fortified by this exhibition of Russian ill-faith towards the Western Democracies. Nevertheless, as a diplomatic *coup*, the Russo-German pact was a strikingly successful and surprising one. It is devoutly to be hoped that it may prove as Pyrrhic as are most diplomatic victories.

At the moment when Herr von Ribbentrop was preparing to fly to Moscow, I received shortly before 9 PM on the 22nd August your Lordship's instructions to convey without delay a personal letter from the Prime Minister to Herr Hitler. I at once got into communication with the Ministry for Foreign Affairs, and in the course of the night an interview was arranged for the following day. I left Berlin at 9.30 on the morning of the 23rd August accompanied by the State Secretary and Herr Hewel, in an aeroplane provided for me by the Ministry for Foreign Affairs.

I reached Salzburg about midday and I had my first audience with Herr Hitler at Berchtesgaden at 1 PM on the 23rd August in the presence of Baron von Weizsäcker and Herr Hewel. I need not say more here than that the three main points of the Prime Minister's letter were (1) insistence on the determination of His Majesty's Government to fulfil their obligations to Poland, (2) their readiness, if a peace atmosphere could be created, to discuss all the problems at issue between our two countries, and (3) their anxiety, during a period of truce, to see immediate direct discussion initiated between Germany and Poland in regard to the reciprocal treatment of minorities.

In Herr Hitler's reply of the 23rd August he declared that Great Britain's determination to support Poland could not modify his policy, as expressed in the German verbal note to the Polish Government of the 9th August; that he was prepared to accept even a long war rather than sacrifice German national interests and honour; and that, if Great Britain persisted in her own measures of mobilisation, he would at once order the mobilisation of the whole of the German forces.

At my first interview with him on that day, Herr Hitler was in a mood of extreme excitability. His language as regards the Poles and British responsibility for the Polish attitude was violent, recriminatory and exaggerated. He referred, for instance, to 100,000 German refugees from Poland, a figure which was at least five times greater than the reality. Again I cannot say whether he was persuaded or persuaded himself of the reality of these figures. At my second interview, when he handed me his reply, he had recovered his calm but was not less uncompromising. No longer, he told me, did he trust Mr Chamberlain. He preferred war, he said, when he was 50 to when he was 55 or 60. He had himself always sought and believed in the possibility of friendship with England. He now realised, he said, that those who had argued the contrary had been right and nothing short of a complete change in British policy towards Germany could ever convince him of any sincere British desire for good relations. My last remark to him was that I could only deduce from his language that my mission to Germany had failed and that I bitterly regretted it.

I flew back from Berchtesgaden to Berlin the same evening. I had in fact little hope that either the Prime Minister's letter or my own language to Herr Hitler, however direct and straightforward, would give him pause. The Russian pact had, I felt, created in his opinion a situation which was favourable to his designs and I believed his mind to be definitely made up. Though he spoke of his artistic tastes and of his longing to satisfy them, I derived the impression that the corporal of the last war was even more anxious to prove what he could do as a conquering Generalissimo in the next.

Nevertheless the visit to Berchtesgaden may after all have postponed the disaster for a week. Herr von Ribbentrop flew back to Germany with the signed Russo-German Agreement and Herr Hitler returned to Berlin the night of the 24th August. I have some reason to believe—though I cannot confirm it—that the order for the German Army to advance into Poland was actually issued for the night of the 25th–26th August. It is difficult otherwise to find justification for the various orders and arrangements which came into force on the 26th and 27th August. In the afternoon of the 25th August itself all telephone communication between Berlin and London and Paris was unexpectedly cut off for several hours. The celebrations at Tannenberg were cancelled on the 26th and the Party Rally at Nuremberg on the 27th August; all Naval, Military and Air Attachés at Berlin were refused permission to leave the city without prior authority being obtained from the Ministry of War. All German airports were closed from that date, and the whole of Germany became a prohibited zone for all aircraft except the regular civil lines. All internal German air services were also suspended. Moreover as from the 27th a system for the rationing of food-stuffs and other commodities throughout Germany came into force. That this latter and—for the public—depressing measure should have been adopted prior to the outbreak of war can scarcely be explained, except on the assumption that war should actually have broken out on the 26th August.

The fact may well be, as I imagine it was, that Herr Hitler had had in consequence of the Prime Minister's letter one last hesitation and countermanded the orders to his Army, whereas the other arrangements were allowed to proceed unchecked. But it was not the horrors of war which deterred him. He had unlimited confidence in the magnificent army and air force which he had re-created and he was certainly not averse to putting them to the test so far as Poland was concerned. In two months, he told me, the war in the East would be ended and he would then, he said, hurl 160 divisions against the Western Front if England was so unwise as to oppose his plans. His hesitation was due rather to one final effort to detach Britain from Poland. Be that as it may, at about 12.45 on the 25th August, I received a message to the effect that Herr Hitler wished to receive me at the Chancellery at 1.30 PM.

Briefly, Herr Hitler's proposals dealt with two groups of questions: (a) the immediate necessity of a settlement of the dispute between Germany and Poland, and (b) an eventual offer of friendship or alliance between Germany and Great Britain. My interview with Herr Hitler, at which Herr von Ribbentrop and Dr Schmidt were also present, lasted on this occasion over an hour. The Chancellor spoke with calm and apparent sincerity. He described his proposals as a last effort, for conscience sake, to secure good relations with Great Britain, and he suggested that I should fly to London myself with them. I told his Excellency that, while I was fully prepared to consider this course, I felt it my duty to tell him quite clearly that my country could not possibly go back on its word to Poland, and that, however anxious we were for a better understanding with Germany, we could never reach one except on the basis of a negotiated settlement with Poland.

Whatever may have been the underlying motive of this final gesture on the part of the Chancellor, it was one which could not be ignored, and, with your Lordship's consent, I flew to London early the following morning (26th August), on a German plane which was courteously put at my disposal. Two days were spent by His Majesty's Government in giving the fullest and most careful consideration to Herr Hitler's message, and on the afternoon of the 28th August I flew back to Berlin with their reply. Therein, while the obligations of His Majesty's Government to Poland were reaffirmed, it was stated that the Polish Government were ready to enter into negotiations with the German Government for a reasonable solution of the matter in dispute on the basis of the safeguarding of Poland's essential interests, and of an international guarantee for the settlement eventually arrived at. His Majesty's Government accordingly proposed that the next step should be the initiation of direct discussions between the Polish and German Governments on that basis and the adoption of immediate steps to relieve the tension in the matter of the treatment of minorities. Furthermore, His Majesty's Government undertook to use all their influence with a view to contributing towards a solution which might be satisfactory to both parties and which would, they hoped, prepare the way for the negotiation of that wider and more complete understanding between Great Britain and Germany which both countries desired. Finally, after a reference to a limitation of armaments, His Majesty's Government pointed out that, whereas a just settlement of the Polish question might open the way to world peace, failure to do so would finally ruin the hopes of a better understanding between our countries and might well plunge the whole world into war.

Before continuing the record of events after my return to Berlin on the evening of the 28th August, it is necessary to give a brief account of what had happened after my meeting with the Chancellor at 1.30 on the 25th August. At 5 PM on that day Herr Hitler had received the French Ambassador and given him a letter for communication to M. Daladier. Its general tenor was a suggestion to France, with whom Germany was stated to have no quarrel, to abstain from further support of Poland. It received a dignified answer from the French Government, which was published on the 27th August. Appeals for peace were made at this time to both the German and Polish Governments as well as to other Powers by the Pope and the President of the United States of America. Though they received a favourable response from the Polish Government, they received scant consideration from Germany.

On the evening of the 25th August the Anglo-Polish Pact had been signed in London. Though it had been under negotiation for several months, its signature gave great offence to Herr Hitler, who was at first inclined to regard it as the reply of His Majesty's Government to his message to them. His immediate retort was the announcement on the morning of the 26th August that Herr Forster had been appointed Reichsoberhaupt, or Head of the State of Danzig. At the same time the German concentrations against Poland began to reach their final stage.

Thereafter there was a lull for two days pending my return to Germany with the reply of His Majesty's Government. I had left London at 5 PM on the 28th August, and at 10.30 PM I was received by Herr Hitler at the Chancellery and handed to him that reply, together with a German translation. I sent to your Lordship a full record of my conversation with the Chancellor the same night.

On this occasion Herr Hitler was again friendly and reasonable and appeared to be not dissatisfied with the answer which I had brought to him. He observed, however, that he must study it carefully and would give me a written reply the next day.

I would mention incidentally that both that evening and the next, when I visited Herr Hitler again and was handed his reply, nothing was left undone to enhance the solemnity of the occasion. A considerable but quite expressionless crowd was waiting outside the Chancellery and a guard of honour awaited me in the courtyard of the main entrance. In view of what has been reported to the contrary, I desire to bear witness here to the fact that throughout the whole of those anxious weeks neither I nor my staff received anything but the utmost courtesy and civility from all Germans, except on one occasion to which I shall refer later.

Such information as reached me during the course of the day of the 29th August tended to represent the atmosphere as not unfavourable and to foreshadow Herr Hitler's readiness to open direct negotiations with the Poles. I was therefore somewhat disappointed on being summoned to the Chancellery at 7.15 that evening to find the Chancellor in a far less reasonable mood than on the previous evening. The German midday press had reported the alleged murder of six German nationals in Poland, and this story, which was probably fabricated by the extremists in fear lest he was weakening, together with the news of the Polish general mobilisation, had probably upset him. I sensed in any case a distinctly more uncompromising attitude on Herr Hitler's part when he handed me his answer. I read it through carefully, and, though it reiterated his demand for the whole Corridor as well as Danzig, I made no comment till I reached the phrase at the end of it, in which, after a grudging acquiescence in direct discussions with the Poles solely by way of proof of Germany's sincerity in her desire for lasting friendship with Great Britain, it was stated that "the German Government counted upon the arrival in Berlin of a Polish Emissary with full powers on the following day, Wednesday, the 30th August." I pointed out to his Excellency that this phrase sounded very much like an ultimatum ("hatte den Klang eines Ultimatums"). This was strenuously and heatedly denied by Herr Hitler himself, supported by Herr von Ribbentrop. According to the former this sentence merely emphasised the urgency of the moment, not only on account of the risk of incidents when two mobilised armies were standing opposite one another, but also when Germans were being massacred in Poland. In this latter connection his Excellency asserted that "I did not care how many Germans were being slaughtered in Poland." This gratuitous impugnment of the humanity of His Majesty's Government and of myself provoked a heated retort on my part and the remainder of the interview was of a somewhat stormy character.

It was closed, however, by a brief and in my opinion quite honest harangue on Herr Hitler's part in regard to the genuineness of his constant endeavour to win Britain's friendship, of his respect for the British Empire, and of his liking for Englishmen generally.

I should like to state here, parenthetically but emphatically, that Herr Hitler's constant repetition of his desire for good relations with Great Britain was undoubtedly a sincere conviction. He will prove in the future a fascinating study for the historian and the biographer with psychological leanings. Widely different explanations will be propounded, and it would be out of place and time to comment at any length in this despatch on this aspect of Herr Hitler's mentality and character. But he combined, as I fancy many Germans do, admiration for the British race with envy of their achievements and hatred of their opposition to Germany's excessive aspirations. It is no exaggeration to say that he assiduously courted Great Britain, both as representing the aristocracy and most successful of the Nordic races, and as constituting the only seriously dangerous obstacle to his own far-reaching plan of German domination in Europe. This is evident in *Mein Kampf*, and, in spite of what he regarded as the constant rebuffs which he received from the British side, he persisted in his endeavours up to the last moment. Geniuses are strange creatures, and Herr Hitler, among other paradoxes, is a mixture of long-headed calculation and violent and arrogant impulse provoked by resentment. The former drove him to seek Britain's friendship and the latter finally into war with her. Moreover, he believes his resentment to be entirely justified. He failed to realise why his military–cum-police tyranny should be repugnant to British ideals of individual and national freedom and liberty, or why he should not be allowed a free hand in Central and Eastern Europe to subjugate smaller and, as he regards them, inferior peoples to superior German rule and culture. He believed he could buy British acquiescence in his own far-reaching schemes by offers of alliance with and guarantees for the British Empire. Such acquiescence was indispensable to the success of his ambitions and he worked unceasingly to secure it. His great mistake was his complete failure to understand the inherent British sense of morality, humanity and freedom.

It must be mentioned here that the concluding passage of the Chancellor's reply to His Majesty's Government had contained a statement to the effect that the German Government would immediately draw up proposals for a solution of the Polish question which it would, if possible, place at the disposal of the British Government before the arrival of the Polish negotiator.

I had at once telegraphed to your Lordship the text of the German note, and in the early hours of the morning of the 30th August (4 AM) I had already conveyed to the Ministry for Foreign Affairs your interim reply, to the effect that it would be carefully considered, but observing that it would be unreasonable to expect that His Majesty's Government could produce a Polish representative at Berlin within twenty-four hours, and that the German Government must not count on this.

Later in the course of the day, I received three messages for communication to the German Government. The first was a personal one from the Prime Minister to the Chancellor notifying the latter of the representations made to Warsaw in regard to the avoidance of frontier incidents, and begging the German Government to take similar precautions. (I transmitted this in the afternoon to its destination in a personal letter to the Minister for Foreign Affairs.) The second similarly notified the German Government of our counsels of restraint to Poland and asked for reciprocation on

Germany's part. The third pointed out that the demand that a Polish Representative with full powers must come to Berlin to receive the German proposals was unreasonable and suggested that the German Government should follow the normal procedure of inviting the Polish Ambassador to call and of handing him the German proposals for transmission to Warsaw with a view to arrangements being made for the conduct of negotiations. This last communication also reminded the German Government that it had promised to communicate its detailed proposals to His Majesty's Government, who undertook, if they offered a reasonable basis, to do their best in Warsaw to facilitate negotiations. The good intentions of His Majesty's Government were, in fact, patently clear and had Herr Hitler honestly desired or preferred a pacific settlement all the arrangements to that end seemed to be in full swing.

I had arranged to see the Minister for Foreign Affairs at 11.30 PM to make these communications to him. Shortly before the appointed time I received in code the considered reply of His Majesty's Government to the German Note of the 29th August. I was accordingly obliged to ask that my meeting with Herr von Ribbentrop should be postponed for half an hour, in order to give me the time to have this last message deciphered.

In the final passages of that communication His Majesty's Government, while fully recognising the need for speed in the initiation of discussions, urged that during the negotiations no aggressive military operations should take place on either side. They further expressed their confidence that they could secure such an undertaking from the Polish Government, if the German Government would give similar assurances. They also suggested a temporary *modus vivendi* at Danzig, such as would obviate the risk of incidents which might render German-Polish relations still more difficult.

I saw Herr von Ribbentrop at exactly midnight, before which hour the German Government had ostensibly counted on the arrival of a Polish emissary at Berlin. I say "ostensibly" since it seems hardly possible that it cannot have occurred to either Herr Hitler or his Minister for Foreign Affairs that it was utterly unreasonable to expect a Polish plenipotentiary [special envoy with full powers] to present himself at Berlin without even knowing in advance the basis of the proposals about which he was expected to negotiate. It is conceivable that the Army Leaders had been representing to their Führer that even 24 hours' delay involved the risk of bad weather holding up the rapidity of the German advance into Poland, but, even so, it is difficult not to draw the conclusion that the proposals in themselves were but dust to be thrown in the eyes of the world with a view to its deception and were never intended to be taken seriously by the German Government itself.

Be that as it may, it is probable that Herr Hitler's mood in the hour when he had to decide between peace or war was not an amiable one. It was reflected in Herr von Ribbentrop, whose reception of me that evening was, from the outset, one of intense hostility, which increased in violence as I made each communication in turn. He kept leaping from his chair in a state

of great excitement, and asking if I had anything more to say. I kept replying that I had, and, if my own attitude was no less unfriendly than his own,
I cannot but say in all sincerity that I had every justification for it. When I
told him that I would not fail to report his remarks to my Government, he
calmed down a little and said that they were his own, and that it was for
Herr Hitler to decide. As for inviting the Polish Ambassador to come and see
him, such a course would, he indignantly said, be utterly unthinkable and
intolerable.

After I had finished making my various communications to him, he produced a lengthy document which he read out to me in German, or rather
gabbled through to me as fast as he could, in a tone of the utmost annoy-
ance. Of the sixteen articles in it I was able to gather the gist of six or seven,
but it would have been quite impossible to guarantee even the exact accuracy of these without a careful study of the text itself. When he had finished,
I accordingly asked him to let me see it. Herr von Ribbentrop refused categorically, threw the document with a contemptuous gesture on the table
and said that it was now out of date ("überholt"), since no Polish Emissary
had arrived at Berlin by midnight.

I observed that in that case the sentence in the German note of the 29th
August to which I had drawn his and his Führer's attention on the preceding
evening had, in fact, constituted an ultimatum in spite of their categorical
denials. Herr von Ribbentrop's answer to that was that the idea of an
ultimatum was a figment of my own imagination and creation.

I do not desire to stress the unpleasant nature of this interview. The hour
was a critical one and Herr von Ribbentrop's excitability at such a moment
was understandable. It seemed to me, however, that he was wilfully throwing away the last chance of a peaceful solution, and it was difficult to remain
indifferent when faced with such a calamity. I would merely add that, contrary to what was subsequently published in the German press, I did not
discuss a single detail of the German proposals with Herr von Ribbentrop,
who flatly declined to do so. While it is true that they were read to me, it
was in such a manner as to make them practically unintelligible.

I returned to His Majesty's Embassy that night with the feeling that the
last hope for peace had vanished. I nevertheless saw the Polish Ambassador
at 2 AM, gave him a brief and studiously moderate account of my conversation with Herr von Ribbentrop, mentioned the cession of Danzig and the
plebiscite in the Corridor as the two main points in the German proposals,
stated that so far as I could gather they were not on the whole too unreasonable, and suggested to him that he might recommend to his Government
that they should propose at once a meeting between Field-Marshals Smigly-
Rydz and Göring. I felt obliged to add that I could not conceive of the
success of any negotiations if they were conducted with Herr von
Ribbentrop.

Though M. Lipski undertook to make this suggestion to his
Government, it would by then probably have been in any case too late. There

was, in fact, for Herr Hitler only one conceivable alternative to brute force, and that was that a Polish plenipotentiary should humbly come to him, after the manner of Dr Schuschnigg or President Hacha, and sign on the dotted line to the greater glory of Adolf Hitler. And even that must happen at once. The Army was asking "Yes" or "No", since the success of its plans depended largely on the rapid occupation of Poland and the conclusion as soon as possible of the war on the Eastern front. Bad weather might otherwise intervene at any time and was likely to prove one of Poland's best defences against the highly mechanised German army. Moreover, a week had already been lost by Herr Hitler's hesitation on the 25th August.

I have no doubt that such and other considerations were present in Herr Hitler's mind on the night of the 30th August. I was consequently not surprised when I received in the early hours of the morning of the 31st reliable information that the actual decision had been taken to order the advance of the German Army by midday or 1 PM if no Polish plenipotentiary had arrived before then. I believe this information to have been accurate, and I attribute the further brief respite which ensued to the twelfth-hour efforts of the Italian Government to restrain Herr Hitler from war.

I had in the meantime obtained from another source more definite, if unauthorised, details of the German proposals, and these I at once communicated through the Counsellor of His Majesty's Embassy to the Polish Ambassador, who spent that morning on the telephone to Warsaw. About the middle of the day I had transmitted to the Ministry for Foreign Affairs a further message from His Majesty's Government to the German Government notifying them that the Polish Government were taking steps to establish contact with them through the Polish Ambassador at Berlin, and asking them to agree to an immediate provisional *modus vivendi* at Danzig, for which purpose M. Burckhardt was suggested as intermediary. To this communication I never received any reply. There was, however, a further delay of some 12 hours. The Polish Government had authorised their Ambassador to establish contact with Herr von Ribbentrop, and Herr Hitler waited to see what message M. Lipski would bring. The question, in fact, was whether his qualifications would be those of a plenipotentiary empowered by the Polish Government to conduct and conclude negotiations or not. On no other terms was Hitler prepared to postpone action. His army was ready and Poland must be taught a lesson. She must crawl or get her whipping.

During the day there had been much activity on the part of Field-Marshal Göring. I think there can be no doubt that Field-Marshal Göring himself would have preferred a peaceful solution, but in matters such as these it was Herr Hitler's decision which alone counted; and whatever Field-Marshal Göring himself might feel, he was merely the loyal and submissive servant of his master. Moreover, he had come down definitely on the side of peace a year before and it may have been difficult for him to adopt this course a second time. He invited me, however, to come and see him that afternoon, and I did so at 5 PM in the company of Sir G. Ogilvie-Forbes.

Inasmuch as I had heard that the text of the proposals which Herr von Ribbentrop had refused to give me was to be announced that evening, my first remark was to point out to the Field-Marshal that this procedure would probably and finally wreck the last prospect of peace and to beg him to do his utmost to prevent their publication. Field-Marshal Göring's reply was that he could not intervene, and that the German Government felt obliged to broadcast their proposals to the world in order to prove their "good faith".

Instead he talked for the best part of two hours of the iniquities of the Poles and about Herr Hitler's and his own desire for friendship with England, and of the benefit to the world in general and the advantage to England in particular of such a friendship. It was a conversation which led nowhere and I could not help feeling that his remarks, which from his point of view were perfectly genuine but which I had heard often before, were chiefly intended for the edification of his listeners. I augured the worst from the fact that he was in a position at such a moment to give me so much of his time. He had a few days before been made president of the new German Defence Council for the Reich (or War Cabinet) and he could scarcely have afforded at such a moment to spare time in conversation if it did not mean that everything down to the last detail was now ready for action.

Incidentally the composition of that council was evidence of Herr Hitler's acumen. He had selected for it all the most respectable of the Nazi leaders, such as Herr Frick, Dr Lammers, Dr Funk, who might be counted upon, with Field-Marshal Göring himself the most popular of them all with the general public, to inspire the confidence of the German people. The worst extremists and the most unpopular with the people were omitted from it. To them was to be confided the less enviable task of dealing with the neutrals, of organising the Interior and of ruthlessly repressing any internal discontent. My general impression of this last talk with Field-Marshal Göring was, in fact, that it constituted a final but forlorn effort on his part to detach Britain from the Poles. Nevertheless the Field-Marshal seemed sincere when, having been called to the telephone, he returned to tell us that M. Lipski was on his way to see Herr von Ribbentrop. He seemed to hope that, provided contact was only established, war might after all prove unnecessary. The meeting between the Polish Ambassador proved, however, quite futile. M. Lipski stated that he was acting solely in his capacity as an Ambassador without plenary powers to discuss or to negotiate, and handed to the Minister for Foreign Affairs a brief communication to the effect that the Polish Government were weighing favourably the proposal of His Majesty's Government for direct discussion and that a formal answer in this matter would be communicated to the German Government in the immediate future. He did not ask for the German proposals and Herr von Ribbentrop did not offer to give them to him. Their meeting lasted but a few minutes.

Early in the morning I had rung up the State Secretary and, after pointing out that the German Government had promised to communicate these proposals to His Majesty's Government, and how helpless I was without the authorised text of them, had asked him to suggest to Herr von Ribbentrop once more that they should be communicated to me. I heard no more from Baron von Weizsäcker until late in the evening, when I received a message asking me to call upon him at 9.15 PM. Similar messages had been sent to the French Ambassador and to the United States Chargé d'Affaires, giving them appointments for 9.30 and 9.45 respectively. I accordingly called on Baron von Weizsäcker at the hour named and received from him the text of the proposals, together with an explanatory statement. As both these documents had already been broadcast at 9 PM, I asked the Secretary of State what was the point now of making these communications to me. Baron von Weizsäcker observed that he was merely carrying out his instructions and that he could make no further statement to me. I could only infer from this reply that Herr Hitler had taken his final decision. I accordingly drafted that night a telegram to your Lordship to the effect that it would be quite useless for me to make any further suggestions since they would now only be outstripped by events and that the only course remaining to us was to show our inflexible determination to resist force by force.

In point of fact the advance into Poland had been ordered that night, and in the early hours of the 1st September without any declaration of war the German army crossed the frontier and the German Air Force proceeded to bomb the Polish aerodromes and lines of communications.

In accordance with Herr Hitler's usual technique everything was done by the German authorities to prove to the German public that it was the Poles who had been the aggressors instead of the aggressed. Cynical notices were communicated at 6 AM to His Majesty's Embassy notifying me that the Bay of Danzig was closed both to navigation and to flying in view of the possibility of military operations "against hostile attacks by Polish naval forces or by Polish aircraft." Field-Marshal Göring also sent me a message to say that the Poles had begun the war by blowing up the bridge across the Vistula at Dirchau, while Herr Hitler himself issued a proclamation to the German army, declaring that the Polish State had refused the settlement which he offered and had appealed to arms, that the Germans in Poland were being persecuted by a bloody terror, and that the Poles were no longer willing to respect the frontier of the German Reich. Every German newspaper repeated the lie that it was the Poles who had begun the fighting. Finally at 10.30 AM Herr Hitler met the Reichstag which had been summoned for that hour, and similarly announced to the assembled Delegates that he had been "forced to take up arms in defence of the Reich." The die had in fact been cast and never can there have been or ever be a case of more deliberate and carefully planned aggression.

Late that evening I was instructed by your Lordship to notify the German Government that the latter by their action had created conditions which called for the implementation by the Governments of the United Kingdom and France of their undertaking to come to Poland's assistance, and that, unless His Majesty's Government received satisfactory assurances that the German Government had suspended all aggressive action and would be prepared to withdraw its forces from Polish territory, His Majesty's Government would, without hesitation, fulfil their obligations to Poland. I was instructed at the same time to request an immediate reply, and was authorised, if asked, to explain that this communication was in the nature of a warning, and was not to be considered as an ultimatum.

I handed this communication in writing to the Minister for Foreign Affairs at 9.30 PM that evening. Herr von Ribbentrop received it without other comment than that the sole blame rested on the Poles, that it was they who had first mobilised and who had first invaded Germany with troops of the regular army. He made no enquiry as to the nature of the communication which he merely said that he must submit to the Führer. I said that I realised that this would be necessary, and that I would be available at whatever hour he might be in a position to give me the Reichschancellor's reply. The French Ambassador, who had been instructed to make a similar communication, did so immediately after me and received a reply on the same lines.

Earlier in the afternoon of that day, in accordance with your Lordship's instructions, I had officially requested the United States Chargé d'Affaires to be good enough to take charge of British interests in the event of war. All cyphers and confidential documents were burnt, and the whole of the Staff left their normal residences and were concentrated in the Adlon Hotel next door or in the Embassy itself. All the arrangements were carried out with a maximum of efficiency and a minimum of confusion, which did the utmost credit to the organisation and competency of the very excellent Staff of His Majesty's Embassy. The chief responsibility for this rested upon Mr Holman, as Head of the Chancery.

The 2nd September was a day of suspense. The Poles were, it was reported, putting up a brave resistance in the face of surprise and over-whelming numbers, and in spite of the vast superiority of the German air force and mechanised forces. No reply was received from the German Government throughout the day to the British and French warnings.

On the other hand, the Italian Government was making one more effort to save the situation. The Italian Ambassador had come to see me at midday on his way to the Ministry for Foreign Affairs. Signor Attolico told me that he must know one thing immediately. Was the communication which I had made the previous evening to Herr von Ribbentrop an ultimatum or not? I told his Excellency that I had been authorised to tell the Minister for Foreign Affairs if he had asked me—which he had not done—that it was not an ultimatum but a warning. I mentioned to Signor Attolico that I under-stood that the Italian Government had put forward a suggestion for the cessation of hostilities and the immediate summoning of a conference of the interested Powers. In this connection I said that I felt bound to express the opinion that such a proposal would never be entertained unless at the same time all the German troops were withdrawn from Polish territory.

The Ambassador retorted that I could not speak for my Government. I admitted that fact, but said that I could not imagine the possibility of ourselves, and much less of the Poles, agreeing to any lesser course. I do not know what reply, if any, was given by the German Government to this proposal. But I should like to put on record here that no one ever worked harder for peace than did Signor Attolico, not only this year but last year also. He was entirely selfless in this his earnest endeavour.

There were, in fact, for Herr Hitler only two solutions: the use of force, or the achievement of his aims by the display of force. "If you wish to obtain your objective by force, you must be strong; if you wish to obtain them by negotiation, you must be stronger still." That was a remark which he made to a foreign Statesman who visited him this year, and it expresses in the concisest possible form the Hitler technique. It was exactly that which he displayed in September 1938. He was no more bluffing then than he was bluffing in August 1939. Up to the middle of August this year the fear of a war on two fronts, with Russia hostile or at least unfriendly, might possibly have deterred him and his military advisers from action against Poland. There was no Eastern front to give him cause for hesitation in 1938, and he could have counted then on Hungarian as well as Polish support in his nefarious plans for the dismemberment of Czecho-Slovakia. But for Munich he would without a shadow of doubt have invaded that country on the 29th September last year, just as surely as he invaded Poland on the 1st September this year, and the war would have come eleven months earlier. In both cases the methods employed were identical: the gradual mobilisation of the German army over a period of months and its secret concentration at the appointed positions, whence the advance could begin at almost any moment and within a very few hours.

So it was again in 1939. If he could have secured his objectives by this display of force he might have been content for the moment, with all the additional prestige which another bloodless success would have procured for him with his own people. But it would only have been to start again once the world had recovered from the shock, and even his own people were beginning to be tired of these repeated crises. Millions of Germans had begun to long for a more peaceful existence. Guns instead of butter were becoming more and more unpopular except with the younger generation, and Hitler may well have wondered what might happen to his Nazi revolution if its momentum were allowed to stop. Moreover the financial and economic position of Germany was such that things could scarcely continue as they were without some form of explosion, internal or external. Of the two alternatives the most attractive from the point of view of his growing personal ambitions, and those of the clique which was nearest to him, was war.

It is scarcely credible that he would have acted as he did if bloody war, rather than a bloodless victory, had not seemed the fairer prospect for him. He had always meant to teach the Poles a lesson for what he regarded as their base ingratitude in refusing the "generous" demands which he had made to them in March. His only manœuvres since that date were with the object of creating circumstances favourable to his plans or of inducing Britain and France to abandon their Polish ally and to leave him a free hand in Central and Eastern Europe.

To this end, encouraged by Herr von Ribbentrop, who apparently advised him up to the last moment that Britain would not fight, he worked unceasingly. In the course of one of the five interviews which I had with him during those last few days, I remarked to him that it was he who was ungenerous to the Poles, in view of the advantages which his treaty of 1934 with Pilsudski had brought him. Herr Hitler denied that that treaty had ever been of any benefit to Germany and asserted that it had merely been unpopular with the Germans. It was a remark which was typical of Herr Hitler's capacity to ignore everything which he might have said, promised or done in the past as soon as it had become contrary to views for the present or the future.

One of Herr Hitler's greatest drawbacks is that, except for two official visits to Italy, he has never travelled abroad. For his knowledge of British mentality he consequently relied on Herr von Ribbentrop as an ex-Ambassador to Britain, who spoke both French and English, and who had spent some years in Canada, and whom he regarded as a man of the world. If report be true Herr von Ribbentrop gave him consistently false counsels in regard to England, while his successes in other spheres induced Herr Hitler to regard him more and more as a second Bismarck, a conviction which Herr von Ribbentrop probably shared to the full.

Even the most absolute Dictator is susceptible to the influence of his surroundings. Nevertheless Herr Hitler's decisions, his calculations, and his opportunisms were his own. As Field-Marshal Göring once said to me, "when a decision has to be taken, none of us count more than the stones on which we are standing. It is the Führer alone who decides." If anything did count, it was the opinion of his Military Advisers. I have always believed that it was they who, in the interests of Germany's strategical security, recommended the establishment of the Protectorate over Bohemia. And again this August, it was they, I fancy, who told Herr Hitler that further delay would be fatal lest the seasonal bad weather in Poland might upset their calculations for her swift overthrow. The army grudged him even the week between the 25th August and the 1st September which his last attempt to secure British neutrality or at least goodwill had cost it.

Yet even so the advice of his soldiers was probably merely cover for the prosecution of Hitler's own plans. His impatience and precipitate action on that last day of August can scarcely have been other than premeditated. All through the summer he had been waiting on events to turn in his favour and had been making his preparations to seize the opportunity, when it was offered to him. The Russian pact appeared to give him the advantage which he was seeking and thereafter there was no time to lose, if mud was not to be added to Poland's allies.

When therefore the Polish Government delayed 48 hours in sending its plenipotentiary to beg for terms at Berlin and even then sent only an Ambassador without plenary powers, Herr Hitler in spite of the expressed readiness of Poland to enter into direct negotiations, finally made up his mind not to keep his army waiting any longer. The order for the advance into Poland was probably given immediately after M. Lipski's interview with Herr von Ribbentrop at 6.30 PM on the 31st August.

Late in the afternoon of the 2nd September I communicated to the Secretary of State for the information of the German Government the verbatim report of the Prime Minister's speech in the House of Commons on that date. Therein Mr Chamberlain stated that while His Majesty's Government could not agree to the proposal of the Italian Government for a conference while Poland was being subjected to invasion, they would be willing, if the German forces were withdrawn from Polish territory, to regard the position as being the same as before the forces had crossed the frontier. It was the last chance of avoiding the great catastrophe of war at the last minute, but the German Government remained silent.

In the early hours (4 AM) of the 3rd September I was accordingly instructed by your Lordship to arrange for a meeting with the Minister for Foreign Affairs at 9 AM. There was some difficulty in establishing contact with the Ministry at that hour, but I was finally informed that Dr Schmidt was authorised by the Minister to accept on his Excellency's behalf any communication which I might make to him. I accordingly handed to Dr Schmidt at 9 AM precisely the final ultimatum from His Majesty's Government, pointing out that over 24 hours had elapsed since I had requested an immediate answer to our warning communication of the 1st September, that since then the attacks on Poland had been intensified, and that, unless satisfactory assurances were received by His Majesty's Government before 11 AM British summer time of the suspension of all aggressive action against Poland and of the withdrawal of the German forces from that country, a state of war would exist between our two countries as from that hour.

Dr Schmidt received this communication and undertook to deliver it immediately to his Chief. As no reply from the German Government was vouchsafed by 11 AM, the German Representative in London was informed in due course at that hour that a state of war existed between Britain and Germany. By 10 minutes past 11 AM every British consular officer in Germany had been advised by the staff of His Majesty's Embassy at Berlin that this was the case.

Shortly after 11 AM I received a final message from Herr von Ribbentrop asking me to call upon him at once. I did so at 11.30 and he handed me this time a lengthy document to read, beginning with a refusal on the part of the German people to accept any demands in the nature of an ultimatum made by the British Government, and stating that any aggressive action by England would be answered with the same weapons and the same form. The rest of the document was pure propaganda with a view to attempting to prove to the German people and the world generally that it was Britain alone who was to blame for everything which had happened. My only comment on reading this completely false representation of events was: "It would be left to history to judge where the blame really lay." Herr von Ribbentrop's answer was to the effect that history had already proved the facts, and that nobody had striven harder for peace and good relations with England than Herr Hitler himself. His last remark to me was that he wished me personally good, to which I could only reply that I deeply regretted the failure of all my efforts for peace, but that I bore no grudge against the German people. Thereafter I saw no further German official except the member of the Protocol, who accompanied our special train as far as Rotterdam. My last official communication to the German Government was a note which I presented on the instructions of His Majesty's Government enquiring whether the German Government would observe the provisions of the Geneva Protocol of 1925 prohibiting the use in war of asphyxiating, poisonous or other gases and of bacteriological methods of warfare—I understand that the German Government have since replied through the Swiss Minister in London giving the required assurance on the understanding that His Majesty's Government would similarly observe the provisions of the Protocol.

The French Ambassador had presented at noon a similar ultimatum to the German Government to expire at 5 PM. For a few hours after 11 AM the telephonic lines of His Majesty's Embassy at Berlin continued to function, but about 4 PM all telephonic lines were cut off and both the staff at the Adlon Hotel and the Embassy itself were isolated from all external contact. Members of my staff, however, had visited the Protocol at 11 AM with a view to arranging for our departure. They were treated with every civility and consideration and were informed that a special train would be placed at our disposal the following morning.

Our only contact thereafter with the outside world was through the American Embassy. Its aid and help was invaluable. No trouble was too great for the Chargé d'Affaires, Mr Alexander Kirk, and the members of his staff. They did everything that was possible to smooth over the difficulties of those last 24 hours, and our pleasantest recollection of them is our appreciation of the great sympathy and willing assistance which we received from the American Embassy.

The French Embassy left Berlin at 9 AM the following morning, Monday, the 4th September. The British Embassy followed in a special train, leaving the Charlottenberg station at 11.20 AM. The whole party consisted of 30 men, 7 women and 2 dogs. A small crowd collected round the Embassy before our departure, but unlike 1914 it evinced no single sign of hostility. Mr Kirk rendered me one more last service by driving me to the station in his own car. The streets of Berlin were practically deserted and there was nothing to indicate the beginning of a war which is to decide whether force

is to be the sole arbiter in international affairs; whether international instruments solemnly and freely entered into are to be modified, not by
negotiation, but by mere unilateral repudiation; whether there is to be any
faith in future in written contracts; whether the fate of a great nation and
the peace of the world is to rest in the future in the hands of one man;
whether small nations are to have any rights against the pretensions of States
more powerful than themselves; in a word, whether government of the
people by the people for the people is to continue in this world, or whether
it is to be replaced by the arbitrary will and ambition of single individuals
regardless of the peoples' will.

Our journey through Germany, if prolonged, was uneventful. At the various stations at which we stopped there was some curiosity but no evidence
of hostility. We reached Rheine, a small station some 20 kilometres from the
German frontier, at about 6 PM on the Monday evening. There our train was
detained for nearly twenty hours pending the safe arrival in Dutch territorial waters of the German mission from London. We eventually left Rheine
at 1.30 PM on Tuesday and were received with great hospitality at the Dutch
frontier. We reached Rotterdam that evening, and after spending a night at
The Hague and one on board the Dutch steamer *Batavier V*, left Rotterdam
in the early hours of Thursday morning, the 7th September. We arrived at
Gravesend about 6 PM that evening.

NEVILE HENDERSON

PART II

⚬⚬◦◦✕◦◦⚬⚬

*DOCUMENTS CONCERNING GERMAN–POLISH
RELATIONS AND THE OUTBREAK OF HOSTILITIES
BETWEEN GREAT BRITAIN AND GERMANY ON
3 SEPTEMBER 1939*

STATEMENTS MADE BY HERR HITLER

The following statements were made since the German–Polish Agreement of 1934. In them, Hitler records his satisfaction at the improvement in German–Polish relations.

Reichstag Speech, 21 May 1935

(Translation)

We recognise, with the understanding and the heartfelt friendship of true Nationalists, the Polish State as the home of a great, nationally conscious people.

The German Reich and, in particular, the present German Government, have no other wish than to live on friendly and peaceable terms with all neighbouring States.

Reichstag Speech, 7 March 1936

(Translation)

I would like the German people to learn to see in other nations historical realities which a visionary may well like to wish away, but which cannot be wished away. I should like them to realise that it is unreasonable to try and bring these historical realities into opposition with the demands of their vital interests and to their understandable claims to live. I would therefore like the German people to understand the inner motives of National Socialist foreign policy, which finds it painful that the outlet to the sea of a people of 35 millions is situated on territory formerly belonging to the Reich, but which recognises that it is unreasonable and impossible to deny a State of such a size as this any outlet to the sea at all ... It is possible that politicians, particularly by invoking might, may carry out such violations of national interests; but the more frequently this happens, the greater becomes the pressure for an outlet of the excited and constrained powers and energies.

Reichstag Speech, 30 January 1937

(Translation)

By a series of agreements we have removed existing tensions and thereby contributed considerably to an improvement in the European atmosphere. I merely recall our agreement with Poland, which has worked out to the advantage of both sides ... And to my own fellow-citizens I would say that the Polish nation and the Polish State have also become a reality ... The peoples of these States (*i.e.*, Italy, Poland and the Balkan States) desire to live and they will live.

Reichstag Speech, 20 February 1938

(Translation)

It fills us, in the fifth year following the first great foreign political agreement of the Reich, with sincere gratification to be able to establish that in our relationship to the State with which we had perhaps the greatest differences, not only has there been a *détente*, but that in the course of these years a constant improvement in relations has taken place. I know perfectly well that this was above all attributable to the circumstance that at the time there was no Western parliamentarism in Warsaw, but a Polish field-marshal [Pilsudski] who as an eminent personality felt the significance, so important to Europe, of such a Germano-Polish *détente*. This good work, which had been doubted by so many at the time, has meanwhile stood the test, and I may say that, since the League of Nations finally gave up its perpetual attempts to unsettle Danzig and appointed in the new commissioner a man of great personal attainments, this most dangerous spot from the point of view of European peace has entirely lost its menacing character. The Polish State respects the national conditions in this State, and both the city of Danzig and Germany respect Polish rights. And so the way to a friendly understanding has been successfully paved, an understanding which, starting from Danzig, has today succeeded in spite of the attempts of certain mischief-makers in finally taking the poison out of the relations between Germany and Poland and transforming them into a sincere, friendly co-operation.

Speech at Nuremberg, 14 September 1938

(Translation)

In Poland a great patriot and a great statesman was ready to make an accord with Germany; we immediately proceeded to action and completed an agreement which was of greater importance to the peace of Europe than all the chattering in the temple of the League of Nations at Geneva.

Speech in the Sportpalast, 26 September 1938

(Translation)

The most difficult problem with which I was confronted was that of our relations with Poland. There was a danger that Poles and Germans would regard each other as hereditary enemies. I wanted to prevent this. I know well enough that I should not have been successful if Poland had had a democratic Constitution. For these democracies which indulge in phrases about peace are the most bloodthirsty war agitators. In Poland there ruled no democracy, but a man; and with him I succeeded, in precisely twelve months, in coming to an agreement which, for ten years in the first instance, entirely removed the danger of a conflict. We are all convinced that this agreement will bring lasting pacification. We realise that here are two peoples which must live together and neither of which can do away with the other. A people of 33 millions will always strive for an outlet to the sea. A way for understanding, then, had to be found; it has been found; and it will be ever further extended. Certainly things were hard in this area. The nationalities and small national groups frequently quarrelled among themselves. But the main fact is that the two Governments, and all reasonable and clear-sighted persons among the two peoples and in the two countries, possess the firm will and determination to improve their relations. It was a real work of peace, of more worth than all the chattering in the League of Nations Palace at Geneva.

Reichstag Speech, 30 January 1939

(Translation)

We have just celebrated the fifth anniversary of the conclusion of our non-aggression pact with Poland. There can scarcely be any difference of opinion today among the true friends of peace with regard to the value of this agreement. One only needs to ask oneself what might have happened to Europe if this agreement, which brought such relief, had not been entered into five years ago. In signing it, this great Polish marshal and patriot rendered his people just as great a service as the leaders of the National Socialist State rendered the German people. During the troubled months of the past year the friendship between Germany and Poland was one of the reassuring factors in the political life of Europe.

DETERIORATION IN EUROPEAN SITUATION

Germany took action against Czecho-Slovakia and invaded that country on 15 *March* 1939.

Speech by the British Prime Minister (Mr Neville Chamberlain) at Birmingham on 17 *March* 1939

I had intended tonight to talk to you upon a variety of subjects, upon trade and employment, upon social service, and upon finance. But the tremendous events which have been taking place this week in Europe have thrown everything else into the background, and I feel that what you, and those who are not in this hall but are listening to me, will want to hear is some indication of the views of His Majesty's Government as to the nature and the implications of those events.

One thing is certain. Public opinion in the world has received a sharper shock than has ever yet been administered to it, even by the present régime in Germany. What may be the ultimate effects of this profound disturbance on men's minds cannot yet be foretold, but I am sure that it must be far-reaching in its results upon the future. Last Wednesday we had a debate upon it in the House of Commons. That was the day on which the German troops entered Czecho-Slovakia, and all of us, but particularly the Government, were at a disadvantage, because the information that we had was only partial; much of it was unofficial. We had no time to digest it, much less to form a considered opinion upon it. And so it necessarily followed that I, speaking on behalf of the Government, with all the responsibility that attaches to that position, was obliged to confine myself to a very restrained and cautious exposition, on what at the time I felt I could make but little commentary. And, perhaps naturally, that somewhat cool and objective statement gave rise to a misapprehension, and some people thought that because I spoke quietly, because I gave little expression to feeling, therefore my colleagues and I did not feel strongly on the subject. I hope to correct that mistake tonight.

But I want to say something first about an argument which has developed out of these events and which was used in that debate, and has appeared since in various organs of the press. It has been suggested that this occupation of Czecho-Slovakia was the direct consequence of the visit which I paid to Germany last autumn, and that, since the result of these events has been to tear up the settlement that was arrived at at Munich, that proves that the whole circumstances of those visits were wrong. It is said that, as this was the personal policy of the Prime Minister, the blame for the fate of Czecho-Slovakia must rest upon his shoulders. That is an entirely unwarrantable conclusion. The facts as they are today cannot change the facts as they were last September. If I was right then, I am still right now. Then there are some people who say: "We considered you were wrong in September, and now we have been proved to be right."

Let me examine that. When I decided to go to Germany I never expected that I was going to escape criticism. Indeed, I did not go there to get popularity. I went there first and foremost because, in what appeared to be an almost desperate situation, that seemed to me to offer the only chance of averting a European war. And I might remind you that, when it was first announced that I was going, not a voice was raised in criticism. Everyone applauded that effort. It was only later, when it appeared that the results of the final settlement fell short of the expectations of some who did not fully appreciate the facts—it was only then that the attack began, and even then it was not the visit, it was the terms of settlement that were disapproved.

Well, I have never denied that the terms which I was able to secure at Munich were not those that I myself would have desired. But, as I explained then, I had to deal with no new problem. This was something that had existed ever since the Treaty of Versailles—a problem that ought to have been solved long ago if only the statesmen of the last twenty years had taken broader and more enlightened views of their duty. It had become like a disease which had been long neglected, and a surgical operation was necessary to save the life of the patient.

After all, the first and the most immediate object of my visit was achieved. The peace of Europe was saved; and, if it had not been for those visits, hundreds of thousands of families would today have been in mourning for the flower of Europe's best manhood. I would like once again to express my grateful thanks to all those correspondents who have written to me from all over the world to express their gratitude and their appreciation of what I did then and of what I have been trying to do since.

Really I have no need to defend my visits to Germany last autumn, for what was the alternative? Nothing that we could have done, nothing that France could have done, or Russia could have done could possibly have saved Czecho-Slovakia from invasion and destruction. Even if we had subsequently gone to war to punish Germany for her actions, and if after the frightful losses which would have been inflicted upon all partakers in the war we had been victorious in the end, never could we have reconstructed Czecho-Slovakia as she was framed by the Treaty of Versailles.

But I had another purpose, too, in going to Munich. That was to further the policy which I have been pursuing ever since I have been in my present position—a policy which is sometimes called European appeasement, although I do not think myself that that is a very happy term or one which accurately describes its purpose. If that policy were to succeed, it was essential that no Power should seek to obtain a general domination of Europe; but that each one should be contented to obtain reasonable facilities for developing its own resources, securing its own share of international trade, and improving the conditions of its own people. I felt that, although that might well mean a clash of interests between different States, nevertheless, by the exercise of mutual goodwill and understanding of what were the limits of the desires of others, it should be possible to resolve all differences by discussion and without armed conflict. I hoped in going to Munich to find out by personal contact what was in Herr Hitler's mind, and whether it was likely that he would be willing to co-operate in a programme of that kind. Well, the atmosphere in which our discussions were conducted was not a very favourable one, because we were in the middle of an acute crisis; but, nevertheless, in the intervals between more official conversations I had some opportunities of talking with him and of hearing his views, and I thought that the results were not altogether unsatisfactory.

When I came back after my second visit I told the House of Commons of a conversation I had had with Herr Hitler, of which I said that, speaking with great earnestness, he repeated what he had already said at Berchtesgaden*—namely, that this was the last of his territorial ambitions in Europe, and that he had no wish to include in the Reich people of other races than German. Herr Hitler himself confirmed this account of the conversation in the speech which he made at the Sportpalast in Berlin, when he said: "This is the last territorial claim which I have to make in Europe." And a little later in the same speech he said: "I have assured Mr Chamberlain, and I emphasise it now, that when this problem is solved Germany has no more territorial problems in Europe." And he added: "I shall not be interested in the Czech State any more, and I can guarantee it. We don't want any Czechs any more."

And then in the Munich Agreement itself, which bears Herr Hitler's signature, there is this clause: "The final determination of the frontiers will be carried out by the international commission"—the *final* determination. And, lastly, in that declaration which he and I signed together at Munich, we declared that any other question which might concern our two countries should be dealt with by the method of consultation.

* Hitler's residence, near Salzburg.

Well, in view of those repeated assurances, given voluntarily to me, I considered myself justified in founding a hope upon them that once this Czecho-Slovakian question was settled, as it seemed at Munich it would be, it would be possible to carry further that policy of appeasement which I have described. But, notwithstanding, at the same time I was not prepared to relax precautions until I was satisfied that the policy had been established and had been accepted by others, and therefore, after Munich, our defence pro-gramme was actually accelerated, and it was expanded so as to remedy certain weaknesses which had become apparent during the crisis. I am con-vinced that after Munich the great majority of British people shared my hope, and ardently desired that that policy should be carried further. But today I share their disappointment, their indignation, that those hopes have been so wantonly shattered.

How can these events this week be reconciled with those assurances which I have read out to you? Surely, as a joint signatory of the Munich Agreement, I was entitled, if Herr Hitler thought it ought to be undone, to that consultation which is provided for in the Munich declaration. Instead of that he has taken the law into his own hands. Before even the Czech President was received, and confronted with demands which he had no power to resist, the German troops were on the move, and within a few hours they were in the Czech capital.

According to the proclamation which was read out in Prague yesterday, Bohemia and Moravia have been annexed to the German Reich. Non-German inhabitants, who, of course, include the Czechs, are placed under the German Protector in the German Protectorate. They are to be subject to the political, military and economic needs of the Reich. They are called self-governing States, but the Reich is to take charge of their foreign policy, their customs and their excise, their bank reserves, and the equipment of the disarmed Czech forces. Perhaps most sinister of all, we hear again of the appearance of the Gestapo, the secret police, followed by the usual tale of wholesale arrests of prominent individuals, with consequences with which we are all familiar.

Every man and woman in this country who remembers the fate of the Jews and the political prisoners in Austria must be filled today with distress and foreboding. Who can fail to feel his heart go out in sympathy to the proud and brave people who have so suddenly been subjected to this inva-sion, whose liberties are curtailed, whose national independence has gone? What has become of this declaration of "No further territorial ambition"? What has become of the assurance "We don't want Czechs in the Reich"? What regard had been paid here to that principle of self-determination on which Herr Hitler argued so vehemently with me at Berchtesgaden when he was asking for the severance of Sudetenland from Czecho-Slovakia and its inclusion in the German Reich?

Now we are told that this seizure of territory has been necessitated by disturbances in Czecho-Slovakia. We are told that the proclamation of this new German Protectorate against the will of its inhabitants has been rendered inevitable by disorders which threatened the peace and security of her mighty neighbour. If there were disorders, were they not fomented from without? And can anybody outside Germany take seriously the idea that they could be a danger to that great country, that they could provide any justification for what has happened?

Does not the question inevitably arise in our minds, if it is so easy to discover good reasons for ignoring assurances so solemnly and so repeatedly given, what reliance can be placed upon any other assurances that come from the same source?

There is another set of questions which almost inevitably must occur in our minds and to the minds of others, perhaps even in Germany herself. Germany, under her present régime, has sprung a series of unpleasant surprises upon the world. The Rhineland, the Austrian *Anschluss*,★ the severance of Sudetenland—all these things shocked and affronted public opinion throughout the world. Yet, however much we might take exception to the methods which were adopted in each of those cases, there was something to be said, whether on account of racial affinity or of just claims too long resisted—there was something to be said for the necessity of a change in the existing situation.

But the events which have taken place this week in complete disregard of the principles laid down by the German Government itself seem to fall into a different category, and they must cause us all to be asking ourselves: "Is this the end of an old adventure, or is it the beginning of a new? Is this the last attack upon a small State, or is it to be followed by others? Is this, in fact, a step in the direction of an attempt to dominate the world by force?"

Those are grave and serious questions. I am not going to answer them tonight. But I am sure they will require the grave and serious consideration not only of Germany's neighbours, but of others, perhaps even beyond the confines of Europe. Already there are indications that the process has begun, and it is obvious that it is likely now to be speeded up.

We ourselves will naturally turn first to our partners in the British Commonwealth of Nations and to France, to whom we are so closely bound, and I have no doubt that others, too, knowing that we are not disinterested in what goes on in South-Eastern Europe, will wish to have our counsel and advice.

In our own country we must all review the position with that sense of responsibility which its gravity demands. Nothing must be excluded from that review which bears upon the national safety. Every aspect of our national life must be looked at again from that angle. The Government, as always, must bear the main responsibility, but I know that all individuals will wish to review their own position, too, and to consider again if they have done all they can to offer their service to the State.

★ Political union of Austria and Germany in 1938.

I do not believe there is anyone who will question my sincerity when I say there is hardly anything I would not sacrifice for peace. But there is one thing that I must except, and that is the liberty that we have enjoyed for hundreds of years, and which we will never surrender. That I, of all men, should feel called upon to make such a declaration—that is the measure of the extent to which these events have shattered the confidence which was just beginning to show its head and which, if it had been allowed to grow, might have made this year memorable for the return of all Europe to sanity and stability.

It is only six weeks ago that I was speaking in this city, and that I alluded to rumours and suspicions which I said ought to be swept away. I pointed out that any demand to dominate the world by force was one which the democracies must resist, and I added that I could not believe that such a challenge was intended, because no Government with the interests of its own people at heart could expose them for such a claim to the horrors of world war.

And, indeed, with the lessons of history for all to read, it seems incredible that we should see such a challenge. I feel bound to repeat that, while I am not prepared to engage this country by new unspecified commitments operating under conditions which cannot now be foreseen, yet no greater mistake could be made than to suppose that, because it believes war to be a senseless and cruel thing, this nation has so lost its fibre that it will not take part to the utmost of its power in resisting such a challenge if it ever were made. For that declaration I am convinced that I have not merely the support, the sympathy, the confidence of my fellow-countrymen and country-women, but I shall have also the approval of the whole British Empire and of all other nations who value peace, indeed, but who value freedom even more.

Speech by the Secretary of State for Foreign Affairs in the House of Lords on 20 March 1939

It is quite true, as both the noble Lord who spoke first and the noble Marquess have said, that recent events have been a profound shock to all thinking people in this country and very far outside it. It may perhaps be of use if with all brevity I give the House a short narrative in order to make sure we have the setting correct of what has actually passed during the last few days. The German military occupation of Bohemia and Moravia began on the morning of the 15th March, and was completed, as we know, without serious incident. It is to be observed—and the fact is surely not without significance—that the towns of Mährisch-Ostrau and Vitkovice were actually occupied by German SS detachments on the evening of the 14th March, while the President and the Foreign Minister of Czecho-Slovakia were still on their way to Berlin and before any discussion had taken place. On the 16th March Herr Hitler issued the decree, to which the noble Marquess has just referred, proclaiming that the former Czecho-Slovak territory occupied by

German troops belonged henceforth to the German Reich and came under its protection under the title of "The Protectorate of Bohemia and Moravia".

It is not necessary to recapitulate the terms of that decree—it has been published—but it should be noted that, while the head of the Administration now to be set up is said to hold the rank of Head of State, and while the protectorate is said to be autonomous and self-administering, a Reich protector is resident in Prague with full powers of veto on legislation. Foreign affairs and the protection of nationals abroad devolve on the German Government, which will also maintain military garrisons and establishments in the protectorate. The protectorate is, further, in the German Customs Union, and, finally, the German Government can issue decrees valid in the protectorate and take any measures for the preservation of security and order. Perhaps I might quote one short article which seems to me to sum up the situation. It says:

> The Protectorate of Bohemia and Moravia shall exercise its sovereign rights in consonance [harmony] with the political, military and economic importance of the Reich.

As to Slovakia, the independence of Slovakia was proclaimed on the 14th March, but at the request of Dr Tiso, the head of the Slovak State, Herr Hitler has undertaken to place Slovakia under German protection and the military occupation of the territory by German troops is now proceeding. As regards Ruthenia, the occupation of Ruthenia by Hungary, which began on the 14th March, has also proceeded. By the 16th March the Hungarian troops had reached the Polish frontier and had virtually completed the occupation of the province. Therefore, as a result of these several actions, the dismemberment of Czecho-Slovakia may be said now to be complete.

Before I come to some of the things that fell from the noble Lord who moved, I would like to say something as to the grounds on which the German Government seek to justify the action that they have taken. The immediate cause of the present crisis in Central Europe originated in Slovakia, and it is claimed that the German Government was entitled to intervene on receiving the request for assistance from the dismissed Slovak Prime Minister. As your Lordships are well aware, there has always been a party in Slovakia which advocated autonomy. That autonomy was, in fact, achieved after Munich in agreement between the various Slovak parties and the Central Government in Prague. The extremist elements in Slovakia, however, were not satisfied with these arrangements, but on all the evidence that is available to me I find it impossible to believe that the sudden decision of certain Slovak leaders to break off from Prague, which was followed so closely by their appeal for protection to the German Reich, was reached independently of outside influence.

It is said that German intervention in Czecho-Slovakia was justified owing to the oppression of the Germany minority by the Czechs. But, as a matter of fact again, it was only very shortly before Herr Hitler's ultimatum to the Czech President that the German press began to renew its campaign of last summer about the alleged Czech brutalities against German citizens. Actually the position of the German minority, which is about 250,000, would appear, since the Munich Agreement, to have been one of what might be termed exceptional privilege. Notwithstanding the right of option which had been accorded by article 7 of that agreement, the members of the German minority were encouraged to remain in Czecho-Slovakia in order that they might form useful centres of German activity and propaganda; and advice to that effect was given to the minority by its leader.

It was as a result of the German-Czecho-Slovak Agreement for the mutual protection of minorities that the German Government obtained the legal right to take a direct interest in the treatment of their minority in Czecho-Slovakia. That minority at once obtained the right to set up separate organisations, and the Czecho-Slovak Government subsequently agreed that the German National Socialist Party in Czecho-Slovakia should be given full liberty to pursue its activities in Bohemia and Moravia. It is difficult to avoid the conclusion that the bulk of the incidents which occurred before the German invasion were deliberately provoked and that the effects were greatly magnified. It must be added in fairness that the Czecho-Slovak authorities received orders to act, and did act, with great restraint in the face of that provocation. It is not necessary, I think, to say much upon the assertion that the Czecho-Slovak President really assented to the subjugation of his people. In view of the circumstances in which he came to Berlin, and of the occupation of Czech territory which had already taken place, I think most sensible people must conclude that there was little pretence of negotiation, and that it is more probable that the Czech representatives were presented with an ultimatum under the threat of violence, and that they capitulated in order to save their people from the horrors of a swift and destructive aerial bombardment.

Finally, it is said that Germany was in some danger from Czecho-Slovakia. But surely the German Government itself can hardly have expected that that contention could be seriously entertained in any quarter. Indeed, if I may sum up my own thoughts on these various explorations, I could wish that, instead of the communications and explanations which have been issued and which carry scant conviction, German superior force had been frankly acknowledged as the supreme arbiter that in fact it was.

In these circumstances, as you are aware, His Majesty's Government thought fit at once to take certain action. Here I touch a point which was touched both by the noble Lord who moved and by the noble Marquess who followed him. His Majesty's Government immediately suspended the visit of the President of the Board of Trade and the Secretary of the Department of Overseas Trade to Berlin, by means of which it had been hoped that His Majesty's Government could directly intervene in those unofficial contacts of industrial representatives which were at that very moment taking place. We felt, and feel, as I think I said in my statement a few days ago, that in the circumstances which have arisen any development of our efforts in that direction was, as the noble Marquess said, frankly out of the question, and that that and many other things had to be and must remain indefinitely postponed. His Majesty's Government, as your Lordships also know, have recalled to report His Majesty's Ambassador in Berlin, and he reached this country yesterday.

Further than those two practical steps, we have lodged a formal protest with the German Government in the sense of informing them that we cannot but regard the events of the last few days as a complete repudiation of the Munich Agreement and a denial of the spirit in which the negotiators of that agreement bound themselves to co-operate for a peaceful settlement. We have also taken occasion to protest against the changes effected in Czecho-Slovakia by German military action, and have said that, in our view, those changes are devoid of any basis of legality. I think, therefore, that we may claim to have left the German Government in no doubt of the attitude of His Majesty's Government, and although I do not cherish any exaggerated hopes of what may be the effect of protests, I think your Lordships will feel it abundantly right that such protests should be registered.

I have from time to time seen efforts made by German apologists to justify the action of their Government by some reference to the past history of the British Empire. It is not necessary to remind you that the principle on which the British Empire is conducted is education in self-government. Wherever we have been in the world, we have left a trail of freedom and of self-government, and our record has nothing in common with the suppression of liberty and independence of people whose political developments had already brought them to the point of enjoyment of those opportunities for self-expression. It has also been objected that what has happened in Czecho-Slovakia is of no interest or concern to this country. It is quite true that we have always recognised that, for reasons of geography, if for no other, Germany must from some points of view be more interested in Czecho-Slovakia or South-Eastern Europe than we are ourselves. It was the natural field for the expansion of German trade. But apart from the fact that changes in any part of Europe produce profound effects elsewhere, the position is entirely changed when we are confronted with the arbitrary suppression of an independent sovereign State by force, and by the violation of what I must regard as the elementary rules of international conduct.

It is natural enough that in the light of these events His Majesty's Government should be told, as the noble Lord told them this afternoon, that the policy of Munich was a tragic mistake. I cannot, of course, claim to correct the noble Lord upon an expression of opinion which he sincerely holds, but I can correct him, I think, on one limited observation that fell from him. He referred to the policy pursued by the Prime Minister as a personal policy. If by that he means that it was a policy to which the Prime Minister had given every ounce of energy, imagination and resolution that he possessed, I should not disagree with him, but if he suggests that it was a policy that was pursued without the fullest co-operation of myself as Foreign Secretary, and of every member of His Majesty's Government, then I must take leave to oppose to what he said the most emphatic contradiction.

My Lords, the Munich Settlement, which was approved by this House and in another place, was accepted by His Majesty's Government for two purposes, quite distinct. The first purpose was to effect a settlement, as fair as might be in all the extremely difficult circumstances of that time, of a problem which was a real one, and of which the treatment was an urgent necessity if the peace of Europe was to be preserved. As to that, I would say, as I have said before in this House, that I have no doubt whatever that His Majesty's Government were right, in the light of all the information available to them, to take the course they did. The second purpose of Munich was to build a Europe more secure, upon the basis of freely accepted consultation as the means by which all future differences might be adjusted; and that long-term purpose, my Lords, has been, as we have come to observe, disastrously belied by events. We are charged with having too readily believed the assurances which were given by Herr Hitler—that after Munich he had no further territorial ambitions, and no desire to incorporate non-German elements in the Reich. The noble Lord referred to the Prime Minister as the "too-simple Prime Minister". I can assure your Lordships that neither the Prime Minister nor I, myself, nor any member of His Majesty's Government, has failed at any moment to be acutely conscious of the difference between beliefs and hope. It was surely legitimate and right to have hopes. But we have always acted—and I challenge any noble Lord to produce any evidence to the contrary—in the knowledge that only with time can hope be converted into sure beliefs.

It is no doubt the case that previous assurances had been broken, whatever justification might have been advanced by Herr Hitler, on the grounds of his mission, as he conceives it, to incorporate ex-German territory and predominantly German areas in the Reich. But in his actions until after Munich a case could be made that Herr Hitler had been true to his own principles, the union of Germans in, and the exclusion of non-Germans from, the Reich. Those principles he has now overthrown, and in including 8 million Czechs under German rule he has surely been untrue to his own philosophy. The world will not forget that in September last Herr Hitler appealed to the principle of self-determination in the interests of 2 million Sudeten Germans. That principle is one on which the British Empire itself has been erected, and one to which accordingly, as your Lordships will recollect, we felt obliged to give weight in considering Herr Hitler's claim. That principle has now been rudely contradicted by a sequence of acts which denies the very right on which the German attitude of six months ago was based, and whatever may have been the truth about the treatment of 250,000 Germans, it is impossible for me to believe that it could only be remedied by the subjugation of 8 million Czechs.

What conclusions, as asked the noble Marquess, are we to draw from this conquest of Czecho-Slovakia? Are we to believe that German policy has thus entered upon a new phase? Is German policy any longer to be limited to the consolidation of territory predominantly inhabited by persons of German race? Or is German policy now to be directed towards domination over non-German peoples? These are very grave questions which are being asked in all parts of the world today. The German action in Czecho-Slovakia has been furthered by new methods, and the world has lately seen more than one new departure in the field of international technique. Wars without declarations of war. Pressure exercised under threat of immediate employment of force. Intervention in the internal struggles of other States. Countries are now faced with the encouragement of separatism, not in the interest of separatist or minority elements but in the imperial interests of Germany. The alleged ill-treatment of German minorities in foreign countries which, it is true, may sometimes, perhaps often, arise from natural causes, but which may also be the subject and result of provocation from outside, is used as a pretext for intervention.

These methods are simple and, with growing experience, quite unmistakable. Have we any assurance that they will not be employed elsewhere? Every country which is Germany's neighbour is now uncertain of the morrow, and every country which values its national identity and sovereignty stands warned against the danger from within, inspired from without. During the last few days there have been rumours that the German Government were adopting a harsh attitude in their negotiations with the Roumanian Government on economic matters. I am glad to say that the Roumanian Government have themselves denied a report that went so far as to speak of an "ultimatum"; but even if there is no menace to Roumania today, or even if that menace has not today developed, and even though it may not develop on these lines, it is not surprising if the Government of Bucharest, like other Governments, should view with the gravest misgivings the happenings of these last few days.

For years past the British people have steadily desired to be on friendly terms with the German people. There is no stronger national instinct among our people than the instinct that leads them, when they have a fight, to shake hands and try to make it up. Our people were not backward in recognising some of the mistakes of the Versailles Treaty that required remedying, but each time during these last years that there has seemed a chance of making progress in understanding, the German Government has taken action which has made that progress impossible. More especially has that been the case in recent months. Very shortly after Munich certain measures were taken by the German Government that gave a profound shock to world opinion. Quite recently it was to be hoped, although there were many clouds still over and below the horizon, that we could look forward to closer economic collaboration, and it was in the hope of developing that economic collaboration into something wider that, as your Lordships know, we had decided on those visits to which I referred a moment ago. All that initiative has been frustrated by the action of the German Government last week, and it is difficult to see when it can be easily resumed.

These affairs, as I said a moment or two ago, have raised wide issues, and the events in Czecho-Slovakia require His Majesty's Government and require every free people to rethink their attitude towards them. Broadly speaking, there have been, at all events since the war, two conflicting theses as to the best method of avoiding conflicts and creating security for the nations of the world. The first thesis is that which upholds the creation of and supports machinery for consultation, conciliation and arbitration with, if possible, the sanction of collective force, and involves an invitation to all States, willing to accept a wide degree of obligation to one another, to agree that an attack on one should be treated as an attack on all. That, your Lordships know well enough, has been the thesis expressed in the Covenant of the League of Nations. Perhaps it is true to say that more precise effect was sought to be given to it in the Geneva Protocol, and it has itself given rise to a number of regional agreements for mutual assistance between the several Powers concerned. That is the first thesis.

The second, which has been in conflict, has been upheld by those who consider that systems seeking to provide collective security, as it has been termed, involved dangerously indefinite commitments quite disproportionate to the real security that these commitments gave. Those who took that view were persuaded that States, conscious of their own pacific purposes, would be wise to refrain from such commitments which might draw them into a war in which their own vital interests were not threatened, and that, therefore, States should not bind themselves to intervene in conflicts unless they themselves were directly attacked.

That is the conflict of philosophy of which your Lordships are very well aware, because in one form or another it has constantly been debated in this House. I have no doubt that in considering these two theses the judgment of many has been influenced by the estimate that they place, rightly or wrongly, upon the probability of direct attack. If it were possible, in their judgment, to rate that probability low, then that low probability of direct attack had to be weighed against what might seem to them the greater risk of States being involved in conflicts that were not necessarily arising out of their own concerns. But if and when it becomes plain to States that there is no apparent guarantee against successive attacks directed in turn on all who might seem to stand in the way of ambitious schemes of domination, then at once the scale tips the other way, and in all quarters there is likely immediately to be found a very much greater readiness to consider whether the acceptance of wider mutual obligations, in the cause of mutual support, is not dictated, if for no other reason than the necessity of self-defence. His Majesty's Government have not failed to draw the moral from these events, and have lost no time in placing themselves in close and practical consultation, not only with the Dominions, but with other Governments concerned upon the issues that have suddenly been made so plain.

It is not possible as yet fully to appraise the consequences of German action. History, to which the noble Marquess always refers us with great profit and enjoyment, records many attempts to impose a domination on Europe, but all these attempts have, sooner or later, terminated in disaster for those who made them. It has never in the long run proved possible to stamp out the spirit of free peoples. If history is any guide, the German people may yet regret the action that has been taken in their name against the people of Czecho-Slovakia. Twenty years ago that people of Czecho-Slovakia recovered their liberties with the support and encouragement of the greater part of the world. They have now been deprived of them by violence. In the course of their long history this will not be the first time that this tenacious, valiant and industrious people have lost their independence, but they have never lost that which is the foundation of independence—the love of liberty. Meanwhile, just as after the last war the world watched the emergence of the Czech nation, so it will watch to-day their efforts to preserve intact their cultural identity and, more important, their spiritual freedom under the last and most cruel blow of which they have been the victims.

Question and the Prime Minister's answer in the House of Commons on 23 March 1939. Mr Attlee asked the Prime Minister whether he had any further statement to make on the European situation.

The Prime Minister: His Majesty's Government have already made clear that the recent actions of the German Government have raised the question whether that Government is not seeking by successive steps to dominate Europe, and perhaps even to go further than that. Were this interpretation of the intentions of the German Government to prove correct, His Majesty's Government feel bound to say that this would rouse the successful resistance of this and other countries who prize their freedom, as similar attempts have done in the past.

I am not yet in a position to make a statement on the consultations which have been held with other Governments as a result of recent developments. I wish to make it clear, however, that there is no desire on the part of His Majesty's Government to stand in the way of any reasonable efforts on the part of Germany to expand her export trade. On the contrary, we were on the point of discussing in the most friendly way the possibility of trade arrangements which would have benefited both countries when the events took place which for the time being at any rate, put a stop to those discussions. Nor is this Government anxious to set up in Europe opposing blocks of countries with different ideas about the forms of their internal administration. We are solely concerned here with the proposition that we cannot submit to a procedure under which independent States are subjected to such pressure under threat of force as to be obliged to yield up their independence, and we are resolved by all means in our power to oppose attempts, if they should be made, to put such a procedure into operation.

Sir N. Henderson to Viscount Halifax

Berlin, 28 May 1939

My Lord,

I paid a short visit to Field-Marshal Göring at Karinhall yesterday.

Field-Marshal Göring, who had obviously just been talking to someone else on the subject, began by inveighing against the attitude which was being adopted in England towards everything German and particularly in respect of the gold held there on behalf of the National Bank of Czecho-Slovakia. Before, however, I had had time to reply, he was called to the telephone and on his return did not revert to this specific question. He complained, instead, of British hostility in general, of our political and economic encirclement of Germany and the activities of what he described as the war party in England, etc.

I told the field-marshal that, before speaking of British hostility, he must understand why the undoubted change of feeling towards Germany in England had taken place. As he knew quite well the basis of all the discussions between Mr Chamberlain and Herr Hitler last year had been to the effect that, once the Sudeten were allowed to enter the Reich, Germany would leave the Czechs alone and would do nothing to interfere with their independence. Herr Hitler had given a definite assurance to that effect in his letter to the Prime Minister of the 27th September. By yielding to the advice of his "wild men" and deliberately annexing Bohemia and Moravia, Herr Hitler had not only broken his word to Mr Chamberlain but had infringed the whole principle of self-determination on which the Munich Agreement rested.

At this point the field-marshal interrupted me with a description of President Hacha's visit to Berlin. I told Field-Marshal Göring that it was not possible to talk of free will when I understood that he himself had threatened to bombard Prague with his aeroplanes, if Dr Hacha refused to sign. The field-marshal did not deny the fact but explained how the point had arisen. According to him Dr Hacha had from the first been prepared to sign everything but had said that constitutionally he could not do so without reference first to Prague. After considerable difficulty telephonic communication with Prague was obtained and the Czech Government had agreed, while adding that they could not guarantee that one Czech battalion at least would not fire on the German troops. It was, he said, only at that stage that he had warned Dr Hacha that, if German lives were lost, he would bombard Prague. The field-marshal also repeated, in reply to some comment of mine, the story that the advance occupation of Witkowitz had been effected solely in order to forestall the Poles who, he said, were known to have the intention of seizing this valuable area at the first opportunity.

I thereupon reminded Field-Marshal Göring that, while I had always appreciated the necessity for the Czechs, in view of their geographical position, to live in the friendliest political and economic relations with Great Germany, he had personally assured me last October that this was all that his

53

Government desired. The precipitate action of Germany on the 15th March, which I again ascribed to the wild men of the party, had consequently, apart from everything and everybody else, been a great shock to me personally and had undone all that I had sought to achieve during my two years at Berlin. Moreover, however indifferent this might seem to him, I could not but regard the destruction of the independence of the Czechs as a major political error, even in Germany's own interests.

The field-marshal appeared a little confused at this personal attack on his own good faith, and assured me that he himself had known nothing of the decision before it had been taken. He would not, he said, have gone to San Remo if he had; nor had his stay there profited him, as he had hoped, owing to the unexpected amount of work which had in consequence been thrust upon him. He then proceeded to give a somewhat unconvincing explanation, though similar to that which Baron von Weizsäcker had furnished me with last March, of the German attempt to come to a satisfactory arrangement with the Czechs and of its failure owing to Czech obstinacy and the revival of what he called the Benes spirit★ as the result of American encouragement.

As my time was limited, I told Field-Marshal Göring that I was well aware of the reasons adduced by his Government to justify its action, but I thought it more important that he himself should understand the British point of view in consequence of it. As the result of the Prague *coup* His Majesty's Government and the British people were determined to resist by force any new aggression. No one desired an amiable arrangement between Germany and Poland in respect of Danzig and the Corridor more than ourselves. But, if Germany endeavoured to settle these questions by unilateral action such as would compel the Poles to resort to arms to safeguard their independence, we and the French as well as other countries would be involved, with all the disastrous consequences which a prolonged world war would entail, especially for Germany, etc. Field-Marshal Göring did not appear to question our readiness to fight and restricted his reply to an attempt to prove that circumstances in 1939 were different to those in 1914, that no Power could overcome Germany in Europe, that a blockade this time would prove unavailing, that France would not stand a long war, that Germany could do more harm to Great Britain than the latter to her, that the history of Germany was one of ups and downs, and that this was one of the "up" periods, that the Poles had no military experience and that their only officers of any value were those who had acquired their training in the German army, that they were not and never had been a really united nation and that, since France and ourselves could not, and Russia out of self-interest would not, give them any effective military assistance, they would be taught a terrible lesson, etc. The field-marshal used, in fact, all the language which might be expected in reply to a statement that Germany was bound

★ Reference to former president of Czecho-Slovakia.

to be defeated. While I was perturbed at his reference to the unreality of Polish unity, which resembled the German arguments last year in regard to Czecho-Slovakia, he gave me the impression, by somewhat over-stating his case, of considerably less confidence than he expressed.

At the end of this tirade, moreover, he asked me whether England, "out of envy of a strong Germany", was really bent on war with her and, if not, what was to be done to prevent it. I said that nobody in their senses could contemplate modern war without horror, but that we should not shrink from it if Germany resorted to another act of aggression. If, therefore, war was to be avoided, patience was necessary and the wild men in Germany must be restrained. Admittedly present-day Germany was in a dynamic condition, whereas England was by tradition the land of compromise. But compromise had its limits, and I did not see how the situation could be saved unless his Government were prepared to wait in order to allow excited spirits to calm down again and negotiations to be resumed in a better atmosphere.

At this point Field-Marshal Göring remarked that if the Poles tried to seize Danzig nothing would stop the Germans from acting at once. As my time was short, I made no comment on this but continued that neither the Prime Minister nor yourself had yet abandoned hope of a peaceful solution either as between Germany and Poland or between Germany and Great Britain, but that everything now entirely depended on Germany's behaviour and actions.

As I had already got up to go, the conversation then took a more amicable turn. Though I was in a hurry, he insisted on showing me with much pride the great structural alterations which he is making to the house at Karinhall and which include a new dining-room to hold an incredible number of guests and to be all of marble and hung with tapestries. He mentioned incidentally that the rebuilding would not be completed before November. He also produced with pride drawings of the tapestries, mostly representing naked ladies labelled with the names of various virtues, such as Goodness, Mercy, Purity etc. I told him that they looked at least pacific, but that I failed to see Patience among them.

NEVILE HENDERSON

GERMAN-POLISH DISCUSSIONS

Extract from Herr Hitler's speech to the Reichstag on 28 *April* 1939
(Translation)

There is little to be said as regards German-Polish relations. Here, too, the Peace Treaty of Versailles—of course intentionally—inflicted a most severe wound on Germany. The strange way in which the Corridor giving Poland access to the sea was marked out was meant, above all, to prevent for all time the establishment of an understanding between Poland and Germany. This problem is—as I have already stressed—perhaps the most painful of all problems for Germany. Nevertheless, I have never ceased to uphold the view that the necessity of a free access to the sea for the Polish State cannot be ignored, and that as a general principle, valid for this case, too, nations which Providence has destined or, if you like, condemned to live side by side would be well advised not to make life still harder for each other artificially and unnecessarily. The late Marshal Pilsudski, who was of the same opinion, was therefore prepared to go into the question of clarifying the atmosphere of German-Polish relations, and, finally, to conclude an agreement whereby Germany and Poland expressed their intention of renouncing war altogether as a means of settling the questions which concerned them both. This agreement contained one single exception which was in practice conceded to Poland. It was laid down that the pacts of mutual assistance already entered into by Poland—this applied to the pact with France—should not be affected by the agreement. But it was obvious that this could apply only to the pact of mutual assistance already concluded beforehand, and not to whatever new pacts might be concluded in the future. It is a fact that the German-Polish Agreement resulted in a remarkable lessening of the European tension. Nevertheless, there remained one open question between

Germany and Poland, which sooner or later quite naturally had to be solved—the question of the German city of Danzig.

Danzig is a German city and wishes to belong to Germany. On the other hand, this city has contracts with Poland, which were admittedly forced upon it by the dictators of the Peace of Versailles. But since, moreover, the League of Nations, formerly the greatest stirrer-up of trouble, is now represented by a High Commissioner—incidentally a man of extraordinary tact—the problem of Danzig must in any case come up for discussion, at the latest with the gradual extinction of this calamitous institution. I regarded the peaceful settlement of this problem as a further contribution to a final loosening of the European tension. For this loosening of the tension is assuredly not to be achieved through the agitations of insane warmongers, but through the removal of the real elements of danger. After the problem of Danzig had already been discussed several times some months ago, I made a concrete offer to the Polish Government. I now make this offer known to you, Gentlemen, and you yourselves will judge whether this offer did not represent the greatest imaginable concession in the interests of European peace. As I have already pointed out, I have always seen the necessity of an access to the sea for this country, and have consequently taken this necessity into consideration. I am no democratic statesman, but a National Socialist and a realist.

I considered it, however, necessary to make it clear to the Government in Warsaw that just as they desire access to the sea, so Germany needs access to her province in the east. Now these are all difficult problems. It is not Germany who is responsible for them, however, but rather the jugglers of Versailles, who either in their maliciousness or their thoughtlessness placed 100 powder barrels round about in Europe, all equipped with hardly extinguishable lighted fuses. These problems cannot be solved according to old-fashioned ideas; I think, rather, that we should adopt new methods. Poland's access to the sea by way of the Corridor, and, on the other hand, a German route through the Corridor have, for example, no kind of military importance whatsoever. Their importance is exclusively psychological and economic. To accord military importance to a traffic route of this kind, would be to show oneself completely ignorant of military affairs. Consequently, I have had the following proposal submitted to the Polish Government:

(1) Danzig returns as a Free State into the framework of the German Reich.
(2) Germany receives a route through the Corridor and a railway line at her own disposal possessing the same extra-territorial status for Germany as the Corridor itself has for Poland.

In return, Germany is prepared:

(1) To recognise all Polish economic rights in Danzig.
(2) To ensure for Poland a free harbour in Danzig of any size desired which would have completely free access to the sea.

(3) To accept at the same time the present boundaries between Germany and Poland and to regard them as ultimate.

(4) To conclude a twenty-five-year non-aggression treaty with Poland, a treaty therefore which would extend far beyond the duration of my own life.

(5) To guarantee the independence of the Slovak State by Germany, Poland and Hungary jointly—which means in practice the renunciation of any unilateral German hegemony in this territory.

The Polish Government have rejected my offer and have only declared that they are prepared (1) to negotiate concerning the question of a substitute for the Commissioner of the League of Nations and (2) to consider facilities for the transit traffic through the Corridor.

I have regretted greatly this incomprehensible attitude of the Polish Government, but that alone is not the decisive fact; the worst is that now Poland, like Czecho-Slovakia a year ago, believes, under the pressure of a lying international campaign, that it must call up troops, although Germany on her part has not called up a single man and had not thought of proceeding in any way against Poland. As I have said, this is in itself very regrettable and posterity will one day decide whether it was really right to refuse this suggestion made this once by me. This—as I have said—was an endeavour on my part to solve a question which intimately affects the German people by a truly unique compromise, and to solve it to the advantage of both countries. According to my conviction Poland was not a giving party in this solution at all but only a receiving party, because it should be beyond all doubt that Danzig will ever become Polish. The intention to attack on the part of Germany, which was merely invented by the international press, led as you know to the so-called guarantee offer and to an obligation on the part of the Polish Government for mutual assistance, which would also, under certain circumstances, compel Poland to take military action against Germany in the event of a conflict between Germany and any other Power and in which England, in her turn, would be involved. This obligation is contradictory to the agreement which I made with Marshal Pilsudski some time ago, seeing that in this agreement reference is made exclusively to existing obligations, that is at that time, namely, to the obligations of Poland towards France of which we were aware. To extend these obligations subsequently is contrary to the terms of the German-Polish non-aggression pact. Under these circumstances I should not have entered into this pact at that time, because what sense can non-aggression pacts have if one partner in practice leaves open an enormous number of exceptions.

There is either collective security, that is collective insecurity and continuous danger of war, or clear agreements which, however, exclude fundamentally any use of arms between the contracting parties. I therefore look upon the agreement which Marshal Pilsudski and I at one time concluded as having been unilaterally infringed by Poland and thereby no longer in existence!

I have sent a communication to this effect to the Polish Government. However, I can only repeat at this point that my decision does not constitute a modification of my attitude in principle with regard to the problems mentioned above. Should the Polish Government wish to come to fresh contractual arrangements governing its relations with Germany, I can but welcome such an idea, provided, of course, that these arrangements are based on an absolutely clear obligation binding both parties in equal measure. Germany is perfectly willing at any time to undertake such obligations and also to fulfil them.

German Government memorandum handed to the Polish Government on 28 April 1939

(Translation)

The German Government have taken note of the Polish–British declaration regarding the progress and aims of the negotiations recently conducted between Poland and Great Britain. According to this declaration there has been concluded between the Polish Government and the British Government a temporary understanding, to be replaced shortly by a permanent agreement which will provide for the giving of mutual assistance by Poland and Great Britain in the event of the independence of one of the two States being directly or indirectly threatened.

The German Government consider themselves obliged to communicate the following to the Polish Government:

When in 1933 the National Socialist Government set about the reshaping of German policy, after Germany's departure from the League of Nations, their first object was to stabilise German–Polish relations on a new plane. The Chancellor of the German Reich and the late Marshal Pilsudski concurred in the decision to break with the political methods of the past and to enter, as regards the settlement of all questions affecting both States, on the path of direct understanding between them.

By means of the unconditional renunciation of the use of force, guarantees of peace were instituted in order to assist the two States in the difficult task of solving all political, economic and cultural problems by means of the just and equitable adjustment of mutual interests. These principles, contained in a binding form in the German–Polish Peace Declaration of the 26th January, 1934, had this aim in view [*sic*] and by their practical success were intended to introduce an entirely new phase of German–Polish relations. The political history of the last five years shows that they proved efficacious in practice for both nations. As recently as the 26th January of this year, on the fifth anniversary of the signature of the declaration, both sides publicly confirmed this fact, while emphasising their united will to maintain in the future their adhesion to the principles established in 1934.

The agreement which has now been concluded by the Polish Government with the British Government is in such obvious contradiction to these solemn declarations of a few months ago that the German

Government can take note only with surprise and astonishment of such a violent reversal of Polish policy. Irrespective of the manner in which its final formulation may be determined by both parties, the new Polish-British Agreement is intended as a regular pact of alliance, which by reason of its general sense and of the present state of political relations is directed exclusively against Germany. From the obligation now accepted by the Polish Government it appears that Poland intends in certain circumstances to take an active part in any possible German-British conflict in the event of aggression against Germany, even should this conflict not affect Poland and her interests. This is a direct and open blow against the renunciation of all use of force contained in the 1934 declaration.

The contradiction between the German-Polish Declaration and the Polish-British Agreement is, however, even more far-reaching in its importance than that. The 1934 declaration was to constitute a basis for the regulation of all differences arising between the two countries, independently of international complications and combinations, by means of direct discussion between Berlin and Warsaw, to the exclusion of external influences. Naturally, such a basis must rest on the mutual confidence of both parties and on the political loyalty of the intentions of one party with regard to the other.

The Polish Government, however, by their recent decision to accede to an alliance directed against Germany, have given it to be understood that they prefer a promise of help by a third Power to the direct guarantee of peace by the German Government. In view of this the German Government are obliged to conclude that the Polish Government do not at present attach any importance to seeking a solution of German-Polish problems by means of direct friendly discussions with the German Government. The Polish Government have thus abandoned the path traced out in 1934 for the shaping of German-Polish relations.

The Polish Government cannot in this connection appeal to the fact that the 1934 declaration was not to affect the obligations previously accepted by Poland and Germany in relation to third parties, and that the Treaty of Alliance between Poland and France maintained its value side by side with that declaration. The Polish-French Alliance already existed in 1934 when Poland and Germany proceeded to reorganise their relations. The German Government were able to accept this fact, since they were entitled to expect that the possible dangers of the Polish-French Alliance, dating from the period of the acutest German-Polish differences, would automatically lose more and more of their significance through the establishment of friendly relations between Germany and Poland. However, the entry of Poland into relations of alliance with Great Britain, which was effected five years after the publication of the declaration of 1934, can for this reason in no way be compared politically with the still valid Polish-French Alliance. By this new alliance the Polish Government have subordinated themselves to a policy inaugurated from another quarter aiming at the encirclement of Germany.

The German Government for their part have not given the least cause for such a change in Polish policy. Whenever opportunity offered, they have furnished the Polish Government, both publicly and in confidential conversations, with the most binding assurances that the friendly development of German-Polish relations is a fundamental aim of their foreign policy, and that, in their political decisions, they will always respect Poland's proper interests. Thus the action taken by Germany in March of this year with a view to the pacification of Central Europe did not, in the opinion of the Government of the Reich, disturb Polish interests in any way. This action led to the creation of a common Polish-Hungarian frontier, which had constantly been described on Poland's side as an important political objective. Moreover, the German Government gave unequivocal expression to their readiness to discuss with the Polish Government in a friendly manner all problems which, in the Polish Government's opinion, might arise out of the changed conditions in Central Europe.

In an equally friendly spirit the German Government tried to regulate yet another question outstanding between Germany and Poland, namely, that of Danzig. The fact that this question required settlement had long been emphasised on the German side, and was not denied on the Polish side. For a long time past the German Government have endeavoured to convince the Polish Government that a solution was certainly possible which would be equitable to the interests of both parties and that the removal of this last obstacle would open a path for a political collaboration of Germany and Poland with the most favourable prospects. In this connection the German Government did not confine themselves to allusions of a general nature, but in March of this year proposed to the Polish Government in a friendly form a settlement of this question on the following basis:

The return of Danzig to the Reich; an extra-territorial railway line and *autostrada* between East Prussia and the Reich; in exchange, the recognition by the Reich of the whole Polish Corridor and the whole of Poland's western frontier; the conclusion of a non-aggression pact for twenty-five years; the maintenance of Poland's economic interests in Danzig and the settlement of the remaining economic and communications problems arising for Poland out of the union of Danzig with the Reich. At the same time, the German Government expressed their readiness to respect Polish interests in ensuring the independence of Slovakia.

Nobody knowing conditions in Danzig and the Corridor and the problems connected therewith can deny, in judging the matter objectively, that this proposal constitutes the very minimum which must be demanded from the point of view of German interests, which cannot be renounced. The Polish Government, however, gave a reply which although couched in the form of counter-proposals, showed in its essence an entire lack of comprehension for the German point of view and was equivalent merely to a rejection of the German proposals. The Polish Government proved that they did not consider their reply suitable for the initiation of friendly discussions by proceeding at the same time, in a manner as unexpected as it was drastic, to effect a partial mobilisation of the Polish army on a large scale. By these entirely unjustified measures, the Polish Government demonstrated the meaning and object of the negotiations which they immediately afterwards entered upon with the British Government. The German Government do not consider it necessary to reply to the partial Polish mobilisation by counter-measures of a military character. They cannot, however, disregard without a word the decisions recently taken by the Polish Government, and are forced, to their own regret, to declare as follows:

(1) The Polish Government did not avail themselves of the opportunity offered to them by the German Government for a just settlement of the Danzig question, for the final safeguarding of Poland's frontiers with the Reich, and thereby for a permanent strengthening of the friendly neighbourly relations between the two countries. The Polish Government even rejected German proposals made with this object.

(2) At the same time the Polish Government accepted, with regard to another State, political obligations which are not compatible either with the spirit, the meaning or the text of the German-Polish Declaration of the 26th January, 1934. Thereby the Polish Government arbitrarily and unilaterally rendered this declaration null and void.

In spite of this necessary statement of fact, the Government of the Reich do not intend to alter their fundamental attitude towards the question of the future of German-Polish relations. Should the Polish Government attach importance to a new settlement of these relations by means of a treaty, the German Government are ready to do this, but on one condition, namely, that such a settlement would have to consist of a clear obligation binding on both parties.

Speech made by M. Beck, the Polish Minister for Foreign Affairs in Parliament on 5 May 1939

(Translation)

The session of the Parliament provides me with an opportunity of filling in some gaps which have occurred in my work of recent months. The course of international events might perhaps justify more statements by a Foreign Minister than my single *exposé* in the Senate Commission for Foreign Affairs.

On the other hand it was precisely that swift development of events that prompted me to postpone a public declaration until such time as the principal problems of our foreign policy had taken on a more definite form.

The consequences of the weakening of collective international institutions and of a complete change in the method of intercourse between nations, which I have reported on several occasions in the Houses, caused many new problems to arise in different parts of the world. That process and its results have in recent months reached the borders of Poland.

A very general definition of these phenomena may be given by saying that relations between individual Powers have taken on a more individual character, with their own specific features. The general rules have been weakened. One nation simply speaks more and more directly to another.

As far as we are concerned, very serious events have taken place. Our contact with some Powers has become easier and more profound, while in some cases serious difficulties have arisen. Looking at things chronologically, I refer, in the first place, to our agreement with the United Kingdom, with Great Britain. After repeated diplomatic contacts, designed to define the scope and object of our future relations, we reached on the occasion of my visit to London a direct agreement based on the principle of mutual assistance in the event of a direct or indirect threat to the independence of one of our countries. The formula of the agreement is known to you from the declaration of Mr Neville Chamberlain of the 6th April, the text of which was drafted by mutual agreement and should be regarded as a pact concluded between the two Governments. I consider it my duty to add that the form and character of the comprehensive conversations held in London give a particular value to the agreement. I should like Polish public opinion to be aware that I found on the part of British statesmen not only a profound knowledge of the general political problems of Europe, but also such an attitude towards our country as permitted me to discuss all vital problems with frankness and confidence without any reservations or doubts.

It was possible to establish rapidly the principles of Polish-British collaboration, first of all because we made it clear to each other that the intentions of both Governments coincide as regards fundamental European problems; certainly, neither Great Britain nor Poland have any aggressive intentions whatever, but they stand equally firmly in defence of certain basic principles of conduct in international life.

The parallel declarations of French political leaders confirm that it is agreed between Paris and Warsaw that the efficacy of our defence pact not only cannot be adversely affected by changes in the international situation, but, on the contrary, that this agreement should constitute one of the most essential elements in the political structure of Europe. The Polish-British Agreement has been employed by the Chancellor of the German Reich as the pretext for unilaterally declaring non-existent the agreement which the Chancellor of the Reich concluded with us in 1934.

Before passing to the present stage of this matter, allow me to sketch a brief historical outline.

The fact that I had the honour actively to participate in the conclusion and execution of that pact imposes on me the duty of analysing it. The pact of 1934 was a great event in 1934. It was an attempt to improve the course of history as between two great nations, an attempt to escape from the unwholesome atmosphere of daily discord and wider hostile intentions, to rise above the animosity which had accumulated for centuries, and to create deep foundations of mutual respect. An endeavour to oppose evil is always the best form of political activity.

The policy of Poland proved our respect for that principle in the most critical moments of recent times.

From this point of view, Gentlemen, the breaking off of that pact is not an insignificant matter. However, every treaty is worth as much as the consequences which follow it. And if the policy and conduct of the other party diverges from the principles of the pact, we have no reason for mourning its slackening or dissolution. The Polish-German Pact of 1934 was a treaty of mutual respect and good neighbourly relations, and as such it contributed a positive value to the life of our country, of Germany and of the whole of Europe. But since there has appeared a tendency to interpret it as limiting the freedom of our policy, or as a ground for demanding from us unilateral concessions contrary to our vital interests, it has lost its real character.

Let us now pass to the present situation. The German Reich has taken the mere fact of the Polish-British understanding as a motive for the breaking off of the pact of 1934. Various legal objections were raised on the German side. I will take the liberty of referring jurists to the text of our reply to the German memorandum, which will be handed today to the German Government. I will not detain you any longer on the diplomatic form of this event, but one of its aspects has a special significance. The Reich Government, as appears from the text of the German memorandum, made its decision on the strength of press reports, without consulting the views of either the British or the Polish Government as to the character of the agreement concluded. It would not have been difficult to do so, for immediately on my return from London I expressed my readiness to receive the German Ambassador, who has hitherto not availed himself of the opportunity.

Why is this circumstance important? Even for the simplest understanding it is clear that neither the character nor the purpose and scope of the agreement influenced this decision, but merely the fact that such an agreement had been concluded. And this in turn is important for an appreciation of the objects of German policy, since if, contrary to previous declarations, the Government of the Reich interpreted the Polish-German declaration of non-aggression of 1934 as intended to isolate Poland and to prevent the normal friendly collaboration of our country with Western Powers, we ourselves should always have rejected such an interpretation.

To make a proper estimate of the situation, we should first of all ask the question, what is the real object of all this? Without that question and our reply, we cannot properly appreciate the character of German statements with regard to matters of concern to Poland. I have already referred to our attitude towards the West. There remains the question of the German proposals as to the future of the Free City of Danzig, the communication of the Reich with East Prussia through our province of Pomorze, and the further subjects raised as of common interest to Poland and Germany.

Let us, therefore, investigate these problems in turn.

As to Danzig, first some general remarks. The Free City of Danzig was not invented by the Treaty of Versailles. It has existed for many centuries as the result—to speak accurately, and rejecting the emotional factor—of the positive interplay of Polish and German interests. The German merchants of Danzig ensured the development and prosperity of that city, thanks to the overseas trade of Poland. Not only the development, but the very *raison d'être* of the city has been due to the formerly decisive fact of its situation at the mouth of our only great river, and today to its position on the main waterway and railway line connecting us with the Baltic. This is a truth which no new formulae can obliterate. The population of Danzig is today predominantly German, but its livelihood and prosperity depend on the economic potential of Poland.

What conclusions have we drawn from this fact? We have stood and stand firmly on the ground of the rights and interests of our sea-borne trade and our maritime policy in Danzig. While seeking reasonable and conciliatory solutions, we have purposely not endeavoured to exert any pressure on the free national, ideological and cultural development of the German majority in the Free City.

I shall not prolong this speech by quoting examples. They are sufficiently well-known to all who have been in any way concerned with the question. But when, after repeated statements by German statesmen, who had respected our standpoint and expressed the view that "this provincial town will not be the object of a conflict between Poland and Germany", I hear a demand for the annexation of Danzig to the Reich, when I receive no reply to our proposal of the 26th March for a joint guarantee of the existence and rights of the Free City, and subsequently I learn that this has been regarded as a rejection of negotiations—I have to ask myself, what is the real object of all this?

Is it the freedom of the German population of Danzig, which is not threatened, or a matter of prestige—or is it a matter of barring Poland from the Baltic, from which Poland will not allow herself to be barred?

The same considerations apply to communication across our province of Pomorze. I insist on the term "province of Pomorze". The word "corridor" is an artificial invention, for this is an ancient Polish territory with an insignificant percentage of German colonists.

We have given the German Reich all railway facilities, we have allowed its citizens to travel without customs or passport formalities from the Reich to East Prussia. We have suggested the extension of similar facilities to road traffic.

And here again the question arises—what is the real object of it all?

We have no interest in obstructing German citizens in their communication with their eastern province. But we have, on the other hand, no reason whatever to restrict our sovereignty on our own territory.

On the first and second points, *i.e.*, the question of the future of Danzig and of communication across Pomorze, it is still a matter of unilateral concessions which the Government of the Reich appear to be demanding from us. A self-respecting nation does not make unilateral concessions. Where, then, is the reciprocity? It appears somewhat vague in the German proposals. The Chancellor of the Reich mentioned in his speech a triple condominium in Slovakia. I am obliged to state that I heard this proposal for the first time in the Chancellor's speech of the 28th April. In certain previous conversations allusions were merely made to the effect that in the event of a general agreement the question of Slovakia could be discussed. We did not attempt to go further with such conversations, since it is not our custom to bargain with the interests of others. Similarly, the proposal for a prolongation of the pact of non-aggression for twenty-five years was also not advanced in any concrete form in any of the recent conversations. Here also unofficial hints were made, emanating, it is true, from prominent representatives of the Reich Government. But in such conversations various other hints were made which extended much further than the subjects under discussion. I reserve the right to return to this matter if necessary.

In his speech the Chancellor of the Reich proposes, as a concession on his part, the recognition and definite acceptance of the present frontier between Poland and Germany. I must point out that this would have been a question of recognising what is *de jure* and *de facto* [by right and in fact] our indisputable property. Consequently, this proposal likewise cannot affect my contention that the German desiderata [wishes] regarding Danzig and a motor road constitute unilateral demands.

In the light of these explanations, the House will rightly expect from me an answer to the last passage of the German memorandum, which says: "Should the Polish Government attach importance to a new settlement of Polish-German relations by means of a treaty, the German Government are prepared to do this." It appears to me that I have already made clear our attitude, but for the sake of order I will make a résumé.

The motive for concluding such an agreement would be the word "peace", which the Chancellor emphasised in his speech.

Peace is certainly the object of the difficult and intensive work of Polish diplomacy. Two conditions are necessary for this word to be of real value: (1) peaceful intentions, (2) peaceful methods of procedure. If the Government of the Reich is really guided by those two pre-conditions in relation to this country, then all conversations, provided, of course, that they respect the principles I have already enumerated, are possible.

If such conversations took place, the Polish Government will, according to their custom, approach the problem objectively, having regard to the experience of recent times, but without withholding their utmost goodwill.

Peace is a valuable and desirable thing. Our generation, which has shed its blood in several wars, surely deserves a period of peace. But peace, like almost everything in this world, has its price, high but definable. We in Poland do not recognise the conception of "peace at any price". There is only one thing in the life of men, nations and States which is without price, and that is honour.

Memorandum communicated to the German Government by the Polish
Government on 5 May 1939, in reply to the German Government memorandum
of 28 April 1939

(Translation)

As appears from the text of the Polish–German Declaration of the 26th January, 1934, and from the course of the negotiations which preceded its conclusion, this declaration had as its object to lay the foundations for a new framing of mutual relations based on the following two principles:

(a) The renunciation of the use of force as between Poland and Germany, and

(b) The friendly settlement by means of free negotiations of any contentious questions which might arise in the relations between the two countries.

The Polish Government have always understood in this manner their obligations under the declaration, and it is in this spirit that they have always been prepared to conduct neighbourly relations with the German Reich.

The Polish Government had foreseen for several years that the difficulties encountered by the League of Nations in carrying out its functions at Danzig would create a confused situation which it was in Poland's and Germany's interest to unravel. For several years the Polish Government had given the German Government to understand that frank conversations should be held on this subject. The German Government, however, avoided these and confined themselves to stating that Polish–German relations should not be exposed to difficulties by questions relating to Danzig. Moreover, the German Government more than once gave assurances to the Polish Government regarding the Free City of Danzig. It is sufficient here to quote the declaration made by the Chancellor of the Reich on the 20th February, 1938.

The Chancellor made publicly in the Reichstag the following declaration regarding Danzig:

> The Polish State respects the national conditions in this State, and the Free City and Germany respect Polish rights. It has thus been possible to clear the way for an understanding which, while arising out of the question of Danzig, has today in spite of the efforts of certain disturbers of the peace succeeded in effectively purifying relations between Germany and Poland and has transformed them into sincere and friendly collaboration.

It was only after the events of September, 1938, that the German Government suggested the opening of Polish–German conversations regarding the alteration in the situation in Danzig and regarding the transit routes between the Reich and East Prussia. In this connexion the German memorandum of the 28th April, 1939, refers to the suggestion put forward by the Reich Minister for Foreign Affairs in his conversation of the 21st March, 1939, with the Polish Ambassador in Berlin. In this conversation emphasis was laid on the German side on the necessity for a rapid settlement of these questions which was a condition of the Reich maintaining its proposals in force in their entirety. The Polish Government, animated by the desire to maintain good relations with the Reich, although surprised at the pressing form in which these proposals were put forward, and by the circumstances in which they were advanced, did not refuse conversations although they considered the German demands thus couched to be unacceptable.

In order to facilitate endeavours to reach an amicable solution of the question, the Polish Government on the 26th March, 1939, formulated their point of view in writing to the German Government, stating that they attached full importance to the maintenance of good neighbourly relations with the German Reich. The Polish point of view was summarised in the following points:

(a) The Polish Government propose a joint guarantee by Poland and Germany of the separate character of the Free City of Danzig, the existence of which was to be based on complete freedom of the local population in internal affairs and on the assurance of respect for Polish rights and interests.

(b) The Polish Government were prepared to examine together with the German Government any further simplifications for persons in transit as well as the technical facilitating of railway and motor transit between the German Reich and East Prussia. The Polish Government were inspired by the idea of giving every possible facility which would permit the citizens of the Reich to travel in transit across Polish territory, if possible without any hindrances. The Polish Government emphasised that their intention was to secure the most liberal treatment possible of the German desiderata in this respect with the sole reservation that Poland could not give up her sovereignty over the belt of territory through which the transit routes would run. Finally, the Polish Government indicated that their attitude in the question of facilitating communications across Pomerania depended on the attitude of the Reich regarding the Free City of Danzig.

In formulating the above proposals the Polish Government acted in the spirit of the Polish-German Declaration of 1934 which, by providing the direct exchanges of views on questions of interest to both countries, authorised each State to formulate its point of view in the course of negotiations.

The Polish Government received no formal reply to their counter-proposals for a month, and it was only on the 28th April, 1939, that they learnt from the Chancellor's speech and from the German Government's memorandum that the mere fact of the formulation of counter-proposals instead of the acceptance of the verbal German suggestions without alteration or reservation had been regarded by the Reich as a refusal of discussions.

It is clear that negotiations in which one State formulates demands and the other is to be obliged to accept those demands unaltered are not negotiations in the spirit of the declaration of 1934 and are incompatible with the vital interests and dignity of Poland.

In this connection it should be pointed out that the Polish Government were unable at that time to express an opinion regarding the Polish–German–Hungarian guarantee of the independence of Slovakia which was alluded to in a general way in the German memorandum and more precisely stated in the Chancellor's speech of the 28th April, 1939, since a proposal of this description and in this form had never been made to them before. It is, moreover, difficult to imagine how such guarantee could be reconciled with the political and military protectorate of the Reich over Slovakia which had been announced a few days previously before the German Reich formulated its proposals towards Poland.

The Polish Government cannot accept such an interpretation of the declaration of 1934 as would be equivalent to a renunciation of the right to conclude political agreements with third States and, consequently, almost a renunciation of independence in foreign policy. The policy of the German Reich in recent years has clearly indicated that the German Government have not drawn conclusions of this sort from the declaration as far as they themselves were concerned. The obligations publicly accepted by the Reich towards Italy and the German–Slovak Agreement of March, 1939, are clear indications of such an interpretation by the German Government of the declaration of 1934. The Polish Government must here recall that in their relations with other States they give and require full reciprocity as being the only possible foundation of normal relations between States.

The Polish Government reject as completely without foundation all accusations regarding the alleged incompatibility of the Anglo–Polish Mutual Guarantee of April, 1939, with the Polish–German Declaration of 1934. This guarantee has a purely defensive character and in no way threatens the German Reich, in the same way as the Polish–French Alliance, whose compatibility with the Declaration of 1934 has been recognised by the German Reich. The declaration of 1934 in its introductory paragraphs clearly stated that both Governments have "decided to base their mutual relations on the principles laid down in the Pact of Paris of the 27th August, 1928." Now the Pact of Paris, which constituted a general renunciation of war as an instrument of national policy, just as the declaration of 1934 constituted such renunciation in bilateral Polish–German relations, contained the explicit reservation that "any signatory Power which shall hereafter seek to promote its national interests by resort to war should be denied the benefits furnished by this treaty." Germany accepted this principle in signing the Pact of Paris and re-affirmed it in the declaration of 1934, together with other principles of the Pact of Paris. It appears from this that the declaration of 1934 would cease to be binding on Poland should Germany have recourse to war in violation of the Pact of Paris. Poland's obligations arising out of the Polish–British understanding would come into operation in the event of German action threatening the independence of Great Britain, and, consequently, in the very circumstances in which the declaration of 1934 and the Pact of Paris had ceased to be binding on Poland as regards Germany.

The German Government in making a complaint against the Polish Government for undertaking obligations to guarantee the independence of Great Britain and in regarding this as a violation by Poland of the declaration of 1934, ignore their own obligations towards Italy of which the Chancellor spoke on the 30th January, 1939, and in particular their obligations towards Slovakia contained in the agreement of the 18th and 23rd March, 1939. The German guarantees of Slovakia did not exclude Poland [*sic*], and, indeed, as appears from the provisions of the above agreement regarding the distribution of garrisons and military fortifications in Western Slovakia, were directed primarily against Poland.

It appears from the above that the Government of the German Reich had no justification for their unilateral decision to regard the declaration of 1934 as not binding. The pact was, indeed, concluded for ten years without any possibility of denunciation during that time. It should be pointed out that the decision to regard the 1934 Declaration as not binding took place after the previous refusal of the German State to accept explanations as to the compatibility of the Anglo-Polish guarantee with the 1934 Declaration, which it was the intention of the Polish Government to furnish to the representative of the Reich in Warsaw.

Although the Polish Government do not share the view of the German Government that the treaty of 1934 has been violated by Poland, nevertheless, should the German Government attach importance to the fresh regulation, by means of a treaty, of Polish-German relations on a good neighbourly basis, the Polish Government would be prepared to entertain suggestions of this kind with the reservation of their fundamental observations contained above in the present memorandum.

ANGLO-POLISH AGREEMENT

Statement by the Prime Minister in the House of Commons on 31 March 1939

The Prime Minister (Mr Chamberlain): The right hon. gentleman the leader of the Opposition asked me this morning whether I could make a statement as to the European situation. As I said this morning. His Majesty's Government have no official confirmation of the rumours of any projected attack on Poland and they must not, therefore, be taken as accepting them as true.

I am glad to take this opportunity of stating again the general policy of His Majesty's Government. They have constantly advocated the adjustment, by way of free negotiation between the parties concerned, of any differences that may arise between them. They consider that this is the natural and proper course where differences exist. In their opinion there should be no question incapable of solution by peaceful means, and they would see no justification for the substitution of force or threats of force for the method of negotiation.

As the House is aware, certain consultations are now proceeding with other Governments. In order to make perfectly clear the position of His Majesty's Government in the meantime before those consultations are concluded, I now have to inform the House that during that period, in the event of any action which clearly threatened Polish independence, and which the Polish Government accordingly considered it vital to resist with their national forces, His Majesty's Government would feel themselves bound at once to lend the Polish Government all support in their power. They have given the Polish Government an assurance to this effect.

I may add that the French Government have authorised me to make it plain that they stand in the same position in this matter as do His Majesty's Government.

Anglo-Polish communiqué issued on 6 April 1939

The conversations with M. Beck have covered a wide field and shown that the two Governments are in complete agreement upon certain general principles. It was agreed that the two countries were prepared to enter into an agreement of a permanent and reciprocal character to replace the present temporary and unilateral assurance given by His Majesty's Government to the Polish Government. Pending the completion of the permanent agreement, M. Beck gave His Majesty's Government an assurance that the Polish Government would consider themselves under an obligation to render assistance to His Majesty's Government under the same conditions as those contained in the temporary assurance already given by His Majesty's Government to Poland.

Like the temporary assurance, the permanent agreement would not be directed against any other country but would be designed to assure Great Britain and Poland of mutual assistance in the event of any threat, direct or indirect, to the independence of either. It was recognised that certain matters, including a more precise definition of the various ways in which the necessity for such assistance might arise, would require further examination before the permanent agreement could be completed.

It was understood that the arrangements above mentioned should not preclude either Government from making agreements with other countries in the general interest of the consolidation of peace.

Agreement of Mutual Assistance between the United Kingdom and Poland
London, 25 August 1939

The Government of the United Kingdom of Great Britain and Northern Ireland and the Polish Government:

Desiring to place on a permanent basis the collaboration between their respective countries resulting from the assurances of mutual assistance of a defensive character which they have already exchanged, have resolved to conclude an Agreement for that purpose and have appointed as their Plenipotentiaries:

The Government of the United Kingdom of Great Britain and Northern Ireland:
The Rt Hon Viscount Halifax, KG, GCSI, GCIE, Principal Secretary of State for Foreign Affairs;

The Polish Government:
His Excellency Count Edward Raczynski, Ambassador Extraordinary and Plenipotentiary of the Polish Republic in London;

Who, having exchanged their Full Powers, found in good and due form, have agreed on the following provisions:

ARTICLE 1

Should one of the Contracting Parties become engaged in hostilities with a European Power in consequence of aggression by the latter against that Contracting Party, the other Contracting Party will at once give the Contracting Party engaged in hostilities all the support and assistance in its power.

ARTICLE 2

(1) The provisions of Article 1 will also apply in the event of any action by a European Power which clearly threatened, directly or indirectly, the independence of one of the Contracting Parties, and was of such a nature that the Party in question considered it vital to resist it with its armed forces.

(2) Should one of the Contracting Parties become engaged in hostilities with a European Power in consequence of action by that Power which threatened the independence or neutrality of another European State in such a way as to constitute a clear menace to the security of that Contracting Party, the provisions of Article 1 will apply, without prejudice, however, to the rights of the other European State concerned.

ARTICLE 3

Should a European Power attempt to undermine the independence of one of the Contracting Parties by processes of economic penetration or in any other way, the Contracting Parties will support each other in resistance to such attempts. Should the European Power concerned thereupon embark on hostilities against one of the Contracting Parties, the provisions of Article 1 will apply.

ARTICLE 4

The methods of applying the undertakings of mutual assistance provided for by the present Agreement are established between the competent naval, military and air authorities of the Contracting Parties.

ARTICLE 5

Without prejudice to the foregoing undertakings of the Contracting Parties to give each other mutual support and assistance immediately on the outbreak of hostilities, they will exchange complete and speedy information concerning any development which might threaten their independence and, in particular, concerning any development which threatened to call the said undertakings into operation.

ARTICLE 6

(1) The Contracting Parties will communicate to each other the terms of any undertakings of assistance against aggression which they have already given or may in future give to other States.

(2) Should either of the Contracting Parties intend to give such an undertaking after the coming into force of the present Agreement, the other Contracting Party shall, in order to ensure the proper functioning of the Agreement, be informed thereof.

(3) Any new undertaking which the Contracting Parties may enter into in future shall neither limit their obligations under the present Agreement nor indirectly create new obligations between the Contracting Party not participating in these undertakings and the third State concerned.

ARTICLE 7

Should the Contracting Parties be engaged in hostilities in consequence of the application of the present Agreement, they will not conclude an armistice or treaty of peace except by mutual agreement.

ARTICLE 8

(1) The present Agreement shall remain in force for a period of five years.

(2) Unless denounced six months before the expiry of this period it shall continue in force, each Contracting Party having thereafter the right to denounce it at any time by giving six months' notice to that effect.

(3) The present Agreement shall come into force on signature.

In faith whereof the above-named Plenipotentiaries have signed the present Agreement and have affixed thereto their seals.

Done in English in duplicate, at London, the 25th August, 1939. A Polish text shall subsequently be agreed upon between the Contracting Parties and both texts will then be authentic.

HALIFAX

EDWARD RACZYNSKI

DEVELOPMENTS IN ANGLO-GERMAN RELATIONS

Speech by Herr Hitler at Wilhelmshaven on 1 *April* 1939
(Translation)
Germans! Volksgenossen und Volksgenossinnen!

Whoever wishes to estimate the decline and regeneration of Germany must look at the development of a city like Wilhelmshaven. A short time ago it was a dead spot almost without any title to existence, without any prospect of a future; today it is filled again with the hum of work and production. It is good if one recalls again to memory this past.

When the city experienced its first rise to prosperity, this coincided with the regeneration of the German Reich after its battle for unification. This Germany was a Germany of peace. At the same time as the so-called peace-loving virtuous nations were carrying on quite a number of wars, the Germany of that time had only one aim, namely, to preserve peace, to work in peace, to increase the prosperity of her inhabitants and thereby to contribute to human culture and civilisation.

This peace-time Germany tried with unceasing industry, with genius and with perseverance to set up its inner life and to assure for itself a proper place in the sun through participation in peaceful rivalry with other nations.

In spite of the fact that this Germany was for decades the surest guarantor of peace and devoted herself only to her own peaceful business, other nations, and particularly their statesmen, could not refrain from persecuting this regeneration with envy and hate and finally answering it with a war.

We know today from historical records how the encirclement policy of that time had been systematically pursued by England. We know from numerous established facts and publications that in that land one was imbued with the conception that it was necessary to crush Germany militarily because its annihilation would assure to every British citizen a larger measure of this world's goods.

Certainly Germany at that time committed errors. Its worst error was to see this encirclement and to take no steps in time to avoid it. The only reproach which we can level at the régime of that day is the fact that it had full knowledge of the devilish plan for a surprise attack on the Reich, and even so was unable to make up its mind to avoid in time such an attack, but allowed this encirclement to mature right up to the outbreak of the catastrophe.

The result was the World War.

In this war the German people, although they were in no way armed the best, fought heroically. No nation can claim for itself the glory of having beaten us to our knees, least of all those whose statesmen today are boasting.

Germany at that time remained unbeaten and unvanquished on land, sea and in the air. And yet we lost the war. We know the power which at that time vanquished Germany. It was the power of falsehood, the poison of a propaganda which did not shrink from distortion and untruthfulness and which caught the German Reich because it was unprepared and defenceless.

When the Fourteen Points of President Wilson were announced many German "*Volksgenossen*", particularly the leading men of the time, saw in those Fourteen Points not only the possibility for ending the World War but for a final pacification of all nations of this world. There would come a peace of reconciliation and understanding, a peace which would recognise neither victors nor vanquished, a peace without war indemnities, a peace of equal rights for all, a peace of equal distribution of colonial territory and of equal consideration for colonial desiderata. A peace which would finally be crowned with a league of free nations. A peace which, by guaranteeing equal rights would make it appear superfluous for nations in future still to endure the burden of armament which, as is known, previously weighed down so heavily on them.

Disarmament, therefore, and in fact disarmament of all nations.

Germany was to give a good example by taking the lead and all undertook to follow her disarmament.

The era of so-called secret diplomacy was to come to an end as well. All problems were to be discussed and negotiated openly and freely.

The right of self-determination for nations was to be finally established and be regarded as the most important factor.

Germany believed these assurances. Relying on these declarations Germany laid down her weapons. And then a breach of faith began such as world history has never seen.

At the moment when our people had laid down their arms a period of blackmail, oppression, pillage and slavery began.

No longer any word of peace without victors and vanquished, but a sentence of condemnation for the vanquished for time without end.

No longer any word of equal rights, but rights for one side and absence of rights and injustice for the other. One robbery after another, one blackmail after another were the results.

No man in this democratic world bothered about the suffering of our people. Hundreds of thousands fell in the war, not through enemy action, but through the hunger blockade. And when the war came to an end this blockade was continued still for months in order to bring still further pressure on our nation. Even the German prisoners of war had to remain in captivity for indefinite periods. The German colonies were stolen from us, German foreign securities were simply confiscated, and our mercantile marine was taken away.

Then came financial pillage such as the world has never up to this day seen. Payments were imposed on the German people which reached astronomical figures, and about which English statesmen said that they could only be effected if the whole German nation reduced its standard of living to the utmost and worked fourteen hours a day.

What German spirit and German diligence had created and saved in decades was now lost in a few years. Millions of Germans were torn away from the Reich, others were prevented from returning into the Reich. The League of Nations was made not an instrument of a just policy of understanding, but a guarantor of the meanest dictate that human beings had ever thought out.

A great people were thus raped and led towards the misery that all of you know. A great people were deprived of their rights by breach of promise and their existence in practice was made impossible. A French statesman gave sober expression to this by declaring: "There are 20 million Germans too many in the world!"

There were Germans who, in despair, committed suicide, others who lethargically submitted to their inevitable fate, and others again who were of the opinion that there was nothing left to do but to destroy everything; others again ground their teeth and clenched their fists in impotent rage, others again believed that the past must be restored as it had been.

Every individual had adopted some sort of attitude. And I at that time, as the unknown soldier of the World War, took up my position.

It was a short and simple programme; it ran: removal of the domestic enemies of the nation, termination of the internal division of Germany, co-ordination of the entire national force of our people in a new community, and the smashing of the Peace Treaty in one way or another ("*so oder so!*"). For as long as this dictate of Versailles weighed upon the German people, it was actually doomed to go under.

When other statesmen talk about the necessity of justice reigning in this world, then I may tell them that their crime is not justice, that their dictate was neither rightful nor legal, and that the permanent vital rights of peoples come before this dictate.

The German people were created by Providence, not in order to obey a law which suits Englishmen or Frenchmen, but to stand up for their vital rights. That is what we are there for!

I was determined to take up this struggle for standing up for German vital rights. I took it up first of all within the nation. The place of a number of parties, classes and associations has now been taken by one single community, the community of the German people!

It is the duty of us all to realise this community and to continue to intensify it. In the course of this time I have had to hurt many an individual. But I believe that the happiness shared today by the entire nation must more than compensate every individual for the things which were dear to him and which he individually had to give up.

You have all sacrificed your parties, your clubs, your associations, but you have instead received a great and strong Reich!

And this Reich is today, thank God, sufficiently strong to take under its protection your rights. We are now no longer dependent upon the favour or disfavour of other States or their statesmen.

When over six years ago I came into power, I took over a pitiful heritage. The Reich appeared to possess no possibilities for existence for its citizens. At that time I began work with the only capital which I possessed. It was the capital of your power to work! It was your power to work, my "*Volksgenossen*", that I began to put into use. I had no foreign exchange and no gold; I only had one thing: my faith and your work! We have now founded a new economic system, a system which is called: capital is power to work, and money is covered by our production. We have founded a system based upon the most noble principle in existence, namely, form your life yourself! Work for your existence! Help yourself, then God will also help you!

We thus began a gigantic work of reconstruction, supported by the confidence of the nation, filled with faith and confidence in its permanent values. In a few years we tore Germany from its despair. The world did not help us in doing so!

If an English statesman today believes that all problems can and must be solved by frank discussion and negotiations, then I would like to say to this statesman: an opportunity to do so existed for fifteen years before our time! If the world today says that one must divide the nations into virtuous and non-virtuous categories—and that the English and French belong in the first place to the virtuous nations and the Germans and Italians to the non-virtuous—then we can only answer: the decision as to whether a nation is virtuous or not virtuous can hardly be made by a mortal human being, and should be left to God!

Perhaps this same British statesman will reply: God has already delivered judgment, for he has given to the virtuous nations one-quarter of the globe and has taken away everything from the non-virtuous! In answer to that, one may be permitted to ask: by what means have the virtuous nations acquired this quarter of the globe? And the answer must be, they have not been virtuous methods!

For 300 years this England has acted only as an unvirtuous nation, and now in old age she is beginning to talk about virtue. It was thus possible that

during the British non-virtuous period 46 million Englishmen have conquered almost a quarter of the world, while 80 million Germans, on account
of their virtue, have to exist at the rate of 140 to the square kilometre.

Yes, twenty years ago the question of virtue was not yet quite clear in
the minds of British statesmen, in so far as it touched conceptions of property. At that time it was still thought to be compatible with virtue simply to
take away from another people the colonies which it had acquired by con-
tract or by purchase because one had the power to do so.

A power which now it is true is to count as something disgusting and
contemptible. In this respect, I can only say one thing to these gentlemen:
we do not know whether they believe that sort of thing themselves or not.
We assume, however, that they do not believe it. For if we were to assume
that they really believed it themselves, then we would lose every feeling of
respect for them.

For fifteen years Germany had borne this fate patiently. I also tried at the
beginning to solve every problem by discussion. At every problem I made
offers, and they were every time refused! There can be no doubt that every
people possesses sacred interests, simply because they are identical with its
life and its vital right.

If a British statesman today demands that every problem concerning
vital German interests should first be discussed with England, then I could
make precisely the same claim and demand that every British problem must
first be discussed with us. Admittedly, this Englishman would answer:
Palestine is none of your business! But, just as Germany has no business in
Palestine, so has England no business in the German *Lebensraum!*★ And if the
problem is claimed to be a question of general rights, then I can only agree
to this opinion if it were regarded as universal and obligatory. One says we
had no right to do this or that. I would like to ask a counter-question: what
right—just to quote only one example—has England to shoot down Arabs
in Palestine, only because they are standing up for their home? Who gives
England the right to do so?

We at any rate have not slaughtered thousands in Central Europe, but
have solved our problems in a peaceful and orderly manner! There is one
thing, however, that I must say: the German people of today, the German
Reich of the present time, are not willing to sacrifice vital interests, and they
are also not willing to stand up to rising dangers without taking action!
When the allies at one time changed the map of Europe with no consideration for expediency, justice, tradition or even common sense, we did not
have the power to prevent them from doing so. But if they expect the
Germany of the present day patiently to allow vassal [subordinate] States,
whose only duty consists in their being set to work against Germany, to
carry on as they like until the day comes when their services are to be
actively employed, then they are confounding present-day Germany with

★ *Lebensraum*: literally, territory for natural expansion.

the Germany of pre-war days. Those who declare that they are prepared to pull chestnuts out of the fire for these Great Powers must also expect to burn their fingers in the course of the process.

We have really no feelings of hatred for the Czech people, we have lived together for years. English statesmen do not know that. They have no idea that the Hradschin was built not by an Englishman but by Germans, and that the St Veit's Cathedral was also not built by Englishmen but by Germans. Frenchmen also were not active there. They do not know that already, at a time when England was still very small, homage was done to a German Emperor on this hill, and that, a thousand years before I did so myself, the first German King stood there and received the homage of this people. This the English do not know, they cannot know it and they need not know it.

It is sufficient that we know it, and that it is true that for a thousand years this area belonged to the *Lebensraum* of the German people. We would, nevertheless, have had nothing against an independent Czech State if this State had not, firstly, oppressed Germans, and, secondly, if it had not been an instrument for a future attack on Germany.

But when a former French Air Minister writes in a newspaper that it is the task of this Czechia, because of her splendid geographical position, to strike at Germany's industry by air attacks in a war, then one will understand that it is not without interest to us, and that we drew certain conclusions therefrom.

It would have been a matter for England and France to defend this air base. It was our affair, at any rate, to prevent the possibility of such an attack taking place. I believed that I could achieve this end in a natural and simple way. It was not until I saw that such an attempt was doomed to fail, and that the anti-German elements would once more gain the upper hand, and it was not until I also saw that this State had for a long time lost its inner capacity to live and that it had already collapsed, that I re-enforced ancient German right and reunited what had to be united by history, geographical position and all rules of common sense.

Not for the purpose of suppressing the Czech people! They will have more freedom than the oppressed peoples of the virtuous nations!

I have, so I believe, thereby rendered a great service to peace, for I have in good time made valueless an instrument that was designed to become effective in time of war against Germany.

If people now say that this is the signal for Germany's desire to attack the whole world, then I do not believe they mean it seriously; such a statement could only be the expression of the very worst of consciences. Perhaps it is anger at the failure of a far-reaching plan; perhaps it is belief that the premises can thereby be created for a new policy of encirclement? Whatever the case may be, I am convinced that I have thereby rendered a great service to peace.

And it is from this conviction that I determined three weeks ago to give the coming Party Rally the name of "Party Rally of Peace". For Germany does not dream of attacking other nations.

What we do not, however, desire to renounce is the extension of our economic relations. To this we have a right, and I do not accept orders in this respect from any statesman inside or outside Europe!

The German Reich is not only a great producer, but also a tremendous consumer. In the same way as we become an irreplaceable commercial partner as consumer, so are we suited as a producer honestly to pay for what we consume.

We do not dream of waging war on other nations, subject, of course, to their leaving us in peace also. The German Reich is, however, in no case prepared permanently to tolerate intimidation, or even a policy of encirclement.

I once concluded an agreement with England—the Naval Agreement. It is based on the ardent desire, shared by us all, never to be forced to fight a war against England. This desire can, however, only be a reciprocal one. If it no longer exists in England, then the practical premises for the agreement have been removed. Germany would accept even a situation of this kind with calm composure! We are so sure of ourselves because we are strong, and we are strong because we are united, and also because we keep our eyes open! And in this town more than elsewhere I can only urge you to look at the world and all happenings therein around us with open eyes. Do not deceive yourselves regarding the most important prerequisite which exists in life, namely, the necessary power at one's own disposal. He who does not possess power loses the right to live! We have had fifteen years' experience of such a condition. That is why I have made Germany strong again and why I have created a defence force on land, on the waters and in the air.

But when there is talk in other countries of present rearmament and of continued and still greater rearmament, then I can only say to these statesmen: it will not be me whom they will tire out!

I am determined to continue to march along this road, and I am convinced that we shall advance faster than the others. No Power in the world will ever wheedle our arms from us by mere words. But should anyone at any time show any desire to measure his strength against ours by force, then the German people will always be in a position and ready and determined to do the same!

And our friends think just as we do, especially the State with which we are closely bound and with which we march, now, and in all circumstances, and for all time. When hostile journalists do not know what else to write about, then they write of cracks in the Axis. They can be at ease.

This Axis is the most natural political instrument in the world. It is a political combination of ideas which owes its existence not only to reason and the desire for justice, but also to strength inspired by idealism.

This structure will hold out better than the present alliances of non-homogeneous bodies on the other side. For if anybody tells me today that there are no differences in world outlook or ideologies between England and Soviet Russia, I can only say: I congratulate you, Gentlemen.

I believe we shall not have long to wait before we see that the unity in world outlook between Fascist Italy and National Socialist Germany is, after all, different from that between democratic Great Britain and the Bolshevik Russia of Stalin.

But if there should really be no ideological difference between them, then I can only say: how right is, after all, my attitude towards Marxism, communism and to democracy! Why two apparitions, when after all they are made of the same substance?

We are experiencing in these days a very great triumph and a feeling of deep inner satisfaction. A country that was also devastated by bolshevism, in which hundreds and thousands of human beings, women, men, children and old people, were slaughtered, has liberated itself, and liberated itself in spite of ideological friends of bolshevism who sit in Great Britain, France and other countries.

We can only too well understand this Spain in her struggle, and we greet her and congratulate her on her victory. We Germans can say so with special pride, for many young German men have done their duty there.

They have helped as volunteers to break a tyrannical régime and to recover for a nation its right to self-determination. We are glad to see how quickly, yes, how extremely quickly, here also a change in the world outlook of the suppliers of war material to the Red side has come about, how extensively one now suddenly understands National Spain and how ready one is to do business with this National Spain, perhaps not ideological business, but at least economic business!

This also is an indication of the direction developments are taking. For I believe that all States will have to face the same problems that we once had to face. State after State will either succumb to the Jewish Bolshevik pest or will ward it off. We have done so, and we have now erected a national German People's State.

This People's State desires to live in peace and friendship with every other State; it will, however, never again permit itself to be forced to its knees by any other State.

I do not know whether the world will become Fascist! I do not believe that the world will become National Socialist! But that the world will in the end ward off this worst form of bolshevistic threat in existence, of that I am absolutely convinced.

And, therefore, I believe in a conclusive understanding among peoples which will come sooner or later. There is no point in bringing about co-operation among nations, based upon permanent understanding, until this Jewish fission-fungus of peoples has been removed.

Today we must depend upon our own power! And we can be satisfied with results of this confidence in ourselves! At home and abroad!

When I came into power, Germany was torn and impotent at home, and abroad a toy of foreign will. Today we have order at home and our economy is flourishing. Abroad we are perhaps not popular, but we are respected. That is the decisive factor. Above all, we have given millions of our "*Volksgenossen*" the greatest happiness they could have wished for: their home-coming into our Great German Reich. And, secondly, we have given great happiness to Central Europe, namely, peace, peace protected by German power. And this power shall not be broken again by any force in the world. That shall be our oath.

We thus realise that the "*Volksgenossen*", more than 2 million in number, who died in the Great War, did not die in vain. From their sacrifice a new Great German Reich has arisen. From their sacrifice this strong young German Reich of the "*Volk*" has been called to life and has now stood its test in life.

And in the face of this sacrifice, we would not fear any sacrifice if it should ever become necessary. This the world should take note of!

They can conclude agreements, make declarations, as many as they like: I put my trust not in scraps of paper, but I put my trust in you, my "*Volksgenossen*".

Germans have been the victims of the greatest breach of promise of all time. Let us see to it that our people at home may never again become easy to break up, then no one in the world will ever be able to threaten us. Then peace will be maintained for our people or, if necessary, it will be enforced. And then our people will flourish and prosper.

It will be able to place its genius, its capability, its diligence, and its perseverance at the disposal of the work of peace and home culture. That is our desire; it is that which we hope and in which we believe.

Twenty years ago the party was founded, at that time a very small structure. Recall the distance covered from that time until today. Recall the extent of the miracle that has been worked upon us. And have faith, therefore, by the very reason of our miraculous progress, in the further road of the German people in the coming great future!

Germany: Sieg-Heil! Sieg-Heil! Sieg-Heil!

Extract from speech by Herr Hitler to the Reichstag on 28 April 1939 (Translation)

I believe that it is a good thing for millions and millions of people that I, thanks to the last-minute insight of responsible men on the other side, succeeded in averting such an explosion, and found a solution which I am convinced has finally abolished this problem of a source of danger in Central Europe.

The contention that this solution is contrary to the Munich Agreement can neither be supported nor confirmed. This agreement could, under no circumstances, be regarded as final, because it admitted that other problems required and remained to be solved. We cannot really be reproached for the fact that the parties concerned—and this is the deciding factor—did not turn to the four Powers, but only to Italy and Germany; nor yet for the fact that the State as such finally split up of its own accord, and there was, consequently, no longer any Czecho-Slovakia. It was, however, understand-able that, long after the ethnographic principle had been made invalid, Germany should take under her protection her interests dating back a thousand years, which are not only of a political but also of an economic nature.

The future will show whether the solution which Germany has found is right or wrong. However, it is certain that the solution is not subject to English supervision or criticism. For Bohemia and Moravia, as the remnants of former Czecho-Slovakia, have nothing more whatever to do with the Munich Agreement. Just as English measures in, say, Northern Ireland, whether they be right or wrong, are not subject to German supervision or criticism, this is also the case with these old German electorates.

However, I entirely fail to understand how the agreement reached between Mr Chamberlain and myself at Munich can refer to this case, for the case of Czecho-Slovakia was settled in the Munich protocol of the four Powers as far as it could be settled at all at that time. Apart from this, provision was merely made that if the interested parties should fail to come to an agreement they should be entitled to appeal to the four Powers, who had agreed in such a case to meet for further consultation after the expiration of three months. However, these interested parties did not appeal to the four Powers at all, but only to Germany and Italy. That this was fully justified, moreover, is proved by the fact that neither England nor France have raised any objections thereto, but have themselves accepted the decision given by Germany and Italy. No, the agreement reached between Mr Chamberlain and myself did not relate to this problem but exclusively to questions which refer to the mutual relationship between England and Germany. This is clearly shown by the fact that such questions are to be treated in future in the spirit of the Munich Agreement and of the Anglo-German Naval Agreement, that is, in a friendly spirit by way of consultation. If, however, this agreement were to be applied to every future German activity of a political nature, England too should not take any step, whether in Palestine or elsewhere, without first consulting Germany. It is obvious that we do not expect this; likewise we refuse to gratify any similar expectation of us. Now, if Mr Chamberlain concludes from this, that the Munich Agreement is for this reason annulled, as if we had broken it, then I shall take cognisance of the fact and proceed accordingly.

During the whole of my political activity I have always expounded the idea of a close friendship and collaboration between Germany and England. In my movement I found innumerable others of like mind. Perhaps they joined me because of my attitude in this matter. This desire for Anglo-German friendship and co-operation conforms not merely to sentiments which result from the racial origins of our two peoples, but also to my realisation of the importance for the whole of mankind of the existence of the British Empire. I have never left room for any doubt of my belief that the existence of this empire is an inestimable factor of value for the whole of human cultural and economic life. By whatever means Great Britain has acquired her colonial territories—and I know that they were those of force and often brutality—nevertheless, I know full well that no other empire has ever come into being in any other way, and that in the final resort it is not so much the methods that are taken into account in history as success, and not the success of the methods as such, but rather the general good which the methods yield. Now there is no doubt that the Anglo-Saxon people have accomplished immeasurable colonising work in the world. For this work I have a sincere admiration. The thought of destroying this labour appeared and still appears to me, seen from a higher human point of view, as nothing but the effluence of human wanton destructiveness. However, this sincere respect of mine for this achievement does not mean forgoing the securing of the life of my own people. I regard it as impossible to achieve a lasting friendship between the German and Anglo-Saxon peoples if the other side does not recognise that there are German as well as British interests, that not only is the preservation of the British Empire the meaning and purpose of the lives of Britishers, but also that for Germans the freedom and preservation of the German Reich is their life purpose. A genuine, lasting friendship between these two nations is only conceivable on the basis of mutual regard. The English people rules a great empire. It built up this empire at a time when the German people was internally weak. Previously Germany had been a great empire. At one time she ruled the Occident. In bloody struggles and religious dissensions, and as a result of internal political disintegration, this empire declined in power and greatness, and finally fell into a deep sleep. But as this old empire appeared to have reached its end, the seeds of its rebirth were springing up. From Brandenburg and Prussia there arose a new Germany, the second Reich, and out of it has grown at last the German People's Reich. And I hope that all English people understand that we do not possess the slightest feeling of inferiority to Britishers. Our historical past is far too tremendous for that!

England has given the world many great men and Germany no fewer. The severe struggle for the maintenance of the life of our people has in the course of three centuries cost a sacrifice in lives which far exceeds that which other peoples have had to make in asserting their existence.

If Germany, a country that was for ever being attacked, was not able to retain her possessions, but was compelled to sacrifice many of her provinces, this was due only to her political misdevelopment and her impotence as a result thereof! That condition has now been overcome. Therefore, we Germans do not feel in the least inferior to the British nation. Our self-esteem is just as great as that of an Englishman for England. In the history of our people, now of approximately two thousand years' standing, there are occasions and actions enough to fill us with sincere pride.

Now, if England cannot understand our point of view, thinking perchance she may look upon Germany as a vassal State, then our love and friendly feelings have, indeed, been wasted on England. We shall not despair or lose heart on that account, but—relying on the consciousness of our own strength and on the strength of our friends—we shall then find ways and means to secure our independence without impairing our dignity.

I have heard the statement of the British Prime Minister to the effect that he is not able to put any trust in German assurances. Under the circumstances I consider it a matter of course that we no longer wish to expect him or the British people to bear the burden of a situation which is only conceivable in an atmosphere of mutual confidence. When Germany became National Socialist and thus paved the way for her national resurrection, in pursuance of my unswerving policy of friendship with England, of my own accord I made the proposal for a voluntary restriction of German naval armaments. That restriction was, however, based on one condition, namely, the will and the conviction that a war between England and Germany would never again be possible. This wish and this conviction are alive in me today.

I am, however, now compelled to state that the policy of England is both unofficially and officially leaving no doubt about the fact that such a conviction is no longer shared in London, and that, on the contrary, the opinion prevails there that no matter in what conflict Germany should some day be entangled, Great Britain would always have to take her stand against Germany. Thus a war against Germany is taken for granted in that country. I most profoundly regret such a development, for the only claim I have ever made, and shall continue to make, on England is that for a return of our colonies. But I always made it very clear that this would never become the cause of a military conflict. I have always held that the English, to whom those colonies are of no value, would one day understand the German situation and would then value German friendship higher than the possession of territories which, while yielding no real profit whatever to them, are of vital importance to Germany.

Apart from this, however, I have never advanced a claim which might in any way have interfered with British interests or have become a danger to the Empire and thus have meant any kind of damage to England. I have always kept within the limit of such demands as are intimately connected with Germany's living space and thus the eternal property of the German nation. Since England today, both by the press and officially, upholds the view that Germany should be opposed under all circumstances, and confirms this by the policy of encirclement known to us, the basis for the Naval Treaty has been removed. I have therefore resolved to send today a communication to this effect to the British Government. This is to us not a matter of practical material importance—for I still hope that we shall be able to avoid an armaments race with England—but an action of self-respect. Should the British Government, however, wish to enter once more into negotiations with Germany on this problem, no one would be happier than I at the prospect of still being able to come to a clear and straightforward understanding.

*Memorandum from the German Government denouncing the Anglo-German
Naval Agreement*

Berlin, 27 April 1939

(Translation)

When in the year 1935 the German Government made the British
Government the offer to bring the strength of the German fleet to a fixed
proportion of the strength of the naval forces of the British Empire by means
of a treaty, it did so on the basis of the firm conviction that for all time the
recurrence of a warlike conflict between Germany and Great Britain was
excluded. In voluntarily recognising the priority of British interests at sea
through the offer of the ratio 100:35 it believed that, by means of this decision, unique in the history of the Great Powers, it was taking a step which
would lead to the establishment of a friendly relationship for all time
between the two nations. This step on the part of the German Government
was naturally conditional on the British Government for their part also
being determined to adopt a political attitude which would assure a friendly
development of Anglo-German relations.

On this basis and under these conditions was the Anglo–German Naval
Agreement of the 18th June, 1935, brought into being. This was expressed
in agreement by both parties on the conclusion of the agreement. Moreover,
last autumn after the Munich Conference the German Chancellor and the
British Prime Minister solemnly confirmed in the declaration, which they
signed, that they regarded the agreement as symbolical of the desire of both
peoples never again to wage war on one another.

The German Government has always adhered to this wish and is still
today inspired by it. It is conscious of having acted accordingly in its policy
and of having in no case intervened in the sphere of English interests or of
having in any way encroached on these interests. On the other hand it must
to its regret take note of the fact that the British Government of late is
departing more and more from the course of an analogous policy towards
Germany. As is clearly shown by the political decisions made known by the
British Government in the last weeks as well as by the inspired anti-German
attitude of the English press, the British Government is now governed by the
opinion that England, in whatever part of Europe Germany might be
involved in warlike conflict, must always take up an attitude hostile to
Germany, even in a case where English interests are not touched in any way
by such a conflict. The British Government thus regards war by England
against Germany no longer as an impossibility, but on the contrary as a capital problem of English foreign policy.

By means of this encirclement policy the British Government has unilaterally deprived the Naval Agreement of the 18th June, 1935, of its basis,
and has thus put out of force this agreement as well as the complementary
declaration of the 17th July, 1937.

The same applies to Part III of the Anglo-German Naval Agreement of
the 17th July, 1937, in which the obligation is laid down to make a mutual

Anglo-German exchange of information. The execution of this obligation rests naturally on the condition that a relationship of open confidence should exist between two partners. Since the German Government to its regret can no longer regard this relationship as existing, it must also regard the provisions of Part III referred to above as having lapsed.

The qualitative provisions of the Anglo-German Agreement of the 17th July, 1937, remain unaffected by these observations which have been forced upon the German Government against its will. The German Government will abide by these provisions also in the future and so make its contribution to the avoidance of a general unlimited race in the naval armaments of the nations. Moreover, the German Government, should the British Government desire to enter into negotiations with Germany, in regard to the future problems here arising, is gladly ready to do so. It would welcome it if it then proved possible to reach a clear and categorical understanding on a sure basis.

Viscount Halifax to Sir N. Henderson (Berlin)
Foreign Office, 16 June 1939

Sir,

The German Ambassador called at the Foreign Office this morning to sign a technical agreement of no great importance between the two Governments, and I had a few moments' conversation with him afterwards. In part this followed the familiar line of assertion on his part of the effect that was being produced in Germany by encirclement. The Ambassador expressed the view that, just as the old phrase "The Fleet in being" suggested pressure even without overt action, so now the regrouping of Powers that we were organising was, in fact, designed to operate as coercive pressure on Germany, and it was this which was resented. His Excellency said, and made the same observation at a later stage in our conversation, that much of the feeling at the present time was due to all the discussion about our anti-aggression negotiations with Russia. In his view the situation would be easier when these negotiations were settled one way or the other. I thought this observation perhaps not without significance.

I replied by saying that, if anybody was encircling Germany, it was herself by the policy that she persisted in pursuing. Whatever might be thought about the policy now being pursued by this country, it seemed to us quite plain that the German Chancellor had broken the china in Europe and it was only he who could put it together again. We repeatedly made efforts from this side to open the way to a diminution of tension and improvement of relations, but this had so far elicited nothing in the nature of response from Herr Hitler.

I told Herr von Dirksen that I hoped he would let me know if at any time he had anything that he might wish to communicate to me that he thought of value, and he replied by expressing a similar wish that I would not hesitate at any time to send for him.

HALIFAX

DETERIORATION IN THE LOCAL SITUATION AT DANZIG

Note from the President of the Danzig Senate to the Polish Commissioner-General of 3 June 1939, *about the question of Polish Customs Inspectors*
(Translation)

Several months ago I had the honour to draw your attention to the fact that the ever-increasing number of Polish Customs Inspectors was not compatible with the execution of their prescribed duties. Since the latest additions there are now well over 100 Polish Customs Inspectors in Danzig territory. Their behaviour, both in their official and their private life, has given rise to increasing complaint. The Danzig population, like the German population, in their local frontier intercourse feel themselves constantly offended by the way in which the Polish Customs officials perform their duty and by their behaviour in private life.

I have no fear that incidents on the part of the population might arise on that account. Still less is the safety of the Polish officials in any way endangered. I have therefore taken steps to ensure that they may, as hitherto, perform their duties absolutely safely and without hindrance. I believe, however, that ways and means must be found to eliminate the constant friction and tension.

For all these reasons I consider it necessary forthwith to restrict the activity of the Polish Customs Inspectors to a general supervision in conformity with the agreement. In particular, I must urge that their official activities be confined to the offices, and not performed outside of them. I can also no longer permit the Danzig Customs officials to take instructions, even in the form of suggestions, from the Polish Customs officials. I will, however, see that questions addressed to officials will be answered officially.

I have directed the President of the Customs Administration of the Free City to instruct his officials accordingly. I have the honour, Mr Minister, to request you to inform your Government accordingly and to exert your influence towards meeting the wishes of the Danzig Government.

I avail myself of this opportunity to revert to our conversation of 8th February last. At that time I explained that I would give instructions to abstain for the present from swearing in the customs officials, and that, should the occasion arise, I would communicate with you before administering the oath.

I have the honour to inform you, with reference to the contents of my letter of the 3rd January last, that I have now left it to the discretion of the Finance Department of the Senate to administer the oath to the customs officials if they regard it as desirable.

GREISER

Sir H. Kennard to Viscount Halifax

Warsaw, 11 June 1939

(Telegraphic)

Following is full summary of note, as published here, addressed on 10th June by Polish Commissioner-General to President of Danzig Senate in reply to latter's note of 3rd June:

President of Senate's complaint of behaviour of Polish Customs Inspectors on and off duty is not supported by any proofs and must be regarded as unfounded. On the other hand, behaviour of certain Danzig elements, including Customs officials, has been highly provocative, as Commissioner-General has frequently pointed out orally and in writing. Polish Inspectors have reacted with dignity and moderation and refused to be provoked. The Polish Government still expect Senate to take measures to secure personal safety of Polish Customs Inspectors to allow free execution of their duty, with reference to Point 3 of Polish-Danzig Agreement of 1922, which lays down that Polish officials in Danzig should receive the same treatment as corresponding Danzig officials.

As regards alleged excessive number of Polish Customs officials, Polish Government, on the contrary, consider it at present rather insufficient. This can be shown by present state of affairs as regards handling of goods in Danzig harbour and passenger traffic between Danzig and Poland, and is partly due to obstruction encountered by officials in execution of their duty.

Polish Government, moreover, cannot agree to any restriction of activity of Polish Inspectors as forecast in note of Danzig Senate. Present treaty arrangements would not permit of Inspectors merely exercising general supervision within customs offices, a restriction which would be contrary to Sections 1 and 4 of Article 204 of the Warsaw Treaty of the 24th October, 1921. In this connection Polish note also quotes Article 10 of Polish-Danzig Customs Agreement of the 6th August, 1934, which lays down that Danzig officials shall conform to instructions of Polish Customs Inspectors in connection with manifest cases of smuggling.

Polish Government must regard Senate as fully responsible for any disputes which may arise in this last connection, and must regard as illegal and contrary to treaty obligations any attempts by Danzig Customs authorities arbitrarily to restrict Polish rights of control. Instructions given to Danzig Customs officials as described in Senate's note must be regarded as a violation of the principle of collaboration between Danzig Customs Administration and Polish Inspectors. Latter have been instructed to continue exercising their functioning within the same limits—which are in conformity with treaty situation—as in the past twenty years, and hope is expressed that they will not meet with obstruction from Danzig authorities.

As regards question of swearing-in Customs officials, Polish note refers to written communications of Senate on this subject and to Commissioner-General's interviews with President. Should Senate not take account of fully justified demands of Polish Government, and should they proceed to swearing-in of officials in spite of assurance by President of Senate that this would not take place except after consultation with Commissioner-General? Polish Government will have to consider question of strengthening customs control, since Danzig Customs officials will in future be giving a less binding guarantee of their respect for, and proper execution of, Polish Customs regulations.

Essence of whole question is that territory of Free City is part of Polish Customs Territory, both legally and in virtue of treaty obligations. Authorities must therefore be assured of thorough-going execution of their Polish Customs policy and regulations on external frontier of their Customs territory. Hence any measures by Danzig authorities which threaten to obstruct, if only in part, the functioning of the Polish Customs system can only provoke reaction by Polish Government in the form of measures designed fully to protect Poland's rightful interest.

Polish Government desire, as before, to regulate all vital questions concerning Free City of Danzig in agreement with Danzig Senate. In the situation recently created, however, they consider it their duty to warn the Senate that any shortcomings or obstructions in functioning of Polish Customs system and administration must react unfavourably on the economic interests of Danzig and its population, a consequence which Polish Government desire to avoid.

Sir H. Kennard to Viscount Halifax

Warsaw, 27 June 1939

(Telegraphic)

I asked the Vice-Minister for Foreign Affairs this morning what information he had regarding the constitution of the Freicorps at Danzig. He told me that according to Polish information a corps of 4,000 was being formed of whom 2,000 would be quartered at barracks in Danzig itself and 2,000 in new buildings which were being constructed at Praust.

As regards the general situation in Danzig it was perhaps a little better. There had been some fifty cases of Danzig officials refusing to carry out the instructions of the Polish Customs Inspectors during the past fortnight, but during the past few days there had been no cases of this kind. This may be due to the fact that the arms for the Freicorps were being surreptitiously introduced into the Free City from East Prussia during the past fortnight and that presumably now that the arms were in Danzig there is less occasion for contravention of the Polish Customs regulations.

M. Arciszewski did not think that Germany would go to the length of risking a general war in connection with Danzig, but felt that she would gradually strengthen her position there, weaken any authority that Poland might still have there and hope that Poland would finally be reduced to such a state of economic exhaustion that she would have to accept some solution as regards Danzig which would be favourable to Germany. Further, Germany would in the meantime, no doubt, assiduously propagate the idea that Great Britain and France would not implement their guarantee as regards Danzig and thereby endeavour still further to undermine Polish morale.

G. Shepherd to Viscount Halifax

Danzig, 28 June 1939

(Telegraphic)

In contrast to calm in Warsaw, the last week has been increasingly eventful here.

For the past fortnight the SA men have been nightly preparing defences around the Free City, and on the night of 26th–27th June were ordered to stand by for a possible emergency, perhaps in connection with celebration in Gdynia of Polish Feast of the Seas or because Polish frontier on Danzig–Gdynia road was closed to traffic from midnight on 26th–27th June until 4 PM on 27th June, presumably in connection with completion of anti-tank defences.

The approaches for a pontoon bridge are in active construction on both sides of the Vistula.

On 23rd June Danzig members of German Automobile Club received an urgent request to complete and return a questionnaire regarding their cars.

All Danzig owners of motor lorries, trucks, etc., were recently ordered to leave them overnight at military police barracks for inspection after which each vehicle was numbered and returned to its owner.

Today several hundred draught and saddle horses have been similarly ordered to barracks nominally for inspection, but as some of them have come from distant parts of the Free City, it seems possible that they may be retained, especially as car-loads of saddles have also been delivered there.

Formation of Freicorps is proceeding rapidly.

In addition to unusually heavily advertised programme of weekend events, nearly 1,000 SS men from East Prussia and a number of high SS officers from Germany arrived here almost unannounced on 25th June ostensibly for sporting contests with local SS.

Dr Boettcher was absent from Danzig and presumably in Berlin on 26th June and 27th June.

In a speech on 25th June Herr Forster said: "Before us lies a new era and for Germany a great epoch. During recent weeks our Danzig has become the centre of political events. We are all aware that we are in the final throes of our fight for freedom. The Free State of Danzig has taken the longest time. Today everyone knows that the Free State will soon come to an end and we also know how it will end."

A considerable number of visiting SS men remained here when others left last Sunday night. Those remaining are reputed to have performed their military service in Germany and to be members of Adolf Hitler's *Verfügungstruppen*. They are readily distinguishable by their deportment and slightly different uniforms from local SS men. About 300 of them are in military police barracks, which are now very full, and others are in other former local barracks which are capable of accommodating from 1,000 to 1,500 men, and have hitherto been occupied by a Danzig social welfare organisation which is being transferred to a hotel that has been requisitioned for the purpose. According to sub-editor of *Dantziger Vorposten*, the largest youth hostel in the world, which is approaching completion here, is to be used as a barracks.

A number of workmen's dwellings at Praust are said to have been requisitioned for storage of ammunition, and my Argentine colleague informs me that he saw a number of military police equipped with gas masks.

All Danzig civil servants and students are required to remain within the Free City during their vacations, and the latter must devote their holidays to harvesting. All categories of military police have been kept in barracks yesterday and today, and tonight members of various National Socialist organisations are apparently again standing by, as remarkably few of them are visible about the City.

Viscount Halifax to Sir H. Kennard (Warsaw)

Foreign Office, 30 June 1939

(Telegraphic)

You should at once seek interview with Minister for Foreign Affairs and ask him how the Polish Government propose to deal with the situation which appears to be impending. It would seem that Hitler is laying his plans very astutely so as to present the Polish Government with a *fait accompli* in Danzig, to which it would be difficult for them to react without appearing in the role of aggressors. I feel that the moment has come where consultation between the Polish, British and French Governments is necessary in order that the plans of the three Governments may be co-ordinated in time. It is in the view of His Majesty's Government essential that these plans shall be so devised as to ensure that Hitler shall not be able so to manage matters as to manœuvre the Polish Government into the position of aggressors.

Mr G. Shepherd to Viscount Halifax

Danzig, 30 June 1939

(Telegraphic)

Horses continued to arrive yesterday, and about 600 of them are being kept in barracks at which large quantities of hay have also been delivered.

For the last few nights the two great shipyards here which normally work all night were closed under strict guard and all workmen evacuated from them.

As from tonight Danzig and suburbs were to be blacked out until further notice and, in case of air raid alarm, all inhabitants were ordered to take refuge in their cellars or public shelters. This order was cancelled this afternoon.

Former local barracks are now occupied by large number of young men with obvious military training who wear uniforms similar to Danzig SS but with deathshead emblem on the right collar and "Heimwehr Danzig" on sleeves. Courtyard is occupied by about fifteen military motor lorries (some with trailers) with East Prussian licences and covered with tarpaulins, also by about forty field kitchens.

Two thousand men are working twenty-four hours a day in three shifts on construction of barracks at Matzkshuter to accommodate 10,000 men. Work is stated to be well advanced.

All dressmakers here are said to be working on bedding, clothing, etc., for barracks and their occupants.

It has just been announced that Tiegenmorse–Einlage section of Danzig–Elbing road is closed for major repairs until 1st August, and it seems unlikely that pontoon bridge will be ready before that date.

My personal impression is that extensive military preparations which are being pressed forward so feverishly are part of large-scale operations but not intended for use before August, unless unexpected developments precipitate matters.

BRITISH ATTITUDE TOWARDS DEVELOPMENTS IN DANZIG

Statement by the Prime Minister in the House of Commons on 10 *July* 1939

Mr Harold Macmillan asked the Prime Minister whether His Majesty's Government will issue a declaration to the effect that any change in the present status of Danzig, other than by an agreement to which the Polish Government is a party, whether brought about externally by military action on the part of Germany or internally by a movement initiated or supported by the German Government, will be regarded as an act of aggression on the part of Germany and, therefore, covered by the terms of our pledge to Poland?

Lieut.-Commander Fletcher asked the Prime Minister whether any attempt to alter the existing régime at Danzig by aggression from outside or penetration from within will be regarded as within the terms of our pledge to maintain the independence of Poland; and has a communication been made to the Polish Government in these terms?

Mr A. Henderson asked the Prime Minister whether he had any statement to make on the situation in Danzig.

Mr V. Adams asked the Prime Minister whether he had any further statement to make on the attitude of His Majesty's Government towards the position of Danzig.

Mr Thurtle asked the Prime Minister whether he is now satisfied that the head of the German Government no longer has any doubt of the intention of this country to discharge to the full the undertaking it has given to Poland; or has he under consideration any further action with a view to removing any possible doubt or misunderstanding which may still exist?

The Prime Minister: I would ask hon. members to be good enough to await the statement which I propose to make at the end of questions.

(Later)

The Prime Minister: I have previously stated that His Majesty's Government are maintaining close contact with the Polish and French Governments on the question of Danzig. I have nothing at present to add to the information which has already been given to the House about the local situation. But I may, perhaps, usefully review the elements of this question as they appear to His Majesty's Government.

Racially Danzig is, almost wholly, a German city; but the prosperity of its inhabitants depends to a very large extent upon Polish trade. The Vistula is Poland's only waterway to the Baltic, and the port at its mouth is therefore of vital strategic and economic importance to her. Another Power established in Danzig could, if it so desired, block Poland's access to the sea and so exert an economic and military stranglehold upon her. Those who were responsible for framing the present statute of the Free City were fully conscious of these facts, and did their best to make provision accordingly. Moreover, there is no question of any oppression of the German population in Danzig. On the contrary, the administration of the Free City is in German hands, and the only restrictions imposed upon it are not of a kind to curtail the liberties of its citizens. The present settlement, though it may be capable of improvement, cannot in itself be regarded as basically unjust or illogical. The maintenance of the *status quo* had in fact been guaranteed by the German Chancellor himself up to 1944 by the ten-year Treaty which he had concluded with Marshal Pilsudski.

Up till last March Germany seems to have felt that, while the position of Danzig might ultimately require revision, the question was neither urgent nor likely to lead to a serious dispute. But in March, when the German Government put forward an offer in the form of certain desiderata accompanied by a press campaign, the Polish Government realised that they might presently be faced with a unilateral solution which they would have to resist with all their forces. They had before them the events which had taken place in Austria, Czecho-Slovakia and the Memelland. Accordingly, they refused to accept the German point of view, and themselves made suggestions for a possible solution of the problems in which Germany was interested. Certain defensive measures were taken by Poland on the 23rd March and the reply was sent to Berlin on the 26th March. I ask the House to note carefully these dates. It has been freely stated in Germany that it was His Majesty's Government's guarantee which encouraged the Polish Government to take the action which I have described. But it will be observed that our guarantee was not given until the 31st March. By the 26th March no mention of it, even, had been made to the Polish Government.

Recent occurrences in Danzig have inevitably given rise to fears that it is intended to settle her future status by unilateral action, organised by surreptitious methods, thus presenting Poland and other powers with a *fait accompli*. In such circumstances any action taken by Poland to restore the situation would, it is suggested, be represented as an act of aggression on her part, and if her action were supported by other Powers they would be accused of aiding and abetting her in the use of force.

If the sequence of events should, in fact, be such as is contemplated on this hypothesis, hon. members will realise, from what I have said earlier, that the issue could not be considered as a purely local matter involving the rights and liberties of the Danzigers, which incidentally are in no way threatened, but would at once raise graver issues affecting Polish national existence and independence. We have guaranteed to give our assistance to Poland in the case of a clear threat to her independence, which she considers is vital to resist with her national forces, and we are firmly resolved to carry out this undertaking.

I have said that while the present settlement is neither basically unjust nor illogical, it may be capable of improvement. It may be that in a clearer atmosphere possible improvements could be discussed. Indeed, Colonel Beck has himself said in his speech on the 5th May that if the Government of the Reich is guided by two conditions, namely, peaceful intentions and peaceful methods of procedure, all conversations are possible. In his speech before the Reichstag on the 28th April the German Chancellor said that if the Polish Government wished to come to fresh contractual arrangements governing its relations with Germany he could but welcome such an idea. He added that any such future arrangements would have to be based on an absolutely clear obligation equally binding on both parties.

His Majesty's Government realise that recent developments in the Free City have disturbed confidence and rendered it difficult at present to find an atmosphere in which reasonable counsels can prevail. In face of this situation, the Polish Government have remained calm, and His Majesty's Government hope that the Free City, with her ancient traditions, may again prove, as she has done before in her history, that different nationalities can work together when their real interests coincide. Meanwhile, I trust that all concerned will declare and show their determination not to allow any incidents in connection with Danzig to assume such a character as might constitute a menace to the peace of Europe.

Sir N. Henderson to Viscount Halifax

Berlin, 15 July 1939

My Lord,

I took the opportunity of a visit to the State Secretary yesterday to mention to him that I had been informed that one of the Under-Secretaries at the Ministry for Foreign Affairs, Dr Keppler, had said that Herr Hitler was convinced that England would never fight over Danzig.

I said to Baron von Weizsäcker that when I was in London I had assured your Lordship and the Prime Minister that Herr Hitler could not possibly be in any doubt as to the facts of the case, namely, that, if Germany by unilateral action at Danzig in any form compelled the Poles to resist,

Britain would at once come to their assistance. He (Baron von Weizsäcker) could not himself be under any misapprehension on the subject, and it seemed to me highly undesirable that a member of his Department should talk in this misleading fashion. That sort of remark would be repeated in London, and would once more make His Majesty's Government wonder what further steps they could take to convince Herr Hitler that they were in earnest. It was solely because they doubted whether Herr Hitler was correctly informed on this point that they continued to reiterate their determination to resist force by force in future. If Herr Hitler wanted war, it was quite simple. He had only to tell the Danzigers to proclaim the re-attachment of the Free City to Germany. Obviously that would put the onus of action on the Poles, but not even that would cause us to hesitate to support them, if Germany attacked them, since we would realise quite well that the Senate at Danzig would only adopt such a resolution on the direct order of the Chancellor.

Baron von Weizsäcker observed that he was not so certain that the Senate would not act one day of its own accord. I told him that I could not possibly believe that, especially as I clearly realised that the Senate would have already so acted if it had not been for Herr Hitler's orders to the con-trary. That he had given those orders was one of the chief grounds for my belief that Herr Hitler still sought a peaceable solution of this question. Nor did the State Secretary demur to this.

As regards my general observations, Baron von Weizsäcker said that Dr Keppler, who had been in the early days a kind of economic adviser of Herr Hitler's and still saw him occasionally at long intervals, was an honest man, who was also in fairly close relations with Herr von Ribbentrop. There were, Baron von Weizsäcker said, so many distinctions about a statement to the effect that England would not go to war over Danzig. Anybody, including Herr Hitler himself, might well say that England did not wish to fight about Danzig, and it would be true. Nor did Germany. Anybody, including Herr Hitler, might say that one day Danzig would revert without war to Germany, and that might equally be true as the result of a pacific settlement with the Poles in their own true interests.

I admitted that there were possibilities of twisting the facts. Yet these were, I said, plain enough, and His Majesty's Government could never be reproached this time, as they had been in 1914, of not having made their posi-tion clear beyond all doubt. If Herr Hitler wanted war, he knew exactly how he could bring it about. Baron von Weizsäcker replied to this that he would also draw a distinction about the position in 1914. He had never reproached Sir Edward Grey for not having publicly announced British intentions at that time. The fault, in his opinion, had been that His Majesty's Government had not made them known privately to the German Government before it was too late. Why did His Majesty's Government today insist all the time upon these public utterances? If something had to be said to Herr Hitler, why could it not be said privately without all the world being kept informed? That had been the mistake last year during the Czech crisis. Public warnings only made it more difficult for Herr Hitler to heed them.

Though I appreciate personally the force of this hint of the State Secretary in favour of the private communication rather than the public warning, I confined myself to replying that one of our main causes for anxiety in England was our belief that disagreeable facts were withheld from Herr Hitler by those who were responsible for making them known to him. To this Baron von Weizsäcker replied that, while he could not tell me what reports the Chancellor read or did not read, Herr Hitler was influenced by nobody, but regarded situations as a whole and was guided solely by his own appreciations of them.

NEVILE HENDERSON

TEMPORARY EASING IN THE DANZIG SITUATION

Mr Shepherd to Viscount Halifax

Danzig, 19 July 1939

(Telegraphic)

Gauleiter* Forster visited the High Commissioner at noon today. The latter has sent me, in a personal and confidential form, notes of conversation, of which the following is a translation:

The Gauleiter told me that the result of his interview with the German Chancellor was as follows:

(1) There is no modification of German claims regarding Danzig and the Corridor as formulated in Chancellor's speech to Reichstag.

(2) Nothing will be done on the German side to provoke a conflict on this question.

(3) Question can wait if necessary until next year or even longer.

(4) The Gauleiter said that the Senate would henceforth seek intervention of High Commissioner in difficult questions which might arise between the Senate and Polish representative. This would, he said, terminate a war of notes which only poisons the situation, but he added that "a single press indiscretion to the effect that the Senate and German Government are having recourse to politics would immediately terminate practice and more direct and consequently more dangerous method would again be applied." He said verbatim: "We are having recourse to High Commissioner and not to Geneva itself."

(5) He requested High Commissioner to intervene officially at once in the matter of military trains not announced beforehand. Non-observance of

---

* Gauleiter: Chief official in the district under Nazi regime.

this rule, which was established by an exchange of letters between the Senate and Polish representative in 1921, would have effect beyond local Danzig question and would, for example, entail a modification of German usage announcing to Polish Government visit of warships to port of Danzig. In addition, according to information at disposal of Senate, there were 300 men at Westerplatte in place of 100 agreed to. Herr Forster gave his word of honour that there were at Danzig only a few anti-aircraft guns, anti-tank guns and light infantry guns—no heavy guns, not an invading German soldier—nobody but Danzigers and four German officers. He claimed that a sharp watch at the frontier was necessary by the extensive importation of weapons for 3,000 Polish reservists resident in the district.

(6) Herr Forster will publish an article which he had already read to me confidentially on the occasion of our last interview, when he said he would submit the question of publication to the Chancellor's decision. This article underlines point of view announced in Reichstag speech. Herr Forster declared that if repercussion of his article is not violent and if there is no incident, this will put an end to all Danzig-Polish polemics and press would be ordered to drop the subject of Danzig completely.

(7) If there is a *détente* in situation, all military measures now taken in Danzig would be dropped.

(8) The Gauleiter promised his loyal collaboration.

(9) High Commissioner would be happy if it were possible to obtain from Poland a positive reaction in any formal matter which might arise in the near future so that new methods may be given a good initiation.

(10) The Gauleiter said that Herr Hitler would have liked to take an opportunity to talk to the High Commissioner about the Danzig situation, but that Herr von Ribbentrop, who was present at the interview at Obersalzberg, had raised objections to which the Chancellor replied evasively: "Well, it will be a little later, I will let you know."

Viscount Halifax to Mr Norton (Warsaw)

Foreign Office, 21 *July* 1939

(Telegraphic)

Danzig telegram of 19th July: I am most anxious that this tentative move from German side should not be compromised by publicity or by any disinclination on part of Polish Government to discuss in friendly and reasonable spirit any concrete question which may be taken up by Senate through High Commissioner.

Unless you see most serious objection, please approach M. Beck in following sense:

His Majesty's Government have learnt with great regret of further incident, but they hope that Polish Government will handle it with same restraint and circumspection which they have hitherto shown, more especially as there is some reason to think that German policy is now to work for a *détente* in the Danzig question. It is nevertheless essential not to destroy possibility of better atmosphere at outset, and I trust that more care than ever will be taken on Polish side to avoid provocation in any sphere and to restrain press. Above all, if any sign is forthcoming of more reasonable attitude on the part of Senate or German Government, it is important that from Polish side this should not be made occasion for provocative assertions that German Government are weakening. Moreover, I hope that if Senate show any sign of desiring to improve atmosphere by discussing concrete questions, the Polish Government for their part will not be slow to respond in a friendly and forthcoming manner.

For your own information, I hope to arrange that we shall be informed through High Commissioner and His Majesty's Consul-General in Danzig when any concrete question is to be taken up by High Commissioner at the request of Senate, and, of course, of the discussions, in order that we may have an opportunity of discreetly urging moderation on Polish Government.

Finally, when newspaper article referred to in telegram under reference appears, please do what you can to ensure that Polish Government and press treat it calmly, perhaps on the lines that it does not introduce any new element into the situation. You might also say that the publication of the proposed article does not modify impression of His Majesty's Government that Senate and the German Government, in fact, desire a *détente* and an improvement in the atmosphere.

Whatever may be the import of this German move, position of Polish Government cannot be worsened in any respect by doing their utmost to make a success of procedure proposed by Gauleiter to High Commissioner.

Mr Norton to Viscount Halifax

Warsaw, 25 July 1939

(Telegraphic)

Your telegram of 21st July: I developed your Lordship's ideas to M. Beck this morning.

M. Beck asked me to assure you that Polish Government were always on the look-out for signs of a German wish for a *détente*. They are inspired by the same principles as your Lordship, since it was in everyone's interest that temperature should be allowed to fall. Polish Commissioner in Danzig had received formal instructions to deal with each question in a purely practical and objective manner. Even shooting of Polish Customs guard, which Polish Government now considered to have been deliberate, was being treated as a local incident.

The most important question was whether new German tendency reported by M. Burckhardt was a manœuvre or not. M. Beck was naturally suspicious since Poland had much experience of German mentality and

Germans' real interest must be by any and every means to attempt to separate Poland from Great Britain. At one moment they tried to achieve this by threats, at another by talk of appeasement. In actual fact Polish Government had not received the slightest concrete sign of a desire for a relaxation of tension. For example, remilitarisation of Danzig was proceeding and identifications of fresh German troops on Polish frontier had been received. Marshal Smigly-Rydz had not decided to counter these for the moment since amongst other things Poland was not so rich as to be able to spend money for military purposes freely.

Words let fall by Herr Forster were not in themselves sufficient evidence of German intentions. Herr Forster had within the last few days complained to M. Burckhardt about Polish intention to put armed guards on their railways in Danzig.

M. Burckhardt had said that such complaint had better be made by Herr Greiser. Latter had at once said that he had no evidence of any such Polish intention. M. Beck feared that this allegation by Herr Forster was only a pretext for increasing militarisation of Danzig.

All in all M. Beck, while entirely understanding and sharing your Lordship's general desire, did not at present see any facts on which to base a forecast of German change of policy.

He said incidentally that he had not given up the idea that *démarche* in the form of warning to Danzig Senate, supported by French and British representations, might be advisable.

Mr F. M. Shepherd to Viscount Halifax

Danzig, 25 July 1939

(Telegraphic)

Herr Forster informed High Commissioner yesterday that Danzig question could, if necessary, wait a year or more, and said that military precautions now being taken would be liquidated in the middle of September.

Meanwhile, there is increasing amount of horse and motor transport visible, and frequent reports reach me of men being called up and of arrival of men and material from East Prussia. While I cannot at present confirm these reports, it would be unwise to ignore them. There are numerous warehouses and other buildings in Danzig where material could be stored and men housed.

I learn that a certain Major-General Eberhard is now in command here.

Sir H. Kennard to Viscount Halifax

Warsaw, 31 July 1939

(Telegraphic)

I asked Minister for Foreign Affairs today what impressions he had brought back from his visit to Gdynia and how far he thought that the *détente* at

Danzig, foreshadowed in the conversation between the Gauleiter and the High Commissioner, should be taken seriously.

M. Beck said that, unfortunately, there were no indications that the Danzig Senate intended to behave more reasonably. They had just demanded that the Polish customs police who accompany the customs officials on their duties should be withdrawn, despite the fact that they had been employed in Danzig by the Polish customs authorities for some years past.

It was possible that the remilitarisation of Danzig was not proceeding so actively, and he had no information as to the intention of the German Government to send a General Officer Commanding to Danzig.

He, further, had no information of a serious increase in German concentrations on the Polish frontier, but he was somewhat perturbed by the reports which he had received from some eight Polish Consular representatives in Germany to the effect that an intensive official propaganda is now being conducted in Germany demonstrating the necessity of an isolated war against Poland without any British or French intervention. This, coupled with the notices which have been sent to German reservists who are to be called up during the second fortnight in August, was somewhat ominous. He said that an intensive propaganda was also being conducted in East Prussia, where reservists up to 58 years old were being called up.

M. Beck did not think that the moment had yet come to convey a serious joint warning to the Danzig authorities, and felt that it would be well to await further developments and see how far the Gauleiter's suggestion of a *détente* was to be taken seriously.

The most essential thing was to show by every possible means the solidarity of the three Governments of Great Britain, France and Poland in their resistance to German aggression in any form.

Sir H. Kennard to Viscount Halifax
Warsaw, 2 August 1939

(Telegraphic)
I discussed the situation at Danzig at some length informally with the Vice-Minister for Foreign Affairs today and asked him more especially for information regarding the controversy respecting the reduction of the Polish customs personnel in the Free State. M. Arciszewski said that three years ago there had only been about thirty Polish customs inspectors, and that in view of the numerous cases of smuggling and so forth, some eighty frontier guards had been added for the purpose of surveillance. The frontier guards wore a different uniform from the customs inspectors, and he thought that provided the Danzig Senate were acting in good faith and any concession would not be interpreted as a sign of weakness, it might be possible to come to some arrangement by which the customs officials and frontier guards should wear the same uniform and the number of the latter might be somewhat reduced. He did not think that any threat of a customs union with Germany should

be taken too seriously as hitherto the Senate had never risked coming too far into the open. He admitted that the general situation might become critical towards the end of this month. He agreed that it was very difficult to fix a limit at which the Polish Government must react seriously to the accentuation of the surreptitious methods by which Germany was endeavouring to bring about a *fait accompli* at Danzig, but he still thought that she would hesitate before going to the length where a serious crisis must develop.

He admitted that the situation might develop within a few hours from the political to the military phase, but felt that the military preparations at Danzig were to some extent exaggerated. If the Reich really did not wish or intend to participate in a European war over the Danzig question, and there were real signs of a *détente*, it might be possible to resume conversations, but he thought that Herr Forster's assertions were in the present circumstances only a manœuvre, and that until there were serious indications that the German Government's intentions were reasonable, it would not be possible to discuss any practical solution.

FURTHER DETERIORATION IN THE SITUATION AT DANZIG

Mr Norton to Viscount Halifax

Warsaw, 4 August 1939

(Telegraphic)

M. Beck tonight, through his "chef de cabinet", informed me that at four customs posts on Danzig–East Prussian frontier Polish customs inspectors were today informed that by decision of Danzig Senate they would henceforth not be allowed to carry out their duties. Polish Government take a very serious view of this step. Previous action of Danzig Senate has been clandestine, but this is an open challenge to Polish interests.

Polish Commissioner-General has therefore been instructed to deliver a note tonight requesting immediate confirmation that Polish customs inspectors will be allowed to carry out their duties, and warning to Senate that if they are interfered with Polish Government will react in the strongest manner. A reply is requested by tomorrow evening, 5th August.

"Chef de cabinet" could not say what steps the Polish Government would take. M. Beck proposed to give me further information tomorrow morning. Meanwhile, he was most anxious that His Majesty's Government should be informed at once of the serious turn events have taken.

Polish note is, I gather, not being published nor its contents revealed to press. M. Burckhardt is being informed by Polish Commissioner-General.

Mr F. M. Shepherd to Viscount Halifax

Danzig, 4 August 1939

(Telegraphic)

Polish representative saw the High Commissioner this morning on his return from Warsaw and read to him a translation of a note which he will hand to the Senate this afternoon. It is polite but firm, and ends on a conciliatory note. Referring to the threat to open the East Prussian frontier M. Chodacki requested the High Commissioner to give the President of the Senate a personal message to the effect that such a move would be for Poland a *casus belli*.

The President of the Senate complained to the High Commissioner that Gauleiter had not passed on to him the desire of the Führer to terminate the war of notes and to work towards a *détente*. Herr Greiser was incensed at having been placed in a false position, and said he would not have sent his notes of 29th July had he been kept *au courant*.

The President and Polish representative will meet at the High Commissioner's house on 7th August.

Sir H. Kennard to Viscount Halifax

Warsaw, 9 August 1939

(Telegraphic)

Polish attitude towards the dispute over recent Danzig attempt to eliminate Polish customs inspection has been firm but studiously moderate. There was at first no attempt to represent the Danzig Senate as having climbed down, but, as was inevitable, the papers have since reproduced comment to this effect from the French and British press. The Polish Government said little to the press about what really passed, and even now nothing has been said of any time limit. Polish attitude to diplomatic conversations is also moderate.

It is true that on 7th August the independent Conservative *Czas* (Polish newspaper), in a commentary on Marshal Smigly-Rydz's speech, said that Poland was ready to fight for Danzig, and that if a *fait accompli* were attempted, then guns would fire. It also emphasised at length the Marshal's insistence that Poland had no aggressive intentions (the German press does not seem to be interested in that point).

The Polish Telegraph Agency today—in a message from its German correspondent—replies to attacks of Deutches Nachrichten-Büro and German press, pointing out that one sentence in the article in *Czas* had been singled out to give a distorted picture of Polish opinion in order to represent Poland as a potential aggressor. "Polish provocations" was the term used in Germany to describe Poland's attempts to defend her just interests. "A volley fired by German guns will be the closing point of the history of modern Poland", that was the pious desire of "peaceful and persecuted Germany". The message concluded by emphasising again that everyone knew that Poland had no aggressive intentions.

I fear that at times of strong national feeling it is almost inevitable that occasional remarks like that of *Czas* should occur in the press. Experience shows that the Germans can wax indignant with anyone and on any subject if Goebbels so desires. And the "provocation" of one article in a small and independent Warsaw newspaper compares strangely with the official utterances of Dr Goebbels and Herr Forster in Danzig and the daily military and civil violation of all the treaties on which Poland's rights are based. Possibly the German campaign is intended to cover up the Senate's withdrawal in Danzig, where the situation is regarded as somewhat easier.

I shall, of course, continue to urge moderation here, both in official and press declarations.

Sir H. Kennard to Viscount Halifax

Warsaw, 10 August 1939

(Telegraphic)

Minister for Foreign Affairs communicated to me today the text of a communication which was made to Polish Chargé d'Affaires at Berlin by State Secretary yesterday and of reply of the Polish Government which was made this afternoon. Both these communications were made verbally though notes were taken of their contents in either case.

M. Beck drew my attention to the very serious nature of German *démarche* as it was the first time that the Reich had directly intervened in the dispute between Poland and Danzig Senate. He had already, through Polish Ambassador in London, warned your Lordship briefly of what he had communicated to me, but he asked me to request you to consider whether you could take any useful action in Berlin to reinforce Polish attitude. He would leave it to your Lordship to decide the nature of any such action, but would be glad in any case to learn your views as to the significance of this *démarche* on the part of the Reich. M. Beck has made a similar communication to my French colleague.

He further told me that the High Commissioner had communicated to him the tenor of a conversation which M. Burckhardt had had with Herr Forster this morning. Conversation was relatively moderate, and Herr Forster said Herr Hitler had told him that no incident should take place at Danzig at present time in view of gravity of the situation. Herr Forster said that he intended in his declaration which he is to make tonight to deal with aggressive tone of Polish press.

M. Beck finally said that he felt that a serious political crisis would develop during the last fortnight of this month, which while it need not necessarily lead to war would require very careful handling. No further military measures were being taken by the Polish Government for the moment, but he would at once inform me if they became necessary. M. Beck stated that while he had not thought it necessary to refer, in his reply to the German Government, to the specific question of Polish customs inspectors, he could have refuted German allegations as the Polish Government had documentary proof that Danzig customs officials had definite instructions to inform Polish inspectors that they could no longer carry out their functions.

Sir H. Kennard to Viscount Halifax

Warsaw, 10 August 1939

(Telegraphic)

Following is translation of German *note verbale*:

German Government have learnt with lively surprise of tenor of note addressed by Polish Government to Senate of Free City of Danzig, in which Polish Government demand in the form of an ultimatum cancellation of an alleged measure whose existence was based on incorrect rumours. This measure, designed to prevent activity of Polish customs inspectors, was not, in fact, decreed by Senate. In case of refusal the threat was expressed that measures of reprisal would be taken.

The German Government are compelled to call attention to the fact that repetition of such demands having the nature of an ultimatum and addressed to the Free City of Danzig as well as of threats of reprisals, would lead to an aggravation of Polish-German relations, for consequences of which responsibility will fall exclusively on Polish Government. Further, the German Government call attention of Polish Government to the fact that steps which latter have taken to prevent export of certain Danzig goods to Poland are of such a nature as to cause heavy economic losses to the population of Danzig.

Should Polish Government persist in maintaining such measures the German Government are of the opinion that the Free City of Danzig would have no choice but to seek other opportunities of exporting and importing goods.

Following is translation of Polish reply:

The Government of Polish Republic have learnt with liveliest surprise of declaration made on 9th August, 1939, by State Secretary to Polish Chargé d'Affaires *ad interim* at Berlin regarding existing relations between Poland and the Free City of Danzig. The Polish Government indeed perceive no juridical basis capable of justifying intervention of Germany in these relations.

If exchanges of views regarding the Danzig problem have taken place between Polish Government and German Government these exchanges were solely based on goodwill of Polish Government and arose from no obligation of any sort.

In reply to above-mentioned declaration of the German Government the Polish Government are obliged to warn the German Government that in future, as hitherto, they will react to any attempt by authorities of the Free City which might tend to compromise the rights and interests which Poland possesses there in virtue of her agreements, by employment of such means and measures as they alone shall think fit to adopt, and will consider any future intervention by German Government to detriment of these rights and interests as an act of aggression.

Sir N. Henderson to Viscount Halifax

Berlin, 16 August 1939

(Telegraphic)

State Secretary, whom I visited yesterday evening, said at once that the situation had very gravely deteriorated since 4th August. When I last saw him he had regarded the position as less dangerous than last year; now he considered it no less dangerous and most urgent. Deterioration was due firstly to Polish ultimatum to Danzig Senate of 4th August, and secondly to last sentence—which he quoted—of Polish reply to German Government of 10th August, but also in general to the unmistakable set policy of persecution and extermination of the German minority in Poland.

I told Baron von Weizsäcker that there was quite another side to the case. Polish note of 4th August had been necessitated by the succession of measures, and particularly military ones, undertaken in Danzig with view to undermining the Polish position there; Polish reply of 10th August had been provoked by German verbal note of 9th August, and moreover only described as aggression "acts to the detriment of Polish rights and interests"; and Polish Ambassador had only the day before complained to me of the number of cases of persecution of Polish minority in Germany.

State Secretary replied with some heat that though isolated cases of persecution of Poles had occurred, there was absolutely no comparison between them and what was being done in Poland. Hitherto, he said, not too much stress had been laid in the German papers on what was happening in this respect, but there was a limit to everything and that limit had now been reached. As he put it the bottle was full to the top. (In other words Herr Hitler's patience was now exhausted.) He admitted the militarisation of Danzig, but said that its object had been entirely defensive in order to protect the town against what should have been its protector.

As regards the Polish note of 10th August he said that if any German intervention to the detriment of Polish rights and interests in Danzig was to be regarded as an act of aggression, it meant asking Germany to disinterest herself altogether in the Free City, since the whole basis of her former negotiations with Poland had been with a view to modifying the position there in favour of Germany. It was a claim which made the whole situation intolerable and even His Majesty's Government had admitted that there might be modifications to be made.

I told Baron von Weizsäcker that the trouble was that Germany could never see but one side to any question, and always wanted everything modified in her favour. We disputed with acrimony about the rights and wrongs of the case without either apparently convincing the other. With these details I need not trouble you. I eventually said that what was done could not now be undone. We seemed to be rapidly drifting towards a situation in which neither side would be in a position to give way and from which war would ensue. Did Herr Hitler want war? I was prepared to believe that Germany would not yield to intimidation. Nor certainly could His Majesty's Government. If Germany resorted to force, we would resist with force. There could be no possible doubt whatsoever about that. The position had been finally defined in your Lordship's speech at Chatham House on 29th June and by the Prime Minister's statement in the House of Commons on 10th July. From that attitude we could not deviate.

In reply to a suggestion of mine, State Secretary observed that whereas it might just have been possible before 5th August, it was absolutely out of the question now to imagine that Germany could be the first to make any gesture. Even apart from the recent Polish ultimatum and the verbal note about aggression, a German initiative could hardly have been possible in view of Colonel Beck's speech on 5th May in which he had deigned to say that if Germany accepted the principles laid down by him Poland would be ready to talk, but not otherwise. That was language which Germany could not admit. I made the obvious retort. State Secretary's only reply was that the fact remained that to talk of German initiative now was completely academic.

Baron von Weizsäcker then proceeded to say that the trouble was that the German Government's appreciation of the situation was totally different from that of His Majesty's Government. Germany, with innumerable cases of the persecution of Germans before her eyes, could not agree that the Poles were showing restraint: Germany believed that Poland was deliberately running with her eyes shut to ruin: Germany was convinced that His Majesty's Government did not realise whither their policy of encirclement and blind assistance to Poland were leading them and Europe: and that finally his own Government did not, would not and could not believe that Britain would fight under all circumstances whatever folly the Poles might commit.

I told Baron von Weizsäcker that the last was a very dangerous theory and sounded like Herr von Ribbentrop who had never been able to understand the British mentality. If the Poles were compelled by any act of Germany to resort to arms to defend themselves there was not a shadow of doubt that we would give them our full armed support. We had made that abundantly clear and Germany would be making a tragic mistake if she imagined the contrary. State Secretary replied that he would put it differently (and he gave me to understand that the phrase was not his own). Germany believed that the attitude of the Poles would be or was such as to free the British Government from any obligation to follow blindly every eccentric step on the part of a lunatic.

I told the State Secretary that we were talking in a circle. The Polish Government had shown extreme prudence hitherto, and would, moreover, take no major step without previous consultation with us; just as in accordance with their military agreement I understood that the German Government would take no irrevocable step without prior consultation with the Italian Government. His Majesty's Government had given their word and must be sole judges of their action. It was consequently hypothetical to speak of "under all circumstances" or of blindly "following Poland's lead".

Baron von Weizsäcker's reply was that Poland had not consulted His Majesty's Government either before M. Chodacki, who could not have so acted without previous authority from Colonel Beck, had addressed his ultimatum to Danzig Senate, or before replying to the German verbal note of 9th August. Yet, in his opinion, both these were major steps fraught with the most serious consequences. He admitted that some of the Poles were, or wished to be, prudent, but they were, unfortunately, not the rulers of Poland today. The real policy of Poland, over which His Majesty's Government had no control and of which they probably were ignorant, was the thousands of cases of persecution and excesses against Germans in Poland. It was a policy based on the Polish belief in the unlimited support of the British and French Governments. Who, he asked, could now induce the Poles to abandon such methods? It was those methods, combined with the Polish press articles, which encouraged them, which made the situation no longer tenable and so extremely dangerous. The matter had since 4th August changed to one of the utmost seriousness and urgency. Things had drifted along till now, but the point had been reached when they could drift no longer.

There is no doubt that Baron von Weizsäcker was expressing, as he assured me very solemnly that he was, the considered views of his Government and the position as he himself sees it. He told me, though he admitted that he could not say anything for certain, that it was likely that Herr Hitler would in fact attend the Tannenberg celebration on 27th August. But he hinted that things might not only depend on a speech. Yet if nothing happens between now and then I fear that we must at least expect there on Herr Hitler's part a warlike pronouncement from which it may well be difficult for him later to withdraw. As Baron von Weizsäcker himself observed, the situation in one respect was even worse than last year as Mr Chamberlain could not again come out to Germany.

I was impressed by one thing, namely, Baron von Weizsäcker's detachment and calm. He seemed very confident, and professed to believe that Russian assistance to the Poles would not only be negligible, but that the USSR would even in the end join in sharing in the Polish spoils. Nor did my insistence on the inevitability of British intervention seem to move him.

Explanatory note on Herr Hitler's meeting with M. Burckhardt on
11 August 1939

M. Burckhardt accepted an invitation from Herr Hitler to visit him at Berchtesgaden. M. Burckhardt accordingly had a conversation of a private character with Herr Hitler on the 11th August, in the course of which it is understood that the Danzig question in its relationship to the general European situation was discussed between them.

Viscount Halifax to Sir H. Kennard (Warsaw)

Foreign Office, 15 August 1939

(Telegraphic)

I have the impression that Herr Hitler is still undecided, and anxious to avoid war and to hold his hand if he can do so without losing face. As there is a possibility of him not forcing the issue, it is evidently essential to give him no excuse for acting, whether or not conversations about Danzig at some future time may be possible. It therefore seems of the first importance to endeavour to get the local issues (customs inspectors, margarine and herrings) settled at once, and not to let questions of procedure or "face" at Danzig stand in the way. It also seems essential that the Polish Government should make every effort to moderate their press, even in the face of a German press campaign and to intensify their efforts to prevent attacks on their German minority.

In dealing with local Danzig issues, I would beg M. Beck to work through the intermediary of the High Commissioner, or at all events after consultation with him, rather than direct with the Senate. I should like M. Beck to treat M. Burckhardt with the fullest confidence, as in my opinion he is doing his best in a very difficult situation.

While the present moment may not be opportune for negotiations on general issues as opposed to local differences, the Polish Government would in my judgment do well to continue to make it plain that, provided essentials can be secured, they are at all times ready to examine the possibility of negotiation over Danzig if there is a prospect of success. I regard such an attitude as important from the point of view of world opinion.

Before speaking to M. Beck on the above lines, please concert with your French colleague who will be receiving generally similar instructions in order that you may take approximately the same line with M. Beck.

Sir H. Kennard to Viscount Halifax

Warsaw, 15 August 1939

(Telegraphic)

I spoke to the Minister for Foreign Affairs in the sense of your telegram of 15th August. M. Beck agreed that Herr Hitler was probably still undecided as to his course of action. German military activity was nevertheless disturbing, though he did not take too alarmist a view at present.

M. Beck agreed that an effort should be made to settle local issues in Danzig and said that he was endeavouring to separate economic from political questions with a view to settling the former quickly and equitably. He hoped that tomorrow's conversation between Polish Commissioner-General and President of the Senate might lead to some results. M. Beck said that if he could not arrive at a direct settlement of new incident which had occurred he would invoke M. Burckhardt's intervention.

This incident was as follows: three Polish customs inspectors, while making their round of harbour in a motor boat, discovered a German vessel entering the harbour without lights, and, as they suspected smuggling of munitions, turned their searchlight on her. On landing, they were arrested by Danzig police. Polish Commissioner-General has sent in a note demanding their release, though not in unduly energetic language. If he did not receive a reply shortly he would invite High Commissioner to settle this incident.

As regards press, he remarked that it was not the Poles but the British and other foreign press who first suggested that firmness of the Polish Government had caused the Senate to yield in the matter of Polish customs inspectors.

TREATMENT OF GERMAN MINORITY IN POLAND

Sir H. Kennard to Viscount Halifax

Warsaw, 24 August 1939

(Telegraphic)

While I am of course not in a position to check all the allegations made by the German press of minority persecutions here, I am satisfied from enquiries I have made that the campaign is a gross distortion and exaggeration of the facts. Accusations of beating with chains, throwing on barbed wire, being forced to shout insults against Herr Hitler in chorus, etc., are merely silly, but many individual cases specified have been disproved.

M. Karletan, for instance, arrested in connection with murder of Polish policeman on 15th August, was alleged by German press to have been beaten to death and his wife and children thrown out of the window. *Manchester Guardian* correspondent tells me that he visited him in prison on Sunday and found him in good health. He had not been beaten or physically injured at all. Story about wife and child was equally devoid of any foundation.

It is true that many of the German minority have left Poland illegally, but I hear both from the Acting British Consul at Katowice and from British Vice-Consul at Lodz that the Germans themselves have told many to leave. There was an initial exodus last May. Many subsequently asked to come back, but the Poles were not anxious to have them, as they had no doubt been trained in propaganda, sabotage and espionage activities, such as Jungdeutsche Partei in Katowice have been conducting. In Lodz area some of those who left recently raised all the money and credit they could before leaving, and the Voivode [head of an administrative division] told Vice-Consul on 20th August that from evidence available he was satisfied that German Consulate had transferred these funds to Germany and was no doubt privy to their departure. Many of those who left, especially from Lodz, are of the *intelligentsia*, and they are said to include Herr Witz, leader of Volksbund. British Vice-Consul at Lodz says many German organisations have been closed there, but they were notoriously conducting Nazi propaganda, and Polish authorities could not ignore it altogether. I think, however, many Germans have lost their jobs, especially in factories of military or semi-military importance, and some 2,000 workmen have left Tomaszów.

Many of those who left their homes undoubtedly did so because they wished to be on German side of the front in event of war, and in general there is by common consent less individual friction with members of the minority now than last May.

Ministry for Foreign Affairs tell me that figure of 76,000 refugees quoted in German press is a gross exaggeration. I should say 17,000 was the absolute maximum. *Gazeta Polska* correspondent in Berlin has asked to be shown refugee camps of the 76,000 and apparently received no answer.

In Silesia the frontier is not fully open, but a special frontier card system is in force and considerable daily traffic is possible. The German authorities having closed frontier in Rybnik area where Poles cross to Poland, Polish authorities closed it elsewhere where Germans cross into Germany. In view of revelations of activities of Jungdeutsche Partei, the Polish authorities feel greater control of frontier traffic is in any case necessary.

Polish press has recently published many complaints of wholesale removal of Poles from frontier districts in Silesia and East Prussia to the interior of Germany, smashing of property, especially in Allenstein district, closing of all Polish libraries in Silesia and other forms of persecution. According to semi-official *Gazeta Polska*, from April to June there were recorded 976 acts of violence against the minority, and since then the number of cases is stated to have increased beyond all bounds. For the last two days, however, no further information has been published, as M. Beck has damped the press down.

In general, responsible organs of the Polish press have not published violent tirades, still less claimed German territory for Poland, and *A.B.C.*, recently quoted in Germany, is a violent Opposition newspaper with little reputation and less influence.

Sir H. Kennard to Viscount Halifax

Warsaw, 26 August 1939

(Telegraphic)

Series of incidents again occurred yesterday on German frontier.

Polish patrol met party of Germans 1 kilometre from East Prussian frontier near Pelta. Germans opened fire. Polish patrol replied, killing leader, whose body is being returned.

German bands also crossed Silesian frontier near Szczyglo, twice near Rybnik and twice elsewhere, firing shots and attacking blockhouses and customs posts with machine guns and hand grenades. Poles have protested vigorously to Berlin.

Gazeta Polska, in inspired leader today, says these are more than incidents. They are clearly prepared acts of aggression of paramilitary disciplined detachments supplied with regular army's arms, and in one case it was a regular army detachment. The attacks are more or less continuous.

These incidents did *not* cause Poland to forsake calm and strong attitude of defence. Facts spoke for themselves and acts of aggression came from German side. This was best answer to ravings of German press.

Ministry for Foreign Affairs state uniformed German detachment has since shot Pole across frontier and wounded another.

Sir H. Kennard to Viscount Halifax

Warsaw, 26 August 1939

(Telegraphic)
Ministry for Foreign Affairs categorically deny story recounted by Herr Hitler to French Ambassador that twenty-four Germans were recently killed at Lodz and eight at Bielsko. Story is without any foundation whatever.

Sir H. Kennard to Viscount Halifax

Warsaw, 27 August 1939

(Telegraphic)
So far as I can judge, German allegations of mass ill-treatment of German minority by Polish authorities are gross exaggerations, if not complete falsifications. There is no sign of any loss of control of situation by Polish civil authorities. Warsaw (and so far as I can ascertain the rest of Poland) is still completely calm. Such allegations are reminiscent of Nazi propaganda methods regarding Czecho-Slovakia last year.

In any case it is purely and simply deliberate German provocation in accordance with fixed policy that has since March exacerbated feeling between the two nationalities. I suppose this has been done with object of (*a*) creating war spirit in Germany, (*b*) impressing public opinion abroad, (*c*) provoking either defeatism or apparent aggression in Poland.

It has signally failed to achieve either of the two latter objects.

It is noteworthy that Danzig was hardly mentioned by Herr Hitler.

German treatment of Czech Jews and Polish minority is apparently negligible factor compared with alleged sufferings of Germans in Poland, where, be it noted, they do not amount to more than 10 per cent of population in any commune.

In face of these facts, it can hardly be doubted that, if Herr Hitler decides on war, it is for the sole purpose of destroying Polish independence.

I shall lose no opportunity of impressing on Minister for Foreign Affairs necessity of doing everything possible to prove that Herr Hitler's allegations regarding German minority are false.

DEVELOPMENTS LEADING IMMEDIATELY TO THE OUTBREAK OF HOSTILITIES BETWEEN GREAT BRITAIN AND GERMANY ON 3 SEPTEMBER 1939

Letter of 22 August 1939, *from the Prime Minister to the German Chancellor*

10 Downing Street, 22 August 1939

Your Excellency will have already heard of certain measures taken by His Majesty's Government, and announced in the press and on the wireless this evening. These steps have, in the opinion of His Majesty's Government, been rendered necessary by the military movements which have been reported from Germany, and by the fact that apparently the announcement of a German-Soviet Agreement is taken in some quarters in Berlin to indicate that intervention by Great Britain on behalf of Poland is no longer a contingency that need be reckoned with. No greater mistake could be made. Whatever may prove to be the nature of the German-Soviet Agreement, it cannot alter Great Britain's obligation to Poland which His Majesty's Government have stated in public repeatedly and plainly, and which they are determined to fulfil.

It has been alleged that, if His Majesty's Government had made their position more clear in 1914, the great catastrophe would have been avoided. Whether or not there is any force in that allegation, His Majesty's Government are resolved that on this occasion there shall be no such tragic misunderstanding. If the case should arise, they are resolved, and prepared, to employ without delay all the forces at their command, and it is impossible to foresee the end of hostilities once engaged. It would be a dangerous illusion to think that, if war once starts, it will come to an early end even if a success on any one of the several fronts on which it will be engaged should have been secured.

Having thus made our position perfectly clear, I wish to repeat to you my conviction that war between our two peoples would be the greatest calamity that could occur. I am certain that it is desired neither by our people, nor by yours, and I cannot see that there is anything in the questions arising between Germany and Poland which could not and should not be resolved without the use of force, if only a situation of confidence could be restored to enable discussions to be carried on in an atmosphere different from that which prevails today.

We have been, and at all times will be, ready to assist in creating conditions in which such negotiations could take place, and in which it might be possible concurrently to discuss the wider problems affecting the future of international relations, including matters of interest to us and to you. The difficulties in the way of any peaceful discussion in the present state of tension are, however, obvious, and the longer that tension is maintained, the harder will it be for reason to prevail.

These difficulties, however, might be mitigated, if not removed, provided that there could for an initial period be a truce on both sides—and indeed on all sides—to press polemics and to all incitement. If such a truce could be arranged, then, at the end of that period, during which steps could be taken to examine and deal with complaints made by either side as to the treatment of minorities, it is reasonable to hope that suitable conditions might have been established for direct negotiations between Germany and Poland upon the issues between them (with the aid of a neutral intermediary, if both sides should think that that would be helpful).

But I am bound to say that there would be slender hope of bringing such negotiations to successful issue unless it were understood beforehand that any settlement reached would, when concluded, be guaranteed by other Powers. His Majesty's Government would be ready, if desired, to make such contribution as they could to the effective operation of such guarantees.

At this moment I confess I can see no other way to avoid a catastrophe that will involve Europe in war.

In view of the grave consequences to humanity, which may follow from the action of their rulers, I trust that Your Excellency will weigh with the utmost deliberation the considerations which I have put before you.

NEVILLE CHAMBERLAIN

Sir N. Henderson to Viscount Halifax (received 24 August)
Berlin, 23 August 1939

(Telegraphic)

Two difficulties were raised last night before visit to Herr Hitler was actually arranged. In first place it was asked whether I would not be ready to wait until Herr von Ribbentrop's return. I said that I could not wait as my instructions were to hand letter myself as soon as possible. An hour or so later I was rung up again by State Secretary on the telephone asking for gist of letter and referring to publication of some private letter addressed to Herr

Hitler last year. I told Baron von Weizsäcker that I had no recollection of publication of any private letter last year and assured him that there was no intention of publishing this one. As regards Prime Minister's letter I said that its three main points were (1) that His Majesty's Government was determined to fulfil their obligations to Poland, (2) that they were prepared, provided a peace atmosphere was created, to discuss all problems affecting our two countries, and (3) that during period of truce they would welcome direct discussions between Poland and Germany in regard to minorities.

State Secretary appeared to regard these replies as likely to be satisfactory, but deferred a final answer till 8 AM this morning. At that hour he telephoned me to say that arrangements made had been confirmed and that he would accompany me to Berchtesgaden, leaving Berlin at 9.30 AM.

We arrived at Salzburg soon after 11 AM and motored to Berchtesgaden, where I was received by Herr Hitler shortly after 1 PM. I had derived the impression that the atmosphere was likely to be most unfriendly and that the probability was that the interview would be exceedingly brief.

In order to forestall this I began conversation by stating that I had been instructed to hand to the Chancellor personally a letter from the Prime Minister on behalf of His Majesty's Government, but before doing so I wished to make some preliminary remarks. I was grateful to his Excellency for receiving me so promptly as it would have been impossible for me to wait for Herr von Ribbentrop's return inasmuch as the fact was that His Majesty's Government were afraid that the situation brooked no delay. I asked his Excellency to read the letter, not from the point of view of the past, but from that of the present and the future. What had been done could not now be undone, and there could be no peace in Europe without Anglo-German co-operation. We had guaranteed Poland against attack and we would keep our word. Throughout the centuries of history we had never, so far as I knew, broken our word. We could not do so now and remain Britain.

During the whole of this first conversation Herr Hitler was excitable and uncompromising. He made no long speeches but his language was violent and exaggerated both as regards England and Poland. He began by asserting that the Polish question would have been settled on the most generous terms if it had not been for England's unwarranted support. I drew attention to the inaccuracies of this statement, our guarantee having been given on 31st March and Polish reply on 26th March. He retorted by saying that the latter had been inspired by a British press campaign, which had invented a German threat to Poland the week before. Germany had not moved a man any more than she had done during the similar fallacious press campaign about Czecho-Slovakia on the 20th May last year.

He then violently attacked the Poles, talked of 100,000 German refugees from Poland, excesses against Germans, closing of German institutions and Polish systematic persecution of German nationals generally. He said that he was receiving hundreds of telegrams daily from his persecuted compatriots. He would stand it no longer, etc. I interrupted by remarking that while I did not wish to try to deny that persecutions occurred (of Poles also in Germany) the German press accounts were highly exaggerated. He had mentioned the castration of Germans. I happened to be aware of one case. The German in question was a sex-maniac, who had been treated as he deserved. Herr Hitler's retort was that there had not been one case but six.

His next tirade was against British support of Czechs and Poles. He asserted that the former would have been independent today if England had not encouraged them in a policy hostile to Germany. He insinuated that the Poles would be tomorrow if Britain ceased to encourage them today. He followed this by a tirade against England, whose friendship he had sought for twenty years only to see every offer turned down with contempt. The British press was also vehemently abused. I contested every point and kept calling his statements inaccurate but the only effect was to launch him on some fresh tirade.

Throughout the conversation I stuck firmly to point (1), namely our determination to honour our obligations to Poland; Herr Hitler on the other hand kept harping on point (3), the Polish persecution of German nationals. Point (2) was not referred to at all and apparently did not interest him. (I had been warned that it would not.)

Most of the conversation was recrimination, the real points being those stressed in his reply in regard to the threat to Poland if persecutions continue and to England and France if they mobilise to such an extent as to constitute a danger to Germany.

At the end of this first conversation Herr Hitler observed, in reply to my repeated warnings that direct action by Germany would mean war, that Germany had nothing to lose and Great Britain much; that he did not desire war but would not shrink from it if it was necessary; and that his people were much more behind him than last September.

I replied that I hoped and was convinced that some solution was still possible without war and asked why contact with the Poles could not be renewed. Herr Hitler's retort was that, so long as England gave Poland a blank cheque, Polish unreasonableness would render any negotiation impossible. I denied the "blank cheque" but this only started Herr Hitler off again and finally it was agreed that he would send or hand me his reply in two hours' time.

Sir N. Henderson to Viscount Halifax (received 24 *August)*

Berlin, 24 August 1939

(Telegraphic)

Following is continuation of my telegram of the 23rd August.

After my first talk yesterday I returned to Salzburg on understanding that if Herr Hitler wished to see me again I would be at his disposal or, if he had nothing new to say, he could merely send me his reply to the Prime Minister by hand.

As in the event he asked to see me, I went back to Berchtesgaden. He was quite calm the second time and never raised his voice once.

Conversation lasted from 20 minutes to half an hour but produced little new, except that verbally he was far more categoric than in written reply as to his determination to attack Poland if "another German were ill-treated in Poland."

I spoke of tragedy of war and of his immense responsibility but his answer was that it would be all England's fault. I refuted this only to learn from him that England was determined to destroy and exterminate Germany. He was, he said, 50 years old; he preferred war now to when he would be 55 or 60. I told him that it was absurd to talk of extermination. Nations could not be exterminated and peaceful and prosperous Germany was a British interest. His answer was that it was England who was fighting for lesser races whereas he was fighting only for Germany: the Germans would this time fight to the last man: it would have been different in 1914 if he had been Chancellor.

He spoke several times of his repeated offers of friendship to England and their invariable and contemptuous rejection. I referred to the Prime Minister's efforts of last year and his desire for co-operation with Germany. He said that he had believed in Mr Chamberlain's good will at the time, but, and especially since encirclement efforts of last few months, he did so no longer. I pointed out fallacy of this view but his answer was that he was now finally convinced of the rightness of the views held formerly to him by others that England and Germany could never agree.

In referring to Russian non-aggression pact he observed that it was England which had forced him into agreement with Russia. He did not seem enthusiastic over it but added that once he made agreement it would be for a long period. (Text of agreement signed today confirms this and I shall be surprised if it is not supplemented later by something more than mere non-aggression.)

I took the line at the end that war seemed to me quite inevitable if Herr Hitler persisted in direct action against Poland and expressed regret at failure of my mission in general to Berlin and of my visit to him. Herr Hitler's attitude was that it was England's fault and that nothing short of complete change of her policy towards Germany could now ever convince him of British desire for good relations.

Sir N. Henderson to Viscount Halifax (received 8.30 PM)

Berlin, 24 August 1939

(Telegraphic)

I have hitherto not made particular reference to the underlined portion in Herr Hitler's reply to the Prime Minister in regard to German general mobilisation as a counter to British and French mobilisations.

When Herr Hitler gave me his reply, readjusted, I asked him what exactly was intended by this sentence, as I would, I said, regard a general German mobilisation as the equivalent to war. The answer I got was confused, as was the actual German text. But the gist was that if the French and British mobilisations convinced Herr Hitler that the Western Powers meant to attack him he would mobilise in self-defence. I pointed out that any British military mobilisation would in any case fall far short of what already existed in Germany. Herr Hitler's reply was that this sentence was more particularly intended as a warning to France, and that, as I gathered, the French Government was being or would be so informed.

I feel that the main objects of inserting this underlined passage [in italics here] in his letter were (*a*) to indicate that Germany could not be intimidated; and (*b*) to serve as an excuse for general mobilisation if and when Herr Hitler decides on it.

Communication from the German Chancellor to the Prime Minister, handed to His Majesty's Ambassador on 23 August 1939

(Translation)

The British Ambassador has just handed to me a communication in which your Excellency draws attention in the name of the British Government to a number of points which in your estimation are of the greatest importance.

I may be permitted to answer your letter as follows:

Germany has never sought conflict with England and has never interfered in English interests. On the contrary, she has for years endeavoured—although unfortunately in vain—to win England's friendship. On this account she voluntarily assumed in a wide area of Europe the limitations on her own interests which from a national-political point of view it would have otherwise been very difficult to tolerate.

The German Reich, however, like every other State, possesses certain definite interests which it is impossible to renounce. These do not extend beyond the limits of the necessities laid down by former German history and deriving from vital economic prerequisites. Some of these questions held and still hold a significance both of a national-political and a psychological character which no German Government is able to ignore.

To these questions belong the German City of Danzig, and the connected problem of the Corridor. Numerous statesmen, historians and men of letters even in England have been conscious of this at any rate up to a few years ago. I would add that all these territories lying in the aforesaid German sphere of interest and in particular those lands which returned to the Reich eighteen months ago received their cultural development at the hands not of the English but exclusively of the Germans and this, moreover, already from a time dating back over a thousand years.

Germany was prepared to settle the questions of Danzig and of the Corridor by the method of negotiation on the basis of a proposal of truly unparalleled magnanimity. The allegations disseminated by England regarding a German mobilisation against Poland, the assertion of aggressive designs towards Roumania, Hungary, etc., as well as the so-called guarantee declarations which were subsequently given had, however, dispelled Polish inclination to negotiate on a basis of this kind which would have been tolerable for Germany also.

The unconditional assurance given by England to Poland that she would render assistance to that country in all circumstances regardless of the causes from which a conflict might spring, could only be interpreted in that country as an encouragement thenceforward to unloosen, under cover of such a charter, a wave of appalling terrorism against the one and a half million German inhabitants living in Poland. The atrocities which since then have been taking place in that country are terrible for the victims, but intolerable for a Great Power such as the German Reich which is expected to remain a passive onlooker during these happenings. Poland has been guilty of numerous breaches of her legal obligations towards the Free City of Danzig, has made demands in the character of ultimata, and has initiated a process of economic strangulation.

The Government of the German Reich therefore recently caused the Polish Government to be informed that it was not prepared passively to accept this development of affairs, that it will not tolerate further addressing of notes in the character of ultimata to Danzig, that it will not tolerate a continuance of the persecutions of the German minority, that it will equally not tolerate the extermination of the Free City of Danzig by economic measures, in other words, the destruction of the vital bases of the population of Danzig by a kind of Customs blockade, and that it will not tolerate the occurrence of further acts of provocation directed against the Reich. Apart from this, the questions of the Corridor and of Danzig must and shall be solved.

Your Excellency informs me in the name of the British Government that you will be obliged to render assistance to Poland in any such case of intervention on the part of Germany. I take note of this statement of yours and assure you that it can make no change in the determination of the Reich Government to safeguard the interests of the Reich as stated above. Your assurance to the effect that in such an event you anticipate a long war is shared by myself. Germany, if attacked by England, will be found prepared and determined. I have already more than once declared before the German people and the world that there can be no doubt concerning the determination of the new German Reich rather to accept, for however long it might be, every sort of misery and tribulation than to sacrifice its national interests, let alone its honour.

The German Reich Government has received information to the effect that the British Government has the intention to carry out measures of mobilisation which, according to the statements contained in your own letter, are clearly directed against Germany alone. This is said to be true of France as well. Since Germany has never had the intention of taking military measures other than those of a defensive character against England or France, and, as has already been emphasised, has never intended, and does not in the future intend, to attack England or France, it follows that this announcement as confirmed by you, Mr Prime Minister, in your own letter, can only refer to a contemplated act of menace directed against the Reich. *I therefore inform your Excellency that, in the event of these military announcements being carried into effect, I shall order immediate mobilisation of the German forces.*

The question of the treatment of European problems on a peaceful basis is not a decision which rests on Germany but primarily on those who since the crime committed by the Versailles dictate have stubbornly and consistently opposed any peaceful revision. Only after a change of spirit on the part of the responsible Powers can there be any real change in the relationship between England and Germany. I have all my life fought for Anglo-German friendship; the attitude adopted by British diplomacy—at any rate up to the present—has, however, convinced me of the futility of such an attempt. Should there be any change in this respect in the future nobody could be happier than I.

ADOLF HITLER

Non-Aggression Pact between Germany and the Union of Soviet Socialist Republics

(Translation)

The Government of the German Reich and the Government of the Union of Soviet Socialist Republics, guided by the desire to strengthen the cause of peace between Germany and the Union of Soviet Socialist Republics, and taking as a basis the fundamental regulations of the Neutrality Agreement concluded in April 1926 between Germany and the Union of Soviet Socialist Republics, have reached the following agreement:

ARTICLE 1

The two Contracting Parties bind themselves to refrain from any act of force, any aggressive action and any attack on one another, both singly and also jointly with other Powers.

ARTICLE 2

In the event of one of the Contracting Parties becoming the object of warlike action on the part of a third Power, the other Contracting Party shall in no manner support this third Power.

ARTICLE 3

The Governments of the two Contracting Parties shall in future remain continuously in touch with one another, by way of consultation, in order to inform one another on questions touching their joint interests.

ARTICLE 4

Neither of the two Contracting Parties shall participate in any grouping of Powers which is directed directly or indirectly against the other Party.

ARTICLE 5

In the event of disputes or disagreements arising between the Contracting Parties on questions of this or that kind, both Parties would clarify these disputes or disagreements exclusively by means of friendly exchange of opinion or, if necessary, by arbitration committees.

ARTICLE 6

The present Agreement shall be concluded for a period of ten years on the understanding that, in so far as one of the Contracting Parties does not give notice of termination one year before the end of this period, the period of validity of this Agreement shall automatically be regarded as prolonged for a further period of five years.

ARTICLE 7

The present Agreement shall be ratified within the shortest possible time. The instruments of ratification shall be exchanged in Berlin. The Agreement takes effect immediately after it has been signed.

For the German Reich Government: RIBBENTROP

For the Government of the USSR: MOLOTOV

Moscow, 23 August 1939

Mr F. M. Shepherd to Viscount Halifax

Danzig, 26 August 1939

(Telegraphic)

Following is translation of decree of Senate dated 23rd August:

> *Decree: Article* 1.—Gauleiter of Danzig is Head of State ("Staatsoberhaupt") of the Free City of Danzig.
> *Article* 2. This decree comes into force on 23rd August, 1939.

Following are translations of letters dated 24th August (*a*) from President of Senate to Herr Forster, and (*b*) of latter's reply:

> (*a*) At its meeting yesterday the Senate passed a resolution according to which you have been declared Staatsoberhaupt of the Free City of Danzig as from yesterday. A copy of the certified resolution is enclosed. In addition, a legal decree has been prepared today and signed making the above-mentioned resolution of the Senate operative. By means of these two acts of the Government the Danzig Constitution has been altered in the above-mentioned sense. The Senate has authorised me to request you, Herr Gauleiter, to accept this office forthwith in order in these difficult but wonderful last decisive days outwardly to give expression to the unity between party and State, which has so often been stressed and which inwardly has always existed.
>
> (*b*) I have taken cognisance of the contents of your letter of the 24th instant and of the enclosed certified copy of the decree regarding the Staatsoberhaupt of the Free City of Danzig of 23rd August, 1939, and of the copy of the Senate's resolution of the 23rd August, 1939, which was also enclosed. It, of course, goes without saying that in my capacity as Leader of the NSDAP of the Danzig district I am prepared in days which are so fateful for Danzig also to conduct the affairs of the State. With this decree promulgated on the 23rd August, 1939, a state of affairs is officially sanctioned which, since the accession to power by the National Socialists in 1933, has in practice been in force.

Sir H. Kennard to Viscount Halifax

Warsaw, 24 August 1939

(Telegraphic)

Following is translation of Polish note to the Danzig Senate:

> Herr Staatsrat Boettcher today informed Councillor of the Polish Commissariat-General of the resolution of the Senate of the Free City conferring on Gauleiter Forster the functions and position of the head of the State ("Staatsoberhaupt") of the Free City, this being confirmed in today's Danzig press. I address myself to the Senate of the Free City as the body which, in accordance with the legally binding Constitution of the Free City, exercises supreme authority in that territory, in order to make on behalf of my Government the following declaration:
>
> My Government sees no legal foundation for the adoption by the Senate of the Free City of a resolution instituting a new State function for which there is no provision whatever in the Constitution of the Free City, and to which, as would appear, the authorities hitherto functioning in the Free City would be subordinated. The Polish Government reserve the right to adopt a further attitude in this respect.
>
> In this connection the Polish Government consider it necessary to remind the authorities of the Free City that they have already more than once warned the Senate of the Free City in the most decisive fashion against a policy of *fait accompli*, the consequence of which might be most serious and the responsibility for which would fall exclusively upon the authorities of the Free City of Danzig.

Speech by the Prime Minister in the House of Commons on 24 August 1939

When at the beginning of this month hon. members separated for the summer recess, I think there can have been few among us who anticipated that many weeks would elapse before we should find ourselves meeting here again. Unfortunately, those anticipations have been fulfilled, and the Government have felt obliged to ask that Parliament should be summoned again, in order to take such new and drastic steps as are required by the gravity of the situation. In the last debate which we had upon foreign affairs, which took place on the 31st July, I observed that the Danzig situation required very careful watching. I expressed my anxiety about the pace at which the accumulation of war weapons was proceeding throughout Europe. I referred to the poisoning of public opinion by the propaganda which was going on, and I declared that if that could be stopped and if some action could be taken to restore confidence, I did not believe there was any question which could not be solved by peaceful discussion. I am sorry to say that there has been no sign since of any such action. On the contrary, the international position has steadily deteriorated until today we find ourselves confronted with the imminent peril of war.

At the beginning of August a dispute arose between the Polish Government and the Danzig Senate as to the position and functions of certain Polish Customs officials. It was not a question of major importance. Many more acute difficulties have been easily settled in the past under less tense conditions and even in this case discussions had actually begun between the parties last week. While those discussions were in progress, the German press opened a violent campaign against the Polish Government. They declared that Danzig could not be the subject of any conference or any compromise and that it must come back to the Reich at once and unconditionally. They went further. They linked up with the Danzig question the question of the Corridor. They attacked the whole policy and the attitude of the Polish Government, and they published circumstantial accounts of the alleged ill-treatment of Germans living in Poland. Now we have no means of checking the accuracy of those stories, but we cannot help being struck by the fact that they bear a strong resemblance to similar allegations that were made last year in respect of the Sudeten Germans in Czecho-Slovakia. We must also remember that there is a large Polish minority in Germany and that the treatment of that minority has also been the subject of bitter complaints by the Polish Government.

There is no subject which is calculated to arouse ill-feeling in any country more than statements about the ill-treatment of people of their own race in another country. This is a subject which provides the most inflammable of all materials, the material most likely to cause a general conflagration. In those circumstances one cannot but deeply regret that such incidents, which, if they were established, would naturally excite sympathy for the victims and indignation against the authors of this alleged ill-treatment, should be treated in a way which is calculated still further to embitter the atmosphere and raise the temperature to the danger point. But I think it will be agreed that, in face of this campaign, declarations by Polish statesmen have shown great calm and self-restraint. The Polish leaders, while they have been firm in their determination to resist an attack upon their independence, have been unprovocative. They have always been ready, as I am sure they would be ready now, to discuss differences with the German Government, if they could be sure that those discussions would be carried on without threats of force or violence, and with some confidence that, if agreement were reached, its terms would be respected afterwards permanently, both in the letter and in the spirit. This press campaign is not the only symptom which is ominously reminiscent of past experience. Military preparations have been made in Germany on such a scale that that country is now in a condition of complete readiness for war, and at the beginning of this week we had word that German troops were beginning to move towards the Polish frontier. It then became evident that a crisis of the first magnitude was approaching, and the Government resolved that the time had come when they must seek the approval of Parliament for further measures of defence.

That was the situation on Tuesday last, when in Berlin and Moscow it was announced that negotiations had been taking place, and were likely soon to be concluded, for a non-aggression pact between those two countries. I do not attempt to conceal from the House that that announcement came to the Government as a surprise, and a surprise of a very unpleasant character. For some time past there had been rumours about an impending change in the relations between Germany and the Soviet Union, but no inkling of that change had been conveyed either to us or to the French Government by the Soviet Government. The House may remember that on the 31st July I remarked that we had engaged upon steps almost unprecedented in character. I said that we had shown a great amount of trust and a strong desire to bring the negotiations with the Soviet Union to a successful conclusion when we agreed to send our soldiers, sailors and airmen to Russia to discuss military plans together before we had any assurance that we should be able to reach an agreement on political matters. Well, Sir, nevertheless, moved by the observation of the Russian Secretary for Foreign Affairs, that if we could come to a successful conclusion of our military discussions, political agreement should not present any insuperable difficulties, we sent the Mission.

The British and French Missions reached Moscow on the 11th August. They were warmly received, in friendly fashion, and discussions were actually in progress and had proceeded on a basis of mutual trust when this bombshell was flung down. It, to say the least of it, was highly disturbing to learn that while these conversations were proceeding on that basis, the Soviet Government were secretly negotiating a pact with Germany for purposes which, on the face of it, were inconsistent with the objects of their foreign policy, as we had understood it. I do not propose this afternoon to pass any final judgment upon this incident. That, I think, would be premature until we have had an opportunity of consulting with the French Government as to the meaning and the consequences of this agreement, the text of which was published only this morning. But the question that the Government had to consider when they learned of this announcement was what effect, if any, this changed situation would have upon their own policy. In Berlin the announcement was hailed, with extraordinary cynicism, as a great diplomatic victory which removed any danger of war, since we and France would no longer be likely to fulfil our obligations to Poland. We felt it our first duty to remove any such dangerous illusion.

The House will recollect that the guarantee which we had given to Poland was given before any agreement with Russia was talked of, and that it was not in any way made dependent upon any such agreement being reached. How, then, could we, with honour, go back upon such an obligation, which we had so often and so plainly repeated? Therefore, our first act was to issue a statement that our obligations to Poland and to other countries remained unaffected. Those obligations rest upon agreed statements made to the House of Commons, to which effect is being given in treaties which are at present in an advanced stage of negotiation. Those treaties, when concluded, will formally define our obligations, but they do not in any way alter, they do not add to or subtract from, the obligations of mutual assistance which have already been accepted. The communiqué which we issued to the press after the meeting of the Cabinet this week spoke also of certain measures of defence which we had adopted. It will be remembered that, as I have said, Germany has an immense army of men already under arms and that military preparations of all kinds have been and are being carried on on a vast scale in that country.

The measures that we have taken up to now are of a precautionary and defensive character, and to give effect to our determination to put this country in a state of preparedness to meet any emergency, but I wish emphatically to repudiate any suggestion, if such a suggestion should be made, that these measures imply an act of menace. Nothing that we have done or that we propose to do menaces the legitimate interests of Germany. It is not an act of menace to prepare to help friends to defend themselves against force. If neighbours wishing to live together peacefully in friendly relations find that one of them is contemplating apparently an aggressive act of force against another of them, and is making open preparations for action, it is not a menace for the others to announce their intention of aiding the one who is the subject of this threat.

There is another action which has been taken today in the financial sphere. Hon. members will have seen the announcement that the Bank Rate, which has remained at 2 per cent for a long time past, has today been raised to 4 per cent, and the House will recognise that this is a normal protective measure adopted for the purpose of defending our resources in a period of uncertainty. There is in this connection a contribution to be made by British citizens generally. The public can best co-operate in reducing as far as possible any demands which involve directly or indirectly the purchase of foreign exchange; next by scrupulously observing the request of the Chancellor of the Exchequer that capital should not at present be sent or moved out of the country; and, finally, by holding no more foreign assets than are strictly required for the normal purpose of business.

In view of the attitude in Berlin to which I have already referred, His Majesty's Government felt that it was their duty at this moment to leave no possible loophole for misunderstanding, and so that no doubt might exist in the mind of the German Government, His Majesty's Ambassador in Berlin was instructed to seek an interview with the German Chancellor and to hand him a message from me on behalf of the British Government. That message was delivered yesterday and the reply was received today. The object of my communication to the German Chancellor was to restate our position and to make quite sure that there was no misunderstanding. His Majesty's Government felt that this was all the more necessary having regard to reports which we had received as to the military movements taking place in Germany and as to the then projected German–Soviet Agreement. I therefore made it plain, as had been done in the communiqué issued after the Cabinet meeting on Tuesday, that if the case should arise His Majesty's Government were resolved and prepared to employ without delay all the forces at their command.

On numerous occasions I have stated my conviction that war between our two countries, admitted on all sides to be the greatest calamity that could occur, is not desired either by our own people or the German people. With this fact in mind I informed the German Chancellor that, in our view, there was nothing in the questions arising between Poland and Germany which could not be, and should not be, resolved without the use of force, if only a situation of confidence could be restored. We expressed our willingness to assist in creating the conditions in which such negotiations could take place. The present state of tension creates great difficulties, and I expressed the view that if there could be a truce on all sides to press polemics and all other forms of incitement, suitable conditions might be established for direct negotiations between Germany and Poland upon the points at issue. The negotiations could, of course, deal also with the complaints made on either side about the protection of minorities.

The German Chancellor's reply includes what amounts to a re-statement of the German thesis that Eastern Europe is a sphere in which Germany ought to have a free hand. If we—this is the thesis—or any country having less direct interest choose to interfere, the blame for the ensuing conflict will be ours. This thesis entirely misapprehends the British position. We do not seek to claim a special position for ourselves in Eastern Europe. We do not think of asking Germany to sacrifice her national interests, but we cannot agree that national interests can only be secured by the shedding of blood or the destruction of the independence of other States. With regard to the relations between Poland and Germany, the German Chancellor in his reply to me has referred again to the situation at Danzig, drawing attention to the position of that city and of the Corridor, and to the offer which he made early this year to settle these questions by methods of negotiation. I have repeatedly refuted the allegation that it was our guarantee to Poland that decided the Polish Government to refuse the proposals then made. That guarantee was not, in fact, given until after the Polish refusal had been conveyed to the German Government. In view of the delicacy of the situation I must refrain for the present from any further comment upon the communications which have just passed between the two Governments. Catastrophe has not yet come upon us. We must, therefore, still hope that reason and sanity may find a way to reassert themselves. The pronouncement we made and what I have said today reflects, I am sure, the views of the French Government, with whom we have maintained the customary close contact in pursuance of our well established cordial relations.

Naturally, our minds turn to the Dominions. I appreciate very warmly the pronouncements made by Ministers in other parts of the British Commonwealth. The indications that have been given from time to time, in some cases as recently as yesterday, of their sympathy with our patient efforts in the cause of peace, and of their attitude in the unhappy event of their proving unsuccessful, are a source of profound encouragement to us in these critical times. The House will, I am sure, share the appreciation with which His Majesty's Government have noted the appeal for peace made yesterday by King Leopold in the name of the heads of the Oslo States, after the meeting in Brussels yesterday of their representatives. It will be evident from what I have said that His Majesty's Government share the hopes to which that appeal gave expression, and earnestly trust that effect will be given to it.

The Foreign Secretary, in a speech made on the 29th June to the Royal Institute of International Affairs, set out the fundamental bases of British foreign policy. His observations on that subject were, I believe, received with general approval. The first basis is our determination to resist methods of force. The second basis is our recognition of the world desire to pursue the constructive work of building peace. If we were once satisfied, my noble Friend said, that the intentions of others were the same as our own, and if we were satisfied that all wanted peaceful solutions, then, indeed, we could discuss problems which are today causing the world so much anxiety. That definition of the basic fundamental ground of British policy still stands. We want to see established an international order based upon mutual understanding and mutual confidence, and we cannot build such an order unless it conforms to certain principles which are essential to the establishment of confidence and trust. Those principles must include the observance of international undertakings when they have once been entered into, and the renunciation of force in the settlement of differences. It is because those principles, to which we attach such vital importance, seem to us to be in jeopardy that we have undertaken these tremendous and unprecedented responsibilities.

If, despite all our efforts to find the way to peace—and God knows I have tried my best—if in spite of all that, we find ourselves forced to embark upon a struggle which is bound to be fraught with suffering and misery for all mankind and the end of which no man can foresee, if that should happen, we shall not be fighting for the political future of a far away city in a foreign land; we shall be fighting for the preservation of those principles of which I have spoken, the destruction of which would involve the destruction of all possibility of peace and security for the peoples of the world. This issue of peace or war does not rest with us, and I trust that those with whom the responsibility does lie will think of the millions of human beings whose fate depends upon their actions. For ourselves, we have a united country behind us, and in this critical hour I believe that we, in this House of Commons, will stand together, and that this afternoon we shall show the world that, as we think, so will we act, as a united nation.

Supplementary communication from the German Chancellor handed to His Majesty's Ambassador on 25 August 1939

The following is a translation of the text of a verbal communication made to Sir Nevile Henderson by Herr Hitler at his interview on the 25th August:

By way of introduction the Führer declared that the British Ambassador had given expression at the close of the last conversation to the hope that, after all, an understanding between Germany and England might yet be possible. He (the Führer) had therefore turned things over in his mind once more and desired to make a move as regards England which should be as decisive as the move as regards Russia which had led to the recent agreement. Yesterday's sitting in the House of Commons and the speeches of Mr Chamberlain and Lord Halifax had also moved the Führer to talk once more to the British Ambassador. The assertion that Germany affected to conquer the world was ridiculous. The British Empire embraced 40 million square kilometres, Russia 19 million square kilometres, America 9½ million square kilometres, whereas Germany embraced less than 600,000 square kilometres. It is quite clear who it is who desires to conquer the world.

The Führer makes the following communication to the British Ambassador:

Poland's actual provocations have become intolerable. It makes no difference who is responsible. If the Polish Government denies responsibility, that only goes to show that it no longer itself possesses any influence over its subordinate military authorities. In the preceding night there had been a further twenty-one new frontier incidents; on the German side the greatest discipline had been maintained. All incidents had been provoked from the Polish side. Furthermore, commercial aircraft had been shot at. If the Polish Government stated that it was not responsible, it showed that it was no longer capable of controlling its own people.

Germany was in all the circumstances determined to abolish these Macedonian conditions on her eastern frontier and, what is more, to do so in the interests of quiet and order, but also in the interests of European peace.

The problem of Danzig and the Corridor must be solved. The British Prime Minister had made a speech which was not in the least calculated to induce any change in the German attitude. At the most, the result of this speech could be a bloody and incalculable war between Germany and England. Such a war would be bloodier than that of 1914 to 1918. In contrast to the last war, Germany would no longer have to fight on two fronts. Agreement with Russia was unconditional and signified a change in foreign policy of the Reich which would last a very long time. Russia and Germany would never again take up arms against each other. Apart from this, the agreements reached with Russia would also render Germany secure economically for the longest possible period of war.

The Führer had always wanted an Anglo-German understanding. War between England and Germany could at the best bring some profit to Germany but none at all to England.

The Führer declared that the German-Polish problem must be solved and will be solved. He is, however, prepared and determined after the solution of this problem to approach England once more with a large comprehensive offer. He is a man of great decisions, and in this case also he will be capable of being great in his action. He accepts the British Empire and is ready to pledge himself personally for its continued existence and to place the power of the German Reich at its disposal if:

(1) His colonial demands which are limited and can be negotiated by peaceful methods are fulfilled and in this case he is prepared to fix the longest time limit.

(2) His obligations towards Italy are not touched; in other words, he does not demand that England gives up her obligations towards France and similarly for his own part he cannot withdraw from his obligations towards Italy.

(3) He also desires to stress the irrevocable determination of Germany never again to enter into conflict with Russia. The Führer is ready to conclude agreements with England which, as has already been emphasised, would not only guarantee the existence of the British Empire in all circumstances as far as Germany is concerned, but also if necessary an assurance to the British Empire of German

assistance regardless of where such assistance should be necessary. The Führer would then also be ready to accept a reasonable limitation of armaments which corresponds to the new political situation, and which is economically tolerable. Finally, the Führer renewed his assurances that he is not interested in Western problems and that a frontier modification in the West does not enter into consideration. Western fortifications which have been constructed at a cost of milliards were the final Reich frontier on the West.

If the British Government would consider these ideas, a blessing for Germany and also for the British Empire might result. If it rejects these ideas there will be war. In no case would Great Britain emerge stronger: the last war proved this.

The Führer repeats that he is a man of *ad infinitum* decisions by which he himself is bound and that this is his last offer. Immediately after solution of the German-Polish question he would approach the British Government with an offer.

Sir N. Henderson to Viscount Halifax (received 7 PM)

Berlin, 25 August 1939

(Telegraphic)

In my immediately preceding telegram I give text of a verbal communication which the Chancellor made to me this morning. He was absolutely calm and normal and spoke with great earnestness and apparent sincerity. Minister for Foreign Affairs was present but took practically no part in the conversation.

Herr Hitler began by saying that he had always and still desired good relations with Great Britain, and his conscience compelled him to make this final effort to secure them. It was his last attempt. He suggested that I should fly to England myself in order in put the case to His Majesty's Government.

Conversation lasted an hour, my attitude being that Russian Pact in no way altered standpoint of His Majesty's Government, and that I must tell him quite honestly that Britain could not go back on her word to Poland and that I knew his offer would not be considered unless it meant a negotiated settlement of the Polish question. Herr Hitler refused to guarantee this on grounds that Polish provocation might at any moment render German intervention to protect German nationals inevitable. I again and again returned to this point but always got the same answer.

I told Herr Hitler that I could not discuss rights and wrongs of mutual provocation and incidents: that was for the Polish Ambassador to discuss with Herr von Ribbentrop and I suggested that he should do so. Herr Hitler's reply was that M. Lipski had seen Field-Marshal Göring, but had not been able to propose anything new.

I told Herr Hitler that we could not abandon Poland to her fate, but I made the entirely personal suggestion that M. Beck and Herr von Ribbentrop should meet somewhere and discuss the way out which alone might save Europe from war. Herr Hitler's reply was that he had invited M. Beck to come and talk the matter over last March only to have his invitation flatly refused. Only intervention by Herr von Ribbentrop in the discussion was to confirm this and to say that M. Lipski, who had had to convey this message, was obliged to put it in other words to soften the abruptness of it.

When I kept saying that His Majesty's Government could not in my opinion consider his offer unless it meant at the same time a peaceful settlement with Poland, Herr Hitler said: "If you think it useless then do not send my offer at all." He admitted the good intentions of M. Beck and M. Lipski, but said they had no control over what was happening in Poland. Only signs of excitement on Herr Hitler's part were when he referred to Polish persecutions. He mentioned that Herr von Ribbentrop on his return to Germany from Russia had had to fly from Königsberg over the sea to avoid being shot at by the Poles, who fired at every German aeroplane that flew over normal routes across Polish territory. He also said that there had been another case of castration.

Among various points mentioned by Herr Hitler were: that the only winner of another European war would be Japan; that he was by nature an artist not a politician, and that once the Polish question was settled he would end his life as an artist and not as a warmonger; he did not want to turn Germany into nothing but a military barracks and he would only do so if forced to do so; that once the Polish question was settled he himself would settle down; that he had no interest in making Britain break her word to Poland; that he had no wish to be small-minded in any settlement with Poland and that all he required for an agreement with her was a gesture from Britain to indicate that she would not be unreasonable.

After I had left, Herr von Ribbentrop sent Dr Schmidt to the Embassy with text of verbal statement and also a message from him to the effect that Herr Hitler had always and still wished for an agreement with Britain and begging me to urge His Majesty's Government to take the offer very seriously.

Viscount Halifax to Sir H. Kennard (Warsaw)
Foreign Office, 25 August 1939, 11 pm

(Telegraphic)
Please sound Polish Government on proposal for corps of neutral observers which, if accepted, would, of course, only come into operation if and when it was found possible to start any negotiations.

Viscount Halifax to Sir H. Kennard (Warsaw)
Foreign Office, 26 August 1939, 5 PM

(Telegraphic)
It is clear that Herr Hitler is laying chief emphasis on ill-treatment of German minority, and may use this at any moment as an excuse for taking some irrevocable action.

Is it not possible for Polish Government to adopt suggestion that they should approach German Government with enquiry as to whether they would contemplate making exchange of populations an element to be considered in any negotiation? It is true this would afford no immediate safeguard as it is a remedy that would take some time to apply, but it would be a pledge that Polish Government recognise the difficulty and are genuinely seeking means to overcome it, and it would give Polish Government some definite and new point on which to open up negotiation.

If action is to be taken by the Polish Government in this sense it ought to be done immediately.

Sir H. Kennard to Viscount Halifax (received 5.05 PM)

Warsaw, 27 August 1939

(Telegraphic)

Your telegrams of 25th and 26th August:

I discussed questions of exchange of populations and neutral observers with M. Beck this morning. As regards first, he said that in principle he saw no objection and was prepared to convey to German Government that he was ready to consider such a proposal, possibly not directly to State Secretary, but in such a manner that he was sure it would reach the highest authorities.

As regards question of neutral observers, he had again consulted President of the Council, but he would let me know his decision in the course of the day.

As he told me that the Pope had during the night, through the Nuncio, asked if there was anything he could do, I suggested to M. Beck that he should inform His Holiness that he was prepared to consider an exchange of populations and also use of neutral observers in order to demonstrate that German accusations of maltreatment were completely without foundation. The Pope could then communicate these proposals to the German Government with approval of Polish Government. M. Beck seemed to consider this favourably and promised he would give it his immediate consideration. I warned him that there was no time to lose.

As regards Danzig, M. Beck did not from his latest information anticipate *fait accompli* there today or in very immediate future. For the moment all was quiet there as far as he knew. I again emphasised to his Excellency importance of his giving sufficient warning to His Majesty's Government of any action which Polish Government or army contemplated taking as result of any *fait accompli* at Danzig. His Excellency again promised to do this, though he made reservation that situation might arise where immediate action would be necessary.

Viscount Halifax to Sir H. Kennard (Warsaw)

Foreign Office, 28 August 1939, 2 PM

(Telegraphic)

Our proposed reply to Herr Hitler draws a clear distinction between the method of reaching agreement on German-Polish differences and the nature of the solution to be arrived at. As to the method we wish to express our clear view that direct discussion on equal terms between the parties is the proper means. Polish Government enjoy protection of Anglo-Polish Treaty.

His Majesty's Government have already made it plain and are repeating in their reply to Herr Hitler today that any settlement of German-Polish differences must safeguard Poland's essential interests and must be secured by international guarantee.

We have, of course, seen reports of Herr Hitler's reply to M. Daladier, but we should not consider intimation by Polish Government of their readiness to hold direct discussions as in any way implying acceptance of Herr Hitler's demands, which would, as made plain above, have to be examined in light of principles we have stated.

As Polish Government appear in their reply to President Roosevelt to accept idea of direct negotiations, His Majesty's Government earnestly hope that in the light of the considerations set forth in foregoing paragraphs Polish Government will authorise them to inform German Government that Poland is ready to enter at once into direct discussion with Germany.

Please endeavour to see M. Beck at once and telephone reply.

Reply of His Majesty's Government dated 28 August 1939, to the German Chancellor's communications of 23 and 25 August 1939

His Majesty's Government have received the message conveyed to them from the German Chancellor by His Majesty's Ambassador in Berlin, and have considered it with the care which it demands.

They note the Chancellor's expression of his desire to make friendship the basis of the relations between Germany and the British Empire and they fully share this desire. They believe with him that if a complete and lasting understanding between the two countries could be established it would bring untold blessings to both peoples.

The Chancellor's message deals with two groups of questions: those which are the matters now in dispute between Germany and Poland and those affecting the ultimate relations of Germany and Great Britain. In connection with these last, His Majesty's Government observe that the German Chancellor has indicated certain proposals which, subject to one condition, he would be prepared to make to the British Government for a general understanding. These proposals are, of course, stated in very general form and would require closer definition, but His Majesty's Government are fully prepared to take them, with some additions, as subjects for discussion and they would be ready, if the differences between Germany and Poland are peacefully composed, to proceed so soon as practicable to such discussion with a sincere desire to reach agreement.

The condition which the German Chancellor lays down is that there must first be a settlement of the differences between Germany and Poland. As to that, His Majesty's Government entirely agree. Everything, however, turns upon the nature of the settlement and the method by which it is to be reached. On these points, the importance of which cannot be absent from the Chancellor's mind, his message is silent, and His Majesty's Government feel compelled to point out that an understanding upon both of these is essential to achieving further progress. The German Government will be aware that His Majesty's Government have obligations to Poland by which they are bound and which they intend to honour. They could not, for any advantage offered to Great Britain, acquiesce in a settlement which put in jeopardy the independence of a State to whom they have given their guarantee.

In the opinion of His Majesty's Government a reasonable solution of the differences between Germany and Poland could and should be effected by agreement between the two countries on lines which would include the safeguarding of Poland's essential interests, and they recall that in his speech of the 28th April last the German Chancellor recognised the importance of these interests to Poland. But, as was stated by the Prime Minister in his letter to the German Chancellor of the 22nd August, His Majesty's Government consider it essential for the success of the discussions which would precede the agreement that it should be understood beforehand that any settlement arrived at would be guaranteed by other Powers. His Majesty's Government would be ready if desired to make their contribution to the effective operation of such a guarantee.

In the view of His Majesty's Government it follows that the next step should be the initiation of direct discussions between the German and Polish Governments on a basis which would include the principles stated above, namely, the safeguarding of Poland's essential interests and the securing of the settlement by an international guarantee.

They have already received a definite assurance from the Polish Government that they are prepared to enter into discussions on this basis, and His Majesty's Government hope the German Government would for their part also be willing to agree to this course. If, as His Majesty's Government hope, such discussion led to agreement the way would be open to the negotiation of that wider and more complete understanding between Great Britain and Germany which both countries desire.

His Majesty's Government agree with the German Chancellor that one of the principal dangers in the German-Polish situation arises from the reports concerning the treatment of minorities. The present state of tension, with its concomitant frontier incidents, reports of maltreatment and inflammatory propaganda, is a constant danger to peace. It is manifestly a matter of the utmost urgency that all incidents of the kind should be promptly and rigidly suppressed and that unverified reports should not be allowed to circulate, in order that time may be afforded, without provocation on either side, for a full examination of the possibilities of settlement. His Majesty's Government are confident that both the Governments concerned are fully alive to these considerations.

His Majesty's Government have said enough to make their own attitude plain in the particular matters at issue between Germany and Poland. They trust that the German Chancellor will not think that, because His Majesty's Government are scrupulous concerning their obligations to Poland, they are not anxious to use all their influence to assist the achievement of a solution which may commend itself both to Germany and to Poland.

That such a settlement should be achieved seems to His Majesty's Government essential, not only for reasons directly arising in regard to the settlement itself, but also because of the wider considerations of which the German Chancellor has spoken with such conviction.

It is unnecessary in the present reply to stress the advantage of a peaceful settlement over a decision to settle the questions at issue by force of arms. The results of a decision to use force have been clearly set out in the Prime Minister's letter to the Chancellor of the 22nd August, and His Majesty's Government do not doubt that they are as fully recognised by the Chancellor as by themselves. On the other hand, His Majesty's Government, noting with interest the German Chancellor's reference in the message now under consideration to a limitation of armaments, believe that, if a peaceful settlement can be obtained, the assistance of the world could confidently be anticipated for practical measures to enable the transition from preparation for war to the normal activities of peaceful trade to be safely and smoothly effected.

A just settlement of these questions between Germany and Poland may open the way to world peace. Failure to reach it would ruin the hopes of better understanding between Germany and Great Britain, would bring the two countries into conflict, and might well plunge the whole world into war. Such an outcome would be a calamity without parallel in history.

Sir N. Henderson to Viscount Halifax (received 2.35 AM 29 *August)*
Berlin, 28 August 1939

(Telegraphic)

I saw the Chancellor at 10.30 this evening. He asked me to come at 10 PM, but I sent word that I could not have the translation ready before the later hour. Herr von Ribbentrop was present, also Dr Schmidt. Interview lasted one and a quarter hours.

Herr Hitler began by reading the German translation. When he had finished, I said that I wished to make certain observations from notes which I had made in the conversations with the Prime Minister and His Majesty's Secretary of State for Foreign Affairs. In the first place I wished to say that we in England regarded it as absurd that Britain should be supposed by the German Government to consider the crushing of Germany as a settled policy. We held it to be no less astonishing that anyone in Germany should doubt for a moment that we would not fight for Poland if her independence or vital interests were menaced.

Our word was our word, and we had never and would never break it. In the old days Germany's word had the same value, and I quoted a passage from a German book (which Herr Hitler had read) about Marshal Blücher's exhortation to his troops when hurrying to the support of Wellington at Waterloo:

"Forward, my children, I have given my word to my brother Wellington, and you cannot wish me to break it."

Herr Hitler at once intervened to observe that things were different 125 years ago. I said not so far as England was concerned. He wanted, I said, Britain's friendship. What value would he place on our friendship if we began it by disloyalty to a friend? Whatever some people might say, the British people sincerely desired an understanding with Germany, and no one more so than the Prime Minister (Herr von Ribbentrop remarked that Mr Chamberlain had once said to him that it was his dearest wish). Today the whole British public was behind the Prime Minister. The recent vote in the House of Commons was an unmistakable proof of that fact. The Prime Minister could carry through his policy of an understanding if, but only if, Herr Hitler were prepared to co-operate. There was absolutely no truth in the idea sometimes held in Germany that the British Cabinet was disunited or that the country was not unanimous. It was now or never, and it rested with Herr Hitler. If he was prepared to sacrifice that understanding in order to make war or immoderate demands on Poland, the responsibility was his. We offered friendship but only on the basis of a peaceful and freely negotiated solution of the Polish question.

Herr Hitler replied that he would be willing to negotiate, if there was a Polish Government which was prepared to be reasonable and which really controlled the country. He expatiated [spoke at length] on misdoings of the Poles, referred to his generous offer of March last, said that it could not be repeated and asserted that nothing other than the return of Danzig and the whole of the Corridor would satisfy him, together with a rectification in Silesia, where 90 per cent of the population had voted for Germany at the post-war plebiscite but where, as a result of the Haller-Korfanti *coup*, what the Plebiscite Commission had allotted had nevertheless been grabbed by Poland.

I told Herr Hitler that he must choose between England and Poland. If he put forward immoderate demands there was no hope of a peaceful solution. The Corridor was inhabited almost entirely by Poles. Herr Hitler interrupted me here by observing that this was only true because a million Germans had been driven out of that district since the war. I again said the choice lay with him. He had offered a Corridor over the Corridor in March, and I must honestly tell him that anything more than that, if that, would have no hope of acceptance. I begged him very earnestly to reflect before raising his price. He said his original offer had been contemptuously refused and he would not make it again. I observed that it had been made in the form of a dictate and therein lay the whole difference.

Herr Hitler continued to argue that Poland could never be reasonable: she had England and France behind her, and imagined that even if she were beaten she would later recover, thanks to their help, more than she might lose. He spoke of annihilating Poland. I said that reminded me of a similar talk last year of annihilation of the Czechs. He retorted that we were incapable of inducing Poland to be reasonable. I said that it was just because we remembered the experience of Czecho-Slovakia last year that we hesitated to press Poland too far today. Nevertheless, we reserved to ourselves the right to form our own judgment as to what was or what was not reasonable so far as Poland or Germany were concerned. We kept our hands free in that respect.

Generally speaking, Herr Hitler kept harping on Poland, and I kept on just as consistently telling Herr Hitler that he had to choose between friendship with England which we offered him and excessive demands on Poland which would put an end to all hope of British friendship. If we were to come to an understanding it would entail sacrifices on our part. If he was not prepared to make sacrifices on his part there was nothing to be done. Herr Hitler said that he had to satisfy the demands of his people, his army was ready and eager for battle, his people were united behind him, and he could not tolerate further ill-treatment of Germans in Poland, etc.

It is unnecessary to recall the details of a long and earnest conversation in the course of which the only occasion in which Herr Hitler became at all excited was when I observed that it was not a question of Danzig and the Corridor, but one of our determination to resist force by force. This evoked a tirade about the Rhineland, Austria and Sudeten and their peaceful reacquisition by Germany. He also resented my references to 15th March.

In the end I asked him two straight questions. Was he willing to negotiate direct with the Poles and was he ready to discuss the question of an exchange of populations? He replied in the affirmative as regards the latter (though I have no doubt that he was thinking at the same time of a rectification of frontiers). As regards the first, he said he could not give me an answer until after he had given reply of His Majesty's Government the careful consideration which such a document deserved. In this connection he turned to Herr von Ribbentrop and said: "We must summon Field-Marshal Göring to discuss it with him."

I finally repeated to him very solemnly the main note of the whole conversation so far as I was concerned, namely, that it lay with him as to whether he preferred a unilateral solution which would mean war as regards Poland, or British friendship. If he were prepared to pay the price of the latter by a generous gesture as regards Poland, he could at a stroke change in his favour the whole of public opinion not only in England but in the world. I left no doubt in his mind as to what the alternative would be, nor did he dispute the point.

At the end Herr von Ribbentrop asked me whether I could guarantee that the Prime Minister could carry the country with him in a policy of friendship with Germany. I said there was no possible doubt whatever that he could and would, provided Germany co-operated with him. Herr Hitler asked whether England would be willing to accept an alliance with Germany. I said, speaking personally, I did not exclude such a possibility provided the developments of events justified it.

Conversation was conducted in quite a friendly atmosphere, in spite of absolute firmness on both sides. Herr Hitler's general attitude was that he could give me no real reply until he had carefully studied the answer of His Majesty's Government. He said that he would give me a written reply tomorrow, Tuesday. I told him that I would await it, but was quite prepared to wait. Herr Hitler's answer was that there was no time to wait.

I did not refer to the question of a truce. I shall raise that point tomorrow if his answer affords any real ground for hope that he is prepared to abandon war for the sake of British understanding.

Sir N. Henderson to Viscount Halifax (received 4.55 PM)

Berlin, 29 August 1939

(Telegraphic)

Following are additional points in amplification of my telegram of 28th August:

Herr Hitler insisted that he was not bluffing, and that people would make a great mistake if they believed that he was. I replied that I was fully aware of the fact and that we were not bluffing either. Herr Hitler stated that he fully realised that that was the case. In answer to a suggestion by him that Great Britain might offer something at once in the way of colonies as evidence of her good intentions, I retorted that concessions were easier of realisation in a good rather than a bad atmosphere.

Speech by the Prime Minister in the House of Commons on 29 August 1939

The Prime Minister (Mr Chamberlain): Since the House met on Thursday last there has been little change in the main features of the situation. The catastrophe, as I said then, is not yet on us, but I cannot say that the danger of it has yet in any way receded. In these circumstances it might perhaps have seemed that it was unnecessary to ask the House to meet again before the date which had been fixed, but in times like these we have felt that it was right that the House should be kept as far as possible continuously informed of all the developments in the situation as they took place. That will continue to be the principle which will guide us in further meetings of this House.

There is one thing that I would like to say at this moment with regard to the press. I think it is necessary once more to urge the press to exercise the utmost restraint at a time when it is quite possible for a few thoughtless words in a paper, perhaps not of particular importance, to wreck the whole of the efforts which are being made by the Government to obtain a satisfactory solution. I have heard that an account purporting to be a verbatim description of the communication of the British Government to Herr Hitler was telegraphed to another country last night or this morning. Such an account could only be an invention from beginning to end. It is, I think, very unfortunate that journalists in the exercise of their profession should take such responsibilities upon themselves, responsibilities which affect not only themselves, but the inhabitants, perhaps, of all the countries in the world.

I hope that it will not be necessary this afternoon to have any long Debate. I will attempt to give the House an account of the events of the last few days, but, of course, there has been no change in the policy of the Government, and, therefore, there would not appear to be any necessity for any lengthy discussion. On the day after the House adjourned—on Friday, that is—we received information in the course of the morning that the German Chancellor had asked the British Ambassador in Berlin to call upon him at half-past one that day, and in the course of the afternoon we were told by telephone that Sir Nevile Henderson had had an interview lasting about an hour and a half with Herr Hitler, that he was sending us an account of that interview, and that Herr Hitler had suggested to him that it would be a good thing if he were to fly over to this country the next morning in order to give us a verbal and more extended account of the conversation. We received the record of the interview from our Ambassador on that evening, on Friday evening, but it was not completely deciphered until after midnight, and I did not myself see the whole of it until the next morning, Saturday morning. On Saturday Sir Nevile Henderson arrived by plane from Berlin shortly before lunch, and we understood from him that in Berlin it was not considered to be necessary that he should go back the same day, as the German Government were very anxious that we should give careful study to the communication he had to make to us. Accordingly, we devoted the whole of Saturday and the Sunday morning to a very careful, exhaustive and thorough consideration of the document which was brought to us by the British Ambassador and of the reply that we proposed to send back, and our final answer was taken by the Ambassador yesterday afternoon, when he flew back to Berlin and delivered it to the Chancellor last night.

I should be glad if I could disclose to the House the fullest information as to the contents of the communications exchanged with Herr Hitler, but hon. members will understand that in a situation of such extreme delicacy, and when issues so grave hang precariously in the balance, it is not in the public interest to publish these confidential communications or to comment on them in detail at this stage. I am, however, able to indicate in quite general terms some of the main points with which they deal. Herr Hitler was concerned to impress upon His Majesty's Government his wish for an Anglo-German understanding of a complete and lasting character. On the other hand, he left His Majesty's Government in no doubt of his views as to the urgency of settling the German-Polish question. His Majesty's Government have also frequently expressed their desire to see the realisation of such an Anglo-German understanding, and as soon as circumstances permit they would naturally welcome an opportunity of discussing with Germany the several issues a settlement of which would have to find a place in any permanent agreement. But everything turns upon the manner in which the immediate differences between Germany and Poland can be handled and the nature of the proposals which might be made for any settlement. We have made it plain that our obligations to Poland, cast into formal shape by the agreement which was signed on 25th August, on Friday last, will be carried out. The House will remember that the Government have said more than once, publicly, that the German–Polish differences should be capable of solution by peaceful means.

Meanwhile, the first prerequisite, if there is to be any general and useful discussion, is that the tension created by frontier clashes and by reports of incidents on both sides of the border should be diminished. His Majesty's Government accordingly hope that both Governments will use their best endeavours to prevent the occurrence of such incidents, the circulation of exaggerated reports, and all other activities that result in dangerous inflammation of opinion. His Majesty's Government would hope that if an equitable settlement of Polish–German differences could be reached by free negotiation, this might in turn lead on to a wider agreement which would accrue to the lasting benefit of Europe and of the world at large. At this moment the position is that we are waiting for the reply of Herr Hitler to our communication. On the nature of that reply depends whether further time can be given for the exploration of the situation and for the operation of the many forces which are working for peace. A waiting period of that kind is often very trying, but nothing, I think, can be more remarkable than the calm which characterises the attitude of the whole British people. It seems to me that there are two explanations of that attitude. The first is that none of us has any doubt of where our duty lies. There is no difference of opinion among us; there is no weakening of our determination. The second explanation is our confidence that we are ready for any eventuality.

The House might like to hear one or two particulars of the preparations which have been made. Obviously, there are many things which I cannot very well say here because they could not be confined to those whom I see before me. My statement must, therefore, be in very general terms. Some of the measures which we had to take, such as those in connexion with requisitioning, necessarily must cause some degree of inconvenience to the public. I am confident that the people of the country generally recognise that the nation's needs must now be paramount and that they will submit willingly, and even cheerfully, to any inconvenience or hardships that may be involved. At any rate, we have not had to begin here by issuing rationing cards. To deal first with the active defence of the country, the air defence of Great Britain has been placed in a state of instant readiness. The ground anti–aircraft defences have been deployed and they are manned by territorial anti–aircraft units. The regular squadrons of the Royal Air Force have been brought up to war strength by the addition of the necessary reservists, including a portion of the Volunteer Reserve. The fighter and general reconnaissance squadrons of the Auxiliary Air Force have been called up and are standing ready and the balloon barrage is in position. The Observer Corps are at their posts, and, indeed, the whole warning system is ready night and day to be brought into instant operation. The coast defences are ready and are manned by the coast defence units of the Territorial Army. Arrangements have also been made for the protection by the National Defence companies, by the Militia and by units of the Territorial Army of a very large number of important points whose safety is essential for the national war effort.

As to the Navy, the House will remember that in July last it was announced that the Reserve Fleet would be called up at the beginning of August in order to take part in combined Fleet and Air exercises. For that purpose a number of reservists were called up under the provisions of the Reserves and Auxiliary Forces Act. As a result, the Navy was in an advanced state of preparedness when the present crisis arose, and the whole of our fighting Fleet is now ready at a moment's notice to take up the dispositions which would be necessary in war. A number of other measures have been taken during the past week to increase the state of our naval preparedness. I need not go into all the details, but the naval officers in charge of the various commercial ports have been appointed and have taken up their duties, and the naval ports and bases have been put into an advanced state of preparedness. As hon. members will be aware, the Admiralty has also assumed control of merchant shipping, acting under the powers conferred by the Emergency Powers Act, and written instructions have already been issued to merchant shipping on various routes. A considerable number of movements have been carried out of units of the armed land forces both at home and overseas. These movements are part of prearranged plans to provide that in order to ensure a greater state of readiness a number of units should, if possible, move to their war stations before the outbreak of war. The Civil Defence regional organisation has been placed on war footing. Regional commissioners and their staffs are at their war stations.

The main responsibility for the organisation of Civil Defence measures generally rests with the local authorities. Instructions have been sent to the local authorities to complete all the preparatory steps so that action can be taken at the shortest notice. Plans for the evacuation of school children, mothers with young children, expectant mothers and blind persons from certain congested areas—plans which have involved an immense amount of detailed thinking—are ready. Those who have to carry out those plans have been recalled for duty, school teachers in evacuation areas have been kept in easy reach of school assembly points since Saturday, and a rehearsal of the arrangements for evacuating school children was carried out yesterday. Nearly a week ago local authorities were warned to make arrangements for the extinction of public lighting and to prepare the necessary aids to movement when the lighting has been extinguished. Arrangements have been completed for calling up at very short notice of the personnel of the Air-Raid Precautions Service, and duty officers are available throughout the twenty-four hours at key posts. The last item I mention is that the necessary preliminary steps have been taken to prepare hospitals for the reception of casualties.

I have given a number of instances of steps which have been taken over and above the measures which have already been put into operation. A complete and continuous survey is being carried out over the whole range of our defence preparations, and preparatory measures are being taken in order to ensure that further precautionary measures, if and when they should be found necessary, can be given effect to as rapidly as possible. The instances I have given to the House are merely illustrations of the general state of readiness, of which the House and the country are aware. I think that they justify and partly account for the general absence of fear, or, indeed, of any violent emotion. The British people are said sometimes to be slow to make up their minds, but, having made them up, they do not readily let go. The issue of peace or war is still undecided, and we still will hope, and still will work, for peace; but we will abate no jot of our resolution to hold fast to the line which we have laid down for ourselves.

> *Reply of the German Chancellor to the communication of 28 August* 1939
> *from His Majesty's Government. This reply was handed to Sir N. Henderson*
> *by Herr Hitler during the evening of 29 August* 1939

(Translation)

The British Ambassador in Berlin has submitted to the British Government suggestions which I felt bound to make in order:

(1) to give expression once more to the will of the Reich Government for sincere Anglo-German understanding, co-operation and friendship;

(2) to leave no room for doubt as to fact that such an understanding could not be bought at the price of a renunciation of vital German interests, let alone the abandonment of demands which are based as much upon common human justice as upon the national dignity and honour of our people.

The German Government have noted with satisfaction from the reply of the British Government and from the oral explanations given by the British Ambassador that the British Government for their part are also prepared to improve the relationship between Germany and England and to develop and extend it in the sense of the German suggestion.

In this connection, the British Government are similarly convinced that the removal of the German–Polish tension, which has become unbearable, is the prerequisite for the realisation of this hope.

Since the autumn of the past year, and on the last occasion in March, 1939, there were submitted to the Polish Government proposals, both oral and written, which, having regard to the friendship then existing between Germany and Poland, offered the possibility of a solution of the questions in dispute acceptable to both parties. The British Government are aware that the Polish Government saw fit, in March last, finally to reject these proposals. At the same time, they used this rejection as a pretext or an occasion for taking military measures which have since been continuously intensified. Already in the middle of last month Poland was in effect in a state of mobilisation. This was accompanied by numerous encroachments in the Free City of Danzig due to the instigation of the Polish authorities; threatening demands in the nature of ultimata, varying only in degree, were addressed to that City. A closing of the frontiers, at first in the form of a measure of customs policy but extended later in a military sense affecting also traffic and communications, was imposed with the object of bringing about the political exhaustion and economic destruction of this German community.

To this were added barbaric actions of maltreatment which cry to Heaven, and other kinds of persecution of the large German national group in Poland which extended even to the killing of many resident Germans or to their forcible removal under the most cruel conditions. This state of affairs is unbearable for a Great Power. It has now forced Germany, after remaining a passive onlooker for many months, in her turn to take the necessary steps for the safeguarding of justified German interests. And indeed the German Government can but assure the British Government in the most solemn manner that a condition of affairs has now been reached which can no longer be accepted or observed with indifference.

The demands of the German Government are in conformity with the revision of the Versailles Treaty in regard to this territory which has always been recognised as being necessary: viz., return of Danzig and the Corridor to Germany, the safeguarding of the existence of the German national group in the territories remaining to Poland.

The German Government note with satisfaction that the British Government also are in principle convinced that some solution must be found for the new situation which has arisen.

They further feel justified in assuming that the British Government too can have no doubt that it is a question now of conditions, for the elimination of which there no longer remain days, still less weeks, but perhaps only hours. For in the disorganised state of affairs obtaining in Poland, the possibility of incidents intervening which it might be impossible for Germany to tolerate, must at any moment be reckoned with.

While the British Government may still believe that these grave differences can be resolved by way of direct negotiations, the German Government unfortunately can no longer share this view as a matter of course. For they have made the attempt to embark on such peaceful negotiations, but, instead of receiving any support from the Polish Government, they were rebuffed by the sudden introduction of measures of a military character in favour of the development alluded to above.

The British Government attach importance to two considerations: (1) that the existing danger of an imminent explosion should be eliminated as quickly as possible by direct negotiation, and (2) that the existence of the Polish State, in the form in which it would then continue to exist, should be adequately safeguarded in the economic and political sphere by means of international guarantees.

On this subject the German Government makes the following declaration: Though sceptical as to the prospects of a successful outcome, they are nevertheless prepared to accept the English proposal and to enter into direct discussions. They do so, as has already been emphasised, solely as the result of the impression made upon them by the written statement received from the British Government that they too desire a pact of friendship in accordance with the general lines indicated to the British Ambassador.

The German Government desire in this way to give the British Government and the British nation a proof of the sincerity of Germany's intentions to enter into a lasting friendship with Great Britain.

The Government of the Reich felt, however, bound to point out to the British Government that in the event of a territorial rearrangement in Poland they would no longer be able to bind themselves to give guarantees or to participate in guarantees without the USSR being associated therewith.

For the rest, in making these proposals the German Government have never had any intention of touching Poland's vital interests or questioning the existence of an independent Polish State. The German Government, accordingly, in these circumstances agree to accept the British Government's offer of their good offices in securing the despatch to Berlin of a Polish Emissary with full powers. They count on the arrival of this Emissary on Wednesday, the 30th August, 1939.

The German Government will immediately draw up proposals for a solution acceptable to themselves and will, if possible, place these at the disposal of the British Government before the arrival of the Polish negotiator.

Sir N. Henderson to Viscount Halifax (received 9.15 PM)

Berlin, 29 August 1939

(Telegraphic)

Herr Hitler handed me German reply at 7.15 this evening. Translation of full text will follow as soon as possible.

In reply to two British proposals, namely, for direct German-Polish negotiations and international guarantee of any settlement, German Government declares:

(1) That, in spite of its scepticism as to the prospect of their success, it accepts direct negotiation solely out of desire to ensure lasting friendship with Britain, and

(2) In the case of any modifications of territory German Government cannot undertake or participate in any guarantees without consulting the USSR.

The note observes that German proposals have never had for their object any diminution of Polish vital interests, and declares that German Government accepts mediation of Great Britain with a view to visit to Berlin of some Polish plenipotentiary. German Government, note adds, counts on arrival of such plenipotentiary tomorrow, Wednesday, 30th August.

I remarked that this phrase sounded like an ultimatum, but after some heated remarks both Herr Hitler and Herr von Ribbentrop assured me that it was only intended to stress urgency of the moment when the two fully mobilised armies were standing face to face. I said that I would transmit this suggestion immediately to His Majesty's Government, and asked whether, if such Polish plenipotentiary did come, we could assume that he would be well received and that discussions would be conducted on footing of complete equality. Herr Hitler's reply was "of course."

German demands are declared to be revision of Versailles Treaty; namely, return of Danzig and the Corridor to Germany, security for lives of German national minorities in the rest of Poland; note concludes with statement that the German Government will immediately elaborate proposals for an acceptable solution, and inform British Government, if possible, before arrival of Polish plenipotentiary.

Sir N. Henderson to Viscount Halifax (received 10.25 PM*)*

Berlin, 29 August 1939

(Telegraphic)

Interview this evening was of a stormy character and Herr Hitler far less reasonable than yesterday. Press announcement this evening that five more Germans had been killed in Poland and news of Polish mobilisation had obviously excited him.

He kept saying that he wanted British friendship more than anything in the world, but he could not sacrifice Germany's vital interests therefor [for that reason], and that for His Majesty's Government to make a bargain over such a matter was an unendurable proposition. All my attempts to correct this complete misrepresentation of the case did not seem to impress him.

In reply to his reiterated statement that direct negotiations with Poland, though accepted by him, would be bound to fail, I told his Excellency that their success or failure depended on his goodwill or the reverse, and that the choice lay with him. It was, however, my bounden duty to leave him in no doubt that an attempt to impose his will on Poland by force would inevitably bring him into direct conflict with us.

It would have been useless to talk of a truce, since that can only depend on whether M. Beck or some other Polish representative came to Berlin or not.

Viscount Halifax to Sir N. Henderson (Berlin)

Foreign Office, 30 August 1939, 2 AM

(Telegraphic)

We shall give careful consideration to German Government's reply, but it is, of course, unreasonable to expect that we can produce a Polish representative in Berlin today, and German Government must not expect this.

It might be well for you at once to let this be known in proper quarters through appropriate channels. We hope you may receive our reply this afternoon.

Sir N. Henderson to Viscount Halifax (received 1 PM)

Berlin, 30 August 1939

(Telegraphic)

Your message was conveyed to the Minister for Foreign Affairs at 4 AM this morning. I had made similar observation to Herr Hitler yesterday evening, his reply being that one could fly from Warsaw to Berlin in one and a half hours.

I repeated the message this morning by telephone to State Secretary, who said that it had already been conveyed to Herr Hitler. He added that something must be done as soon as possible.

While I still recommend that the Polish Government should swallow this eleventh-hour effort to establish direct contact with Herr Hitler, even if it be only to convince the world that they were prepared to make their own sacrifice for preservation of peace, one can only conclude from the German reply that Herr Hitler is determined to achieve his ends by so-called peaceful fair means if he can, but by force if he cannot. Much, of course, may also depend on detailed plan referred to in last paragraph of the German reply.

Nevertheless, if Herr Hitler is allowed to continue to have the initiative, it seems to me that result can only be either war or once again victory for him by a display of force and encouragement thereby to pursue the same course again next year or the year after.

Viscount Halifax to Sir N. Henderson (Berlin)

Foreign Office, 30 August 1939, 2.45 PM

(Telegraphic)

We are considering German note with all urgency and shall send official reply later in afternoon. We are representing at Warsaw how vital it is to reinforce all instructions for avoidance of frontier incidents, and I would beg you to confirm similar instructions on German side.

I welcome the evidence in the exchanges of views, which are taking place, of that desire for Anglo-German understanding of which I spoke yesterday in Parliament.

Sir H. Kennard to Viscount Halifax (received 10 AM)

Warsaw, 30 August 1939

(Telegraphic)

I feel sure that it would be impossible to induce the Polish Government to send M. Beck or any other representative immediately to Berlin to discuss a settlement on basis proposed by Herr Hitler. They would certainly sooner fight and perish rather than submit to such humiliation, especially after examples of Czecho-Slovakia, Lithuania and Austria.

I would suggest that if negotiations are to be between equals it is essential that they should take place in some neutral country or even possibly Italy, and that the basis for any negotiations should be some compromise between the clearly defined limits of March proposals on the German side and *status quo* on the Polish side.

Considering that the Polish Government, standing alone and when they were largely unprepared for war, refused the March terms it would surely be impossible for them to agree to proposals which appear to go beyond the March terms now that they have Great Britain as their ally. France has confirmed her support and world public opinion is clearly in favour of direct negotiations on equal terms and is behind Poland's resistance to a dictated settlement.

I am, of course, expressing no views to the Polish Government, nor am I communicating to them Herr Hitler's reply till I receive instructions which I trust will be without delay.

Viscount Halifax to Sir H. Kennard (Warsaw)
Foreign Office, 30 August 1939, 5.30 PM

(Telegraphic)
Atmosphere may be improved if strict instructions are given or confirmed by Polish Government to all their military and civil authorities:

(1) Not to fire on fugitives or members of the German minority who cause trouble, but to arrest them;
(2) To abstain themselves from personal violence to members of German minority, and to prevent similar violence on the part of the population;
(3) To allow members of the German minority wishing to leave Poland to pass freely;
(4) To stop inflammatory radio propaganda.

Please inform M. Beck, adding that I realise that Herr Hitler is using reports to justify immoderate action, but I am anxious to deprive him of this pretext. I am requesting German Government to reciprocate; and warning them that Polish Government can only be expected to maintain such instructions if no provocation is offered by members of the German minority.

Sir H. Kennard to Viscount Halifax (received 8.15 PM)
Warsaw, 30 August 1939

(Telegraphic)
M. Beck has asked me to say:

(1) His Majesty's Government may rest absolutely assured that Polish Government have no intention of provoking any incidents. On the other hand, they point out that German provocation at Danzig is becoming more and more intolerable.
(2) In connection with proposed British answer to Herr Hitler, Polish Government feel sure that His Majesty's Government will not express any definite views on problems concerning Poland without consulting Polish Government.

Viscount Halifax to Sir N. Henderson (Berlin)
Foreign Office, 30 August 1939, 5.30 PM
(Telegraphic)

In informing German Government of the renewed representations which have been made in Warsaw, please make it clear that Polish Government can only be expected to maintain an attitude of complete restraint if German Government reciprocate on their side of frontier and if no provocation is offered by members of German minority in Poland. Reports are current that Germans have committed acts of sabotage which would justify the sternest measures.

Viscount Halifax to Sir N. Henderson (Berlin)
Foreign Office, 30 August 1939, 6.50 PM
(Telegraphic)

We understand that German Government are insisting that a Polish representative with full powers must come to Berlin to receive German proposals.

We cannot advise Polish Government to comply with this procedure, which is wholly unreasonable. Could you not suggest to German Government that they adopt the normal procedure, when their proposals are ready, of inviting Polish Ambassador to call and handing proposals to him for transmission to Warsaw and inviting suggestions as to conduct of negotiations.

German Government have been good enough to promise they will communicate proposals also to His Majesty's Government. If latter think they offer reasonable basis they can be counted on to do their best in Warsaw to facilitate negotiations.

Reply of His Majesty's Government to the German Chancellor's communication of 29 August 1939. This reply was handed by Sir N. Henderson to Herr von Ribbentrop at midnight on 30 August 1939

His Majesty's Government appreciate the friendly reference in the Declaration contained in the reply of the German Government to the latter's desire for an Anglo-German understanding and to their statement of the influence which this consideration has exercised upon their policy.

His Majesty's Government repeat that they reciprocate the German Government's desire for improved relations, but it will be recognised that they could not sacrifice the interests of other friends in order to obtain that improvement. They fully understand that the German Government cannot sacrifice Germany's vital interests, but the Polish Government are in the same position and His Majesty's Government believe that the vital interests of the two countries are not incompatible.

His Majesty's Government note that the German Government accept the British proposal and are prepared to enter into direct discussions with the Polish Government. His Majesty's Government understand that the German Government accept in principle the condition that any settlement should be made the subject of an international guarantee. The question of who shall participate in this guarantee will have to be discussed further, and His Majesty's Government hope that to avoid loss of time the German Government will take immediate steps to obtain the assent of the USSR, whose participation in the guarantee His Majesty's Government have always assumed.

His Majesty's Government also note that the German Government accept the position of the British Government as to Poland's vital interests and independence.

His Majesty's Government must make an express reservation in regard to the statement of the particular demands put forward by the German Government in an earlier passage in their reply. They understand that the German Government are drawing up proposals for a solution. No doubt these proposals will be fully examined during the discussions. It can then be determined how far they are compatible with the essential conditions which His Majesty's Government have stated and which in principle the German Government have expressed their willingness to accept.

His Majesty's Government are at once informing the Polish Government of the German Government's reply. The method of contact and arrangements for discussions must obviously be agreed with all urgency between the German and Polish Governments, but in His Majesty's Government's view it would be impracticable to establish contact so early as today.

His Majesty's Government fully recognise the need for speed in the initiation of discussion, and they share the apprehensions of the Chancellor arising from the proximity of two mobilised armies standing face to face. They would accordingly most strongly urge that both parties should undertake that, during the negotiations, no aggressive military movements will take place. His Majesty's Government feel confident that they could obtain such an undertaking from the Polish Government if the German Government would give similar assurances.

Further, His Majesty's Government would suggest that a temporary *modus vivendi* might be arranged for Danzig, which might prevent the occurrence of incidents tending to render German-Polish relations more difficult.

Viscount Halifax to Sir H. Kennard (Warsaw)
(Sent to Sir H. Kennard on 30 August and acted on in the early morning
of 31 August)

Foreign Office, 30 August 1939

(Telegraphic)

My telegram to Berlin gives the text of the reply of His Majesty's Government to the German communication which has been repeated to you. Please communicate it to M. Beck. In doing so, you should point out that, whilst the first part of the German Government's reply consists of an indefensible and misleading presentation of the German case, the really important part of the reply consists of Germany's acceptance of the proposal for direct discussion, of the suggestion of the proposed international guarantee, and Germany's assertion that she intends to respect Poland's vital interests.

It is perhaps unnecessary to take exception at this stage to much that finds place in the German reply, of which His Majesty's Government would be as critical as, they have no doubt, would be the Polish Government, but His Majesty's Government have made an express reservation in regard to statement of the particular demands put forward in the German note. The point that seemed to call for immediate comment was the German demand that a Polish representative should present himself at Berlin today. M. Beck will see the line we took last night on this (see my telegram to Berlin) and the further reference we have made to point in our reply to German Government's latest communication. German Government are now drawing up proposals for a solution, and it will be in the light of these, and of other developments, that the decision as to future procedure, including place and conditions of discussion, will have to be taken.

M. Beck will see from the reply of His Majesty's Government that the proposal has been made for a military standstill during discussions, to which His Majesty's Government earnestly hope that the Polish Government will have no objection.

His Majesty's Government would be glad to have the views of the Polish Government urgently. In view of the fact that the Polish Government have authorised His Majesty's Government to say that they are prepared to enter into direct discussions with the German Government, His Majesty's Government hope that, provided method and general arrangement for discussions can be satisfactorily agreed, Polish Government will be prepared to do so without delay. We regard it as most important from the point of view of the internal situation in Germany and of world opinion that, so long as the German Government profess themselves ready to negotiate, no opportunity should be given them for placing the blame for a conflict on Poland.

You should, of course, emphasise that His Majesty's Government have made it quite clear to Herr Hitler that they are irrevocably determined to implement their obligations without reserve. On this point there is no misunderstanding in Berlin. The position of the Polish Government is very different from that which they occupied last March, since it is now supported both by direct British guarantee and promise of British participation in guarantee of any settlement reached on bases we have indicated, and the conversations would be carried on against this background.

Sir N. Henderson to Viscount Halifax (received 2.45 AM 31 *August)*
Berlin, 30 August 1939

(Telegraphic)

I informed Herr von Ribbentrop tonight of the advice given to the Polish Government in your telegram of 30th August to Warsaw. Practically his only comment was that all provocation came from the side of Poland. I observed that His Majesty's Government had constantly warned the Polish

Government that all provocative action should be vigorously discouraged and that I had reason to believe that the German press accounts were greatly exaggerated. Herr von Ribbentrop replied that His Majesty's Government's advice had had cursed ("verflucht") little effect. I mildly retorted that I was surprised to hear such language from a Minister for Foreign Affairs.

Sir N. Henderson to Viscount Halifax (received 9.30 AM 31 August)
Berlin, 30 August 1939

(Telegraphic)

I told Herr von Ribbentrop this evening that His Majesty's Government found it difficult to advise Polish Government to accept procedure adumbrated [foreshadowed] in German reply, and suggested that he should adopt normal contact, i.e., that when German proposals were ready to invite Polish Ambassador to call and to hand him proposals for transmission to his Government with a view to immediate opening of negotiations. I added that if basis afforded prospect of settlement His Majesty's Government could be counted upon to do their best in Warsaw to temporise negotiations.

Herr von Ribbentrop's reply was to produce a lengthy document which he read out in German aloud at top speed. Imagining that he would eventually hand it to me I did not attempt to follow too closely the sixteen or more articles which it contained. Though I cannot therefore guarantee accuracy the main points were: restoration of Danzig to Germany; southern boundary of Corridor to be line Marienwerder, Graudenz, Bromberg, Schönlanke; plebiscite to be held in the Corridor on basis of population on 1st January, 1919, absolute majority to decide; international commission of British, French, Italian and Russian members to police the Corridor and guarantee reciprocal communications with Danzig and Gdynia pending result of the plebiscite; Gdynia to be reserved to Poland; Danzig to be purely commercial city and demilitarised.

When I asked Herr von Ribbentrop for text of these proposals in accordance with undertaking in the German reply of yesterday, he asserted that it was now too late as Polish representative had not arrived in Berlin by midnight.

I observed that to treat matter in this way meant that request for Polish representative to arrive in Berlin on 30th August constituted, in fact, an ultimatum in spite of what he and Herr Hitler had assured me yesterday. This he denied, saying that idea of an ultimatum was figment of my imagination. Why then I asked could he not adopt normal procedure and give me copy of proposals and ask Polish Ambassador to call on him, just as Herr Hitler had summoned me a few days ago, and hand them to him for communication to Polish Government? In the most violent terms Herr von Ribbentrop said that he would never ask the Ambassador to visit him. He hinted that if Polish Ambassador asked him for interview it might be different. I said that I would naturally inform my Government so at once. Whereupon he said while those were his personal views he would bring all that I had said to Herr Hitler's notice. It was for Chancellor to decide.

We parted on that note, but I must tell you that Herr von Ribbentrop's whole demeanour during an unpleasant interview was aping Herr Hitler at his worst. He inveighed incidentally against Polish mobilisation, but I retorted that it was hardly surprising since Germany had also mobilised as Herr Hitler himself had admitted to me yesterday.

Sir H. Kennard to Viscount Halifax (received 8 AM)

Warsaw, 31 August 1939

(Telegraphic)

I have communicated to M. Beck the reply of His Majesty's Government to Herr Hitler and made the comments therein in the sense of your telegram of 30th August. M. Beck stated that before giving me a definite reply he would have to consult his Government but he could tell me at once that he would do everything possible to facilitate the efforts of His Majesty's Government which he greatly appreciated. I think he was greatly relieved to know that His Majesty's Government had not in any way committed themselves as regards demands put forward by German Government and he fully realised the main importance which His Majesty's Government attaches to the necessity for not giving the German Government any opportunity for placing the blame on Poland in any refusal to enter into direct negotiations.

He has promised me the considered reply of his government by midday tomorrow. I took the opportunity of impressing upon him again the necessity of avoiding any incidents in the meantime and asked him whether any had recently occurred. He said he had just heard that there had been a clash between German and Polish military forces but as at present informed he did not think it had amounted to more than an exchange of shots without serious casualties.

Viscount Halifax to Sir H. Kennard (Warsaw)

Foreign Office, 31 August 1939, 12 noon

(Telegraphic)

You should concert with your French colleague in suggesting to Polish Government that they should now make known to the German Government, preferably direct, but if not, through us, that they have been made aware of our last reply to German Government and that they confirm their acceptance of the principle of direct discussions.

French Government fear that German Government might take advantage of silence on part of Polish Government.

Viscount Halifax to Sir H. Kennard (Warsaw)

Foreign Office, 31 August 1939, 1.45 PM

(Telegraphic)

Berlin telegram of 30th August:

Please at once inform Polish Government and advise them, in view of fact that they have accepted principle of direct discussions, immediately to instruct Polish Ambassador in Berlin to say to German Government that, if latter have any proposals, he is ready to transmit them to his Government so that they may at once consider them and make suggestions for early discussions.

Sir H. Kennard to Viscount Halifax (received 7.15 PM)
Warsaw, 31 August 1939

(Telegraphic)

M. Beck has just handed me in writing Polish reply to my *démarche* last night; translation is in my immediately following telegram. He particularly asked that it should be treated as most confidential.

I asked M. Beck what steps he proposed to take in order to establish contact with the German Government. He said he would now instruct M. Lipski to seek an interview either with the Minister for Foreign Affairs or State Secretary in order to say Poland had accepted British proposals. I urged him to do this without delay.

I then asked him what attitude Polish Ambassador would adopt if Herr von Ribbentrop or whoever he saw handed him the German proposals. He said that M. Lipski would not be authorised to accept such a document as, in view of past experience, it might be accompanied by some sort of ultimatum. In his view it was essential that contact should be made in the first instance, and that then details should be discussed as to where, with whom, and on what basis negotiations should be commenced.

As regards Danzig he pointed out that the situation there was becoming extremely serious. Polish officials were being arrested, railway traffic was suspended, and he thought it essential that immediate steps should be taken to secure a *modus vivendi* as a result of which those arrested would be released and railway traffic would be resumed. He suggested M. Burckhardt might be able to effect this.

He confirmed that no other serious incidents had occurred, but stated that he feared that in connection with any negotiations he would have to appeal to the intervention of His Majesty's Government.

He added that if invited to go to Berlin he would of course not go, as he had no intention of being treated like President Hacha.

Sir H. Kennard to Viscount Halifax (received 6.30 PM)
Warsaw, 31 *August* 1939

(Telegraphic)

Following is text of Poland's reply dated 31st August, 1939:

(1) Polish Government confirm their readiness which has previously been expressed for a direct exchange of views with the German Government on the basis proposed by British Government and communicated to me by Lord Halifax's telegram of 28th August addressed to the British Ambassador, Warsaw.

(2) Polish Government are also prepared on a reciprocal basis to give a formal guarantee that in the event of negotiations taking place Polish troops will not violate the frontiers of the German Reich provided a corresponding guarantee is given regarding non-violation of frontiers of Poland by troops of the German Reich.

(3) In the present situation it is also essential to create a simple provisional *modus vivendi* in the Free City of Danzig.

(4) As regards the suggestions communicated to Polish Government on 28th August through the intermediary of the British Ambassador at Warsaw, an explanation of what the British Government understands by international guarantee would be required in regard to relations between Poland and the German Reich. In default of an answer to this fundamental question the Polish Government are obliged completely to reserve their attitude towards this matter until such time as full explanations are received.

(5) Polish Government express hope that in the event of conversations with the German Reich being initiated, they will continue to be able to take advantage of good offices of His Majesty's Government.

Message which was communicated to HM Ambassador in Berlin by the State Secretary on 31 August 1939, at 9.15 PM

(Translation)

His Majesty's Government informed the German Government, in a note dated the 28th August, 1939, of their readiness to offer their mediation towards direct negotiations between Germany and Poland over the problems in dispute. In so doing they made it abundantly clear that they, too, were aware of the urgent need for progress in view of the continuous incidents and the general European tension. In a reply dated the 29th August, the German Government, in spite of being sceptical as to the desire of the Polish Government to come to an understanding, declared themselves ready in the interests of peace to accept the British mediation or suggestion. After considering all the circumstances prevailing at the time, they considered it necessary in their note to point out that, if the danger of a catastrophe was to be avoided, then action must be taken readily and without delay. In this sense they declared themselves ready to receive a personage appointed by the Polish Government up to the evening of the 30th August, with the proviso that the latter was, in fact, empowered not only to discuss but to conduct and conclude negotiations.

Further, the German Government pointed out that they felt able to make the basic points regarding the offer of an understanding available to the British Government by the time the Polish negotiator arrived in Berlin.

Instead of a statement regarding the arrival of an authorised Polish personage, the first answer the Government of the Reich received to their readiness for an understanding was the news of the Polish mobilisation, and only towards 12 o'clock on the night of the 30th August, 1939, did they receive a somewhat general assurance of British readiness to help towards the commencement of negotiations.

Although the fact that the Polish negotiator expected by the Government of the Reich did not arrive removed the necessary condition for informing His Majesty's Government of the views of the German Government as regards possible bases of negotiation, since His Majesty's Government themselves had pleaded for *direct* negotiations between Germany and Poland, the German Minister for Foreign Affairs, Herr von Ribbentrop, gave the British Ambassador on the occasion of the presentation of the last British note precise information as to the text of the German proposals which would be regarded as a basis of negotiation in the event of the arrival of the Polish plenipotentiary.

The Reich Government considered themselves entitled to claim that in these circumstances a Polish personage would immediately be nominated, at any rate retroactively. For the Reich Government cannot be expected for their part continually not only to emphasise their willingness to start negotiations, but actually to be ready to do so, while being from the Polish side merely put off with empty subterfuges and meaningless declarations.

It has once more been made clear as a result of a *démarche* which has meanwhile been made by the Polish Ambassador that the latter himself has no plenary powers either to enter into any discussion, or even to negotiate.

The Führer and the German Government have thus waited two days in vain for the arrival of a Polish negotiator with plenary powers. In these circumstances the German Government regard their proposals as having this time too been to all intents and purposes rejected, although they considered that these proposals, in the form in which they were made known to the British Government also, were more than loyal, fair and practicable.

The Reich Government consider it timely to inform the public of the bases for negotiation which were communicated to the British Ambassador by the Minister for Foreign Affairs, Herr von Ribbentrop. The situation existing between the German Reich and Poland is at the moment of such a kind that any further incident can lead to an explosion on the part of the military forces which have taken up their position on both sides. Any peaceful solution must be framed in such a way as to ensure that the events which lie at the root of this situation cannot be repeated on the next occasion offered, and that thus not only the East of Europe, but also other territories shall not be brought into such a state of tension. The causes of this development lie in: (1) the impossible delineation of frontiers, as fixed by the Versailles dictate; (2) the impossible treatment of the minority in the ceded territories.

In making these proposals, the Reich Government are, therefore, actuated [motivated] by the idea of finding a lasting solution which will remove the impossible situation created by frontier delineation, which may assure to both parties their vitally important line of communication, which may—as far as it is at all possible—remove the minority problem and, in so far as this is not possible, may give the minorities the assurance of a tolerable future by means of a reliable guarantee of their rights.

The Reich Government are content that in so doing it is essential that economic and physical damage done since 1918 should be exposed and repaired in its entirety. They, of course, regard this obligation as being binding for both parties.

These considerations lead to the following practical proposals:

(1) The Free City of Danzig shall return to the German Reich in view of its purely German character, as well as of the unanimous will of its population;

(2) The territory of the so-called Corridor which extends from the Baltic Sea to the line Marienwerder–Graudenz–Kulm–Bromberg (inclusive) and thence may run in a westerly direction to Schönlanke, shall itself decide as to whether it shall belong to Germany or Poland;

(3) For this purpose a plebiscite shall take place in this territory. The following shall be entitled to vote: all Germans who were either domiciled in this territory on the 1st January, 1918, or who by that date have been born there, and similarly of Poles, Kashubes, etc., domiciled in this territory on the above day (the 1st January, 1918) or born there up to that date. The Germans who have been driven from this territory shall return to it in order to exercise their vote with a view to ensuring an objective plebiscite, and also with a view to ensuring the extensive preparation necessary therefor. The above territory shall, as in the case of the Saar territory, be placed under the supervision of an international commission to be formed immediately, on which shall be represented the four Great Powers—Italy, the Soviet Union, France and England. This commission shall exercise all the rights of sovereignty in this territory. With this end in view, the territory shall be evacuated within a period of the utmost brevity, still to be agreed upon, by the Polish armed forces, the Polish Police, and the Polish authorities;

(4) The Polish port of Gdynia, which fundamentally constitutes Polish sovereign territory so far as it is confined territorially to the Polish settlement, shall be excluded from the above territory. The exact frontiers of this Polish port should be determined between Germany and Poland, and, if necessary, delimited by an international committee of arbitration;

(5) With a view to assuring the necessary time for the execution of the extensive work involved in the carrying out of a just plebiscite, this plebiscite shall not take place before the expiry of twelve months;

(6) In order to guarantee unrestricted communication between Germany and East Prussia and between Poland and the sea during this period, roads and railways shall be established to render free transit traffic possible. In this connection only such taxes as are necessary for the maintenance of the means of communication and for the provision of transport may be levied;

(7) The question as to the party to which the area belongs is to be decided by simple majority of the votes recorded;

(8) In order to guarantee to Germany free communication with her province of Danzig-East Prussia, and to Poland her connection with the sea after the execution of the plebiscite—regardless of the results thereof—Germany shall, in the event of the plebiscite area going to Poland, receive an extra-territorial traffic zone, approximately in a line from Bütow to Danzig or Dirschau, in which to lay down an autobahn and a 4-track railway line. The road and the railway shall be so constructed that the Polish lines of communication are not affected, i.e., they shall pass either over or under the latter. The breadth of this zone shall be fixed at 1 kilometre, and it is to be German sovereign territory. Should the plebiscite be favourable to Germany, Poland is to obtain rights, analogous to those accorded to Germany, to a similar extra-territorial communication by road and railway for the purpose of free and unrestricted communication with Gdynia;

(9) In the event of the Corridor returning to the German Reich, the latter declares its right to proceed to an exchange of population with Poland to the extent to which the nature of the Corridor lends itself thereto;

(10) Any special right desired by Poland in the port of Danzig would be negotiated on a basis of territory against similar rights to be granted to Germany in the port of Gdynia;

(11) In order to remove any feeling in this area that either side was being threatened, Danzig and Gdynia would have the character of exclusively mercantile towns, that is to say, without military installations and military fortifications;

(12) The peninsula of Hela, which as a result of the plebiscite might go either to Poland or to Germany, would in either case have similarly to be demilitarised;

(13) Since the Government of the German Reich has the most vehement complaints to make against the Polish treatment of minorities, and since the Polish Government for their part feel obliged to make complaints against Germany, both parties declare their agreement to have these complaints laid before an international committee of enquiry, whose task would be to examine all complaints as regards economic or physical damage, and any other acts of terrorism. Germany and Poland undertake to make good economic or other damage done to minorities on either side since 1918, or to cancel expropriation as the case may be, or to provide complete compensation to the persons affected for this and any other encroachments on their economic life;

(14) In order to free the Germans who may be left in Poland and the Poles who may be left in Germany from the feeling of being outlawed by all nations, and in order to render them secure against being called upon to perform action or to render services incompatible

with their national sentiments, Germany and Poland agree to guarantee the rights of both minorities by means of the most comprehensive and binding agreement, in order to guarantee to these minorities the preservation, the free development and practical application of their nationality (*Volkstum*), and in particular to permit for this purpose such organisation as they may consider necessary. Both parties undertake not to call upon members of the minority for military service;

(15) In the event of agreement on the basis of these proposals, Germany and Poland declare themselves ready to decree and to carry out the immediate demobilisation of their armed forces;

(16) The further measures necessary for the more rapid execution of the above arrangement shall be agreed upon by both Germany and Poland conjointly.

Viscount Halifax to Sir N. Henderson (Berlin)
Foreign Office, 31 August 1939, 11 PM

(Telegraphic)

Please inform German Government that we understand that Polish Government are taking steps to establish contact with them through Polish Ambassador in Berlin.

Please also ask them whether they agree to the necessity for securing an immediate provisional *modus vivendi* as regards Danzig. (We have already put this point to German Government.) Would they agree that M. Burckhardt might be employed for this purpose if it were possible to secure his services?

Viscount Halifax to Sir H. Kennard (Warsaw)
Foreign Office, 1 September 1939, 12.50 AM

(Telegraphic)

I am glad to learn that Polish Ambassador at Berlin is being instructed to establish contact with German Government. I fully agree as to the necessity for discussing detailed arrangements for the negotiations and as to the undesirability of a visit by M. Beck to Berlin.

On the other hand, I do not see why the Polish Government should feel difficulty about authorising Polish Ambassador to accept a document from the German Government, and I earnestly hope that they may be able to modify their instructions to him in this respect. There was no mention of any ultimatum in the report on the German proposals which has been furnished to us, and the suggestion that the demand for the presence of a Polish plenipotentiary at Berlin on 30th August amounted to an ultimatum was vigorously repudiated by Herr von Ribbentrop in conversation with His Majesty's Ambassador. If the document did contain an ultimatum, the Polish Government would naturally refuse to discuss it until the ultimatum was withdrawn. On the other hand, a refusal by them to receive proposals would be gravely misunderstood by outside opinion.

I should have thought that the Polish Ambassador could surely be instructed to receive and transmit a document and to say (*a*) if it contained anything like an ultimatum, that he anticipated that the Polish Government would certainly be unable to discuss on such a basis, and (*b*) that, in any case, in view of the Polish Government, questions as to the venue of the negotiations, the basis on which they should be held, and the persons to take part in them, must be discussed and decided between the two Governments.

If negotiations are initiated, His Majesty's Government will at all times be ready, if desired, to lend any assistance in their power to achieve a just settlement. As regards an international guarantee, this will no doubt have to be fully discussed. What His Majesty's Government had in mind was a guarantee of the full and proper observance of any settlement reached.

As regards Danzig, we fully share the view of M. Beck as to the importance of establishing some *modus vivendi*. We have already made a suggestion in this sense to the German Government and will in the light of paragraph 4 of your telegram of 31st August do so again. If German Government agree, I will at once approach M. Burckhardt.

Please speak to M. Beck immediately in the above sense.

Sir H. Kennard to Viscount Halifax (dated 7.43 PM 1 September and received 2 AM 2 September)

Warsaw, 1 September 1939

(Telegraphic)
Your telegram of 1st September was deciphered at 4 AM today. M. Lipski had already called on the German Foreign Minister at 6.30 PM yesterday. In view of this fact, which was followed by German invasion of Poland at dawn today, it was clearly useless for me to take the action suggested.

Sir N. Henderson to Viscount Halifax (received 12.10 AM 1 September)

Berlin, 31 August 1939

(Telegraphic)
Following is translation from text of communication handed by Polish Ambassador to German Minister for Foreign Affairs this evening:

> During the course of the night the Polish Government received from the British Government news of the exchange of information with the German Government regarding the possibility of direct discussion between the Government of the Reich and the Polish Government.
>
> The Polish Government are weighing favourably the British Government's suggestion; a formal answer in this matter will be communicated to them in the immediate future.

I understand that no discussion took place.

Explanatory note upon the actual course of events

The Polish Ambassador in Berlin (M. Lipski) was not received by Herr von Ribbentrop until the evening of 31st August. After this interview the German Government broadcast their proposals forthwith. M. Lipski at once tried to establish contact with Warsaw but was unable to do so because all means of communication between Poland and Germany had been closed by the German Government.

Speech by the Prime Minister in the House of Commons on 1 September 1939

The Prime Minister (Mr Chamberlain): I do not propose to say many words tonight. The time has come when action rather than speech is required. Eighteen months ago in this House I prayed that the responsibility might not fall upon me to ask this country to accept the awful arbitrament of war. I fear that I may not be able to avoid that responsibility. But, at any rate, I cannot wish for conditions in which such a burden should fall upon me in which I should feel clearer than I do today as to where my duty lies. No man can say that the Government could have done more to try to keep open the way for an honourable and equitable settlement of the dispute between Germany and Poland. Nor have we neglected any means of making it crystal clear to the German Government that if they insisted on using force again in the manner in which they had used it in the past we were resolved to oppose them by force. Now that all the relevant documents are being made public we shall stand at the bar of history knowing that the responsibility for this terrible catastrophe lies on the shoulders of one man—the German Chancellor, who has not hesitated to plunge the world into misery in order to serve his own senseless ambitions.

I would like to thank the House for the forbearance which they have shown on two recent occasions in not demanding from me information which they recognised I could not give while these negotiations were still in progress. I have now had all the correspondence with the German Government put into the form of a White Paper. On account of mechanical difficulties I am afraid there are still but a few copies available, but I understand that they will be coming in in relays while the House is sitting. I do not think it is necessary for me to refer in detail now to these documents, which are already past history. They make it perfectly clear that our object has been to try and bring about discussions of the Polish–German dispute between the two countries themselves on terms of equality, the settlement to be one which safeguarded the independence of Poland and of which the due observance would be secured by international guarantees.

There is just one passage from a recent communication, which was dated the 30th August, which I should like to quote, because it shows how easily the final clash might have been avoided had there been the least desire on the part of the German Government to arrive at a peaceful settlement. In this document we said:

> His Majesty's Government fully recognise the need for speed in the initiation of discussions and they share the apprehensions of the Chancellor arising from the proximity of two mobilised armies standing face to face. They would accordingly most strongly urge that both parties should undertake that during the negotiations no aggressive military movements should take place. His Majesty's Government feel confident that they could obtain such an undertaking from the Polish Government if the German Government would give similar assurances.

That telegram, which was repeated to Poland, brought an instantaneous reply from the Polish Government, dated the 31st August, in which they said:

> The Polish Government are also prepared on a reciprocal basis to give a formal guarantee in the event of negotiations taking place that Polish troops will not violate the frontiers of the German Reich provided a corresponding guarantee is given regarding the non-violation of the frontiers of Poland by troops of the German Reich.

We never had any reply from the German Government to that suggestion, one which, if it had been followed, might have saved the catastrophe which took place this morning. In the German broadcast last night, which recited the 16 points of the proposals which they have put forward, there occurred this sentence:

> In these circumstances the Reich Government considers its proposals rejected.

I must examine that statement. I must tell the House what are the circumstances. To begin with let me say that the text of these proposals has never been communicated by Germany to Poland at all. The history of the matter is this. On Tuesday, the 29th August, in replying to a Note which we had sent to them, the German Government said, among other things, that they would immediately draw up proposals for a solution acceptable to themselves and

> will, if possible, place these at the disposal of the British Government before arrival of the Polish negotiator.

It will be seen by examination of the White Paper that the German Government had stated that they counted upon the arrival of a plenipotentiary from Poland in Berlin on the 30th, that is to say, on the following day. In the meantime, of course, we were awaiting these proposals. The next evening, when our Ambassador saw Herr von Ribbentrop, the German Foreign Secretary, he urged upon the latter that when these proposals were ready—for we had heard no more about them—he should invite the Polish Ambassador to call and should hand him the proposals for transmission to his

Government. Thereupon, reports our Ambassador, in the most violent terms Herr von Ribbentrop said he would never ask the Ambassador to visit him. He hinted that if the Polish Ambassador asked him for an interview it might be different.

The House will see that this was on Wednesday night, which, according to the German statement of last night, is now claimed to be the final date after which no negotiation with Poland was acceptable. It is plain, therefore, that Germany claims to treat Poland as in the wrong because she had not by Wednesday night entered upon discussions with Germany about a set of proposals of which she had never heard.

Now what of ourselves? On that Wednesday night, at the interview to which I have just referred, Herr von Ribbentrop produced a lengthy document which he read out in German, aloud, at top speed. Naturally, after this reading our Ambassador asked for a copy of the document, but the reply was that it was now too late, as the Polish representative had not arrived in Berlin by midnight. And so, Sir, we never got a copy of those proposals, and the first time we heard them—*we* heard them—was on the broadcast last night. Well, Sir, those are the circumstances in which the German Government said that they would consider that their proposals were rejected. It is not clear that their conception of a negotiation was that on almost instantaneous demand a Polish plenipotentiary should go to Berlin—where others had been before him—and should they receive a statement of demands to be accepted in their entirety or refused? I am not pronouncing any opinion upon the terms themselves, for I do not feel called upon to do so. The proper course, in our view—in the view of all of us—was that these proposals should have been put before the Poles, who should have been given time to consider them and to say whether, in their opinion, they did or did not infringe those vital interests of Poland which Germany had assured us on a previous occasion she intended to respect.

Only last night the Polish Ambassador did see the German Foreign Secretary, Herr von Ribbentrop. Once again he expressed to him what, indeed, the Polish Government had already said publicly, that they were willing to negotiate with Germany about their disputes on an equal basis. What was the reply of the German Government? The reply was that without another word the German troops crossed the Polish frontier this morning at dawn and are since reported to be bombing open towns. [An hon. member: "Gas?"] In these circumstances there is only one course open to us. His Majesty's Ambassador in Berlin and the French Ambassador have been instructed to hand to the German Government the following document:

> Early this morning the German Chancellor issued a proclamation to the German Army which indicated clearly that he was about to attack Poland. Information which has reached His Majesty's Government in the United Kingdom and the French Government indicates that German troops have crossed the Polish frontier and that attacks upon Polish towns are proceeding. In these circumstances it appears to the Governments of the United Kingdom and France that by their action the

German Government have created conditions, namely, an aggressive act of force against Poland threatening the independence of Poland, which call for the implementation by the Governments of the United Kingdom and France of the undertaking to Poland to come to her assistance. I am accordingly to inform your Excellency that unless the German Government are prepared to give His Majesty's Government satisfactory assurances that the German Government have suspended all aggressive action against Poland and are prepared promptly to withdraw their forces from Polish territory, His Majesty's Government in the United Kingdom will without hesitation fulfil their obligations to Poland.

[An hon. member: "Time limit?"] If a reply to this last warning is unfavourable, and I do not suggest that it is likely to be otherwise, His Majesty's Ambassador is instructed to ask for his passports. In that case we are ready. Yesterday, we took further steps towards the completion of our defensive preparations. This morning we ordered complete mobilisation of the whole of the Royal Navy, Army and Royal Air Force. We have also taken a number of other measures, both at home and abroad, which the House will not perhaps expect me to specify in detail. Briefly, they represent the final steps in accordance with pre-arranged plans. These last can be put into force rapidly, and are of such a nature that they can be deferred until war seems inevitable. Steps have also been taken under the powers conferred by the House last week to safeguard the position in regard to stocks of commodities of various kinds.

The thoughts of many of us must at this moment inevitably be turning back to 1914, and to a comparison of our position now with that which existed then. How do we stand this time? The answer is that all three Services are ready, and that the situation in all directions is far more favourable and reassuring than in 1914, while behind the fighting Services we have built up a vast organisation of Civil Defence under our scheme of Air Raid Precautions. As regards the immediate man-power requirements, the Royal Navy, the Army and the Royal Air Force are in the fortunate position of having almost as many men as they can conveniently handle at this moment. There are, however, certain categories of service in which men are immediately required, both for Military and Civil Defence. These will be announced in detail through the press and the BBC. The main and most satisfactory point to observe is that there is today no need to make an appeal in a general way for recruits such as was issued by Lord Kitchener 25 years ago. That appeal has been anticipated by many months, and the men are already available.

So much for the immediate present. Now we must look to the future. It is essential in the face of the tremendous task which confronts us, more especially in view of our past experiences in this matter, to organise our man-power this time upon as methodical, equitable and economical a basis as possible. We, therefore, propose immediately to introduce legislation directed to that end. A Bill will be laid before you which for all practical purposes will amount to an expansion of the Military Training Act. Under its operation all fit men between the ages of 18 and 41 will be rendered liable to military service if and when called upon. It is not intended at the outset that any considerable number of men other than those already liable shall be called up, and steps will be taken to ensure that the man-power essentially required by industry shall not be taken away.

There is one other allusion which I should like to make before I end my speech, and that is to record my satisfaction, and the satisfaction of His Majesty's Government, that throughout these last days of crisis Signor Mussolini also has been doing his best to reach a solution.

It now only remains for us to set our teeth and to enter upon this struggle, which we ourselves earnestly endeavoured to avoid, with determination to see it through to the end. We shall enter it with a clear conscience, with the support of the Dominions and the British Empire, and the moral approval of the greater part of the world. We have no quarrel with the German people, except that they allow themselves to be governed by a Nazi Government. As long as that Government exists and pursues the methods it has so persistently followed during the last two years, there will be no peace in Europe. We shall merely pass from one crisis to another, and see one country after another attacked by methods which have now become familiar to us in their sickening technique. We are resolved that these methods must come to an end. If out of the struggle we again re-establish in the world the rules of good faith and the renunciation of force, why, then even the sacrifices that will be entailed upon us will find their fullest justification.

Speech by Herr Hitler to the Reichstag on 1 September 1939
(Translation)

For months we have been suffering under the torture of a problem which the Versailles *Diktat* created—a problem which has deteriorated until it becomes intolerable for us. Danzig was and is a German city. The Corridor was and is German. Both these territories owe their cultural development exclusively to the German people. Danzig was separated from us, the Corridor was annexed by Poland. As in other German territories of the East, all German minorities living there have been ill-treated in the most distressing manner. More than 1,000,000 people of German blood had in the years 1919–20 to leave their homeland.

As always, I attempted to bring about, by the peaceful method of making proposals for revision, an alteration of this intolerable position. It is a lie when the outside world says that we only tried to carry through our revisions by pressure. Fifteen years before the National Socialist Party came to power there was the opportunity of carrying out these revisions by peaceful settlements and understanding. On my own initiative I have, not once but several times, made proposals for the revision of intolerable conditions. All these proposals, as you know, have been rejected—proposals for limitation of armaments and even, if necessary, disarmament, proposals for the limitation of war-making, proposals for the elimination of certain methods of modern warfare. You know the proposals that I have made to fulfil the necessity of restoring German sovereignty over German territories. You know the endless attempts I made for a peaceful clarification and understanding of the problem of Austria, and later of the problem of the Sudetenland, Bohemia, and Moravia. It was all in vain.

It is impossible to demand that an impossible position should be cleared up by peaceful revision and at the same time constantly reject peaceful revision. It is also impossible to say that he who undertakes to carry out these revisions for himself transgresses a law, since the Versailles *Diktat* is not law to us. A signature was forced out of us with pistols at our head and with the threat of hunger for millions of people. And then this document, with our signature, obtained by force, was proclaimed as a solemn law.

In the same way, I have also tried to solve the problem of Danzig, the Corridor, etc., by proposing a peaceful discussion. That the problems had to be solved was clear. It is quite understandable to us that the time when the problem was to be solved had little interest for the Western Powers. But that time is not a matter of indifference to us. Moreover, it was not and could not be a matter of indifference to those who suffer most.

In my talks with Polish statesmen I discussed the ideas which you recognise from my last speech to the Reichstag. No one could say that this was in any way an inadmissible procedure or undue pressure. I then naturally formulated at last the German proposals, and I must once more repeat that there is nothing more modest or loyal than these proposals. I should like to say this to the world. I alone was in the position to make such proposals, for I know very well that in doing so I brought myself into opposition to millions of Germans. These proposals have been refused. Not only were they answered first with mobilisation, but with increased terror and pressure against our German compatriots and with a slow strangling of the Free City of Danzig—economically, politically, and in recent weeks by military and transport means.

Poland has directed its attacks against the Free City of Danzig. Moreover, Poland was not prepared to settle the Corridor question in a reasonable way which would be equitable to both parties, and she did not think of keeping her obligations to minorities.

I must here state something definitely; Germany has kept these obligations; the minorities who live in Germany are not persecuted. No Frenchman can stand up and say that any Frenchman living in the Saar territory is oppressed, tortured, or deprived of his rights. Nobody can say this.

For four months I have calmly watched developments, although I never ceased to give warnings. In the last few days I have increased these warnings. I informed the Polish Ambassador three weeks ago that if Poland continued to send to Danzig notes in the form of ultimata, if Poland continued its methods of oppression against the Germans, and if on the Polish side an end was not put to Customs measures destined to ruin Danzig's trade, then the Reich could not remain inactive. I left no doubt that people who wanted to compare the Germany of today with the former Germany would be deceiving themselves.

An attempt was made to justify the oppression of the Germans by claiming that they had committed acts of provocation. I do not know in what these provocations on the part of women and children consist, if they themselves are maltreated, in some cases killed. One thing I do know—that no great Power can with honour long stand by passively and watch such events.

I made one more final effort to accept a proposal for mediation on the part of the British Government. They proposed, not that they themselves should carry on the negotiations, but rather that Poland and Germany should come into direct contact and once more to pursue negotiations.

I must declare that I accepted this proposal, and I worked out a basis for these negotiations which are known to you. For two whole days I sat with my Government and waited to see whether it was convenient for the Polish Government to send a plenipotentiary or not. Last night they did not send us a plenipotentiary, but instead informed us through their Ambassador that they were still considering whether and to what extent they were in a position to go into the British proposals. The Polish Government also said that they would inform Britain of their decision.

Deputies, if the German Government and its Leader patiently endured such treatment Germany would deserve only to disappear from the political stage. But I am wrongly judged if my love of peace and my patience are mistaken for weakness or even cowardice. I, therefore, decided last night and informed the British Government that in these circumstances I can no longer find any willingness on the part of the Polish Government to conduct serious negotiations with us.

These proposals for mediation have failed because in the meanwhile there, first of all, came as an answer the sudden Polish general mobilisation, followed by more Polish atrocities. These were again repeated last night. Recently in one night there were as many as twenty-one frontier incidents; last night there were fourteen, of which three were quite serious. I have, therefore, resolved to speak to Poland in the same language that Poland for months past has used towards us. This attitude on the part of the Reich will not change.

The other European States understand in part our attitude. I should like here above all to thank Italy, which throughout has supported us, but you will understand that for the carrying on of this struggle we do not intend to appeal to foreign help. We will carry out this task ourselves. The neutral States have assured us of their neutrality, just as we had already guaranteed it to them.

When statesmen in the West declare that this affects their interests, I can only regret such a declaration. It cannot for a moment make me hesitate to fulfil my duty. What more is wanted? I have solemnly assured them, and I repeat it, that we ask nothing of these Western States and never will ask anything. I have declared that the frontier between France and Germany is a final one. I have repeatedly offered friendship and, if necessary, the closest co-operation to Britain, but this cannot be offered from one side only. It must find response on the other side. Germany has no interests in the West, and our western wall is for all time the frontier of the Reich on the west. Moreover, we have no aims of any kind there for the future. With this assurance we are in solemn earnest, and as long as others do not violate their neutrality we will likewise take every care to respect it.

I am happy particularly to be able to tell you of one event. You know that Russia and Germany are governed by two different doctrines. There was only one question that had to be cleared up. Germany has no intention of exporting its doctrine. Given the fact that Soviet Russia has no intention of exporting its doctrine to Germany, I no longer see any reason why we should still oppose one another. On both sides we are clear on that. Any struggle between our people would only be of advantage to others. We have, therefore, resolved to conclude a pact which rules out for ever any use of violence between us. It imposes the obligation on us to consult together in certain European questions. It makes possible for us economic co-operation, and above all it assures that the powers of both these powerful States are not wasted against one another. Every attempt of the West to bring about any change in this will fail.

At the same time I should like here to declare that this political decision means a tremendous departure for the future, and that it is a final one. Russia and Germany fought against one another in the World War. That shall and will not happen a second time. In Moscow, too, this pact was greeted exactly as you greet it. I can only endorse word for word the speech of the Russian Foreign Commissar, Molotov.

I am determined to solve (1) the Danzig question; (2) the question of the Corridor; and (3) to see to it that a change is made in the relationship between Germany and Poland that shall ensure a peaceful co-existence. In this I am resolved to continue to fight until either the present Polish Government is willing to bring about this change or until another Polish Government is ready to do so. I am resolved to remove from the German frontiers the element of uncertainty, the everlasting atmosphere of conditions resembling civil war. I will see to it that in the East there is, on the frontier, a peace precisely similar to that on our other frontiers.

In this I will take the necessary measures to see that they do not contradict the proposals I have already made known in the Reichstag itself to the rest of the world, that is to say, I will not war against women and children. I have ordered my air force to restrict itself to attacks on military objectives. If, however, the enemy thinks he can from that draw *carte blanche* on his side to fight by the other methods he will receive an answer that will deprive him of hearing and sight.

This night for the first time Polish regular soldiers fired on our own territory. Since 5.45 AM we have been returning the fire, and from now on bombs will be met with bombs. Whoever fights with poison gas will be fought with poison gas. Whoever departs from the rules of humane warfare can only expect that we shall do the same. I will continue this struggle, no matter against whom, until the safety of the Reich and its rights are secured.

For six years now I have been working on the building up of the German defences. Over 90 milliards have in that time been spent on the building up of these defence forces. They are now the best equipped and are above all comparison with what they were in 1914. My trust in them is unshakable. When I called up these forces and when I now ask sacrifices of the German people and if necessary every sacrifice, then I have a right to do so, for I also am today absolutely ready, just as we were formerly, to make every personal sacrifice.

I am asking of no German man more than I myself was ready throughout four years at any time to do. There will be no hardships for Germans to which I myself will not submit. My whole life henceforth belongs more than ever to my people. I am from now on just first soldier of the German Reich. I have once more put on that coat that was the most sacred and dear to me. I will not take it off again until victory is secured, or I will not survive the outcome.

Should anything happen to me in the struggle then my first successor is Party Comrade Göring; should anything happen to Party Comrade Göring my next successor is Party Comrade Hess. You would then be under obligation to give to them as Führer the same blind loyalty and obedience as to myself. Should anything happen to Party Comrade Hess, then by law the Senate will be called, and will choose from its midst the most worthy—that is to say the bravest—successor.

As a National Socialist and as German soldier I enter upon this struggle with a stout heart. My whole life has been nothing but one long struggle for my people, for its restoration, and for Germany. There was only one watchword for that struggle: faith in this people. One word I have never learned: that is, surrender.

If, however, anyone thinks that we are facing a hard time, I should ask him to remember that once a Prussian King, with a ridiculously small State, opposed a stronger coalition, and in three wars finally came out successful because that State had that stout heart that we need in these times. I would, therefore, like to assure all the world that a November 1918 will never be repeated in German history. Just as I myself am ready at any time to stake my life—anyone can take it for my people and for Germany—so I ask the same of all others.

Whoever, however, thinks he can oppose this national command, whether directly or indirectly, shall fall. We have nothing to do with traitors. We are all faithful to our old principle. It is quite unimportant whether we ourselves live, but it is essential that our people shall live, that Germany shall live. The sacrifice that is demanded of us is not greater than the sacrifice that many generations have made. If we form a community closely bound together by vows, ready for anything, resolved never to surrender, then our will will master every hardship and difficulty. And I would like to close with the declaration that I once made when I began the struggle for power in the Reich. I then said: "If our will is so strong that no hardship and suffering can subdue it, then our will and our German might shall prevail."

Herr Hitler's Proclamation to the German Army on 1 *September* 1939
(Translation)
The Polish State has refused the peaceful settlement of relations which I desired, and has appealed to arms. Germans in Poland are persecuted with bloody terror and driven from their houses. A series of violations of the frontier, intolerable to a great Power, prove that Poland is no longer willing to respect the frontier of the Reich.

In order to put an end to this lunacy, I have no other choice than to meet force with force from now on. The German Army will fight the battle for the honour and the vital rights of reborn Germany with hard determination. I expect that every soldier, mindful of the great traditions of eternal German soldiery, will ever remain conscious that he is a representative of the National-Socialist Greater Germany. Long live our people and our Reich!

Viscount Halifax to Sir N. Henderson (Berlin)
Foreign Office, 1 September 1939, 4.45 PM
(Telegraphic)
My immediately following telegram contains the text of a communication that you should, in conjunction with your French colleague, make at once to the German Government.

You should ask for immediate reply and report result of your interview. I shall then send you further instructions.

In reply to any question you may explain that the present communication is in the nature of warning and is not to be considered as an ultimatum.

For your own information. If the German reply is unsatisfactory the next stage will be either an ultimatum with time limit or an immediate declaration of war.

Viscount Halifax to Sir N. Henderson (Berlin)
Foreign Office, 1 September 1939, 5.45 PM
(Telegraphic)
Following is text referred to in my immediately preceding telegram:

On the instructions of His Majesty's Principal Secretary of State for Foreign Affairs, I have the honour to make the following communication:

Early this morning the German Chancellor issued a proclamation to the German army which indicated clearly that he was about to attack Poland. Information which has reached His Majesty's Government in the United Kingdom and the French Government indicates that German troops have crossed the Polish frontier and that attacks upon Polish towns are proceeding.

In these circumstances, it appears to the Governments of the United Kingdom and France that by their action the German Government have created conditions (viz., an aggressive act of force against Poland threatening the independence of Poland) which call for the implementation by the Governments of the United Kingdom and France of the undertaking to Poland to come to her assistance.

I am accordingly to inform your Excellency that unless the German Government are prepared to give His Majesty's Government satisfactory assurances that the German Government have suspended all aggressive action against Poland and are prepared promptly to withdraw their forces from Polish territory, His Majesty's Government in the United Kingdom will without hesitation fulfil their obligations to Poland.

Sir N. Henderson to Viscount Halifax (received 10.30 PM*)*

Berlin, 1 September 1939

(Telegraphic)

I was received by Herr von Ribbentrop at 9.30 this evening, and handed him the communication from His Majesty's Government. After reading it, he said that he wished to state that it was not Germany who had aggressed Poland, that on the contrary it was Poland who had provoked Germany for a long time past; that it was the Poles who had first mobilised and that yesterday it was Poland that had invaded German territory with troops of the regular army.

I said that I was instructed to ask for immediate answer. The Minister replied that he would submit the British communication to the Head of the State. I replied that I realised that this would be necessary, and that I was at his disposal at whatever time he might be in a position to give the Chancellor's answer. Herr von Ribbentrop then remarked that if His Majesty's Government had been as active, *vis-à-vis* Poland, as they had been *vis-à-vis* Germany, a settlement would have been reached at an early stage.

French Ambassador saw Herr von Ribbentrop immediately after and received an identic reply.

As I was leaving Herr von Ribbentrop gave me long explanation of why he had been unable to give me text of German proposals two nights ago. I told him that his attitude on that occasion had been most unhelpful and had effectively prevented me from making a last effort for peace, and that I greatly deplored it.

He was courteous and polite this evening. I am inclined to believe that Herr Hitler's answer will be an attempt to avoid war with Great Britain and France, but not likely to be one which we can accept.

Sir H. Kennard to Viscount Halifax (received 2 PM*)*

Warsaw, 1 September 1939

(Telegraphic)

Minister for Foreign Affairs has just telephoned to me in the middle of an air raid to beg me to point out to your Lordship that various cases of armed

German aggression, which have occurred this morning on Polish soil, cannot be taken longer as mere isolated cases but constitute acts of war. Various open towns have been bombed from the air, with heavy civilian casualties, and his Excellency drew my attention to desirability of some military action from the air this afternoon.

His Excellency pointed out that at 6.30 PM Polish Ambassador saw Herr von Ribbentrop and expressed readiness of Polish Government to enter into direct negotiations. At dawn this morning, without any further diplomatic development or declaration of war, Germany had committed various acts of unprovoked aggression on a major scale, and thus, while Polish Government had made every effort to avoid serious clashes, German forces had deliberately attacked Polish territory and already caused deaths of numerous innocent civilians. Polish Government had, therefore, no course but to break off relations with German Government, and Polish Ambassador at Berlin has asked for his passports.

His Excellency failed to see what measures could now be taken to prevent European war, and while he did not say so in so many words it is obvious that he hopes His Majesty's Government will take some action of a military character to relieve the pressure on this field of operations. M. Beck has also given me a categorical and official denial that any Polish act of aggression occurred last night as stated by Deutsches Nachrichten-Büro.

French Ambassador has suggested to me that French and British wireless should repeatedly point out that Germany has openly and flagrantly attacked Poland without warning.

Viscount Halifax to Sir H. Kennard (Warsaw)

Foreign Office, 1 September 1939

The Polish Ambassador called to see me at his request at 10.30 this morning. Count Raczynski said that he had been officially informed from Paris that German forces had crossed the frontier at four points. He added that the towns of Vilno, Grodno, Brest-Litovsk, Lodz, Katowice and Cracow were being bombed and that at 9 AM an air attack had been made on Warsaw, as a result of which there were many civilian victims, including women and children. As regards the German attack, he understood, although he had no official information, that the points at the frontier which had been crossed were near Danzig, in East Prussia and Upper Silesia. His Excellency said that he had few words to add, except that it was a plain case as provided for by the treaty. I said that I had no doubt on the facts as he had reported them that we should take the same view.

Sir H. Kennard to Viscount Halifax (received 8 PM)

Warsaw, 2 September 1939

(Telegraphic)

M. Beck requested French Ambassador and me to see him today and points out while the Polish army was sternly resisting the German attack it found itself much hampered by German superiority in the air. It was possible for German Air Force to throw whole of their weight on this front at present, and he very discreetly suggested it was essential that there should be some diversion as soon as possible in the West.

He hoped, therefore, we would inform him as soon as possible of entry of the two countries into the war and that our aircraft would find it possible to draw off a considerable proportion of German aircraft operating on this front.

His Excellency also drew our attention to the fact that German aircraft had not confined themselves strictly to military objectives. They have bombed factories not engaged in war work, villages not near military objectives, and have caused severe losses among civilian population.

I trust I may be informed at the earliest possible moment of our declaration of war and that our air force will make every effort to show activity on western front with a view to relieving pressure here.

Viscount Halifax to Sir N. Henderson (Berlin)
Foreign Office, 3 September 1939, 5 AM

(Telegraphic)

Please seek interview with Minister for Foreign Affairs at 9 AM today, Sunday or, if he cannot see you then, arrange to convey at that time to representative of German Government the following communication:

> In the communication which I had the honour to make to you on 1st September I informed you, on the instructions of His Majesty's Principal Secretary of State for Foreign Affairs, that, unless the German Government were prepared to give His Majesty's Government in the United Kingdom satisfactory assurances that the German Government had suspended all aggressive action against Poland and were prepared promptly to withdraw their forces from Polish territory, His Majesty's Government in the United Kingdom would, without hesitation, fulfil their obligations to Poland.
>
> Although this communication was made more than twenty-four hours ago, no reply has been received but German attacks upon Poland have been continued and intensified. I have accordingly the honour to inform you that, unless not later than 11 AM, British Summer Time, today 3rd September, satisfactory assurances to the above effect have been given by the German Government and have reached His Majesty's Government in London, a state of war will exist between the two countries as from that hour.

If the assurance referred to in the above communication is received, you should inform me by any means at your disposal before 11 AM today, 3rd September. If no such assurance is received here by 11 AM, we shall inform the German representative that a state of war exists as from that hour.

Memorandum handed to Sir N. Henderson at 11.20 AM *on 3 September* 1939, *by Herr von Ribbentrop*

(Translation)

The German Government have received the British Government's ultimatum of the 3rd September, 1939. They have the honour to reply as follows:

The German Government and the German people refuse to receive, accept, let alone to fulfil, demands in the nature of ultimata made by the British Government.

On our eastern frontier there has for many months already reigned a condition of war. Since the time when the Versailles Treaty first tore Germany to pieces, all and every peaceful settlement was refused to all German Governments. The National Socialist Government also has since the year 1933 tried again and again to remove by peaceful negotiations the worst rapes and breaches of justice of this treaty. The British Government have been among those who, by their intransigent attitude, took the chief part in frustrating every practical revision. Without the intervention of the British Government—of this the German Government and German people are fully conscious—a reasonable solution doing justice to both sides would certainly have been found between Germany and Poland. For Germany did not have the intention nor had she raised the demands of annihilating Poland. The Reich demanded only the revision of those articles of the Versailles Treaty which already at the time of the formulation of that Dictate had been described by understanding statesmen of all nations as being in the long run unbearable, and therefore impossible for a great nation and also for the entire political and economic interests of Eastern Europe. British statesmen, too, declared the solution in the East which was then forced upon Germany as containing the germ of future wars. To remove this danger was the desire of all German Governments and especially the intention of the new National Socialist People's Government. The blame for having prevented this peaceful revision lies with the British Cabinet policy.

The British Government have—an occurrence unique in history—given the Polish State full powers for all actions against Germany which that State might conceivably intend to undertake. The British Government assured the Polish Government of their military support in all circumstances, should Germany defend herself against any provocation or attack. Thereupon the Polish terror against the Germans living in the territories which had been torn from Germany immediately assumed unbearable proportions. The Free City of Danzig was, in violation of all legal provisions, first threatened with destruction economically and by measures of customs policy, and was finally subjected to a military blockade and its communications strangled. All these violations of the Danzig Statute, which were well known to the British Government, were approved and covered by the blank cheque given to Poland. The German Government, though moved by the sufferings of the German population which was being tortured and treated in an inhuman manner, nevertheless remained a patient onlooker for five months, without undertaking even on one single occasion any similar aggressive action against Poland. They only warned Poland that these happenings would in the long run be unbearable, and that they were determined, in the event of no other kind of assistance being given to this population, to help them themselves. All these happenings were known in every detail to the British Government. It would have been easy for them to use their great influence in Warsaw in order to exhort those in power there to exercise justice and humaneness and to keep to the existing obligations. The British Government did not do this. On the contrary, in emphasising continually their obligation to assist Poland under all circumstances, they actually encouraged the Polish Government to continue in their criminal attitude which was threatening the peace of Europe. In this spirit, the British Government rejected the proposal of Signor Mussolini, which might still have been able to save the peace of Europe, in spite of the fact that the German Government had declared their willingness to agree to it. The British Government, therefore, bear the responsibility for all the unhappiness and misery which have now overtaken and are about to overtake many peoples.

After all efforts at finding and concluding a peaceful solution had been rendered impossible by the intransigence of the Polish Government covered as they were by England, after the conditions resembling civil war, which had existed already for months at the eastern frontier of the Reich, had gradually developed into open attacks on German territory, without the British Government raising any objections, the German Government determined to put an end to this continual threat, unbearable for a great Power, to the external and finally also to the internal peace of the German people, and to end it by those means which, since the Democratic Governments had in effect sabotaged all other possibilities of revision, alone remained at their disposal for the defence of the peace, security and honour of the Germans. The last attacks of the Poles threatening Reich territory they answered with similar measures. The German Government do not intend, on account of any sort of British intentions or obligations in the East, to tolerate conditions which are identical with those conditions which we observe in Palestine, which is under British protection. The German people, however, above all do not intend to allow themselves to be ill-treated by Poles.

The German Government, therefore, reject the attempts to force Germany, by means of a demand having the character of an ultimatum, to recall its forces which are lined up for the defence of the Reich, and thereby to accept the old unrest and the old injustice. The threat that, failing this, they will fight Germany in the war, corresponds to the intention proclaimed for years past by numerous British politicians. The German Government and the German people have assured the English people countless times how much they desire an understanding, indeed close friendship, with them. If the British Government hitherto always refused these offers and now answer them with an open threat of war, it is not the fault of the German people and of their Government, but exclusively the fault of the British Cabinet or of those men who for years have been preaching the destruction and extermination of the German people. The German people and their Government do not, like Great Britain, intend to dominate the world, but they are determined to defend their own liberty, their independence and above all their life. The intention, communicated to us by order of the British Government by Mr King-Hall, of carrying the destruction of the German people even further than was done through the Versailles Treaty is taken note of by us, and we shall therefore answer any aggressive action on the part of England with the same weapons and in the same form.

Speech by the Prime Minister in the House of Commons on 3 September 1939

The Prime Minister: When I spoke last night to the House I could not but be aware that in some parts of the House there were doubts and some bewilderment as to whether there had been any weakening, hesitation or vacillation on the part of His Majesty's Government. In the circumstances, I make no reproach, for if I had been in the same position as hon. members not sitting on this Bench and not in possession of all the information which we have, I should very likely have felt the same. The statement which I have to make this morning will show that there were no grounds for doubt. We were in consultation all day yesterday with the French Government and we felt that the intensified action which the Germans were taking against Poland allowed no delay in making our own position clear. Accordingly, we decided to send to our Ambassador in Berlin instructions which he was to hand at 9 o'clock this morning to the German Foreign Secretary [see p. 175 for text of instructions].

That was the final Note. No undertaking was received by the time stipulated, and, consequently, this country is at war with Germany. I am in a position to inform the House that, according to arrangements made between the British and French Governments, the French Ambassador in Berlin is at this moment making a similar *démarche*, accompanied also by a definite time limit. The House has already been made aware of our plans. As I said the other day, we are ready.

This is a sad day for all of us, and to none is it sadder than to me. Everything that I have worked for, everything that I have hoped for, everything that I have believed in during my public life, has crashed into ruins. There is only one thing left for me to do; that is, to devote what strength and powers I have to forwarding the victory of the cause for which we have to sacrifice so much. I cannot tell what part I may be allowed to play myself; I trust I may live to see the day when Hitlerism has been destroyed and a liberated Europe has been re-established.

*Herr Hitler's proclamations of 3 September 1939 to the German people and the
German Army*

(Translation)

APPEAL TO THE GERMAN PEOPLE

Great Britain has for centuries pursued the aim of rendering the peoples of
Europe defenceless against the British policy of world conquest by proclaiming a balance of power, in which Great Britain claimed the right to attack on
threadbare pretexts and destroy that European State which at the moment
seemed most dangerous. Thus, at one time, she fought the world power of
Spain, later the Dutch, then the French, and, since the year 1871, the German.

We ourselves have been witnesses of the policy of encirclement which
has been carried on by Great Britain against Germany since before the war.
Just as the German nation had begun, under its National Socialist leadership,
to recover from the frightful consequences of the *Diktat* of Versailles, and
threatened to survive the crisis, British encirclement immediately began
once more.

The British war inciters spread the lie before the War that the battle was
only against the House of Hohenzollern or German militarism; that they
had no designs on German colonies; that they had no intention of taking the
German mercantile fleet. They then oppressed the German people under the
Versailles *Diktat*, the faithful fulfilment of which would have sooner or later
exterminated 20 million Germans.

I undertook to mobilise the resistance of the German nation against this,
and to assure work and bread for them. But as the peaceful revision of the
Versailles *Diktat* of force seemed to be succeeding, and the German people
again began to live, the new British encirclement policy was resumed. The
same lying inciters appeared as in 1914. I have many times offered Great
Britain and the British people the understanding and friendship of the
German people. My whole policy was based on the idea of this understanding. I have always been repelled. I had for years been aware that the aim of
these war inciters had for long been to take Germany by surprise at a
favourable opportunity.

I am more firmly determined than ever to beat back this attack.
Germany shall not again capitulate. There is no sense in sacrificing one life
after another and submitting to an even worse Versailles *Diktat*. We have
never been a nation of slaves and will not be one in the future. Whatever
Germans in the past had to sacrifice for the existence of our realm, they shall
not be greater than those which we are today prepared to make.

This resolve is an inexorable one. It necessitates the most thorough measures, and imposes on us one law above all others: if the soldier is fighting at
the front, no one shall profit by the war. If the soldier falls at the front no
one at home shall evade his duty.

As long as the German people was united it has never been conquered. It
was the lack of unity in 1918 that led to collapse. Whoever offends against this

unity need expect nothing else than annihilation as an enemy of the nation. If our people fulfils its highest duty in this sense, that God will help us who has always bestowed His mercy on him who was determined to help himself.

APPEAL TO THE GERMAN ARMY ON THE WESTERN FRONT

Soldiers of the Western Army: just as before the War, so after the War Great Britain has pursued the policy of Germany's encirclement. In spite of the fact that Germany has no demands to make on any other State to the west of the Reich; in spite of the fact that Germany claims no territorial revision in this territory; and in spite of the fact that Germany has made, above all to Great Britain just as to France, the offer of a cordial understanding, indeed of friendship. The British Government, driven on by those warmongers whom we knew in the last War, have resolved to let fall their mask and to proclaim war on a threadbare pretext.

The German people and your comrades in the East now expect from you, soldiers of the Western Front, that you shall protect the frontiers of the Reich, unshakable as a wall of steel and iron, against every attack, in an array of fortifications which is a hundred times stronger than that western front of the Great War, which was never conquered.

If you do your duty, the battle in the East will have reached its successful conclusion in a few months, and then the power of the whole National Socialist State stands behind you. As an old soldier of the World War, and as your Supreme Commander, I am going, with confidence in you, to the Army on the East. Our plutocratic enemies will realise that they are now dealing with a different Germany from that of the year 1914.

ADOLF HITLER

D DAY TO VE DAY, 1944–45

GENERAL EISENHOWER'S REPORT ON THE INVASION OF EUROPE

CONTENTS

MAPS

The clear reporting of war by military leaders to Parliament is a tradition that seems to have ended since this report was prepared by General Eisenhower for the US Senate and the British Parliament.

There is a fashionable view that the decisive battle to finish the Second World War took place in a few days of hard fighting on the French coast and some difficult encounters on the Dutch–German border. General Eisenhower's account of the invasion of Europe in 1944 presents the story of a far more arduous struggle against forces whose tenacity he admired and whose skills he feared. It is a tactical account of his understanding of enemy manoeuvres, and his attempts to counter their actions.

The formality of the document is coloured by many personal touches, and the reader senses Eisenhower's growing determination to complete the task. Hindsight would have had the general take more notice of Russian activity, but that this was not obvious to him is one of the fascinations of such a contemporary document.

General Eisenhower went on to become President of the United States from 1953 to 1961, during one of the most difficult periods of the Cold War. In this edition we have retained his American spelling and reproduced the maps as they were presented in the original report.

DIRECTIVE TO SUPREME COMMANDER ALLIED EXPEDITIONARY FORCE

(*Issued* 12 *February* 1944)

1. You are hereby designated as Supreme Allied Commander of the forces placed under your orders for operations for liberation of Europe from Germans. Your title will be Supreme Commander Allied Expeditionary Force.

2. *Task* You will enter the Continent of Europe and, in conjunction with the other United Nations, undertake operations aimed at the heart of Germany and the destruction of her armed forces. The date for entering the Continent is the month of May 1944. After adequate channel ports have been secured, exploitation will be directed towards securing an area that will facilitate both ground and air operations against the enemy.

3. Notwithstanding the target date above you will be prepared at any time to take immediate advantage of favorable circumstances, such as withdrawal by the enemy on your front, to effect a re-entry into the Continent with such forces as you have available at the time; a general plan for this operation when approved will be furnished for your assistance.

4. *Command* You are responsible to the Combined Chiefs of Staff and will exercise command generally in accordance with the diagram given. Direct communication with the United States and British Chiefs of Staff is authorized in the interest of facilitating your operations and for arranging necessary logistic support.

5. *Logistics* In the United Kingdom the responsibility for logistics organization, concentration, movement, and supply of forces to meet the requirements of your plan will rest with British Service Ministries so far

CHAIN OF COMMAND

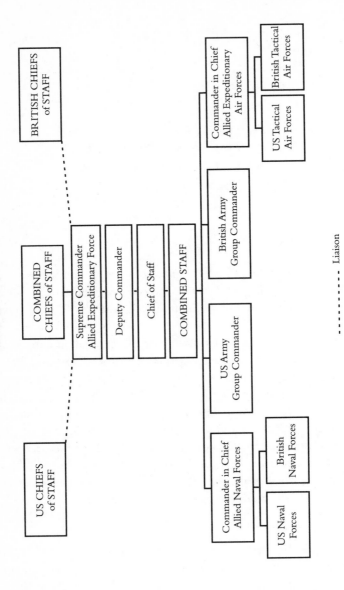

CHAIN OF COMMAND

BRITISH CHIEFS of STAFF

COMBINED CHIEFS of STAFF

US CHIEFS of STAFF

Supreme Commander Allied Expeditionary Force

Deputy Commander

Chief of Staff

COMBINED STAFF

US Army Group Commander

British Army Group Commander

Commander in Chief Allied Naval Forces

US Naval Forces

British Naval Forces

Commander in Chief Allied Expeditionary Air Forces

US Tactical Air Forces

British Tactical Air Forces

- - - - - - - - Liaison

as British Forces are concerned. So far as United States Forces are concerned, this responsibility will rest with the United States War and Navy Departments. You will be responsible for the coordination of logistical arrangements on the Continent. You will also be responsible for coordinating the requirements of British and United States forces under your command.

6. *Coordination of operations of other forces and agencies* In preparation for your assault on enemy-occupied Europe, sea and air forces, agencies of sabotage, subversion, and propaganda, acting under a variety of authorities, are now in action. You may recommend any variation in these activities which may seem to you desirable.

7. *Relationship to United Nations forces in other areas* Responsibility will rest with the Combined Chiefs of Staff for supplying information relating to operations of the forces of the USSR for your guidance in timing your operations. It is understood that the Soviet Forces will launch an offensive at about the same time as Overlord with the object of preventing the German forces from transferring from the Eastern to the Western front. The Allied Commander in Chief, Mediterranean Theater, will conduct operations designed to assist your operation, including the launching of an attack against the south of France at about the same time as Overlord. The scope and timing of his operations will be decided by the Combined Chiefs of Staff. You will establish contact with him and submit to the Combined Chiefs of Staff your views and recommendations regarding operations from the Mediterranean in support of your attack from the United Kingdom. The Combined Chiefs of Staff will place under your command the forces operating in southern France as soon as you are in a position to assume such command. You will submit timely recommendations compatible with this regard.

8. *Relationship with Allied Governments—the re-establishment of Civil Governments and Liberated Allied Territories and the administration of enemy territories* Further instructions will be issued to you on these subjects at a later date.

SUMMARY OF OPERATIONS IN NORTHWEST EUROPE

The broad strategy behind our main effort against the German war machine included as a highly desirable preliminary the successful conclusion of operations in North Africa and their extension across Sicily to the Italian mainland. With these accomplished, with the Mediterranean "flank" freed for Allied shipping, and with the necessary special equipment built or in sight, we were at last in a position to prepare for the final cross-Channel assault which had been agreed upon since April 1942 as our main operation against Germany. It was correctly believed that only on the historic battlefields of France and the Low Countries could Germany's armies in the west be decisively engaged and defeated.

America and England—the Western Allies—could not be sufficiently strong to undertake the assault against France until June 1944, but the broad tactical plans for the operation were completed and approved by the Combined Chiefs of Staff in August 1943, prior to my assumption of command of the European Theater in February 1944.

As part of our basic strategy, and in accordance with the task given to the Strategic Air Force under the Casablanca Directive in January 1943, the bombing of Germany, begun early in the war by the British Bomber Command, was intensified in May 1943 and continued with mounting strength to the end of the campaign. Neither the contemplated invasion of Europe nor the direct attack on the German industrial and economic system would be feasible until we had achieved supremacy over the German Air Force. This struggle for air supremacy, which had been going on throughout the war, was given added impetus by a new directive (known as Pointblank) in January 1943 which aimed at subjugating the enemy air force by the spring of 1944. In the event, German air might was thoroughly dominated by D Day and we were free to apply the immense strength of the Allied air forces in the manner we wished and to launch the invasion confident that our plans could not be seriously upset by the German Air Force. In addition, air bombardment had disrupted the German communications system, immeasurably aiding our ground forces by impeding enemy movements.

Our main strategy in the conduct of the ground campaign was to land amphibious and airborne forces on the Normandy coast between Le Havre and the Cotentin Peninsula and, with the successful establishment of a beachhead with adequate ports, to drive along the lines of the Loire and the Seine Rivers into the heart of France, destroying the German strength and freeing France. We anticipated that the enemy would resist strongly on the line of the Seine and later on the Somme, but once our forces had broken through the relatively static lines of the beachhead at St-Lô and inflicted on him the heavy casualties in the Falaise pocket, his ability to resist in France was negligible. Thereafter our armies swept east and north in an unimpeded advance which brought them to the German frontier and the defenses of the Siegfried Line.

Here enemy resistance stiffened, due primarily to the fact that he had fallen back on long-prepared defenses. At the same time our own offensive capabilities were lessened because our forces had, in their extremely rapid advance, outdistanced supply lines which had been maintained only by herculean efforts. By mid-September our armies in the north and center were committed to relatively static warfare and faced the threat of stabilization. This was true also on our southern flank, where forces landed from the Mediterranean against the south of France in mid-August had swept north through the Rhône Valley to link with the Central Group of Armies and close the Belfort Gap.

At this time we planned to attack quickly on the northern front in an effort to establish a bridgehead over the lower Rhine while the German armies were still reeling from our blows, but the airborne operation launched at Arnhem was not altogether successful in this respect, although considerable ground was gained and our positions in this area improved. Coincidentally with approving the Arnhem operation, it was directed that operations be undertaken to clear Antwerp as a supply port, essential to our continued offensive action. This was accomplished in November.

While our forces moved slowly in attacks launched at selected points on the front to close to the Rhine, the enemy on 16 December launched a desperate and last counter-attack designed to throw our campaign into disorder and to delay our planned advance deep into Germany. The attack was not without its immediate effect upon us, but the sturdy defense by our forces followed by our rapid and continuous counter-attacks brought home clearly to Germany's military leaders that this last effort had failed completely and that the Nazi war machine faced inevitable disaster.

My plan was to destroy the German forces west of the Rhine along the entire length of the front in a series of heavy blows beginning in the north, and it was my expectation that the enemy would, as he had done in Normandy, stand without giving ground in a futile attempt to "fight it out" west of the Rhine. Moreover, the air forces were used intensively to destroy his mobility. By March, when our forces crossed the river north of the Ruhr, at Remagen, and at various points to the south, resistance on the eastern bank was again reduced to resemble that in France following the breakthrough, particularly because the enemy, mistaking our intentions, crowded a great part of his remaining forces into the Ruhr area.

Our attack to isolate the Ruhr had been planned so that the main effort would take place on the front of the Northern Group of Armies with a secondary effort on the Central Group of Armies' front. This secondary effort was to be exploited to the full if success seemed imminent. Clearing the left bank of the Rhine throughout its length released the means required to strengthen this secondary effort. With the capture of the Remagen bridgehead and the destruction of enemy forces west of the Rhine, the anticipated opportunity became almost a certainty.

Our forces were now able to bridge the Rhine in all sectors and they fanned out in great mobile spearheads through western Germany, disrupting communications, isolating one unit from another, and in the area of the Ruhr completing perhaps the largest double envelopment in history, rendering that great industrial area useless to support what was left of the Nazi armies.

As our forces moved rapidly eastward with the main effort in the center, to establish contact with the advancing Russian armies at the Elbe, and in turn to swing swiftly north and south to cut off any remaining refuge, the German High Command reluctantly recognized defeat and belatedly initiated negotiations which terminated with unconditional surrender on 7 May 1945.

In these campaigns the United States of America and Great Britain worked as one nation, pooling their resources of men and material. To the Combined Chiefs of Staff, through whom the directives of the two governments were expressed, we constantly accorded our admiration for their well-devised system of command by which they applied the concerted national efforts. Their political leaders, the President of the United States and the Prime Minister, also contributed immeasurably to the success of our armies in the field; once they had committed themselves to a course of action they never failed to give us unstinted support.

References in this document to the operations of Allied and enemy units are based upon contemporary reports received at SHAEF [Supreme Headquarters Allied Expeditionary Force]. Often these reports were not clear or were fragmentary. The narration of our operations in full and accurate detail will be more adequately performed by historians, who, aided by the complete records, will be able to present in their true perspective the magnificent achievements of each of the manifold units which composed the Allied Expeditionary Force.

PLANNING AND PREPARATION

THE COSSAC PLAN

In June 1942, I was ordered to England with instructions to begin preparations for United States participation in a cross-Channel attack against Fortress Europe which had been agreed upon by the American and British governments in April of that year as the Allied principal effort in the defeat of Germany. Some planning, in cooperation with Admiral Sir Bertram H. Ramsay, General Sir Bernard C. T. Paget, and Air Chief Marshal Sir Sholto Douglas, all of the British forces, was undertaken immediately following my arrival, but this had not proceeded beyond the informal, conversational stage when I received orders to take command of the Allied attack in Northwest Africa, decided upon on 26 July. As a result of these conversations it seemed clear that the Normandy region offered the greatest chance of success in an invasion of Europe, although some individuals favored a more direct attack against the Calais area.

The successful conclusion of the campaign in North Africa was necessary before the attention of the Allies could be devoted to a full-scale attack upon Europe, but at the Casablanca Conference, in January 1943, the Combined Chiefs of Staff felt that the time had come at least to evolve the outline tactical plans for cross-Channel operations. They directed that preparations be undertaken for an emergency return to the Continent in the event that Germany suddenly should weaken sufficiently to permit our landing in the face of light or negligible resistance. While preparations for such a hoped-for contingency were necessary, the chief problem was the planning for the full-scale assault to be launched against the Continent as early as possible in 1944. Some consideration was given to the possibility that a return to the Continent in force might take place late in 1943, but a review of the build-up figures of

United States forces in the United Kingdom indicated that this would be impossible and that no large-scale attack could be undertaken until 1944.

Accordingly, in preparation for the day when a Supreme Commander should be appointed to command the Allied forces, the Combined Chiefs of Staff named Lieut. Gen. Sir F. E. Morgan to the post of Chief of Staff to the Supreme Allied Commander (designate). Using the initials of this title, the organization was called Cossac, and, with a staff composed of both United States and British personnel, work began upon the creation of the assault plan against Fortress Europe. By July 1943 the Outline Plan for Overlord, as the operation was called, was ready for presentation to the Combined Chiefs of Staff. In August of the same year the Combined Chiefs, with the concurrence of President Roosevelt and Prime Minister Churchill, approved the plan at the Quebec Conference and ordered the completion of its details insofar as this was possible prior to the arrival of a Supreme Commander.

In the creation of the plan, Cossac had been instructed on 25 May, through a supplementary directive from the Combined Chiefs of Staff, that the target date for the operation was to be 1 May 1944, and that simultaneous landing-craft lift for the assault forces would be limited to craft sufficient to load five divisions. A total of 29 divisions in all was to be available for the assault and immediate build-up. Of these, five infantry divisions were to be simultaneously loaded in the landing craft, three to assault initially with two in the immediate follow-up. In addition, two airborne divisions were to be employed and two other infantry divisions were to follow as quickly as turn-around shipping became available. In all, then, nine divisions were to be initially employed in the assault and immediate follow-up period. The remaining 20 divisions were to be available for movement to the lodgement area as quickly as the build-up could be achieved.

The fact that simultaneous landing-craft lift for only five divisions had been allotted made mandatory a definite concentration of effort. The basic factor in determining where the initial assault was to be made lay in the requirement that the lodgement area should contain sufficient port facilities to maintain a force of some 26 to 30 divisions and enable that force to be augmented by follow-up shipments from the United States or elsewhere of additional divisions and supporting units at the rate of three to five divisions per month.

For such purposes, the Pas-de-Calais region offered advantages in that its proximity to England would facilitate air support and a quick turn-around for shipping. On the other hand, its beaches, while favorable to the actual landing, lacked good exits to the hinterland. Also the area was the most formidably defended on the whole French coast and was a focal point of the enemy fighter air forces disposed for defense. Moreover, the area did not offer good opportunities for expansion of the lodgement zone, and it would have been necessary to develop the beachhead to include either the Belgian ports as far as Antwerp or the Channel ports westward to include Le Havre and Rouen.

A second area considered was the Cotentin Peninsula where it was recognized that the assaulting forces would initially have a reasonable chance of success and would additionally gain the valuable port of Cherbourg. This area, however, lacked suitable airfields, and might have become a trap for the assault troops, since the enemy could, with relatively light forces, defend the neck of the peninsula, bottling Allied troops within the beachhead and denying them any expansion into the interior of France.

In the Caen sector the defenses were relatively light and the beaches were of high capacity and sheltered from the prevailing winds. The terrain, moreover, was suitable for airfield development and for the consolidation and subsequent expansion of the beachhead. Air support to the initial area at such a distance from the English coast presented the chief difficulty. From a beachhead in the Caen sector it was believed that it would be possible to seize the Brittany ports between Cherbourg and Nantes, and through them to build up sufficient forces for the subsequent advance eastward.

In view of these considerations, it was decided that the initial landing on the Continent should be effected in the Caen area with the subsequent seizure of a lodgement area comprising the Cherbourg–Brittany ports.

The assault itself, according to the Cossac plan, was to be launched with a short air bombardment of the beach defenses, after which three assault divisions would be landed on the Caen beaches, followed by the equivalent of two tank brigades and a regimental combat team. At the same time, airborne forces were earmarked for the capture of the town of Caen, while subsidiary operations were to be undertaken by commandos and airborne units to neutralize certain coast defenses and to seize important river crossings. The object of the assault forces was to occupy the general line Grandcamp–Bayeux–Caen.

Action subsequent to the assault and early build-up was to take the form, under this initial plan, of a strong thrust southward and southwestward with a view to destroying enemy forces, acquiring sites for airfields, and gaining depth for a turning movement into the Cotentin Peninsula directed on Cherbourg. When sufficient depth had been gained, a force was to advance into the Cotentin and seize Cherbourg. At the same time a thrust was to be made to deepen the beachhead southeastward to cover the establishment of additional airfields in the area southeast of Caen. It was estimated that within 14 days of the initial assault Cherbourg would be taken and the beachhead extended to include the general line Trouville–Alençon–Mont-St-Michel. By that time it should have been possible to land some 18 divisions and to have in use about 14 airfields from which 28 to 33 fighter-type squadrons could operate.

Later operations based upon this plan were necessarily to be dictated to a large extent by enemy reactions. If he proved sufficiently weak, an immediate advance might be undertaken to seize Le Havre and Rouen. More probably, however, it was felt that it would be necessary to take and bring into use the Brittany ports first in order to build up forces sufficient to breach the line of the Seine upon which it was expected the enemy would make a stand with the bulk of his forces. For this purpose a thrust southward would be made to seize Nantes and St-Nazaire, followed by Brest and the smaller Brittany ports. The beachhead would be consolidated on the left flank along the Eure River from Dreux to Rouen and thence along the Seine to the sea, while Chartres, Orléans, and Tours were occupied. As soon as lines of communications in this area were developed and sufficient air forces established, operations would be instituted against Paris and the Seine ports, with subsidiary operations to clear the Biscay ports for the reception of additional United States troops and supplies.

In broad outline, this was the plan proposed for the assault upon Nazi Europe. Following approval by the Combined Chiefs of Staff and in accordance with their instructions, the Cossac organization proceeded with more detailed planning, and by 29 November sufficient progress had been made to permit of directives being issued to 21 Army Group and to the United States First Army.

DEVELOPMENT OF PLAN OVERLORD

During the period of this staff planning for Overlord, I was personally occupied with the Mediterranean campaigns and was not in close touch with the plans evolved for the campaign in Northwest Europe, nor did I during this period know that I would ultimately be connected with the operation. In December, however, I was notified by the Combined Chiefs of Staff that I had been appointed Supreme Commander of the Allied Expeditionary Force and that prior to assuming command in England early in January I was to return briefly to Washington for conferences with General Marshall and the Combined Chiefs.

Prior to leaving my Headquarters in North Africa, I was able early in December 1943 to see a copy of the Outline Plan of Overlord and to discuss it with Field Marshal (then General) Sir Bernard L. Montgomery, who was to command 21 Army Group, and with my Chief of Staff, Lieut. Gen. (then Maj. Gen.) Walter B. Smith. I instructed them to consider the plan in detail upon their arrival in England because, while agreeing with the broad scope of the operation and the selection of the assault area, I nevertheless felt that the initial assaulting forces were being planned in insufficient strength and committed on too narrow a front. This they did, and shortly after my arrival in London on 15 January, I was able, with them and my other commanders, to reach an agreement which altered the Overlord operation in this respect.

While my appointment as Supreme Commander did not become official until the receipt of a directive★ from the Combined Chiefs of Staff on

★ The text of the directive is reproduced at the beginning of this report, along with the organization chart. It should be noted that the US Strategic Air Forces in Europe and the RAF Bomber Command remained under the control of the Combined Chiefs of Staff.

14 February, and while the status of my Headquarters—to be known as SHAEF—was not recognized until the following day, the basic work of planning continued during this transitional period. The staff brought into being as Cossac came under my control was greatly expanded as the pressure of time and the vast scope of our work required.

I patterned my Headquarters upon the closely integrated Allied establishment which it had been my policy to maintain at AFHQ in the Mediterranean, and in this respect I was fortunate in obtaining for my staff men whose proved ability had already been demonstrated in previous campaigns—Air Chief Marshal Sir Arthur W. Tedder as my Deputy Supreme Commander, General Walter B. Smith as my Chief of Staff, and Lieut. Gen. Sir Humfrey M. Gale as Chief Administrative Officer. General Morgan remained as Deputy Chief of Staff, his detailed knowledge of tactical plans making him absolutely indispensable.

Relationship between SHAEF and the Headquarters of my Commanders-in-Chief for the Navy, Army, and Air Forces was established on the operational planning level through a Joint Planning Staff which closely integrated the work of all. The Headquarters of Cossac had been located at Norfolk House, St James' Square, with an annex at 80, Pall Mall, and it was here initially that my own Headquarters came into being. However, I was convinced by past experience that a Headquarters located in the heart of a great city would not be as unified as one located elsewhere. Accordingly SHAEF was moved in March to Bushy Park, near Kingston-on-Thames. Here we studied the operation in detail and ironed out all the numerous and frequently vexing problems relating to so vast an undertaking.

The chief changes which we were to make in the assault plan were considered at the first meeting which I held with my Commanders-in-Chief at Norfolk House on 21 January. Field Marshal Montgomery (Commanding General, 21 Army Group), Admiral Sir Bertram H. Ramsay (Commander of the Allied Naval Expeditionary Force), and Air Chief Marshal Sir Trafford Leigh-Mallory (Commander of the Allied Expeditionary Air Force) reviewed operation Overlord as a whole with me and were in agreement upon certain amendments to the plan.

The Cossac plan called for an initial assaulting force of three divisions. I had felt when I originally read the Overlord plan that our experiences in the Sicilian campaign were being misinterpreted, for, while that operation was in most respects successful, it was my conviction that had a larger assault force been employed against the island beachheads our troops would have been in a position to overrun the defenses more quickly. Against the better prepared defenses of France I felt that a three-division assault was in insufficient strength, and that to attain success in this critical operation a minimum of five divisions should assault in the initial wave. Field Marshal Montgomery was in emphatic agreement with me on this matter, as were also Admiral Ramsay and Air Chief Marshal Leigh-Mallory, even though a larger assault force raised great new problems from both the naval and air points of view.

In addition to increasing the assault force from three to five divisions, I felt that the beach area to be attacked should be on a wider front than that originally envisaged. Particularly, it was considered that an attack directly against the Cotentin Peninsula should be included in the plan, with a view to the speedy conquest of Cherbourg. In the event that our troops were able to attain a high degree of surprise in the attack, they would be in a better position to overwhelm the strung-out defenses before the enemy could regroup or mass for a counter-attack. Conversely, in the event of strong resistance, we would be more advantageously situated, on a wider front and in greater force, to find "soft spots" in the defense.

The original Cossac plan included the beachhead areas from Courseulles in the east to Grandcamp in the west. We decided to extend this area eastward to include the Ouistreham beaches, feeling that this would facilitate the seizure—by rapidly securing the eastern flank—of the important focal point of Caen and the vital airfields in the vicinity. Westward, we decided that the assault front should be widened to include the Varreville beaches on the eastern side of the Cotentin Peninsula itself. A strong foothold on the peninsula and a rapid operation to cut its neck would greatly speed up the capture of the port of Cherbourg.

For the operation against the neck of the Cotentin to be successful, it was believed that two airborne divisions should be employed in support of the troops assaulting the Varreville beaches, still leaving one airborne division to hold vital bridges in the Orne–Dives Rivers area to the northeast of Caen. Field Marshal Montgomery and Admiral Ramsay were in agreement on this point, but Air Chief Marshal Leigh-Mallory saw technical difficulties which it was necessary to consider closely.

It was his feeling, both then and subsequently, that the employment of airborne divisions against the South Cotentin would result in landing losses to aircraft and personnel as high as 75–80%. In the face of this estimate, however, I was still convinced of the absolute necessity of quickly overrunning the peninsula and attaining the port of Cherbourg, vital to the support and maintenance of our land forces. Without the airborne divisions an assault against the Varreville beaches would have been most hazardous, since our attack here could only be on a one-division front. Behind the landing beach was a lagoon, traversed only by a few causeways; the exits of these had to be captured from the rear, or else the strip of beach would quickly become a death trap. In addition, this beach was separated from the other four beaches to be assaulted by an estuary and marsh lands which would have effectively prevented the junction and link-up of the forces for several days, permitting the enemy in this sector more easily to dislodge us and threaten our right flank. Support by the airborne troops was essential, and I ultimately took upon myself the heavy responsibility of deciding that the airborne operation against the Cotentin be carried out. The decision, once taken, was loyally and efficiently executed by the airborne forces, and it is to them that immeasurable credit for the subsequent success of the western operation belongs. The airborne landing losses proved only a fraction of what had been feared, amounting in fact to less than 10%.

Our decisions to strengthen the forces employed in the initial assault, to widen the area of attack, and to employ the airborne forces in the Cotentin rather than at Caen, were communicated to the Combined Chiefs of Staff on 23 January, and at the same time I brought up the subject of the target date for the operation.

In the original plan, the target date for the D-Day assault had been 1 May. A new factor, however, which made me doubt that the date could be adhered to was our deficiency in assault craft for the larger five-division attack. In the Cossac plan, three divisions in the assault and two immediate follow-up divisions, a total of five, were to be preloaded in assault craft. Sufficient craft for five divisions had been planned. The new plan, calling for five divisions in the assault, still retained the two follow-up divisions, requiring therefore sufficient craft to preload seven divisions. There was considerable doubt that the additional craft could be made available by 1 May, and I informed the Combined Chiefs of Staff that, rather than risk failure with reduced forces on that date, postponement of the target date for a month would be preferable if I could be assured of then obtaining the strength required. My planners had advised me that a month's additional production of assault craft in both Great Britain and the United States would go far toward supplying the deficiency they then foresaw for the earlier date.

From the air point of view, the extension of the target date would afford a longer opportunity for the strategic bombing of Germany and the wearing down of German air strength. In addition, the tactical bombing of railheads and transportation centers, the preliminary softening of fortifications on the Channel coast, and the diversionary heavy air attacks in the Pas-de-Calais could be undertaken with greater thoroughness. The training of the invasion forces, and particularly the troop-carrier crews for the airborne operations, could also be carried on more thoroughly.

The Navy, moreover, desired additional time for the training of the assault craft crews and for the delivery and assembly of the extra vessels needed in the enlarged attack. From the naval viewpoint a postponement of the target date to the first of June was preferable to any briefer postponement, say of two weeks, since an early June date guaranteed the favorable tides necessary for the beach operations as well as a full moon.

From the strategic point of view the postponement seemed desirable, since weather conditions at the end of May would be likely to be more favorable for the mounting of a large-scale Russian offensive to assist the Overlord operation. Additionally, the situation in the Mediterranean might be sufficiently resolved by that time to preclude the necessity of an operation against the south of France closely coordinated with our western assault. The German forces in that theater might be so heavily engaged by our armies that a diversionary and containing assault would not be required in direct and immediate assistance to Overlord.

The Combined Chiefs of Staff agreed on 1 February that Overlord would be mounted with a target date not later than 31 May. We indicated that the exact date of the assault should be left open and subject to weather conditions prevailing during the first week of June. Later, on 17 May, I set 5 June as the "final" date for the assault, subject, of course, to last-minute revision if the weather should prove unfavorable. The selection of this date was based primarily on tidal and light conditions. It was necessary that the tide be sufficiently low to enable the initial assault elements to land and prepare lanes through the heavy obstacles which were above water only at or near a low tide. Also, this tidal condition had to coincide with a period of sufficient light to permit visual bombing by aircraft of the beach defenses and bombardment by the naval vessels. The dates of 5, 6, and 7 June were all acceptable on this basis, but any postponement beyond these dates would have necessitated waiting until 19 June for a similar favorable tidal period. This later date would have necessitated the acceptance of moonless conditions.

Strategically, the postponement of the target date proved to be a sound measure. By 1 May, the original date, our forces in Italy were still encountering heavy resistance south of Rome along the Gustav Line, while Russian forces were occupied in the Crimea and still forming for a western attack. By the first week in June, however, Rome had fallen, Kesselring's forces were in retreat, the Crimea had been cleared, and Germany was nervously predicting an all-out Russian offensive. Furthermore, the enemy had been keyed up to a 1 May Allied offensive from the United Kingdom, to judge from his "invasion any day now" feelers. The month's delay served perhaps to lull him into believing that we would now not attack until some time in July. The month's postponement also guaranteed, as events proved, the availability of assault craft and shipping to move the staggering number of men and vehicles required for the D-Day assault.

It should be noted here, however, that had it been possible to adhere to the initial date, the weather would have been much superior for the invasion than was the weather encountered during the first week of June. During the first week of May, in the full-moon period, the Channel was consistently calm and the skies cloudless, ideal both for naval and air operations. The weather was strikingly similar to that which favored England during the disastrous days of Dunkirk. In the first week of June, on the other hand, the Channel was choppy at best, with heavy seas running most of the time. The skies were overcast, and days of rain hampered air operations. The full extent to which this unfavorable weather influenced our operations will be considered later in this report.

With the settlement of the basic problems essential to firm planning—the size of the assault and the target date—the Army, Navy, and Air Forces were in a position to develop their final plans for the attack against the

Normandy beaches. The best method of controlling the effort of the Strategic Air Forces was still under discussion and will be referred to later in the section on "Preparatory Operations." Immediately under my command in the pre-D-Day period were the Commanders-in-Chief already mentioned, Field Marshal Montgomery, Admiral Ramsay, and Air Chief Marshal Leigh-Mallory.

Within 21 Army Group, Field Marshal Montgomery had under his command the Canadian First Army (2 Corps) under Lieut. Gen. H. D. G. Crerar; the British Second Army (1, 8, 12, and 30 Corps) under Lieut. Gen. (then Maj. Gen.) Sir M. C. Dempsey; the British airborne troops (1 and 6 Divisions) under Lieut. Gen. F. A. M. Browning; and the United States First Army (V, VII, VIII, and XIX Corps, with the attached airborne troops of the 82nd and 101st Divisions) under General (then Lieut. Gen.) Omar N. Bradley. While plans called for eventual organization of American and British ground forces each under their own commander, directly responsible to me, the initial assault was foreseen as a single battle, closely interrelated in all its parts, and requiring the supervision of a single battle-line commander. All agreed on this necessity.

The army plans for the assault and subsequent build-up period were prepared, pursuant to periodical directives from Supreme Headquarters, by the planning staffs of the American and British Army Headquarters, coordinated by 21 Army Group Headquarters, and subsequently reviewed by the G-3 Division of my staff under Maj. Gen. H. R. Bull and his deputy, Maj. Gen. J. F. M. Whiteley. Constant revision of the plans was necessary throughout the early months of 1944, due primarily to the continuing uncertainty as to the exact number of assault craft to be made available for the loading of the troops. Even with the extra month's production of craft in both the United States and the United Kingdom, it seemed that sufficient lift would not be forthcoming, and it became necessary during this period to consider drawing craft from either the Mediterranean or the Pacific to round out the figure needed. This entailed a constant exchange of views between theaters and between my Headquarters and the Combined Chiefs of Staff until the problem was finally settled—as late as 24 March. Since the problem also was related to the mounting of operation Anvil, the assault against southern France from the Mediterranean, reference will be made to the matter again in this report. Suffice it to say here, however, that before firm planning can be undertaken on any major amphibious operation, involving, as such an operation does, the forces of both the Army and the Navy, the primary factor of assault craft must be definitely determined. This decision should be made as early as humanly possible, for it is a matter of the first priority.

Based upon the Cossac plan for the assault, together with the revisions as to date and size of attack which have been mentioned, the final plan produced by 21 Army Group and approved by Supreme Headquarters thus came into being.

Broadly, the army plan of attack involved a D-Day assault on a five-divisional front on the beaches between Ouistreham and Varreville with the immediate purpose of establishing beachheads to accommodate follow-up troops. The initial objectives of the attack included the capture of Caen, Bayeux, Isigny, and Carentan, with the airfields in their vicinity, and the essential port of Cherbourg. Thereafter our forces were to advance on Brittany with the object of capturing the ports southward to Nantes. Our next main aim was to drive east on the line of the Loire in the general direction of Paris and north across the Seine, with the purpose of destroying as many as possible of the German forces in this area of the west.

Because it was ultimately intended to supply the United States forces engaged in Europe directly from American ports, American troops were assigned the right flank in the operations. They were to take Cherbourg and the Brittany ports as supply bases, while the British, driving east and north along the coast, were to seize the Channel ports, as far north as Antwerp, through which they were to be supplied directly from England.

On the right, American forces of General Bradley's First Army were to assault the Varreville (Utah) beach and the St-Laurent (Omaha) beach. Lieut. Gen. (then Maj. Gen.) J. Lawton Collin's VII Corps was to land with the 4th Infantry Division in the assault on Utah beach just north of the Vire Estuary. During the early morning hours of D Day the 82nd and 101st Airborne Divisions were to drop in the area southeast and west of Ste-Mère-Eglise where their mission was to capture the crossings of the Merderet River, secure the line of the Douve River as a barrier, and assist the landing of the 4th Infantry Division at the beach. By the end of D Day, we anticipated that VII Corps, with the airborne divisions under command, would control the area east of the Merderet from just south of Montebourg to the Douve.

Lieut. Gen. (then Maj. Gen.) Leonard T. Gerow's V Corps planned its attack on a 7,000-yard stretch of beach known as Omaha, on the northern coast of Calvados near St-Laurent. One combat team of the 29th Infantry Division on the right and one combat team of the 1st Infantry Division on the left, both under the command of the 1st Infantry Division, were to assault in the initial wave.

The primary objective of VII Corps, supported by the airborne divisions, was to cut the Cotentin Peninsula against attack from the south, and, driving northward, to seize the port of Cherbourg—we hoped by D plus 8. While Cherbourg was being taken, troops of V Corps and follow-up forces were to drive south towards St-Lô, seizing the city by D plus 9. With the reduction of the Cotentin Peninsula, the forces engaged there and follow-up forces subsequently landed were also to turn south, join with the forces landed over Omaha, and drive to a line Avranches–Domfront by approximately D plus 20.

Forces of General (then Lieut. Gen.) George S. Patton's Third Army were, during this period, to be landed across the American beaches and initially come under the operational control of First Army, passing to the control of Third Army when its headquarters moved to the Continent at about D plus 30. While First Army was to make an initial turning movement into the Brittany Peninsula in the direction of St-Malo, it was planned that Third Army, with its growing forces, would take over the reduction of the peninsula and the Brittany ports from First Army on this same date. First Army, then, freed of the responsibility for Brittany, was to turn its forces south and east along the Loire, reaching a line beyond Angers–Le Mans on the Sarthe River by D plus 40.

British and Canadian forces, landing on the Ouistreham (Sword), Courseulles (Juno), and Asnelles (Gold) beaches were in the meantime to protect the left flank of the Allied forces against what was expected to be the main German counter-attack from the east. An additional important task was to gain the ground south and southwest of Caen, favorable for the development of airfields and for the use of our armor. The first assault was to be made by three divisions of General Dempsey's British Second Army; the 3 Canadian and 3 British Infantry Divisions of 1 Corps, and the 50 Infantry Division of 30 Corps. British 6 Airborne Division was to be dropped behind the beach defenses to secure the vital bridges over the Caen Canal and the Orne River between Caen and the sea, together with certain other objectives in that locality. These forces with follow-up troops, advancing southward, were to occupy territory inland to a line Vire–Falaise, including the Caen road center, by about D plus 20.

After occupation of this area, the British forces were to continue expansion along the general line of the Seine, advancing on the left of the American divisions until, by D plus 90, the general Allied front was to stand on the Seine from Le Havre to Paris on the north, and along the Loire from Nantes to Orléans, Fontainebleau and Paris on the south and east. In the west the Brittany Peninsula was to be fully occupied. By D plus 90 the armies were to be ready to take Paris, force the crossing of the Seine in strength in an advance northward to the Somme, and continue east along the Marne in a drive toward the German frontier.

Early in May 1944 after I had approved Field Marshal Montgomery's plans for establishing our forces on the Continent, and for placing them in position prepared for eruption from the lodgement area, the planning staff presented their visualization of the several lines of action which might be followed for the continuance of the campaign, up to and including the final period, for a drive into the heart of Germany. The favored line of action was sketched on a map of the Continent. It contemplated an advance on a broad front with the main effort constantly on the left (north) flank and with another thrust toward Metz, passing north and south of Paris in the event the Germans determined to hold it as a fortress, joining up with General Devers' forces coming from the south to cut off southwest France; penetration of the Siegfried Line, still with the main effort in the north; elimination of the German forces west of the Rhine either by decisive defeat or by pressure which would force their withdrawal, with particular emphasis on the area from Cologne–Bonn to the sea; a power crossing of the Rhine north of the Ruhr, coupled with a secondary effort via the Frankfurt Corridor, the two thrusts to join in the general area of Kassel, encircling the Ruhr. Thereafter it was anticipated that the destruction of remaining German strength would be easy.

This estimate made at this early date is particularly interesting since the proposed scheme of maneuver was practically identical with that which was followed during the campaign.

Later in this report is described the supporting air plan, success in which was vital to the attainment of the ambitious objectives prescribed for the land forces. Also necessary to an understanding of the whole battle is a knowledge of the information we possessed, prior to the assault, regarding the enemy dispositions, a summary of which is also included in a subsequent section.

In the initial phases of Overlord, Field Marshal Montgomery, whom I had designated as tactical commander of the early land battles, was to have operational control of all land forces, including the United States First Army, until the growing build-up of the American forces made desirable the establishment of an independent Army Group. When sufficient forces had disembarked on the Continent, a United States Army Group was to come into being, equal both operationally and administratively to the British 21 Army Group, which latter was to continue under Field Marshal Montgomery's command. Although no definite time was set for this, it was estimated that it would take place when Third Army had become fully operational; the date was also dependent, of course, upon the progress of the initial land battles beyond the beachhead area where, as already pointed out, simplicity of command in a narrow space was desirable.

In the matter of command, it can be said here that all relationships between American and British forces were smooth and effective. Because of certain fundamental national differences in methods of military supply and administration, it was early agreed that no unit lower than a corps of one nationality would be placed under command of the other nationality except where unavoidable military necessity made this imperative.

To carry out the mission of invading Western Europe, there were to be available, by D Day, in the United Kingdom 37 divisions: 23 Infantry, 10 armored, and 4 airborne. These were to be employed in the assault and subsequent build-up period in France. As the campaign progressed, the flow of divisions to the Continent was to be maintained at a rate of three to five divisions per month, and this flow was to be augmented by the divisions entering the European Theater with the assault against southern France from the Mediterranean. Ultimately, at the time of the German surrender, I had under command a total of 90 divisions: 61 American, 13 British, 5 Canadian, 10 French, and 1 Polish. These divisions, with anti-aircraft, anti-tank, and tank units habitually attached, averaged about 17,000 in combat strength, well over twice the strength of Russian divisions. In addition there were three French divisions which were not completely equipped, and lesser units of Czech, Belgian, and Dutch forces on the Continent, as well as the units of the French Forces of the Interior. Our Headquarters estimated that, at times, the value of these latter French forces to the campaign amounted in manpower to the equivalent of 15 divisions, and their great assistance in facilitating the rapidity of our advance across France bore this out.

The initial success of the land forces in the assault against Northwest Europe was dependent upon the operations of the Allied Naval Expeditionary Force under the command of Admiral Ramsay. In his operational orders issued on 10 April, he clearly defined the Navy's mission to those under his command: "The object of the Naval Commander-in-Chief is the safe and timely arrival of the assault forces at their beaches, the cover of their landings, and subsequently the support and maintenance and the rapid build-up of our forces ashore." To accomplish this mission successfully months of detailed planning and training, closely coordinated with the ground and air forces, were necessary.

Reports on the North African and Sicilian Campaigns have made mention of the magnitude of the naval forces involved, but the sea power displayed there was to fade by comparison with the forces to be employed in this great amphibious assault. The extent of the problem of berthing, loading, and moving the forces involved may be realized with the knowledge that over 5,000 ships and 4,000 additional "ship-to-shore" craft were to be engaged in the Channel operations during the assault and build-up period. That everything went according to plan is a remarkable tribute to the hard work, coordinated effort, and foresight of the thousands engaged in the initial planning and training and, as Admiral Ramsay stated in his report, to the "courage of the tens of thousands in the Allied navies and merchant fleets who carried out their orders in accordance with the very highest traditions of the sea."

With the expansion of the assault from a three-divisional to a five-divisional attacking force, increased naval forces were necessary both to protect the invasion fleet *en route* and to bring added fire power to bear on the beaches. These were allotted by the Combined Chiefs of Staff on 15 April 1944. The chief units in the final naval forces included 6 battleships, 2 monitors, 22 cruisers, and 93 destroyers.

Under the naval plan the assault area for the naval forces was bounded on the north by the parallel of 49° 40′ N, and on the west, south and east by the shores of the Bay of the Seine. This area was subdivided into two Task Force Areas, American and British, the boundary between them running from the root of the Port-en-Bessin western breakwater in an 025° direction to the meridian of 0° 40′ W, and thence northward along this meridian to latitude 49° 40′ N. Within these defined areas, the Western Task Force, operating in the American zone, was under the command of Rear Adm. A.G. Kirk, and the Eastern Task Force, operating in the British zone, under the command of Rear Adm. Sir P. L. Vian. The Western and Eastern Task Forces were again subdivided to include, altogether, five assault forces, each responsible for the landing of an assault division upon one of the five beach areas, and two follow-up forces. The assault forces were known for the American zone as Force "U" and Force "O" (Utah and Omaha) and were under the command respectively of Rear Adm. D. P. Moon and Vice Adm. (then Rear Adm.) J. L. Hall, Jr. For the British zone the assault forces were similarly known as Force "S," Force "J," and Force "G" (Sword, Juno, and Gold), and were commanded by Rear Adm. A. G. Talbot, Commodore G. N. Oliver, and Rear Adm. C. Douglas-Pennant.

In order to ensure the safe arrival of the assault troops on the beaches, the Navy was to provide adequate covering forces to protect the flanks of the routes of our assault and was, with mine-sweeping vessels, to clear the Channel ahead of the assault craft. For this latter purpose 12 mine-sweeping flotillas were to be employed. Once within range of the beachhead area, the heavy naval guns were to neutralize the enemy coastal batteries, supplementing the work of the air forces, and then, as the landing craft drove inshore, there was to be an intense bombardment of the beach defenses by every gun that could be brought to bear.

Some consideration had initially been given to the possibility of assaulting at night in order to obtain the maximum surprise, but it was decided that the lessons of the Pacific should be adhered to, and that, possessing superiority in air and naval forces, the assault against strong defenses should take place by day. This was palpably advantageous to the Navy in the coordinated movement of a vast fleet in relatively narrow waters. H Hour varied for most of the five assault forces, due to varying beach conditions such as the necessity for higher tide to cover certain rock obstacles and the length of time needed to remove enemy obstructions. Force "U" was to touch down at 0630 hours while Force "J" was not to land until 35 minutes later.

With the success of the assault determined, the naval forces were to maintain swept channels between France and England through which supplies and reinforcements could be shuttled to the Continent. In view of the initial limited port facilities and the fact that we did not anticipate seizing the Brittany ports for some time after the assault, the Navy was also charged with providing for the establishment off the French coast of five artificial anchorages (Gooseberries). Two of these were subsequently to be expanded into major artificial harbors (Mulberries); through these the bulk of our stores were to be unloaded during the early stages of the campaign. To provide oil and gasoline in bulk, the Navy was also to set up tanker discharge points off the French coast and to establish cross-Channel submarine pipe lines.

By 26 April, the five naval assault forces were assembled in the following areas: Force "U," Plymouth; Force "O," Portland; Force "S," Portsmouth; Force "G," Southampton; and Force "J," Isle of Wight. The two follow-up forces, Force "B" and Force "L," were assembled in the Falmouth–Plymouth and Nore areas. In addition to the berthing problems inherent in the assembly of these seven forces, other space had to be found for the many ships and craft which were assigned the tasks of supply, maintenance, repair, and reinforcement. The berthing problem was one of major proportions, but it was solved, as Admiral Ramsay reported, by making use of every available berth from Milford Haven to Harwich. Many units had, additionally, to be berthed in the Humber, at Belfast, and in the Clyde.

The concentration of ships in southern ports was bound, we felt, to be detected by the enemy and would thus give him some indication that our assault was about to be launched. In order to confuse him in this respect, arrangements were made with the British Admiralty to have the large number of commercial ships destined for the Thames and also the ships to be used in later supply convoys to our forces on the Continent held in Scottish ports until the operation was under way. The concentration of shipping thus spread itself automatically throughout the whole British Isles and was not confined to a single area. As was the case against Sicily, we did not believe that the growing preparations and the size of our forces could be entirely concealed from the enemy. We hoped, though, to be able to confuse him as to the time of the assault and the exact beachhead area of attack. In this we were to be successful for a variety of reasons which I shall consider later.

The air plan in support of the amphibious operation consisted of two parts, the preparatory phase and the assault phase, and was brought into being under the direction of Air Chief Marshal Leigh-Mallory, commanding the Tactical Air Forces. These forces, composed of the British Second Tactical Air Force and the US Ninth Air Force, were to operate in direct support of the land armies. The Strategic Air Forces also would be given definite tactical responsibilities during critical periods, although their principal mission would be to continue their attacks on the industrial potential of Germany, with emphasis now placed on the facilities for aircraft production.

Until January 1944, the view had been held that the heavy bombers of the Strategic Air Forces could make sufficient direct contribution to the assault in a period of about a fortnight before D Day. Further consideration, however, indicated the need to employ them for a much longer period— about three months—and a plan was finally adopted which aimed at the crippling of the French and Belgian railway systems and the consequent restriction of the enemy's mobility. The plan had a wider conception than the dislocation of the enemy's lines of communication in the zone in which the land forces were to be deployed. It was looked upon as the first of a series of attacks, which as they spread eastward, would ultimately affect the whole German war effort. The adoption of this plan entailed a major effort by the Strategic Air Forces.

In the preparatory phase, the striking power of the Tactical Air Forces was to be directed against rail targets, bridges, airfields in the vicinity of the assault area, coastal batteries, radar stations, and other naval and military targets. In addition to reserve aircraft, these forces had operationally available 2,434 fighters and fighter-bombers, and 700 light and medium bombers.

The program of attack on rail centers and bridges was designed to deprive the enemy of the means for the rapid concentration of men and material and to hinder his efforts to maintain an adequate flow of reinforcements and supplies, forcing him to move by road with resultant delay, increased wastage in road transport and fuel, and increased vulnerability to air attack. Blows against the railroad centers were to be started about D minus 60 and were to cover a wide area so as to give the enemy no clue to our proposed assault beaches. Shortly before D Day, however, the attacks would be intensified and focused on key points more directly related to the assault area but still so controlled as not to indicate to the enemy the area itself.

Attacks against coastal batteries, airfields, bridges, and other targets in the preparatory period were planned in such a manner that only one-third of the effort expended would be devoted to the targets threatening the success of our assault. The preliminary attacks upon the bridges in northwestern France were scheduled to begin on D minus 46 and to be intensified in tempo as D Day approached. The ultimate purpose of these attacks was to isolate the battle area from the rest of France by cutting the bridges over the Seine and the Loire below Paris and Orléans, respectively. The attacks upon the airfields had a similar purpose. Within a 130-mile radius of the battle area, all enemy airfields and air installations were to be attacked beginning not later than D minus 21. By neutralizing the fields, we were certain to limit the maneuvrability of German fighter forces, compelling them to enter the battle from fields situated a considerable distance from the Normandy beaches.

This preparatory bombing program was placed in effect as scheduled and, as D Day approached, the intensity of our attacks increased and the preparatory phase gave way to the assault phase. In the assault itself, the air forces were assigned the tasks, in conjunction with the navies, of protecting the cross-Channel movement of our forces from enemy air and naval attack. They were also to prepare the way for the assault by destroying the enemy's radar installations and by neutralizing coastal batteries and beach defenses between Ouistreham and Varreville, the area of our attack. Additionally, the air forces were to provide protective cover over the landing beaches and, by attacking the enemy, reduce his ability to reinforce and counter-attack. Subsequent to the establishment of the beachhead, the Tactical Air Forces were to support the land troops in their advance inland from the assault beaches.

During the assault it was planned to maintain a sustained density of ten fighter squadrons to cover the beach area, five over the British sector and five over the American. An additional six squadrons were to be maintained in readiness to support the beach cover if necessary. Over the main naval approach channels we agreed upon a sustained density of five squadrons centered at 60 miles and three at 80 miles from the south coast of England. Additionally, a striking force of 33 fighter squadrons was to be held in reserve for use as the air situation might require, subsequent to its initial employment as escort to the airborne formations.

The total fighter aircraft which we allocated for the D-Day assault was as follows:

Beach Cover	54	squadrons
Shipping Cover	15	squadrons
Direct Air Support	36	squadrons
Offensive Fighter Operations and Bomber Escort	33	squadrons
Striking Force	33	squadrons
Total	171	squadrons

The photographic reconnaissance units of the Allied Air Forces were the first to begin active and direct preparations for the invasion of Europe from the west. For more than a year, much vital information was accumulated which contributed very greatly to the ultimate success of the assault. The variety, complexity, and the detailed accuracy of the information gathered was of great importance in the preparatory phase of the operation. One of the most remarkable tasks accomplished was the series of sorties flown to obtain low-level obliques of underwater beach defenses.

LOGISTICAL PROBLEMS

In support of operation Overlord it had been proposed at the Casablanca Conference that an assault against southern France be mounted from the Mediterranean to coincide closely with the timing of the assault against northwest France. I had been engaged in the planning phase of this operation, known initially as Anvil and subsequently as Dragoon, prior to leaving my command in the Mediterranean, and felt then that its contribution to the downfall of the enemy would be considerable. I continued to recognize its importance after leaving the Mediterranean Theater, fully conscious not only of the psychological effect upon the enemy and upon Europe as a whole of the double assault, but of the great military value the southern blow would have in splitting all enemy forces in France and of thus assisting Overlord.

Initially we had hoped that the Anvil assault could be mounted with three divisions or, at the worst, with two divisions, building up to a strength of ten divisions in the follow-up. However, on 23 January 1944, it became necessary to recommend to the Combined Chiefs of Staff that some consideration be given to reducing the Anvil assault to one division, maintaining it as a threat until enemy weakness justified its employment. This recommendation was necessary because of our shortage of assault craft for the enlarged Overlord operation. We hoped that craft in the Mediterranean, originally allocated for Anvil, would thus be freed for our use.

The Combined Chiefs of Staff did not agree with this proposal and on the basis of planning data available to them stated that sufficient craft would be on hand to mount an Overlord assault of seven divisions (including the two follow-up divisions) and an Anvil of two divisions. These figures did not coincide with those of my own planners and the discrepancy was explained to the planners at Washington by my Chief of Staff. It was pointed out that the divisions involved in the assault each actually represented a division plus a regimental combat team and included the armor attached to it. Additionally, a number of subsidiary assaults by Commandos and Rangers necessitated craft for 5,000 personnel. Beyond this, the nature of the terrain, the heavy beach defenses, and the large rise and fall of tide in the Channel demanded the use of a very much larger number of engineer personnel and personnel for work on the beaches than would have otherwise been necessary. The scale of the problem may be understood more readily, perhaps, by the fact that we intended on D Day and D plus 1 to land 20,111 vehicles and 176,475 personnel. The vehicles included 1,500 tanks, 5,000 other tracked fighting vehicles, 3,000 guns of all types, and 10,500 other vehicles from jeeps to bulldozers.

This explanation helped to clarify our needs, and the Combined Chiefs of Staff recognizing the situation, met it by suggesting that the Anvil assault be postponed rather than mounted simultaneously with Overlord. Field Marshal (then General) Sir Maitland Wilson, as Supreme Commander in the Mediterranean Theater, and the British Chiefs of Staff in London, had at one time suggested that the Anvil operation be cancelled, chiefly because of weakness in the initial assault and the length of time required to build up sufficient forces. However, this was held to be inadvisable from the strategic point of view and contrary to the decisions reached at Teheran. The military advantages to be gained through a force of an additional ten or more divisions operating on our right flank after clearing Southern France would, I believed, be of extraordinary value later in the campaign. Accordingly, on 24 March, Anvil was postponed from a target date of 31 May to one of 10 July, some four weeks after the Overlord assault, and the craft necessary to round out our full needs were in part drawn from Mediterranean resources and allocated to our use. Although the question of Anvil was to reappear and the target date to be again postponed to 15 August, our problem in the mounting of Overlord had been settled and the priority of our needs in the larger operation established.

While the problem of assault craft was being resolved, the build-up of American troops and supplies in the United Kingdom continued under the direction of Lieut. Gen. John C. H. Lee. Planning for Bolero, the name by which this logistical program was known, had begun in the United Kingdom as early as April 1942. The small original staff was divided for the North African (Torch) operation, but expanded in 1943 and 1944 as the Overlord task became larger until, by D Day, the Communications Zone establishment contained 31,500 officers and 350,000 enlisted personnel. By July 1943 some 750,000 tons of supplies were pouring through English ports each month and this amount was steadily increased until in June 1944 1,900,000 tons were received from the United States. Much of this material was used to supply the troops already arrived in England, and other amounts were stored for use as Overlord progressed, but the stock pile earmarked for the American forces, over and above basic loads and equipment, was a full 2,500,000 tons for the invasion alone. By 1 June also, the number of US Army troops in the United Kingdom had risen from 241,839 at the end of 1942 to 1,562,000.

The operation of transporting supplies from the United States to the United Kingdom was facilitated by the fact that cargoes were discharged through established ports and over established rail lines. Additionally, large quantities of materials for the invasion were made directly available from British resources within the United Kingdom itself. These conditions could not, of course, exist on the Continent and plans were accordingly made to overcome the difficulties envisaged. It was recognized that the major tonnage reception on the Continent would be over the Normandy beaches during the first two months, with the port of Cherbourg being developed at an early date. Successively, it was anticipated that port development would proceed in Brittany, the major effort in that area to be an artificial port at Quiberon Bay with complementary development of the existing ports of Brest, Lorient, St-Nazaire, and Nantes. While these were being brought into use the flow of supplies over the beaches was to be aided by the two artificial harbors (Mulberry "A" and Mulberry "B"). As the campaign progressed, it was anticipated that the bulk of American supplies would flow directly from the United States through the Brittany ports, while the Channel ports to the north, including Ostend and Antwerp, would be developed for the British armies. These expectations, however, did not materialize, due primarily to enemy strategy and the vicissitudes of the campaign. That both the American and British supply systems were able, in spite of this, to support the armies to the extent they did is a remarkable tribute to the flexibility of their organizations and to their perseverance in a single purpose.

The importance of the steady supply of our forces, once landed, may be gauged by reference to German strategy. This was intended to ensure that our supplies should never be permitted to begin flowing into the beachheads. The German philosophy was: "Deny the Allies the use of ports and they will be unable to support their armies ashore." For this reason the chain of Atlantic and Channel ports from Bordeaux to Antwerp was under orders from Hitler himself to fight to the last man and the last round of ammunition. The Germans fully expected us to be able to make a landing at some point on the Channel coast, but they were nevertheless certain that they could dislodge us before supplies could be brought ashore to maintain the troops. They had no knowledge of our artificial harbors, a secret as closely guarded as the time and place of our assault. The impossible was accomplished and supplies came ashore, not afterwards to support a force beleaguered on the beachheads, but actually with the troops as they landed. The Germans were, by virtue of our initial supply, denied the opportunity of dislodging us and were subsequently, throughout the campaign, under sustained attack as the result of the feats of maintenance performed by our administrative organizations.

A captured enemy document, written by a division commander, perhaps pays as great a tribute to all the forces responsible for supply of the front-line troops as could be found. He wrote:

> I cannot understand these Americans. Each night we know that we have cut them to pieces, inflicted heavy casualties, mowed down their transport. We know, in some cases, we have almost decimated entire battalions. But—in the morning, we are suddenly faced with fresh battalions, with complete replacements of men, machines, food, tools, and weapons. This happens day after day. If I did not see it with my own eyes, I would say it is impossible to give this kind of support to frontline troops so far from their bases.

GERMAN MISCALCULATIONS

While our plans developed and the build-up of supplies and men in readiness for the operation continued with regularity, we had been studying the possible action which the enemy might take in the expectation of an assault against him mounted from the United Kingdom. In any operation as large as Overlord it was palpably impossible to keep from the enemy the fact that we intended, during 1944, to launch an attack against Europe. Where, when, and in what strength the attack would be launched was another matter, and I was not without hope that he would not necessarily appreciate that our target was the Normandy beaches. Indeed we had some reason to believe that the enemy expected numerous attacks from many quarters and was continually uncertain as to the strength of any of them, unable in his own mind to determine or distinguish between a threat which we had no intention of launching, a diversion in strength, or an all-out main assault. In consequence he was stretched to the utmost in every theater.

We thought that to the German High Command an assault upon the Pas-de-Calais would be the obvious operation for the Allies to undertake. Not only was this the shortest sea journey where the maximum air cover would be available, but a lodgement in the Pas-de-Calais would lead the Allies by the shortest road directly to the Ruhr and the heart of Germany. Such an operation would have to be mounted mainly from southeast England and the Thames area. Concentrated in the Pas-de-Calais was the German Fifteenth Army, which had the capability both of shifting its forces to Normandy prior to the assault if the intended area of the attack were to become known and also of quickly reinforcing the divisions in Normandy, after the assault.

Acting on the assumption that this would be the German estimate we did everything possible to confirm him in his belief. Without departing from the principle that the efficient mounting of the operation remained at all times the first consideration, we took every opportunity of concentrating units destined ultimately for the Normandy beachhead in the east and southeast rather than in the southwest. In this way it was hoped that the enemy, by his observations based on aerial reconnaissance and radio interception, would conclude that the main assault would take place farther to the east than was in fact intended. As a result of these measures, we also felt that had an enemy agent been able to penetrate our formidable security barrier, his observations would have pointed to the same conclusion.

Shipping arrangements were made with the same end in view. Surplus shipping was directed to the Thames Estuary where an enormous concentration was already assembled in preparation for the invasion; while landing craft were moored at Dover, in the Thames, and at certain East Anglian ports.

Further support was afforded by the aerial bombing program. The distribution of bombing effort was so adjusted as to indicate a special interest in the Pas-de-Calais. It was also hoped that the bombing of the V-1 sites would be misinterpreted in our favor. Finally the large and very visible components of the artificial harbors, which were subsequently set up on the Normandy beaches, were anchored in Selsey Bay immediately before the invasion, a point farther east than originally proposed.

After the assault had gone in on 6 June we continued to maintain, for as long as possible, our concentrations in the southeast and our displays of real and dummy shipping, in the hope that the enemy would estimate that the Normandy beachhead was a diversionary assault and that the main and positive blow would fall on the Pas-de-Calais when the diversion had fulfilled its purpose.

The German Fifteenth Army remained immobile in the Pas-de-Calais, contained until the latter part of July by what we now know from high-level interrogation was the threat of attack by our forces in the southeast of England. Not until 25 July did the first division of the Fifteenth Army advance westward in a belated and fruitless attempt to reinforce the crumbling Normandy front.

Every precaution was taken against leakage of our true operational intentions against Normandy. The highest degree of secrecy was maintained throughout all military establishments, both British and American, but additional broader measures affecting the general public were necessary as D Day approached.

On 9 February, all civilian travel between Britain and Ireland was suspended to prevent the leakage of information through Dublin, where German agents continued officially to represent their government. On 1 April, also as a result of a request made by me, the British Government imposed a visitors' ban on the coastal areas where our assault was being mounted and extending inland to a depth of ten miles.

Because even the most friendly diplomats might unintentionally disclose vital information which would ultimately come to the ears of the enemy, the British Government took the further unprecedented step of restricting diplomatic privileges. On 17 April it banned the movement of diplomats or their couriers into and out of the United Kingdom and subjected hitherto immune correspondence to censorship. At my request this ban was maintained until 19 June.

Lastly, it was considered expedient on 25 May to impose an artificial delay of ten days on the forwarding of all American mail to the United States and elsewhere and to deny to American personnel trans-Atlantic telephone, radio, and cable facilities. The mail of all British military personnel due to take part in the Normandy operation had been, even within England itself, subject to strict censorship since April.

PREPARATORY OPERATIONS

Preparatory operations incident to the assault were already under way. These were the special concern of the Air Forces and the Navy, and consisted, apart from the Tactical Air Forces' operations already considered, primarily of the strategic bombing of Germany and the Channel exercises designed to afford training to the assault forces.

By a decision taken by the Combined Chiefs of Staff, prior to my arrival in the theater, command of the strategic bombing forces—the RAF Bomber Command and the United States Strategic Air Forces (composed of the Fifteenth Air Force in the Mediterranean Theater and the Eighth Air Force in the European Theater)—ultimately rested with the Combined Chiefs themselves. This decision had been taken with the purpose of coordinating strategic bombing against Germany from all sides. Within the European Theater overall command of the United States Strategic Air Forces rested with General (then Lieut.-General) Carl A. Spaatz and command of the RAF Bomber Command with Air Chief Marshal Sir Arthur Harris. The Strategic Air Forces were thus not under my direct orders, their commanders being instead responsible directly to the Combined Chiefs in Washington. While understanding the long-range motives which brought this decision into being, I was nevertheless dissatisfied with the arrangement, feeling that, since responsibility for the principal effort against Germany fell upon my Headquarters, all the forces to be employed within the theater—by land, sea, and air—should be responsible to me and under my direction, at least during the critical periods preceding and succeeding the assault.

I stated these views to the Combined Chiefs of Staff. At the same time I set forth the necessity for concentrated bombing of the rail network of Northwest Europe and particularly France, to which there was considerable opposition, the reasons for which will be considered shortly. I felt strongly about both these matters.

In a review of the matter, the Combined Chiefs of Staff, who were aware of my problems, gave me operational control of the air forces from 14 April. The Strategic Air Forces after this date were to attack German military, industrial, and economic targets in an order of priority established within the Theater and approved by the Combined Chiefs. Additionally, they were to be available to me upon call for direct support of land and naval operations when needed. This was a role for which they had not previously been normally used, but the Salerno campaign had afforded convincing evidence of their effectiveness for the purpose.

In the final command set-up of the air forces, then, the commanders of the Strategic Air Forces (RAF Bomber Command and the United States Strategic Air Forces) reported to Supreme Headquarters independently as did also Air Chief Marshal Leigh-Mallory, commanding the tactical forces which comprised the Allied Expeditionary Air Force. The effort of the three separate commands was coordinated, under my direction, through the Deputy Supreme Commander, Air Chief Marshal Tedder.

Prior to my arrival in the theater, the Combined Chiefs of Staff had approved a combined bomber offensive plan against Germany which included the strategic bombing of critical industrial and military targets in the Reich. It had been determined that Germany's vulnerability lay primarily in six industrial systems indispensable to the German war effort: submarines, aircraft, ball bearings, oil, rubber, and communications. Of these six targets, aircraft, oil, and communications became the three which were to occupy the continuing attention of the Strategic Air Forces throughout the war. The bombing attacks upon these targets were to assist materially in weakening the enemy's potentiality to resist our offensives and immeasurably to aid our ground forces in their advance.

An indispensable condition to the success of our Normandy assault was, at the very least, sufficient control of the air to ensure the build-up in England and subsequently on the beachhead of our invasion forces and supplies. In anticipation of D Day, therefore, the Allied forces were first concerned with weakening the German Air Force through attacks upon its installations and resources on the ground and on the force itself in the air. Quite apart from the direct assistance these attacks lent to the success of our landings, they were essential also as a preliminary to the intensive bombing of German industry.

We were aware that the Germans had planned, as far back as July 1942, to develop an air force equal to the task of smashing any invasion. Their aircraft expansion program had as its ultimate goal the production of some 3,000 combat aircraft per month. It was also estimated that the enemy planned to have a first-line strength of 10,000 aircraft, adequately supplied by reserves in depth and a steady flow of replacements. Considerable progress had been made with this program before the growth of Allied aircraft strength in this Theater permitted the intensive scale of air fighting which began in May 1943. Commencing with that date, our attacks upon German aircraft production centers checked the projected increase of manufacture, but the German Air Force was able, nevertheless, to survive 1943 with its front-line strength little changed. In December 1943 the Germans planned to produce 3,000 single-engine fighters per month, thus indicating that their production program was influenced as much by the necessity for countering the allied bombing offensive as for stopping a possible ground invasion.

Beginning in January 1944, however, the assaults upon aircraft production centers were intensified and the effect of these attacks was such that the German Air Force had been robbed by mid-summer of most of its production capacity and also deprived of the adequate reserves necessary to maintain its front-line strength. These conditions resulted not only from damage to production centers but also from such other factors as attrition of aircraft and crews in air battles, shortage of aviation gasoline for training purposes, and disruption of communications. As the invasion date approached, a clear sign of our superiority in the air was the obvious unwillingness of the enemy to accept the challenge to combat which we initiated with large-scale fighter sweeps over his territory. Our D-Day experience was to convince us that the carefully laid plans of the German High Command to oppose Overlord with an efficient air force in great strength were completely frustrated by the strategic bombing operations. Without the overwhelming mastery of the air which we attained by that time our assault against the Continent would have been a most hazardous, if not impossible, undertaking.

This mastery of the air was maintained throughout 1944 and 1945 by continuing attacks against production centers. But the enemy was able, through factory reconstruction and dispersal, together with the development of jet aircraft, to maintain into 1945 a fighter force of a theoretical strength by no means negligible. Nevertheless, it still was not qualitatively good and proved incompetent to perform successfully for any substantial period any of the normal missions of an air force.

By D Day the Strategic Air Forces together with the Tactical Air Forces had so successfully performed their mission of disrupting enemy communications that there was a chronic shortage of locomotives and cars, repair facilities were inadequate, coal stocks were reduced to a six days' supply, and 74 bridges and tunnels leading to the battle area were impassable. The communications chaos thus produced had fatal effects upon the enemy's attempts at reinforcement of the threatened areas after our landings.

The initial attacks upon the communications system in France were undertaken as the result of an extremely difficult decision for which I assumed the full responsibility. I was aware that the attacks upon the marshalling yards and rail centers, by both the Strategic and Tactical Air Forces, would prove costly in French lives. In addition, a very important part of the French economy would for a considerable period be rendered useless. On separate occasions both Prime Minister Churchill and General Koenig, Commander of the French Forces of the Interior, asked that I reconsider my decision to bomb these particular targets. General Koenig requested once that he be permitted to participate as a member of a review board to determine the relative necessity of bombing centers of population; with regard to the loss of French lives, however, he took a stern and soldierly attitude, remarking: "It is war." I was aware of all the implications inherent in my decision, even of the heartrending possibility that our French Allies might be alienated from us. Nevertheless, for purely military reasons, I considered that the communications system of France had to be disrupted. The fate of a Continent depended upon the ability of our forces to seize a foothold and to maintain that foothold against everything we expected the enemy to throw against us. No single factor contributing to the success of our efforts in Normandy could be overlooked or disregarded. Military events, I believe, justified the decision taken, and the French people, far from being alienated, accepted the hardships and suffering with a realism worthy of a far-sighted nation.

With mastery of the air achieved in the spring of 1944, it became more readily possible for the Allied Strategic Air Forces to concentrate their power over-whelmingly against the declining oil reserves of Germany. The attack against the German oil industry commenced in April and continued until the termination of operations. Within the first month of attack German production fell to 80% of its previous normal capacity, and by December 1944 it had fallen to a mere 30%. This 30% itself was only produced as the result of herculean efforts which diverted manpower and labor hours from other equally essential industries, such as, for example, the production of the new and ingenious weapons of war with which Germany hoped to decide the issue of the conflict.

The subsequent shortage of oil brought on by our operations contributed to the complete collapse of the German bomber force and must have had its effect upon the decline of the U-boat [German submarine] menace. Immobility from oil shortage caused the capture of tens of thousands of German soldiers and the destruction of their vehicles. Lack of oil and communications shattered by air bombardment retarded divisions arriving to reinforce the Normandy front in June. By December, when von Rundstedt's forces attacked in the Battle of the Ardennes, many units had to set out with extremely limited supplies of fuel, hoping desperately to overrun our positions so quickly that captured stocks would support their further advance. Within Germany the oil situation was so desperate that the recovery and repair program for the shattered industry was given the highest priority in the national war effort, above aircraft and submarine production and all other activities.

In addition to the strategic bombing of oil, aircraft, and communications targets, we were, during the campaign, to call upon the Strategic Air Forces for tactical support. At the time of the breakthrough in Normandy and several times later, including the Battle of the Ardennes, strategic bombers were employed in strength to attack enemy positions, supply bases immediately supporting the enemy front, and strongpoints and communication centers within the battle area. In these instances of tactical assistance, the Strategic Air Forces aided immeasurably in turning the decision of battle in our favor.

While the preparatory air operations of both the Strategic and Tactical Air Forces were growing in intensity as D Day approached, the naval and assault forces were engaged in Channel exercises designed not only to afford final training to the troops and crews but also to test enemy reaction to our mounting preparations. During the assembly of the five assault forces in the areas of Plymouth, Portland, Portsmouth, Southampton, and the Isle of Wight, which was completed on 26 April, considerable enemy E-boat★ activity was noted which was primarily reconnaissance rather than offensive in nature. On 26 April the first full-scale exercise, Tiger, involving Force "U" under the command of Admiral Moon, took place from the Plymouth area. Owing to the fact that one of the escorting destroyers was damaged in a collision during the night of 26/27 April and was not on hand when the assault convoy was attacked by E-boats, there was an unfortunate loss of life in the sinking of two LSTs.† In other respects the exercises were successful and valuable lessons were learned, relating not only to the movement and handling of the task force ships, but also to the assault against beaches. Areas such as Slapton Sands in southwest England, similar to those which the troops would encounter in France, were used for practice purposes.

Subsequent to Exercise Tiger, further Channel exercises involving the other task forces were undertaken during the first week of May. Considerable enemy reaction had been anticipated, but the exercises proceeded without any undue interference or even attention from the enemy. In certain cases it seemed apparent that he lacked information as to the extent and nature of the exercises. Our air superiority had driven his reconnaissance planes from the skies, the watch kept by our naval forces was unceasing, and the security precautions taken effectively neutralized the efforts of any agents whom he may have employed. Following the E-boat attack upon Force "U," the German radio had, for example, simply announced that ships of a Channel convoy had been torpedoed and sunk, indicating that the German command was unaware that the ships were assault craft and not the usual merchant ships in convoy. We also knew that the enemy was aware in other instances of our purposes, but preferred to reserve his forces for use on D Day itself rather than to expend them against local exercises.

ENEMY CAPABILITIES

In our planning for the assault, it was necessary—and increasingly so as D Day approached—to take into consideration the normal enemy capabilities which he might employ against our attack. We assumed that the enemy, once aware that a full-scale invasion was under way, would throw everything he possessed on the land, sea, and in the air against the assault. We accordingly

★ Small German torpedo boat.
† Tank landing ships.

made preparations to counter his reaction. Mention has already been made of the enemy's capability in the air and the overall disruption of his plans as the result of strategic bombing of the German Air Force production resources and of the tactical bombing of air-fields in the vicinity of the assault area. In spite of his losses, nevertheless, it was anticipated that he might, by carefully husbanding the fighters and bombers remaining to him, attack the invasion forces with furious—if brief—air effort. Against this, our covering squadrons of fighters were allocated as already outlined in the air plan for the assault.

In addition to air attack, the ruthless and even reckless employment of all enemy naval forces was also expected. We estimated that the enemy was capable of employing within the first few days of the assault the following forces: 5 destroyers, 9–11 torpedo boats, 50–60 E-boats, 50–60 R-boats, 25–30 "M" class mine sweepers, and 60 miscellaneous local craft. In addition to the surface craft available, the enemy was also in a position to use 130 U-boats forthwith and to reinforce these by D plus 14 to a total of 200. Against the anticipated attacks from these craft, the Navy was to undertake preliminary minelaying outside the channels of our approach. Aircraft of RAF Coastal Command also were to maintain a constant patrol in sufficient density and over such an extended stretch of the Channel that no U-boat would be capable of reaching the battle area without first surfacing and becoming vulnerable to attack. In the event that any enemy vessels proved capable, in spite of these measures, of reaching the task forces and assault convoys, the Navy's protective screen of ships, together with the considerable air umbrella supporting the task forces, was felt to be in sufficient strength to neutralize any serious threat.

The enemy had, as early as February, disposed of 53 divisions in the west under the Supreme Command of Field Marshal von Rundstedt. By 3 June his strength in France, Belgium, and Holland had been increased to 60 divisions, including 10 panzer type and 50 infantry divisions. Of these, 36 infantry and 6 panzer divisions were located in the general coastal area opposite England, from Holland to Lorient in Western France. In the immediate area of our Normandy assault the Germans had concentrated nine infantry divisions and one panzer division, while their greatest strength—the Fifteenth Army—remained in the Pas-de-Calais. The bombing of the Seine bridges and other communications served to isolate the battle zone from immediate reinforcement and the diversionary plans were responsible for holding strategic reserves away from the Normandy beaches. Thus, although disposing of 60 divisions, the enemy's immediate capabilities for their employment were considerably reduced.

Apart from the estimates of normal enemy capabilities, one unusual danger hung as a threat over Overlord from July 1943 through D Day. The Germans were emplacing what appeared to be rocket or pilotless aircraft sites on the Channel coast, and while the weapons appeared to be largely oriented on London, there was the possibility that our concentration of shipping in the ports of southern England would prove an attractive target and that the mounting of the operation would meet with interference from the new menace. The staff consequently gave some consideration to changing the areas where the amphibious forces were to be mounted, but, because other places did not have adequate facilities and the whole naval plan would have had to be altered, we adhered to our original plans. Defensive and offensive countermeasures against the threat were taken, and the Pas-de-Calais area, where the majority of the sites were located, was subjected to severe and continual bombing which served to delay the employment of the "V" weapons until after our assault had been launched.

With our land forces assembled in the area where the assault was to be mounted and with the Channel exercises under way, I felt that the final decision as to the launching of the assault should be made from a forward command post located near the invasion bases on the Channel coast and, accordingly, my tactical headquarters were set up in the vicinity of Portsmouth. As 1 June approached I had visited the greater part of the divisions to be engaged in the operations as well as air force installations and several of the larger naval ships. Without exception, the morale of the men was extraordinarily high, and they looked forward to the immediate task confronting them with sober confidence. This same confidence, born of the long hours of arduous preparatory toil, existed within all echelons of the services and was noticeably present when the final plans of all the commanders were formally presented at St Paul's School, 21 Army Group Headquarters in London, on 15 May.

With the planning and preparatory period completed, it now became necessary to make the supreme decision for which I was responsible—the designation of the exact day for the assault against the Continent of Europe.

THE ASSAULT

June 1944 saw the highest winds and roughest seas experienced in the English Channel in June for 20 years.

From 1 June onward, my commanders and I met daily to correlate our last-minute preparations and to receive the weather forecasts upon which we had to base our final decision as to the date of launching the assault. The provisional D Day was 5 June, but the meteorological predictions which came in on the 3rd were so unfavorable that at our meeting on the morning of the 4th I decided that a postponement of at least 24 hours would be necessary. By that time part of the American assault force had already put out into the Channel, but so heavy were the seas that the craft were compelled to turn about and seek shelter.

By the morning of 5 June conditions in the Channel showed little improvement, but the forecast for the following day contained a gleam of hope. An interval of fair conditions was anticipated, beginning late on the 5th and lasting until the next morning, with a drop in the wind and with broken clouds not lower than 3,000 feet. Toward evening on the 6th, however, a return to high winds and rough seas was predicted, and these conditions were then likely to continue for an indefinite period.

The latest possible date for the invasion on the present tides was 7 June, but a further 24-hour postponement until then was impracticable as the naval bombardment forces which had already sailed from their northern bases on the 3rd would have had to put back into port to refuel and the whole schedule of the operation would thus have been upset. I was, therefore, faced with the alternatives of taking the risks involved in an assault during what was likely to be only a partial and temporary break in the bad weather, or of putting off the operation for several weeks until tide and moon should again be favorable. Such a postponement, however, would have

The Assault

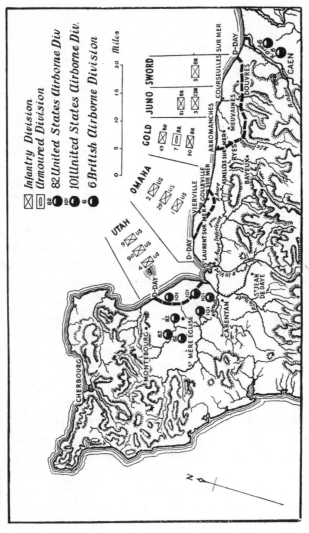

been most harmful to the morale of our troops, apart from the likelihood of our losing the benefits of tactical surprise. At 0400 hours on 5 June I took the final and irrevocable decision: the invasion of France would take place on the following day.

On D Day the wind had, as forecast, moderated and the cloud was well broken, with a base generally above 4,000 feet. This afforded conditions which would permit of our airborne operations, and during the hour preceding the landings from the sea large areas of temporarily clear sky gave opportunities for the visual bombing of the shore defenses. The sea was still rough, and large numbers of our men were sick during the crossing. The waves also caused some of the major landing craft to lag astern, while other elements were forced to turn back.

As events proved, the decision to launch the assault at a time when the weather was so unsettled was largely responsible for the surprise which we achieved. The enemy had concluded that any cross–Channel expedition was impossible while the seas ran so high and, with his radar installations rendered ineffective as a result of our air attacks, his consequent unpreparedness for our arrival more than offset the difficulties which we experienced.

The weather was not the only circumstance surrounding the Allied landings which was contrary to the enemy's expectations. Apparently he had assumed that we should make our attempt only when there was a new moon and on a high tide, and that in choosing the place of main assault we should pick the immediate neighborhood of a good harbor and avoid cliffs and shallow, dangerous waters. In point of fact, we assaulted shortly after low tide, when the moon was full; we landed away from large harbors and at some points below sheer cliffs; and the waters through which we approached the shore were so strewn with reefs and subjected to strong currents that the German naval experts had earlier declared them to be impassable for landing craft.

While our assault forces were tossing on the dark waters of the Channel en route for France, the night bombers which were to herald our approach passed overhead. Shortly after midnight the bombing commenced, and by dawn 1,136 aircraft of RAF Bomber Command had dropped 5,853 tons of bombs on ten selected coastal batteries lining the Bay of the Seine between Cherbourg and Le Havre. As the day broke, the bombers of the US Eighth Air Force took up the attacks, 1,083 aircraft dropping 1,763 tons on the shore defenses during the half-hour preceding the touchdown. Then medium, light, and fighter-bombers of the Allied Expeditionary Air Force (AEAF) swarmed in to attack individual targets along the shores and artillery positions farther inland. The seaborne forces bore witness to the inspiring morale effect produced by this spectacle of Allied air might and its results as they drew in toward the beaches.

During the remainder of the day, the heavy bombers concentrated their attacks upon the key centers of communication behind the enemy's lines, through which he would have to bring up his reinforcements. Fighters and fighter-bombers of the AEAF roamed over the entire battle area, attacking the German defensive positions, shooting up buildings known to house headquarters, strafing troop concentrations, and destroying transport. During the 24 hours of 6 June, the Strategic Air Forces flew 5,309 sorties to drop 10,395 tons of bombs, while aircraft of the tactical forces flew a further 5,276 sorties.

The lightness of the losses which we sustained on all these operations is eloquent of the feeble enemy air reactions and testifies to the effectiveness of our diversionary operations. Such reconnaissance and defense patrols as were flown by the Germans were mainly over the Pas-de-Calais area while over the assault beaches and their approaches only some 50 half-hearted sorties were attempted. Our heavy bombers were permitted to carry out their allotted tasks without any interference from enemy fighters. One result of this absence of opposition was that our own fighter-bombers were able to operate in small units of one or two squadrons, thus permitting their all-important harassing attacks to be more continuously maintained and their activities to cover a wider field. Not until two days after the initial landings did the enemy reinforce his air strength over the invasion zone to any appreciable extent.

As the night bombers were finishing their work in the early hours of 6 June, the Allied sea armada drew in toward the coast of France. The crossing had, as Admiral Ramsay reported, an air of unreality about it, so completely absent was any sign that the enemy was aware of what was happening. No U-boats were encountered, the bad weather had driven the enemy surface patrol craft into port, the German radar system was upset as a result of our air attack and scientific countermeasures, and no reconnaissance aircraft put in an appearance. Not until after the naval escort fleets had taken up their positions and commenced their bombardment of the shore defenses was there any enemy activity, and then, taken unprepared as the Germans were, it was mainly ineffective. We achieved a degree of tactical surprise for which we had hardly dared to hope. The naval operations were carried out almost entirely according to plan. The damage to his communications by the Allied bombing caused the enemy to remain in the dark as to the extent and significance of the airborne landings which had already been carried out. He was still uncertain as to whether he had to deal with invasion or merely a large-scale raid while our first assault wave was plunging shoreward to discover the truth about the vaunted Atlantic Wall.

The layout of the defenses which the Allied armies had to breach in order to establish their beachheads on French soil had been largely determined by the Germans' experience at the time of the Dieppe raid in 1942. This raid convinced the enemy that any attempt at invasion could, and should, be destroyed on the beaches themselves, and the defense system subsequently constructed on this principle was lacking in depth.

Appreciating that one of our chief initial objectives would be the capture of a port, the enemy had developed heavy frontal defenses during 1943 at all the principal harbors from Den Helder to Brest. As the invasion threat grew, Cherbourg and Le Havre were further strengthened, while heavy guns were installed to block the entrance to the Bay of the Seine. Between the ports stretched a line of concrete defense positions, and coastal and flak batteries, each self-contained, heavily protected against air bombing and lavishly equipped. These positions were usually designed for all-round defense, their frontal approaches were mined, and where possible artificial flooding was used to guard the rear approaches. Fixed heavy and medium guns, intended to bombard approaching shipping, were sited well forward at the rear of the beaches, while divisional artillery of light and medium guns, which were to lay down a barrage on the beaches themselves, were located some two to three miles inland. Behind these defenses, however, there was no secondary defense line to check our invading armies if they should succeed in penetrating beyond the beach areas. The enemy was so confident in the strength of his "wall" that when our landings came upon him he had not the mobile reserves necessary to stem our advance and prevent our establishment of a lodgement area. Therein lay the main factor behind our successes following the disembarkations.

The assumption of command in France by Field Marshal Erwin Rommel during the winter of 1943–1944 was marked by a vigorous extension and intensification of the defensive work already in progress, and this continued up to the very day on which our landings took place. While the coastal guns were casemated and the defense posts strengthened with thicker concreting against the threat of air attack, a program was commenced in February 1944 of setting up continuous belts of underwater obstacles against landing craft along the entire length of all possible invasion beaches. It was intended by this means to delay our forces at the vital moment of touchdown, when they were most vulnerable, and thus to put them at the mercy of devastating fire from the enemy positions at the rear of the beaches. These obstacles—including steel "hedgehogs", tetrahedrons, timber stakes, steel "Element C" curved rails and ramps—were developed to cover high and lowtide contingencies, and most of them had affixed mines or improvised explosive charges. The program was not completed by 6 June, and the obstacles which our men encountered, though presenting considerable difficulties, nevertheless fell short of current German theory. Few mines were laid on the actual beaches, while the minefields at their exits were often marked and proved less troublesome to our troops than we had feared might be the case.

Despite the massive air and naval bombardments with which we prefaced our attack, the coastal defenses in general were not destroyed prior to the time when our men came ashore. Naval gunfire proved effective in neutralizing the heavier batteries, but failed to put them permanently out of action, thanks to the enormous thickness of the concrete casemates. Air bombing proved equally unable to penetrate the concrete, and after the action no instances were found of damage done by bombs perforating the covering shields. Such of the guns as were silenced had been so reduced by shellfire through the ports. The pre-D-Day bombing had, nevertheless, delayed the completion of the defense works, and the unfinished state of some of the gun emplacements rendered them considerably less formidable than anticipated.

The defenses on the beaches themselves were also not destroyed prior to H Hour as completely as had been hoped. The beach-drenching air attacks, just before the landing, attained their greatest success on Utah beach, where the Ninth Air Force bombed visually below cloud level. But elsewhere patches of cloud forced the aircraft to take extra safety precautions to avoid hitting our own troops, with the result that their bombs sometimes fell too far inland, especially at Omaha beach.

Nevertheless, the air and naval bombardments combined did afford invaluable assistance in ensuring the success of our landings, as the enemy himself bore witness. Although the strongly protected fixed coastal batteries were able to withstand the rain of high explosives, the field works behind the beaches were largely destroyed, wire entanglements were broken down, and some of the minefields were set off. Smoke shells also blinded the defenders and rendered useless many guns which had escaped damage. The enemy's communications network and his radar system were thrown into complete confusion, and during the critical period of the landings the higher command remained in a state of utter ignorance as to the true extent, scope, and objectives of the assault. The German gun crews were driven into their bomb-proof shelters until our forces were close inshore, and the sight which then confronted them was well calculated to cause panic. The terrible drum-fire of the heavy naval guns especially impressed the defenders, and the morale effect of this bombardment following a night of hell from the air was perhaps of greater value than its material results. Such return fire as was made from the heavy batteries was directed mainly against the bombarding ships, not the assault forces, and it was generally inaccurate. The close-support fire from destroyers, armed landing craft, rocket craft, and craft carrying self-propelled artillery, which blasted the beaches as the infantry came close to shore, was particularly effective.

The men who manned the static beach defenses were found to be a very mixed bag. A large proportion of them were Russians and other non-Germans, but with a Teutonic stiffening, and under German officers. Of the German troops, many companies were found to be composed of men either under 20 or over 45 years of age, and a large proportion were of low medical categories. Their morale was not of the best: the lavishness of the defenses and the concrete protection to their underground living quarters had produced a "Maginot Line complex," and, having gone below when the bombing began, they were not prepared for so prompt a landing when the bombs stopped falling. The field troops who manned the mobile artillery and many of the works between the heavy batteries, on the other hand, were of a different caliber and offered a stout resistance to our landings. By themselves, however, they were powerless to prevent our gaining a foothold.

The high seas added enormously to our difficulties in getting ashore. Awkward as these waters would have been at any time, navigation under such conditions as we experienced called for qualities of superlative seamanship. Landing craft were hurled on to the beaches by the waves, and many of the smaller ones were swamped before they could touch down. Others were flung upon and holed by the mined underwater obstacles. Numbers of the troops were swept off their feet while wading through the breakers and were drowned, and those who reached the dry land were often near exhaustion. It was, moreover, not possible on every beach to swim in the amphibious DD tanks upon which we relied to provide fire support for the infantry clearing the beach exits. These were launched at Sword, Utah, and Omaha beaches, and, although late, reached land at the two former; at Omaha, however, all but two or three foundered in the heavy seas. At the remaining beaches the tanks had to be unloaded direct to the shore by the LCTs, which were forced, at considerable risk, to dry out for the purpose. Fortunately the beaches were sufficiently flat and firm to obviate damage to the craft.

Despite these difficulties, the landings proceeded, and on all but one sector the process of securing the beachheads went according to plan. Meanwhile, four and a half hours before the first seaborne troops set foot upon the shore of France at 0630 hours, the air transport commands had commenced dropping the airborne assault forces on either flank of the invasion zone. In this operation, the biggest of its kind ever to date attempted, 1,662 aircraft and 512 gliders of the US IX Troop Carrier Command and 733 aircraft and 355 gliders of 38 and 46 Groups, RAF, participated.

In the British sector, the very accurate work of the Pathfinder force enabled the RAF groups to overcome the difficulties arising from the use of different types of aircraft, carrying various loads at various speeds, and the 6 Airborne Division troops were dropped precisely in the appointed areas east of the Orne River. Thanks to this good start, all the main military tasks were carried out, and at a lower cost than would have been paid in using any other arm of the service. The party charged with the mission of securing the Bénouville bridges over the Orne and the Caen Canal was particularly successful. Landing exactly as planned, in a compact area of just over one square kilometer, the troops went into action immediately and secured the bridges intact, as required, by 0850 hours. The tactical surprise achieved, coupled with the confusion created by the dropping of explosive dummy parachutists elsewhere, caused the enemy to be slow to react, and it was not until midday that elements of 21st Panzer Division counter-attacked. By that time our men had consolidated their positions and the enemy's efforts to dislodge them were in vain. During the day reinforcements were safely landed by gliders, against which the German pole obstructions proved ineffective; the operation went off like an exercise, no opposition was encountered, and by nightfall the division had been fully resupplied and was in possession of all its heavy equipment. This formation continued to hold the flank firmly until our lodgement area had been consolidated and the breakout eastward across France relieved it of its responsibility.

On the western flank, at the base of the Cotentin Peninsula, the American airborne forces of the 82nd and 101st Divisions were faced with greater initial difficulties. Owing to the cloud and atmospheric conditions, the Pathfinders failed to locate the exact areas fixed for the parachute drops, and the inexperience of some of the pilots led to wide dispersal of troops and supplies. The 6,600 parachute elements of 101st Division were scattered over an area 25 miles by 15 miles in extent, and 60% of their equipment was lost in consequence. Nevertheless, the operation represented an improvement upon those undertaken in Sicily, and the great gallantry with which the troops fought enabled them in general to accomplish their mission successfully. Gliders flown in during the day suffered considerable casualties, but reinforcements were introduced during the night of 6/7 June. While 101st Division held the exits to Utah beach and struck southward toward Carentan, the 82nd Division, despite heavy shelling in the Ste-Mère-Eglise area, also established contact with the troops pushing inland from Utah beach early on 7 June. The element of surprise was as effective in the western as in the eastern sector, and the enemy himself bore witness to the confusion created by the American troops in cutting communications and disorganizing the German defense. The success of the Utah assault could not have been achieved so conspicuously without the work of the airborne forces.

The seaborne assault on the British–Canadian sector was carried out according to plan, and despite the rough approach, substantial beachheads were established on D Day. In the 1 Corps area, on the left flank, British 3 Division assaulted Sword beach, west of Ouistreham. The initial opposition ashore was only moderate, although light batteries shelled the landing craft as they came in to beach. The obstacles were forced, the DD tanks swam ashore to give fire support, and by 1050 hours the powerful coast defense battery in this sector was taken and elements of the assault force had advanced to Colleville-sur-Orne. By evening a considerable penetration inland had been made and reinforcements were coming in over the beaches. To the west, Canadian 3 Division landed on Juno beach, in the region of Courseulles-sur-Mer and Bèrnières-sur-Mer. Though met by considerable shelling and mortar fire, the troops succeeded in clearing the beaches by 1000 hours and pushed inland towards Caen.

In the 30 Corps sector, British 50 Division landed on Gold beach, near Asnelles-sur-Mer. Although strongpoints on the left flank caused some trouble, the enemy opposition as a whole was found to be less than anticipated, and the defenses at the rear of the beaches were successfully overcome. During the day Arromanches, Meuvaines, and Ryes were occupied and a firm footing was obtained inland.

It was in the St-Laurent-sur-Mer sector, on Omaha beach, where the American V Corps assault was launched, that the greatest difficulties were experienced. Not only were the surf conditions worse than elsewhere, causing heavy losses to amphibious tanks and landing craft among the mined obstacles, but the leading formations—the 116th Infantry of the 29th Division at Vierville-sur-Mer and the 16th Infantry of the 1st Division at Colleville-sur-Mer—had the misfortune to encounter at the beach the additional strength of a German division, the 352nd Infantry, which had recently reinforced the coastal garrison. Against the defense offered in this sector, where the air bombing had been largely ineffective, the naval guns were hampered by the configuration of the ground which made observation difficult and were able to make little impression. Exhausted and disorganized at the edge of the pounding breakers, the Americans were at first pinned to the beaches but, despite a murderous fire from the German field guns along the cliffs, with extreme gallantry, they worked their way through the enemy positions. The cost was heavy; before the beaches were cleared some 800 men of the 116th had fallen and a third of the 16th were lost, but by their unflinching courage they turned what might well have been a catastrophe into a glorious victory.

The American 4th Division (VII Corps) assault on the Utah beaches just west of the Vire Estuary, met with the least opposition of any of our landings. Moreover, an error in navigation turned out to be an asset, since the obstacles were fewer where the troops actually went ashore than on the sector where they had been intended to beach. The enemy had apparently relied upon the flooding of the rear areas here to check any force which might attempt a landing, and the beaches themselves were only lightly held. Complete surprise was achieved and a foothold was obtained with minimum casualties, although it was here that we had expected our greatest losses. The airborne troops having seized the causeways through the inundated hinterland and prevented the enemy from bringing up reinforcements, the 4th Division struck northwest toward Montebourg, on the road to Cherbourg.

Apart from the factor of tactical surprise, the comparatively light casualties which we sustained on all the beaches except Omaha were in large measure due to the success of the novel mechanical contrivances which we employed and to the staggering morale and material effect of the mass of armor landed in the leading waves of the assault. The use of large numbers of amphibious tanks to afford fire support in the initial stages of the operation had been an essential feature of our plans, and, despite the losses they suffered on account of the heavy seas, on the beaches where they were used they proved conspicuously effective. It is doubtful if the assault forces could have firmly established themselves without the assistance of these weapons. Other valuable novelties included the British AVRE (Armoured Vehicle Royal Engineers) and the "flail" tank which did excellent work in clearing paths through the minefields at the beach exits.

The enemy's confusion in the face of our assault was very clearly shown in the telephone journal of the German Seventh Army Headquarters which subsequently fell into our hands. Although Field Marshal von Rundstedt claimed on 20 June that the Germans were not taken by surprise, the evidence of this document told a very different story. Convinced that the main Allied assault would be delivered in the Pas-de-Calais, the Army HQ was at first of the opinion that the Normandy operations were of a diversionary nature and unlikely to include seaborne landings, even after the airborne operations had been followed by the opening of the naval bombardment. When, on 8 June, an operation order of the US VII Corps fell into the Germans' hands, they concluded that while this unit was in charge of all the Cotentin operations, the V Corps mentioned in the order must embrace all the Anglo-American forces assaulting the Calvados area from the Vire to the Seine. The enemy assumed, in view of the anticipated further landings in the Pas-de-Calais, that the Allies could not afford to employ more than two corps elsewhere.

On D Day, because of the chaos in communications produced by our bombing, the Seventh Army HQ did not hear of the Calvados landings until 0900 hours, and then the information was both meager and inaccurate. It was not until 1640 hours that the Army learned of the Utah seaborne assault, having previously received reassuring reports as to the progress being made against the airborne forces dropped in that area. Meanwhile at noon, the German LXXXIV Corps had optimistically, but prematurely, announced that the attempted landings by the V Corps troops at St-Laurent had been completely smashed. Thanks to such misinformation and to a faulty estimate of the situation, Seventh Army decided by the evening of D Day that the landings near the Orne constituted the chief danger in the area so far invaded, and took steps to commit its strongest and most readily available reserves in that sector. Little was known of the strength or objectives of the American landings, and the operations in the Cotentin continued to be regarded simply as a diversionary effort which could easily be dealt with. This estimate of the situation dominated the enemy's policy, with fatal results, during the ensuing days.

On 7 June I toured the assault area by destroyer, in company with Admiral Ramsay, and talked with Field Marshal Montgomery, General Bradley, and the Naval Force Commanders. All were disappointed in the unfavorable landing conditions and longed for an improvement in the weather that would enable our troops to exploit to the full their initial successes. After noon on this day the weather did show some signs of moderating, and a chance was offered for us to catch up in part with our delayed unloading schedule. On Omaha beach, which continued to cause us most anxiety, General Bradley reported some improvement, but in view of the check received here I decided to alter the immediate tactical plan to the extent of having both V and VII Corps concentrate upon effecting a link-up through Carentan, after which the original plan of operations would be pursued. Of the morale of the men whom I saw on every sector during the day I cannot speak too highly. Their enthusiasm, energy, and fitness for battle were an inspiration to behold.

During the next five days our forces worked to join up the beachheads into one uninterrupted lodgement area and to introduce into this area the supplies of men and material necessary to consolidate and expand our foothold.

In the British–Canadian sector, chief interest centered in the thrust by the British 3 and Canadian 3 Divisions toward Caen. Exploiting the success achieved on D Day, they pushed southward, and, despite heavy casualties, succeeded on 7 June in reaching points some two or three miles north and northwest of the city. However, the enemy fully appreciated the danger in this sector and, employing the tanks of 21st Panzer and 12th SS Panzer Divisions, counter-attacked successfully in ideal tank country. This counter-attack penetrated nearly to the coast, and drove a wedge between the two Allied divisions, preventing a combined attack upon Caen for the time being. Subsequent events showed that the retention of the city was the key to the main enemy strategy, and during the struggles of the following weeks the Germans fought furiously to deny us possession and to prevent our breaking out across the Orne toward the Seine. Further west Bayeux was taken on 8 June and the beachhead expanded inland.

Meanwhile the Allies had their first experience of the enemy's skill and determination in holding out in fortified strongpoints behind our lines. Although German claims of the effect of these strongpoints in delaying the development of our operations were greatly exaggerated, it was undeniably difficult to eliminate the suicide squads by whom they were held. The biggest of these points was at Douvres in the Canadian sector, where the underground installations extended to 300 feet below the surface. It was not until 17 June that the garrison here was compelled to surrender.

In the American sector the V Corps assault forces, having overcome their initial difficulties, reached the line of the Bayeux–Carentan road by midday on 7 June, and on the next day established contact with the British 50 Division on their left flank. On 9 June, reinforced by the 2nd Infantry Division, V Corps advanced rapidly to the south and west, reaching the line Caumont–Cerisy Forêt–Isigny by 11 June. Reinforcements then stiffened the German defenses, particularly in the hills protecting St-Lô. At the other end of the American zone, the enemy rushed forces to bar the Cherbourg road at Montebourg. In the center there was a stern struggle to link the two beachheads across the marshlands of the Vire Estuary. The prevention of this junction was regarded by the enemy as second in importance only to the defense of Caen, but on 10 June patrols of the two American corps made contact, and on the 12th Carentan fell. The Germans made desperate but fruitless efforts to recover the town and re-establish the wedge between our forces. Our initial lodgement area was now consolidated, and we held an unbroken stretch of the French coast from Quinéville to the east bank of the Orne.

Meanwhile, on and off the beaches, the naval, mercantile marine, and land force supply services personnel were performing prodigies of achievement under conditions which could hardly have been worse. Enormous as was the burden imposed upon these services even under the best of conditions, the actual circumstances of our landings increased the difficulties of their task very considerably. The problems of unloading vast numbers of men and vehicles and thousands of tons of stores over bare beaches, strewn with mines and obstacles, were complicated by the heavy seas which would not permit the full use of the special landing devices, such as the "Rhino" ferries, which had been designed to facilitate unloading at this stage of operations. The beaches and their exits had to be cleared and the beach organizations set up while the fighting was still in progress close by, and on either flank the unloading had to be carried on under fire from German heavy artillery. Off shore, enemy aircraft, although absent by day, laid mines each night, requiring unceasing activity by our mine sweepers. By 11 June, despite these complications, the machinery of supply over the beaches was functioning satisfactorily. Initial discharges of stores and vehicles were about 50% behind the planned schedule, but against this we could set the fact that consumption had been less than anticipated. Reserves were being accumulated and the supply position as a whole gave us no cause for concern. The artificial harbor units were arriving and the inner anchorages were already in location. During the first six days of the operation, 326,547 men, 54,186 vehicles and 104,428 tons of stores were brought ashore over the beaches. These figures gave the measure of the way in which all concerned, by their untiring energy and courage, triumphed over the difficulties which confronted them.

On 11 June, with the linking up of the beachheads, the stage was set for the battles of the ensuing two months during which the fate of France was to be decided. The enemy never succeeded fully in recovering from the confusion into which he was plunged by the surprise of our attack and the effects of our air and naval bombardment. During the first five days of the campaign all the symptoms developed which were to characterize the Germans' resistance in the subsequent battles. Desperate attempts to repair the shattered communications system met with little success while the Allied air forces continued their onslaught against the enemy lines and far to the rear. At some critical moments the Army lost touch with corps, corps with divisions, and divisions were ignorant of the fate of their regiments. Already the panzer divisions were reporting that they were halted through lack of fuel, reinforcements were unable to reach the battle area for the same reason, and by 13 June the Seventh Army had no fuel dump nearer than Nantes from which issues could be made. Ammunition was also scarce, and the fall of Carentan was explained as due to the fact that the defending forces lacked shells. These things were lacking, not because the Germans did not possess the means to wage war, but because the movement of supplies to the fighting zone was practically impossible when the Allied domination of the skies was so complete. All this explains the enemy's failure to regain the initiative following his loss of it when our forces broke through the Atlantic Wall defenses upon which Rommel had, with such fatal misjudgment, pinned his faith.

From 11 June onward the enemy strove desperately but vainly to contain the beachheads which he had been unable to prevent us from securing. The orders of 7 June that the Allies were to be driven back into the sea were already obsolete; the aim now was to save Cherbourg, to attempt to re-establish the wedge between the Cotentin and Calvados at Carentan, and to hold fast on the eastern flank by denying us possession of the city of Caen. The next six weeks were to see the failure of all three of these aims before the moral and material superiority of the Allied armies.

ESTABLISHMENT OF THE LODGEMENT AREA

After the success of the assault operations had gained us a foothold on French soil, there followed six weeks of gruelling struggle to secure a lodgement area of sufficient depth in which to build up a striking force of such magnitude as to enable us to make full use of our potential material superiority. The process took longer than we had expected, largely owing to the adverse weather conditions which repeatedly interrupted the flow of men and stores across the Channel. The enemy fought tenaciously to contain our beachheads, though he was at no time able to collect the strength to constitute a serious offensive threat. Consequently our operations fell somewhat behind the planned schedule, but we were able to build up our armies to a power which made it possible, when the breakthrough came, not only to regain the time lost but to outstrip the anticipated rate of advance.

Our immediate need was to expand our shallow beachhead inland to a depth sufficient to secure the beaches from enemy gunfire in order that the build-up might proceed without interruption. We also had to capture the port of Cherbourg, which was essential to permit of the rapid inflow of the vast stocks of war material required for future operations.

Then, as our strength grew, we needed space in which to maneuver and so dispose our forces that the best use could be made of our material assets and a decisive blow be delivered at the enemy. To this end we had to secure Caen and establish bridgeheads across the Orne and Odon Rivers, to eliminate the possibility of the enemy's driving a wedge between the Allied sectors east and west of the Vire River, and to extend our hold upon the southern part of the Cotentin Peninsula.

Meanwhile, the enemy found himself in a dilemma. He had pinned his faith on Rommel's policy of concentrating upon the beach defenses, and when they failed to prevent the establishment of the Allied beachheads, he

Establishment of the lodgement area

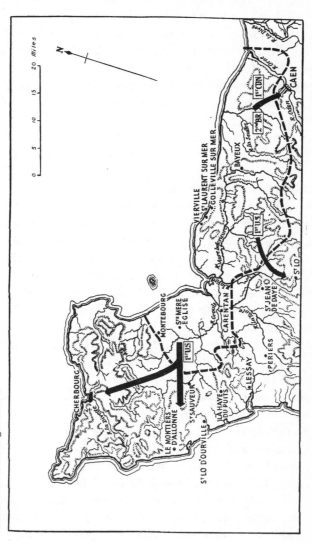

lacked any alternative means of combatting the threat offered. Rommel's confidence in his mines and concrete was indeed to have disastrous results for the German Army. There being no system of defense in depth, when the beaches were forced the enemy lost the initiative and never subsequently succeeded in regaining it. The hand of von Rundstedt, endeavoring to remedy the errors of his lieutenant, became apparent after the first two or three weeks of the campaign, when desperate attempts were made to form a mobile armored striking force in reserve; but it was too late. The enemy had been forced, by reason of his shortage of infantry, to use his armor in purely defensive roles. Once this armor was so committed, our constant pressure made it impossible for the enemy to withdraw his mobile forces for more appropriate employment until early in August, when the breakthrough of the US forces on the west flank had already sealed the fate of the German Seventh Army.

Lack of infantry was the most important cause of the enemy's defeat in Normandy, and his failure to remedy this weakness was due primarily to the success of the Allied threats levelled against the Pas-de-Calais. This threat, which had already proved of so much value in misleading the enemy as to the true objectives of our invasion preparations, was maintained after 6 June, and it served most effectively to pin down the German Fifteenth Army east of the Seine while we built up our strength in the lodgement area to the west. I cannot overemphasize the decisive value of this most successful threat, which paid enormous dividends, both at the time of the assault and during the operations of the two succeeding months. The German Fifteenth Army, which, if committed to battle in June or July, might possibly have defeated us by sheer weight of numbers, remained inoperative throughout the critical period of the campaign, and only when the breakthrough had been achieved were its infantry divisions brought west across the Seine—too late to have any effect upon the course of victory.

A certain amount of reinforcement of the Normandy front from other parts of France and from elsewhere in Europe did take place, but it was fatally slow. The rate of the enemy's build-up in the battle area during the first six weeks of the campaign averaged only about half a division per day. By 16 June he had committed his four nearest panzer divisions to battle, and his six nearest infantry divisions were brought in by 19 June. But it was not until the beginning of July, when the scale of the Allied effort was no longer in any doubt, that reinforcements began to arrive from more distant locations.

This process of reinforcement was rendered hazardous and slow by the combined efforts of the Allied air forces and the French patriots. Despite the comparative speed with which tracks could be repaired, our prolonged bombing campaign against rail centers and marshalling yards had effected a marked reduction in the operating efficiency of the rail systems of northeast France and Belgium, and by D Day 27% of the locomotive servicing facilities, 13% of the locomotives themselves, and 8% of the other rolling stock had been destroyed. All but two of the Seine bridges below Paris were cut by Allied bombers before D Day, and during the subsequent weeks these surviving ones were also demolished, together with the principal road and rail bridges across the Loire. Thus the battle area in Normandy was virtually isolated except for the routes which led into it through the Paris–Orléans "gap" between the two rivers; there the roads and railroads inevitably became congested and afforded rich opportunities for sabotage and bombing. The Tactical Air Forces also, by a series of concentrated attacks against junctions on the edge of the tactical area during the first few days following the assault, drew a line beyond which all enemy rail movement was impossible by day. This line of interdiction originally ran through Pontaubault, Fougères, Mayenne, Alençon, Dreux, and Evreux, but was subsequently adjusted as the ground situation developed.

The consequence of these attacks upon enemy communications was that the Germans were compelled to detrain their reinforcement troops in eastern France, after a circuitous approach over a disorganized railway system, and then to move them up to the front by road. Road movement, however, was difficult by reason of the critical oil shortage, apart from the exposure of the columns to Allied bombing and strafing. During the first six months of 1944 the German oil production was reduced by at least 40% as a result of the bombing of the plants by the Strategic Air Forces, and the outcome was seen in the trials of the enemy reinforcements and supply columns as they struggled toward Normandy. Whole divisions were moved on seized bicycles, with much of their impedimenta on horse transport, while the heavy equipment had to follow as best it could by rail, usually arriving some time after the men. The 275th Infantry Division, for instance, took a week to move 150 miles from Fougères. It began the journey by train but was halted by bombing, then the French seized the horses which had been collected to move the division by road, and the destination was eventually reached on foot, movement being possible only at night because of the perils of air strafing by day. The 9th and 10th SS Panzer Divisions took as long to travel from eastern France to Normandy as from Poland (where they had been stationed) to the French frontier; while the men of the 16th GAF Division, having left the Hague by train on 18 June, were forced to make a grand tour of Holland, Belgium, the Rhineland, and eastern France before they eventually reached the front on 3 July. Travelling under such conditions, the reinforcements arrived in Normandy in a piecemeal fashion, and were promptly thrown into battle while still exhausted and unorganized. By mid-July, units had been milked from Brittany, the southwest and west of France, Holland, Poland, and Norway; only the Fifteenth Army in the Pas-de-Calais, waiting for a new invasion which never came, was still untouched.

Meanwhile the Allied air forces enjoyed absolute supremacy over the battle area, as indeed over the whole of Nazi-occupied Western Europe. During fine weather, a normal total of over 1,000 US heavy bombers by day and over 1,000 RAF heavy bombers by night was dispatched on strategic missions. Their top-priority targets were the German oil refineries, synthetic oil production plants, and dumps, but they were also available for use, at my request, against tactical targets connected with the Normandy front. Unfortunately the prevalent bad weather prevented our full use of the air weapon, operations being repeatedly reduced or cancelled for this cause.

The weather, however, failed to stop the AEAF (Allied Expeditionary Air Force) from constantly hammering its tactical targets. While in fine weather as many as 4,000 sorties a day were flown by aircraft of this command, the attacks were continued on the maximum scale possible even under the most adverse conditions. During the first week of the campaign the Tactical Air Forces flew some 35,000 sorties in direct support of ground troops, and by their persistent blows in subsequent weeks against their targets behind the enemy lines—transport, communications, strongpoints, airfields, fuel dumps, and troop concentrations—they caused a degree of confusion and disloca-tion that was essential to the success of our breakthrough in late July. So complete was our air mastery that in fine weather all enemy movement was brought to a standstill by day, while at night the attacks were continued with the aid of flares. Von Rundstedt himself reported that the Allied tactical air-craft controlled not only the main battlefield areas but also the approach routes to a depth of over 100 miles. Even a single soldier, he claimed, was not immune from attack.

An important factor in ensuring the success of our close-support air operations lay in the establishment of landing strips on French soil, from which our fighter planes could operate. Work began on the preparation of these strips as soon as we obtained a footing on shore, and, thanks to the bril-liant work of our engineer services, I was able to announce on the morning of 9 June that for the first time since 1940 Allied air forces were operating from France. Within three weeks of D Day, 31 Allied squadrons were oper-ating from the beachhead bases.

All this extremely effective use of our great air superiority was possible despite the very considerable diversion of our striking power against the enemy's preparations to attack the United Kingdom by means of flying bombs and heavier rocket projectiles. The first flying bombs fell on England during the night of 12–13 June, and the regular attacks commenced three days later. Attacks upon the V-1 sites were difficult by reason of their small-ness, the effective nature of their camouflage, their comparative mobility and the ease with which they could be repaired. For this reason it was consid-ered more profitable to attack the supply dumps, transport facilities and services. Blows designed to delay progress on the larger, massive concrete structures, of the exact purpose of which we were at the time still uncertain, also required the attentions of large formations of heavy planes, dropping the biggest types of bombs.

In contrast to the intensity of the Allied air effort, the activities of the German Air Force (GAF) apart from sporadic fighter-bomber attacks by flights of 20 to 30 aircraft on the assault area, were limited to cautious patrolling by day and sea-mining by a small number of heavy bombers at night. We were now to reap the fruits of the long struggle for air supremacy which had cost the Allied air forces so much effort since the start of the war. Following the enemy's failure to take effective action against our forces during the initial stages of the assault, he remained on the defensive, being chiefly concerned with the protection of his bases, stores, and lines of communication. Aggressive support of his ground forces was noticeably lacking, and even defense of their positions against our fighter-bomber attacks was weak and desultory. The enemy was, in fact, in an awkward predicament. To take the offensive when his numerical strength was so inferior to that of the Allies was to court disaster; yet to remain always on the defensive would mean slow attrition and a decline in ground force morale because of the absence of the air cover which had played so large a part in the victories of 1940.

The number of GAF planes available for employment in the invasion area had been built up during the six weeks prior to the assault, but this increase in strength was neutralized by our air forces, and post-D-Day reinforcement proved less than expected. The GAF fighter bases, from Bordeaux to Belgium, were subjected to attacks of such scope that the enemy was unable to concentrate his fighter resources over the battle zone, and his planes were thus denied effective employment. Normally the Luftwaffe fighter activities were limited to defensive patrolling behind the Germans' own lines, an average of 300–350 sorties per day being flown in fine weather with a maximum of about 450. There was also some enemy activity against the beaches, and bombing and torpedo attacks against shipping. It was a reflection of this enemy weakness that on 14 June RAF Bomber Command was able to send some 350 heavy bombers against Le Havre and Boulogne in daylight, the first daylight operation in force by the Command since early in the war, and lost only one aircraft on the operation.

When the enemy planes did come up, they showed a marked tendency to avoid combat. Only on 12 June did they react in any considerable strength when a mass onslaught was made on French airfields by 1,448 Fortresses and Liberators of the US Eighth Air Force—the largest force of heavy bombers hitherto airborne on a single mission. On this occasion the enemy suffered severely at the hands of the Allied fighters and failed to reach the bombers. The reluctance normally shown to engage our planes was doubtless in part dictated by the need to conserve a depleted strength; but there was also noticeable a lack of organization and experience on the part of the German pilots. The persistent RAF night bombing attacks of the past had led the German command to concentrate on the training and development of night fighters, with the result that day fighter pilots were generally of a poorer standard and rarely a match for their Allied opponents. As a consequence of this weakness, our forces—both on operations over the battle area and on long-range strategic daylight missions—frequently encountered no air opposition whatsoever, and the overall weekly Allied losses averaged only about 1% of the aircraft employed.

The quality of the German ground forces with whom our armies came in contact varied considerably. At the top of the scale came the troops of SS panzer and parachute units, considerably better than those of the ordinary infantry divisions. Their morale, backed by a blind confidence in ultimate Nazi victory, was extremely good, and whether in attack or defense they fought to a man with a fanatical courage. But in the infantry divisions we found opponents inferior, both physically and morally, to those against whom we had fought in North Africa. The lack of air and artillery support, the breakdown of ration supplies, the non-arrival of mail, the unsoldierly behaviour of some of the officers, the bombing of home towns—all tended to lower the men's spirits. Perhaps two-thirds of them were under 19 or over 30 years of age, and many were obviously tired of the war. Nevertheless they had not yet reached the dangerous state of indifference. Their inborn Teutonic discipline and their native courage enabled them to fight on stubbornly, and it was only toward the end of the campaign in France that their morale broke momentarily. Many who were so-called non-Nazis saw no hope for Germany other than through Hitler, and thought it better to go down fighting than to suffer a repetition of 1918. Moreover, it cannot be doubted that the governmental propaganda on "V" weapons had a considerable effect in strengthening morale in these early stages of the campaign. At the bottom of the scale came the foreigners who had either volunteered for, or been pressed into, the service of Germany. These men were dispersed throughout fixed garrisons and infantry divisions in order that adequate supervision could be exercised over them, but it was from their ranks almost exclusively that deserters came.

The abortive plot of the German military clique to assassinate Hitler, which astonished the world on 20 July, seemed to have little effect upon enemy morale. The details were little publicized by the German authorities, and the majority of the soldiers apparently regarded the facts as presented to them by the Allies as mere propaganda. Nor did the subsequent Himmler purge of non-Nazi elements in the army produce any marked change in the outlook of the enemy rank and file.

The struggle which took place during this period of the establishment of the lodgement area, following the success of our initial assault, took the form of a hard slugging match on the British sector of the front, with the city of Caen as its focal point. Here the enemy concentrated the bulk of his strength, while the men of the US First Army fought their way up the Cherbourg Peninsula to capture the port itself, subsequently regrouping and consolidating their position to the south in preparation for what was to prove the decisive breakthrough at the end of July.

By his anxiety to prevent the capture of Caen and the eastward extension of our beachhead, the enemy to some extent contributed to the accomplishment of our initial plan insofar as the capture of Cherbourg was concerned, and from D plus 6 or 7 the battle developed in general as foreseen. This enemy anxiety in the east was manifested from D plus 1 onwards, following the failure of our attempt to seize the city of Caen in our first rush inland. It was vital for the enemy to deny us the Seine basin: partly as it afforded the last natural barrier defending the V-1 and V-2 sites; partly because he needed the river ferries to bring over supplies and reinforcements to his divisions in Normandy; partly because he feared a thrust on Paris which would cut off all his forces to the west; partly because he foresaw a threat to Le Havre, which was an invaluable base for his naval craft operating against the approaches to the assault area; but perhaps most of all because he wished to avoid the possibility of a link-up between those Allied forces already ashore and those which he expected to land in the Pas-de-Calais.

For these reasons, therefore, he committed all his available armor and a considerable part of his infantry to the battle in the Caen sector, thus rendering easier the task of the Allied troops in the west but denying us access to the good tank and airfield country toward Falaise. His secondary aims, which crystallized as our strategy became clear to him, were to maintain a wedge threatening to divide the US forces in the Cotentin from those in Calvados, to prevent the cutting of the Cherbourg Peninsula and to block the way to Cherbourg itself. He fully appreciated the importance to us of securing this port—indeed, he overestimated the necessity of it, being ignorant of our artificial harbors project and probably underestimating our ability to use the open beaches—but his shortage of infantry and preoccupation with the Caen sector impaired his ability to defend it.

Our strategy, in the light of these German reactions, was to hit hard in the east in order to contain the enemy main strength there while consolidating our position in the west. The resulting struggle around Caen, which seemed to cost so much blood for such small territorial gains, was thus an essential factor in ensuring our ultimate success. The very tenacity of the defense there was sufficient proof of this. As I told the press correspondents at the end of August, every foot of ground the enemy lost at Caen was like losing ten miles anywhere else. At Caen we held him with our left while we delivered the blow toward Cherbourg with our right.

The enemy's tenacity in the east did not mean that the Allied forces in the west enjoyed a walk-over. The terrain through which they fought was overwhelmingly favorable to the defense. In the close "bocage" countryside, dotted with woods and orchards, and with its fields divided by high tree-topped embankments, each in itself a formidable anti-tank obstacle, armor was of little value, and the infantry had to wage a grim struggle from hedgerow to hedgerow and bank to bank, harassed by innumerable snipers and concealed machine-gun posts. For this type of warfare, experience gained by some of our units in their intensive pre-invasion exercises in battle-training areas of southwest England proved valuable, as they had there been taught to fight in country resembling that in which they found themselves at grips with the real enemy.

After the fall of Carentan on 12 June, marking the effective junction of the two American beachheads, the enemy became anxious concerning the drive of the 82nd Airborne and 9th Infantry Divisions which, striking towards St-Sauveur-le-Vicomte, threatened to cut the neck of the peninsula and thus isolate Cherbourg. Although the enemy's 77th Infantry Division had been brought up from Brittany to assist, his available forces were not sufficient to cope with this thrust as well as with the more direct threat to Cherbourg levelled by our 4th and 90th Infantry Divisions which were pushing north on both sides of the Montebourg road. The enemy concentrated, therefore, on counter-attacks from the south in an unsuccessful endeavor to recapture Carentan and re-establish the "wedge," while deploying a considerable mass of artillery to bar the way north at Montebourg. The town eventually fell on 19 June, but meanwhile the enemy weakness in the center led to the evacuation of St-Sauveur on 16 June. Patrols of 82nd Airborne Division entered the town on that day, and on 17 June the 9th Infantry Division reached the west coast at Les-Moitiers-d'Allone and St-Lô-d'Ourville, north and south of Barneville. The enemy had formed two battle groups, one of which was to defend Cherbourg and the other to escape to the south, but when the peninsula was cut, part of the "escape" force was trapped. The forces isolated to the north included the bulk of two infantry divisions, parts of two others, and the naval and garrison personnel employed in Cherbourg itself. Once VII Corps had reached the west coast, the enemy was unable to reopen his corridor to the north.

The Montebourg defense having been broken by 19 June, the advance on Cherbourg continued. Valognes fell on the following day, and three infantry divisions (the 4th on the right, 79th in the center, and 9th on the left) under VII Corps closed in on the city. The German attempt to hold us at Montebourg, as personally ordered by Hitler, proved to be an error of judgment, since, when the line was forced, the units which retreated to Cherbourg were in no state of organization to maintain a protracted defense of the city. Had the withdrawal taken place earlier, Cherbourg might have been able to hold out as long as Brest did subsequently. The lesson had been learned by the time the fighting reached Brittany.

An attack on Cherbourg was launched on the afternoon of 22 June, following an 80-minute bombardment of the outer defenses, but the enemy at first fought back stoutly. By 25 June, however, our men were fighting in the streets while the thunder of the German demolitions in the port area reverberated from the surrounding hills. At 1500 hours on 26 June, the joint commanders, Maj. Gen. von Schlieben (land forces) and Rear Adm. Hennecke (naval forces), despite having previously exacted no-surrender pledges from their men, gave themselves up. The Arsenal held out until next morning, and other fanatical groups which even then continued to resist had to be eliminated one by one. A certain number of the enemy still remained to be rounded up in the northwest corner of the peninsula, but on 1 July their commander, Colonel Keil, was captured with his staff and all resistance in the northern Cotentin came to an end.

It was the judgment of Rommel himself that, with Cherbourg in our hands, elimination of the beachhead was no longer possible. The admission was tantamount to a confession of the failure of his own policy of relying on a concrete "wall" to frustrate an invasion on the very beaches. The next few weeks were to see the enemy making a frantic but unavailing effort, under von Rundstedt's supervision, to create the mobile striking force necessary for a policy of elastic defense. But it was too late now.

This inability of the enemy, after the initial success of our landings, to form an adequate reserve with which to regain the initiative and drive us into the sea became very apparent during the fighting in the British–Canadian sector. While the US V Corps pushed inland from its Calvados beachhead to the south and east of Caumont, a heavy, see-saw battle was fought by the Second Army in the Tilly area, with two panzer divisions initially providing the bulk of the opposition. As our pressure increased, reinforcements were introduced by the enemy from two other armored divisions, but these proved inadequate. On 28 June, the British 8 Corps established a bridgehead some 4,000 yards wide and 1,000 yards deep beyond the Odon River near Mondrainville. The greater part of eight armored divisions was now flung into the battle by the enemy in a fruitless attempt to halt the advance and to cut the Allied corridor north of the river. Despite the bad weather, which deprived us of full air support, the bridgehead was reinforced and stood firm. The cream of the SS panzer troops failed to dislodge us, not because they were lacking in fighting spirit, but because they were put into the battle piecemeal as soon as they could be brought to the scene. In his efforts to prevent a break-through, the enemy found it necessary to employ his forces in small groups of about 200 infantry supported by 15 to 20 tanks, a process which proved both ineffective and expensive. The British forces compelled the enemy to continue these tactics, until by 1 July any chance he may have had of mounting a large-scale blow at any one point had been completely destroyed. By their unceasing pressure they had never allowed the initiative to pass to the enemy and had never given him the respite necessary to withdraw and mass his armored resources.

Nevertheless, in the east we had been unable to break out toward the Seine, and the enemy's concentration of his main power in the Caen sector had prevented us from securing the ground in that area we so badly needed. Our plans were sufficiently flexible that we could take advantage of this enemy reaction by directing that the American forces smash out of the lodgement area in the west while the British and Canadians kept the Germans occupied in the east.

Incessant pressure by the Second Army to contain the enemy's strength was therefore continued by Field Marshal Montgomery during July. Simultaneously, the US forces in the Cotentin proceeded to fight their way southward, alongside those who had landed east of the Vire, to win ground for mounting the attack which was to break through the German defenses at the end of the month. Field Marshal Montgomery's tactical handling of this situation was masterly. By this time, I was in no doubt as to the security of our beachhead from any immediate enemy threat, and the chief need was for elbow room in which to deploy our forces, the build-up of which had proceeded rapidly. We were already approaching the stage when the capacity of Cherbourg, the beaches, and the artificial ports would no longer be adequate to maintain us, and it was imperative that we should open up other ports, particularly those in Brittany, so that we might make our great attack before the enemy was able to obtain substantial equality in infantry, tanks, and artillery. The danger we had to meet was one of a position of stalemate along the whole front, when we might be forced to the defensive with only a slight depth of lodgement area behind us.

The indomitable offensive spirit animating all sections of the Allied forces prevented such a situation from arising; but it was hard going all along the front, and the first half of July was a wearing time for both sides. While the Second Army battled furiously against the enemy's armored strength to the east, the First Army struggled forward on both sides of the Vire.

It had been my intention that General Bradley's forces should strike south as soon as Cherbourg had fallen, but the need to reorganize and regroup prevented a start being made until 3 July. Then the advance was a laborious business owing to the close nature of the country and the atrocious weather. The enemy resisted fiercely along the whole front. In the VIII Corps sector violent fighting raged in the La-Haye-du-Puits area from 4 to 10 July, when the enemy's strongly organized positions were finally broken. VII Corps, attacking in terrain restricted by swampy land, suffered heavy losses for small gains along the Carentan–Périers highway. XIX Corps attacked across the Vire and established a bridgehead at St-Jean-de-Daye, then struck southward. The Germans, for the first time, transferred some armor from the eastern to the western sector, when the 2nd SS Panzer Division had been the only armored unit in action. Panzer Lehr now joined it west of the Vire. On 11 July, Panzer Lehr's counter-attack was smashed by the 9th and 30th Infantry Divisions, and on the same day, the US First Army opened a new drive east of the Vire and directly toward St-Lô. Promising gains were made but the German 2nd Parachute Corps rallied to prevent any breakthrough to St-Lô.

In view of the strength of this opposition to the First Army, which caused the advance to be disappointingly slow although General Bradley attacked unceasingly with everything he could bring into action, Field Marshal Montgomery had decided to redouble the efforts on the eastern flank and, as he said, to "put the wind up the enemy by seizing Caen" in preparation for establishing a bridgehead across the Orne. When this had been done, the Second Army could either drive south with its left flank on the Orne or else take over the Caumont sector in order to free more American troops for the thrust toward Brittany.

In spite of his reinforcement of the western part of the front, it was evident that the enemy continued to regard the defense of Caen as the matter of greatest importance, and 700 of his available 900 tanks were still located in this sector. They were now under command of Panzer Group West, which held the sector east of the Drôme River, facing the British Second Army. Following the establishment of the Odon bridgehead, interest in the Second Army area was focused on a Canadian thrust towards Caen from the west which led to bitter resistance by the Germans at Carpiquet, where a three-day duel (4–6 July) for the possession of the airfield was fought between the Canadian 3 Infantry Division and the 12th SS Panzer Division.

On 8 July, Field Marshal Montgomery mounted his full-scale assault upon Caen. Applying the principles which he had first employed with such success in North Africa, he concentrated a maximum of striking power on one sector to achieve a breakthrough. The attack was preceded by an air bombardment of nearly 500 RAF "heavies," supplemented by effective naval fire from HMS *Rodney, Roberts* and *Belfast*, and by land artillery. Although six hours elapsed between the air bombing and the ground attack, the result was to paralyse the enemy, who broke before our attack. The bombing having cut off their supplies, they ran out of ammunition and rations, and we occupied the whole of the town north and west of the Orne. Our advance was made difficult by the debris and cratering resulting from the bombing, and the enemy still held the Faubourg de Vaucelles across the river.

The entry into Caen was followed by a renewed thrust to extend the Odon bridgehead, and the capture of Maltôt on 10 July threatened to trap the enemy in the triangle between the Orne and the Odon. The threat produced vigorous enemy reaction again, the fighting for possession of Hill 112 being especially bitter. Once more the enemy was forced to bring back into the battle the armored elements which he had been in process of replacing in the line by infantry and withdrawing to form a strong striking force in reserve. A few days later he made another attempt, withdrawing two SS panzer divisions, but the Second Army attack on Évrecy on 16–17 July forced him, not only to bring the armor hurriedly back, but to adopt the dangerous and uneconomical policy of dividing an SS panzer division into two battle groups. Only the 12th SS Panzer Division, weary from a long period of activity culminating in its defeat before Caen, now remained in reserve, and the big attack south and east of Caen which materialized on 18 July put an end to its relaxation.

This continuing failure by the enemy to form an armored reserve constitutes the outstanding feature of the campaign during June and July: to it we owed the successful establishment of our lodgement area, safe from the threat of counter-attacks which might have driven us back into the sea. Every time an attempt was made to replace armor in the line with a newly arrived infantry division a fresh attack necessitated its hasty recommittal. These continual Allied jabs compelled the enemy to maintain his expensive policy of frantically "plugging the holes" to avert a breakthrough. So long as the pressure continued, and so long as the threat to the Pas-de-Calais proved effective in preventing the move of infantry reinforcements from there across the Seine, the enemy had no alternative but to stand on the defensive and see the Seventh Army and Panzer Group West slowly bleed to death. All that he could do was play for time, denying us ground by fighting hard for every defensive position.

Meanwhile, to the west, the steady pressure of the First Army forced the enemy gradually back through the close countryside, strewn with mines, toward the line of the Lessay–Périers–St-Lô road, where he had decided to make his main stand. His defence was weakest at the western extremity of this line, but in the St-Lô sector he showed a lively anxiety to hold this important road junction, the capture of which was essential to the success of our plan for a breakthrough. On 18 July, however, St-Lô fell to the 29th Division, and the 9th and 30th Infantry Divisions, west of St-Lô and across the Vire, had reached high ground suitable for launching the breakthrough attempt.

Thus, by 18 July, both the First and Second Armies had taken up the positions from which the breakthrough attacks were to be started. We now had the requisite room to maneuver, and our divisions in the field had been built up to 15 US (including 3 armored) and 15 British and Canadian (including 4 armored), against which the enemy had 27, 8 of which were armored. On account of the losses which we had inflicted, however, the actual strength of the enemy was no more than the equivalent of six panzer or panzer-grenadier and ten full-strength infantry divisions. He had committed 540,000 men to battle and had lost at least 160,000 of them, killed, wounded, and prisoners; of 1,200 tanks committed, 30% had been lost. His reinforcement prospects were not rosy, for only four of his panzer divisions in the west (outside the Pas-de-Calais) had not yet been committed to the battle, and these were not ready for combat. His six divisions in Brittany had already been bled to help hold the line in Normandy, while in the southern half of France there were only 12 divisions left, of which but seven or eight were actually available to guard the coasts, thanks to the action of the Maquis inland. The southwestern part of the country had been practically evacuated of effective field units. Only the Fifteenth Army in the Pas-de-Calais, 19 divisions strong, was still left substantially intact, waiting for the expected further landings, which the commencement of the flying bomb attacks on 12 June may have made appear more likely than ever to the Germans.

Although the process had taken somewhat longer than we had anticipated, we had undeniably won the first and second rounds. In the first round we had gained our footing in France; in the second we had retained the initiative while expanding and consolidating our lodgement area and building up our strength in men and materials in readiness for the decisive blow to follow.

The enemy never succeeded in remedying the fatal situation into which Rommel's reliance on the Atlantic Wall had led him following the achievement of our landings. It was a coincidence that our old opponent of Africa should be struck down on the eve of the Second Army attack across the Orne, which was to be the precursor of the breakthrough in the west.

THE BREAKTHROUGH

From the beginning of the campaign in Normandy, I agreed with Field Marshal Montgomery and General Bradley that our basic policy should be so to maneuver and attack as to pin down and destroy substantial portions of the enemy in our immediate front in order later to have full freedom of action. The alternative would have been merely a pushing-back, with consequent necessity for slowly battling our way toward the ultimate geographical objectives. By the third week in July, our forces were in position to launch the all-out attack, which, in accordance with this strategic idea, was to break through and destroy the enemy divisions then with difficulty attempting to contain us in our lodgement area. By throwing all our weight into an offensive at this stage, I felt confident that we should not only achieve our objectives but that, in the long run, the cost of our victory would be the less.

The enemy's reaction had convinced us that we should strike hard with our left and then follow through promptly with a right-hand blow. In both cases, the whole weight of our air power was to be employed to support the ground attacks. We agreed also that the main attacks were to be supported by aggressive action all along the line to pin down the enemy's local reserves. He had no major reserves immediately available, and we did not fear any serious counter-offensive.

In the Second Army sector, vigorous thrusts in the Évrecy–Esquay area through the Odon bridgehead on 16–17 July were to be in the nature of a feint to distract the enemy's attention and to cause him to withdraw more of his armor westward across the Orne to meet the threat. Then on 18 July, the main British–Canadian thrust was to take the form of a drive across the Orne from Caen toward the south and southeast, exploiting in the direction of the Seine basin and Paris. On the following day, General Bradley would launch his major attack across the Périers–St-Lô. Having achieved a

The breakthrough

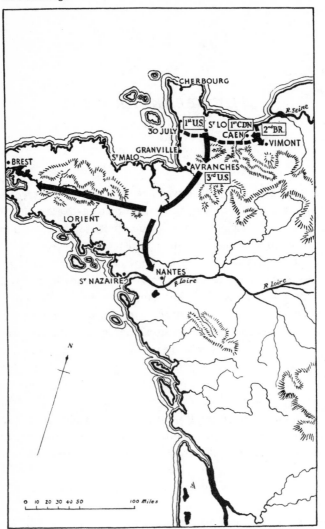

breakthrough, he was to swing his spearheads westward to Coutances, in order to isolate the enemy divisions between St-Lô and the coast, and then strike down through Avranches, creating if possible an open flank. By this means we could then operate into the Brittany Peninsula to open up the much-needed ports, while the German Seventh Army and at least part of Panzer Group West could be encircled and crushed between the US forces to the west and the British and Canadians to the east.

The execution of this plan opened promisingly. The enemy, as we had hoped, was deceived as to our intentions on the Second Army front by the operations in the Évrecy–Esquay area on 16 and 17 July. The reserve which he had been trying to form with two armored divisions was hurriedly broken up and part of one of them was brought westward over the Orne to counter our threat. Consequently our drive to the south and southeast of Caen across the river on 18 July achieved complete tactical surprise.

The attack was preceded at dawn on that day by what was the heaviest and most concentrated air assault hitherto employed in support of ground operations. The operation was a fine example of Anglo-American air cooperation, in which over 2,000 aircraft of RAF Bomber Command and the US Eighth and Ninth Air Forces took part, dropping a total of over 7,000 tons of bombs. While RAF Halifaxes and Lancasters dropped over 5,000 tons of bombs in less than 45 minutes on the area south of the river over which the ground assault was to be made, US planes attacked the enemy concentrations to the rear and on the flanks. In the carpet bombing, fragmentation bombs were used to break the enemy resistance without causing extensive cratering which would have hindered the advance of our tanks. At the same time, a strong naval bombardment was made to supplement the air effort.

Although only temporary in effect, the results of the bombing were decisive so far as the initial ground attack was concerned. Actual casualties to the enemy, in his foxholes, were comparatively few, but he was stunned by the weight of the bombing and a degree of confusion was caused which rendered the opposition to our advance negligible for some hours. At the same time, the spectacle of our mighty air fleets roaring in over their heads to attack had a most heartening effect upon our own men. The attack was led by the 7, 11, and Guards Armoured Divisions under 8 Corps, commanded by Lieut. Gen. O'Connor. These struck across the river at 0745 hours, followed by the infantry of 1 Corps and Canadian 2 Corps on either flank. The enemy at first proved unable to regroup his armor to meet the thrust, while the 21st Panzer and 16th GAF Divisions, which bore the brunt of the attack, were too disorganized by the bombing to offer much resistance. By the afternoon, the 11 Armoured Division had reached the Bourguébus area, the Guards were at Vimont, and the 7 Armoured Division had advanced to the south beyond Démouville. Toward evening, however, enemy resistance stiffened and he was able to counter-attack with 50 tanks south and southeast of Bourguébus. By nightfall, he succeeded in establishing a strong anti-tank screen with guns which had escaped the bombing, and this effectively halted our advance on the line Emiéville–Cagny–Soliers. On the following days the weather, which had relented to permit the massive air effort of the 18th, broke once more, turning the low-lying country of the battle area into a sea of mud which afforded an effective check to further tank operations.

This break in the weather also delayed the First Army attack which was scheduled for 19 July. Here, as at Caen, General Bradley and I had decided that an overwhelming air bombardment was a necessary prerequisite to the success of our plans. It was not, however, until 25 July that the skies cleared sufficiently to permit this air effort. Meanwhile the men of the First Army were compelled to huddle in their foxholes under the dripping hedgerows in conditions of extreme discomfort, while the enemy, similarly entrenched behind the natural defenses of the country, was alert to every movement. It was not until after six days of waiting, more miserable to the American troops than any others in this campaign, that the opportunity for action came on 25 July.

The plan of the attack was that, following a heavy air bombardment of the enemy positions, the First Army was to advance on a 3-divisional front west of St-Lô, with the general line Marigny–St-Gilles as the primary objective. Three more divisions were then to pass through the first wave, turn westward, and strike for Coutances and Granville, thus cutting off the enemy in the area Périers–Lessay. These first two waves were to be launched by VII Corps, with VIII Corps subsequently taking up the battle in the Lessay sector and advancing along the coast on our right.

As the outcome of the British–Canadian–American joint operations, I envisaged three possibilities. First, given a spell of fine weather, there was good reason to hope for such measure of success by both the First and Second Armies that our forces might encircle the enemy west of Vire and so eliminate his units as practically to create an open flank. In this case, it would be unnecessary to detach any large forces for the conquest of Brittany and the bulk of our strength could be devoted to completing the destruction of the enemy forces in Normandy. As a second possibility, the enemy might succeed in establishing a defensive line running from Caen to Avranches, in which case the task of gaining Brittany would require another large-scale thrust on the right flank. Thirdly, if, as seemed very unlikely, the enemy could manage to block our advance beyond this Caen–Avranches line, we had ready a special amphibious–airborne operation designed to seize Brittany in the enemy's rear. As the situation stood at that time, the conquest of Brittany was still an all-important aim of our policy in order that through its ports we might receive and maintain the additional divisions with which we planned to pursue the battle across France. We could not then envisage the full extent of the defeat which the enemy was to sustain in Normandy.

On the morning of 25 July an area five miles long and one mile wide to the west of St-Lô was blasted by 1,495 heavy bombers of the Eighth Air Force and 388 aircraft of AEAF dropping over 4,700 tons of bombs. At the same time, medium bombers attacked troops and gun concentrations southeast of Caen, and fighter-bombers with bombs and rocket projectiles attacked targets behind the American assault area. The total of AEAF sorties for this day was 4,979. Of all the planes employed in these massive operations, only 6 heavy bombers, 4 light bombers, and 19 fighters were lost. These were chiefly the victims of flak; the enemy fighters offered more combat than usual, but did not succeed in penetrating our fighter screen and reaching the bombers.

As in the case of the bombardment of Caen a week earlier, the air blow preceding the ground attack west of St-Lô did not cause a large number of casualties to the enemy sheltering in their dug-in positions, but it produced great confusion. Communications broke down and supplies from the rear were cut off. During the actual bombing the bewilderment of the enemy was such that some men unwittingly ran toward our lines and four uninjured tanks put up white flags before any ground attack was launched. Again, as at Caen, this stunning effect was only temporary.

The closeness of the air support given in this operation, thanks to our recent experiences, was such as we should never have dared to attempt a year before. We had indeed made enormous strides forward in this respect; and from the two Caen operations we had learned the need for a quicker ground follow-up on the conclusion of the bombing, for the avoidance of cratering, and for attacks upon a wider range of targets to the rear and on the flanks of the main bombardment area. Our technique, however, was still not yet perfected, and some of our bombs fell short, causing casualties to our own men. Unfortunately, perfection in the employment of comparatively new tactics, such as this close-support carpet bombing, is attainable only through the process of trial and error, and these regrettable losses were part of the inevitable price of experience. Among those who lost their lives on this occasion was Lieut. Gen. Lesley J. McNair, who was watching the preparations for the attack from a foxhole in the front line. His death was a heavy blow to the United States Army and a source of keen sorrow to me personally.

At the commencement of the ground battle, VII Corps, in the sector west of St-Lô, had under command the 2nd and 3rd Armored Divisions and the 1st, 4th, 9th, and 30th Infantry Divisions; while VIII Corps, in the Périers–Lessay sector had the 8th, 79th, 83rd, and 90th Infantry Divisions with the 4th Armored Division. The battle began with the advance of VII Corps at midday on 25 July; the 9th Division was on the right flank, 4th Division in the center, and 30th Division on the left, with 1st Division and the armor in the rear. At the same time our VIII, XIX, and V Corps maintained their pressure along the remainder of the army front. South of Caen, the Canadian 2 Corps simultaneously advanced southward astride the Falaise road.

The American advance was met with intense artillery fire, from positions not neutralized by the air bombing, on the left flank, while on the right German parachute units resisted fiercely. The ordinary infantry opposition, provided by elements of three infantry divisions, and of one panzer division, was not so severe. The enemy was still weak in armor in the sector fronting the US armies: although three panzer divisions were there, the bulk of his armored strength was still concentrated under Panzer Group West, with one panzer division west of the Orne, and five east of the river.

The advance at first made slow progress, but by midnight VII Corps had crossed the Périers–St-Lô road, and on 26 July its 1st Infantry and 2nd and 3rd Armored Divisions took up the attack. Lozon, Marigny, and St-Gilles were taken and the St-Lô–Coutances road cut. On the same day VIII Corps attacked across the Périers–St-Lô road to the west of VII Corps. The Germans continued to counter-attack vigorously, and, as the Allied thrust swung westward toward Coutances, it became clear that the enemy intended to retain that town as long as possible in order that he might extricate his troops from the north.

During 27 July the towns of Périers and Lessay were taken, and despite many mines and booby-traps the advance on Coutances was pushed ahead, led by the armored units. Pockets of resistance were by-passed by the tanks and left to be mopped up by the infantry. The enemy meanwhile struggled to withdraw his forces through Coutances, but the infantry elements in the coastal sector had commenced their retreat too late, and our air forces took heavy toll of the vehicles streaming southward along the roads converging on the city. The enemy forces north of Coutances at this time comprised elements of three infantry divisions (77th, 243rd, and 353rd), 2nd SS Panzer and 17th SS Panzer Grenadier Divisions, and battle groups of the 265th, 266th, and 275th Infantry Divisions. The German Command concentrated primarily on evacuating the SS formations, leaving the remainder to their fate.

On 28 July the escape route through Coutances was sealed with the capture of the city by the 4th Armored Division, which, with the 6th Armored Division, formed the spearhead of VIII Corps. These two formations then pressed on southward with gathering speed to the Sienne River, while VII Corps, spearheaded by the 2nd and 3rd Armored Divisions, continued to attack southwestward toward Granville and Avranches. The enemy withdrawal, following the loss of Coutances, began to degenerate into a disorderly retreat, and 4,500 prisoners were taken during the 24 hours of 28 July. Although minefields were laid to slow the pursuit, and German armored units fought a stubborn rearguard action, the advance was not checked. The 5th Parachute Division, Panzer Lehr Division, and 353rd Infantry Division were almost completely accounted for by this time, although, in accordance with German practice, they were reconstituted at a later stage of the campaign.

Meanwhile, on 28 July, XIX Corps, advancing south from St-Lô, reached Tessy-sur-Vire, while V Corps attacked south of the Forêt de Cerisy against stiff resistance by 3rd Parachute Division. Further east, in the British–Canadian sector, Canadian 2 Corps' advance toward Falaise had been halted by a strong defensive belt of anti-tank guns, dug-in tanks and mortars.

The Canadians were probing the defenses, with the aid of magnificent support by the RAF 83 Group, and considerable losses were inflicted on the enemy. Our pressure on this sector was not, however, able to prevent the move of 2nd Panzer Division from the east bank of the Orne across to the Tessy area, where it made a stand to cover the general withdrawal from Coutances. Elements of two infantry divisions with a small proportion of the 2nd Parachute Division were also being brought to the battle area from Brittany to bolster up the enemy's front. Prior to the arrival of these reinforcements, the enemy troops opposing the US sector, while nominally consisting of nine infantry, two parachute, one panzer grenadier, and two panzer divisions, had an estimated combat strength of only three and a half infantry, one parachute, and three panzer-type divisions. Against the British sector, from Caumont to Cabourg, were nominally eight infantry and five panzer divisions, of a real strength not exceeding that of five and a half infantry and three and a half panzer divisions.

If further reinforcements were to be provided for the Seventh Army, and Panzer Group West, the majority of them would have to be drawn from the Fifteenth Army in the Pas-de-Calais. Of the Seventh Army itself, only the infantry division in the Channel Islands and parts of the two divisions in Brittany remained uncommitted. In the southwest of France, the German First Army had only two limited-employment infantry divisions, three training divisions, and a panzer division (which was engaged against the Maquis). The Nineteenth Army, in the southeast, had already sent three infantry divisions to the battle area, only one of which had been replaced; one field-type infantry division, six limited-employment infantry divisions, and a panzer division remained. The double threat of the Maquis and of Allied landings on the Mediterranean coast made it unlikely that much more would be forthcoming for Normandy from this source, with the possible exception of elements of the panzer division. Holland had contributed three limited-employment divisions to Normandy, and its coast-guarding units were seriously stretched. Replacements from within Germany had begun to arrive in the battle area, but the strength of the divisions opposing the Allies continued to decrease. Many units had been compelled in the recent fighting to use service elements, engineers, and artillery personnel as infantry, and others had been cannibalized to maintain the stronger divisions.

It was at this time that the effectiveness of our threat to the Pas-de-Calais began to decrease as the Germans found themselves faced with a more immediate danger in the shape of the breakthrough in Normandy. We were anxious to maintain the threat for as long as possible, although its greatest function—that of keeping the Fifteenth Army inactive during the crucial period of the assault and establishment of the lodgement area—had already been completed with such extraordinary success. The first moves from the Fifteenth Army area westward over the Seine coincided with the launching of the US First Army attack on 25 July, when the German 363rd Infantry Division began to cross the river, while others prepared to follow it.

Following the success of our initial breakthrough in the west I considered that, in order fully to exploit our advantages, the time had come for the establishment of the US Third Army. This officially came into existence under General Patton on 1 August, taking over command of VIII, XII, XV, and XX Corps, while V, VII, and XIX Corps remained with First Army. The two armies were placed under command of General Bradley, whose leadership of the First Army had been so brilliantly successful. General (then Lieut. Gen.) C. H. Hodges succeeded him as Commanding General, First Army.

Earlier, on 23 July, the Canadian First Army under General Crerar had also become operational, having under command initially the British 1 Corps, to which was joined the Canadian 2 Corps on 31 July. The army took over the easternmost coastal sector of the entire front. With the British Second Army, under General Dempsey, it now formed 21 Army Group, commanded by Field Marshal Montgomery.

My own operational headquarters was at this time in process of moving to the Continent, and in order to ensure unified control during this critical stage of our operations General Montgomery continued to act as my representative, with authority, under my supervision, over the entire operation as coordinator of activities. This arrangement continued from 1 August until 1 September, when my operations staff and communications were established and I assumed personal direction of the two army groups.

Following the capture of Coutances our plan was for the Third Army to drive south in the western sector, breaking through Avranches into Brittany and seizing the area Rennes–Fougères, thence turning westward to secure St-Malo, the Quiberon Bay area and Brest, and clearing the entire peninsula. Meanwhile the First Army would advance south to seize the area Mortain–Vire.

At the same time the Second Army was to concentrate on a thrust in the Caumont area, side by side with that of the First Army on Vire. The enemy in this part of the front had only some four regiments in the line, reinforced with an occasional dug-in tank, and a great opportunity appeared here for a striking blow which, with General Bradley's offensive in the west, might bring decisive results. Rapidity of action was the vital factor now. We could not afford to wait either for weather or for perfection in the details of our preparations. The enemy was reeling and it was imperative that we should not allow him time to readjust his lines, shift his units, or bring up reserves. Our policy must be to indulge in an all-out offensive and, if necessary, throw caution to the winds.

Our advance in the west continued. On 29 July VIII Corps' armor crossed the Sienne, south of Coutances; two days later Avranches fell to the 4th Armored Division; and on 31 July the 6th Armored Division reduced the elements resisting at Granville. No effective barrier now lay between us and Brittany, and my expectations of creating an open flank had been realized. The enemy was in a state of complete disorganization and our fighters and fighter-bombers swarmed over the roads, shooting up the jammed columns of German transport to such effect that our own advance was slowed by the masses of knocked-out vehicles. The enemy infantry was in no condition to resist us, and only the weary, badly battered armor put up any considerable fight.

At the same time the British launched their thrust south of Caumont. The enemy was attempting, with two armored divisions, to establish a hinge in the Percy–Tessy area on which to conduct operations designed to prevent a collapse of the entire Normandy front. In this, however, he was defeated by the combined First Army frontal attacks and the Second Army flank drive toward Vire. The British offensive in the Caumont sector was preceded by another smashing air bombardment by nearly 700 RAF heavy bombers, supported by over 500 AEAF light and medium bombers, which, as usual, had a paralysing effect upon the enemy. Prisoners stated that the confusion was so great that effective unit fighting was rendered impossible for at least 12 hours, although the Allies lost some part of this advantage through not launching the ground attack immediately after the cessation of the bombing. Enemy attempts to deny us the high ground west of Mont Pinçon and the valley of the Vire were frustrated; Le Bény-Bocage was captured by the 11 Armoured Division (8 Corps) on 1 August and, following heavy fighting, Vire was entered on 2 August only to be temporarily recaptured by two SS panzer divisions on the next day. There was a bitter struggle for some days before the enemy was finally forced back from this sector. Farther to the northeast, Villers-Bocage was taken on 5 August and Évrecy and Esquay, southwest of Caen, on the 4th.

By these combined efforts of the First and Second Armies, the flank of the American salient was safeguarded. The enemy, having finally decided to use his Fifteenth Army resources to reinforce the Normandy front, was now at last replacing, with the newly acquired infantry, the armor which he had hitherto kept massed east of the Orne to prevent any possibility of a breakthrough there toward Paris and the Seine. The armor so freed he proceeded to transfer westward toward the Vire area in support of the Seventh Army troops struggling to prevent a collapse of the front there, and to provide the necessary weight to hurl against the flanks of the Third Army. Resistance accordingly stiffened as four panzer divisions arrived from east of the Orne, followed by a further panzer division and an infantry division from across the Seine.

Following the capture of Granville and Avranches, the Third Army advance continued against negligible resistance into Brittany. The passage of the Selune River was assured by the 4th Armored Division's capture of its dams on 1 August and then this division struck southward to cut the neck of the Brittany Peninsula, while the 6th Armored Division turned westward toward Brest. The airborne operation which we had prepared to assist in "turning the corner" into Brittany was rendered unnecessary by the unimpeded rapidity of the ground force advances. On 2 August the 4th Armored

Division was in the suburbs of Rennes, and the 6th Armored Division reached Dinan, by-passing St-Malo. Combat commands of these two divisions, followed by the 8th, 79th, and 83d Infantry Divisions, now proceeded quickly to overrun the peninsula. On 4 August Rennes was in our hands, and while one column drove on from there toward Nantes another secured Fougères and Vitre, continuing southward toward the Loire. By 6 August the line of the Vilaine River was held from Rennes to the sea, thus completing the cutting off of the peninsula, while to the east the 5th Infantry Division reached the Loire River between Nantes and Angers, Nantes itself falling on 10 August. Meanwhile the 6th Armored Division had traversed Brittany to the west and was standing before Brest.

The opposition encountered by General Patton's flying columns in the course of this sweep was negligible, for the enemy's flank had collapsed so completely that there was hardly any resistance offered by organized units above company strength. The Germans, realizing the impossibility of forming any defensive line on which to hold the peninsula, accepted the inevitable and abandoned the interior of Brittany in order to concentrate their available strength to defend Brest, St-Nazaire, St-Malo, and Lorient, the ports which they estimated to be our principal objectives. The forces left to them for this purpose consisted of some 45,000 garrison troops, together with elements of the 2nd Parachute Division and three infantry divisions—in all some 75,000 men. Inland, only small pockets of resistance remained, and these were by-passed by the armored columns and left to be mopped up by the infantry and the local French Forces of the Interior (FFI). By the end of the first week of August the enemy had been forced everywhere to fall back into the ports under siege by the troops of VIII Corps.

Special mention must be made of the great assistance given us by the FFI in the task of reducing Brittany. The overt resistance forces in this area had been built up since June around a core of SAS troops of the French 4th Parachute Battalion to a total strength of some 30,000 men. On the night of 4/5 August the État-Major was dispatched to take charge of their operations. As the Allied columns advanced, these French forces ambushed the retreating enemy, attacked isolated groups and strongpoints, and protected bridges from destruction. When our armor had swept past them they were given the task of clearing up the localities where pockets of Germans remained, and of keeping open the Allied lines of communication. They also provided our troops with invaluable assistance in supplying information of the enemy's dispositions and intentions. Not least in importance, they had, by their ceaseless harassing activities, surrounded the Germans with a terrible atmosphere of danger and hatred which ate into the confidence of the leaders and the courage of the soldiers.

BATTLE OF THE FALAISE–ARGENTAN POCKET

During the first week of August, the completeness of the enemy collapse on his western flank was such that my best hopes were realized and we were presented with the opportunity of operating toward the rear of his forces in Normandy to effect an encirclement. I felt that the chances of delivering a knockout blow there were so favorable that, despite our need for the Brittany ports, I was unwilling to detach for their capture major forces from the main armies fighting in Normandy. Into the ranks of the German Seventh Army and Panzer Group West had been drawn the cream of the enemy forces in Western Europe. Our tactics must again be adapted to take advantage of the enemy's reactions. The encirclement and destruction of these armies would afford us complete freedom of action throughout France. Therefore it was decided virtually to turn our backs upon Brittany. The VIII Corps of the Third Army alone would be left with the task of reducing Brittany ports, while the remainder of our troops, supported by the maximum weight of our air effort, could concentrate on the annihilation of the main body of the enemy.

XV Corps of the Third Army, striking south on the left flank of VIII Corps, occupied the towns of Mayenne and Laval on 6 August, and our plan was for this corps to advance thence to the east, supported by XII Corps and XX Corps as these became operational. From Le Mans a spearhead was to turn northward, advancing through Alençon toward Argentan. At the same time the Canadian First Army would continue its thrust on Falaise with a view to an eventual link-up with the Americans at Argentan, thus drawing a net around the bulk of the enemy forces to the west. Meanwhile the British Second Army and US First Army would close in from the north and west respectively.

Battle of Falaise–Argentan pocket

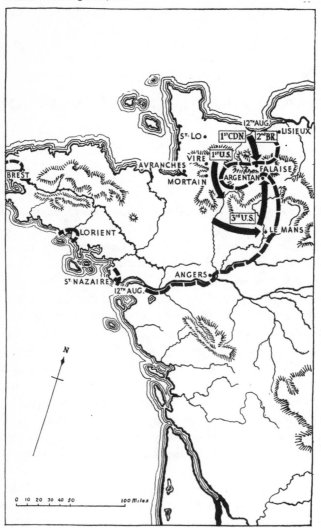

Our greatest difficulty and danger in the execution of this plan lay in the problem of supply to the Third Army. General Patton's lightning armored thrusts, exploiting the enemy's open flank, had already imposed upon our Services of Supply an immense burden. This was successfully shouldered only by dint of gallant and unceasing efforts by the personnel of the transport columns, the capacity of which was heavily strained. Moreover, because of the enemy's stubborn resistance in the Brittany ports, these supplies had to be brought from the beaches and from Cherbourg all the way down the west side of the Cotentin and through our still narrow corridor at Avranches.

It was the precarious nature of this supply route that now dictated the enemy's strategy, a strategy which, while initially it appeared sound, ultimately helped us to accomplish our object of shattering the two German armies in Normandy. As has been shown, the arrival in the Caen sector of infantry reinforcements from east of the Seine at the end of July enabled the enemy to move armor toward the Vire, to prevent an immediate collapse of his entire front when our breakthrough was achieved west of St-Lô. This armor was now massed in the Mortain area and brought under unified command, with the intention of driving westward through Avranches to the coast and thus cutting off the US Third Army from its supply bases. This was the first occasion since the commencement of the campaign two months earlier that the enemy had been able to assemble his armor into a strong striking force of the traditional panzer type; and it was destined to be his last panzer offensive until von Rundstedt launched his desperate thrust from the Siegfried Line against the First Army on 16 December. The group assembled east of Mortain for the drive on Avranches consisted of the 1st SS, 2nd SS, 2nd and 116th Panzer Divisions, with elements of the 17th SS Panzer Grenadier Division, and supporting infantry: a formidable force. The importance which the enemy attached to the operation was shown by the withdrawal of his long-range bombers from night mine-laying off the beaches (almost their sole employment since 6 June) for use in support of the ground thrust.

The attack was launched on 7 August, while other elements of the Seventh Army counter-attacked at Vire to safeguard the flanks of the armored drive. General Bradley had correctly estimated the enemy intentions, had taken his own dispositions in ample time, and had no concern as to the result. When the blow fell, the 4th, 9th, and 30th Infantry Divisions, the 3rd Armored Division, and part of the 2nd Armored Division were near Mortain. In stern defensive battle these units of VII Corps stemmed the attack. Great assistance in smashing the enemy's spearhead was given by the rocket-firing Typhoon planes of the Second Tactical Air Force. They dived upon the armored columns, and, with their rocket projectiles, destroyed and damaged many tanks in addition to quantities of "soft-skinned" vehicles. The result of the vigorous reaction by ground and air forces was that the enemy attack was effectively brought to a halt, and a threat was turned into a great victory. For once, the weather was on our side, and conditions were ideal for our air operations. If our planes had been grounded, the enemy might have succeeded in reaching Avranches in his first rush, and this would then have forced us to depend for a time on air supply to our troops south and east of the Avranches corridor, necessarily restricting their capacity to maneuver.

Despite this check and the high losses sustained, the enemy persisted for the time being in his efforts to break through to Avranches, and the battle continued during the following days. The fierce attacks of the panzer divisions were met with stubborn resistance by US VII Corps, while our tactical air forces continued to afford magnificent support in bombing and strafing the enemy concentrations. To maintain the weight of his attack, the enemy brought up further armored reinforcements, and the fighting continued heavy and confused around the hills at Mortain. From there the Germans could look westward over the level plain across which they had hoped to drive to Avranches, and perhaps the fact that they thus had their objective within view contributed to the persistence of their efforts.

It was not until 12 August that the first signs became evident that the enemy had resigned himself to the impossibility of attaining his objective and at last was contemplating a withdrawal. As on former occasions, the fanatical tenacity of the Nazi leaders and the ingrained toughness of their men had led the Germans to cling too long to a position from which military wisdom would have dictated an earlier retreat. Already by 10 August it was difficult to see how the enemy's counter-attacks, admitted that they represented a desperate effort to stabilize temporarily a most dangerous general situation, could achieve decisive results.

By 10 August, following a conference at General Bradley's Headquarters, it was decided to seize the opportunity for encirclement offered by the enemy tactics. XV Corps of the Third Army already had pushed eastward to capture Le Mans on 9 August and had thence turned north according to plan to threaten the rear of the armored forces battling at Mortain. At the same time XX Corps drove beyond Châteaubriant toward the Loire and captured Angers on 10 August, thus effectively guarding the southern flank of our encircling movement. On 11 August XV Corps was north of the Sées–Carrouges road, and on the night of 12 August the US 5th Armored Division was in the outskirts of Argentan and the French 2nd Armored Division at Ecouche, with the 79th and 90th Infantry Divisions in support.

Meanwhile the US First Army pushed southwest from Vire against stubborn resistance while the British Second Army forced the enemy from his dominating position on Mont Pinçon (south of Aunay-sur-Odon) and on 13 August occupied Thury-Harcourt. Six days earlier, the Second Army had established a bridgehead across the Orne below Thury-Harcourt at Grimbosq, in the teeth of furious opposition. This salient was created in support of the Canadian First Army thrust down the Caen–Falaise road. Still, as ever, the Caen sector remained the most sensitive part of the front in the north, and the Allied progress was slow and dearly bought against the strongest defenses yet encountered in the campaign. The Fifth Panzer Army, replacing Armored Group West, now defended this sector. On 7 August, over 1,000 heavy bombers of the RAF were employed to soften up enemy concentrations between Caen and Bretteville, and on the following day nearly 500 heavies of the Eighth Air Force laid a carpet in front of a Canadian attack which reached Bretteville itself. The enemy fell back to the line of the Laison River between Potigny and Maizières, where he successfully held the Canadians for several days. Not until 14 August was this line broken, following a further heavy air onslaught, and on 17 August Falaise was finally occupied. From our landings in June until that day, the enemy resistance in this sector had exacted more Allied bloodshed for the ground yielded than in any other part of the campaign. Without the great sacrifices made here by the Anglo-Canadian armies in the series of brutal, slugging battles, first for Caen and then for Falaise, the spectacular advances made elsewhere by the Allied forces could never have come about.

With the Third Army forces at Argentan and the Canadians at Falaise, the stage was set for the "Battle of the Pocket," with the enemy struggling to keep open the gap between the two towns through which to extricate his forces from the west. By 13 August, the withdrawal from Mortain eastward toward Argentan was under way. Infantry reinforcements were being brought hurriedly across the Seine—five divisions crossed during the week preceding 12 August—but it was too late now for them to be able to save the situation. In the pocket, the enemy's strategy was to line the southern lip through Argentan with his armor to defend against the American forces as he extricated what he could through the gap, while a strong defensive barrier against the Canadians was established with the 12th SS Panzer and 21st Panzer Divisions at Falaise. By this means, resisting fiercely, he managed to hold open the jaws of our pincers long enough to enable a portion of his forces to escape. As usual, he concentrated on saving his armor and left the bulk of the infantry to their fate—a subject of bitter comment by prisoners from the latter units who fell into our hands. A considerable part of the 1st SS Panzer, 2nd SS Panzer, 9th SS Panzer, 12th SS Panzer, Panzer Lehr, 2nd Panzer, 9th Panzer, and 116th Panzer Divisions managed thus to get away; but the 326th, 353rd, 363rd, 271st, 276th, 277th, 89th, and part of the 331st Infantry Divisions, with some of the 10th SS Panzer and 21st Panzer Divisions, were trapped. Those armored forces which did escape, however, only did so at the cost of losing a great proportion of their equipment.

Until 17 August, there was a steady seep eastward through the gap, but then came a convulsive surge to get out on the part of all ranks; and the orderliness with which the retreat had hitherto been carried out collapsed suddenly. The 12th SS Panzer Division, aided by the other elements which had managed to escape, counter-attacked from outside the pocket to assist the remainder, but as the gap narrowed they were forced to abandon their efforts and look to their own safety as the advance of the Third Army to the Seine threatened a new trap behind them. All became chaos and confusion as the remaining forces in the pocket struggled to get out through the diminishing corridor by Trun, which was all that remained of the escape route. Road discipline among the columns fleeing toward the Seine became non-existent, and vehicles plunged madly across the open country in an effort to avoid the blocked roads. Our air forces swept down upon the choked masses of transport, and there was no sign of the Luftwaffe to offer any opposition. With the US Third Army on the Seine, the German fighter force had been compelled to retire to airfields in the east of France, too far away for them to be able now to give any assistance to the ground troops in Normandy.

Back inside the pocket, the confusion was still greater, and the destruction assumed immense proportions as our aircraft and artillery combined in pounding the trapped Germans. Allied guns ringed the ever-shrinking "killing-ground," and, while the SS elements as usual fought to annihilation, the ordinary German infantry gave themselves up in ever-increasing numbers. By 20 August the gap was finally closed near Chambois, and by 22 August the pocket was eliminated. The lovely, wooded countryside west of Argentan had become the graveyard of the army which, three months earlier, had confidently waited to smash the Allied invasion on the Normandy beaches. What was left of the Seventh and Fifth Panzer Armies was in headlong flight toward the Seine, and a further stand west of the river was impossible.

THE ADVANCE TO THE SEINE

My decision, following the collapse of the enemy's western flank at the end of July, to concentrate upon the encirclement and destruction of his forces in Normandy, and to use almost the whole of our available strength in order to attain this object, marked a considerable departure from the original Allied plan of campaign. Under this, as already explained, a primary objective had been the capture of the Brittany ports, through which it was intended to introduce the further divisions from the United States necessary to ensure the completion of the German defeat. The capture of these ports had been envisaged as a task for the Third Army as a whole, but in order to accomplish our new plans for the Normandy battle it was necessary to move the bulk of General Patton's forces eastward to carry out the great encircling movement.

The prospect of inflicting a decisive and annihilating defeat upon the Seventh Army and Panzer Group West had been so good that I had no hesitation in making my decision. If their units could be shattered in Normandy, then I knew that there was no further German force in France capable of stopping us, particularly after the Franco-American Dragoon forces landed on the Mediterranean coast on 15 August and proceeded to occupy all the attention of the German Nineteenth Army. In the event that we obtained the victory which I anticipated, the Brittany ports would be isolated without hope of relief, and they would no longer represent a vitally important factor in our build-up considerations, since our rapid advance eastward would be assured and our reinforcements could be introduced through the Channel ports nearer to the front line as these were cleared.

Events demonstrated that the decision to throw the maximum weight into the Normandy struggle rather than detach substantial forces to lay siege to the Brittany ports was fully justified. Even though the battle of the

Advance to the Seine

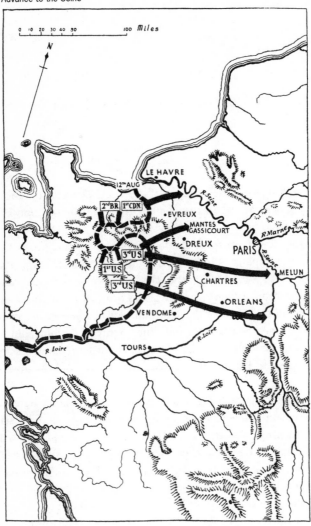

Falaise–Argentan pocket did not accomplish the utter annihilation of the German armies in Normandy, they were broken as an effective fighting force, and our way across France was opened. While Franco-American armies forced their way up the valley of the Rhône from the south, our forces swept across the north of France and through Belgium without a check by any major delaying action until they stood upon the frontiers of Germany.

The enemy, appreciating our need for the Brittany ports under the terms of our original plan, fortified them and rejected all appeals to surrender. Although the progress of our eastward advance must have made the garrisons realize that the ports they held were no longer necessary to the maintenance of our forces, they continued to hold out in their usual tenacious fashion, no doubt with the intention of proving thorns in our flesh after the manner of the British stand at Tobruk in 1941.

The desperate defense which the enemy was prepared to offer was revealed in the violent and bitter struggle to secure the capitulation of St-Malo, and still more so in the fighting which took place at Brest. By 8 August practically all resistance in the peninsula had ceased outside the ports, and our forces had taken up their positions preparatory to attempting the reduction of these strongholds. At St-Malo, the town was occupied on 14 August, but the garrison held on grimly in the Citadel, which did not capitulate until the 17th. Even after that the enemy batteries on the Ile de Cézembre, commanding the harbor approaches, continued to resist until 2 September despite bombardment by HMS *Malaya* on 31 August.

At Brest the resistance of the garrison of 30,000 men under General Ramcke was more prolonged notwithstanding the air and naval bombardments which we used to supplement the land attacks. Determined to hold on to the great port, which had been his chief Atlantic base for the U-boat campaign against Allied shipping, the enemy had to be driven back in house-to-house fighting before he finally gave in on 18 September. When at last the Allies gained possession, they found the port installations so completely wrecked as to be capable of rehabilitation only to a minor degree, and our plans for the introduction of trans-Atlantic troop convoys to the once magnificent harbor had to be abandoned.

The heavy price which the enemy's resistance had compelled us to pay for this barren prize convinced me that the further employment of large numbers of our troops to secure the reduction of the remaining enemy garrisons in Brittany—at Lorient, St-Nazaire, and Quiberon Bay—was not worth while. At that time our advance to the east had progressed so rapidly that our men were on the threshold of the enemy's homeland, and I wished to employ all the weight we could muster to deliver a knockout blow which might bring Germany to her knees before her exhausted armies could reform and renew the struggle on the Siegfried Line. Already, on 5 September, Third Army had been freed from the embarrassment of commitments in the west, far from the areas where its main forces were operating, by the transfer of VIII Corps to the newly created Ninth Army, under Lieut. Gen. W. H. Simpson. After the fall of Brest, however, this army also was moved into the line on the German border, leaving the task of containing the remaining enemy in Brittany to the French Forces of the Interior who maintained the siege during the succeeding months, under difficult conditions, with such equipment as it was in our power to provide. Although these troops might not be able to secure the capitulation of the German garrisons, I felt certain that the latter were now in no condition to adopt a policy of aggression.

While VIII Corps was occupied in Brittany, XV Corps of the Third Army pushed eastward and then north to Argentan in the move to encircle the German forces in Normandy. While the enemy was still struggling to escape through the Falaise–Argentan gap, General Patton with XII and XX Corps began his dash eastward across France north of the Loire in another wider encircling movement. As the battle of the pocket drew to a close, XV Corps also joined in this advance, leaving V Corps of the First Army to complete the task of closing the gap north of Argentan. With his main forces trapped and broken in Normandy, the enemy had no means of checking the Third Army drive, the brilliant rapidity of which was perhaps the most spectacular ever seen in modern mobile warfare. The three corps, each spearheaded by an armored division, raced headlong toward Paris and the Seine with an impetus and spirit characteristic of their leader, at once guarding the flank of the armies to the north and seeking fresh objectives of their own.

The primary objective of the Third Army advance was to deny to the enemy the use of the key lines of communication running through the Paris–Orléans gap, between the Seine and Loire Rivers. As has already been seen, the cutting of the bridges over these rivers had compelled the enemy to route part of his supplies and reinforcements from the east to Normandy through this gap, and now it was vital that we should cut it, not only to prevent the German forces in Normandy from receiving their necessary supplies, but also to bar the most convenient line of retreat from their doomed positions. We had prepared an airborne operation designed to accomplish the seizure of this strategic area ahead of the land advances, but, as events proved, General Patton's rapid moves made this unnecessary. By 17 August—two days before the earliest possible date for the airborne operation—Chartres and Dreux were captured, and the routes running to the south of Paris were virtually blocked. On the 19th the process was completed when XV Corps reached the Seine at Mantes-Gassicourt; with this important communications center in Allied hands, the roads to Normandy from Paris itself were severed. Below this point, no bridges across the river remained open, and the enemy, deprived of all hope of supplies from the southeast, had to retreat toward the ferries lower down the river as his only means of escape.

Meanwhile XII Corps, on the southern flank of the Third Army, pushed through Vendôme to reach Orléans on 17 August, by-passing the small groups of the enemy mustered at the Loire crossings upstream from Tours. Advancing parallel with XII Corps, on its left flank, was XX Corps, whose patrols reached Fontainebleau on 20 August. During the following days the tanks swept like a sickle around the southeast of Paris to Melun, driving the enemy back across the Seine. Other elements forced their way past the strongpoints defending the Loing and Yonne Rivers, and by 25 August the spearhead of XII Corps was 40 miles east of Troyes. The pursuit toward Germany continued, so that within one month of the day on which the Third Army became operational in France it had not only broken out of Normandy and through Brittany but had secured the line of the Loire and had advanced 140 miles beyond Paris to within 60 miles of the German border.

Air power again played an important part in making the rapidity of this advance possible. To each of the armored divisions was attached a fighter-bomber group belonging to XIX Tactical Air Command of the US Ninth Air Force, providing the "eyes" of the columns and smashing the enemy's troop concentration, armor, and supply system in advance of the ground forces. The closeness of the air–ground liaison in this work was one of the remarkable features of the advance and produced extraordinarily successful results. The air arm also took over the task of watching the long flank of the Loire and of preventing any dangerous concentration of the enemy there. Strafing and bombing of the small parties of Germans prevented their coalescing into an effective force, and the Third Army was thus able to pursue its advance untrammeled by the necessity of detaching troops to protect its flank.

The chief difficulty in the drive eastward arose not so much from the armed opposition encountered as from the problems of supply. Already at the beginning of August, when General Patton's men were overrunning the interior of Brittany, the necessity of transporting from Cherbourg and the beaches the gasoline, ammunition, and other supplies needed to maintain the flying armored columns had, as previously mentioned, imposed a severe strain upon our supply organization. Now that the spearheads were far on their way across France to the east, these difficulties were multiplied a hundredfold. With the Brittany ports either wrecked or remaining in German hands, all the materials of war had still to pass through the overworked Normandy bases. As the Third Army neared the Seine, truck transportation became utterly inadequate to cope with the situation, and we were compelled to have recourse to air lift, by troop carrier planes supplemented by heavy bombers, in order to enable the speed of the advance to be maintained. It was at first planned to allot planes for this task sufficient to lift an average of 1,000 tons per day to the Third Army forward bases, but when the capture of Dreux rendered the projected airborne operation in the Paris–Orléans gap unnecessary, this figure was increased to 2,000 tons per day.

Invaluable as this air lift proved, however, the use of the planes for such a purpose was inevitably attended by other drawbacks. The required numbers could only be provided by withdrawing craft from the newly created First Allied Airborne Army. This army had been instructed to prepare for operations, not only to seize the Paris–Orléans gap, but also to assist in crossing the Seine and the Somme should the enemy attempt a stand on the lines of the rivers, and later in breaching the Siegfried Line and in crossing the Rhine. Because of the obligation of making ready for these undertakings, the withdrawing of the planes caused considerable embarrassment to the Airborne Army's commander, Lieut. Gen. L. H. Brereton, whose program of training was thereby interrupted. He justly pointed out that there was a risk that continued cargo carrying would render the troop-carrier commands unfit for a successful airborne operation. Since the procedure and training required for the two functions were in many respects diametrically opposed, combined exercises by airborne troops and the air transport personnel were of the utmost importance. I consider, however, that my decision to use the planes for ground resupply purposes was justified by the fact that thereby the speed of our armies' advances was maintained, and as a consequence of this the projected airborne operations in France were rendered unnecessary.

When our troops had reached the Seine at Melun below and Mantes-Gassicourt above the city, the position of the German garrison in Paris became intolerable. Not only were they faced with a threat of encirclement, but the Allies were at Versailles, threatening a frontal attack. Within the city, the police went on strike and defied the German authorities when the latter laid siege to the Prefecture of Police on the Ile-de-la-Cité on 19 August. The traditional barricades appeared in the streets, the resistance movement came into the open, and for over a week a strange, skirmishing battle was fought through the city. While General von Choltitz, the German commander, made no attempt to destroy the bridges or other installations, a truce to enable the garrison of 10,000 men to withdraw broke down, and the enemy troops retired into the hotels and public buildings which they had turned into strongpoints.

For the honor of being the first Allied troops to re-enter Paris, the French 2nd Armored Division was brought up from the Argentan sector where it had formed part of the Third Army spearhead in the original encircling move resulting in the battle of the pocket. On 24 August the division's tanks were in the outskirts of the city, and on 25 August their commander, General Leclerc, received the surrender of the German commander. During the past four years this division had fought its way from Lake Chad, across the torrid wastes of the Sahara, to play a notable part in the victorious Tunisian campaign, had been brought to England, and had come thence to assist in the liberation of Metropolitan France. For these men to accept in Paris the surrender of the enemy, under whose dominion their country had lain for so long, was a fitting triumph in the odyssey which took them from Central Africa to Berchtesgaden.

Meanwhile, following the XV Corps thrust to the Seine at Mantes-Gassicourt on 19 August, the 79th Infantry Division had established the first bridgehead across the river at the nearby village of Rollebois on 20 August. The remainder of the Corps proceeded to press down the west bank in an endeavor to deny to the enemy the lower crossings and thus to cut off the only remaining escape routes of the elements which had struggled through the jaws of the Falaise–Argentan gap. In this operation our forces encountered stiffening resistance as they advanced, and at Elbeuf the enemy made a desperate stand to guard his last ferries as the remainder of his beaten army streamed across the river.

Following the elimination of the Falaise pocket, the US First Army took over from the Third Army the forces attacking northward toward the mouth of the Seine, while the British and Canadians closed in from the west. Day by day the enemy-held territory west of the river shrank. The Canadians having overcome fierce resistance in Cabourg and other coastal strongpoints, the enemy attempted a delaying action on the line of the Touques River. But that barrier was forced on 24 August, and, supported by the naval guns off-shore, the eastward advance continued. Evreux had fallen on the preceding day, and now Lisieux was cleared. On 25 August Elbeuf was captured, and by the 30th the last remaining pockets had been eliminated; apart from the beleaguered garrisons in Brittany, no German soldier remained west of the Seine who was not in Allied hands. Our bridgeheads were linked up along the whole length of the river, and our forces were pouring over in continued pursuit. The enemy's disorganization was such that any attempt to make a stand on the eastern bank was out of the question, particularly with the Third Army providing yet a further threat to his line of retreat. Once again, therefore, the accomplishments of our ground forces had rendered unnecessary a projected airborne operation designed to facilitate the overcoming of a potentially difficult obstacle. The battle of western France was over, and the liberation of the entire country had been assured. On 31 August General Hans Eberbach, commander of the ill-fated German Seventh Army, was captured with his staff while at breakfast at Amiens.

That the enemy was able to extricate a considerable portion of his forces via the few crossings left to him following our advance to Elbeuf was due to the skill with which he organized his system of ferries and pontoons. These had been established earlier, following our bombing of the bridges, as a means of transporting supplies and reinforcements to Normandy, and now they were to prove invaluable as a means of escape. Some of the pontoons were cunningly hidden under camouflage against the banks by day to avoid detection from the air, and then swung across the stream at night. By such means, 27,000 troops were transported over the river at a single crossing in three days.

Nevertheless, the losses sustained by the Germans at the Seine were enormous. The dense concentrations of tanks and vehicles along the roads leading to the crossings afforded ideal targets for strafing and bombing attacks from the air, and whole columns were annihilated thus. On the river itself, during the seven days preceding 23 August when the exodus was at its peak, 166 barges were destroyed, 10 probably destroyed and 116 damaged, and 3 large river steamers were sunk. Over 2,000 sorties a day were flown by aircraft of AEAF on these missions, while hundreds of planes of the Strategic Air Forces added their weight to the attacks. These attacks were not carried out entirely without opposition, for since the beginning of the battle of the Falaise pocket the Luftwaffe had come up in greater strength than for some time past in a desperate effort to assist the German ground forces. The enemy suffered severely in this air effort, however, and the losses sustained—coupled with the effects of the Third Army's thrust eastward which necessitated a rapid withdrawal to more distant bases on the part of the German fighter squadrons—were such as to produce a marked decline in the scale of the air opposition subsequently encountered.

Although the rush crossing of the lower Seine, planned to be made by 21 Army Group and the US First Army in phase with the Third Army advance through the Paris–Orléans gap, had been somewhat delayed by the stubborn nature of the enemy's rearguard actions, the elimination of the last German pocket west of the river nevertheless marked the completion of a great victory. The German Seventh Army and the Fifth Panzer Army had been decisively defeated, and into the debacle had been drawn the bulk of the fighting strength of the First and Fifteenth Armies. Since our landings on 6 June, of the enemy's higher commanders, three field marshals, and one army commander had been dismissed or incapacitated by wounds, and one army commander, three corps commanders, fifteen divisional commanders, and one fortress commander had been killed or captured.

The enemy's losses in men and equipment since the commencement of the campaign had been enormous. Of his panzer divisions, the equivalent of five had been destroyed and a further six severely mauled. The equivalent of twenty infantry divisions had been eliminated and twelve more (including three crack parachute divisions) had been badly cut up. One parachute and two infantry divisions were trapped in Brittany and another infantry division was isolated in the Channel Islands.

By 25 August the enemy had lost, in round numbers, 400,000 killed, wounded, or captured, of which total 200,000 were prisoners of war. One hundred and thirty-five thousand of these prisoners had been taken since the beginning of our breakthrough on 25 July. Thirteen hundred tanks, 20,000 vehicles, 500 assault guns, and 1,500 field guns and heavier artillery pieces had been captured or destroyed, apart from the destruction inflicted upon the Normandy coast defenses.

The German Air Force also had taken a fearful beating. Two thousand three hundred and seventy-eight aircraft had been destroyed in the air and 1,167 on the ground, in addition to 270 probably destroyed and 1,028 probably damaged in the air. These figures are all the more remarkable when one considers the depleted strength of the Luftwaffe and the feebleness of its attempts to counter the Allied operations.

By the end of August the morale of the enemy, as revealed in the prisoners who passed through the Allied cages, was distinctly lower than it had been a month earlier. A lack of determination was particularly noticeable among the infantry, whose outlook, for the most part, was one of bewilderment and helplessness. This state of mind was produced by the rapidity of the Allies' movements, their overwhelming superiority in equipment (both on the ground and in the air), and by the Germans' own losses of arms and transport which had left them without the necessary means of mounting an adequate defense. Our air strafing attacks had especially contributed toward breaking the enemy's spirit. The great majority of the enlisted men from the ordinary infantry divisions stated that they were glad to be out of the war, but the élite of the SS formations still retained something of their former arrogant self-confidence. Many of the senior officers were now prepared to recognize the inevitability of defeat, but the younger ones, in whom the Nazi spirit was strongest, still proclaimed the invincibility of the German cause. The army as a whole, despite its losses, had clearly not yet reached the stage of mass morale collapse, and, as events subsequently showed, the escaping elements were still capable, when given a pause for breath, of renewing the struggle with all their old determination on the threshold of the Fatherland. Of the generals participating in the Normandy campaign, it is interesting to note that all appeared on the list prepared by the Russians of those guilty of atrocities in the east; it was not likely that surrender would be forthcoming from such men. In fact, although we might have reached the military conditions of 1918, the political conditions which produced the German collapse in that year were still remote.

Behind the strategic reasons for our success lay the many factors embodied in the excellence of the Allied teamwork. This, as in the Mediterranean campaigns, again demonstrated its ability, extending through all services, to overcome the most adverse conditions. Despite difficulties due to the enforced separation of commanders and the burden of maintaining signal communications over long distances and in rapidly changing situations, the command system, based upon complete inter-Allied confidence, functioned smoothly throughout the campaign.

In assessing the reasons for victory, one must take into account not only the achievements in the field but the care and foresight which was applied to the preparations before D Day. It was to the meticulous care in planning and preparation by my staff, supported resolutely in all important aspects by the Combined Chiefs of Staff, that we owed such essential factors as the degree of surprise achieved in our landings, the excellence and sufficiency of our amphibious equipment, and the superb organization which lay behind the miraculous achievements of our supply and maintenance services. While it is true that we had hoped that the tactical developments of the first few days would yield us the territory south and southeast of Caen, so suitable for the construction of necessary airfields and for exploitation of our strength in armor, the fact remains that in the broad strategic development we attained our anticipated line of D plus 90 two weeks prior to that date and in substantial accordance with our planned strategic program. Moreover, I am convinced that without the brilliant preparatory work of our joint air forces—a belief in the effectiveness of which was the very cornerstone of the original invasion conception—the venture could never logically have been undertaken.

The greatest factor of all, however, lay in the fighting qualities of the soldiers, sailors, and airmen of the United Nations. Their valor, stamina, and devotion to duty had proved beyond praise, and continued to be so as the Battle of France gave place to the Battle of Germany.

THE BUILD-UP AND THE
ALLIED NAVIES

The landing in Northwest Europe being the largest amphibious operation ever undertaken, the problem of supply to the armies on the far shore entailed an organization of unprecedented magnitude and complexity. I have already indicated the obstacles which faced my logistical planning staff during the months of preparatory effort. There was a struggle to acquire the necessary shipping and landing craft, a struggle to collect the requisite tugs, a struggle against time to prepare the novel devices, such as the various elements of the artificial harbors upon which we so greatly relied; eventually there was the herculean pre-D-Day task of assembling the vast armada in the ports of southern England in such a manner that it might be loaded and sailed to schedule and yet achieve the seemingly impossible in escaping the attention of the enemy. Events were to show the success with which these and many other difficulties were overcome. I must also acknowledge the work of my Chief Administrative Officer, General Gale, of whose abilities I had received full evidence during the campaign in North Africa and Italy, but whose achievements in that theater were dwarfed by his accomplishments in the invasion and liberation of Northwest Europe.

When the anxieties of D Day were over, the burden of responsibility of those in charge of our logistical services was in no way lightened. Some problems might be solved by experience, but new ones were ever arising. The smooth running of the shuttle service across the Channel, the efficient transfer of supplies to the armies over the beaches and through the ports, the protection of the supply routes, and safeguarding of the packed anchorages as the build-up progressed, remained the responsibility of the Allied Naval Commander, Admiral Ramsay. His untimely death on 2 January 1945 was a great loss to the Allied cause. The handling of the large number of varied craft employed was a most praiseworthy feat on the part of Admiral Ramsay and the Task Force Commanders responsible for the execution of his orders. Over 5,000 ships and craft were employed in the actual assault, and in addition over 2,000 Allied merchantmen, with an aggregate displacement of some 4,000,000 tons, had to be prepared and fitted into the complex plan of the subsequent build-up. These merchant ships presented a peculiarly delicate problem, as the 70,000 men who sailed them were not under direct naval discipline. Nevertheless, their crews surrendered many of the age-old privileges of the sailor in their willingness to become part of the great invasion machine, and during the months following D Day they served the cause with consistent courage and devotion to duty.

The lightness of our losses at sea and in the anchorages compared with the number of ships involved is the best measure of the success with which the Allied navies kept the seas and held the enemy at bay from the invasion area. Behind this success lay in part the experience gained in the expedition to North Africa in 1942, but off France, operating in much more difficult waters, the problems facing them were often new and always far more complex than those encountered earlier. In this operation we staked our all in many respects upon unknown factors, and to the skill with which the navies met the unexpected our initial victory was largely due. New enemy defense devices and weather of unprecedented foulness even for the capricious English Channel alike failed to overcome this ingenuity and determination. Such adverse factors might prevent our supply from attaining the theoretical maximum, but from D plus 2 onward, except for the great storm later in June, there was never any real danger of our maintenance failing, and the armies never went short of food for men or ammunition for guns. On 1 July the Chief Administrative Officer was able to report that the commanders in the field had complete freedom of action as far as supply arrangements were concerned.

By D plus 5 we had in the main successfully overcome the initial struggle to get the beachheads organized. We had cleared the enemy from all the beaches; the Allies had linked up along the whole of the invasion coastline; the first units of the artificial harbors were in position and the build-up forged ahead steadily. The enemy was still in a position to bring gunfire to bear upon the beaches and anchorages on either flank; his coastal forces were massing at Cherbourg and Le Havre to prey upon the approaches; and his aircraft were nightly engaged in laying mines. It was, moreover, not only with the human antagonist that our navies and mercantile marines had to contend. The weather during June 1944, was the worst experienced for that month during the present century. The gales which had threatened us with disaster on D Day itself continued to hamper our operations throughout subsequent weeks, culminating in the great storm of 19–22 June, the effects of which were so serious as to imperil our very foothold upon the Continent. After the gales came the fogs of July, which once more held up the cross-Channel shuttle services. Through all this the perseverance of the seamen kept the armies in the field.

The principal handicap to the build-up after D Day sprang from the shortage of landing and ferry craft following the serious losses among the mines and obstacles during the assault. Also, apart from the invaluable dukws,★ many of the minor landing craft proved too lightly built for continuous service in waters as rough as we experienced, and this was particularly true of the rhino ferries, the serviceability of which rarely rose above 50%. Another major worry arose from the losses we suffered in motor transport ships from mechanical defects and enemy action.

To overcome these difficulties we were compelled to resort to "drying out" LSTs and coasters on the beaches. Such a process had previously been thought too dangerous to attempt, but having been adopted as a desperate expedient on D plus 1, it proved so successful as to be continued as a regular practice. The only drawback was a slower turn-around and consequent tendency for shipping to accumulate off the far shore.

By thus profiting from the lessons of experience, the Allied navies and mercantile marine were able to land over 500,000 men by D plus 9, and the millionth man stepped ashore in France on D plus 28. Apart from the personnel landed, a million tons of stores and nearly 300,000 vehicles were put ashore by D plus 38. At the end of August, when the German armies were in flight eastward beyond the Seine, but while we were still basically dependent for our build-up on the beaches, Cherbourg, and the artificial harbors, the Allied armies under my command exceeded two million men. For them over three million tons of stores had been brought across the Channel, together with over 400,000 vehicles.

Thus, despite the trials of wind and weather and the persistent attacks of an ingenious enemy, the necessary rate of reinforcement to our land forces was maintained. Our build-up outstripped that of the Germans, deceived as they were by our latent threat to the Pas-de-Calais and hampered by our air attacks upon their communications.

A great part of the men and supplies were landed over the beaches by the splendid effort of naval and engineer personnel who handled this difficult operation. Despite the delays occasioned by unfavorable weather, the rate of discharge over the beaches was maintained at a high level. At Omaha beach, for example, the daily average of supplies unloaded from D Day to 30 September was 10,000 tons, the daily rate reaching nearly 12,000 tons for the critical period of July and August. At the smaller Utah beach, the daily average from D Day through September was 5,000 tons, and during this period upward of 750,000 men disembarked at this one point. Since Cherbourg did not begin to function in volume until August, and only approached a 10,000-ton daily average in September, the importance of the beaches to our supply is easy to appreciate.

Another factor of importance was the novel expedient upon which we staked much of our chances of success, the artificial harbors. Although our

★ Amphibious trucks.

plan of operations called for the seizure of Cherbourg at an early date, we realized that the Germans might leave the port in such a condition as to preclude its full use for many weeks following its capture. The Mulberry artificial harbors were judged essential to ensure the discharge of cargo, under conditions that would be relatively independent of weather during the crucial early stages of the campaign. When the time came for the execution of the scheme, the Mulberries were subjected to strains of a severity far greater than we had believed likely. Nevertheless, although the American harbor had eventually to be written off as a total loss, the British Mulberry, which suffered less, was repaired and continued to function. It was of tremendous aid to our operations during the summer.

In the months of continued experiment and feverish constructional activity following the Quebec Conference in August 1943, when the outline of the harbor project was approved, the Mulberry scheme occasioned me and my staff many a headache. Some of the prototype units evolved promptly sank when tried out at sea (although their models had behaved excellently in the storms of experimental tanks), labor difficulties caused hold-ups in construction, and securing the necessary tug allocations was in doubt up to the last moment. Confusion, moreover, was occasioned by the division of responsibility between the Admiralty, the War Office, and the British Ministry of Supply. The Minister of Labour performed the miracle of raising the necessary workmen from a labor-exhausted Britain, however, and the construction of the huge concrete caissons in pits beside the rivers, into which on completion they were floated by breaching the retaining banks, was typical of the ingenuity and resource by which difficulties were met and overcome. Not least of our anxieties was the fear that the enemy should learn of our intentions, particularly in view of the large amount of casual labor which had to be employed, but events proved that the secret was well kept, a remarkable achievement considering the thousands of men and women who had a hand in the work of construction. Indeed, so complete was the ignorance of the enemy as to our intentions, and so lacking was he in air reconnaissance when the plans were being put into effect, that it was not until mid-July, when the scheme was practically completed, that he realized the existence and purpose of the Mulberry. Then he failed to appreciate its true significance, assuming it to be an improvised measure forced upon us by the extent of his demolitions at Cherbourg and the ravages of the storms.

Under the final scheme, five sheltered anchorages, known as Gooseberries, where landing craft could operate when an on-shore wind might otherwise hamper their unloading, were to be constructed with sunken blockships, one Gooseberry to each of the five assault beaches. Two of these anchorages were subsequently to be expanded into complete Mulberry harbors, each the size of Dover and costing some $100,000,000. A Mulberry was to consist of a breakwater of sunken blockships, supplemented with sunken concrete caissons, each 200 feet long, known as a Phoenix. Within the shelter thus provided, LSTs and coasters could discharge their cargoes on to floating Whale piers, so constructed that at low tide they would rest firmly on the rock foreshore. Seven miles of pier with 15 pierheads were planned. Outside the ring of Phoenix caissons and Corncob blockships was to be a further floating breakwater of 200-foot steel Bombardon units, designed to provide a sheltered anchorage for Liberty ships, within which they might transfer their cargoes to ferry craft. The enclosed area at each Mulberry was to extend some two miles in length and one mile in width. In all, 400 units, totalling 1,500,000 tons, had to be towed across the Channel, and 160 tugs were required to make 35 heavy tows daily in order to complete the installation by the target date of D plus 18.

The accurate and successful planting of the Mulberry units represented a triumph of skill for the two navies respectively responsible for the installations off the American and British beaches. The sinking of the Gooseberry blockships began on D plus 1, and by the following day the first Mulberry tows, which had set out on the morning of D Day, had arrived off the French shores. The installation of the harbors in acutely congested waters, under enemy action, during the early stages of our whole gigantic enterprise was a task of extreme complexity, but it was expeditiously and accurately carried out, and in the course of the two weeks following 6 June the ports rapidly took shape. By the morning of D plus 5 the blockship breakwaters in both harbors were completed, and all the Gooseberries were in full use except that at Utah beach, work on which had been hindered by enemy gunfire. By D plus 10 all the Gooseberries were completed and the Mulberries 50% so. The towing of the huge, cumbersome caissons and the sections of piers and pierheads was considerably hampered by the continued bad weather, and nearly a third of the Whale units was lost in transit through this cause. By 19 June, however, lengths of pier were already in use; the Mulberries as a whole were about 90% completed, and over 2,000 tons of stores a day were being handled in the British harbor alone.

On that day, 19 June, broke the great storm which at one time seemed certain to bring all our work to disaster. The weather had been unsettled since D Day, but the on-shore gale which now blew up was the worst known in June for 40 years past. The Mulberries took the full force of the mountainous seas driven by the gale, and the situation was all the worse since the storm had not been expected and no forecasts of it were received. All unloading, except for a few ammunition and fuel cargoes which were taken off by intrepid dukw crews, had to be suspended, and shipping in the congested anchorages was soon in difficulties. The storm continued for four days. During that time, tows caught in passage were lost, and craft and ships off the beaches dragged their anchors and were dashed ashore. To add to our troubles, the enemy's new Oyster mines were activated by the movement of the waters and caused further casualties. By 21 June the Mulberries themselves began to disintegrate, particularly the US installation, which was in an even more exposed position off St-Laurent than the British one at Arromanches. The Bombardons of the outer breakwaters broke adrift and sank; the Phoenix caissons shifted; and the angry seas poured through the gaps, pounding the ferry craft against the piers and smashing them to pieces. Only the blockships saved the situation from becoming one of complete disaster.

During 22 June the fury of the gale gradually abated, but the seas continued to run high and hinder the work of salvage. After the Mulberries had been so near completion and the beach organization had got into its stride, it was appalling to contemplate the damage wrought by the gale. Despite the gallant efforts of the tug crews and other personnel to save the shipping, efforts which cost them heavy loss of life, some 800 craft were stranded on the beaches, and the greater part of these suffered damage. Wreckage was strewn over the sands along the whole invasion coastline. Some 600 craft were eventually refloated on the 8 July spring tides and a further 100 a fortnight later, but the resulting shortage of ferry craft was a serious blow which hampered us throughout the summer.

Of the Mulberries themselves, that at St-Laurent was so shattered as to be irreparable. Due to the scour and sea action, the main Phoenix breakwater at St-Laurent was broken and the blockships had sunk some 10 to 12 feet below their original level. At Arromanches the Phoenix breakwater would be made good, at least temporarily, and the line of blockships had held. The great value of these latter was such that on 23 June, while the seas still ran high, 4,500 tons of much needed supplies were unloaded under the shelter still afforded. The outer Bombardon breakwaters were completely wrecked and had to be abandoned at both anchorages.

On 26 June it was decided that in view of the damage sustained the original plan for the St-Laurent Mulberry would have to be abandoned, although the remaining blockships could be strengthened to provide a shallow anchorage for barges and small craft. The Arromanches Mulberry, having suffered less, could be repaired and completed; moreover, by decking in the caissons and making other modifications, it was thought that it could be made to last until October or possibly longer. Salvaged material from St-Laurent was available to complete the three damaged piers. This scheme for the rehabilitation and winterization of the Arromanches harbor was approved and the work was at once commenced.

In the accomplishment of the work I was given loyal and effective help by the British authorities, although the difficulties facing them were legion. The supply of labor was a particularly serious problem at a time when the repair of V-bombed houses in London drew heavily upon the resources. US general service troops and naval construction personnel were made available to assist in this respect. By great efforts and sacrifices on the part of all concerned, the work was accomplished. Although the winterization modifications had yet to be finished, the harbor was virtually completed and the storm damage repaired by 20 July. At the end of that month nearly 4,000 men, over 400 vehicles, and over 11,000 tons of supplies were disembarked within its shelter during a single period of 24 hours. Throughout the summer and autumn the achievements of the Mulberry exceeded our best hopes, for, although the planned rate of supply discharge was 6,000 tons a day, the actual average, from 20 June to 1 September, was 6,765 tons.

The course of our military fortunes was to make the utmost demands upon the means upon which we were so completely dependent for supply. Although by September we had defeated the enemy decisively in Normandy, he, knowing our necessities, clung obstinately to the western ports of St-Nazaire and Lorient, as well as to the Quiberon Bay area (which we had planned to develop into a major harbor), while demolishing the installations at Cherbourg and Brest so thoroughly that it required many weeks' work before they could be restored to full capacity. Under these circumstances, the open beaches and the Mulberry continued to be the main channels of supply to our armies during the period when their drive eastward across France forced logistical demands to a peak. It was not until Antwerp had been captured and the Scheldt made safe for our shipping that the beach installations and the Mulberry became superfluous. Throughout the summer of 1944 they represented an essential factor in the success of our operations. Without them our armies could not have been adequately maintained in the field, and the men who worked them with so much gallantry and devotion deserve the gratitude of liberated Europe for their share in our victory.

Of the natural ports which fell into our hands before the opening of Antwerp, only Cherbourg, third biggest port of France, had a capacity that would appreciably lighten our supply problems. The small harbors along the Norman coast, such as Ouistreham, Courseulles, and Port-en-Bessin, had their value, particularly during the early days of the campaign, but their capacities were small, and the same was true of Granville, St-Malo, Morlaix, and the other harbors uncovered by our subsequent drive south through the Cotentin and into Brittany. Brest, when it eventually fell to us after stubborn resistance, was so fully destroyed that, in view of its remoteness from the main battle front, it was considered useless to attempt any major rehabilitation.

Cherbourg, however, represented a cardinal factor in our basic logistical plans. The sea and airborne landings in the Cotentin, as has been shown, had been expressly designed to facilitate its early capture so that we might use its valuable harbor as an all-weather base through which to introduce supplies. The enemy, on the other hand, fully appreciated the importance to us of an early seizure of the port, and when his attempt to defend the city failed he undertook the task of rendering the harbor unusable with typical Teutonic thoroughness.

Cherbourg's commander surrendered on 26 June, and the US Port Clearance party began the work of tidying-up on the following day, although nests of resistance among the dockyards were yet unsubdued and the guns of the breakwater forts prevented mine sweeping. While certain major facilities survived, such as the breakwaters enclosing the great anchorage and some of the drydocks, the extent of the enemy demolitions presented a formidable task to the clearance personnel. Seventy-five per cent of the cranes had been destroyed, over a dozen vessels had been sunk to block the dock entrances, and quantities of every kind of mine had been sown. Such equipment as was not destroyed had been immobilized by the removal of vital parts and the skilled labor had been evacuated.

The task of mine sweeping was fraught with difficulties and dangers, even when the forts had been reduced, but by 19 July the port came into use and unloading began. At first the disembarkation of stores was mainly by dukws, but through the summer work on the harbor installations went on at a feverish pace. By the end of August, Cherbourg was handling an average of over 10,000 tons a day, and by the beginning of October, when the work of reconstruction was completed, its capacity was as great as, if not greater than, had been the case before the war.

The cross-Channel supply of fuel for our armies in Operation Overlord constituted a special problem. Although the lines of communication over which the fuel had to be brought, from the United Kingdom to the battle front, were not as long as those to North Africa, the rate of consumption was far higher. During the assault phase we had naturally to rely upon canned gasoline, but by 3 July bulk supply was being introduced by ship-to-shore pipeline from tankers to storage dumps, thus affording a considerable saving of time and tonnage. For the period when the armies had attained the strength to enable them to break out from their lodgement area and sweep across France, however, as well as for the later stages of the campaign against Germany, novel devices were employed, the experimental character of which was second in daring only to the artificial harbors project.

The scheme, developed jointly under naval and military auspices, was known by the name of Pluto. In order to save shipping, to increase the rate of supply, and to prevent interference with the armies' maintenance by bad weather, submarine pipelines were to be laid across the Channel. The pipes were of two types: the Hais and the Hamel, each of which was 3 inches in diameter and expected to discharge 250 tons of gasoline a day. The first lines were planned from the Isle of Wight to the vicinity of Cherbourg—a distance of 56 miles. It was hoped to have ten lines operative by D plus 75, giving 2,500 tons of gasoline daily.

As was to be expected with so experimental a scheme, many obstacles were encountered. The laying of the lines was a hazardous process, and the storms of June and July repeatedly interrupted the work. The first Hais line was completed by 12 August, and a second by the 21st, but leaks and stoppages resulted in further delay before either line could be operated, bad weather preventing clearance work. Subsequently, however, these teething troubles were overcome and further lines were laid over the shorter route from Dungeness to Boulogne. These provided our main supplies of fuel during the winter and spring campaigns.

For the protection of our cross-Channel shipping routes—and hence for the successful maintenance of the armies in France—we were dependent upon the ceaseless work of the Allied navies, assisted by RAF Coastal Command. These kept constant watch, to such good effect that the shipping losses which we sustained due to direct enemy action were extremely small in proportion to the vast tonnage involved.

The enemy concentrated his main efforts against the beaches and anchorages. From landward, although our penetrations soon ensured the freedom of the central beaches from artillery fire, the flank ones remained objects of attack. The reduction of the Cotentin Peninsula removed this menace on the west, but Sword beach—the easternmost of the British sector—continued to be exposed to enemy shelling as well as to attacks by E-boats, explosive motor boats, and human torpedoes based in the Seine area. The resultant losses were considerably greater than those in other sectors, and, after restrictions had been repeatedly imposed for these reasons, the decision was taken on 13 July to abandon the beach permanently for unloading purposes.

To counter the menace of enemy shelling and to afford support to our troops advancing inland, the navies carried out many heavy bombardments of the enemy batteries, defensive positions, communications, and supply dumps. On the eastern flank the configuration of the ground made observation difficult, but the armies were warm in their praise of the support given to them by the heavy naval guns. The characteristic ingenuity of the Navy was seen in the device of rocking the ships to raise the angle of the guns so that they might engage targets beyond normal range; and the effectiveness of the firing was seen when the capture of the strongly casemated battery at Houlgate (which had been primarily responsible for the shelling of Sword beach) revealed that three out of its four guns had sustained direct hits. The ships intervened vigorously in the battles ashore, both to break up enemy concentrations for counter-attacks and to supplement the barrages preparatory to our own advances, and this intervention was continued until the breakthrough came at the end of July and the enemy retired eastward.

During the early stages of the campaign the enemy made some daylight attacks upon the anchorages with bomber and fighter-bomber planes, but these proved very ineffective and were soon abandoned. Night raiding (sometimes in conjunction with surface craft attacks) continued and caused casualties. We found in this connection that, although naval anti-aircraft fire was good, fire discipline was not easy to enforce among the large and diverse fleet of merchant shipping assembled for the build-up. Blind firing without orders resulted in the loss of some friendly planes, and eventually the Allied Naval Commander was forced to prohibit all night anti-aircraft fire by merchant ships.

Although both bombs and torpedoes were dropped by the night raiders, their chief effort was devoted to mine-laying, supplementing the activities in this respect of the surface craft based on Le Havre. The mining aircraft were awkward enemies with which to cope; they frequently operated in single sorties, up to a total of 50 a night, the planes flying in low and dropping their mines out of range of the shore defenses. Such attacks were carried out on every night but one from 6 to 30 June and took toll of our shipping by reason of their persistence.

The mines laid by the enemy off our anchorages provided the biggest problem facing the Allied navies, since they included two novel, pressure-actuated types, one of which could not be swept at all with the gear available and the other only under certain weather conditions. The task of the mine-sweeping flotillas was thus often thankless and always hazardous, for, though they detonated large numbers of mines and worked tirelessly with their accustomed bravery under often appalling weather conditions, some mines inevitably remained and our shipping necessarily suffered casualties. Serious as these losses might be, they were, nevertheless, not so heavy in proportion to the total number of ships we employed as materially to affect our build-up. The losses reached their peak in the days immediately following the great storm of 19–21 June, which had the effect of "ripening" many of the mines; but subsequently the casualty rate gradually declined. Despite the depletion of the mine-sweeper strength through the losses incurred, the development of "explosive sweeps" and the use of nets to catch drifting mines partially reduced the dangers. It was not, however, until August, when the land advances forced the enemy to abandon his air bases for others farther east that his mining activity effectively died down. The extent of the menace may be seen from the fact that by three months after D Day the number of mines swept off our invasion ports and beaches totalled one-tenth those swept in all theaters combined from the beginning of the war to 6 June.

The threat to our supply routes from enemy destroyers was virtually removed on 9 June when Force 26 met and annihilated four enemy vessels off the Ile de Batz following their interception by RAF Coastal Command aircraft. Attacks by light coastal craft, however—E- and R-boats based initially at Cherbourg and Le Havre—were carried out against the assault area with a persistence equal to that of the air-mining effort. Although the enemy never dared to interfere with our build-up by day, his craft made forays against our anchorages almost nightly from D Day onwards. A certain number of E-boats were transferred to Brest following the fall of Cherbourg, but the chief menace thereafter became concentrated in Le Havre, from which operations were directed primarily against the British anchorages. To guard against this, a protective screen was established on our eastern flank, and it was but rarely that the raiders succeeded in penetrating this barrier and destroying our shipping within. Our own coastal forces were continually engaged in repelling the enemy, and the pursuit was often followed under the guns of the hostile shore batteries. The German forces suffered severely from attrition, our close blockade effectively preventing any appreciable reinforcement. Successful air attacks were also made by Bomber Command against the docks at Le Havre, sinking a number of E-boats and other craft at their moorings. When Le Havre finally fell to our forces in September, the danger to our western Channel routes and anchorages from surface attack was practically ended.

The German fondness for war gadgets was as marked in the naval as in the military and aeronautical spheres; on one occasion the naval commander on our eastern flank reported that his protective net was "bulging with secret weapons." Among these devices, in addition to the mines already mentioned, were human torpedoes, explosive motor boats, radio–controlled glider bombs, and even an occasional V-1 flying bomb, the latter arriving probably more by accident than design. As was inevitable in our crowded anchorages, we suffered a number of casualties from these devices, used in conjunction with more orthodox weapons, but the enemy also paid heavily for his use of them. On 2/3 August, for instance, a determined attack was launched on the British anchorages by human torpedoes and explosive motor boats, under cover of diversionary air raids and E-boat assaults. We lost a destroyer, a trawler, and an LCG, while other craft were damaged; but on the German side at least 20 explosive motor boats, 30 human torpedoes, and 1 E-boat were destroyed, and 2 more human torpedoes were caught in the net.

The submarine threat proved markedly less serious than we had antici-pated. When the assault was first launched, the enemy U-boats were concentrated in the Biscay area, but at once began to move toward the Channel. RAF Coastal Command, however, had established a system of air patrols covering the whole of the Western Approaches to guard against this menace, and its operations were highly successful. U-boats approaching our supply routes were spotted, sunk, or forced to abandon their missions, and during the critical first ten days of the invasion there was no evidence of penetration by a single craft. Later on, occasional U-boats got through under cover of bad weather, but the results obtained were insignificant.

In close liaison with the air watchers, Allied naval forces maintained a constant blockade along the Biscay and Channel coasts from the Gironde to Den Helder. From the outset of the campaign the Allied naval supremacy off Western Europe was not seriously challenged, and apart from the raiding of the assault area by locally based small craft the enemy was compelled to restrict his activities to attempts by blockade runners to sneak from port to port, hugging the shores, under cover of darkness or foul weather. Several such convoys were intercepted and broken up, and by the end of the year 68 enemy vessels, from destroyers to small merchantmen, had been sunk at sea, while over 200 more had been scuttled, sunk, or immobilized in ports. Considering the enormous quantities of shipping which we employed, our own losses were negligible. By mid-July the position was sufficiently satis-factory to permit release of some US destroyers for service in other theaters, and on 25 July the Admiralty resumed general control of the Channel from Admiral Ramsay (Allied Naval Commander Expeditionary Force) who, however, retained operational authority over the actual assault area.

Against the bases in England from which our convoys sailed across the Channel the enemy made no piloted air raids, but did make some use of flying bombs. A few of these missiles which fell in the Portsmouth–Southampton area early in July hit landing-craft bases but failed to cause any damage to the shipping itself. The primary object of attack, from 13 June onwards, was always London, the bombs being employed essentially as terror weapons. Two LSTs were damaged there at Deptford docks, but there was little direct interference with our build-up, and the work of loading proceeded without undue interruption. The gigantic concrete "secret weapon" installations in the Cherbourg Peninsula and the Pas-de-Calais, designed to enable "V" missiles to be assembled and launched under conditions of immunity from Allied air attack, were captured before completion.

For our freedom from effective interference by "V" weapons we were indebted to the air forces, whose persistent attacks—first upon the experimental establishment at Peenemünde and subsequently upon the operational installations in France and the Low Countries—successfully delayed the enemy's preparations until they were too late to check our operations. The attacks against London were regarded as a serious menace and one of my tasks while I had control of all the air forces was to allot air effort to reducing the enemy scale of attack against the capital. In spite of the many tasks imposed on the air forces in connection with Overlord it was still possible to make many successful attacks on the "V" weapon organization, and the apparently large diversion of effort was in fact reduced, as far as possible, by selecting opportunities for attack when the weather was unfavorable for higher priority targets. The bombardment of London following our landings was a desperate and ill-conceived measure, for more profitable results would certainly have been achieved had the main weight of the attack even then been directed against the ports along the south coast. The enemy's vindictive hatred of the British people and his underestimation of the Londoners' powers of endurance, together with his own blind overconfidence in the effects of the new weapon, enabled us to continue our build-up and successfully to establish ourselves on the soil of France.

Our communications system was satisfactory. The Admiralty, the Royal Corps of Signals, and the British Post Office jointly achieved the feat of laying a cross-Channel cable, giving three telephone and six telegraph circuits, as early as D plus 4, and a number of further cables were subsequently installed, affording adequate signal facilities with our bases in the United Kingdom. When the breakthrough came in France at the end of July the speed of the advances imposed a heavy strain on the communications personnel. Although the spearhead units necessarily relied largely on radio, a line network of great complexity was required in their rear to cope with the amount of traffic involved. Existing civilian communications were of limited value in consequence of lack of maintenance during recent years aggravated by war destruction, and within four months of D Day the Allies laid over 100,000 circuit miles of line.

Within France, the organization of our supply system did not present any major problems until our armies achieved their breakthrough. While we were consolidating our hold upon the lodgement area, the supply dumps to maintain the forces when the fighting became mobile were steadily built up, and the coastal area from the Cotentin to Caen developed into one immense depot, the biggest in history ever assembled on an invaded territory. When the breakthrough came, however, a great strain was imposed upon the maintenance system, not through any inherent fault in that system but by reason of the unexpected circumstances under which the advances occurred. The enemy's tenacious defense of the Brittany ports and my decision to concentrate all available strength fully to exploit the opportunity for a decisive victory offered in Normandy necessitated, as already indicated, the abandonment of the original plan for these harbors to be brought rapidly into use as the main arteries through which to supply the American armies on the right flank.

This meant that we had to rely for our maintenance at a most vital period of the campaign upon the original supply lines through Cherbourg, the Arromanches Mulberry, and the Normandy beaches. Some cargoes were unloaded through the minor harbors and over the beaches of northern Brittany, but they represented only a small fraction of our total needs. The bulk of the supplies for the Third Army had to be transported by the long, roundabout route down through the Cotentin and then eastward around the German pocket resisting at Falaise and Argentan. The Third Army, when it got into its stride in the dash across France, was advancing at a speed of up to 40 miles a day, and our transport services were taxed to the limit. The incentive offered by the chance of a smashing victory, however, drove the men in whose hands the maintenance of supply rested to feats of superhuman accomplishment. In the light of the difficulties they had to overcome, it seems, when one looks back upon those amazing days, well-nigh incredible that at no period up to the time when we stood upon the threshold of Germany was the momentum of the drive retarded through lack of essential needs. The spectacular nature of the advance was due in as great a measure to the men who drove the supply trucks as to those who drove the tanks.

The three essentials were food, ammunition, and gasoline; and to get these up to the armored spearheads in as expeditious a manner as possible the system known as the "Red Ball Express" was instituted. By this, a circular one-way traffic route was established across France from the beachheads to the fighting zone and back again. All civilian and local military traffic was debarred from using the "Red Ball Highway," and along it the convoys swept at high speed day and night, in an unending stream. Similarly on the railroads, many of them single-track lines never intended for such heavy usage, the trains, each loaded to capacity, pushed eastward, travelling nose to tail in a manner that defied all the normal rules of safety.

To keep all this traffic rolling would have been impossible but for the very fine work of the Engineers, who had to contend with the damage caused not only by the enemy but by our own attacks preceding the advance. The roads were strewn with mines which had to be detected, wrecked German vehicles which had to be pushed aside, and bomb craters which had to be filled. There were bridges which had to be rebuilt and the rubble of ruined towns and villages through which paths had to be driven. On the railroads there were again bridges to be constructed as well as wrecked trains to be cleared, torn-up rails to be replaced, and the frightful chaos produced by our bombing at every major junction and marshalling yard to be remedied. So greatly had the French railroads suffered that over 900 locomotives and a third of the rolling stock used had to be shipped over from Allied sources in England. Thanks to the untiring efforts of the men and the excellence of their mechanical equipment, all this work was successfully accomplished at an unprecedented rate. Bridge-building parties especially performed remarkable feats, and work which under normal conditions would have required months was completed in a matter of days.

With the resistance offered by the retreating enemy at a minimum, fuel was a more vital requisite than ammunition. Approximately a million gallons of gasoline were needed at the front every day to enable the armored columns to maintain the headlong rate of their advance. Trucked supplies could not by themselves cope with this enormous demand, but pipelines, both for aviation and ordinary purposes, were laid in the wake of the armies from the beachhead storage tanks. Our experiences in North Africa and Italy had taught us much in the matter of pipelines, and as many as 30 miles of 6-inch pipe were now laid in a single day. By early October the system was delivering 4,500 tons of gasoline daily from the main distributing point near Paris, apart from the considerable quantities being drawn from it at other points intermediate between there and Cherbourg.

Despite all these efforts and accomplishments, however, my anxiety over the successful maintenance of supplies essential to support our continued advance increased as the lines of communication lengthened. The Third Army maintenance in particular was stretched to the limit, and, as previously described, we had to employ transport aircraft to carry over 2,000 tons a day to keep the spearheads going. The enemy's failure to make a successful stand on any of the river lines freed us momentarily from the necessity for air-borne operations which would have taken away the planes from the task of keeping the ground forces supplied, but it was evident that sooner or later such a situation would arise when we came up against the main frontier defenses of the Reich.

As will be indicated in due course, the difficulties of supply eventually forced a halt upon us when we reached Germany, but the very rapidity of our advance across France had made that inevitable. In consequence of the enemy's denial to us of the Brittany ports and the unexpected situation of having to support a dash of such length and speed entirely from our bases on the Normandy shore, only a miracle of hard work and brilliant improvisation by the supply services had carried our armored spearheads so far. Without the magnificent work performed by these men in coping with peculiarly arduous problems, the sweeping victory which liberated France would not have been possible.

THE ADVANCE FROM THE SEINE TO THE GERMAN BORDER

As our armies swept north through the Pas-de-Calais and into Belgium and east toward the German border, the size of our forces and the extent of our front made it necessary for me to take direct control of the land forces operating on the Continent. Until 1 September the command system had functioned effectively, exactly as planned and in accordance with the developments of the tactical and strategic situation. Full credit for this was due to the Commanders-in-Chief, to all Senior Commanders, and to the higher staffs of all services, who consistently worked together as an efficient Allied team. Change in the command set-up was necessary, however, due to the diverging lines of operation and the need for having a commander on each of the main fronts capable of handling, with a reasonable degree of independence, the day-to-day operations in each sector. These operations were to be guided by directives issued from my Headquarters.

Therefore, when on 1 September my operational Headquarters opened officially on the Continent and Field Marshal Montgomery's responsibility for arranging for coordination between 21 Army Group and General Bradley's forces terminated, Field Marshal Montgomery continued to command 21 Army Group which was also designated the Northern Group of Armies. As from this date General Bradley's command was known as the 12th or Central Group of Armies and consisted of the United States First Army under General Hodges, the United States Third Army under General Patton, and the United States Ninth Army under General Simpson.

The Franco-American forces coming from the south were not at this time under my control, but I planned with the approval of the Combined Chiefs of Staff to assume command of them on 15 September, when it was estimated that contact would have been securely established with the Central

Advance from the Seine to the German border

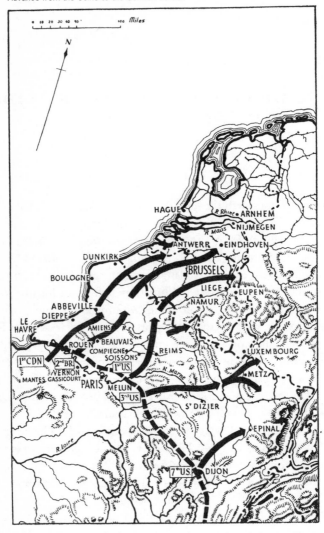

Group of Armies. Actually, first contact was reached prior to this on 11 September when troops of the French 1st Armored Division met troops of the French 2nd Armored Division in the vicinity of Sombernon, but formal command did not pass to my Headquarters until the 15th. These forces, consisting of the French First Army under General de Lattre de Tassigny and the United States Seventh Army under Lieut. Gen. Alexander E. Patch, were designated the 6th or Southern Group of Armies, under command of General (then Lieutenant-General) Jacob L. Devers.

Each of these three Groups of Armies was supported by its own Tactical Air Force. The Northern Group of Armies was accompanied by the Second Tactical Air Force under Air Marshal Sir Arthur Coningham and the Central Group of Armies by the Ninth Air Force under Lieut. Gen. (then Maj. Gen.) Vandenberg. The Southern Group of Armies had, in the advance from the south, been supported by one Fighter Group and auxiliary units of XII Tactical Air Command. When the Southern Group of Armies came under my control, this Air Command was augmented with units of the Ninth Air Force, but later the air support of the Southern Group of Armies was to be constituted as the First Tactical Air Force.

The Tactical Air Forces in support of the Army Groups reported to my headquarters through Air Chief Marshal Leigh-Mallory, while the remaining overall air control exercised by me continued as it had originally been planned in April, the United States Strategic Air Forces and the RAF Bomber Command reporting independently. Air matters were, as already stated, coordinated through my Deputy, Air Chief Marshal Tedder.

There was no change in the Naval Command system at this time, except that Admiral Ramsay's headquarters were moved to France early in September. Later in September control of the Strategic Air Forces passed from me to the Commanding General of the USAAF and the Chief of the Air Staff jointly.

By 1 September also a new and important command unit had been formed within our Expeditionary Forces. All British and American Airborne Forces were placed under the single command of General Brereton on 8 August to form the First Allied Airborne Army. Chief components of this Army included the United States XVIII Corps (82nd, 101st, and 17th Airborne Divisions), the British Airborne Troops Command (6 and 1 Airborne Divisions), the United States IX Troop Carrier Command, and RAF 38 and 46 Groups. In view of the important roles that the airborne divisions were to play in the development of our campaign, and also in order to unify the highly specialized and integrated planning and training, I felt that an Army designation rightly belonged to General Brereton's headquarters and to the troops, even though, in the strict sense of the word, the divisions did not operate as an independent army unit once they had been committed to action. Our first use of the airborne divisions under the newly constituted command set-up was to be on 17 September, to assist in seizing the Rhine crossings at Nijmegen and Arnhem after the rapid advance by our land armies.

Although it was originally intended to employ the airborne units to close the Paris–Orléans gap against the enemy retreating from Normandy, General Patton's advance had been so rapid that the area was completely overrun by our land forces and an airborne operation was unnecessary. We had subsequently considered employing them to assist in seizing successively the crossings over the Seine and the Somme, and lastly in the Pas-de-Calais area to cut off the retreat of the German Fifteenth Army. All these areas were rapidly gained by our ground forces, a clear indication of the tremendous forward strides being made by our armor and infantry. By the time the Airborne Army was first employed in the Arnhem–Nijmegen area, enemy resistance had stiffened and we had begun the long and gruelling grind, in part unexpected, which was ultimately to take us in force across the Rhine.

It was our plan to attack northeastward in the greatest strength possible. This direction had been chosen for a variety of reasons. First, the great bulk of the German Army was located there. Secondly, there was the great desirability of capturing the flying bomb area, not only to remove this menace to England, but also to deny to the enemy the propaganda value which he enjoyed on the home front and in the army from the attacks on London and talk of new weapons which would "decide the war." A third reason for the northeastward attack was our imperative need for the large port of Antwerp, absolutely essential to us logistically before any deep penetration in strength could be made into Germany. Fourthly, we wanted the airfields in Belgium. Finally, and most important, I felt that during the late summer and early autumn months the lower Rhine offered the best avenue of advance into Germany, and it seemed probable that through rapidity of exploitation both the Siegfried Line and the Rhine River might be crossed and strong bridgeheads established before the enemy could recover sufficiently to make a definite stand in the Arnhem area. In furtherance of this plan strong United States forces marched abreast of the Northern Group of Armies to the northeast, while three United States divisions were completely immobilized in order to supply additional logistical support for the Northern Group. At the same time the entire airborne forces were made available to Field Marshal Montgomery.

Secondary to this main effort in the north was the desirability of pushing eastward with some force in order to link up with the French and American forces advancing from the south, so as to clear all southwest France as the cheapest way of protecting our flanks and rear. In addition, a drive along the Verdun–Metz axis would enhance the opportunity for surprise and maneuver, thus requiring the enemy to extend his forces, and leaving him in doubt as to the direction of the Allied main thrust.

From the time when our armies first crossed the Seine in force to the employment of the Airborne Army in Holland on 17 September, our ground forces made prodigious strides. Along the Channel coast the Canadian First Army began advancing on 30 August from the Elbeuf bridgehead above Rouen on the Seine and from bridgeheads below the city. On 1 September both Rouen and Dieppe were taken, the forces first entering Dieppe consisting of battalions of the Essex Scottish Regiment, the Royal Hamilton Light Infantry and the Royal Regiment of Canada which had fought there on 19 August 1942.

Le Havre was cut off, but the garrison rejected an ultimatum to surrender on 4 September and the city was invested. Attacks against it were supported by heavy aerial bombing during which more than 11,000 tons were dropped on the city, half this total being dropped on the 10th. On 10 September also the final ground attack was launched by the British 49 Infantry Division operating with the Canadian First Army. This attack was supported by naval forces including the battleship *Warspite* and the monitor *Erebus*, which bombarded enemy installations with 300 rounds of 15-inch shell. By noon on the 11th the northern and eastern outskirts of Le Havre had been reached and at 1130 hours on the 12th the city surrendered with its garrison of 7,000 troops.

Meanwhile other forces of the Canadian First Army had swept northeastward along the coast, taking, in addition to Dieppe, the small ports of Fecamp, St-Valery-en-Caux, Le Treport, and Abbeville. Etaples fell on 4 September and the Somme River, which we had anticipated as a possible barrier, was crossed in force. Calais was surrounded and the outskirts of Boulogne reached on the 6th. On the 8th the Canadians overran Ostend and after capturing the port turned east towards Bruges which was entered by patrols on the 9th. In the meantime other troops of Canadian 2 Corps had driven toward Dunkirk, investing that city by the 11th. On the 11th also Blankenberghe, between Ostend and Zeebrugge, was taken by the Canadian 4 Armored Division.

Thus, within two weeks of the Seine crossings the Canadians had driven north, clearing large sections of the "flying bomb coast," and northeast toward the Scheldt estuary. Along the coast they had forced the enemy to hole up in a few ports which he was to defend tenaciously. Boulogne, with its garrison of 10,000, did not fall until 23 September and Calais until the 30th, both to the Canadian 2 Corps, after heavy bombardment by Bomber Command. Dunkirk was surrounded, but since the use of the small harbor as a port was not essential, I did not feel that a strong effort should be made to take it. As in the case of the Brittany ports, I decided that it would be preferable to contain the enemy, estimated at 12,000 troops, with the minimum forces necessary rather than to attempt an all-out attack. In the northeast, the Canadian advance toward the Scheldt estuary formed the lower jaw of a trap closing on the Germans, the other jaw consisting of British forces which had captured Antwerp.

The British advance on the right of the Canadians to Antwerp and the Dutch border had been spectacular during this period. From their bridgehead at Vernon their armor swept to Antwerp, a distance of some 195 miles as the crow flies, in less than four days. The advance began on 30 August and Antwerp, with its port installations virtually intact, was occupied on 4

September by the 11 Armoured Division of 30 Corps. By 29 August the British bridgehead at Vernon had extended, at its deepest penetration, 12 miles north of the Seine. On the 30th they made an advance of 25 miles from this point, taking Beauvais, while another column of the 11 Armoured Division reached a point only 25 miles south of Amiens after a 30-mile advance. On the following day they raced on to Amiens, took the town, established bridgeheads across the Somme, and pushed farther to the north-east. At the same time other British units turned northwest and attacked toward the Channel. On the morning of 1 September, British armor took Albert, about 12 miles northeast of Amiens, and Bapaume, 28 miles northeast of Amiens, while later in the day Arras was captured by the Guards Armoured Division of 30 Corps. Meanwhile Amiens was turned over to the infantry, which had come up from the south, and another armored column of the Guards Armoured Division moved north to take Doullens, about 23 miles east of Abbeville.

A part of the armored column which took Arras turned east on the next morning and captured Douai, while the main force continued to the north. On the morning of 2 September it made slow progress, but during that afternoon and the following day it gathered speed and advanced 60 miles in 36 hours, crossing the Belgian border east of Lille, taking Tournai, where the Lille–Brussels road was cut, and then turning east along this road. At noon on the 3rd this column was 28 miles from Brussels, and late on that same day it reached the capital, which had been hastily evacuated by the enemy. On 4 September part of this column turned east and reached Louvain, the rest continuing north and entering Antwerp with the 11 Armoured Division, which had moved rapidly north from the Arras area, taking Lille on the way. By evening the dock area was being cleared, and on the 5th, with Antwerp firmly in their hands, the British spread out to the west and reached the outskirts of Ghent, which fell the following day.

Still farther west another armored division which had begun an attack northwest from the Amiens area on the morning of 2 September made rapid progress in the direction of Calais and Dunkirk and on the 3rd reached Aire, 27 miles south of the latter town. This area was subsequently taken over by the Canadians moving up from the south.

As the British forces approached closer to the German homeland, resistance stiffened and the rapid advances which had made the capture of Antwerp possible came to an end. However, by attacking northeast from Louvain on 7 September, 30 Corps was able to establish a deep bridgehead over the Albert Canal, seize Bourg Leopold after a bitter and fluctuating battle, and by the 12th cross the Dutch border to reach a point seven miles from Eindhoven. Driving east from Bourg Leopold, elements of 30 Corps advanced almost to the Meuse.

While the Canadians and British thus moved northeastward in a great sweeping drive which stretched inland from the Channel coast to Vernon, and northward to Antwerp and Eindhoven, the American First Army under

General Hodges poured across the Seine bridgeheads between Mantes-Gassicourt and Melun to the east, beginning an equally spectacular drive on a three-corps front toward Namur, Liége, and the German frontier. On the right, VII Corps crossed the Aisne on 29 August, and Soissons was cleared of enemy forces by the 3rd Armored Division, which also liberated Laon the next day after stiff fighting. This division continued its rapid advance, while infantry supported it and protected its flank, and on 1 September reached a point 30 miles northeast of Laon. In the next two days the column advanced 40 miles, crossing the Belgian border in the Hirson area and reaching Charleroi and Mons.

On the First Army's left, a similar drive northward from the Mantes bridgehead area had been accomplished by a rapidly moving column of XIX Corps, spearheaded by the 2nd Armored Division. Gaining momentum, on 30 August this force advanced 13 miles, and the next day another spurt of 20 miles carried it close to Montdidier. By 2 September XIX Corps had reached the Belgian border south of Tournai, registering an advance of more than 60 miles in two days.

As a result of these operations, VII and XIX Corps cut off a large German force in the pocket that lay between their advancing columns. This pocket extended from Mons to the forest of Compiègne, where German infantry resisted stubbornly the advance of V Corps. The latter unit, forming the center of the First Army's drive northward, nevertheless made good progress on the axis Compiègne–St-Quentin, reaching a line east of Cambrai on the 2nd. During the next three days some 25,000 prisoners were captured at the top of the pocket in the Mons area.

On 4 September the First Army began a wheel to the east, V Corps moving to the right flank and crossing the Meuse north of Sedan on 5–6 September. That town fell to the 5th Armored Division on 6 September, and in the next few days advance was rapid across Belgium and Luxembourg, on a 65-mile front. The same division liberated the city of Luxembourg on 10 September, and by the 11th, V Corps had reached the German frontier and the Siegfried defenses. Farther north, VII Corps units captured Namur and the Meuse crossings near Dinant on 4–5 September, then continued to advance down both banks of the river toward Liége. Stiff resistance in this area was broken; Liége fell on 8 September and by noon on the 9th our forces reached Limbourg, 13 miles southwest of Aachen. Here resistance increased, and extensive mining and numerous road blocks with anti-tank guns were encountered. Nevertheless, on 10 September further advances were made, and at 1723 hours VII Corps artillery for the first time shelled German territory. On the 11th both Eupen and Malmedy were captured. XIX Corps had paralleled this advance; by 11 September it was at the edge of Maastricht, and farther south had crossed the Meuse.

In less than two weeks, then, the First Army had crossed the Seine in force, swept across France, Belgium, and Luxembourg, and brought the war to the threshold of Germany. The bitter struggle for Aachen and the Roer bridgeheads was to follow.

In the Third Army zone of advance, on the right of our forces, General Patton's troops had crossed the upper Marne in the vicinity of Vitry-le-François on 29 August. On the 30th, 4th Armored Division of XII Corps moved on to St-Dizier, 17 miles to the east, while to the north the 80th Infantry Division captured Châlons-sur-Marne and advanced 8 miles northward. On the 31st the column which took St-Dizier pushed on to Commercy on the Meuse, while the XX Corps turned east on the axis Reims–Verdun–Metz. The following morning units of the XX Corps entered Verdun, and crossed the Meuse to reach a point six miles to the east on the road to Metz. On the 2nd this column pushed on another seven miles to Etain, while the XII Corps advanced to the vicinity of Nancy. Meanwhile, between these two columns, other crossings of the Meuse were effected, and on 2 September St-Mihiel was taken. On the 4th patrols operating up to the Moselle failed to find the enemy in any strength, except at Pont-â-Mousson, about 13 miles south of Metz. Here, after patrol clashes in the morning, the Germans withdrew to the right bank of the river and shelled the town as we moved up to it. On the 5th we reached the important communications center of Nancy, on the left bank about 28 miles above Metz.

Crossings of the Moselle were made against enemy opposition beginning on 7 September. By the 11th we had established ourselves in strength on the east bank of the river between Metz and Nancy. While some of General Patton's forces moved southward from Toul for a distance of 30 miles to compress the Belfort area through which the German Nineteenth Army was withdrawing, other forces crossed the Moselle on the 12th and began the turning movement northeast of Nancy which was to result in the fall of the city to the XII Corps on 15 September.

In the Metz area General Patton's forces had captured Aumetz on the 11th and driven to Thionville, 12 miles north of Metz, by the 13th. The city itself was stubbornly defended and the siege was to be long and arduous.

The Third Army's rapid advance involved herculean tasks in the matter of supply. At the Moselle enemy resistance had stiffened and the problem of supply became increasingly acute, to the extent that General Patton's forces were partially immobilized and physically incapable of mounting assaults on a large scale or of continuing a pursuit had the opportunity offered. This was in a measure also true of the whole front facing east against Germany and our positions here became relatively stable on a line running from the First Army's sector in the Aachen area south along the German border to Metz, Nancy, and Epinal.

On 11 September patrols from General Patch's Seventh Army had established contact with patrols of General Patton's Third Army west of Dijon, but contact in force was not finally established until a Seventh Army column, driving north against enemy opposition, joined forces with the right wing of the Third Army west of Epinal on 21 September. This action reduced the size of the pocket west of the Belfort Gap and straightened the line which as a result now extended almost due south from Epinal to the Swiss frontier. In spite of the fact that use of the Belfort Gap as an escape route was now prevented, the enemy continued to hold on stubbornly in this whole area, evidently pursuing his usual policy of not yielding an inch except under pressure. This policy reacted to our advantage since it kept the enemy fully engaged and unable to withdraw forces to aid in the north, where the airborne operation against the lower Rhine was taking place. Along the whole line the war was to resolve itself into slow, hard fighting (with the few exceptions which I shall now consider) until after the German counter-attack in December and the opening of our own offensive in February.

CONSOLIDATION ON
THE FRONTIER

In part the slowdown along the front facing Germany was due to my decision to employ our greatest strength in the north to attain flanking bridgeheads across the lower Rhine beyond the main fortifications of the Siegfried Line. In view of the fact, however, that the main highway to Berlin—the plains and level fields of northern Germany—lay beyond the Rhine in the north, and that the southern country was unsuitable for the desired rapid advance and continued exploitation by reason of its mountainous and forested terrain, my commanders and I were in full agreement as to the desirability of exerting our strongest pressure in the north. The attractive possibility of quickly turning the German north flank led me to approve the temporary delay in freeing the vital port of Antwerp, the seaward approaches to which were still in German hands.

The operation to seize the bridges over the Rhine was made up of two parts. The airborne operation, known as Market, had as its purpose the capture of the vital bridges over the Maas, the Waal, and the Lower Rhine at Grave, Nijmegen, and Arnhem. The forces employed in the airborne operation included the US 82nd Airborne Division, the 101st Airborne Division, the British 1 Airborne Division, and the Polish 1st Paratroop Brigade. The British 1 Airborne Division was to be dropped farthest north in the Arnhem area, the US 82nd Airborne Division in the Nijmegen area, and the US 101st Division in the St Oedenrode area north of Eindhoven. In rapid support of the airborne troops, armor and infantry of the British Second Army were to advance northward from the general line of the Albert and Escaut Canals. Passing over the bridges held by the airborne troops, the armor was to push on to the Zuider Zee and thus, if successful, cut off the land exit of enemy troops in western Holland. The land operation, known as Garden, was to take place on a very narrow front with only one road as a line of communication

Consolidation on the frontier

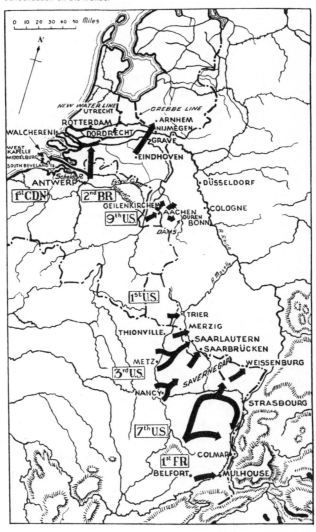

for a considerable part of the way. The axis of advance lay through Eindhoven, St Oedenrode, Veghel, Uden, Grave, Nijmegen, Arnhem, and Apeldoorn.

The first landings of the main airborne forces were made on 17 September and follow-up troops and reinforcements continued to be flown in on succeeding days in spite of unfavorable weather on several occasions. Initial losses *en route* and at the dropping zones were very slight and bore out General Brereton's contention that heavy bomber effort on flak positions immediately preceding an airborne operation would greatly reduce casualties. These attacks had been undertaken by "heavies" of both the RAF Bomber Command and the US Eighth Air Force, which neutralized enemy airfields in the vicinity of the dropping zones and flak positions *en route*. By the 19th, British Second Army ground forces, advancing from the south, had made contact with all of the airborne troops except those to the north of the lower Rhine in the Arnhem area. Here the British 1 Airborne Division was holding out heroically against greatly superior forces, including a quantity of armor, the presence of which in the area had been estimated by my intelligence staff. This, in the outcome, proved to be effective against the tactical power we could apply.

The British Guards Armoured Division had pushed north on 17 September, but met heavy resistance slowing its advance into Eindhoven, which had been taken by the 101st Airborne Division. Firm contact was established between the two forces on the 18th, and the Guards Armoured pushed rapidly north to Grave, which had fallen to the 82nd Airborne Division. The area between Grave and Nijmegen was held by this latter division and the armored advance to the town was consequently rapid. Nijmegen itself, however, was held by the enemy, as was also the extremely important road bridge crossing the Waal. This bridge, a modern five-span structure of steel and concrete, some 6,000 feet in length, was a valuable prize, since, without it, the river would have been a formidable obstacle. An attempt by armor to get through to the bridge failed on the 19th in the face of heavy fire from anti-tank guns sited in houses near the approaches. On the following day, however, a regiment of the 82nd Airborne Division crossed the river in assault boats upstream from the bridge and surprised and overcame the German forces holding the northern approaches. The British meanwhile had seized the southern end, and that evening, after mines had been removed, the armor crossed the bridge and advanced two miles to the north where it was held up by an anti-tank screen.

During the next few days there was confused and heavy fighting in the area between Nijmegen and Arnhem, and it was not until the 24th that British infantry reached the lower Rhine in force and artillery began lending fire support to the beleaguered 1 Airborne Division on the northern bank of the river.

By 23 September the position of the 1 Airborne Division had become so precarious that the Second Army gave 30 Corps permission to withdraw the division if the situation did not improve. 30 Corps ordered every risk to be taken to relieve the division on the 24th, by which date the forces on the northern bank had been forced into a steadily contracting perimeter approximately 1,000 yards by 1,500 yards. The shelling, mortaring, and strafing of this area by the enemy was incessant, and on 25 September, 30 Corps finally ordered the withdrawal of all forces across the lower Rhine. This was effected that night and 2,163 men of the 1 Airborne Division withdrew under cover of darkness, infiltrating in small groups through the enemy lines and across the river. Casualties had been heavy, the division losing in killed, wounded and missing some 7,000 men.

While the crossing of the lower Rhine was not completed, the operation brought very positive and important advantages to our forces. Repeated enemy attacks against the thin line of communications had temporarily necessitated withdrawal of armor from Nijmegen to keep the single road open, but the line was ultimately held and supplies went through even under constant shelling. As the line was strengthened with the arrival of stronger infantry units, the corridor was gradually widened on both sides. British forces pushed west in conjunction with northward attacks by other British and Canadian forces to establish a firm line eventually running along the Waal and Mass. To the east the corridor was also widened to bring the Northern Group of Armies into line with the Central Group and within striking distance of Kleve. Bridgeheads had been firmly secured across the Maas and Waal and the watershed between the two was to serve as a valuable corridor for a later advance to the Rhine.

Operation Market had been the largest airborne operation undertaken by the Allied forces up to this time. Between 17 and 30 September, 20,190 troops had been dropped from aircraft by parachute, 13,781 had landed in gliders, and 905 were air-landed on a strip made ready by the preceding airborne troops. In addition to this total of 34,876 troops, 5,230 tons of equipment and supplies, 1,927 vehicles, and 568 artillery pieces were transported by air. In all, the supporting air forces, who showed great gallantry in continuing to fly supplies to the isolated forces, flew over 7,800 sorties.

My decision to concentrate our efforts in this attempt to thrust into the heart of Germany before the enemy could consolidate his defenses along the Rhine had resulted in a delay in opening Antwerp and in making the port available as our main supply base. I took the full responsibility for this, and I believe that the possible and actual results warranted the calculated risk involved. Had our forces not pushed north and east to hold the line of the Maas and Waal well north of Antwerp, the port itself would have been in constant danger not only from a blow possibly synchronized with the later breakthrough in the Eifel but from independent attacks launched at close range from Holland.

With the completion of the Market-Garden operation the Northern Group of Armies was instructed to undertake the opening of Antwerp as a matter of the first priority. While the city and port installations had fallen virtually intact to 30 Corps on 4 September, the harbor had proved and was to continue to prove useless to us until the Scheldt estuary had been cleared of mines and South Beveland and Walcheren Island, commanding the sea lane to the harbor, had been reduced. The operation to achieve this involved the employment of amphibious forces, and the joint naval, air, and ground force planning was immediately undertaken and worked out during the latter part of September and early October at the headquarters of the Canadian First Army.

As an integral part of the operation, and in support of the amphibious elements, Canadian forces attacked north of Antwerp toward the South Beveland Isthmus in mid-October. On 24 October, having overcome resistance at Woensdrecht and thus ensured their flank protection, the Canadian 2 Division turned west and advanced slowly across the narrow neck connecting South Beveland with the mainland. Progress here was particularly difficult, the troops often having to fight waist-deep in water while the Germans offered strong resistance.

The Canadian forces continued their advance, however, and by midday on 27 October had reached the line of the canal at the west end of the isthmus. Crossing this at its southern extremity, they pressed forward to within 2½ miles of troops of the British 52 Division who had been landed on the south shore of South Beveland on the night of the 25th/26th, and by the 29th they effected a juncture with them. By the 30th the whole of South Beveland had been cleared and the British and Canadians continued their attack against the causeway connecting the isthmus with Walcheren.

On Walcheren the enemy consisted of the remnants of a division, forced back with severe losses from South Beveland, and elements of the German Fifteenth Army which had made their escape by sea across the Scheldt from the trap in which they had been caught with the seizure of Antwerp. Against Walcheren the Canadians attacked from the west, while amphibious forces, landed on 1 November at both Westkapelle and Vlissingen, moved east and north, converging on the strongpoints of the island. These forces, consisting of the Royal Marine 4 SS Brigade (Commandos) and two battalions of the 52 Infantry Division, had been successfully landed from naval assault craft under heavy fire. Great credit for the success of the amphibious operation is due to the support craft of the British Navy, which unhesitatingly and in the highest traditions of the service attracted to themselves the point-blank fire of the land batteries, thus permitting the commandos and assault troops to gain the shore with much lighter casualties than otherwise would have been the case. The air forces also, operating in great strength despite appallingly difficult weather conditions, lent invaluable support throughout the operation, a feature of this support being the accurate bombing by aircraft of the Bomber Command which succeeded in breaching the dykes.

The three converging ground forces, attacking over terrain made extremely difficult by flooding, and suffering heavy casualties, advanced with great gallantry against stiff enemy resistance to capture the strongpoints of

Veere and Middelburg and wipe out enemy opposition. By 9 November all resistance had ceased and some 10,000 troops had been captured, including a division commander.

With the capture of South Beveland and Walcheren the land approaches to Antwerp were now freed, but the Scheldt estuary had still to be swept of mines before the port could become useful. This work was at once undertaken by the Navy and Antwerp became a port of supply for our forces with the unloading of the first ships on 26 November. The enemy, however, recognizing the importance of the harbor to us as a supply base, began at this time the launching in considerable strength of V-1 and V-2 weapons against the dock and town area. While the weapons were erratic in about the same degree as those launched against the London area, they nevertheless caused considerable damage in the district, killing both civilian and military personnel as well as disrupting communications and supply work for brief periods. Great credit is due to the citizens of Antwerp for sustaining the attacks as London had done and for unflinchingly going about their tasks which were of assistance to us in forwarding the war effort. In addition to attacks from the V-weapons against docks and shore installations, the enemy also employed large numbers of E-boats and midget submarines against our naval craft and shipping, but all these attempts at disrupting our flow of supplies were successfully countered by vigorous naval and air measures.

While the Arnhem–Nijmegen operation and the attack upon the approaches to Antwerp were the more spectacular successes during the latter part of September, the month of October and early November, the slugging matches along the rest of the front facing north and east were equally important for the general development of the campaign. Our two immediate objectives during this period were, first, to advance east to the Rhine and north to the Maas and, second, to use the space between our front and the Rhine as a "killing ground" in which to engage the enemy either in a large decisive battle or so to maul him that when the Rhine had been reached he would have little left with which to resist our crossings and prevent a breakthrough leading to mobile warfare.

Although we were not to reach the Rhine as quickly as we had hoped, or yet to engage the enemy in a decisive battle except as he himself created it in his December counter-offensive, the continued daily losses which he suffered in both personnel and equipment contributed to weakening him so that when our main blows ultimately fell victory was inevitable. By the end of September total enemy casualties, including killed, wounded, and prisoners, totalled approximately 1,000,000 men, including those swept into our net with the rapid advance of General Devers' forces from the south and their junction with General Bradley's troops west of the Belfort Gap. The isolated remnants of the German First Army in southwest France gave themselves up in piecemeal groups to the French Forces of the Interior and to our own forces, the largest single body consisting of 20,000 troops who surrendered without even attempting resistance after being trapped south of the

Loire. Our continued hard-fought battles during the next three months were to increase this total by mid-January to 1,500,000, a figure indicative of the steady attrition being inflicted on the enemy. In spite of these losses, however, German troops continued to put up strong resistance, battling with a stubbornness and Teutonic fury born of the desperate knowledge that they were fighting on their own "holy soil." Our logistical situation, coupled with the fact that the terrain was suitable to the defense, aided the enemy. Additionally, during this period we experienced weather conditions which admirably suited him. The rains which fell in November were the worst known on the Continent in many years and created flood conditions along our whole front, reducing the lesser roads to quagmires and impeding tank operations and vehicular movement. All these factors made it more easily possible for the enemy, exploiting a comparatively static situation, to mine and booby-trap the areas ahead of us, contributing further to our problems.

In spite of these difficulties we achieved much. The First Army troops had entered Germany in the Trier region on 11 September and in the Aachen area east of Eupen on the 12th. At Aachen the enemy resisted bitterly but by the 20th the city was under attack from three sides and subject to heavy shelling. On the north side, which was still open, the First Army launched an attack across the German border on 2 October and in the first two days breached the Siegfried Line on a 3-mile front, the southern point of the breakthrough being about eight miles north of Aachen. Within the next few days the two remaining main roads into Aachen from the north were cut and the defenders isolated. Concurrently with these attacks the First Army attacked eastward against Stolberg, where heavy house-to-house fighting took place. On 13 October the First Army troops entered Aachen from the east and by the 19th, in spite of resistance from fortified cellars and buildings, had cleared half the city, which was now in ruins as a result of our bombing and shelling. Following the success of our assault, enemy resistance gradually weakened and the final surrender of the first large German city to Allied forces took place on 21 October when the garrison gave in to troops of the 1st Infantry Division of VII Corps. After the fall of Aachen the First Army's offensive operations were curtailed until the November offensives which were mounted along the entire front.

On the Third Army's front Nancy had fallen on 15 September, but Metz, strongly defended by its outer ring of forts, was to remain in enemy hands until our offensive ultimately reduced it on 22 November. South of Metz, along the line of the Moselle, the Third Army pushed eastward slowly until its line extended roughly parallel with the river to a depth of 20 to 25 miles. Farther south the Seventh Army and the French First Army, probing slowly into the area of the High Vosges across the Moselle from Epinal and against the Belfort Gap area, brought their line up to conform with that of the Third Army.

The relatively static warfare of October had thus brought us into position for the limited offensives which we were mounting for November.

During the month of October an administrative change had been placed in effect which was to bring the Tactical Air Forces more closely under the control of my Headquarters. Prior to 15 October the Allied Expeditionary Air Force, under Air Chief Marshal Leigh-Mallory, had maintained its separate Headquarters, reporting to me through my deputy, Air Chief Marshal Tedder. In October, however, we were informed that the Air Ministry desired to transfer Air Chief Marshal Leigh-Mallory to a post of greater responsibility in the China–Burma–India Theater, where, because of his long experience, his presence could be best employed to further the ends of the war. It was with great reluctance that I agreed to this change, but once it had been made I felt that the AEAF, without Air Chief Marshal Leigh-Mallory, might better function as an integral part of my own headquarters. SHAEF Air Staff thus came into being on 15 October and the planning and operational staffs became part of my headquarters. Shortly after this, on 14 November, Air Chief Marshal Leigh-Mallory, *en route* to his new command, was reported missing. His loss to the common war effort came as a keen personal blow to me and to the members of my staff.

With the opening of Antwerp our supply problem was considerably eased, but the Germans had profited by our earlier logistical handicap to reinforce their Siegfried defenses with hurriedly formed Volksgrenadier divisions. These divisions initially had very low combat value, but both General Bradley and I felt that unless the Siegfried positions could be speedily attacked the relative strength of the opposing forces would gradually become more favorable to the enemy.

My plan of campaign at this period included an advance on the fronts of the Northern and Central Groups of Armies to the Rhine, which it was necessary to hold from its mouth to Düsseldorf at least, if not to Bonn or Frankfurt, before a large-scale penetration beyond the river into Germany could be attempted. With the strong defensive barrier which the Rhine would afford our armies, it would become more easily possible to concentrate power at one point for the breakthrough, leaving relatively thinly held positions along the rest of the front.

The eastward drive by 21 Army Group began on 15 November, but progress was slow over ground made extremely difficult by the severe weather and it was not until 4 December that the last enemy pocket on the west bank of the Maas was cleared. A direct advance across the Maas to the Rhine was judged impracticable and extensive regrouping would have been necessary for a drive southeast from the Nijmegen area along the relatively dry watershed separating the two rivers. To accomplish this latter penetration it would have been necessary to reduce the frontage of the Northern Group of Armies in order to gather strength at the point of attack. Due to limitations in strength, 21 Army Group itself was incapable of holding the whole of its frontage and attacking at the same time, and 12th Army Group would have had to take over a portion of the line. This could only have been done by 12th Army Group at the expense of weakening the Aachen attack, a course which was not acceptable to me. I therefore decided to postpone further major operations by 21 Army Group until the drive toward Cologne had made adequate progress in the central sector.

In the Aachen sector the offensive by the First and Ninth Armies was launched on 16 November after an hour and a half of intensive air and artillery bombardment. Over 1,200 US heavy bombers dropped bombs on fortified positions north of Eschweiler and west of Düren. Later in the day RAF bombers also attacked Düren itself and Jülich, practically obliterating these towns. The offensive was launched in two main directions, eastward from Aachen toward Eschweiler and northeastward toward Geilenkirchen. East of Aachen the enemy was driven entirely out of Stolberg, which he had partially held for some six weeks while our own forces were entrenched in the remainder of the town. By the 21st our troops had penetrated into Eschweiler, which fell after heavy fighting on the following day. Meanwhile the fighting had moved farther along the right flank into the Hürtgen Forest, southeast of Aachen, and gains in this sector placed our troops within attacking range of Düren.

To the north Geilenkirchen had fallen on the 19th and the Ninth Army continued advancing slowly until 3 December it had reached the Roer River. The First Army was conforming to the south more slowly still. Fourteen at first, and eventually seventeen, divisions were employed in the Aachen sector by the First and Ninth Armies, and at the height of the offensive no fewer than ten divisions were in the line together on a 24-mile front, this being the maximum which it was practicable to deploy. In spite of this concentration and the very large-scale strategic and tactical air attacks, the progress had been slow and the fighting bitter. The delay imposed on our advance here was a testimony to the improved defense works which the enemy had constructed following our breakthrough of the Siegfried Line in September.

While the Ninth Army had reached the Roer by 3 December, General Bradley considered it imprudent to cross the river while the Schmidt Dams, which controlled the flooding of the Roer Valley, remained intact in enemy hands. The German Sixth Panzer Army had moved west of the Rhine by this time, and had the American forces crossed the Roer the enemy, releasing the flood waters, would have been in a position to trap the attackers. Air attacks on the dams were called for at short notice and accurately executed; direct hits were secured on the structures. These attacks, however, failed to destroy the dams, partly because bad weather precluded the concentration of the necessary weight of bombs and also because of the enemy's ability to adjust the water level. General Bradley therefore ordered the First Army to maneuver to capture them. The First Army began the attack for the dams on 13 December and the attack was still in progress when the subsequent enemy counter-offensive was launched in the Eifel.

Meanwhile, south of the Ardennes, the Third Army offensive toward the Saar which started on 8 November made excellent progress. North of Metz several bridgeheads established across the Moselle in the Thionville area were linked together by the 14th, and four days later troops operating from the bridgehead crossed the German frontier in several places. To the south Metz was surrounded and cut off, but, while the city itself fell on 22 November, seven of the forts continued to resist and the difficult task of mopping them up was not accomplished until 13 December. By 5 December, also, the Third Army's right flank had pushed eastward from the Metz–Nancy area to the Saar in conformity with the advance from Thionville, closing a stretch of the river over 16 miles in length. Three bridgeheads were secured in the Saarlautern area and contact was made with the main Siegfried defenses. These defenses at the Third Army's front of attack south of Merzig on the Saar River were the strongest sections of the line, guarding the triangle between the Moselle and the Rhine. The forward line, continuous but of no very great depth, closely followed the east bank of the Saar. The rear line, of greater strength, consisted of a zone of forts about two and a half miles deep, passing in front of Lebach and continuing through the Saarbrücken Forest to rejoin the forward line ten miles east of Saarbrücken itself. Following the Third Army's rapid advance, these defenses slowed the attack so that some regrouping and additional logistical support was necessary prior to reassuming the offensive. While I had hoped that the Third Army would have been able to achieve complete victory in the Saar, I had nevertheless set a time limit for the operation. The Third Army's final attack was to begin on 19 December, after which, regardless of results, divisions were to be transferred to the north to assist in the main effort against the Rhine and into Germany. The German counter-offensive through the Ardennes on 16 December upset these plans, and made the final offensive on the 19th an impossibility in view of the need for the Third Army to contain and subsequently counter-attack on the southern flank of the breakthrough.

On the 6th Army Group front the November offensive of the French First Army was launched on the 14th. Within a week the Belfort Gap had been breached and our troops had reached the Rhine. Belfort was cleared of all resistance by the 22nd. The breakthrough, accomplished on the 18th, turned the flank of the German positions in the Vosges and forced a general withdrawal in front of the Seventh Army sector to the north, where Seventh Army troops, after launching their attack simultaneously with that of French First Army, had been struggling slowly forward along the roads leading through the Vosges passes. The towns of Blâmont, Raon-l'Etape, Gérardmer, and St-Dié, with other lesser villages which controlled the passes through the hills, had been stubbornly defended by the enemy, for as long as they remained in his hands the High Vosges stood as an impassable wall protecting the Rhine plain to the east. With the outflanking movement to the south these towns fell to advancing Seventh Army troops, and the 44th Infantry Division, rapidly exploiting the strategic possibilities, advanced to Saarebourg, which fell on the 21st. Meanwhile, the French 2nd Armored Division, operating on the right of the 44th Infantry, by-passed Saarebourg and penetrated the defenses in front of the Saverne Gap, capturing the town itself the following day. Also on the 22nd, columns pushed both north and east of the town and broke out into the Rhine plain. On the 23rd, the French 2nd Armored Division reached Strasbourg, but, while the city was rapidly and easily cleared, some of the outer ring of forts continued to offer resistance until the 27th.

On the 24th the enemy launched a counter-attack from the northeast, directed against Saarebourg, with the seeming expectation of being able to cut the corridor which Seventh Army had rapidly extended to the Rhine. Initially some ground was lost, but the 44th Infantry Division fought the enemy to a standstill and regained earlier positions. To the east the 79th Division, which had been mopping up in the rear of the French 2nd Armored Division, resumed a northward advance and, with the 44th, made rapid progress toward Haguenau, which was taken on 12 December.

On the right flank the French First Army's advance down the Rhine plain was slowed by enemy counter-attacks across its lines of communication. After reaching the Rhine on the 20th, French armor turned north and by the 22nd cleared Mulhouse in an advance so rapid that part of the staff of the German Nineteenth Army was captured as it fled from the city. The German counter-attacks against the advancing columns' lines of communication forced a temporary withdrawal from positions gained along the Rhine east of Mulhouse, but by the 27th this ground was recaptured.

Between the northern columns of the Seventh Army which had reached the Rhine in the Strasbourg area and the southern columns of the French First Army which had approached the river near Mulhouse, troops of both armies advanced steadily through the Vosges to tighten the ring around German forces stubbornly defending their positions in the area about Colmar.

On 27 November, in view of the strategic opportunity afforded our armies to attack into the Saar Basin, I directed the Seventh Army, after rapid regrouping, to attack northward to breach the Siegfried Line west of the Rhine, launching the attack west of the Pfalzerwald in conjunction with the southern flank of the Central Group of Armies. This advance from the south and southwest directly aided the Third Army's operations against the Saar. By mid-December the Seventh Army had crossed the German frontier on a 22-mile front and penetrated well into the Siegfried defenses northeast of Wissembourg. Our progress in the Saar and Wissembourg sectors contained 14 enemy divisions, and had it been possible to continue the advance the enemy would have been compelled to divert forces from the north, thus directly aiding our main effort in that sector. Meantime, the enemy forces driven from the Vosges maintained their bridgehead west of the Rhine in the Colmar area, which the French First Army, weakened by their recent offensive operations and short of trained infantry replacements, were unable to liquidate. This bridgehead area, which was to become known as the "Colmar Pocket," later exerted a profound and adverse effect on our operations until it was finally eliminated.

THE ARDENNES
COUNTER-OFFENSIVE

As a result of the decision to deploy our maximum effort in the Aachen sector and to sustain the successful progress of the Saar–Wissembourg operations with the balance of available forces, other stretches of the front were weakly held. In particular the Eifel sector of some 75 miles between Trier and Monschau was held by no more than four divisions. In this disposition of our forces I took a calculated risk, based on the absence of strategic objectives or large depots in the area and also on the relatively difficult terrain.

When the attacks from Aachen towards the Roer had to be suspended pending the capture of the river dams and the southern thrusts began to slow down, however, it was noticeable that the German panzer units started to withdraw from the line, their places being taken by Volksgrenadier divisions. All intelligence agencies assiduously tried to find out the locations and intentions of these panzer units, but without complete success. My headquarters and 12th Army Group had felt for some time that a counter-attack through the Ardennes was a possibility, since American forces were stretched very thinly there in order to provide troops for attack elsewhere and because Field Marshal von Rundstedt had gradually placed in this quiet sector six infantry divisions, a larger number than he required for reasonable security. However, we did not consider it highly probable that von Rundstedt would, in winter, try to use that region in which to stage a counter-offensive on a large scale, feeling certain that we could deal with any such effort and that the result would ultimately be disastrous to Germany. Nevertheless, this is exactly what the enemy did, employing for a second time the plan of campaign and strategy which had made his first breakthrough in 1940 a complete success, and taking advantage of a period of bad weather which prevented our air power

The Ardennes counter-offensive

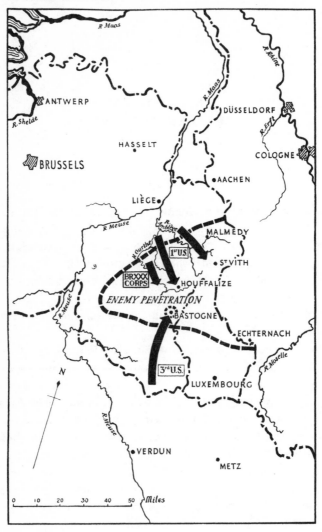

from operating. In order fully to appraise the desperate risk which the enemy undertook in making this venture it must be recognized that he aimed his blow, above all, at the will of the Allied Command. If he could weaken our determination to maintain that flaming, relentless offensive which, regardless of his reaction, had carried us from the beaches to the Siegfried Line, his sacrifices would not be altogether futile.

The attack started, after preparations of the very greatest secrecy, on Saturday, 16 December. General Bradley had just arrived at my headquarters for a conference on replacements when we received word that some penetrations of the American line had been effected, with the enemy using tanks. Sensing that this was something more than a mere local attack, I immediately advised General Bradley to move the 10th Armored Division from the south and the 7th Armored Division from the north, both toward the flanks of the attack. Army Commanders on both flanks were directed to alert what divisions they had free for instant movement toward that region if necessary. My own staff acted at once to move our reserve divisions forward. Of these movements, the most significant and important was that of the 101st Airborne Division, which was in SHAEF reserve and which was directed to Bastogne.

The following morning, the 17th, General Bradley returned to his own headquarters to keep a close grip on the situation, and during that day and the next it became clear that the enemy was making an all-out effort to split us and throw our campaign into disorder.

The enemy's general plan, as we initially analysed it and as events subsequently confirmed, was to break through our thin line of defenses in a sudden blitz drive to the Meuse in the Liége–Namur area. Having seized Liége, which was our key maintenance and communication center feeding 12th Army Group from the north, the enemy hoped to drive rapidly and with as much strength as possible to Antwerp, our great port of supply. Seizing or destroying this, he would have made our supply position practically untenable and would at the same time have split the British armies, together with the American Ninth Army and part of the First, in the north from the American and French forces in the south, isolating them and making possible their destruction in detail by attacks from Holland in the north and by his striking force in Belgium. The attack upon Antwerp itself would probably have been coordinated with an assault by paratroopers and infantry from Holland.

In all the enemy employed three armies for the battle, the Fifth Panzer Army and the Sixth Panzer Army supported by the Seventh Army, totalling some 14 infantry and 10 panzer and panzer grenadier divisions. Field Marshal von Rundstedt was in personal charge, and from field orders subsequently captured we obtained confirmation of our belief that this attack was in the nature of a final, desperate blow into which every available reserve was thrown. In addition to the main attacking forces, the enemy employed one panzer brigade which operated in American equipment with the mission of spearheading German combat units and spreading panic and confusion in and immediately behind our front line. Parties of paratroops were dropped throughout the battle area and particularly in the Malmedy area where about one battalion was employed, while small paratroop units and agents who had remained behind during our advance were active in attempting to sabotage key bridges and headquarters as far to the rear as Paris. For the first time also since our landing the Luftwaffe rose to give active combat support to the ground forces, not only by engaging our air forces off the ground but by attacking the airfields and installations throughout Belgium. On 1 January, for example, the German Air Force attacked our airfields in Holland and Belgium with the largest concentration of planes employed since D Day. Some 800 sorties were flown in an all-out air offensive and losses to our planes on the ground were considerable, although on this one day alone German losses amounted to 200 aircraft.

As soon as confirmation had been received of the extent of the enemy's effort to bring about a breakthrough, I immediately ordered the cessation of all attacks along the whole front and the gathering up of every possible reserve to strike the penetration on both flanks. My plan was to hold firmly the shoulders of the penetration, particularly the Monschau area on the north and the Bastogne area on the south, prevent enemy penetration west of the Meuse or in the Liége–Namur area, and then to counter-attack with General Patton's Army in the general direction of Bastogne–Cologne. This counter-attack was to be followed by an attack by the forces under Field Marshal Montgomery, directed as the result and progress of General Patton's operations should indicate. I directed General Devers also to reach out as far as possible to his left to relieve Third Army, and to make available every single United States Division that he could, retaining as his own mission merely the covering of vital communications. He was told to give ground if necessary in order to keep his thus-stretched forces intact. This order was given verbally on the morning of 19 December at Verdun, where I had directed all interested ground and air commanders to assemble. Later I amplified this order by directing him to be ready to move back to the general line Belfort–Vosges in order to save the troops in the pocket lying between the Vosges, the Rhine, and the Siegfried Line. The same general instructions were given to Field Marshal Montgomery with respect to the northern flank.

On 19 December, when it became apparent that General Bradley's left flank was badly separated from his right and that the situation of his own Headquarters, located at Luxembourg, limited his command and communication capabilities to the area south of the penetration, I realized that it would be impracticable for him to handle the American forces both north and south of the large salient which was being created. I therefore fixed a boundary running east and west through the breach in our lines, generally on the axis Givet–Prüm, giving both places inclusive to the Northern Group. All forces north of the boundary, including the major part of the US

First and Ninth Armies and part of the Ninth Air Force, I placed respectively under the operational command of Field Marshal Montgomery and Air Marshal Coningham, Commander in Chief of the Second Tactical Air Force. This left General Bradley suitably located to command the forces on the southern flank of the salient, comprising mainly the US Third Army and XIX Tactical Air Command, considerably reinforced.

The full brunt of the enemy assault was met first by the four divisions deployed along the thinly held Eifel–Ardennes sector: the 4th, 28th, and 106th Infantry Divisions and the 9th Armored Division. In spite of being by-passed and divided by the penetration, these forces slowed the enemy thrust and the 7th Armored Division denied him the important area of St-Vith during the critical early days. The momentum of the breakthrough was further reduced by the arrival in the battle area on 18 December of the 101st and 82nd Airborne Divisions moved from reserve in the Reims area to the command of 12th Army Group. The 101st Airborne Division, reinforced by armor, then held the vital road center at Bastogne although completely surrounded for five days and under constant attack by forces many times superior in strength. The commitment of these divisions, however, removed the last Theater Reserve and the 11th Armored Division, newly arrived from England, was directed to assemble rapidly in the Reims area to protect the center and to meet a head-on attack on the Meuse if necessary. The 17th Airborne Division was also ordered over from England to help the 11th Armored Division secure the Meuse line south of Givet. To re-establish and maintain a reserve, additional infantry divisions then in England were brought to the Continent in advance of planned schedule.

As the week wore on we succeeded in bolstering up the northern shoulder of the penetration, at the same time collecting a United States Corps under General Collins for use in counter-attack. From the south, General Patton began a transfer of six divisions to the north of the Moselle. 21 Army Group likewise collected reserves and placed a corps under Lieut. Gen. Horrocks in the Brussels area. The flanks of the penetration at Monschau and Echternach were held and the salient gradually stabilized by these measures. However, the penetration directly westward was still moving and, while on the north it had been possible with the 17th Airborne Division and the 11th Armored Division to cover the Meuse bridges adequately down as far as Givet, south of that the crossings remained alarmingly weak. To defend them I issued instructions that all available rear echelon troops and service units as well as six French infantry battalions be moved to the Meuse to protect the crossings at all costs and in no event to permit any bridge to fall intact into the hands of the enemy.

Because of the difficult situation in the region of Bastogne, where the 101st Airborne Division and other elements were steadfastly holding out against greatly superior forces, General Bradley felt that he should start General Patton's Third Army attacking to the northward from the Arlon–Luxembourg area no later than Friday, 22 December. General Patton was authorized to begin the attack, but prior to launching it he was instructed to make absolutely certain of the safety of his right flank in the Trier region from which a new offensive by the German Seventh Army still threatened. He was also to attack by phase lines, holding all forces carefully together in order to avoid any risk of dispersion or wastage of strength before Field Marshal Montgomery was in a position to join the attack from the north.

Prior to the 22nd the weather had been most unfavorable. From the 16th to the 22nd the enemy had the advantage of being able to attack under cover of a thick ground fog which deprived us of practically all air assistance apart from limited and extremely hazardous missions. His ground troops were able, as a result, to move against our defending forces with maximum surprise. On the 22nd, however, the weather began to improve and our air forces commenced their paralysing attacks upon enemy communications at the same time that the Third Army attack was launched northeastward from the Arlon–Luxembourg area. Since the enemy initiated the attack, prior planning of air operations (such as for the Normandy battle) was impossible. The object of our air attacks against the enemy's rail system, carried out in spite of the bad weather (both in the target area and over the bases in England), was to force back the enemy's railheads; the mounting of their offensive and the continued supply of the German forces were largely dependent on rail communications. The heavy bomber attacks achieved their object and made the closer-range attacks against road movements all the more effective in helping to strangle von Rundstedt's efforts. Throughout the period the Strategic Air Forces battered marshalling yards east of the Rhine and blocked centers of movement such as St-Vith, while the medium and light bombers of the Tactical Air Forces destroyed bridges, headquarters, dumps, and other targets in the battle area. The fighter-bombers ranged far and wide in and beyond the battle area creating havoc in enemy road and rail movement, their efficacy in starving the enemy of fuel, food, and ammunition being amply testified to by prisoners. A concerted attack on the German Air Force airfields on 24 December helped to reduce the activity of the enemy fighters and thus afforded our fighter-bombers still greater opportunity for concentration on ground targets rather than on air fighting, which had up to this time been as intense as any the enemy had proved capable of offering since D Day.

The 4th Armored Division of the Third Army, attacking northward against heavy resistance toward Bastogne, was able by 26 December to make firm contact with the defenders of the important road net there, who had meanwhile been supplied by air, and to check the enemy's advance on that flank. This attack also drew strong enemy forces away from the north of the salient. By the 26th also, additional reserves had been so disposed along the Meuse as to relieve anxiety over this sector, and it was then clear that the enemy had failed in his main intention. By the time the German drive was halted the enemy had breached a 45-mile gap in our lines from Echternach to Monschau and had penetrated over 60 miles westward to within 4 miles of the Meuse near Celles.

As soon as the enemy's advance had been checked, my intention was to cut his lines of communication into the salient and if possible to destroy him by launching ground attacks from both north and south in close coordination with continued heavy air attacks designed to extend paralysis of movement and communication over a large area. Simultaneously the strategic air effort which had been employed so effectively in the battle area was released to resume its normal tasks.

The counter-attack from the north, aimed at Houffalize in the center of the salient, was launched by the First Army on 3 January on a two-corps front, with a corps of the British Second Army conforming on the west flank. On 9 January, the Third Army, which had been maintaining strong pressure in the Bastogne area, launched a fresh attack also directed towards the Houffalize road net. Both these attacks were hampered by adverse weather over snow-covered minefields and were met by stubborn enemy resistance. Slow progress was made, however, and the gap between the attacking armies had by 10 January been narrowed to some ten miles. By this time the enemy had begun to withdraw from the western tip of his salient, but still strongly opposed our pressure against his northern and southern flanks. Nevertheless, on the 16th, attacking forces of the First and Third Armies established firm contact at Houffalize and turned their full strength eastward against the retreating enemy. St-Vith fell to the First Army forces on the 23rd and by the end of the month our line was approximately what it had been at the beginning of the breakthrough, while advance forces attacked beyond this in the direction of Bonn.

With the establishment of contact between the First and Third Armies and the reopening of direct communications between General Bradley's Headquarters and General Hodge's First Army, the operational command of the First Army reverted to the Central Group of Armies. The US Ninth Army was retained within the Northern Group of Armies under Field Marshal Montgomery.

The German counter-offensive had opened on 16 December and had been brought under control by the 26th. The initiative in the battle had passed to our forces shortly thereafter, and by 16 January, one month after the initial attack, our forces were in a firm position astride the Houffalize road network, ready to counter-attack strongly into enemy territory. Within this month, the enemy, although failing to reach even his initial objectives on the Meuse, had nevertheless succeeded in stopping our attacks against the Ruhr and the Saar. Operations to deal with the enemy offensive had occupied a full four weeks and were not, even by the 16th, completed. A certain regrouping was essential prior to the mounting of a full-scale offensive by our forces, and at that time I estimated that the enemy attack had delayed our offensive operations by at least six weeks. In addition to this disruption of our effort, the Strategic Air Forces had of necessity been drawn into the battle, thus leaving oil, aircraft, and communication targets deeper in Germany free of attack for nearly a month.

The counter-offensive, however, was not without its effects upon the enemy. Land and air forces had been carefully built up for months, and supplies, particularly of fuel, had been carefully hoarded for this all-out effort. During the month ending 16 January, my commanders estimated that the enemy suffered 120,000 serious casualties and lost 600 tanks and assault guns. He also lost about 1,620 planes—a severe blow—and his fuel stocks, after nearly a month of large-scale effort, were reduced to a bare minimum. The Tactical Aircraft claims for the month included also over 6,000 motor transport destroyed and 7,000 damaged, together with some 550 locomotives destroyed and over 600 damaged. By the end of our own counter-offensive the enemy had lost 220,000 men, including 110,000 prisoners of war. More serious in the final analysis was the widespread disillusionment within the German Army and Germany itself which must have accompanied the realization that the breakthrough had failed to seize any really important objective and had achieved nothing decisive.

During the progress of the Battle of the Ardennes, the enemy had also, as a diversionary and containing measure, mounted an attack on the 6th Army Group front with the apparent purpose of regaining the Alsace-Lorraine plains westward to the Vosges. It had initially been our plan to press the attacks against the enemy in this sector and to establish an easily held defensive line on the Rhine in order to be in a position to move forces northward for the main attack into Germany. The Battle of the Ardennes had made it immediately necessary to transfer to the north strong forces under command of General Patton prior to attaining our full objectives in the south. 6th Army Group had, as a result of the shift northward of these forces, been compelled to abandon the plans to clear the territory west of the Rhine, and was left with only the minimum forces required to maintain the defensive on its original line. Moreover, it was faced with an unhealthy situation in the area of the Colmar pocket.

After General Devers' troops had broken through the Vosges Mountains in November, it had appeared to him that the remaining German forces around the Colmar pocket could and would be quickly mopped up by the French Army. Consequently he had, according to plan, turned north with the bulk of his forces to assist General Patton who had fundamentally the same offensive role of securing the Rhine line. It was expected that as soon as the Colmar pocket had been reduced, the French Army itself would be capable of holding all Alsace-Lorraine and the entire Seventh Army could be employed north and east of the Vosges sector. As time went on, however, the enemy was able to stabilize the Colmar pocket, and to reinforce the area. Consequently, when the German thrust came through the Ardennes in great strength, we had on our extreme right flank, instead of the strong, easily defended line we expected, a situation that was inherently weak from a defensive standpoint. The entire VI Corps was lying to the east of the Vosges facing north, while the US 3rd Infantry Division had to be maintained with the French First Army in order to sustain the integrity of our lines in the Colmar pocket. The danger, clearly recognized by all of us from the start, was that the enemy would attempt to drive southward along the west of the Vosges and at the same time possibly try to erupt with a secondary attack from the Colmar pocket. In this event, VI Corps would not only have been unable to provide us with any reserves for the rest of the front, but would actually have had to turn and fight its way out of an awkward situation.

In view of this unsatisfactory position, and because General Devers' local reserves should manifestly be stationed west of the protective mountain barrier, I ordered a general withdrawal of the VI Corps line to the Vosges, retaining in the area north of Strasbourg only light reconnaissance elements that would have had to withdraw under any sizeable enemy advance. This move would, of course, have exposed Strasbourg to occupation by enemy forces and would have forced the left flank of the French Army to swing back into the mountains. It would, however, give General Devers the strongest possible defensive line along his eastern flank, since our forces had failed to gain the Rhine, and he would be enabled to collect into his own reserves at least two armored divisions in the regions south of the Siegfried Line and west of the Vosges. This would have given us opportunity to employ two US divisions as a SHAEF reserve farther to the north, leaving General Bradley free to devote his entire power to the offensive.

General Devers planned to execute this movement by stages, and until it could be completed we obviously had to leave the two divisions scheduled for SHAEF reserve under his control. Throughout the planning of the movement the French were kept informed. As the plans crystallized, however, the French became convinced that a withdrawal from the Strasbourg area would have unfortunate political repercussions in their country, bringing about perhaps even the downfall of the de Gaulle Government. They were so convinced of the necessity of at least putting up a fight for Strasbourg, rather than of voluntarily withdrawing to a better defensive line, that they were prepared to defend the city with the few French troops that could be hurriedly gathered together. These troops would have been so unready for battle and so inadequately equipped, however, that nothing could have been accomplished.

After closely studying the French views in the matter, and recognizing the political importance of Strasbourg, I felt compelled to alter the original plan for withdrawal. Originally, I had considered that the matter of Strasbourg was merely a conflict between military and political considerations and that I was completely justified in handling the question on a purely military basis. However, as I studied the French views, it became evident that the execution of the original plans for withdrawal might have such grave consequences in France that all our lines of communication and our vast rear areas might become seriously affected through interference with the tasks of the service troops and through civil unrest generally. Clearly, the prevention of such a contingency became a matter of military as well as of political necessity.

The plan was accordingly altered so that VI Corps merely withdrew from its sharp salient and its left rested in the Vosges with its right extending toward Strasbourg. In the meantime, preparation of defensive positions in the Vosges went on, conducted mainly by service troops. In view of my orders to go over to the defensive, to withdraw from the salient, and to place in reserve or send northward all available divisions, the enemy made some progress against our lines with a total force estimated at 14 divisions. Between Saarguemines and Neunhofen attacks shaping up into two prongs were made on 1 January in the direction of Rohrbach and toward the Saverne Pass, southeast of Bitche. Six days later the enemy succeeded in pushing troops across the Rhine, a few miles north of Strasbourg, and gained ground in a thrust northward from the Colmar pocket. This latter drive threatened to overrun the Alsatian Plain and to isolate Strasbourg. General Devers' forces inflicted heavy losses upon the enemy and with vigorous counter-measures, in spite of the difficulties under which they labored, succeeded in stabilizing the line so that no militarily essential ground in the Vosges was lost and Strasbourg itself no more than threatened.

PLANS FOR THE 1945 CAMPAIGN

By early 1945, the German oil supply was critically short and there was a growing transportation crisis which was already affecting every aspect of the German war effort. Our successful land advances had disrupted the German air defense system, had enabled us to install blind-bombing aids on the Continent, and had increased the depth to which fighter escorts could accompany the bombers into Germany. All these factors greatly increased our bombing power and reduced the capacity of the German Air Force to resist attacks.

By 16 January, the Battle of the Ardennes was substantially concluded. The First and Third Armies had joined hands through the salient at Houffalize, and their junction marked the achievement of tactical victory. At midnight on 17/18 January, the First Army reverted to the command of General Bradley's 12th Army Group, and the Allied line once more took up the order in which it was ranged along the threshold of Germany at the time when von Rundstedt's offensive interrupted our invasion preparations a month earlier. The task now was to regrasp the strategic initiative and resume the advance.

In planning our forthcoming spring and summer offensives, I envisaged the operations which would lead to Germany's collapse as falling into three phases: first, the destruction of the enemy forces west of the Rhine and closing to that river; second, the seizure of bridgeheads over the Rhine from which to develop operations into Germany; and third, the destruction of the remaining enemy east of the Rhine and the advance into the heart of the Reich. This was the same purpose that had guided all our actions since early 1944.

The immediate aim was to be the smashing of the enemy west of the Rhine, in order to reduce to a minimum the forces which would be available to oppose our crossing of the river and subsequent advance. A secondary purpose was to give us a maximum ability for concentration along chosen avenues across the Rhine, with maximum economy of security troops on other portions of the front. The form which these operations west of the Rhine were to take was largely dependent upon the geographical factors which would condition our progress in the later phases.

Once we had crossed the Rhine, there were two main avenues by which we could advance to the heart of Germany and defeat such enemy forces as were left to oppose us. The first of these was from the lower Rhine, north of the Ruhr and into the North German Plain; the second was from the Mainz–Karlsruhe area and thence northeast through Frankfurt toward Kassel. The former axis of advance, apart from offering the most suitable terrain for mobile operations—the type of warfare which we wished to force upon the enemy in order to exploit our superior mobility—afforded the quickest means of denying to the Germans the vital Ruhr industries. The northern and eastern exits of the Ruhr could be cut by enveloping action on the part of the ground forces, while the southern ones could be interrupted by air action. On the other hand, the importance of the Ruhr to the enemy was such that he was likely to accord it first priority in his defense plans, so that the rapid development of a superior force across the Rhine would be essential to Allied success. An advance on the southern axis from Mainz toward Kassel would also secure to us an industrial zone, in the Frankfurt area, and would therefore also be likely to afford us an opportunity of destroying considerable enemy forces. It would, moreover, offer suitable airfield sites from which to support further advances. On the debit side, however, the advance would be over terrain less suitable for armored operations, although once Kassel had been reached the Allies could either push north to complete the encirclement of the Ruhr, or northeast toward Berlin, or eastward toward Leipzig.

From the Mainz–Karlsruhe sector, a thrust might also be eastward toward Nürnberg, but this, important as it was later to become, was not of immediate concern in the long-term planning on which we were engaged in January. We still held on to the hope for an opportunity to effect a massive double envelopment of the Ruhr, to be followed by a great thrust to join up with the Russians, but we could not then foresee to what extent the forthcoming Russian offensive, in its sweeping advances, might influence our strategy in this direction.

With respect to the local geographical factors governing our choice of Rhine crossing-sites, the Mainz–Karlsruhe sector was more favorable than that north of the Ruhr. In the latter, between Emmerich and Wesel, there were sites suitable for three divisional assaults on a 20-mile front, in addition to one possible, though difficult, further site. Flooding conditions west of Emmerich would quite likely preclude any extension of this assault area until after June. In the Mainz–Karlsruhe sector there were sites for five divisional assaults, with a possible sixth south of Karlsruhe. In addition to these two main sectors, there was one site on each side of Cologne which would accommodate a single divisional assault crossing, but this would prove tactically difficult, and, once across the river, the forces would be faced with unfavorable terrain. The nature of the country likewise militated against the use of sites between Coblenz and Bonn except under conditions of very light opposition.

Another factor which had to be taken into account in planning the Rhine assault operations was the technical opinion of the Engineers that until March there would be a danger of ice hampering the crossings and bridging. Below Mainz summer floods, following the melting of the Alpine snows, would make it imperative to complete the construction of permanent bridges by May. This estimate differed from earlier technical reports in that it indicated the advisability of a March–April attack, whereas the Engineers originally believed that conditions on the Rhine would render unwise any such attempt between 20 November and late May.

From the logistical aspect, there was available to the Allied armies sufficient bridging equipment and personnel to launch nine assault crossings, and, in addition, one unopposed crossing of the Rhine. After the crossings had been effected, it was estimated that our lines of communication would enable us to build up to a maximum of some 35 divisions north of the Ruhr, leaving some 55 divisions (counting scheduled arrivals) for holding and secondary operations.

None of the considerations mentioned above indicated any change in the decision arrived at during our pre-D-Day planning, that is that the main thrust of the Allied armies for the crossing of the Rhine and the isolation of the Ruhr should be on the axis north of the Ruhr. Without that vast industrial region, Germany would be incapable of continuing to wage war, especially when the expected Russian offensive had engulfed the Silesian industrial area which alone was comparable to the Ruhr in productive capacity. Since we could not attack the Ruhr frontally, we must by-pass it; and the most favorable terrain lay to its north. I was equally certain that this main effort on the north should be accompanied by a secondary effort as strong as our means permitted after the main, northern thrust had been provided for, from the Mainz–Karlsruhe area in the general direction of Kassel. Thus the maneuver would constitute a great double envelopment, which would encircle the Ruhr and the mass of the enemy forces which were certain to concentrate in its defense.

With this in mind, the first task must be to initiate operations west of the Rhine and north of the Moselle which should destroy the enemy in that zone and bring our armies on to the Rhine north of Düsseldorf to permit preparation for the ensuing main attack. That done, we must direct our main effort to eliminating other enemy forces west of the Rhine which might still constitute an obstacle or a potential threat to our subsequent crossing operations. When the enemy had thus been cleared from the west bank, we must seize bridgeheads over the river both in the north and the south. North of the Ruhr, we must deploy east of the Rhine the maximum number of divisions which we were capable of maintaining there, while to the south, on the axis Mainz–Frankfurt–Kassel, we must deploy such forces as might be available after providing the estimated 35 divisions required for the principal thrust north of the Ruhr.

The primary task of the southern force was to draw away enemy units which might otherwise oppose the main advance in the north. It was essential to force the enemy to disperse his strength, so that we might use all possible crossings and lines of communication to establish in western Germany a concentrated force of sufficient size to complete the conquest. Flexibility had to be an essential of our plans, as the possibility of failure to secure the necessary bridgeheads in one or another sector could not be overlooked. Logistical preparations must therefore be made rapidly to switch the main effort from north to south if this should prove necessary. Whatever the opposition might be, the fact remained that in any case the crossing of the Rhine, on the narrow frontages available, would be a tactical and engineering feat of the greatest magnitude. Use of airborne forces, air support, and amphibious equipment on the maximum scale would be required if the successful passage of the main Allied armies was to be assured.

The strength of our land forces, at the time of planning in January, was 71 divisions, but this figure did not accurately represent their effective value. Many of the American divisions were seriously under strength in infantry, and, although strenuous efforts were being made to find the necessary replacements both by accelerating the flow of reinforcements from the United States and by taking fit men from rear echelon employment, it was obvious that some time must elapse before these men could become available for front-line duty. For the moment the French divisions on our southern flank were depleted to relatively low combat effectiveness. By the time at which we estimated we should be ready to cross the Rhine, in March, the Allied strength would, under the existing build-up program, have risen to 85 divisions, including 6 airborne, with 5 to 8 new French divisions organizing, training and equipping for possible later employment. It was also hoped that the existing French divisions would have their combat value largely restored.

As against the Allied power, it was difficult, as the situation then stood, to calculate the likely strength of the enemy in the spring. This depended partly upon the extent to which he might be able to draw reinforcements from Italy and Norway for the Western Front. It would depend also upon the destructive effects of our continuing winter operations, which, as always, I was determined to pursue vigorously. Finally, it depended upon the degree to which events on the Eastern Front would engross the enemy's attention. If the worst happened and the anticipated Russian spring offensive proved weak and ineffectual, the enemy was estimated to be capable of maintaining as many as 100 divisions in the west. But if the Russian offensive proved as successful as we hoped, it seemed unlikely that more than 80 divisions could be spared to meet our attack, while the German logistical potentialities would be correspondingly impaired.

Now that the time was approaching for what, we trusted, would be the final blow to Nazi Germany a closer coordination with the Russian High Command and mutual understanding of our respective plans became essential. Our first liaison with Moscow had been effected late in 1944 when air operations necessitated the establishment of a coordinated bomb-line, but little further had been accomplished. The only link between my headquarters and that of Marshal Stalin was through the medium of the Allied Military Mission in Moscow, and it appeared most difficult to learn of Soviet intentions. Up to the end of 1944 I had received no information on matters affecting the Russian grand strategy, although I had expressed my willingness to afford any such information concerning my own overall plans as the Red Army might desire. At Christmas time, however, following upon a message which I sent to the Combined Chiefs of Staff explaining the difficulty with which I was faced in attempting to evolve plans while still ignorant of the Russian intentions, President Roosevelt secured from Marshal Stalin his agreement to receive our representative in order to discuss the correlation of our respective efforts in the forthcoming spring.

Accordingly, in January, my deputy, Air Chief Marshal Tedder, accompanied by Major-General Bull (G-3) and Brig. Gen. Betts (G-2), journeyed to Moscow for this purpose. The conference proved conspicuously successful. In the course of a discussion ranging over many aspects of the forthcoming campaigns, Marshal Stalin was acquainted with the nature of our own plans, including the timing. He, in turn, responded with a full explanation of the great four-pronged offensive, involving from 150 to 160 divisions, which the Red Army was preparing to launch. He further gave us an assurance that, in the event of the main offensive being halted by bad weather, the Red Army would still conduct local operations which he believed would so pin down German armies as to permit no major movement of divisions from east to west during the difficult period of the spring thaw. As events showed, the success of this gigantic offensive proved even greater than had been anticipated. In the meantime, fortified by Marshal Stalin's assurances, we were able to proceed with our own operational planning.

In addition to his preoccupation with the Russian forces, the enemy was certain to be seriously hampered in the forthcoming operations on our front by the logistical difficulties which had been imposed upon him by the attacks of the Allied Strategic Air Forces from the west, while in the east the vital Silesian industrial region was soon to be overrun by the Soviet armies. Despite superhuman efforts to keep the lines open, the German railroad system was gradually breaking down under the weight of ever-increasing air blows. The attacks upon the facilities behind the Ardennes front had forced the railheads back nearly to the Rhine. Heavy destruction had also been inflicted upon the enemy's airplane industries, although dispersion of plants and the construction of underground factories had enabled him to make some progress with his jet aircraft production—the most serious threat with which we were faced. But planes would be of little avail without fuel, and it was against the German refineries and synthetic plants that our greatest effort was directed. Although some recovery had been effected during the autumn and early winter, the heavy blows struck at the end of the year once more brought production down to an extremely critical figure. The gasoline produced during January was likely to be no more than 100,000 tons (20% of the pre-raid amount), and there was a prospect of a further drop to about half this figure with the intensification of our attacks in the near future. In fact, with the immobilization of probably the whole Ruhr synthetic fuel industry, the simultaneous stoppage of the great installations at Bruz, Leuna, and Politz, and the threat of the Russian advances to the synthetic plants in Silesia, the German oil industry was facing a graver crisis than ever before, and this at a time when operational requirements were likely to rise to a point higher than in any previous period of the past six months.

It was to this oil offensive that we pinned our faith to counterbalance the numerical superiority which the enemy enjoyed over us in respect to his jet aircraft. Had the program of production which the Luftwaffe envisaged been put into effect, our air mastery in the spring of 1945 would have been precarious, for our own production had not enabled us to meet the jets on equal terms. Fortunately our bombing campaign, both upon the production centers and upon the airfields from which the jet planes operated, so limited their numbers and potentialities that the German effort was too little and too late. So far as orthodox aircraft were concerned, despite a numerical strength that was still considerable, the fuel situation and the growing dearth of trained pilots were so acute that the German Air Force was never in a position seriously to interfere with our operations after the great but costly effort made on New Year's Day, when some 800 aircraft raided Allied airfields in Belgium and Holland.

On the Allied side, I was satisfied that our Tactical Air Forces were strong enough to fulfil the tasks which would face them when our offensives began, and that the Strategic Air Forces were fully capable of carrying out their planned programs. Attacks on oil installations, jet aircraft and armament factories, and naval and communications targets were to be the chief objectives of the heavy bombers, with an overriding priority of coordination with the ground force offensive operations. The air staff fully explored the possibility of destroying the 31 Rhine bridges behind the enemy armies west of the river, in the same way that in the previous summer we had cut the lines of communication over the Seine and Loire behind the German Seventh Army in Normandy, but did not consider such a program practicable. It was believed that to undertake the destruction of so many bridges as an additional target system would involve too great a diversion from the existing strategic effort, and that the weather was unlikely to afford the requisite number of visual bombing days. Certain key bridges were to be attacked, however, in conjunction with a transverse blocking of communications within each battle area which would limit the enemy's tactical mobility.

In the latter respect, the enemy was favored by the advantages accruing from his strong defensive lines, first the Siegfried fortifications, and behind them the great barrier of the Rhine itself. These defenses were extremely formidable, and apart from the cost of piercing them on a selected front, their chief value to the enemy lay in the fact that they would enable him to concentrate safely for counter-attack at our lines of communication. That capability was well demonstrated when the Ardennes thrust had been launched, and, although that attempt had been defeated, the possibility of further, though necessarily weaker, offensives remained. To meet this we would have to station all along our extended line more troops than we could afford, and any concentration on our part for an attack on a given point would entail a dangerous weakening of other sectors, *unless* before striking our decisive blow at the heart of Germany we ourselves possessed such a defensive line as the enemy himself enjoyed. I was convinced that only the Rhine could fulfil this requirement. Once we held the Rhine substantially throughout its length we should possess such a line as could be held with minimum forces along the inactive sectors. Thus we could safely concentrate the great strength required for our intended main thrust across the river north of the Ruhr and, by the exercise of economy elsewhere, provide reasonable strength for a secondary effort. Moreover, the enemy would find himself at the same disadvantage as that at which the possession of the Siegfried Line had formerly placed us. We would have the opportunity of threatening him at a number of points along the line, forcing him to disperse his defending forces and thus making easier the task of our troops invading the Reich at the points selected for our attack.

For these reasons, we considered that before attempting any major operations east of the Rhine it was essential to destroy the main enemy armies west of the river, although it might not be worth the time and cost to indulge in protracted operations to reduce any strong but constricted bridgeheads that might remain in German hands. When the Combined Chiefs of Staff expressed doubts as to our ability to maintain two thrusts—north of the Ruhr and in the Mainz–Frankfurt area—with the forces at my disposal, it was pointed out that such would indeed be the case if we did not clear to the Rhine before embarking on a major offensive to the east of that river. Given a situation, however, where we could operate without fear for the security of our flanks and without expending for defensive purposes more strength than we could afford, I felt confident of our ability to carry out the plans already indicated, putting the chief weight into the northern thrust but at the same time striking in the south and retaining flexibility enough to switch the main effort if the situation so required. Moreover, the simple fact remained that destruction of enemy forces should be easier on the west of the Rhine than on the east.

Of the 85 divisions which were to be at my disposal, 35 were tentatively allocated for the northern thrust. Of the remainder, I estimated that only 25 were necessary for defense and reserve purposes if we held the line of the

Rhine, whereas as many as 45 would be required were the northern assault to be attempted while the rest of the front was substantially west of the river, with the enemy capable of striking at us from behind his Siegfried fortifications.

Together with their suggestion that I should concentrate upon the single heavy drive in the north rather than run what might, except in the circumstances described, have proved a dangerous risk of weakening the Allied efforts of overdispersal, the Combined Chiefs of Staff submitted for my consideration a proposal by the British Chiefs of Staff that a single ground commander for the whole front north of Luxembourg be appointed to exercise, under me, operational control and coordination of all ground forces involved in the offensive which was to take us across the Rhine. This suggestion was based upon the assumption that all the remainder of the front would remain on the defensive, contrary to my plans. I pointed out that, under these plans, the Ruhr marked the logical division of command zones, and that Field Marshal Montgomery would be in charge of all the forces—the Canadian Army, British Army, and US Ninth Army—that were to participate in the northern offensive to capture the Ruhr. In the center, during the operations preceding the Rhine crossing, General Bradley's 12th Army Group, comprising the US First and Third Armies, would concentrate primarily on an offensive through the Siegfried Line along the axis Prüm–Bonn with its left swinging north to support the Ninth Army and its right swinging south to flank the Saar. South of the Moselle General Devers' 6th Army Group, with the US Seventh and French First Armies, would remain on the defensive at first, subsequently operating to clear the Saar Basin and close the Rhine when the Germans had been driven out of the zone north of the Moselle.

The existing Army Group system of command thus fitted naturally into the operational plans which we had evolved, and I could not see how the appointment of a C-in-C of Ground Forces over the Army Group Commanders to direct the forthcoming battles would in any way secure better coordination of effort. On the contrary, the appointment would, in fact, have necessitated a duplication of personnel and communications which could have resulted only in decreased efficiency, while such functions as the allocation of forces and supplies between the Army groups were already performed by my own headquarters.

In this connection, my views as to the place of a so-called "ground" C-in-C in a theater commanded by a single Supreme Commander are roughly as follows: ground forces should ordinarily be commanded according to the possibilities, frequently determined by geography, of close battlefield supervision. Battlefield command extends upward through the Division, Corps, Army, and Army Group Commander. This last commander is the highest ground commander who has a logical function separate from that of the Theater Commander and who, at the same time, can be sufficiently freed from broad strategic, logistic, and civil problems to give his entire attention to the battle. The next higher commander above the Army Group Commander, by whatever name he is called, such as Supreme or Theater Commander, necessarily controls broad strategy and commands air and sea forces, and therefore is the only one in position to bring additional strength to bear to influence the action. When the ground front is such that configuration and extent permit close battle supervision by a single Army Group Commander, then this officer is also known as the Ground Commander of the entire force. But when there is more than one Army Group in a single theater, there cannot logically be an overall "ground commander" separate from the Theater or Supreme Commander. Each Army Group should normally occupy a well defined channel of strategic advance. A special case would be one where a series of armies would be operating, each in a distinctly separate geographical area and without close tactical relationship, one to the other. In this case each Army Commander would be directly subordinate to the Theater Commander, since an Army Group Commander could serve no useful function.

These convictions, together with the outline operational plans which had been worked out, were explained to the Combined Chiefs of Staff when they met at the Malta Conference in the last week of January, on their way to the Tripartite Conference in the Crimea. My Chief of Staff, who attended the Malta Conference as my representative, assured the Combined Chiefs that we would seize the west bank of the Rhine at the crossing sites in the north as soon as this was feasible and without waiting to come up to the river throughout its length. We undertook further to advance across the Rhine in the north with maximum strength and complete determination as soon as the situation in the south allowed us to collect the necessary forces and carry out the assault without incurring unreasonable risks.

OPERATIONS TO REACH
THE RHINE

In conformity with our strategic plans for operations into the heart of Germany, the main effort in the Allied operations west of the Rhine was to be in the northern sector, with a view to seizing the crossings north of the Ruhr. All our other operations were designed primarily to assist this northern operation, to gain secure flanks so as to permit of the heaviest concentration with which to force a crossing in the north, and eventually to provide the bases for our secondary effort.

Operations west of the Rhine were to be developed in three distinct phases. Phase I was to consist primarily of the operations known as Veritable and Grenade, by which respectively the Canadian Army and the US Ninth Army were to advance to the Rhine below Düsseldorf. In addition, the US First Army was to seize the line of the Erft west and northwest of Cologne, thus ensuring the security of our communications between Aachen and München-Gladbach. As soon as these operations began, the existing offensive in the Ardennes was to give place to a policy of aggressive defense designed to contain the German divisions fighting there and to widen the breaches made in the Siegfried Line. South of the Moselle our forces were to remain on the defensive, such local operations as were necessary to contain the German forces on their front being conducted with the maximum economy both of personnel and of ammunition.

During Phase II, while the Rhine-crossing operations were prepared and instituted in the north, the enemy was to be driven back to the river north of its confluence with the Moselle in order that the main bridgehead's lines of communication should be absolutely secure. On completion of these operations our southern forces were to initiate an offensive to capture the Saar Basin and begin their advance to the Rhine in that sector.

Operations to reach the Rhine

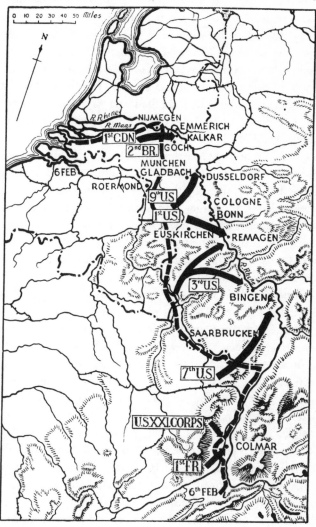

Finally, in Phase III, while the northern bridgehead was consolidated and expanded and the Central Group of Armies remained on the defensive north of the Moselle, the remaining forces in the south were to complete their operations to reach the Rhine so that the Allies would hold the entire left bank.

During the latter half of January and the beginning of February the Central Group of Armies continued to fight hard in the Ardennes sector to take advantage of the check we had imposed upon the enemy there. General Bradley was instructed to inflict the maximum losses upon the Germans, to seize any opportunity of breaching the Siegfried Line and, if successful, to advance northeast on the axis Prüm–Euskirchen. The attack was to be pressed with all vigor as long as there was any reasonable chance of securing a decisive success, but, as an alternative, we had to be ready to pass quickly to the defensive in the Ardennes and to launch the new attacks in the northern sector.

The latter offensive, comprising operations Veritable and Grenade, was to be under the control of 21 Army Group. The US Ninth Army was to remain under the command of Field Marshal Montgomery for this purpose and was to be built up to a strength of four corps, totalling twelve divisions, the rate of build-up being determined by the progress of operations in the Ardennes. In operation Veritable, the target date for which was to be not later than 8 February, the Canadian First Army was to conduct a strong offensive from the Nijmegen area southeast between the Rhine and the Maas, carrying the thrust as far as the general line Xanten–Geldern, clearing the whole area and establishing a firm flank along the Rhine. The attack was to be made on a two-corps front, British 30 Corps on the right and Canadian 2 Corps on the left, while British 1 Corps was also to be under command of the Canadian Army. In all, seven infantry and four armored divisions, with four infantry and five armored brigades, were to be employed. If, as was hoped, dry ground conditions prevailed, the basis of the operation was to be speed and violence, the armored columns passing through the enemy lines and disrupting his rear areas. As events turned out the state of the country was the very reverse of what had been desired.

In order that operation Grenade might be launched, 12th Army Group was to extend its left wing northward as far as Jülich, and the Ninth Army would then hold a front on the Roer River from Jülich to Roermond. From the right portion of this front it was to launch a strong attack toward the Rhine, with its right flank on the line Jülich–Neuss. The offensive was to be carried up to the Rhine between Düsseldorf and Mors. 12th Army Group was initially to protect the Ninth Army's right flank. It was hoped to commence Grenade not later than 10 February.

Operation Veritable was duly launched on the target date of 8 February, but the weather conditions could hardly have been more unfavorable. January had been exceptionally severe, with snow lying on the ground through the month, and when the thaw set in at the beginning of February, the ground became extremely soft and water-logged, while floods spread far and wide in the area over which our advance had been planned to take place. The difficulties thus imposed were immense, and the men had sometimes to fight waist-deep in water. The privations which they underwent were appalling, but their spirit was indomitable, and they overcame their personal hardships with great gallantry to inflict a major defeat upon the enemy in some of the fiercest fighting of the whole war.

Under such conditions it was inevitable that our hopes for a rapid breakthrough should be disappointed, and the fighting soon developed into a bitter slugging match in which the enemy had to be forced back yard by yard. When the attack was first launched the enemy's reaction was slow, but our own difficulties gave him a chance to consolidate his defenses. The Germans' trouble lay, as usual, in their lack of mobility, for the stocks of gasoline which they had laboriously accumulated for the Ardennes offensive were now exhausted and the incessant Allied air attacks upon the fuel-producing plants, the roads, and the railways caused the situation daily to deteriorate still further.

Apart from the German army's logistical difficulties, moreover, it was considerably weakened in numerical strength on the Western Front by the date when Veritable was launched, as compared with that army's state at the beginning of January. During the closing stages of the Ardennes battle, when the failure of the offensive was seen to be inevitable, the Sixth Panzer Army had been withdrawn from the line to commence a weary and unhappy trek across Germany to the Eastern Front. With it went the remnants of some seven panzer and panzer grenadier divisions, two panzer brigades, and three infantry divisions, a force which included considerably over half the armor which had confronted us when von Rundstedt launched his attack in mid-December. As against these departures and some 150,000 serious battle casualties, the reinforcements sent to the Western Front were insignificant in both quality and quantity. Now that the Allies were once more on the general offensive, all hope of any renewed major offensive by the enemy disappeared, and it soon became merely a question of how long von Rundstedt's skill and the stubborn spirit of his depleted forces could maintain a purely defensive battle west of the Rhine. Again the desperate commitment of formations piecemeal to the fighting, which we had first witnessed in Normandy, was repeated. The enemy's chief assets for the moment lay in the weather and the terrain, but these could never compensate for the seasoned fighting forces which he had lost.

During the first days of Veritable good progress was made through the forest called Reichswald and to the outskirts of Kleve, but fierce resistance was then encountered. The opposition on the southern edge of the forest was particularly violent. Nevertheless, Kleve fell by 12 February and on the 13th the forest was cleared. On the following day the Rhine was reached opposite Emmerich, and on the 16th the Kalkar–Goch road was crossed, although German forces of the First Parachute Army continued to resist strongly in the Goch sector. The town itself fell on 21 February, two days before operation Grenade was launched.

Despite the comparative slowness of our progress, Veritable achieved its strategic objectives. We gained a footing on the west bank of the Rhine in the area where our major crossing operations were subsequently to be launched, and, equally important, heavy losses were inflicted on the Germans west of the river. Moreover, the offensive steadily drew in the enemy's slender reserves and thus cleared the way for very rapid progress by the Ninth Army when operation Grenade was initiated on 23 February.

Grenade had of necessity been repeatedly postponed on account of the ground conditions. The Ninth Army was ready to strike on the target date appointed, 10 February, but the state of the terrain enforced delay until the floods should subside. Apart from the effects of the thaw, aggravated by the heavy rains which followed the melting of the snow, the enemy was in a position to flood the area further by reason of his control of the Roer dams. The First Army was instructed to concentrate on the capture of these prior to the launching of Grenade, and in heavy fighting its forces pushed hard toward their objectives through extremely difficult country of broken hills covered with forests. The first of the seven dams was reached on 4 February and the last and most important one—the Schwammenauel Dam—on 10 February. The controls on some of the dams had been hit by our air bombing in December, but the damage had been partially repaired, and before the enemy was compelled to abandon the Schwammenauel Dam, he opened the sluices. The water poured down the valley, causing the level of the Roer to rise about four feet, and it was not until 23 February that the flood subsided sufficiently to permit the launching of Grenade across the river.

The attack was begun, in clear moonlight, by VII Corps of the First Army, over the Roer south of Düren at 0330 hours. An hour later, XIX and XIII Corps of the Ninth Army commenced their crossing of the river in the Jülich sector. The attacks were preceded by 45 minutes' intensive artillery bombardment which effectively reduced enemy interference with our initial assault, but considerable difficulties were experienced from the mines sown in the river and from the swiftness of the current which rendered the passage of the assault boats extremely hazardous. However, bridgeheads were speedily gained and consolidated. Once across the river, our forces met their chief opposition from the German artillery, which also bombarded the bridging sites, while the enemy infantry generally fell back after rallying for only one real counterattack. The enemy also made a considerable air bombing and strafing effort against the bridges, but they were unable to hold the advance.

Our offensive rapidly gathered momentum. VII Corps cleared Düren by 25 February, Jülich had fallen the day before, and the enemy recoiled north and northeast of Linnich as the Ninth Army armor passed through the infantry to thrust forward its spearheads. While the First Army forces pushed towards Cologne, those of the Ninth Army were directed towards München-Gladbach and Grevenbroich. The speed of the advance increased daily, and whole units of the German Fifteenth Army surrendered as their losses in both men and ground began to tell. By 1 March the industrial center of München-Gladbach had been cleared, Grevenbroich had fallen, Neuss was entered, Venlo reached, and Roermond found abandoned by the enemy. With General Simpson, the Ninth Army Commander, I visited München-Gladbach to catch a glimpse of the fighting north and east of that city. The troops definitely sensed ultimate victory and were irresistible.

Meanwhile, the First Parachute Army had been fighting stubbornly to hold the continued pressure by the Canadian Army between the Rhine and the Maas farther north, but the advance of the Ninth Army now threatened its rear and its withdrawal became inevitable. Although an armored division fought hard to retain the wooded area south of Marienbaum and keep us back from the Rhine, on 4 March the two Allied armies made contact in the Geldern area and the success of the combined Veritable–Grenade operations was assured. By 5 March there were no enemy left west of the Rhine between Neuss and Homberg, but the Parachute Army struggled bitterly to retain its last bridgehead across the river in the Wesel–Xanten area. It was not until 10 March that this bridgehead finally collapsed, the enemy blowing the bridges behind him as his last forces withdrew to the east bank. On the following day the task of mopping up the whole area on the west bank was completed. The prisoners brought our total captured since D Day to over 1,000,000.

While the Ninth Army was pushing to the Rhine in its sector, the First Army was exploiting its successful crossing of the Roer and thrusting towards Cologne. This operation, however, may more correctly be considered as part of those which comprised Phase II of the whole campaign west of the Rhine. It was intended that the First Army should close in upon the river from the northwest and the Third Army from the southwest, eliminating the enemy north of the Moselle. While these operations, known under the general name of Lumberjack, were being executed, 6th Army Group, south of the Moselle, would remain basically on the defensive, while in the north 21 Army Group would complete its preparations for the forthcoming major assault across the Rhine north of the Ruhr.

The plan of operation Lumberjack was for the First Army to seize the high ground east of the Erft River northwest of Cologne and to close to the Rhine south of Düsseldorf. Farther south, the road center of Euskirchen was to be captured, bridgeheads established over the Erft in that sector, and forces concentrated for an advance to the southeast. Cologne was then to be invested from the northwest, and, at the appropriate moment, a strong attack on a narrow front was to be driven southeast from Euskirchen to converge with the Third Army advance, and the Rhine was to be reached in the army zone. The Third Army was to seize bridgeheads over the Kyll River, on which its forces at present stood, and then, when so ordered, to drive hard eastward to seize the Mayen–Coblenz area and complete the clearance of the enemy from the west bank of the Rhine between the Moselle and the Ahr.

If the enemy defenses proved weak, the Third Army was also, in a subsequent stage, to obtain a bridgehead over the Moselle to the southeast, to facilitate the operations which were to be initiated in that sector.

We had good reason to hope for sweeping success in these operations, for the enemy's forces, reduced as they were both by their contributions to the Eastern Front and by the heavy casualties inflicted on them by our armies, had, in the Veritable–Grenade campaign, shown themselves inadequate to contain simultaneous Allied attacks on a broad front. The same policy of converging major thrusts which had proved successful in 21 Army Group sector was now about to be repeated by 12th Army Group. Apart from the damaging losses which the enemy had incurred, the fighting spirit of his armies, taken as a whole, had undergone a decline, and at certain points his defensive system was manifestly disorganized. Few—if any—trained reserves outside the west were believed to be available, and in the hard fighting which had taken place since the New Year virtually all the reserves in the west had been committed to the defensive battle. Under the circumstances, it seemed to me that the enemy's only course would be to do as he had done in the north and make as orderly a retreat as possible to the east of the Rhine, though it appeared likely that he would try to hold small bridgeheads on the west bank. Our plans were designed to prevent a safe withdrawal over the river.

Meanwhile, the increased hammering of the fuel installations in Germany, which followed the improvement in weather conditions after January, had made the enemy's situation more grave than ever in this respect. The February output fell to a total only 14% of normal, representing barely half the minimum requirements to maintain full-scale military effort. The effects of this and of the transportation crisis in Germany were seen not only on our own front but also on that facing the Russians, where, despite the transfer of the Sixth Panzer Army, the enemy had shown himself incapable of mounting an effective counter-attack to stem the growing tide of Soviet successes.

Operation Lumberjack fulfilled expectations. In the First Army drive, with VII Corps, toward Cologne, heavy opposition was for a time encountered east of the Erft Canal, but the three armored formations brought up to block our advance were dispersed by our air attacks, carried out in strength. The Erft bridgeheads were expanded, and on 5 March the advance elements of VII Corps were entering Cologne. By the afternoon of the 7th the city was entirely in our hands, the enemy resistance having collapsed once the Allied forces had reached the outskirts. The untrained Volkssturm left as a forlorn hope when the regular forces withdrew over the Rhine, blowing the bridges behind them, were capable of little fight. On the same day that Cologne fell, the remainder of the enemy evacuated the west bank north to Düsseldorf. This success had a profound effect on our subsequent operations, as the divisions which would have been used to invest Cologne became available to assist in exploiting the great opportunity we were shortly to be offered.

Farther south, the progress of the First Army was even more spectacular. III Corps attacked southeast in accordance with the operational plan, rolled up the disorganized enemy confronting it and closed to the Rhine at Remagen on 7 March. It was here on that day that occurred one of those rare and fleeting opportunities which occasionally present themselves in war, and which, if grasped, have incalculable effects in determining future success. In his confusion before the rapidity of the Allied thrust, the enemy failed to complete the destruction of the Ludendorff railroad bridge across the Rhine. Before he could rectify his mistake, a small spearhead of 9th Armored Division with the greatest determination and gallantry had seized the bridge—the only one to be left intact by the Germans throughout the entire length of the river.

The Remagen bridge was not in a sector from which it had been intended to launch a major thrust eastward, but I at once determined, at the expense of modifying details of the plan of campaign, to seize the golden opportunity offered to us. It was obvious that possession of a foothold over the Rhine here would constitute the greatest possible threat as a supporting effort for the main attack north of the Ruhr. In order, therefore, to exploit the situation and establish an adequate bridgehead, consolidated in readiness for an offensive therefrom as soon as the progress of our operations south of the Moselle permitted, I ordered General Bradley, when he telephoned me to report the occurrence, to put not less than five divisions on to the far bank.

Partially anticipating this decision, General Bradley had begun the exploitation of the bridgehead immediately the bridge fell into his hands. A combat command was rapidly passed across, and by 9 March we held a lodgement area some three miles deep. It was several days before the enemy recovered sufficiently from his surprise and overcame his transport difficulties to send reinforcements to the threatened sector, and by the time they arrived the bridgehead had been enlarged and strengthened to a degree which rendered its elimination impossible. Enemy armored forces were again, as in Normandy, committed to battle piecemeal as they arrived on the scene, and no concerted major attack was mounted on a scale sufficient to effect a serious penetration. Such efforts as the enemy did make were unable to check the further expansion of the bridgehead; and as its area grew, the north–south autobahn east of the river, so vital to the enemy, was severed. By 24 March, when our main attacks eastward from the Rhine began in the north, the area held by the First Army at Remagen was 25 miles long and 10 miles deep, and within it three corps were poised ready to strike.

In the meantime the enemy had made desperate efforts to destroy the bridge while the security lodgement area was still dependent upon it. Long-range artillery was brought to bear on it, and the German Air Force put up the strongest effort of which it was capable in attempts to cut the structure by bombs, rocket projectiles, and cannon fire. All these efforts proved equally unsuccessful. The air battles over Remagen provided the Luftwaffe with its greatest test, and it failed. The umbrella established over the vital area by the US Ninth Air Force effectively disrupted the attacks, and the enemy's losses, both to our fighter planes and to the heavy concentration of anti-aircraft guns established on the river banks, were severe.

The enemy onslaught nevertheless made the area extremely uncomfortable, especially for the Engineers who carried out, with conspicuous gallantry and determination, the dangerous work of repairing damage and of strengthening the bridge to bear the enormous strains to which it was subjected and which it had never been intended to undergo. These strains eventually proved too much for the damaged structure, and on 17 March the center span (which had been damaged in the Germans' unsuccessful last-minute attempts at demolition on the 7th) collapsed into the river. Although a disappointment, this had no serious effect upon our operations, for by this time a number of supplementary floating bridges had been constructed, and the build-up of the forces on the east bank continued without interruption.

While III Corps of the First Army was establishing the bridgehead at Remagen, V Corps, on its right flank, struck to the south to make contact with the advancing spearheads of the Third Army. The German Fifth Panzer Army, disorganized, offered little resistance, and the Allied thrust made rapid progress. Bad Godesberg and Bonn fell on 9 March, and on the following day the link-up along the Rhine with the Third Army forces which had closed to the river in the Andernach area was accomplished. Considerable elements of the Fifth Panzer Army were cut off to the west by these converging drives; they fought courageously to the last, but it was the courage of despair, and they made no organized attempt to force a way out of the trap.

During February, the Third Army had been engaged in making the necessary preparations for its subsequent push to the Rhine. XX Corps had eliminated enemy resistance in the Saar–Moselle triangle by 23 February, and bridgeheads had been established over the Saar at Ockfen and Serrig in the teeth of violent opposition. The Siegfried defenses were penetrated, and Trier fell on 2 March. Farther north, the German Seventh Army had been forced back successively over the Our and Prüm Rivers, despite extensive minefields and obstacles, and on 4 March the first bridgeheads were gained across the Kyll.

The Third Army advance to the Rhine now began. VIII Corps, spearheaded by 11th Armored Division, broke through north of Kyllburg on 7 March. Advancing northeast with increasing rapidity, it reached the Rhine at Andernach on the 9th and linked up with the First Army, as already described, on the following day. To the south of VIII Corps, on 5 March, 4th Armoured Division of XII Corps, with great boldness, charged along the north bank of the Moselle, parallel to VIII Corps, toward its confluence with the Rhine. This objective was attained on 10 March, large quantities of enemy equipment being captured in the process. By the next day, the left bank of the Rhine from Coblenz to Andernach had been cleared, and the enemy had virtually been eliminated along its length north of the Moselle, thus accomplishing Phase II of the operations to close the river in its entirety through German territory.

The stage was now set for the initiation of the joint offensive operations by the Third and Seventh Armies south of the Moselle which had been anticipated as Phase III of the campaign west of the Rhine. In the 6th Army Group sector, operations during January and February had, in accordance with our overall plan, been mainly of a defensive nature. Such local operations as had been conducted were designed to eliminate the dangerous situation created in the south, as I have earlier described, following the enemy attacks in support of his Ardennes offensive and our weakening of 6th Army Group when divisions had to be moved northward to meet the major threat.

Chief among the tasks which had to be accomplished was the destruction of the Colmar pocket. An attack was launched by the French I Corps against the southern edge of the pocket on 20 January, but this at first made little progress, partly because of bad weather. North of the pocket the French II Corps fared similarly. However, we had assembled and turned over to the French First Army the US XXI Corps, composed of the 3rd, 28th, and 75th Infantry Divisions, and the 12th Armored Division, under Maj. Gen. Frank W. Milburn, to carry the brunt of the battle by an attack between the two French corps. Its efforts quickly became effective. Lack of reinforcements caused the enemy resistance to crumble at the end of the month and at the same time the weather improved. Before our three-corps attack the German disintegration developed rapidly: Colmar itself fell on 3 February, and by the 6th the enemy was mainly east of the Rhine–Rhône canal. The evacuation of the disorganized remnants across the Rhine was then in progress, and with the collapse of opposition at Neuf Brisach on 9 February all organized resistance west of the Rhine in that zone ceased. In the course of the operation the enemy suffered over 22,000 casualties and considerable losses of equipment: the German Nineteenth Army was virtually destroyed.

After the elimination of the Colmar pocket, interest in the 6th Army Group area centered in the Seventh Army zone, in front of the Siegfried defenses. The French Army maintained the defensive along the Rhine, and its left wing assumed responsibility for the front as far north as Bischweiler. During the latter half of February and early March the chief activity on the Seventh Army front was in the Saarbrücken-Forbach area, where bitter fighting took place and restricted Allied advances were made.

Following the Third Army successes north of the Moselle, the time had arrived for launching operation Undertone, the major offensive south of the Moselle, with the objectives of destroying the enemy west of the Rhine and closing on that river from Coblenz southward. By this means crossing-sites for the establishment of bridgeheads would be obtained in the Mainz–Mannheim sector and more enemy forces would be drawn away from the area where our main effort was shortly to be made in the north. To this end, the Seventh Army was to assume control of elements of the

French forces known as the Groupement Montsabert and then to attack in the general direction Homberg–Kaiserslautern–Worms. It was to breach the Siegfried Line, destroy the enemy in its zone, close on the Rhine and seize a bridgehead. Meanwhile the French Army was to protect the right flank of the Seventh Army and to conduct an aggressive defense along the Rhine. In cooperation with the Seventh Army effort, General Bradley was instructed to launch a thrust by the Third Army forces southeast across the lower reaches of the Moselle, with the object of turning the German line and thrusting deep into the rear areas of the forces facing the Seventh Army. He was also to attack the nose of the Saar salient.

On 15 March the offensive began. While XX Corps of the Third Army struck from the Allied bridgeheads over the Saar and Moselle into the forested hills of the Hunsruck from the west, VI and XV Corps of the Seventh Army, with the French elements under command, attacked north between Haguenau and Saarbrücken. The former attack met with stiff opposition from the enemy's prepared positions, but the southern thrust took the German First Army by surprise and, following the capture of Haguenau on the first day, a number of deep penetrations were made. Zweibrucken and Saarbrucken were occupied by 20 March and resistance in the western portion of the front became disorganized; but the defenders in the Siegfried Line farther to the east stood firm against the Allied attacks.

It was at this point that the intervention of the Third Army across the lower Moselle became devastatingly effective. XII Corps had attacked across the river on 14 March, and the bridgehead gain was rapidly expanded. The Germans were, in fact, completely misled by the Allied tactics. Following the Third Army's swift arrival on the Rhine north of the Moselle they had expected its forces to erupt through the Remagen bridgehead. Instead, when the Third Army turned southeast, the enemy was taken off balance, being utterly unprepared for such a development. No real opposition to the XII Corps drive was offered, and the unready enemy forces were brushed aside as the Allies swept up the Rhine. At the same time, Coblenz was occupied, and by 19 March the river bank was cleared from there as far as the Bingen bend. On the 22nd all resistance ceased in Mainz and on the following day Speyer was reached.

The enemy was still holding out in the Siegfried positions in the Rhine valley west of Karlsruhe, but, with the escape routes across the river cut by the Third Army advances in their rear, his situation was now hopeless. General Patton's aggressive tactics culminated in a surprise night crossing of the Rhine on 22 March. He sent over the US 5th Division without formal preparations of any kind and with negligible losses. Thus, before our main "power" crossing of the Rhine was attempted by 21 Army Group, we were already in possession of two sizeable bridgeheads in the south. Farther west the German units were in a state of chaos and their positions were rapidly overrun and enveloped. By 25 March an end came to all organized resistance west of the Rhine, and Phase III of the operations to close the river was over, with the added accomplishment of two Rhine crossings completed as Phase III closed; while we were rounding up the broken remnants of the enemy the First Army surrounded to the west, we had launched our carefully prepared main effort in the north in our invasion of the German hinterland over the last great barrier remaining to its defenders.

All these operations west of the Rhine had, like those in France, been greatly assisted by the vast weight of Allied air power which we had been able to bring to bear in their support. While the long-range strategic effort was maintained against the fuel and industrial targets in the heart of Germany, a steady offensive was kept up against the enemy lines of communication westward across the Rhine. In addition, the heavy bombers were also employed in direct support of the ground tactical operations whenever the weather conditions permitted. They were further, during this period, engaged in the extensive and remarkable Ruhr interdiction program, which will be mentioned later.

The weather, although persistently bad, could not halt the operations of the tactical air forces, whose performance was never more magnificent than during this time. The ground advances were supported resolutely by these tactical forces; their operations at once warded off the German Air Force attempts at interference and at the same time greatly contributed to the disorganization of the German armies opposing us, strafing and bombing the enemy positions and causing havoc in his supply system. Particularly noteworthy was the work of the First Tactical Air Force in support of the Saar offensive, when 8,320 sorties were flown in a single week, with claims of 2,400 motor vehicles, 85 armored vehicles, 146 locomotives and 1,741 railroad cars. In addition, over 2,000 motor vehicles and 100 armored vehicles were damaged and over 300 rail cuts made. These great efforts played an important part in assuring the success of the ground campaign in the southern sector.

By this time the broad pattern of air-ground operations had become almost a fixed one—subject to adjustment of details to terrain, weather, hostile communications, and so on. Faith in the ability of the Air Force to intervene effectively in the ground battle was the vital feature of the original invasion plan; the general scheme thus used for the isolation of the battlefield, for direct action against selected targets, for air cover and for other important missions, including supply, had by now been so perfected that teamwork was easy and the results obtained were regularly decisive in the area of attack.

In connection with the Allied air activities during the early months of 1945, the operation known as Clarion, carried out on 22 February, is worthy of special mention. Nearly 9,000 aircraft, from bases in England, France, Holland, Belgium, and Italy, took part in this gigantic onslaught, which involved targets covering an area of a quarter of a million square miles, extending from Emden to Berlin, Dresden, Vienna, and Mulhouse. The aim was to attack incidental communications facilities, such as railroad signal points and grade crossings, canal locks, and junctions, in order to aggravate the growing difficulties experienced in keeping open the German life-lines. It had been found by experience that such local attacks, complementary to large ones, had far-reaching effects in slowing down enemy movement, and it was hoped that Clarion would spread the paralysis throughout Germany. It was a bold scheme, demanding great skill and daring on the part of all involved. Confounded by the widespread nature of the blow, the enemy's attempts at defense were completely ineffective.

The whole of the Allied campaign west of the Rhine had gone according to plan to an extraordinary degree, and my fullest hopes were realized. Two features of the operations upon which I had not originally calculated were the rapid capture of the Cologne area and the seizure of the Remagen bridge. Both these events turned wholly to our profit, for, thanks to the flexibility of our plans, we were able to take full advantage of the opportunity which the prizes offered without sacrifice of our planned objectives. In each of the three phases of the campaign, two converging armies had thrust to the Rhine and cut off and destroyed the German forces which had been disposed to bar their way. We had attained along the whole length of the Rhine in German territory the economically defensible front upon which I had insisted as an essential prerequisite to the launching of the concentrated thrusts over the river which were to strike at the heart of Germany, and in the process we had eliminated her own future defensive abilities. The armies which she now so sorely needed to man the last great natural barrier left to her had been broken to pieces in fruitless attempts to halt our slashing blows among the floods of the lower Rhineland, in the Eifel, and amid the hills and forests of the Saar Palatinate.

Field Marshal Montgomery's attack, in the extreme north, got off on 8 February, exactly as planned. The Ninth Army was to join this attack on 10 February, and was ready to do so. Field Marshal Montgomery and I had already agreed that while the ideal situation would be for the Second Army and the US Ninth Army to attack almost simultaneously, yet realizing that flood conditions on the Roer River might hold up the Ninth Army indefinitely, we were fully prepared to accept a two-weeks' delay in the Ninth Army attack in the confidence that the shifting of German reserves to the north would facilitate victory in that sector. Events fully justified this estimate. The Ninth Army's attack across the Roer River on the 23rd rapidly converged with the Canadian Army and we held the Rhine in the Wesel region.

In the 12th Army Group General Bradley's plan for supporting the Ninth Army and then for the destruction of the German forces north of the Moselle by swift converging blows materialized in almost exact accordance with his diagrammatic plans. Moreover, his constant concern was to see that at the culmination of each offensive his forces were so situated as to undertake the next succeeding step without delay for regrouping, and from such direction as to surprise and confuse the enemy. He went into the attack with instructions for each unit to look for and to seize any opportunity to cross the Rhine.

Finally, the 6th Army Group, which had been confined heretofore largely to a holding, protecting, and supporting role, was suddenly unleashed with the Seventh Army brought up to a strength of 15 US divisions. We knew that the enemy was at that time discounting the strength of the Seventh Army and that he felt relatively safe lying in the Siegfried Line facing General Patch's forces. No defeat the Germans suffered in the war, except possibly Tunisia, was more devastating in the completeness of the destruction inflicted upon his forces than that which he suffered in the Saar Basin. Yet this attack was conducted by portions of two Army Groups and, though a boundary between such large forces is ordinarily considered one of the weakest tactical spots in a major front, no real difficulty was encountered in coordination and unification of the battle. Although I personally kept in touch with details and was in position to make tactical decisions when such proved necessary, the real reason for this lack of confusion and for the incisiveness of the whole operation is to be found in the identity of tactical training, organization, and mutual confidence among all the divisions and commanders participating in the battle. The whole operation was characterized by boldness, speed, and determination, and the victory was so complete that when General Patton thrust a division across the Rhine on the night of 22/23 March, he was able to do so with almost no reaction from the enemy.

I unhesitatingly class General Bradley's tactical operations during February and March, which witnessed the completion of the destruction of the German forces west of the Rhine, as the equal in brilliance of any that American forces have ever conducted. The cooperation during the latter part of this period between General Bradley's 12th Army Group and General Devers' 6th Army Group was a superb example of grand tactical cooperation on the battlefield.

CROSSING THE RHINE

When the time came for launching the main assault across the Rhine, the Allied armies under my command had been built up to a total strength on the Continent of nearly four million men. The difficult manpower situation with which we had been confronted during the Ardennes battle had been remedied and we were once more at full strength, with every unit demonstrating an unbelievably high morale and battle effectiveness.

In the 6th Army Group sector the French divisions had been reformed and strengthened, while the passing of winter facilitated the re-employment of the colonial troops for whom active operations had been impracticable during the very severe weather. To the American armies had been added fresh divisions from the United States; and to 21st Army Group had come British and Canadian reinforcements from the Mediterranean Theater. The Combined Chiefs of Staff decided, at their Malta conference at the end of January, that the situation on the Italian Front was such as to permit the transfer of up to five divisions from the Eighth Army to the Western Front. The move of three divisions was to commence forthwith, and two more were to follow as soon as the situation in Greece allowed. In addition, a corresponding proportion of the Twelfth Air Force was to be transferred with the ground forces. The complicated process of moving the units to France and northward across the lines of communication of the Southern and Central Groups of Armies (called Operation Goldflake) was carried out efficiently and smoothly, and the security precautions taken were completely successful in concealing from the Germans what was afoot. By the time the 21st Army Group offensive across the Rhine came to be launched, these latest units to arrive were ready to play their part in it.

The enemy now found himself in an unenviable position. He had, as we had hoped, and attempted to compel, elected to stand and fight west of the

Crossing the Rhine

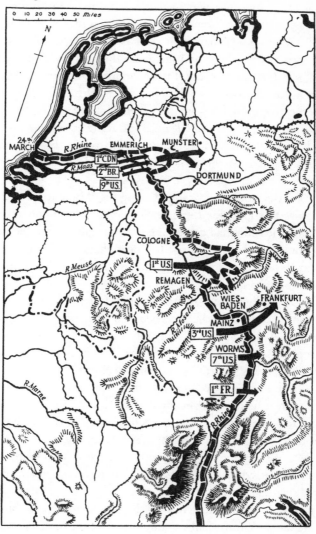

Rhine, and the results had been disastrous to him. Beaten in the open field and behind his frontier fortifications, he was now in no condition to hold fast in the defensive line to which he had been compelled to retreat. His powers of resistance had been reduced by increasing shortages of weapons, ammunition and oil which resulted from our attacks against his war economy. His losses in battle had been crippling, and these inevitably caused a deterioration in the morale of all but his élite units. The SS and the armored divisions were for the most part made up of fanatical Nazis whose faith in the cause they served could be shaken by little less than annihilation; yet the time was soon to come when even their commanders, realizing the fruitlessness of further struggle, would surrender their units rather than see their men slaughtered to no purpose. In the ordinary infantry divisions, spirits were again as low as when they had fled eastward from France to gain the shelter of the Siegfried Line in the preceding autumn. Moreover, as his losses grew, the enemy was forced more and more to entrust his defense to the ragged army of the local Volkssturm who might, in some cases, fight courageously enough in the protection of their homes, but as field units were at times as much a liability as an asset.

Such were the troops now ranged along the Rhine to bar our crossing. The front was too long for them, shrunken as their numbers were since January. While the Allies had gained the economically defensible line behind which to concentrate in safety for the overwhelming thrusts about to be launched in the selected sectors, the enemy, lacking the reconnaissance to obtain definite information as to our intentions, could only spread his forces as far as they would go and wait for the blow to fall.

Under these conditions the success of our operations appeared certain, a conviction which I felt was undoubtedly shared by the German General Staff. Continuance of the struggle was now merely evidence of Hitler's fanaticism. The enemy's northern sector, where our chief weight was to be brought to bear, had been weakened by his movement of forces southward to meet the threat which had already developed from the Remagen bridgehead. Even had the situation there been such as to allow the enemy to disengage and return his forces to the north (which was far from being the case), his lack of mobility was too greatly reduced to enable them to arrive in time to meet us while our foothold on the east bank north of the Ruhr was still precarious.

The plan of campaign for crossing the Rhine and establishing a strong force on the far bank was, thanks to the success of the operations west of the river, basically the same as that envisaged in our long-term planning in January, and even before D Day. Its fundamental features were the launching of a main attack to the north of the Ruhr, supported by a strong secondary thrust from bridgeheads in the Frankfurt area, directed initially on Kassel to complete the envelopment of the Ruhr. Subsequently, offensives would strike out from the bridgeheads to any remaining organized forces and complete their destruction.

In the execution of this plan, the seizure of the Remagen bridgehead was a factor of great significance. Apart from the effect its existence had already produced upon the German defenses, it afforded us a base from which we might the more rapidly accomplish the aim of encircling the Ruhr. Moreover, its existence forced the Germans to man an east–west line along the Sieg River, because of the immediate threat imposed upon the industries of the Ruhr. The forces now gathered within the bridgehead could maintain a pressure to the north, squeezing the Ruhr frontally while enveloping it on the eastern flank, and at the same time strike southeast to Frankfurt. In the latter area the crossing of our forces over the Mainz sector of the river would thus be assisted, and our general build-up for the southern attack would be accomplished rapidly. Consequently we were able to launch a southern supporting offensive in strength on a much earlier date than we had originally expected to be feasible; and this, in turn, had an important effect in determining the future Allied strategy within the interior of Germany.

The plan of Operation Plunder, the great assault across the Rhine north of the Ruhr which was to constitute our main effort, involved the use of three Allied armies. Under the command of Field Marshal Montgomery, the US Ninth Army on the right and the British Second Army on the left were to attack over the river between Rheinberg and Rees. They were to capture the communications center of Wesel and then to expand their initial lodgement area on the east bank southward to a distance sufficient to secure the roads through Wesel from enemy ground action, northward to enable the river to be bridged at Emmerich, and eastward and northeastward to secure a firm bridgehead of adequate size from which further offensive operations could be developed. The Ninth Army's assault was to be launched south of Wesel, with its main bridging area at Rheinberg, and its principal initial task was to be the protection of the Army Group right flank. The Second Army was to assault north of Wesel and to concentrate first on the capture of that town in order that the Ninth Army might commence bridging there. The Second Army was also to bridge the river at Xanten and Rees.

To assist the advance of the Second Army, the First Allied Airborne Army was to drop XVIII Airborne Corps (comprising the US 17th and British 6th Airborne Divisions) north and northwest of Wesel to seize the key terrain in that area. This airborne operation (known as Varsity) was, unlike those previously conducted by the Allies, timed to follow the commencement of the ground assault, it being hoped thereby to achieve an additional element of surprise.

The Canadian Army, on the left flank, was to take no active part in the assault, but was to hold firmly the line of the Rhine and Maas from Emmerich westward to the sea, to ensure the absolute security of the existing bridgehead over the Rhine at Nijmegen, and to guard the Scheldt estuary, the port of Antwerp being now practically the only place where effective enemy interference behind our lines could be achieved. Following the successful establishment of the Second Army bridgehead, the Canadian 2nd Corps was to be passed over the Rhine at Rees by Second Army and to operate to secure Emmerich, where the Canadian Army would then be responsible for the construction of another bridge.

It will be seen from the nature of these operations that the cutting of communications from the Ruhr was a matter of the first importance in facilitating the establishment of a bridgehead on the east bank of the Rhine north of the industrial area. I shall deal in due course with the progress of the land forces in accomplishing its encirclement and reduction, but it must here be noted that already, when the attack was launched over the river in the north, the Allied air forces had achieved the practical denial to the enemy of the Ruhr resources and at the same time had isolated the battle area from the rest of Germany.

The plan of the air forces' Ruhr isolation program was that, prior to the establishment of the 21st Army Group bridgehead, the northwestern area of Germany should be cut off from the central and southern regions by the drawing of a line of interdiction running in a rough curve southward from Bremen to the Rhine at Coblenz. In principle, it was a repetition of the air plan for the original invasion. Along this line were 18 vital railroad bridges and viaducts, the destruction of which would, it was estimated, cut every main rail route from the Ruhr to the remainder of the country. Three of the lines, running through the targets at Bielefeld, Altenbeken, and Armsberg, carried about half of the total traffic between them and were thus of particular importance.

Some of the bridges had earlier received incidental damage, but the main interdiction program began on 21 February. During the next month, 40 major blows were struck by heavy and medium bombers, apart from many fighter-bomber attacks designed to cut the bridge approaches and hamper the Germans' frantic efforts to carry out repairs. In the course of the attacks the RAF used, for the first time, its 22,000-pound monster bombs, with devastating results. The operations proved singularly successful: by 24 March, ten of the bridges had been destroyed, two seriously damaged, and two more were damaged, though possibly passable. The aim in view, that of interrupting the enemy's all-important traffic out of the Ruhr and at the same time preventing the large-scale movement of supplies from central and southern Germany to the armies in the threatened area on the lower Rhine, was fully realized, and the results were immediately evident when our ground forces set foot on the east bank.

The German communications network running west of the interdiction line toward the Rhine was also heavily attacked from the air during the weeks preceding the assault across the river. A very important operation comprised blows delivered by Bomber Command on 11 and 12 March. On the 11th a record was established for the load of bombs dropped on a single target in one raid when 1,079 heavy bombers rained some 5,000 tons on the Essen rail center. The record was surpassed on the 12th when 1,108 heavies dropped 5,487 tons on Dortmund. These communications attacks were also energetically supported by fighters and fighter-bombers of the RAF Second Tactical Air Force and the US XXIX Tactical Air Command. The resulting chaos was such as to prove far beyond the powers of the Reichsbahn repair organization to remedy, despite its immense efforts to keep the lines open.

Mention should be made of the excellent work performed, in preparation for the ground assault, by the Allied photographic reconnaissance aircraft. Now, as throughout the campaign in Europe, their work provided the armies with extremely full and accurate intelligence information. Conversely, the enemy's failure, from D Day onward, was partly due to his own lack, by reason of his air weakness, of the facilities which the Allies enjoyed in this respect.

As 23/24 March approached, the target date for Operation Plunder, the strategic and tactical air force attacks upon the communications in the battle area were intensified. In addition, during the 72 hours preceding the assault, a number of attacks were made upon enemy barracks and camps in the vicinity of the planned bridgehead. Defenses which the Germans were observed to be constructing around the towns and villages, with a view to turning them into strongpoints, were also bombed and strafed. Individual targets of particular importance were allotted to the pilots of rocket-firing Typhoons especially experienced in the technique of pinpoint attacks. Among the buildings destroyed in the course of these operations was one believed to house the headquarters of the German Twenty-fifth Army. Apart from the casualties inflicted in such attacks, it cannot be doubted that they produced a serious morale effect upon the enemy, who, after enduring three days of unremitting hell from the air, was in no condition to meet the frontal assault when it was launched.

Important in the aerial preparation for Operation Plunder were the Allied attacks upon the enemy air force bases in northwest Germany. As earlier stated, the chief threat which the enemy could exercise against our air power lay in his jet aircraft. The Allied production of these machines lagged behind that of our opponents, and in the air it was difficult to counter their attacks. We therefore decided that the best insurance against their possible interference with our Rhine-crossing operations was to employ our heavy bombers to render the enemy's jet airfields unusable. A number of fields possessing the extra-long runways necessary to enable jet planes to take off were located within range of the battle area, and reconnaissance revealed that the Germans were concentrating their machines on them. These fields were accordingly subjected to severe blows from 21 March onward, while the fuel dumps and auxiliary installations were attacked at the same time. The consequence was that the enemy lost a large number of planes on the ground, and the runways were cratered and rendered temporarily unusable. Before repairs could be effected our ground forces were across the Rhine. On 24 March the Allied air forces flew some 8,000 aircraft and 1,300 glider sorties while sighting fewer than 100 enemy planes in the air.

In all these preparatory operations, as on 24 March itself, our air forces were favored with excellent weather conditions, clear skies, and perfect visibility permitting visual bombing and greatly assisting the tactical forces in picking out their targets for pinpoint attacks.

Apart from the airborne landing operations, which I shall consider below, the air force blows reached their peak on 24 March. Prior to the arrival of the transport planes and gliders, the Ninth Air Force and the Second Tactical Air Force planes attacked the enemy flak positions, with the result that interference with the airborne elements from this source was considerably reduced. Also, in immediate cooperation with the armies, medium bombers attacked 18 towns which were either strongpoints or communication centers. Gun and mortar sites and the enemy forward positions generally were relentlessly strafed and bombed, while armed reconnaissance was maintained against the German supply lines. The whole weight of the Eighth Air Force bombers, apart from one division of Liberators used for airborne resupply, was employed in the attacks on the jet airfields.

Two major diversionary air operations were also conducted during the day. One hundred and fifty bombers of the Fifteenth Air Force, with five groups of fighters, flew 1,500 miles from their Italian bases to Berlin and back, while other forces from Italy were raiding airfields in the south. Over Berlin itself fighters of the Eighth Air Force provided cover. This raid successfully fulfilled its object of drawing enemy fighters away from the Rhine battle area. The second diversion was carried out by RAF Bomber Command, which attacked the rail center of Sterkrade as well as oil targets in the Ruhr. In all, during the four days, 21–24 March, American and British air forces, based in Britain, Western Europe and Italy, flew over 42,000 sorties against Germany.

The task of the armies assaulting across the Rhine represented the largest and most difficult amphibious operation undertaken since the landings on the coast of Normandy. The width of the Rhine and the nature of its currents indeed were such that, without the operations already mentioned which were to reduce enemy resistance on the far bank to a minimum, the success of the crossing might well have been a matter of doubt. The variations in the river level also presented unusually difficult problems for, apart from the seasonal fluctuations, there was a danger of artificial floods being created by the enemy's ability to demolish the dams located on the eastern tributaries. A special flood-warning system was instituted to guard against this threat.

It was therefore necessary to treat the assault as an amphibious operation in the fullest sense, involving naval as well as military forces, since the equipment available to the engineer elements of the armies was alone insufficient to cope with the task. Months previously, exhaustive experiments had been carried out on rivers in Britain giving bank and current conditions similar to those of the Rhine in order to determine what ferry craft were most suitable and what loads they could carry. The LCM and LCV(P) craft were chosen for the purpose and these were transported to the Rhine, partly by waterway and partly overland on special trailers built to stand the great strains involved in transit across roads ravaged by war. The immense difficulty of this feat may be judged from the fact that the craft measured as much as 45 feet in length and were 14 feet wide. British and American naval forces were built up to operate the ferry service, and valuable experience was gained when some of the craft were used in the Remagen area early in March. The fact that an LCM could take such loads as a Sherman tank or 60 men, and an LCV(P) a bulldozer or 35 men, may serve to indicate their value in the initial stages of our main assault in the north.

The offensive was heralded, at 2000 hours on 23 March, with a great artillery barrage of an hour's duration, directed against the east bank of the Rhine and extending through the zone where the airborne forces were to be dropped and landed on the next day. At 2100 hours, as soon as the barrage lifted, the British I Commando Brigade commenced the assault on Wesel. This town had been so heavily and accurately bombed by Bomber Command that it was captured with only 36 casualties. During the night the main attacks went in. In the Second Army zone, 15 Division led the 12 Corps assault north of Xanten, and 51 Division crossed in the 30 Corps sector astride Rees. South of the Lippe Canal, 30th and 79th Divisions launched the Ninth Army assault under the command of XVI Corps.

After spending the night on the west bank of the river in the Ninth Army area I met, next day, the Prime Minister of Great Britain, who was accompanied by the Chief of the Imperial General Staff, Field Marshal Brooke. We toured the west bank of the river to witness the ferrying of troops and supplies and to visit troops, all of whom reflected the highest state of enthusiasm and morale. Both the Prime Minister and Field Marshal Brooke, who expressed themselves as extraordinarily delighted with the complete success of our operations of the past 45 days, made a brief visit that afternoon to the east bank of the river.

The initial crossings, thanks to the weight of the preparatory artillery fire and bombing, were generally effected against only slight opposition, and firm footholds were obtained on the far bank of the river. On 24 March, while the ferrying of further troops proceeded steadily, the Allied bridgeheads were expanded and contact was made with the airborne forces flown in during the morning. Wesel was successfully cleared, and in most sectors the enemy's confusion and disorganization were reflected in the uncoordinated resistance offered. Only at Rees did the defenders hold out stubbornly and bring heavy and accurate fire to bear upon the bridging sites.

The airborne landings in the Wesel area, coordinated by the First Allied Airborne Army, commenced just before 1000 hours and continued until 1300 hours. The 6 Airborne Division was flown from bases in East Anglia in 669 planes and 429 gliders of the RAF 38 and 46 Groups and the US IX Troop Carrier Command, while the 17th Airborne Division was brought from the Paris area in 903 planes and 897 gliders of the IX Troop Carrier

Command. Fighter escorts on the approach flights were provided by the 213 RAF Fighter Command and by 676 Ninth Air Force planes. Nine hundred aircraft of the British Second Tactical Air Force provided cover over the target area, while 1,253 fighters of the Eighth Air Force established a screen east of the Rhine. As a result of this protection, coupled with the measures taken against enemy airfields, not one transport was molested by hostile aircraft. Some losses were sustained from anti-aircraft fire over the target, but the total of 46 planes destroyed (3.98% of those employed) was remarkably low considering the fact that, to ensure accuracy of dropping and landing, no evasive action was taken. I witnessed as much of this operation as could be seen from observation posts west of the river and was struck by the courage of transport pilots flying relatively slow aircraft steadily along their allotted routes in spite of heavy flak barrages.

The two divisions established contact with each other during the afternoon and with the 15 Division by nightfall. Their positions were rapidly consolidated, and on the 25th, the 6 Airborne Division commenced a swift advance eastward with 15 Division, while the 17th Airborne Division, after linking with the main forces of Ninth Army, followed suit.

Operation Varsity was the most successful airborne operation carried out to date, and its brilliant results reflected the great strides made in this aspect of warfare since the landings on D Day, nine months earlier. Much of this was due to the coordination secured by the units of the First Allied Airborne Army. The glider landings and parachute drops had been carried out with accuracy, while the supplies dropped shortly after the main landings were virtually 100% recovered. The timing of the attack had achieved the element of surprise which had been planned, and the rapidity with which the forces reformed and established their positions after landing also resulted in the casualties being extremely low. As may be seen from the composition of the forces involved, Varsity was an Allied operation in the fullest sense, and the victory won represented yet another triumph in the annals of Anglo-American cooperation in the common fight.

From 25 March onward the success of our assault north of the Ruhr was assured. Rees was reduced on that day and the Allied bridgeheads were quickly expanded. Enemy resistance was stiffest on the flanks, but during the following week XVI Corps of the Ninth Army, on the right, began to press south into the Ruhr, while on the left Emmerich was cleared by Canadian 2 Corps by 30 March. The Allied troops continued to pour across the Rhine, and, with the airborne units coming under command of the Second and Ninth Armies, the main thrusts eastward to encircle the Ruhr and strike into the heart of Germany began. The great operation of forcing the lower Rhine had proved successful to the fullest extent of my desire.

Meanwhile, in the sector of the Central Group of Armies, operations were proceeding equally well. There, as has been stated earlier, the main object was to establish a firm lodgement area in the Frankfurt region from which an advance in strength could be made toward Kassel. This lodgement area was to extend from the Neckar River in the south to the Sieg River in the north, and eastward as far as Eberbach, Hanau, Giessen, and Siegen. To create this base for our future operations, the First Army was to undertake an offensive south from the Remagen bridgehead, while the Third Army and the Seventh Army crossed the Rhine mainly between Mainz and Mannheim. This direction of movement from the Remagen bridgehead had been decided upon promptly after the securing of that foothold. It completely surprised the German High Command.

In the execution of these plans we were again greatly aided by the results of the dash and daring with which the operations west of the Rhine had been carried out. The sweep which General Patton had conducted across the lower Moselle and up the west bank of the Rhine, together with the heavy blows of the Seventh Army and the continued aggressiveness in the First Army bridgehead, had so utterly disorganized the enemy and so largely destroyed his forces in the region that, although he had managed to blow the last bridges as the escaping remnants struggled across, he was in no condition to defend the east bank. General Patton, as before mentioned, seized the opportunity thus offered, and on the night of 22/23 March, as our main, carefully prepared crossing in the north was poised for its massive blow, 5th Division of XII Corps crossed the Rhine in the neighbourhood of Oppenheim, south of Mainz. The bridgehead gained grew swiftly, and by the evening of 24 March it was 9 miles long and 6 miles deep, while 19,000 prisoners were taken in 24 hours. The remainder of XII Corps crossed the river, seized Darmstadt on the 25th, and swept on to capture intact the main bridges at Aschaffenburg.

While this success was being exploited, the First Army steadily expanded the Remagen bridgehead with advances by V, III, and VII Corps. The enemy's efforts against the northern flank continued to prove fruitless, and by 26 March he was compelled to withdraw over the Sieg River. On the same day the resistance on the southern flank of this bridgehead, which had previously been light, collapsed completely. In a rapid thrust by V Corps to the southeast, Limbourg was overrun and the advance continued toward the Main River. At the same time, the Third Army was clearing this river from Frankfurt to the Rhine.

These sweeping advances completed the demoralization of the enemy forces in the sector. Taking advantage of this, VIII Corps of the Third Army established new bridgeheads over the Rhine at Boppard and north of Brauback on 25 March. The Rhine here flows between hills which fall sharply to the banks of the river, presenting country more difficult for a crossing operation than any which can be well imagined. Despite the advantages thus offered to the defense, the enemy's resistance, though initially heavy, was short-lived. On the following day two more crossings at St Goarshausen and Oberwesel were effected with equal success by VIII Corps. The forces thus put across the Rhine struck hard to the east and, after Bad Schwalbach had been taken on 28 March and Wiesbaden on the 29th, all enemy activity in the area soon ceased. Farther east, Aschaffenburg and Frankfurt were also cleared by 29 March, and the whole Allied lodgement area in the Frankfurt region was securely established. Marburg had been taken by VII Corps, and the armored advance on Kassel was already under way.

The success of the Undertone operations west of the Rhine had equally favored the Seventh Army in its river crossings. Plans had been prepared for an airborne operation in this zone, by the US 13th Airborne Division, to assist the frontal assault, but the weakness of the enemy following his defeat in the Saar rendered it unnecessary. I intended that this situation should be so exploited as to enable the Seventh Army to take over the sector south of the Main, and its first bridgeheads were accordingly established near Worms on 26 March. Once again, initially heavy opposition on the east bank dwindled in the face of Allied superiority, and the four small footholds gained by XV Corps were swiftly consolidated into a firm lodgement area extending southward to the Neckar, a link-up with the Third Army being effected south of Darmstadt on the 27th. On 28 March the Neckar was crossed, and on the following day Mannheim surrendered. The advances from this bridgehead also into Germany had begun.

Finally, on 1 April, the French II Corps established a bridgehead for the French Army at Philippsburg, and there built up a base on the east bank from which subsequently to strike southeast toward Stuttgart and to clear the right bank of the Rhine as far as the Swiss border.

Thus the Rhine barrier, the greatest natural obstacle with which the Allied armies had been faced since the landings in France, had been breached all along the line, and the cost to our forces had been fantastically small. The enemy had committed the same error as in Normandy, and with the same fatal results. His characteristic refusal to admit tactical defeat had proved his undoing. Instead of carrying out a planned withdrawal to the strong defensive positions afforded by the great river, which his inferiority in men and equipment indicated as the logical course, he had chosen to stand and fight a hopeless battle in front of the Rhine. The result was that he was then too weak, when the withdrawal was eventually forced upon him, to hold the line which Nature had offered to him. Spread out along the vast front, his broken and depleted forces could not hope to withstand the overwhelming weight hurled against them in the concentrated Allied assaults. Moreover, once we had gained a bridgehead his lack of mobility rendered him incapable of rushing reinforcements to the threatened area, and the breach once made could never be closed. The élan of the Allied armies had sealed Germany's fate in the operations which had preceded the crossing of the Rhine, and now they were pouring over the river to surge with the same victorious impetus to the innermost parts of the country.

Von Rundstedt had failed in Normandy and had been removed from his command as the penalty. Later he had been reinstated to conduct the ill-fated offensive in the Ardennes where, in 1940, he had achieved his most spectacular success in the invasion of France. Now, with the Allies over the Rhine, he was again dismissed; and with him went the last hopes of Germany's survival. Kesselring was brought from Italy to assume the forlorn task of holding together the beaten armies of the west in the last month of their existence.

THE ENVELOPMENT OF THE RUHR AND THE JUNCTION WITH THE RUSSIANS

If the Nazi leaders, in appointing Kesselring to the command of the German forces in the west, expected him to repeat his defensive successes of Italy, they were to be sadly disappointed. With the Rhine crossed, he had here no Gustav Line, no Monte Cassino, upon which to make a stand. So completely had the Germans relied upon their ability to hold out in the Siegfried Line that east of the Rhine there were no artificial barriers ready to halt our progress other than hastily constructed local defense works. Any other defenses on a larger scale existed only as plans, now never to be realized.

Nor had Kesselring the unified resolute forces which had withstood the Allied attacks in his former command. During March, an average of 10,000 prisoners had fallen into our hands every day, apart from the heavy losses in killed and wounded, and the divisions which had been weak when the Rhineland battles began were now reduced to mere skeletons. The total of enemy casualties from the opening of the Allied spring offensive on 8 February represented the destruction of a score of full divisions.

Within a week of the crossing of the Rhine, the Allied spearheads were thrusting eastward, isolating corps and divisions, and cutting off one army from another. Despair gripped the German forces as never before, and the disintegration of the entire Western Front developed rapidly. Already the task of exercising unified command over the German detachments was becoming almost an impossibility. Communications were breaking down, and reports filtered through so slowly that Kesselring could never be sure what the position at a given moment might be. By the time information had been received and instructions sent back to the armies, the Allied advance guards had probably pressed forward 50 miles and the entire situation had been transformed. Under such circumstances, the local commanders were increasingly compelled to

Envelopment of the Ruhr

make their own decisions, irrespective of what might be happening elsewhere, and to act independently of the higher command. In consequence, Kesselring found himself increasingly unable to exercise any real control over the situation, and the organization of the Western Front collapsed completely. Only one thing was certain: by Hitler's order, the fight was to go on.

It thus seemed evident that the enemy had no hope of ever re-establishing a line in Germany capable of withstanding the Allied avalanche. His only chance of prolonging resistance for any length of time lay in retreating to the so-called "National Redoubt" in the Alps, where he might be able to hold the immensely strong natural defenses against our attacks for a considerable period. At the same time, he would probably continue to resist in the "fortresses" of western France and Dunkirk, where his troops were still under siege, in the Channel Islands, in the Frisian Islands, in Norway, and behind the floods of Holland. Knowing the Nazi mentality, I had little expectation of an immediate all-embracing collapse and an abrupt termination of the struggle through complete surrender while these outposts remained unsubdued.

The task which the Allies had now to undertake lay in so exploiting the success of the Rhine crossings as to effect, in the shortest possible time, the complete defeat of the broken armies immediately before us. We had to thrust forward our armored spearheads with the maximum speed that logistics would permit, and to divide and destroy the enemy before he could withdraw into such defensible positions as those afforded by the mountains of the Redoubt.

In order fully to carry out this policy of speed and violence, however, our attacking armies had, as far as possible, to be freed from the responsibility of holding down the ever-growing rear areas in Germany. There was a danger that the detachment of forces for security purposes in the overrun territory would so weaken the combat formations as seriously to limit their powers of rapid advance. For this reason, on 30 March the US Fifteenth Army was activated, its function being to occupy, organize, and govern the parts of Germany already conquered and thus permit the other armies to concentrate on their task of bringing the war to the speediest possible conclusion. At first the Fifteenth Army was responsible, under the 12th Army Group, for the administration of territory west of the Rhine between Bonn and Homberg, together with command of the reinforced 66th Division containing the enemy garrisons in Lorient and St-Nazaire. Later it was to extend the area under its control as the other armies advanced eastward. The Allied military government organization was working smoothly and, apart from isolated outbreaks by individual Nazi fanatics, was experiencing little trouble with the population.

The Ruhr had been isolated by air action early in 1945. In addition to the direct damage to factories, the transportation system had been wrecked, and the coal and steel produced there, on which the German war economy largely depended, had been, for the time being, denied the enemy. Before operations deep into the German interior could safely be undertaken, however, the Allies had, following the Rhine crossings, to complete the encirclement of the Ruhr and the elimination of any danger from the pocket which would be thus created. With this vast armory in Allied hands, and the Russians in control of its Silesian counterpart, Germany's power of continuing to wage war would be destroyed even were her armies to be preserved intact. The essential weapons, ammunition, and fuel produced by the Ruhr would be denied to them, and even the local factories dispersed about Germany to escape the Allied bombs would be brought to a standstill through lack of raw materials, for the bulk of which they were yet dependent upon the Ruhr and Silesian resources.

I determined, therefore, before launching any further offensive eastward into Germany, to carry out the policy originally envisaged of enveloping the Ruhr by converging thrusts from the two bridgeheads at Wesel and Frankfurt. The southern drive, thanks to the rapidity of the 12th Army Group build-up east of the Rhine which our position upon the river line had permitted, was now capable of being made in far greater strength than would otherwise have been possible. Accordingly 21st Army Group and 12th Army Group were instructed to concentrate on achieving a junction in the Kassel–Paderborn area, while 6th Army Group was to protect the right flank as far north as the Hohe–Rhön hill mass. The First Allied Airborne Army was to be prepared to assist the advances by carrying out a one-division air drop in the Kassel area to seize the airfields there and the Eder River dam. The rapidity with which the ground forces progressed rendered this relatively small airborne operation unnecessary. Previously we had seriously considered the greatest airborne operation yet attempted. The outline plan was to employ about seven airborne and infantry divisions in seizing a large area in the Kassel region, where by blocking all roads and operating on remaining German units from the rear, all these could be destroyed in place. The rapidity and decisiveness of our air–ground operations made this operation completely unnecessary. Under the Ninth Army in the north, while XVI Corps probed southward into the industrial area, XIX Corps swung around its left flank and drove eastward. Meanwhile VII Corps of the First Army, spearheaded by the 3rd Armored Division, struck north from Marburg, which had been taken on 28 March. On 1 April the two armies made contact near Lippstadt, and the encirclement of the Ruhr, which might be said to have begun with the air forces' interdiction program in February, was completed.

The operation constituted the largest double envelopment in history. Inside the pocket we had trapped the whole of the German Army Group B and two corps of Army Group H, including the picked troops who had been massed in March to defend the southern approaches of the Ruhr against the immediate offensive which the enemy had erroneously expected us to launch northward from the Remagen bridgehead.

The decision of the High Command to hold on in the Ruhr can be explained only by the German's innate insistence upon fighting where he stood in preference to carrying out a withdrawal, no matter what the odds against him; and coupled with this, perhaps, went some realization of the difficulties which any move would entail in the armies' present condition. The tactics of the battle of the Falaise pocket were therefore repeated on a far greater scale. Yet in the Ruhr there was no objective like the cutting of the Avranches corridor to justify the German obstinacy; here our armies were in strength all around the enemy, and there could be no question of a threat to our supply lines. As for the Ruhr resources, even though still in German hands these were obviously of no value to the bulk of the armies which were now cut off from them to the east.

The enemy may have entertained ideas of holding out in the Ruhr for some time and thus constituting a threat in our rear which would prevent our further progress while his remaining armies regrouped. If so, he had seriously miscalculated. Events were to show that the Ruhr could not support its defenders, despite its armament works and fuel production plants, while the armies to the east were in no condition to regroup and reform any sort of effective line. Each of them was hard put to maintain its own position, and there was no hope of filling the gap in the center of the front created by the trapping of the 21 divisions of Army Groups B and H. Through that gap the Allied armies were shortly to pour eastward, since the German troops which should have been barring their path were, instead, on the march to Allied prison camps.

Immediately the encircling move had been completed, operations were instituted to render innocuous the forces in the pocket. The densely built-up Ruhr area offered many advantages to the defense, and it was my intention, should the enemy continue to resist firmly, to content myself with compressing him into a small area where only a few divisions would be needed to contain him, and there to starve him into surrender. Even if the Ruhr itself could supply its garrison with adequate means of defense, it was clear that so populated an area, containing many hungry civilian mouths, could not also feed indefinitely the huge armies which it suddenly found in its midst. Meanwhile the remainder of our forces would devote themselves to the more important tasks facing them farther east.

At first the trapped enemy showed spirit, and Field Marshal Model, who was in command, attempted to strike out from Hamm in the north and Siegen in the south. These attempts, however, like the cooperating counter-attacks by the enemy armies outside the pocket, were abortive, and were forced back everywhere except along the bank of the Rhine. Meanwhile the ammunition factories ceased production, and what little was available could not be transported to the front. Fuel and food likewise could not be supplied where they were needed; the rail system was ineffective for this purpose since, apart from the damage it had suffered, the network was thinnest where the fighting was hottest, in the southern Sauerland. The shortage of weapons was as grave as elsewhere in the German armies; rear echelons were stripped to arm the forward ones, but even then the latter often lacked ammunition of the correct calibers.

By 13 April, signs of disintegration were evident, resistance becoming scattered and the enemy giving themselves up in such numbers that the disposal of the prisoners constituted a difficulty. It was clear now that there would be no question of starving a stubborn remnant into submission. The main industrial towns in the north were cleared, and on 14 April the pocket was split in two at Hagen. The eastern half collapsed on 16 April, when 80,000 prisoners were taken in the 24 hours, and on 18 April the pocket was finally liquidated. The total bag of prisoners reached the immense figure of 325,000 including 30 general officers. Originally we had estimated that only 150,000 could be taken. Twenty-one divisions were destroyed, including three panzer, one panzer grenadier and three parachute divisions, and enormous quantities of booty fell into our hands. What Hitler may have expected to prove a fortress to hold us back from central Germany had given way after 18 days, and by now the main front was over 100 miles distant to the east.

Once the process of eliminating the enemy forces in the Ruhr had reached a stage when they presented no potential threat to our security, three main avenues by which we could thrust deeper into Germany lay before us.

In the north, a route lay across the North German Plain toward the Baltic and Berlin. Berlin was the symbol of victory before the eyes of every Allied soldier from the day we set foot in Normandy; but other gains would spring from an advance to the northern sector, gains which were at least as important as those to be derived from capture of the German capital. By a thrust to the Baltic, we should cut off from the main enemy armies those elements which were located in Denmark, Norway, northwest Germany, and Holland, at once depriving them of supplies and preventing their coming to the assistance of the forces in the center of Germany. Furthermore, we should gain the north German ports and thus deny the enemy use of his naval bases and ship-building yards, bringing to an end the activities of the submarines and other craft which had for so long preyed upon our supply routes. Finally, we should link hands with the Russian forces sweeping across Pomerania to the north of Berlin.

In central Germany, a route was open to us through the gap in the enemy's line created by the trapping of Army Group B in the Ruhr. An easy advance was thus offered from Kassel, through Erfurt and Leipzig, to Dresden. This would again bring our forces to an important industrial area, the richest still left to the Germans after their loss of the Ruhr and Silesia. There also we should be able to meet the advancing Red Army, and in so doing we should cut in half what remained of Hitler's Reich.

In the south, an axis of advance was available through Nürnberg and Regensburg, by the Danube Valley into Austria, where the Russians were already threatening Vienna. A thrust on this axis would also enable us to isolate, and then penetrate, the Redoubt in western Austria into which we now knew the enemy intended eventually to withdraw as many of his forces as possible. The prevention of such a withdrawal was a major objective in any operations which we might execute in the south.

Weighing the relative advantages which would accrue from an advance in strength in either north, center, or south, I decided that an offensive first in the center would prove the most effective. With Germany once cut in two, the enemy remaining in each portion could then more economically be eliminated. Such a central thrust, moreover, would afford us the maximum degree of flexibility for future operations, as we could subsequently switch forces rapidly to the north or to the south as the situation should indicate.

General Bradley was accordingly instructed to launch an offensive with the Central Group of Armies from the Kassel area, where he now stood, toward Leipzig, establishing the right flank of his advance on the line Bayreuth–Erzgebirge. He was to seize any opportunity of capturing a bridgehead over the Elbe River and to be prepared for operations farther east, but it was anticipated that these would be unnecessary as the speed of the Russian advance would probably lead to a junction with them on the Elbe, if not west of the river. To assist the First and Third Armies in executing this thrust, Ninth Army reverted from 21st Army Group to the operational command of 12th Army Group on 4 April.

While General Bradley's forces were thus engaged in the center, the operations of the Allied army groups in the north and south were to be of a limited nature, designed primarily to support the principal offensive. Field Marshal Montgomery's 21st Army Group, after completing its present operations to the Leine River and Bremen was to strike toward the Elbe on the northern flank of 12th Army Group. It was also to be prepared to establish bridgeheads over the river. General Devers' 6th Army Group was to protect the southern flank of the central advance west of Bayreuth, and meanwhile to prepare for a later thrust of its own along the axis Nürnberg–Regensburg–Linz to prevent any concentration of German resistance in the south.

When the central thrust had achieved its object, the principal task was to be an advance to the Baltic and the cleaning out of the whole northern area from Kiel and Lübeck westward by 21st Army Group. The Ninth Army would, if necessary, again be used to assist Field Marshal Montgomery in this work. After the requirements for these northern operations had been met, we should be able to direct 6th Army Group, with perhaps the Third Army, southeastward down the Danube Valley and into the Redoubt.

It will have been observed that in all the possible lines of advance into Germany following the Ruhr encirclement the question arose of effecting a junction with the Russians. In fact, with the approach of our respective forces from east and west, it was now essential that operations on the two fronts should be coordinated, and necessary to learn something of the Russians' intentions in order to know best how to exploit such success as our own plan of campaign might achieve. I therefore informed Marshal Stalin of my general plan to strike first in the center and subsequently to effect a link-up with his forces in the Regensburg–Linz area with a view to neutralizing the Redoubt. Marshal Stalin replied that this scheme coincided entirely with the Russian plans in respect to both the central and southern sectors.

The decision to concentrate first upon a major thrust in the center nevertheless gave rise to some misgivings. The desirability of bringing the U-boat war to an end, of opening up supply lines through the north German ports, of acquiring the use of Swedish shipping, of relieving the Dutch, and of occupying Denmark and Norway, and the political and psychological effects of an early entry into Berlin were all advanced as reasons in favor of early operations in the 21st Army Group sector.

Our reply pointed out that we had not forgotten the important advantages to be gained by the conquest of north Germany. It was merely a question of timing that was at issue. Our plan for an advance in the center was itself intended to facilitate such a conquest which, I was convinced, could more easily be achieved once Germany was cut in two. It was vital that we should concentrate for each effort in turn rather than allow our power to be dispersed by attempting to undertake too many projects at once.

Despite appearances on the map, the North German Plain does not in reality afford such favorable terrain for a rapid advance as does the central sector at this time of year. Between Kassel and Leipzig we should be moving over a plateau with no major river obstacles, whereas the northern area is intersected with water-ways and the ground was in a condition to make heavy going. Previous experience of the Germans' thoroughness in bridge destruction also served to indicate the advisability of advancing across headwaters rather than the lower reaches of rivers when speed was an essential factor.

Berlin, I was now certain, no longer represented a military objective of major importance. The Russian advance and the Allied bombing had largely destroyed its usefulness, and even the governmental departments were understood to be in process of evacuation. Military factors, when the enemy was on the brink of final defeat, were more important in my eyes than the political considerations involved in an Allied capture of the capital. The function of our forces must be to crush the German armies rather than to dissipate our own strength in the occupation of empty and ruined cities. Moreover, the Russians were practically on its outskirts (30 miles away) and it was a matter of serious concern to avoid entangling of forces in areas where, due to difficulties of communication and difficulties in language, unfortunate incidents might occur.

Kassel was cleared on 4 April, and within the following week the main Allied advances to the east were begun. On the southern flank, the Third Army, headed by XX Corps, encountered only scattered opposition, with little more than road blocks to bar its progress in the country north of the Thuringian Forest. Weimar was reached on 11 April and Erfurt cleared the next day. By the 13th, Jena had been cleared and the 4th Armored Division was at the outskirts of Chemnitz. The enemy retired southeast into the

Erzgebirge along the frontier of Czechoslovakia, although he still clung to the town of Chemnitz as a pivot to the north, where the south Saxon cities were putting up a stiff resistance to the First Army. At the same time that XX Corps was advancing to the north of Czechoslovakia, XII and VIII Corps of Third Army, farther south, pushed through Bayreuth and Neustadt toward the mountains of the Bohemian Forest forming the southwestern border of the country. On 18 April the Allied armies set foot in Czechoslovakia.

On the left flank of the First Army, Ninth Army continued the advance to the northeast which it had commenced under 21 Army Group following its successful envelopment of the north of the Ruhr. XIX Corps established a bridgehead over the Weser at Hameln on 6 April and pushed rapidly ahead, south of Brunswick, to reach the Elbe south of Magdeburg on 11 April. On the next day, Brunswick fell and the first bridgehead was gained on the east bank of the Elbe by the 2nd Armored Division. A second bridgehead, south of Wittenberge, was achieved by the 5th Armored Division of XIII Corps on 13 April.

From Magdeburg to Wittenberge, the enemy showed himself ready to evacuate the west bank of the river, but he fought hard to deny us possession of Magdeburg itself, which only fell to XIX Corps on 18 April. Very strong counter-attacks were also launched against the bridgeheads, and these were so severe as to compel the Ninth Army, on 14 April, to abandon the two footholds originally obtained. But a third, at Barby, held firm, as enemy attempts to destroy the bridges by floating mines down the river proved abortive. So rapid had been the thrust to reach the Elbe that a number of German pockets had been by-passed on the way. The forces in these, before being mopped up, attempted to harass the Allied lines of communication, but with little success.

The First Army offensive, south of the Harz Mountains, got under way by 11 April, and rapid progress was made against generally disorganized resistance. On 14 April, the 3rd Armored Division of VII Corps reached Dessau, just south of the confluence of the Elbe and Mulde Rivers. In the course of this thrust, the Harz Mountains, containing some 10,000 enemy troops, were almost encircled, but attempts to reduce this pocket met with strong resistance. The garrison succeeded for some time, with the aid of the difficult terrain, in holding the Allied inroads to a minimum, while striving to keep open a corridor to the east near Bernburg. The encirclement was nevertheless completed when this corridor was severed on 18 April. A desperate attempt by the von Clausewitz Panzer Division to relieve the garrison by a dash across some 50 miles of Allied-held territory was foiled, and opposition within the pocket soon weakened. The last organized resistance in the Harz ceased on 21 April.

Meanwhile, although the Allies had penetrated to the southeast of Leipzig, the enemy fought back strongly to its west and southwest. After two days of bitter struggle, the 69th Division of V Corps cleared the city on 19 April. The enemy salient which had extended westward from the line of the

Mulde to the Leipzig–Halle area had now disappeared and Allied elements cleared to the river.

On 25 April patrols of the 273rd Regiment, 69th Division, under V Corps, which had probed eastward from the Mulde, met elements of the Russian 58th Guards Division in the Torgau area, on the Elbe. The junction of the Eastern and Western Fronts had been effected, and Germany was cut in two. The object of the central thrust had been achieved.

The problem of liaison with the Russians had grown more pressing during the advance across central Germany, strategical questions being replaced by tactical ones as the time of junction approached; but solutions were not forthcoming until the last minute. One of our principal anxieties concerned the mutual identification of our respective force, both in the air and on the ground. Already, at the beginning of April, our tactical air forces had come into contact and shots had been mistakenly exchanged, and we considered it of the utmost importance that all possible arrangements should be made to ensure proper recognition in order to prevent errors and possibly tragic incidents which might result in later recriminations. Following recommendations by the Army Group Commanders, a system of recognition signs and signals was eventually arranged by 20 April.

In regard to the territorial questions affecting the junction of the fronts it did not seem to me practicable to restrict our operations to a demarcation line prepared in advance, either on the basis of the subsequent occupational zones or otherwise. Both fronts should be free to advance until contact was imminent, after which an agreement should be reached between the local commanders concerned as to any readjustment of lines which operational considerations might render desirable. This policy met with the approval of the Combined Chiefs of Staff and of the Soviet High Command, and instructions accordingly were issued to the armies under my command. The arrangement worked smoothly and, in accordance with an agreement reached with the Soviet High Command when contact was imminent, the boundary was temporarily fixed in the central sector along the easily identified line of the Elbe and Mulde Rivers. The subsequent readjustment to the zonal boundaries for occupational purposes was carried through without incident after the cessation of hostilities.

While the Central Group of Armies had been pushing eastward to divide Germany, the Northern and Southern Groups had each in their respective sectors been carrying out the operations assigned to them during this period.

Under 21st Army Group, Second Army was, by my instructions, to advance towards Bremen and Hamburg, thereafter thrusting to the Elbe (gaining a bridgehead if the opportunity offered) and thereby protecting the northern flank of the Ninth Army in the 12th Army Group. Meanwhile the Canadian Army was to open up a supply route to the north through Arnhem and then to operate to clear northeast Holland, the coastal belt eastward to the Elbe, and west Holland, in that order of priority. The operations were, in many respects, similar to those carried out in France by the same Army Group in the preceding summer, when the Second Army drove across the rear to the Pas-de-Calais while the Canadian Army mopped up the enemy along the coast.

The Second Army advance was made with 30 Corps on the left flank, 12 Corps in the center, and 8 Corps on the right. Resistance at first was slight and good progress was made. North of Münster, the German First Parachute Army troops were scattered, Rheine was taken on 3 April, and enemy hopes of a stand on the Weser–Ems Canal were frustrated. On 6 April, 8 Corps established a bridgehead over the Weser on the southern flank, and continued the advance to the Elbe, which 11 Armoured Division reached at Lauenburg on 19 April. Farther north, 12 Corps, against stiffer resistance, reached Harburg, on the south bank of the Elbe opposite Hamburg, on 20 April. South of Bremen, the advance of 30 Corps was stoutly contested. The Allies were at the outskirts of the city by 22 April, but very bitter fighting took place before 3 and 52 Divisions finally crushed all opposition on the 26th.

Meanwhile the Canadian Army was probing into Holland. In a thrust northward, Canadian 2 Corps, conforming with the Second Army on its right, initially met heavy opposition from the First Parachute Army, but broke out on 6 April and, while some elements turned northwest, others advanced northeast toward Oldenburg. Resistance in north Holland collapsed and the sea was reached on 15 April. By the 21st, the whole area, apart from a small tip in the northeast, was cleared as far south as Harderwijk on the eastern shore of the Ijssel Meer. To the west, the Ijssel River line was stubbornly defended at Deventer and Zutphen, but the former town fell on 10 April and a bridgehead was established over the river. In the southern sector of the army zone, Canadian 1 Corps attacked from Nijmegen, clearing to the lower Rhine by 5 April, and Arnhem was captured on the 15th. The enemy now withdrew into "Fortress Holland" behind the Grebbe and New Water Lines, protected by the floods, beyond which no further Allied advance was made in this sector. It was rightly felt by Field Marshal Montgomery that an advance into Holland would occasion great additional suffering for that unhappy country and that the quickest and most economical way to free the country was to complete the destruction of the enemy forces elsewhere.

The principal task of 6th Army Group during the first half of April was, as previously indicated, the protection of the right flank of the 12th Army Group thrust as far east as Bayreuth. To accomplish this, Seventh Army was ordered to advance with all speed to a line Ludwigsburg–Crailsheim–Nürnberg–Bayreuth, linking with Third Army in the Bayreuth area. The Bayreuth–Nürnberg autobahn was to be cut and Nürnberg itself captured, after which the army was to be prepared to attack towards Regensburg and Linz. The French First Army was to advance its Rhine bridgehead force to the line Lichtenau–Pforzheim–Ludwigsburg, capturing

Karlsruhe and Pforzheim. When the principal bridgehead had been adequately built up, the area east of the Rhine was to be cleared far enough south to enable a new bridgehead to be established at Strasbourg. The troops there would then cross the Rhine, after which the main effort would be an advance on Stuttgart from the Pforzheim–Ludwigsburg areas.

In the execution of these plans the opposition encountered was generally steady, despite the losses incurred by the enemy. While XXI Corps, in the Seventh Army sector, penetrated to Schweinfurt by 11 April, stiff resistance met the Allied thrusts at Würzburg and Heilbronn. At the latter place the enemy defended the Neckar River line against VI Corps for some days and then fought in the town for a week before it was cleared on 12 April. A salient thrust as far as Crailsheim by the 10th Armored Division on 7 April had to be temporarily abandoned in the face of enemy pressure. By 16 April XV Corps reached Nürnberg, but again several days' hard fighting was required before the city was cleared.

In the French Army sector, resistance in the Rhine Valley was initially stiff, but soon weakened. Karlsruhe fell on 4 April and Baden-Baden on the 12th. The enemy defenses to the south now collapsed before French I Corps. By 15 April, Kehl was taken and the way cleared for bridging to be started at Strasbourg. As the withdrawal to the south up the right bank of the Rhine continued, the enemy was forced to conform by retiring in the Black Forest to the east, and the situation was prepared for the capture of Stuttgart by Allied pincers converging from northeast and southwest.

THE FINAL PHASE

The division of Germany accomplished by the junction with the Russians at Torgau produced immediate and far-reaching consequences. The enemy's difficulties of command which followed the loss of Army Group B in the Ruhr now reached their climax, and all chance of restoring effective unity to the armies facing the Western Allies irrevocably disappeared. The enemy found himself split into virtually independent commands in the north and south, with no means of coordinating the operations in the two zones. Each had to fight its own battle as best it could.

The morale effect of this situation was immense, and a weakening of the resistance previously offered in both north and south was at once evident. During the first three weeks of April over a million prisoners were taken by our armies, and losses sustained at such a rate inevitably brought on collapse in every sector. The Russians, moreover, were now fighting their way into Berlin, and the government, already partly evacuated, was rendered powerless.

At the same time, the paralysis of the German administrative system as a whole, which had set in as a result of Allied air action, and since spread rapidly as 12th Army Group advanced eastward, gripped the entire country. The autocratic nature of the system was such that, with its mainspring disabled in Berlin, the parts throughout the rest of Germany automatically ceased to function. Communications finally broke down, the postal services came to a standstill, and the complete isolation from his home in which the German soldier now found himself sapped his last powers of resistance. With his world collapsing about him, he lost all heart in the fight. The horror pictures which the Nazis had painted with such lurid colors in their anti-Bolshevik propaganda began to have an effect very different from that envisaged by their originators. Instead of being steeled to a last superhuman effort, the soldier, confused and disillusioned by the helplessness of the units to which he had once been proud to belong, became concerned solely with his individual desire to be with his family in whatever fate might be overtaking them.

Prior to the Allied advance across central Germany, evidence had been received that the government was preparing to evacuate Berlin and move southward, ultimately perhaps to Berchtesgaden in the National Redoubt. Some of the departments had already left the city, but the main body now found that, with the Allied link-up on the Elbe, it was too late. An impassable barrier had been drawn across the country, and the way to the Redoubt was cut off. In consequence, Hitler and his intimate henchmen stayed on in Berlin.

Although the Redoubt was not, therefore, to be the last seat of the Nazi government, the possibility remained that it would still be the scene of a desperate stand by the fanatical elements of the armies south of the dividing line, together with those which might retreat northward out of Italy. These armies, totalling about 100 nominal divisions, included the bulk of the remaining German armored and SS formations, and up to 30 panzer divisions might conceivably be concentrated behind the mountain barriers. In addition, most of the surviving German jet fighter plane strength was located in the south. The conquest of the Redoubt area thus remained as an important objective of the Allies, despite the collapse of the rest of Germany. In the event of determined resistance, its reduction would constitute a formidable problem, and speed of movement was therefore essential to forestall the enemy's retiring into the area in time to fortify it against our attacks.

Extending some 240 miles in length and 80 miles in depth, the Redoubt comprised the western half of Austria, with small portions of Germany to the north and Italy to the south. It was bounded on the north by the Bavarian plains, on the south by the Dolomites and Carnic Alps, on the west by the Swiss frontier and the Rhine Valley, and on the east by the Lageneurt Basin and the eastern extremity of the Niedere Tauern. Within it lay Berchtesgaden and Hitler's "Eagle's Nest".

The whole area was extremely mountainous and thus unsuitable for large-scale airborne operations, while the roads into it followed narrow valleys which could easily be held by determined defenders. The snows and danger of avalanches limited the possibility of any military operations to the summer months between May and October. Although there was no evidence of any completed system of defenses along the natural ramparts, some progress appeared to have been made in this respect along the northern flank. Air reconnaissance also revealed underground constructional activity. It was believed that some subterranean factories had been established in the area, but if any considerable numbers of troops were to be maintained there they would have to rely for their supplies, both of food and ammunition, upon previously accumulated stocks.

North of the dividing line in central Germany some 50 enemy divisions were likely to remain to be mopped up, and of these the only formidable elements were those of the First Parachute Army. Although it was not conceivable that resistance could long be maintained in the North German Plain, it was possible that some withdrawal might be attempted into Denmark and Norway with a view to make a last stand in those countries, while "Fortress Holland" would also continue to hold out behind the water barriers. The prevention of such a withdrawal, by means of a rapid Allied advance to the Baltic, thus became the primary objective of our operations in the northern sector.

For the subsequent reduction of Norway, in the event that the German garrison there continued to hold after its isolation had been effected, a task force was assembled in Scotland under the command of Lieut. Gen. Sir Andrew Thorne.

On the Central German Front, although elements pushed forward, as described, to meet the Russians at Torgau, it was necessary to halt the main Allied forces on the lines of the Elbe and Mulde Rivers and the Erzgebirge. For this decision logistical factors were mainly responsible, as well as the aim of concentrating forces now on the north and south flanks. The rapidity of our advance and the large scale upon which the operation was conducted had strained our supply organization to an unprecedented degree, and it could not, at the moment, be further stretched.

As in the dash across France in 1944, it was possible now to maintain the momentum of the armored columns in their swift advances only by the expedient of airborne supply. In executing this task, the carrier planes accomplished remarkable feats, and, invaluable as they had proved throughout the campaign in Northwest Europe, the "flying boxcars" were never more essential than in these concluding stages of the war. Landing on improvised airfields close to the front line and sometimes within pockets temporarily surrounded by the enemy, 1,500 IX Troop Carrier Command C-47s, supplemented by heavy bombers stripped for the purpose, flew over 20,000 sorties during April to carry nearly 60,000 tons of freight (including 10,255,509 gallons of gasoline) to the forward elements of the ground forces. Making their outward flights from French bases in the mornings, the planes returned in the afternoons bearing thousands of evacuated casualties and Allied prisoners of war who had been liberated during the advances. Without such assistance it would have been impossible for the armored divisions to achieve the sweeping successes which attended their operations.

While our forces in the center were halted on the Mulde and Elbe Rivers, we turned to the completion of operations in the north and south, concentrating upon the two principal objectives of further subdividing the enemy's remaining armies and of neutralizing the areas already described where he might the most effectively make his last stands.

Accordingly, in the northern sector 21 Army Group with US XVIII Airborne Corps under command, was directed to fulfil the tasks upon which it was at present engaged west of the Elbe, to seize crossings over that river in the British Second Army zone, secure Hamburg, and advance with the utmost speed on the general area of Kiel–Lübeck. This done, Field Marshal Montgomery was to be prepared to conduct operations northward to liberate Denmark, using, if necessary, an airborne assault to force the Kiel Canal. Meanwhile operations were to continue to achieve the clearing of the coastal belt, and to reduce the enemy naval bases and fortifications which threatened the approaches to Hamburg. The Allied naval and air forces were to assist in these operations, but the nature of the defenses made it possible that their reduction might prove lengthy and difficult, in which case the availability to the Allies of the German ports might be delayed. The question of the subsequent opening of either Hamburg or Bremen, or both, was also dependent upon the condition in which we should find their port installations, but first priority was to be accorded to Hamburg. On the eastern flank of 21 Army Group, operations toward Berlin would have to await the developments of the situation following the accomplishment of the more important tasks outlined above.

In view of the great importance of the opening up of the port of Bremen, Bomber Command carried out a heavy attack on Heligoland on 18 April in order to neutralize its defenses and thus facilitate a Commando landing if such an operation became necessary.

At the same time that 21 Army Group concentrated on its principal thrust to Lübeck, a similar advance was to be made in the southern zone down the Danube Valley toward Linz with the object of effecting a further junction with the Russians. The static situation in the center now permitted the use of the Third Army for this purpose, while 6th Army Group devoted the whole of its attention to the problem of the Redoubt farther south and west.

Even when the Danube offensive had subdivided the enemy's forces in the south, it might still be possible for the Redoubt to hold out, and Third Army was therefore instructed, in addition to its principal thrust, to seize Salzburg, while the Seventh Army, under 6th Army Group, was to advance along the axis Würzburg–Munich, penetrate the mountains, and subsequently to occupy the fortress area. We made available to General Devers the use of the US 13th Airborne Division to assist in these operations if it should prove necessary. Farther west, the French Army was to mop up the Black Forest region and clear along the Swiss frontier, and subsequently to enter Austria if the situation required.

In the execution of the 21 Army Group operations in the north, the resistance encountered by the British Second Army in its attacks toward Bremen and Hamburg was persistent. Following the fall of Bremen on 26 April, however, the situation changed. The main Allied effort was now transferred to the sector of 8 Corps, which launched an attack across the Elbe at Lauenburg on 29 April. Weak opposition only was offered—chiefly by local defense battalions and labor services—and across the river the bridgehead was quickly enlarged. Simultaneously the US XVIII Airborne Corps, now fighting in a ground role, effected a crossing to the south and was attached to the Second Army to provide flank protection for further advances. On 1 May, 11 Armoured Division broke out of the British 8 Corps bridgehead to dash across Schleswig-Holstein to the Baltic and entered Lübeck on the afternoon of 2 May, thereby sealing off the enemy in Denmark. On the same day, the British 6 Airborne Division, under XVIII Corps, reached Wismar, farther east along the coast, while inland Schwerin was attained.

While the hold thus gained on the neck of the Danish peninsula was being consolidated, other forces crossed the Elbe and turned down its right bank toward Hamburg, which surrendered and was occupied by 7th Armored Division on 3 May. At the same time, 30 Corps completed clearance of the area between the Elbe and the Weser.

On 3 May, US XVIII Airborne Corps was in contact with the Russians along the general line Wismar–Schweriner–Lake Grabow. While Berlin was in flames, a new offensive by the Red Army during the last week of April had taken Stettin and swept rapidly westward across Mecklenburg, driving the disorganized remnants of German armies before it. Now, with the junction of the Allied fronts, all resistance in northern Germany ceased.

By the end of April the enemy had finally abandoned all attempts to stem the Allied advances from east and west simultaneously. He turned his back upon the western Allies to concentrate all his remaining forces in a last desperate effort to hold back the Russians, but it was too late. As his armies were forced farther and farther back, the troops gave themselves up in thousands to the Anglo-American armies in their rear. While the Second Army was thrusting unopposed to the Baltic, the American units standing on the Elbe were receiving wholesale surrenders from the enemy retreating westward across the river and into their arms. One corps alone took 300,000 prisoners in the course of a single day.

In northeast Holland and along the coastal belt eastward, the Canadian Army continued its operations to clear the area, taking Oldenburg on 2 May, after overcoming stiff resistance, and driving on beyond. In western Holland, however, no further ground advances were made across the flood barriers behind which the German Twenty-fifth Army lay entrenched.

The situation confronting us in western Holland was one of peculiar difficulty. Civilian conditions there had deteriorated steadily for some months, and after the advances of our armies to the east had isolated the area from Germany, the position of the population became desperate. It was imperative, therefore, that steps should be taken by the Allies to relieve the growing distress before wholesale starvation took place. The strength of the German defenses was such, however, that to mount an operation on a sufficiently large scale to ensure success would have necessitated a serious weakening of the main armies in Germany just at the time when it was all-important that we should press home the attacks which were bringing about the final collapse of the enemy there. Moreover, even had we been able to launch an offensive against western Holland at this moment, the enemy would have opened the dykes to flood the whole country, ruining its fertility for many years to come, and bringing further miseries to its people.

We warned General Blaskowitz, the German commander, that the opening of the dykes would constitute an indelible blot upon his military honor and that of the German Army, and pointed out to him that the retention of Holland could not impede the coming collapse of Germany before our advances. Meanwhile, Seyss-Inquart, the Nazi commissioner for Holland, offered a solution by proposing a truce. If the Allied forces were to continue to stand on the Grebbe Line as at present, no further flooding would take place and the Germans would cease all repressive measures against the Dutch, at the same time cooperating in the introduction of relief supplies. The Combined Chiefs of Staff having accorded me a free hand in the matter, my Chief of Staff met Seyss-Inquart on 30 April, a Russian representative being present and concurring in the action taken on behalf of his government. Methods of introducing food by land, sea, and air routes were agreed upon, and the movement of the supplies which the Allies had held ready commenced forthwith; the free dropping of food had indeed already begun.

Seyss-Inquart was impressed by the arguments put forward by the Allies that, recognizing the hopelessness of the position, the German garrison should surrender at once instead of waiting for the inevitable; but that, he said, was a decision for the military commander, over whom he had no control. Blaskowitz would not consider capitulation so long as any form of resistance continued in Germany.

With the relief of the Dutch thus assured, no useful purpose could be served by attempting inroads into "Fortress Holland" at this time when the final collapse of all German resistance was imminent. The Canadians accordingly held fast on the Grebbe Line until the enemy garrison surrendered with the remainder of the forces in northern Germany.

In the south, the thrust of the Third Army down the Danube Valley began on 22 April and made rapid progress against a tottering enemy. Although the defenders held out at Regensburg until 26 April, XX Corps established bridgeheads across the Danube east and west of the city on the 25th, and then advanced southeast down the right bank while XII Corps did likewise north of the river. By 2 May the north bank had been cleared of the enemy as far as Passau, and the 11th Armored Division shot ahead to receive the surrender of Linz on 5 May. With this lengthening of the XII Corps line, the Third Army took command of V Corps, from the First Army, for operations into Czechoslovakia on its northern flank. By an attack eastward across the frontier, Pilsen was captured on 6 May.

These operations were carried out in full coordination with the Russians approaching from the east. The American troops advanced to the line Budejovice–Pilsen–Karlsbad, but were there halted while the Red Army cleared the east and west banks of the Moldau River and occupied Prague. South of Czechoslovakia, the agreed provisional line of junction ran down the Budejovice–Linz railroad and thence along the valley of the Enns, where contact was effected in due course.

South of the Danube, XX Corps crossed the Isar River on 29 April, at the same time clearing the north bank to the Danube confluence. On 1 May the corps reached the Inn River at Braunau and proceeded to close that river in its sector. On its right flank, III Corps crossed the Danube in the Ingolstadt area on 26 April, and, advancing southeast, established bridgeheads over the Isar on the 28th, in conformity with the Seventh Army offensive farther west. On 2 May III Corps reached the Inn at Wasserburg, securing the Mühldorf bridges intact, after which the sector was taken over by the Seventh Army.

The final thrust by the Seventh Army also began on 22 April, following the fall of Nürnberg two days earlier. On the right flank, XV Corps moved down the Danube and then struck south to Munich, which was captured, in the face of some opposition, on 30 April. The enemy attempted to move an SS Panzer Division to block the Allied advance along the Alpine foothills, but was powerless to check our progress. On 4 May, the 3rd Division of XV Corps cleared Berchtesgaden, while other troops occupied Salzburg, and the entire enemy sector between there and Linz fell apart.

Meanwhile XXI and VI Corps had crossed the Danube in the Dillingen area on 22 April, and at Donauwörth two days later. Pockets of the enemy created south of the river by the converging advances were eliminated, and Augsburg was cleared by XXI Corps on the 28th. Farther west, the Ulm area was reached by VI Corps, which, after a pause occasioned by the moves of the flanking French units, drove on toward the Alpine foothills. The infantry passed through the armor to penetrate the mountains, where the terrain served to slow progress more than did the opposition of the enemy. On 3 May, Innsbruck was taken, and the 103rd Division of VI Corps pushed on to the Brenner Pass.

Here, at Vipiteno on the Italian side of the border, a junction was effected during the morning of 4 May with the 88th Division of the US Fifth Army which, after the defeat of the enemy forces in Italy, had struck into the Alps from the south. The danger of a last stand by the enemy in the Redoubt was finally eliminated, and on the following day the enemy Nineteenth Army capitulated, followed by the whole of Army Group G on 6 May. Among the prisoners taken in the course of the Alpine campaign was the most formidable of my former antagonists, the now retired Field Marshal von Rundstedt.

While the Seventh Army was smashing its way into the Redoubt, the French First Army was completing the destruction of the enemy farther west. Following the collapse of the German resistance in the Black Forest sector, the French broke through with great speed. On 22 April, French I Corps thrust to the east of the Black Forest to reach Lake Constance, and the corridor was widened on the next day. Then, turning northeast, an advance was made to Ulm, where contact was made with Seventh Army forces on 24 April. This action created three pockets of the enemy: one in the southern Black Forest, one in the Stuttgart area, and one north of Sigmaringen. Meanwhile another French force drove up the right bank of the Rhine to the Swiss frontier at Basel and then east to complete the process of encirclement. By 26 April, the Allies were along the Swiss border from Basel to Lake Constance. Stuttgart itself had been cleared on 21 April, and by the 27th organized resistance had ceased in all the pockets despite the strong opposition offered in some places, aided by difficult terrain.

After being relieved by the Seventh Army in the Ulm sector, the French armor now drove along the northern shore of Lake Constance and turned south across the Austrian border on 30 April. Feldkirch was captured on 4 May, and the advance was continued up the Ill and Kloster Valleys to penetrate the western end of the Redoubt and to make contact with the Seventh Army there as the enemy capitulated.

Apart from the main activities of the French First Army, operations were also carried out at this time by French forces under the control of 6th Army Group on the Franco-Italian border and against the German pocket which had continued to hold out at the mouth of the Gironde. Extensive air operations supported the latter offensive. The penetrations over the Alps into northwest Italy were executed as a diversionary measure to assist 15th Army Group in its breakthrough across the plain of Lombardy. As such, they fulfilled all that was expected of them. The operations against the Gironde enclave were launched on 14 April, after repeated postponements since October 1944 necessitated by the demands of the more important battles elsewhere. Long isolated, and now demoralized by the Allied successes on the main fronts, the defenders were incapable of any extended resistance. Fighting ceased in the Royan sector north of the river on 18 April and three days later the Pointe de Grave on the south bank fell. The final elimination of the enemy in the area was achieved with the reduction of the Island of Oléron on 1 May. Farther north, however, the St-Nazaire–Lorient "fortress" held out until the final surrender of all the German armies.

In these concluding stages of the war, the Allied air forces continued to afford the invaluable support which had been such a vital factor in ensuring our successes throughout the entire campaign. As the Eastern and Western Fronts closed together, however, the opportunities for employment of the strategic bomber forces grew more and more limited, former strategic targets having now become tactical ones. The chief occupation of Bomber Command and the Eighth Air Force by the beginning of May consequently consisted of flying food supplies to the Dutch civilian population and of evacuating casualties and liberated Allied prisoners.

The Tactical Air Forces' work in close support of the advancing armies in the north and south went on, but their operations also were restricted by the danger of hitting advanced Russian elements and the large bodies of prisoners who, having broken loose from their camps, were streaming westward along the roads. The last major offensive by the tactical planes was in the south, where attacks were concentrated ahead of the Third Army advance down the Danube Valley, destroying the enemy's remaining dumps of fuel and other supplies in that area, and cutting the few communications still available for their distribution.

Of enemy offensive activity in the air there was no sign. As the area left to the Germans decreased, the congestion of planes on the remaining airfields grew worse, and the number of aircraft destroyed on the ground amounted in proportion. The demoralization of the German Air Force personnel was too far developed for any suicidal effort to be made with the jet aircraft squadrons left in Austria and Czechoslovakia, and by the beginning of May practically the only flights undertaken were for the purpose of desertion.

The end of the German Navy was even more unspectacular. Having put to sea only on rare occasions throughout the war, then invariably to be hounded to their destruction or driven crippled back to their bases where the Allied air forces repeatedly undid any repair work attempted, the heavy units lay helpless in the northern ports as these fell into the hands of the advancing armies. Only three of the larger ships were in anything approaching a condition for effective action when the last naval bases surrendered. The coastal craft had ceased to operate during April, and it was left to the submarine forces—the only truly successful naval weapon of which the enemy had enjoyed the use—to carry on the fight to the end.

By 5 May the principal objectives of the Allies had been achieved in every sector, and the war in Europe was virtually at an end. Nowhere on the Continent was there still in existence a German army capable of continuing the fight.

To the east, the armies under my command were joining hands with their Russian allies from the Baltic to the Alps. To the south, they had linked with their comrades in Italy, where already the enemy had made formal surrender. Of the Nazi "fortresses," the National Redoubt had been penetrated while its intended garrison lay dispersed and broken outside its walls; Norway was isolated and doomed; Dunkirk, the Brittany ports, and the Channel Islands were helpless; and Holland and Denmark had just capitulated.

The German war machine which had sought to dominate the world lay overwhelmed and crushed to a degree never before experienced in the history of modern armies. The moment had come for Germany to make her final acknowledgment of defeat.

THE SURRENDER

During the spring of 1945, as the sky grew darker over Germany, the Nazi leaders had struggled desperately, by every means in their power, to whip their people into a last supreme effort to stave off defeat, hoping against hope that it would be possible, if only they could hold on long enough, to save the day by dividing the Allies. Blinded as they were by their own terror and hatred of "Bolshevism", they were incapable of understanding the strength of the bond of common interest existing between Britain, the United States, and the Soviet Union.

As soon as it became clear that a war on two fronts had become impossible to maintain, the Nazi government set itself to obtain, if possible, a truce in the west in order that all its remaining forces might be concentrated in an attempt to check the rolling tide of the Russian advances in the east. In March an approach was made to this end through the British Embassy in Stockholm, but the offer was, of course, rejected out of hand.

Even after this rebuff, however, the Germans clung to their fond hopes of an Allied rift, and a last desperate attempt to create a schism between the Anglo-Americans and the Russians came as late as the last week in April. Himmler, claiming that he spoke for the German government because Hitler was now "incapacitated", approached the Swedish government, through Count Bernadotte, with an offer to surrender all the forces now fighting on the Western Front. Once more the Allies replied that the only acceptable terms were of immediate and unconditional surrender on all fronts simultaneously. Whereupon Himmler disappeared from the scene until, after the final capitulation, he was apprehended as a fugitive from justice and met his death by suicide.

Hitler and his close followers determined to carry on the fight. They personally had everything to lose, nothing to gain, by peace now. Amid the disillusionment of their armies and the ruins which daily multiplied in Germany, they deliberately chose to sacrifice the remnants of their country.

Not all of their henchmen, however, followed their lead. Waffen SS General Karl Wolff, the chief SS officer in northern Italy, in mid-February approached Allied representatives with a view to a capitulation in the Mediterranean Theater. Negotiations with AFHQ made clear to the Germans that the Allies would discuss no terms and would accept unconditional surrender only. By 26 April the deterioration of the enemy's position which followed the Allies' splitting of his armies in Lombardy and Venetia led to renewed approaches; and, on the 29th German representatives signed the terms of surrender, by which all hostilities in Italy were to cease on 2 May.

This capitulation by the German armies facing south in the Alps led inevitably to an abandonment of the struggle by those who, behind them, had been driven back into the mountains before the Allied 6th Army Group offensive. On 2 May Wolff asked with whom the surrender of the North Alpine area should be negotiated. He was told to apply to General Devers, but warned that only unconditional submission would be acceptable. On 5 May the representative of General Schulz, commanding Army Group G, accepted the Allied terms at Haar, in Bavaria, and the German First and Nineteenth Armies accordingly laid down their arms. The surrender was officially to take effect at noon on 6 May, but both sides at once announced the termination of hostilities in order to obviate further loss of life.

Rumors of an impending local capitulation in the north also reached the Allies in mid-April. Field Marshal Busch, commanding the Hamburg area, was stated to be anti-Nazi and willing to surrender, but unable to do so until the Western Allies reached the Baltic and cut him off from the possibility of the arrival of die-hard SS formations from central Germany. General Lindemann, the commander in Denmark, was also understood to be ready to yield at the same time as Busch, and on 30 April an emissary appeared in Stockholm to confirm this. It was urged that the British Army should make all speed to reach the Baltic before the Russians did so, for the Germans would under no circumstances surrender to the Red Army.

By 3 May, however, when the capture of Lübeck had severed Denmark and northwest Germany from the remainder of the country, more important figures came within our reach. As the Red Army had drawn nearer to the Western Allies, Admiral Doenitz, upon whom the mantle of the Führer had now fallen, had instructed his armies which had been facing east to turn about and surrender to the Anglo-American forces.

While thousands of Germans fleeing westward gave themselves up daily, Admiral Friedeburg, the new head of the German Navy, accompanied by Field Marshal Busch's chief of staff and two other officers, appeared at Field Marshal Montgomery's headquarters on 3 May. They asked to be allowed to surrender the Third Panzer, Twelfth, and Twenty-first Armies, which had been fighting the Russians, and to be permitted to pass refugees through the Allied lines into Schleswig-Holstein. Their sole desire was to avoid the necessity of surrendering to the Russians. Field Marshal Montgomery, however, refused to discuss capitulation with them on these terms, though he informed them that individual soldiers who gave themselves up would be treated as prisoners of war. The German representatives then sent back to Field Marshal Keitel, the Chief of the German High Command, for further instructions, meanwhile urging the Allies to follow the retreating German armies closely to avoid chaos.

On 4 May Friedeburg announced that he had received permission from his superiors to make unconditional surrender of all German armed forces, land, sea, and air, in northwest Germany (including the Frisian Islands, Heligoland, and all other islands), Holland, Schleswig-Holstein, and Denmark. I had instructed Field Marshal Montgomery that a capitulation covering these areas might be regarded as a tactical matter and, as such, be dealt with by him. It was arranged that a Russian officer should be present to accept the German submission on behalf of his government. The instrument of surrender was accordingly signed on 4 May, and it became effective at 0800 hours on 5 May.

As laid down in my directive from the Combined Chiefs of Staff, no commitments of any nature were made on the Allied side in accepting these local capitulations, and their terms were made subject to the provisions of the subsequent general unconditional surrender of all the German armed forces. The time for this final yielding had now arrived: unlike Hitler, Admiral Doenitz was ready to bow to the inevitable.

On 4 May it was learned that Doenitz was sending a representative to my headquarters on the following day, and that he had already ordered the German U-boats to return to port in earnest of his intention to bring the war to a close as speedily as possible. I at once notified the Russian High Command of this fact, and they agreed with my suggestion that a Red Army officer should be appointed to join with me in handling the surrender in order that a simultaneous capitulation on all fronts might be arranged. General Suslaparov was accordingly delegated to act on behalf of the Soviet High Command for this purpose.

At the same time that Doenitz's emissary was coming to Reims, Field Marshal Kesselring, as Commander-in-Chief West, transmitted a message stating that he desired to send a plenipotentiary to discuss terms of capitulation. He was informed that unless his surrender covered all German forces facing east as well as west, in addition to those isolated elsewhere, negotiation was out of the question.

Meanwhile Admiral Friedeburg arrived at my headquarters on the evening of 5 May. He began by stating that he wished to clarify a number of points, but was bluntly told that only unconditional surrender was acceptable. To this he replied that he had no power to sign any document of capitulation. The hopelessness of the German military position was pointed out to him, and he was shown the act of military surrender which had been drafted.

Friedeburg cabled a report of his interview to the government, and was informed by Doenitz that General Jodl was on his way to assist in the negotiations. Jodl arrived on the evening of 6 May. It was at once obvious that the Germans were merely playing for time so that meanwhile they could evacuate the largest possible number of soldiers and civilians from the Russian front to behind our lines. They persisted even now in attempting to surrender the Western Front separately, going so far as to say that, whatever my answer might be, they intended to order their armies to cease firing upon the Anglo-Americans. They asked for an adjournment for 48 hours before signing the final surrender, allegedly to enable them to get the necessary orders to their outlying units, but actually, it was clear, only to gain further respite for the purpose above mentioned.

They were informed that unless they agreed to my terms forthwith I would break off all negotiations and seal my front, preventing, by force if necessary, any further westward movement of German soldiers and civilians. They then drafted a cable to Doenitz, asking for authority to make full surrender, but specifying that actual fighting would cease 48 hours after signing. Since this solution obviously placed the decision as to when fighting should cease in the hands of the Germans, I refused to accept it; and finally told them that unless all hostilities should terminate on both fronts within 48 hours of midnight that night, my threat to seal the Western Front would be carried out.

This declaration at last had the desired effect. Doenitz gave his approval for acceptance of my terms, and at 0241 hours on the morning of 7 May the act of surrender was signed by Jodl on behalf of the German High Command. My Chief of Staff signed for me, and Maj. Gen. Ivan Suslaparov signed for the Soviet High Command. General Savez of the French Army, Deputy Chief of Staff for National Defense, signed as witness. The terms were to become effective at midnight, 8/9 May.

In addition to the act of military surrender, Jodl signed an undertaking that the Chief of the German High Command, with the Commanders-in-Chief of the Army, Navy, and Air Force, would appear at a time and place to be designated by the Soviet High Command and myself for the purpose of executing formal ratification of the unconditional surrender on behalf of the German High Command. This meeting was held in Berlin on the night of 9 May, when Air Chief Marshal Tedder signed on my behalf, and Marshal Zhukov for the Soviet High Command. General Spaatz of the US Air Forces and General de Lattre de Tassigny (representing the French Government) were present as witnesses.

With this final capitulation by the German leaders, the mission of the Allied Expeditionary Force placed under my supreme command on 14 February 1944 was accomplished.

CONCLUSION

In attempting very briefly to assess the factors underlying the Allied success in this campaign, I would stress the importance of three episodes as being the most decisive in ensuring victory.

The first of these was the battle of the Normandy beaches. We sailed for France, possessed of all the tactical information which an efficient intelligence service could provide, but we had yet to take the measure of the foe we were to meet. We were embarking upon the largest amphibious operation in history against a coastline bristling with all the defenses modern ingenuity could devise, and behind the beaches lay the German armies of the west which had not been tried in full-scale battle since the dark days of 1940.

As we struggled first to gain and then to hold our footing in Normandy, we learned the strength and also the weakness of these armies. We learned that the German soldier was still the same stubborn fighter whom we had met in Africa and in Italy, but we saw, too, how slender was the thread upon which his existence in France depended. During the months of June and July all the difficulties of communications and supply which were ultimately to prove his undoing became manifest. It was thus that we were enabled to establish ourselves on the Continent and to build up the great armies necessary to achieve the liberation of Europe. We learned also, at this time, how inadequate was the enemy's intelligence concerning the Allied intentions. Thanks to his air weakness and consequent lack of reconnaissance, he was completely misled by our diversionary operations, holding back until too late the forces in the Pas-de-Calais which, had they been rushed across the Seine when first we landed, might well have turned the scales against us.

The second vital battle was that of the Falaise pocket. Here the enemy showed that fatal tendency to stand and fight when all the logic of war demanded a strategic withdrawal. By so doing, he allowed his Seventh Army to be encircled and ground to pieces, and the battle for France was decided among the bloody orchards and hedgerows of Normandy. As the broken forces fled eastward we strained every effort to complete their overthrow before they could reach the shelter of the Siegfried Line, but the logistical burden was too great, and we had to wait until the weary winter drew to a close before we could strike the final blow.

The third decisive phase in the campaign consisted of the battles west of the Rhine during February and March. Once again the enemy played into our hands by his insistence upon fighting the battle where he stood. In the lowland country between the Rhine and the Meuse, in the Eifel, and in the Saar, the armies which had been intended to defend Germany were shattered beyond recovery. The potential barrier of the Rhine lay practically undefended before us, and from that time onwards there was no German force in existence capable of halting our forward march. The war was won before the Rhine was crossed.

Throughout the struggle, it was in his logistical inability to maintain his armies in the field that the enemy's fatal weakness lay. Courage his forces had in full measure, but courage was not enough. Reinforcements failed to arrive, weapons, ammunition, and food alike ran short, and the dearth of fuel caused their powers of tactical mobility to dwindle to the vanishing point. In the last stages of the campaign they could do little more than wait for the Allied avalanche to sweep over them.

For this state of affairs we had, above all, to be grateful to the work of the Allied air forces. Long before we landed in France, the heavy bombers had begun their task of destroying the centers of production upon which the enemy relied, and the fruits of this effort were evident immediately the land campaign began. Following the invasion, these strategic blows at the heart of German industry were continued, and the task was also undertaken of cutting the supply lines which linked the factories to the fronts. Meanwhile the tactical aircraft, by their incessant bombing and strafing of the enemy before us in the field, broke his powers of resistance and prepared the way for the ground advances which struck toward the center of Germany. Those thrusts, moreover, were made with a rapidity which only the expedient of airborne supply could support. The overwhelming Allied superiority in the air was indeed essential to our victory. It at once undermined the basis of the enemy's strength and enabled us to prepare and execute our own ground operations in complete security.

It is difficult even for a professional soldier to appreciate the tremendous power which was achieved on the battlefields and in the skies of Western Europe by the concerted efforts of the Allied Nations. As stated earlier in this report, most of the 90 divisions which fought in the later phases of our operations were habitually reinforced to a strength of 17,000 men by tank, tank destroyer, and anti-aircraft attachments. An idea of their shattering impact upon the Nazi war machine comes from consideration of the terrific firepower which they represent, of the mass of heavier Corps and Army artillery which supported them, of the inexhaustible supply system that sustained them, and of the flexibility with which their efforts could be applied by means of the efficient communications system. For behind the combat units the efforts of three millions of other men and women in uniform were devoted to maintaining them in action. We could, in effect, apply against the enemy on the Continent a force 30 times as large as the Allied armies which defeated Napoleon on the battlefield at Waterloo. In addition, we had available nearly 11,000 fighter and bomber airplanes whose mobile firepower could be applied at virtually any point we desired, as I have just described, and whose annihilating effects are evidenced by the wreckage of a powerful nation's cities, industries and communications, and by the destruction of the air forces which defended them. To this power was added the striking and strangling force of two formidable naval fleets working as one.

Mention has already been made of the skill and devotion of our service forces whose efforts, both in the field and at home, made an essential contribution to our victory. To them, and to the civilian workers of factory and farm who provided us with unstinted means, we are forever indebted. Our enormous material superiority gave us an unchallengeable advantage over our foes. While Germany's own war potential crumbled, that of the Allies rose to heights unprecedented. No army or navy was ever supported so generously or so well. Never, during the entire campaign, were we forced to fight a major battle without the weapons that were needed.

More important even than the weapons, however, was the indomitable fighting spirit of the men of the Allied nations who wielded them. The courage and devotion to duty which they exhibited throughout the campaign, in the grim days of the Ardennes counter-offensive as well as in the excitement of the dash across France and later the advances into the midst of Germany, were unsurpassable. It was the spirit that had enabled them to withstand the shocks of Dunkirk and Pearl Harbor which brought us at the last to Lübeck, to Torgau, and to Berchtesgaden.

Underlying this invincibility of spirit was the confidence in Allied unity and the justice of the common cause which permeated all who were engaged, directly or indirectly, in the struggle. The comradeship which had been first exemplified in North Africa carried us to new triumphs in Northwest Europe. Within my own headquarters the American and British personnel worked harmoniously together, obliterating all distinction of national outlook in their zealous service to a single organization, while in the field of battle the men of the Allied armies fought shoulder to shoulder under my supreme command.

Those civilian volunteers who shared the rigors and dangers of campaign that they might brighten the existence of our men have the assurance of our warmest gratitude.

The United States of America and Great Britain have worked, not merely as Allies, but as one nation, pooling their resources of men and material alike, in this struggle against the forces of evil engendered by Hitler's Germany. In the Expeditionary Forces which it has been my privilege to lead, both in the Mediterranean Theater and in Northwest Europe, an Allied experiment unprecedented in the history of the world has been carried out with decisive results.

In concluding this report it is with regret that I am unable to record here the details of my personal and official obligations and gratitude to those who served so devotedly at Supreme Headquarters and at the other headquarters which cooperated so loyally and effectively with us. Nor can I make adequate recognition of the collaboration of those many individuals in civil and military positions in Great Britain and the United States with whom my duties brought me into contact, and whose efforts aided in a major degree the accomplishment of our common task. Yet I know that all these would have me pay a final tribute to the memory of two very senior and gallant officers who started the campaign with us and who lost their lives before its conclusion. These were Admiral Sir Bertram H. Ramsay of the Royal Navy, and Air Chief Marshal Sir Trafford Leigh-Mallory of the Royal Air Force. At the beginning of the operation these officers were respectively my Naval Commander-in-Chief and my Air Commander-in-Chief. The former lost his life in an airplane accident near Versailles, France, while still serving in the same capacity. The latter, relieved from my Command to take over the Allied Air Forces in Southeast Asia, was lost in an airplane accident near Grenoble, France. The war service, the devotion to duty, and the sacrifice of these two outstanding men typify the irreplaceable cost of the campaign represented in the lives of thousands of officers and enlisted men and members of the women's services, of the American, British, and French forces.

All of them died in the spirit of that unity which joined the Allies in our common ideals. To them, and to those who still bear the wounds of battle, we, their comrades in arms, render most grateful and humble tribute.

Under the arrangements made by the Combined Chiefs of Staff for the control of the field forces, General of the Army George C. Marshall acted as their executive in transmitting to me their orders and instructions. Moreover, under that most distinguished Secretary of War, Henry L. Stimson, General Marshall was always my direct administrative superior in my capacity as a Commander of United States Army forces. To this great soldier-statesman, I owe a particular debt for his friendly counsel and constant support. There was nothing throughout the war so morally sustaining as the knowledge that General Marshall concurred in the plans I was adopting and the means I was taking to put them into effect.

Dwight D. Eisenhower

Dwight D. Eisenhower,
Supreme Commander,
Allied Expeditionary Force

13 *July*, 1945

THE JUDGMENT
OF NUREMBERG, 1946

THE INTERNATIONAL MILITARY TRIBUNAL FOR THE
TRIAL OF GERMAN MAJOR WAR CRIMINALS

CONTENTS

SELECTED GLOSSARY

AB action
Code name for the liquidation of Polish intellectuals and leaders after the German invasion of Poland (*Ausserordentliche Befriedungsaktion*; Extraordinary Pacification Action)

Abwehr
Intelligence service of the Wehrmacht

Allgemeine SS
General SS, the SS organisation as a whole

Anschluss
German annexation of Austria, March 1938

APA
Office of Foreign Affairs (of the NSDAP)

Bullet (Kugel) Decree
March 1944; under which certain categories of prisoners of war who were recaptured were not treated as prisoners of war but taken to Mauthausen concentration camp in secret and shot

Case Barbarossa
Code name for military onslaught on the USSR

Case Grün
see Fall Grün

Case Otto
Code name for the Austrian campaign

Case Yellow
see Fall Gelb

Commando Order
18 October 1942; directive, authorised by Hitler, ordering that all members of Allied commando units, often when in uniform and whether armed or not, were to be "slaughtered to the last man", even if they attempted to surrender

Commissar Order
6 June 1941; Hitler's decree ordering execution of all Soviet political workers and Soviet intellectuals

DAF
German Labour Front (*Deutsche Arbeitsfront*)

Einsatzgruppe
Special task force of the SIPO and SD

Einsatzkommando
Subdivision of an Einsatzgruppe

Einsatzstab Rosenberg
Centre for National Socialist Ideological and Educational Research, headed by Alfred Rosenberg; originally designed for the establishment of a research library, it developed into a project for the seizure of cultural treasures from German occupied territories

Fall Gelb
Code name for operation against the Netherlands

Fall Grün
Code name for attack on Czechoslovakia

Fall Weiss
Code name for the invasion of Poland

Gau
Territorial administrative political unit of the NSDAP

Gauleiter
NSDAP official in charge of a Gau

General-Government
Especially, portion of Poland occupied by Germany prior to invasion of USSR in June 1941; not administratively annexed to Third Reich

Geneva Convention
1929; providing international rules for the humane treatment of prisoners of war

Geneva Protocol
League of Nations 1924 Protocol for the Pacific Settlement of International Disputes

Gestapo
German State Secret Police under Hitler (*Geheime Staatspolizei*)

Grenzpolizei
Frontier Police

Grossadmiral
Admiral of the Fleet

Hitler Jugend
Hitler Youth Organisation

Hoszbach Conference
Meeting held in Reich Chancellery on 5 November 1937 at which Hitler revealed plans for future and at which Lt.-Col. Hoszbach, Hitler's personal adjutant, took notes

Kommissarbefehl
see Commissar Order

Kripo
Criminal Police (*Kriminalpolizei*)

Lebensraum
Living space; territory for natural expansion

Luftwaffe
German Air Force

Marita
Code name for invasion of Greece

MEFO
Bill system that enabled the Reich to obtain credit from the Reichsbank which, under existing statutes, it could not have obtained directly; bills were drawn by armament contractors and accepted by a limited liability company, the *Metallurgische Forschungsgesellschaft* (MEFO), a dummy organisation

Munich Agreement/Pact
September 1938; accord formulated and signed by Germany, Italy, France and Great Britain, securing acceptance by Great Britain and France of Hitler's demand that Sudetenland be ceded to Germany

Nacht und Nebel (Erlass)
see Night and Fog

Night and Fog (Decrees)
Series of related decrees introduced in late 1941 under which persons who committed offences against the Reich or the German forces in occupied territories were either executed within a week or taken

secretly to Germany and handed over to the SIPO and SD for trial or punishment in Germany, without being permitted to communicate with family and friends

NSDAP
National Socialist German Workers' Party (*Nationalsozialistische Deutsche Arbeiter Partei*) = Nazi Party

Nuremberg Laws / Nürnberg Decrees
September 1935; most important effect of which was to deprive Jews of German citizenship

Oberbefehlshaber
Commander-in-Chief

Obergruppenführer
SS rank equivalent to that of General in the army

OKH
Army High Command (*Oberkommando des Heeres*)

OKL
Supreme Command of the Air Force (*Oberkommando der Luftwaffe*)

OKM
Navy High Command (*Oberkommando der Kriegsmarine*)

OKW
High Command of the Armed Forces (*Oberkommando der Wehrmacht*)

Operation Grün
see Fall Grün

Order Police
Uniformed police, consisting of national, rural and local police (*Ordnungspolizei*)

Organisation Todt
German labour and construction organisation; functioning principally in the occupied areas on such projects as the Atlantic Wall and the construction of military highways

pogrom
An organised massacre, especially of the Jews

Putsch
Secret and sudden attempt to depose a government

Reichsführer–SS
Reich Leader of the SS; SS Chief Himmler's official title

Reichsstatthalter
Reich Governor

Reichsregierung
Reich Cabinet

Reichstag
German parliamentary legislative chamber

RSHA
Reich Security Head Office (*Reichssicherheitshauptamt*)

SA
Storm Troopers; para-military force of the NSDAP (*Sturmabteilung*)

Schmundt Notes
Notes taken by Lt.-Col. Schmundt, adjutant of Hitler, at military conference held on 23 May 1939

SD
Security Service of the SS (*Sicherheitsdienst des Reichführers–SS*); intelligence agency of the NSDAP and SIPO

SIPO
Security Police, including Kripo and Gestapo (*Sicherheitspolizei*)

SKL
Naval War Staff (*Seekriegsleitung*)

SS
Protection or guard detachment (*Schutzstaffel*) of the NSDAP

Standartenführer
SS rank equivalent to that of Colonel in the army

Sudetenland
German-speaking region of Czechoslovakia bordering Germany

Totenkopfverbände
Death's Head Detachments; special troops employed to guard concentration camps

Verfügungstruppe
SS members who volunteered for four years armed service in lieu of compulsory service with the army

Volksdeutschmittelstelle
Office for repatriation of racial Germans

Volkssturm
German Home Guard

Waffen–SS
Armed SS; under tactical command of the Army, but equipped and supplied through the administrative branches of the SS and under SS disciplinary control

Wehrmacht
German Armed Forces

Weser Exercise
Operation against Norway and Denmark

WVHA
Economic Administration Main Office of the SS (*Wirtschafts- und Verwaltungshauptamt*)

Zollengrenzschutz
Border and Customs Protection

Europe 1939 (showing the boundary realignments after World War I)

1. Great Britain
2. Irish Free State
3. Norway
4. Denmark
5. Sweden
6. Finland
7. Estonia
8. Latvia
9. Lithuania
10. East Prussia
11. Netherlands
12. Belgium
13. Luxemburg
14. Switzerland
15. Austria
16. Czechoslovakia
17. Hungary
18. Bulgaria
19. Albania
20. Greece
21. Italy
22. Portugal

Scale in miles

0   200   400   600

Adolf Hitler's rise to power in Germany in 1933 and his ruthless establishment of the Nazi regime led to European upheaval, culminating in the Second World War. During the 12 years of Hitler's dictatorship, 30 million people were to lose their lives, not only on the battlefields, but by mass shooting, in forced labour camps, and in the gas ovens of the concentration camps, in line with Nazi theories of racial purity.

Such was the revulsion of the world at the atrocities committed by the Nazis, that the Allies were determined that its leaders would not go unpunished. The International Military Tribunal (IMT) was established in 1945, with the Allies signing the Charter of the IMT on 6 August which would govern the laws and procedures of the trial. The American Robert Jackson was appointed Chief Prosecutor, with the British judge Sir Geoffrey Lawrence as president. The location of the war crimes trials was to be Nuremberg in Germany, one of the few German cities which still held a standing courthouse.

Twelve trials were held in Nuremberg from 1945 to 1949, but attention focused mainly on the first trial of 21 major war criminals. This trial opened on 20 November 1945, and lasted 315 days. It began with the reading of the indictments, which concerned four counts. Count One was conspiracy to wage aggressive war, and addressed crimes committed before war began. Count Two was crimes against peace or waging an aggressive war in violation of international treaties and assurances. Count Three was concerned with war crimes such as the killing or mistreatment of prisoners of war, while Count Four, crimes against humanity, addressed crimes committed against Jews, ethnic minorities, civilians in other countries, and the physically and mentally disabled.

The verdict was finally read out on 1 October 1946. The text of this uncovered edition *is the summation and verdict of that trial.*

INTRODUCTION

On 8th August, 1945, the Government of the United Kingdom of Great Britain and Northern Ireland, the government of the United States of America, the Provisional Government of the French Republic, and the Government of the Union of Soviet Socialist Republics entered into an Agreement establishing this Tribunal for the trial of war criminals whose offences have no particular geographical location. The following Governments of the United Nations have expressed their adherence to the Agreement: Greece, Denmark, Yugoslavia, the Netherlands, Czechoslovakia, Poland, Belgium, Ethiopia, Australia, Honduras, Norway, Panama, Luxemburg, Haiti, New Zealand, India, Venezuela, Uruguay and Paraguay.

By the Charter annexed to the Agreement, the constitution, jurisdiction and functions of the Tribunal were defined.

The Tribunal was invested with power to try and punish persons who had committed crimes against peace, war crimes and crimes against humanity.

The Charter also provided that at the trial of any individual member of any group or organisation, the Tribunal may declare that the group or organisation of which the individual was a member was a criminal organisation.

In Berlin, on 18th October 1945, an Indictment was lodged against the defendants, who had been designated by the Committee of the Chief Prosecutors of the signatory Powers as major war criminals. A copy of the Indictment in the German language was served upon each defendant in custody at least thirty days before the Trial opened.

This Indictment charges the defendants with crimes against peace by the planning, preparation, initiation and waging of wars of aggression, which were also wars in violation of international treaties, agreements and assurances; with war crimes; and with crimes against humanity. The defendants are also charged with participating in the formulation or execution of a common plan or conspiracy to commit all these crimes. The Tribunal was further asked by the Prosecution to declare all the named groups or organisations to be criminal.

The defendant Robert Ley committed suicide in prison on 25th October, 1945. On 15th November, 1945, the Tribunal decided that the defendant Gustav Krupp von Bohlen und Halbach could not then be tried because of his physical and mental condition, but that the charges against him in the Indictment should be retained for trial thereafter, if the physical and mental condition of the defendant should permit On 17th November, 1945, the Tribunal decided to try the defendant Bormann in his absence under the provisions of Article 12 of the Charter. After argument, and consideration of full medical reports, and a statement from the defendant himself, the Tribunal decided on 1st December, 1945, that no grounds existed for a postponement of the trial against the defendant Hess because of his mental condition. A similar decision was made in the case of defendant Streicher.

In accordance with Articles 16 and 23 of the Charter, Counsel were either chosen by the defendants in custody themselves, or at their request were appointed by the Tribunal. In his absence the Tribunal appointed Counsel for the defendant Bormann, and also assigned Counsel to represent the named groups or organisations.

The Trial which was conducted in four languages – English, Russian, French and German – began on 20th November, 1945, and pleas of "Not Guilty" were made by all the defendants except Bormann.

The hearing of evidence and the speeches of Counsel concluded on 31st August, 1946.

Four-hundred-and-three open sessions of the Tribunal have been held. Thirty-three witnesses gave evidence orally for the Prosecution against the individual defendants, and 61 witnesses, in addition to 19 of the defendants, gave evidence for the Defence.

A further 143 witnesses gave evidence for the Defence by means of written answers to interrogatories.

The Tribunal appointed Commissioners to hear evidence relating to the organisations, and 101 witnesses were heard for the Defence before the Commissioners, and 1,809 affidavits from other witnesses were submitted. Six reports were also submitted, summarising the contents of a great number of further affidavits.

Thirty-eight-thousand affidavits, signed by 155,000 people, were submitted on behalf of the Political Leaders, 136,213 on behalf of the SS, 10,000 on behalf of the SA, 7,000 on behalf of the SD, 3,000 on behalf of the General Staff and OKW, and 2,000 on behalf of the Gestapo.

The Tribunal itself heard 22 witnesses for the organisations. The documents tendered in evidence for the prosecution of the individual defendants and the organisations numbered several thousands. A complete stenographic record of everything said in court has been made, as well as an electrical recording of all the proceedings.

Copies of all the documents put in evidence by the Prosecution have been supplied by the Defence in the German language. The applications made by the defendants for the production of witnesses and documents raised serious problems in some instances, on account of the unsettled state of the country. It was also necessary to limit the number of witnesses to be called, in order to have an expeditious hearing. The Tribunal, after examination, granted all those applications which in their opinion were relevant to the defence of any defendant or named group or organisation, and were not cumulative. Facilities were provided for obtaining those witnesses and documents granted through the office of the General Secretary established by the Tribunal.

Much of the evidence presented to the Tribunal on behalf of the Prosecution was documentary evidence, captured by the Allied armies in German army headquarters, Government buildings, and elsewhere. Some of the documents were found in salt mines, buried in the ground, hidden behind false walls and in other places thought to be secure from discovery. The case, therefore, against the defendants rests in a large measure on documents of their own making, the authenticity of which has not been challenged except in one or two cases.

THE CHARTER PROVISIONS

The individual defendants are indicted under Article 6 of the Charter, which is as follows:

> Article 6. The Tribunal established . . . for the trial and punishment of the major war criminals of the European Axis countries shall have the power to try and punish persons who, acting in the interests of the European Axis countries, whether as individuals or as members of organisations, committed any of the following crimes:
>
> The following acts, or any of them, are crimes coming within the jurisdiction of the Tribunal for which there shall be individual responsibility:
>
> (a) Crimes against Peace: namely, planning, preparation, initiation or waging of a war of aggression, or a war in violation of international treaties, agreements or assurances, or participation in a common plan or conspiracy for the accomplishment of any of the foregoing.
>
> (b) War Crimes: namely, violations of the laws or customs of war. Such violations shall include, but not be limited to, murder, ill-treatment or deportation to slave labour or for any other purpose of civilian population of or in occupied territory, murder or ill-treatment of prisoners of war or persons on the seas, killing of hostages, plunder of public or private property, wanton destruction of cities, towns or villages, or devastation not justified by military necessity.

(c) Crimes against Humanity: namely, murder, extermination, enslavement, deportation, and other inhumane acts committed against any civilian population, before or during the war, or persecutions on political, racial or religious grounds in execution of or in connection with any crime within the jurisdiction of the Tribunal, whether or not in violation of the domestic law of the country where perpetrated.

Leaders, organisers, instigators and accomplices participating in the formulation or execution of a common plan or conspiracy to commit any of the foregoing crimes are responsible for all acts performed by any persons in execution of such plan.

For the purpose of showing the background of the aggressive war and war crimes charged in the Indictment, the Tribunal will begin by reviewing some of the events that followed the First World War and, in particular, by tracing the growth of the Nazi Party under Hitler's leadership to a position of supreme power from which it controlled the destiny of the whole German people and paved the way for the alleged commission of all the crimes charged against the defendants.

THE NAZI RÉGIME IN GERMANY

ORIGIN AND AIMS OF THE NAZI PARTY

On 5th January, 1919, not two months after the conclusion of the Armistice which ended the First World War and six months before the signing of the peace treaties at Versailles, there came into being in Germany a small political party called the German Labour Party. On 12th September, 1919, Adolf Hitler became a member of this party, and at the first public meeting held in Munich, on 24th February, 1920, he announced the party's programme. That programme, which remained unaltered until the party was dissolved in 1945, consisted of twenty-five points, of which the following five are of particular interest on account of the light they throw on the matters with which the Tribunal is concerned:

> Point 1. We demand the unification of all Germans in the Greater Germany, on the basis of the right of a self-determination of peoples.
>
> Point 2. We demand equality of rights for the German people in respect to the other nations; abrogation of the peace treaties of Versailles and Saint Germain.
>
> Point 3. We demand land and territory for the sustenance of our people, and the colonisation of our surplus population.
>
> Point 4. Only a member of the race can be a citizen. A member of the race can only be one who is of German blood, without consideration of creed. Consequently no Jew can be a member of the race.
>
> Point 22. We demand abolition of the mercenary troops and formation of a national army.

Of these aims, the one which seems to have been regarded as the most important, and which figured in almost every public speech, was the removal of the "disgrace" of the Armistice and the restrictions of the peace treaties of Versailles and Saint Germain. In a typical speech at Munich on 13th April, 1923, for example, Hitler said with regard to the Treaty of Versailles:

> The treaty was made in order to bring 20 million Germans to their deaths, and to ruin the German nation . . . At its foundation our movement formulated three demands:
>
> 1. Setting aside of the Peace Treaty.
>
> 2. Unification of all Germans.
>
> 3. Land and soil to feed our nation.

The demand for the unification of all Germans in the Greater Germany was to play a large part in the events preceding the seizure of Austria and Czechoslovakia; the abrogation of the Treaty of Versailles was to become a decisive motive in attempting to justify the policy of the German Government; the demand for land was to be the justification for the acquisition of "living space" at the expense of other nations; the expulsion of the Jews from membership of the race of German blood was to lead to the atrocities against the Jewish people; and the demand for a national army was to result in measures of rearmament on the largest possible scale, and ultimately to war.

On 29th July, 1921, the Party which had changed its name to Nationalsozialistische Deutsche Arbeiter Partei (NSDAP) was reorganised, Hitler becoming the first "Chairman". It was in this year that the Sturmabteilung or SA was founded, with Hitler at its head, as a private paramilitary force, which allegedly was to be used for the purpose of protecting NSDAP leaders from attack by rival political parties and preserving order at NSDAP meetings, but in reality was used for fighting political opponents on the streets. In March, 1923, the defendant Goering was appointed head of the SA.

The procedure within the Party was governed in the most absolute way by the leadership principle (Führerprinzip).

According to the principle, each Führer has the right to govern, administer or decree, subject to no control of any kind and at his complete discretion, subject only to the orders he received from above.

This principle applied in the first instance to Hitler himself as the Leader of the Party, and in a lesser degree to all other party officials. All members of the Party swore an oath of "eternal allegiance" to the Leader.

There were only two ways in which Germany could achieve the three main aims above-mentioned, by negotiation or by force. The twenty-five points of the NSDAP programme do not specifically mention the methods on which the leaders of the party proposed to rely, but the history of the Nazi régime shows that Hitler and his followers were only prepared to negotiate on the terms that their demands were conceded, and that force would be used if they were not.

On the night of 8th November, 1923, an abortive Putsch took place in Munich. Hitler and some of his followers burst into a meeting in the Bürgerbräu Cellar, which was being addressed by the Bavarian Prime Minister Kehr, with the intention of obtaining from him a decision to march forthwith on Berlin. On the morning of 9th November, however, no Bavarian support was forthcoming, and Hitler's demonstration was met by the armed forces of the Reichswehr and the Police. Only a few volleys were fired; and after a dozen of his followers had been killed, Hitler fled for his life, and the demonstration was over. The defendants Streicher, Frick and Hess all took part in the attempted rising. Hitler was later tried for high treason, and was convicted and sentenced to imprisonment. The SA was outlawed. Hitler was released from prison in 1924, and in 1925 the Schutzstaffel, or SS, was created, nominally to act as his personal bodyguard, but in reality to terrorise political opponents. This was also the year of the publication of *Mein Kampf*, containing the political views and aims of Hitler, which came to be regarded as the authentic source of Nazi doctrine.

THE SEIZURE OF POWER

In the eight years that followed the publication of *Mein Kampf*, the NSDAP greatly extended its activities throughout Germany, paying particular attention to the training of youth in the ideas of National Socialism. The first Nazi youth organisation had come into existence in 1922, but it was in 1925 that the Hitler Jugend was officially recognised by the NSDAP. In 1931 Baldur von Schirach, who had joined the NSDAP in 1925, became Reich Youth Leader of the NSDAP.

The Party exerted every effort to win political support from the German people. Elections were contested both for the Reichstag and the Landtage. The NSDAP leaders did not make any serious attempt to hide the fact that their only purpose in entering German political life was in order to destroy the democratic structure of the Weimar Republic, and to substitute for it a National Socialist totalitarian régime which would enable them to carry out their avowed policies without opposition. In preparation for the day when he would obtain power in Germany, Hitler in January, 1929, appointed Heinrich Himmler as Reichsführer–SS with the special task of building the SS into a strong but elite group which would be dependable in all circumstances.

On 30th January, 1933, Hitler succeeded in being appointed Chancellor of the Reich by President von Hindenburg. The defendants Goering, Schacht and von Papen were active in enlisting support to bring this about. Von Papen had been appointed Reich Chancellor on 1st June, 1932. On the 14th June he rescinded the decree of the Brüning Cabinet of 13th April, 1932, which had dissolved the Nazi para-military organisations, including the SA and the SS. This was done by agreement between Hitler and von Papen, although von Papen denies that it was agreed as early as 28th May, as Dr Hans Volz asserts in "Dates from the History of the NSDAP"; but that it was the result of an agreement was admitted in evidence by von Papen.

The Reichstag elections of the 31st July, 1932, resulted in a great accession of strength to the NSDAP, and von Papen offered Hitler the post of Vice-Chancellor, which he refused, insisting upon the Chancellorship itself. In November, 1932, a petition signed by leading industrialists and financiers was presented to President Hindenburg, calling upon him to entrust the Chancellorship to Hitler; and in the collection of signatures to the petition Schacht took a prominent part.

The election of 6th November, which followed the defeat of the Government, reduced the number of NSDAP members, but von Papen made further efforts to gain Hitler's participation, without success. On 12th November, Schacht wrote to Hitler:

> I have no doubt that the present development of things can only lead to your
> becoming Chancellor. It seems as if our attempt to collect a number of signatures
> from business circles for this purpose was not altogether in vain.

After Hitler's refusal of 16th November, von Papen resigned, and was succeeded by General von Schleicher; but von Papen still continued his activities. He met Hitler at the house of the Cologne banker von Schröder on 4th January, 1933, and attended a meeting at the defendant Ribbentrop's house on 22nd January, with the defendant Goering and others. He also had an interview with President Hindenburg on 9th January, and from 22nd January onwards he discussed officially with Hindenburg the formation of a Hitler Cabinet.

Hitler held his first Cabinet meeting on the day of his appointment as Chancellor, at which the defendants Goering, Frick, Funk, von Neurath and von Papen were present in their official capacities. On 28th February, 1933, the Reichstag building in Berlin was set on fire. This fire was used by Hitler and his Cabinet as a pretext for passing on the same day a decree suspending the constitutional guarantees of freedom. The decree was signed by President Hindenburg and countersigned by Hitler and the defendant Frick, who then occupied the post of Reich Minister of the Interior. On 5th March elections were held, in which the NSDAP obtained 288 seats of the total of 647. The Hitler Cabinet was anxious to pass an "Enabling Act" that would give them full legislative powers, including the power to deviate from the Constitution. They were without the necessary majority in the Reichstag to be able to do this constitutionally. They therefore made use of the decree suspending the guarantees of freedom and took into so-called "protective custody" a large number of Communist deputies and party officials. Having done this, Hitler introduced the "Enabling Act" into the Reichstag, and after he had made it clear that if it was not passed, further forceful measures would be taken, the Act was passed on 24th March, 1933.

THE CONSOLIDATION OF POWER

The NSDAP, having achieved power in this way, now proceeded to extend its hold on every phase of German life. Other political parties were persecuted, their property and assets confiscated, and many of their members placed in concentration camps. On 26th April, 1933, the defendant Goering founded in Prussia the Gestapo as a secret police, and confided to the deputy leader of the Gestapo that its main task was to eliminate political opponents of National Socialism and Hitler. On 14th July, 1933, a law was passed declaring the NSDAP to be the only political party, and making it criminal to maintain or form any other political party.

In order to place the complete control of the machinery of Government in the hands of the Nazi leaders, a series of laws and decrees were passed which reduced the powers of regional and local governments throughout Germany, transforming them into subordinate divisions of the Government of the Reich. Representative assemblies in the Länder were abolished and with them all local elections. The Government then proceeded to secure control of the Civil Service. This was achieved by a process of centralisation, and by a careful sifting of the whole Civil Service administration. By a law of 7th April it was provided that officials "who were of non-Aryan descent" should be retired; and it was also decreed that "officials who because of their previous political activity cannot be guaranteed to exert themselves for the national state without reservation shall be discharged". The law of 11th April, 1933, provided for the discharge of "all Civil Servants who belong to the Communist Party". Similarly, the Judiciary was subjected to control. Judges were removed from the Bench for political or racial reasons. They were spied upon and made subject to the strongest pressure to join the Nazi Party as an alternative to being dismissed. When the Supreme Court acquitted three of the four defendants charged with complicity in the Reichstag fire, its jurisdiction in cases of treason was thereafter taken away and given to a newly established "People's Court", consisting of two judges and five officials of the Party. Special courts were set up to try political crimes and only party members were appointed as judges. Persons were arrested by the SS for political reasons, and detained in prisons and concentration camps; and the judges were without power to intervene in any way. Pardons were granted to members of the Party who had been sentenced by the judges for proved offences. In 1935 several officials of the Hohenstein concentration camp were convicted of inflicting brutal treatment upon the inmates. High Nazi officials tried to influence the Court, and after the officials had been convicted, Hitler pardoned them all. In 1942 "Judges' letters" were sent to all German judges by the Government, instructing them as to the "general lines" that they must follow.

In their determination to remove all sources of opposition, the NSDAP leaders turned their attention to the trade unions, the churches and the Jews. In April, 1933, Hitler ordered the late defendant Ley, who was then staff director of the political organisation of the NSDAP, "to take over the trade unions". Most of the trade unions of Germany were joined together in two large federations, the "Free Trade Unions" and the "Christian Trade Unions". Unions outside these two large federations contained only 15 per cent of the total union membership. On 21st April, 1933, Ley issued an NSDAP directive announcing a "co-ordination action" to be carried out on 2nd May against the Free Trade Unions. The directive ordered that SA and SS men were to be employed in the planned "occupation of trade union properties and for the taking into protective custody of personalities who come into question". At the conclusion of the action the official NSDAP press service reported that the National Socialist Factory Cells Organisation had "eliminated the old leadership of Free Trade Unions" and taken over the leadership themselves. Similarly, on 3rd May, 1933, the NSDAP press service announced that the Christian trade unions "have unconditionally subordinated themselves to the leadership of Adolf Hitler". In place of the trade unions the Nazi Government set up a German Labour Front (DAF), controlled by the NSDAP, and which, in practice, all workers in Germany were compelled to join. The chairmen of the unions were taken into custody and were subjected to ill-treatment, ranging from assault and battery to murder.

In their effort to combat the influence of the Christian churches, whose doctrines were fundamentally at variance with National Socialist philosophy and practice, the Nazi Government proceeded more slowly. The extreme step of banning the practice of the Christian religion was not taken, but year by year efforts were made to limit the influence of Christianity on the German people, since, in the words used by the defendant Bormann to the defendant Rosenberg in an official letter, "the Christian religion and National Socialist doctrines are not compatible". In the month of June, 1941, the defendant Bormann issued a secret decree on the relation of Christianity and National Socialism. The decree stated that:

> For the first time in German history the Führer consciously and completely has the leadership in his own hand. With the Party, its components and attached units, the Führer has created for himself, and thereby the German Reich Leadership, an instrument which makes him independent of the Treaty ... More and more the people must be separated from the churches and their organs, the Pastor ... Never again must an influence on leadership of the people be yielded to the churches. This influence must be broken completely and finally. Only the Reich Government and by its direction the Party, its components and attached units, have a right to leadership of the people.

From the earliest days of the NSDAP, anti-Semitism had occupied a prominent place in National Socialist thought and propaganda. The Jews, who were considered to have no right to German citizenship, were held to have been largely responsible for the troubles with which the nation was afflicted following on the war of 1914–18. Furthermore, the antipathy to the Jews was intensified by the insistence which was laid upon the superiority of the Germanic race and blood. The second chapter of Book 1 of *Mein Kampf* is dedicated to what may be called the "Master Race" theory, the doctrine of Aryan superiority over all other races, and the right of Germans in virtue of this superiority to dominate and use other peoples for their own ends. With the coming of the Nazis into power in 1933, persecution of the Jews became official state policy. On 1st April, 1933, a boycott of Jewish enterprises was approved by the Nazi Reich Cabinet, and during the following years a series of anti-Semitic laws were passed, restricting the activities of Jews in the Civil Service, in the legal profession, in journalism and in the armed forces. In September, 1935, the so-called Nuremberg Laws were passed, the most important effect of which was to deprive Jews of German citizenship. In this way the influence of Jewish elements on the affairs of Germany was extinguished, and one more potential source of opposition to Nazi policy was rendered powerless.

In any consideration of the crushing of opposition, the massacre of 30th June, 1934, must not be forgotten. It has become known as the "Röhm Purge" or "the bloodbath", and revealed the methods which Hitler and his immediate associates, including the defendant Goering, were ready to employ to strike down all opposition and consolidate their power. On that day Röhm, the Chief of Staff of the SA since 1931, was murdered by Hitler's orders, and the "Old Guard" of the SA was massacred without trial and without warning. The opportunity was taken to murder a large number of people who at one time or another had opposed Hitler. The ostensible ground for the murder of Röhm was that he was plotting to overthrow Hitler, and the defendant Goering gave evidence that knowledge of such a plot had come to his ears. Whether this was so or not it is not necessary to determine.

On 3rd July the Cabinet approved Hitler's action and described it as "legitimate self-defence by the State".

Shortly afterwards Hindenburg died, and Hitler became both Reich President and Chancellor. At the Nazi-dominated plebiscite which followed, 38 million Germans expressed their approval, and with the Reichswehr taking the oath of allegiance to the Führer, full power was now in Hitler's hands.

Germany had accepted the Dictatorship with all its methods of terror and its cynical and open denial of the rule of law.

Apart from the policy of crushing the potential opponents of their régime, the Nazi Government took active steps to increase its power over the German population. In the field of education, everything was done to ensure that the youth of Germany was brought up in the atmosphere of National Socialism and accepted National Socialist teachings. As early as 7th April, 1933, the law reorganising the Civil Service had made it possible for the Nazi Government to remove all "subversive and unreliable teachers"; and this was followed by numerous other measures to make sure that the schools were staffed by teachers who could be trusted to teach their pupils the full meaning of National Socialist creed. Apart from the influence of National Socialist teaching in the schools, the Hitler Youth Organisation was also relied upon by the Nazi Leaders for obtaining fanatical support from the younger generation. The defendant von Schirach, who had been Reich Youth Leader of the NSDAP since 1931, was appointed Youth Leader of the German Reich in June, 1933. Soon all the youth organisations had been either dissolved or absorbed by the Hitler Youth, with the exception of the Catholic Youth. The Hitler Youth was organised on strict military lines, and as early as 1933 the Wehrmacht was co-operating in providing pre-military training for the Reich Youth.

The Nazi Government endeavoured to unite the nation in support of their policies through the extensive use of propaganda. A number of agencies were set up whose duty was to control and influence the press, radio, films, publishing firms, etc., in Germany, and to supervise entertainment and cultural and artistic activities. All these agencies came under Goebbels' Ministry of the People's Enlightenment and Propaganda, which, together with a corresponding organisation in the NSDAP and the Reich Chamber of Culture, was ultimately responsible for exercising this supervision. The defendant Rosenberg played a leading part in disseminating the National Socialist doctrines on behalf of the Party, and the defendant Fritzsche, in conjunction with Goebbels, performed the same task for the State.

The greatest emphasis was laid on the supreme mission of the German people to lead and dominate by virtue of their Nordic blood and racial purity, and the ground was thus being prepared for the acceptance of the idea of German world supremacy.

Through the effective control of the radio and the press, the German people, during the years which followed 1933, were subjected to the most intensive propaganda in furtherance of the régime. Hostile criticism, indeed criticism of any kind, was forbidden, and the severest penalties were imposed on those who indulged in it.

Independent judgment, based on freedom of thought, was rendered quite impossible.

MEASURES OF REARMAMENT

During the years immediately following Hitler's appointment as Chancellor, the Nazi Government set about reorganising the economic life of Germany, and in particular the armament industry. This was done on a vast scale and with extreme thoroughness.

It was necessary to lay a secure financial foundation for the building of armaments, and in April, 1936, the defendant Goering was appointed co-ordinator for raw materials and foreign exchange, and empowered to supervise all State and Party activities in these fields. In this capacity he brought together the War Minister, the Minister of Economics, the Reich Finance Minister, the

President of the Reichsbank and the Prussian Finance Minister to discuss problems connected with war mobilisation, and on 27th May, 1936, in addressing these men, Goering opposed any financial limitation of war production and added that "all measures are to be considered from the standpoint of an assured waging of war". At the Party Rally in Nuremberg in 1936, Hitler announced the establishment of the Four Year Plan and the appointment of Goering as the Plenipotentiary in charge. Goering was already engaged in building a strong air force, and on 8th July, 1938, he announced to a number of leading German aircraft manufacturers that the German Air Force was already superior in quality and quantity to the English. On 14th October, 1938, at another conference, Goering announced that Hitler had instructed him to organise a gigantic armament programme, which would make insignificant all previous achievements. He said that he had been ordered to build as rapidly as possible an air force five times as large as originally planned, to increase the speed of the rearmament of the navy and army, and to concentrate on offensive weapons, principally heavy artillery and heavy tanks. He then laid down a specific programme designed to accomplish these ends. The extent to which rearmament had been accomplished was stated by Hitler in his memorandum of 9th October, 1939, after the campaign in Poland. He said:

> The military application of our people's strength has been carried through to such an extent that within a short time at any rate it cannot be markedly improved upon by any manner of effort . . .

> The warlike equipment of the German people is at present larger in quantity and better in quality for a greater number of German divisions than in the year 1914. The weapons themselves, taking a substantial cross-section, are more modern than in the case with any other country in the world at this time. They have just proved their supreme war worthiness in their victorious campaign . . . There is no evidence available to show that any country in the world disposes of a better total ammunition stock than the Reich . . . The AA artillery is not equalled by any country in the world.

In this reorganisation of the economic life of Germany for military purposes, the Nazi Government found the German armament industry quite willing to co-operate, and to play its part in the rearmament programme. In April, 1933, Gustav Krupp von Bohlen submitted to Hitler on behalf of the Reich Association of German Industry a plan for the reorganisation of German industry, which he stated was characterised by the desire to co-ordinate economic measures and political necessity. In the plan itself, Krupp stated that "the turn of political events is in line with the wishes which I myself and the board of directors have cherished for a long time". What Krupp meant by this statement is fully shown by the draft text of a speech which he planned to deliver in the University of Berlin in January, 1944, though the speech was in fact never delivered. Referring to the years 1919 to 1933, Krupp wrote:

> It is the one great merit of the entire German war economy that it did not remain idle during those bad years, even though its activity could not be brought to light, for obvious reasons. Through years of secret work, scientific and basic groundwork was laid in order to be ready again to work for the German armed forces at the appointed hour, without loss of time or experience ... Only through the secret activity of German enterprise, together with the experience gained meanwhile through production of peace time goods, was it possible after 1933 to fall into step with the new tasks arrived at, restoring Germany's military power.

In October, 1933, Germany withdrew from the International Disarmament Conference and League of Nations. In 1935, the Nazi Government decided to take the first open steps to free itself from its obligations under the Treaty of Versailles. On 10th March, 1935, the defendant Goering announced that Germany was building a military air force. Six days later, on 16th March, 1935, a law was passed bearing the signatures, among others, of the defendants Goering, Hess, Frank, Frick, Schacht and von Neurath, instituting compulsory military service and fixing the establishment of the German Army at a peace time strength of 500,000 men. In an endeavour to reassure public opinion in other countries, the Government announced on 21st May, 1935, that Germany would, though renouncing the disarmament clauses, still respect the territorial limitations of the Versailles Treaty, and would comply with the Locarno Pacts. Nevertheless, on the very day of this announcement, the secret Reich Defence Law was passed and its publication forbidden by Hitler. In this law, the powers and duties of the Chancellor and other Ministers were defined, should Germany become involved in war. It is clear from this law that by May of 1935 Hitler and his Government had arrived at the stage in the carrying out of their policies when it was necessary for them to have in existence the requisite machinery for the administration and government of Germany in the event of their policy leading to war.

At the same time that this preparation of the German economy for war was being carried out, the German armed forces themselves were preparing for a rebuilding of Germany's armed strength.

The German Navy was particularly active in this regard. The official German naval historians, Assmann and Gladisch, admit that the Treaty of Versailles had only been in force for a few months before it was violated, particularly in the construction of a new submarine arm.

The publications of Captain Schüssler and Oberst Scherf, both of which were sponsored by the defendant Raeder, were designed to show the German people the nature of the Navy's effort to rearm in defiance of the Treaty of Versailles. The full details of these publications have been given in evidence.

On the campaign trail: Adolf Hitler (1889–1945) greets the SA at Berchtesgarten, c. 1932.
Hulton Archive.

Troop inspection: in 1939 Adolf Hitler salutes one of the officers as he reviews the SS troops
in Hamburg. Hulton Archive.

An aerial view of Hitler's inspection of the Condo Legion in the Lustgarten, Berlin, on 6 June 1939. Hulton Archive.

Admiral Erich Raeder (1876–1960), the commander-in-chief of the German navy, seen here boarding a ship c. 1940, after reports that he had handed in his resignation to Hitler. Hulton Archive.

Planning war: the German chief of staff, General Alfred Jodl, seen here planning troop dispositions with Adolf Hitler, Benito Mussolini and General Keitel, c. 1942. Hulton Archive.

German chief of staff Alfred Jodl, flanked by his aide on the left and Grand Admiral von Friedeburg on the right, signs the unconditional surrender document imposed by the Allies at General Eisenhower's headquarters in Reims, France. Hulton Archive.

British commandos who landed in Normandy on 6 June 1944 set out to capture a Nazi gun site, which is protected by enemy snipers. Hulton Archive.

Towards Cherbourg: on 13 June 1944, Americans pass through the devastated town of Valognes in France. Hulton Archive.

On 6 June 1944, the US infantry wade to the Normandy shore at Omaha beach during the D Day invasion. Hulton Archive.

Full-length view of US soldiers disembarking from one of two American landing crafts on the Normandy beachhead during the Allied invasion of France in June 1944. Hulton Archive.

High-altitude photograph showing the landing craft and troop activity on the Normandy coast in June 1944. Public Record Office.

General Dwight D. Eisenhower (1890–1969) smiles while speaking to the men of the US 101st Airborne Division (the "Screaming Eagles"), as they prepare for the D Day invasion on 6 June 1944. Hulton Archive.

Winnie and Dwight: on 14 November 1944 British Prime Minister Winston Churchill (smoking a cigar) listens while General Dwight D. Eisenhower shows him round his trailer. Hulton Archive.

Left to right: Air Chief Marshal Tedder (1890–1967), General Eisenhower and Field Marshal Montgomery (1887–1976). These men were the supreme commanders of the Allied Expeditionary Force during World War II. Hulton Archive.

The War Crimes Trial: Nazi leaders in the dock at Nuremberg on 21 September 1946.
Back row (from left to right): Raeder (just visible); Schirach (speaking); Sauckel (behind Schirach);
Jodl; von Papen; Seyss-Inquart; Speer; Neurath; Fritzche.
Front row (from left to right): Goering; Hess; Ribbentrop; Keitel; Kaltenbrunner; Rosenberg; Frank;
Frick; Streicher; Funk; Schacht. Hulton Archive.

On 22 November 1945, members of Hitler's Third Reich sit in the courtroom at Nuremberg wearing
headsets. Front row (left to right): Goering (writing); Hess; Ribbentrop; Keitel. Back row (left to right):
Doenitz; Raeder; Schirach; Sauckel. Military police stand behind them. Hulton Archive.

On 12th May, 1934 the defendant Raeder issued the Top Secret armament plan for what was called the Third Armament Phase. This contained the sentence:

> All theoretical and practical A-preparations are to be drawn up with a primary view to readiness for a war *without any alert period*.

One month later, in June, 1934, the defendant Raeder had a conversation with Hitler, in which Hitler instructed him to keep secret the construction of U-boats and of warships over the limit of 10,000 tons which was then being undertaken.

And on 2nd November, 1934, the defendant Raeder had another conversation with Hitler and the defendant Goering, in which Hitler said that he considered it vital that the German Navy "should be increased as planned, as no war could be carried on if the Navy was not able to safeguard the ore imports from Scandinavia".

The large orders for building given in 1933 and 1934 are sought to be excused by the defendant Raeder on the ground that negotiations were in progress for an agreement between Germany and Great Britain, permitting Germany to build ships in excess of the provisions of the Treaty of Versailles. This agreement, which was signed in 1935, restricted the German Navy to a tonnage equal to one-third of that of the British, except in respect of U-boats where 45 per cent was agreed, subject always to the right to exceed this proportion after first informing the British Government and giving them an opportunity of discussion.

The Anglo-German Treaty followed in 1937, under which both Powers bound themselves to notify full details of their building programme at least four months before any action was taken. It is admitted that these clauses were not adhered to by Germany.

In capital vessels, for example, the displacement details were falsified by 20 per cent, whilst in the case of U-boats, the German historians Assmann and Gladisch say:

> It is probably just in the sphere of submarine construction that Germany adhered the least to the restrictions of the German–British Treaty.

The importance of these breaches of the Treaty is seen when the motive for this rearmament is considered. In the year 1940 the defendant Raeder himself wrote:

> The Führer hoped until the last moment to be able to put off the threatening conflict with England until 1944–5. At that time, the Navy would have had available a fleet with a powerful U-boat superiority, and a much more favourable ratio as regards strength in all other types of ships, particularly those designed for warfare on the High Seas.

The Nazi Government, as already stated, announced on 21st May, 1935, their intention to respect the territorial limitations of the Treaty of Versailles. On 7th March, 1936, in defiance of that Treaty, the demilitarised zone of the Rhineland was entered by German troops. In announcing this action to the German Reichstag, Hitler endeavoured to justify the re-entry by references to the recently concluded alliances between France and the Soviet Union, and between Czechoslovakia and the Soviet Union. He also tried to meet the hostile reaction which he no doubt expected to follow this violation of the Treaty by saying:

We have no territorial claims to make in Europe.

THE COMMON PLAN OR CONSPIRACY AND AGGRESSIVE WAR

The Tribunal now turns to the consideration of the crimes against peace charged in the Indictment. Count One of the Indictment charges the defendants with conspiring or having a common plan to commit crimes against peace.

Count Two of the Indictment charges the defendants with committing specific crimes against peace by planning, preparing, initiating and waging wars of aggression against a number of other States. It will be convenient to consider the question of the existence of a common plan and the question of aggressive war together, and to deal later in this Judgment with the question of the individual responsibility of the defendants.

The charges in the Indictment that the defendants planned and waged aggressive wars are charges of the utmost gravity. War is essentially an evil thing. Its consequences are not confined to the belligerent states alone, but affect the whole world.

To initiate a war of aggression, therefore, is not only an international crime; it is the supreme international crime differing only from other war crimes in that it contains within itself the accumulated evil of the whole.

The first acts of aggression referred to in the Indictment are the seizure of Austria and Czechoslovakia, and the first war of aggression charged in the Indictment is the war against Poland begun on 1st September, 1939.

Before examining that charge it is necessary to look more closely at some of the events which preceded these acts of aggression. The war against Poland did not come suddenly out of an otherwise clear sky; the evidence has made it plain that this war of aggression, as well as the seizure of Austria and Czechoslovakia, was pre-meditated and carefully prepared, and was not undertaken until the moment was thought opportune for it to be carried through as a definite part of the pre-ordained scheme and plan.

For the aggressive designs of the Nazi Government were not accidents arising out of the immediate political situation in Europe and the world; they were a deliberate and essential part of Nazi foreign policy.

From the beginning, the National Socialist movement claimed that its object was to unite the German people in the consciousness of their mission and destiny, based on inherent qualities of race, and under the guidance of the Führer.

For its achievement, two things were deemed to be essential: the disruption of the European order as it had existed since the Treaty of Versailles, and the creation of a Greater Germany beyond the frontiers of 1914. This necessarily involved the seizure of foreign territories.

War was seen to be inevitable, or, at the very least, highly probable, if these purposes were to be accomplished. The German people, therefore, with all their resources, were to be organised as a great political-military army, schooled to obey without question any policy decreed by the State.

PREPARATION FOR AGGRESSION

In *Mein Kampf* Hitler had made this view quite plain. It must be remembered that *Mein Kampf* was no mere private diary in which the secret thoughts of Hitler were set down. Its contents were rather proclaimed from the house-tops. It was used in the schools and universities and among the Hitler Youth, in the SS and the SA, and among the German people generally, even down to the presentation of an official copy to all newly married people. By the year 1945 over 6½ million copies had been circulated. The general contents are well known. Over and over again Hitler asserted his belief in the necessity of force as the means of solving international problems, as in the following quotation:

> The soil on which we now live was not a gift bestowed by Heaven on our
> forefathers. They had to conquer it by risking their lives. So also in the future, our
> people will not obtain territory, and therewith the means of existence, as a favour
> from any other people, but will have to win it by the power of a triumphant sword.

Mein Kampf contains many such passages, and the extolling of force as an instrument of foreign policy is openly proclaimed.

The precise objectives of this policy of force are also set forth in detail. The very first page of the book asserts that "German-Austria must be restored to the great German Motherland", not on economic grounds, but because "people of the same blood should be in the same Reich".

The restoration of the German frontiers of 1914 is declared to be wholly insufficient, and if Germany is to exist at all, it must be as a world power with the necessary territorial magnitude. *Mein Kampf* is quite explicit in stating where the increased territory is to be found:

> Therefore we National Socialists have purposely drawn a line through the line of
> conduct followed by pre-war Germany in foreign policy. We put an end to the

perpetual Germanic march towards the South and West of Europe, and turn our eyes towards the lands of the East. We finally put a stop to the colonial and trade policy of the pre-war times, and pass over to the territorial policy of the future ... But when we speak of new territory in Europe to-day, we must think principally of Russia and the border states subject to her.

Mein Kampf is not to be regarded as a mere literary exercise, nor as an inflexible policy or plan incapable of modification. Its importance lies in the unmistakable attitude of aggression revealed throughout its pages.

THE PLANNING OF AGGRESSION

Evidence from captured documents has revealed that Hitler held four secret meetings to which the Tribunal proposes to make special reference because of the light they shed upon the question of the common plan and aggressive war.

These meetings took place on 5th November, 1937, 23rd May, 1939, 22nd August, 1939, and 23rd November, 1939. At these meetings important declarations were made by Hitler as to his purposes, which are quite unmistakable in their terms. The documents which record what took place at these meetings have been subject to some criticism at the hands of defending Counsel.

Their essential authenticity is not denied, but it is said, for example, that they do not purport to be verbatim transcripts of the speeches they record, that the document dealing with the meeting on 5th November, 1937, was dated five days after the meeting had taken place, and that the two documents dealing with the meeting of August 22nd, 1939, differ from one another, and are unsigned.

Making the fullest allowance for criticism of this kind, the Tribunal is of the opinion that the documents are documents of the highest value, and that their authenticity and substantial truth are established.

They are obviously careful records of the events they describe, and they have been preserved as such in the archives of the German Government, from whose custody they were captured. Such documents could never be dismissed as inventions, nor even as inaccurate or distorted; they plainly record events which actually took place.

CONFERENCES OF 23RD NOVEMBER, 1939, AND 5TH NOVEMBER, 1937

It will perhaps be useful to deal first of all with the meeting of 23rd November, 1939, when Hitler called his Supreme Commanders together. A record was made of what was said, by one of those present. At the date of the meeting, Austria and Czechoslovakia had been incorporated into the

German Reich, Poland had been conquered by the German armies, and the war with Great Britain and France was still in its static phase. The moment was opportune for a review of past events. Hitler informed the Commanders that the purpose of the Conference was to give them an idea of the world of his thoughts, and to tell them his decision. He thereupon reviewed his political task since 1919, and referred to the secession of Germany from the League of Nations, the denunciation of the Disarmament Conference, the order for rearmament, the introduction of compulsory armed service, the occupation of the Rhineland, the seizure of Austria and the action against Czechoslovakia. He stated:

> One year later, Austria came; this step also was considered doubtful. It brought about a considerable reinforcement of the Reich. The next step was Bohemia, Moravia and Poland. This step also was not possible to accomplish in one campaign. First of all, the western fortification had to be finished. It was not possible to reach the goal in one effort. It was clear to me from the first moment that I could not be satisfied with the Sudeten German territory. That was only a partial solution. The decision to march into Bohemia was made. Then followed the erection of the Protectorate and with that the basis for the action against Poland was laid, but I wasn't quite clear at that time whether I should start first against the East and then in the West or vice versa ... Basically I did not organise the armed forces in order not to strike. The decision to strike was always in me. Earlier or later I wanted to solve the problem. Under pressure it was decided that the East was to be attacked first.

This address, reviewing past events and re-affirming the aggressive intentions present from the beginning, puts beyond any question of doubt the character of the actions against Austria and Czechoslovakia, and the war against Poland. For they had all been accomplished according to plan; and the nature of that plan must now be examined in a little more detail.

At the meeting of 23rd November, 1939, Hitler was looking back to things accomplished; at the earlier meeting now to be considered, he was looking forward, and revealing his plans to his confederates. The comparison is instructive.

The meeting held at the Reich Chancellery in Berlin on 5th November, 1937, was attended by Lieut.-Colonel Hoszbach, Hitler's personal adjutant, who compiled a long note of the proceedings, which he dated the 10th November, 1937, and signed.

The persons present were Hitler; the defendants Goering, von Neurath and Raeder, in their capacities as Commander-in-Chief of the Luftwaffe, Reich Foreign Minister and Commander-in-Chief of the Navy, respectively; General von Blomberg, Minister of War; and General von Fritsch, the Commander-in-Chief of the Army.

Hitler began by saying that the subject of the conference was of such high importance that in other States it would have taken place before the Cabinet. He went on to say that the subject matter of his speech was the result of his detailed deliberations, and of his experience during his four and a half years of Government. He requested that the statements he was about to make should be looked upon in the case of his death as his last will and testament. Hitler's main theme was the problem of living space, and he discussed various possible solutions, only to set them aside. He then said that the seizure of living space on the continent of Europe was therefore necessary, expressing himself in these words:

> It is not a case of conquering people, but of conquering agriculturally useful space. It would also be more to the purpose to seek raw material producing territory in Europe directly adjoining the Reich and not overseas, and this solution would have to be brought into effect for one or two generations . . . The history of all times – Roman Empire, British Empire – has proved that every space expansion can only be effected by breaking resistance and taking risks. Even setbacks are unavoidable: neither formerly nor today has space been found without an owner; the attacker always comes up against the proprietor.

He concluded with this observation:

> The question for Germany is where the greatest possible conquest could be made at the lowest cost.

Nothing could indicate more plainly the aggressive intentions of Hitler, and the events which soon followed showed the reality of his purpose. It is impossible to accept the contention that Hitler did not actually mean war; for after pointing out that Germany might expect the opposition of England and France, and analysing the strength and the weakness of those powers in particular situations, he continued:

> The German question can be solved only by way of force, and this is never without risk . . . If we place the decision to apply force with risk at the head of the following expositions, then we are left to reply to the questions "when" and "how". In this regard we have to decide upon three different cases.

The first of these three cases set forth a hypothetical international situation, in which he would take action not later than 1943 to 1945, saying:

> If the Führer is still living then it will be his irrevocable decision to solve the German space problem not later than 1943 to 1945. The necessity for action before 1943 to 1945 will come under consideration in Cases 2 and 3.

The second and third cases to which Hitler referred show the plain intention to seize Austria and Czechoslovakia, and in this connection Hitler said:

> For the improvement of our military-political position, it must be our first aim in every case of entanglement by war to conquer Czechoslovakia and Austria

simultaneously in order to remove any threat from the flanks in case of a possible advance westwards.

He further added:

> The annexation of the two states to Germany militarily and politically would constitute a considerable relief, owing to shorter and better frontiers, the freeing of fighting personnel for other purposes, and the possibility of reconstituting new armies up to a strength of about twelve divisions.

This decision to seize Austria and Czechoslovakia was discussed in some detail; the action was to be taken as soon as a favourable opportunity presented itself.

The military strength which Germany had been building up since 1933 was now to be directed at the two specific countries, Austria and Czechoslovakia.

The defendant Goering testified that he did not believe at that time that Hitler actually meant to attack Austria and Czechoslovakia, and that the purpose of the conference was only to put pressure on von Fritsch to speed up the rearmament of the Army.

The defendant Raeder testified that neither he, nor von Fritsch, nor von Blomberg believed that Hitler actually meant war, a conviction which the defendant Raeder claims that he held up to 22nd August, 1939. The basis of this conviction was his hope that Hitler would obtain a "political solution" of Germany's problems. But all that this means, when examined, is the belief that Germany's position would be so good, and Germany's armed might so overwhelming, that the territory desired could be obtained without fighting for it. It must be remembered too that Hitler's declared intention with regard to Austria was actually carried out within a little over four months from the date of the meeting, and within less than a year the first portion of Czechoslovakia was absorbed, and Bohemia and Moravia a few months later. If any doubts had existed in the minds of any of his hearers in November, 1937, after March of 1939 there could no longer be any question that Hitler was in deadly earnest in his decision to resort to war. The Tribunal is satisfied that Lt.-Col. Hoszbach's account of the meeting is substantially correct, and that those present knew that Austria and Czechoslovakia would be annexed by Germany at the first possible opportunity.

ACTS OF AGGRESSION

THE INVASION OF AUSTRIA

The invasion of Austria was a pre-meditated aggressive step in furthering the plan to wage aggressive wars against other countries. As a result Germany's flank was protected, that of Czechoslovakia being greatly weakened. The first step had been taken in the seizure of *Lebensraum*; many new divisions of trained fighting men had been acquired; and with the seizure of foreign exchange reserves, the re-armament programme had been greatly strengthened.

On 21st May, 1935, Hitler announced in the Reichstag that Germany did not intend either to attack Austria or to interfere in her internal affairs. On 1st May, 1936, he publicly coupled Czechoslovakia with Austria in his avowal of peaceful intentions; and so late as 11th July, 1936, he recognised by treaty the full sovereignty of Austria.

Austria was in fact seized by Germany in the month of March, 1938. For a number of years before that date, the National Socialists in Germany had been co-operating with the National Socialists of Austria with the ultimate object of incorporating Austria into the German Reich. The Putsch of July 25th, 1934, which resulted in the assassination of Chancellor Dollfuss, had the seizure of Austria as its object; but the Putsch failed, with the consequence that the National Socialist Party was outlawed in Austria. On 11th July, 1936, an agreement was entered into between the two countries, Article 1 of which stated:

> The German Government recognises the full sovereignty of the Federated State of Austria in the spirit of the pronouncements of the German Führer and Chancellor of the 21st May, 1935.

Article 2 declared:

> Each of the two Governments regards the inner political order (including the
> question of Austrian National Socialism) obtaining in the other country as an
> internal affair of the other country, upon which it will exercise neither direct nor
> indirect influence.

The National Socialist movement in Austria, however, continued its illegal
activities under cover of secrecy; and the National Socialists of Germany
gave the Party active support. The resulting "incidents" were seized upon by
the German National Socialists as an excuse for interfering in Austrian
affairs. After the conference of 5th November, 1937, these "incidents" rapidly
multiplied. The relationship between the two countries steadily worsened,
and finally the Austrian Chancellor Schuschnigg was persuaded by the
defendant von Papen and others to seek a conference with Hitler, which
took place at Berchtesgaden on 12th February, 1938. The defendant Keitel
was present at the conference, and Dr Schuschnigg was threatened by Hitler
with an immediate invasion of Austria. Schuschnigg finally agreed to grant
a political amnesty to various Nazis convicted of crime, and to appoint the
Nazi Seyss-Inquart as Minister of the Interior and Security with control of
the Police. On 9th March, 1938, in an attempt to preserve the independence
of his country, Dr Schuschnigg decided to hold a plebiscite on the question
of Austrian independence, which was fixed for 13th March, 1938. Hitler, two
days later, sent an ultimatum to Schuschnigg that the plebiscite must be
withdrawn. In the afternoon and evening of 11th March, 1938 the defendant Goering made a series of demands upon the Austrian Government,
each backed up by the threat of invasion. After Schuschnigg had agreed to
the cancellation of the plebiscite, another demand was put forward that
Schuschnigg must resign, and that the defendant Seyss-Inquart should be
appointed Chancellor. In consequence, Schuschnigg resigned, and President
Miklas, after at first refusing to appoint Seyss-Inquart as Chancellor, gave way
and appointed him.

Meanwhile Hitler had given the final order for the German troops to
cross the border at dawn on the 12th of March and instructed Seyss-Inquart
to use formations of Austrian National Socialists to depose Miklas and to
seize control of the Austrian Government. After the order to march had been
given to the German troops, Goering telephoned the German Embassy in
Vienna and dictated a telegram which he wished Seyss-Inquart to send to
Hitler to justify the military action which had already been ordered. It was:

> The provisional Austrian Government, which, after the dismissal of the Schuschnigg
> Government, considers its task to establish peace and order in Austria, sends to the
> German Government the urgent request to support it in its task and to help it to
> prevent bloodshed. For this purpose it asks the German Government to send
> German troops as soon as possible.

Keppler, an official of the German Embassy, replied:

> Well, SA and SS are marching through the streets, but everything is quiet.

After some further discussion, Goering stated:

> Please show him [Seyss-Inquart] the text of the telegram, and do tell him that we are asking him – well, he doesn't even have to send the telegram. All he needs to do is to say "Agreed".

Seyss-Inquart never sent the telegram; he never even telegraphed "Agreed".

It appears that as soon as he was appointed Chancellor, some time after 10 pm, he called Keppler and told him to call up Hitler and transmit his protests against the occupation. This action outraged the defendant Goering, because "it would disturb the rest of the Führer, who wanted to go to Austria the next day". At 11.15 pm an official in the Ministry of Propaganda in Berlin telephoned the German Embassy in Vienna and was told by Keppler: "Tell the General Field Marshal that Seyss-Inquart agrees."

At daybreak on 12th March, 1938, German troops marched into Austria and met with no resistance. It was announced in the German press that Seyss-Inquart had been appointed the successor to Schuschnigg, and the telegram which Goering had suggested, but which was never sent, was quoted to show that Seyss-Inquart had requested the presence of German troops to prevent disorder. On 13th March, 1938, a law was passed for the reunion of Austria in the German Reich. Seyss-Inquart demanded that President Miklas should sign this law, but he refused to do so, and resigned his office. He was succeeded by Seyss-Inquart, who signed the law in the name of Austria. This law was then adopted as a law of the Reich by a Reich Cabinet decree issued the same day, and signed by Hitler and the defendants Goering, Frick, von Ribbentrop and Hess.

It was contended before the Tribunal that the annexation of Austria was justified by the strong desire expressed in many quarters for the union of Austria and Germany; that there were many matters in common between the two peoples that made this union desirable; and that in the result the object was achieved without bloodshed.

These matters, even if true, are really immaterial, for the facts plainly prove that the methods employed to achieve the object were those of an aggressor. The ultimate factor was the armed might of Germany, ready to be used if any resistance was encountered. Moreover, none of these considerations appear from the Hoszbach account of the meetings of 5th November, 1937, to have been the motives which actuated Hitler; on the contrary, all the emphasis is there laid on the advantage to be gained by Germany in her military strength by the annexation of Austria.

THE SEIZURE OF CZECHOSLOVAKIA

The conference of 5th November, 1937, made it quite plain that the seizure of Czechoslovakia by Germany had been definitely decided upon. The only question remaining was the selection of the suitable moment to do it. On 4th March, 1938, the defendant Ribbentrop wrote to the defendant Keitel with regard to a suggestion made to Ribbentrop by the Hungarian Ambassador in Berlin, that possible war aims against Czechoslovakia should be discussed between the German and Hungarian armies. In the course of this letter Ribbentrop said:

> I have many doubts about such negotiations. In case we should discuss with Hungary possible war aims against Czechoslovakia, the danger exists that other parties as well would be informed about this.

On 11th March, 1938, Goering made two separate statements to Mastny, the Czechoslovak Minister in Berlin, assuring him that the developments then taking place in Austria would in no way have any detrimental influence on the relations between the German Reich and Czechoslovakia, and emphasised the continued earnest endeavour on the part of the Germans to improve those mutual relations. On 12th March, Goering asked Mastny to call on him, and repeated these assurances.

This design to keep Czechoslovakia quiet whilst Austria was absorbed was a typical manoeuvre on the part of the defendant Goering, which he was to repeat later in the case of Poland, when he made the most strenuous efforts to isolate Poland in the impending struggle. On the same day, 12th March, the defendant von Neurath spoke with Mastny, and assured him on behalf of Hitler that Germany still considered herself bound by the German–Czechoslovak Arbitration Convention concluded at Locarno in October, 1925.

The evidence shows that after the occupation of Austria by the German Army on 12th March, and the annexation of Austria on 13th March, Conrad Henlein, who was the leader of the Sudeten German Party in Czechoslovakia, saw Hitler in Berlin on 28th March. On the following day, at a conference in Berlin, when Ribbentrop was present with Henlein, the general situation was discussed, and later the defendant Jodl recorded in his diary:

> After the annexation of Austria the Führer mentions that there is no hurry to solve the Czech question, because Austria has to be digested first. Nevertheless, preparations for Case Grün (that is, the plan against Czechoslovakia) will have to be carried out energetically; they will have to be newly prepared on the basis of the changed strategic position because of the annexation of Austria.

On 21st April, 1938, a discussion took place between Hitler and the defendant Keitel with regard to "Case Grün", showing quite clearly that the preparations for the attack on Czechoslovakia were being fully considered. On 28th May, 1938, Hitler ordered that preparations should be made for military action against Czechoslovakia by 2nd October, and from then onwards the plan to invade Czechoslovakia was constantly under review. On 30th May, 1938, a directive signed by Hitler declared his "unalterable decision to smash Czechoslovakia by military action in the near future".

In June, 1938, as appears from a captured document taken from the files of the SD in Berlin, an elaborate plan for the employment of the SD in Czechoslovakia had been proposed. This plan provided that "the SD follow, if possible, immediately after the leading troops, and take upon themselves the duties similar to their tasks in Germany".

Gestapo officials were assigned to co-operate with the SD in certain operations. Special agents were to be trained beforehand to prevent sabotage, and these agents were to be notified:

> before the attack in due time ... in order to give them the possibility to hide themselves, avoid arrest and deportation. ... At the beginning, guerrilla or partisan warfare is to be expected, therefore weapons are necessary.

Files of information were to be compiled with notations as follows: "To arrest" ... "To liquidate" ... "To confiscate" ... "To deprive of passport", etc.

The plan provided for the temporary division of the country into larger and smaller territorial units, and considered various "suggestions", as they were termed, for the incorporation into the German Reich of the inhabitants and districts of Czechoslovakia. The final "suggestion" included the whole country, together with Slovakia and Carpathian Russia, with a population of nearly 15 million.

The plan was modified in some respects in September after the Munich Conference, but the fact that the plan existed in such exact detail and was couched in such war-like language indicated a calculated design to resort to force.

On 31st August, 1938, Hitler approved a memorandum by Jodl, dated 24th August, 1938, concerning the timing of the order for the invasion of Czechoslovakia and the question of defence measures. This memorandum contained the following:

> Operation Grün will be set in motion by means of an "incident" in Czechoslovakia, which will give Germany provocation for military intervention. The fixing of the exact time for this incident is of the utmost importance.

These facts demonstrate that the occupation of Czechoslovakia had been planned in detail long before the Munich Conference.

In the month of September, 1938, the conferences and talks with military leaders continued. In view of the extraordinarily critical situation which had arisen, the British Prime Minister, Mr Chamberlain, flew to

Munich and then went to Berchtesgaden to see Hitler. On 22nd September Mr Chamberlain met Hitler for further discussions at Bad Godesberg. On 26th September, 1938, Hitler said in a speech in Berlin, with reference to his conversation:

> I assured him, moreover, and I repeat it here, that when this problem is solved there will be no more territorial problems for Germany in Europe; and I further assured him that from the moment when Czechoslovakia solves its other problems, that is to say, when the Czechs have come to an arrangement with their other minorities, peacefully and without oppression, I will be no longer interested in the Czech State, and that as far as I am concerned I will guarantee it. We don't want any Czechs.

On the 29th September, 1938, after a conference between Hitler and Mussolini and the British and French Prime Ministers in Munich, the Munich Pact was signed, by which Czechoslovakia was required to acquiesce in the cession of the Sudetenland to Germany. The "piece of paper" which the British Prime Minister brought back to London, signed by himself and Hitler, expressed the hope that for the future Britain and Germany might live without war. That Hitler never intended to adhere to the Munich Agreement is shown by the fact that a little later he asked the defendant Keitel for information with regard to the military force which in his opinion would be required to break all Czech resistance in Bohemia and Moravia. Keitel gave his reply on 11th October, 1938. On 21st October, 1938, a directive was issued by Hitler, and countersigned by the defendant Keitel, to the armed forces on their future tasks, which stated:

> Liquidation of the remainder of Czechoslovakia: It must be possible to smash at any time the remainder of Czechoslovakia if her policy should become hostile towards Germany.

On 14th March, 1939, the Czech President Hácha and his Foreign Minister Chvalkovsky came to Berlin at the suggestion of Hitler, and attended a meeting at which the defendants Ribbentrop, Goering and Keitel were present, with others. The proposal was made to Hácha that if he would sign an agreement consenting to the incorporation of the Czech people in the German Reich at once, Bohemia and Moravia would be saved from destruction. He was informed that German troops had already received orders to march and that any resistance would be broken with physical force. The defendant Goering added the threat that he would destroy Prague completely from the air. Faced by this dreadful alternative, Hácha and his Foreign Minister put their signatures to the necessary agreement at 4.30 in the morning, and Hitler and Ribbentrop signed on behalf of Germany.

On 15th March German troops occupied Bohemia and Moravia, and on 16th March the German decree was issued incorporating Bohemia and

Moravia in the Reich as a Protectorate, and this decree was signed by the defendants Ribbentrop and Frick.

THE AGGRESSION AGAINST POLAND

By March, 1939, the plan to annex Austria and Czechoslovakia, which had been discussed by Hitler at the meeting of 5th November, 1937, had been accomplished. The time had now come for the German leaders to consider further acts of aggression, made more possible of attainment because of that accomplishment.

On 23rd May, 1939, a meeting was held in Hitler's study in the new Reich Chancellery in Berlin. Hitler announced his decision to attack Poland and gave his reasons, and discussed the effect the decision might have on other countries. In point of time, this was the second of the important meetings to which reference has already been made, and in order to appreciate the full significance of what was said and done, it is necessary to state shortly some of the main events in the history of German–Polish relations.

As long ago as the year 1925 an Arbitration Treaty between Germany and Poland had been made at Locarno, providing for the settlement of all disputes between the two countries. On 26th January, 1934, a German–Polish declaration of non-aggression was made, signed on behalf of the German Government by the defendant von Neurath. On 30th January, 1934, and again on 30th January, 1937, Hitler made speeches in the Reichstag in which he expressed his view that Poland and Germany could work together in harmony and peace. On 20th February, 1938, Hitler made a third speech in the Reichstag in the course of which he said with regard to Poland:

> And so the way to a friendly understanding has been successfully paved, an understanding which, beginning with Danzig, has today, in spite of the attempts of certain mischief makers, succeeded in finally taking the poison out of the relations between Germany and Poland and transforming them into a sincere, friendly co-operation. Relying on her friendships, Germany will not leave a stone unturned to save that ideal which provides the foundation for the task which is ahead of us – peace.

On 26th September, 1938, in the middle of the crisis over the Sudetenland, Hitler made the speech in Berlin which has already been quoted, and announced that he had informed the British Prime Minister that when the Czechoslovakian problem had been solved there would be no more territorial problems for Germany in Europe. Nevertheless, on 24th November of the same year, an OKW directive was issued to the German armed forces to make preparations for an attack upon Danzig; it stated:

> The Führer has ordered:
>
> 1. Preparations are also to be made to enable the Free State of Danzig to be occupied by German troops by surprise.

In spite of having ordered military preparations for the occupation of Danzig, Hitler, on 30th January, 1939, said in a speech in the Reichstag:

> During the troubled months of the past year, the friendship between Germany and Poland has been one of the most reassuring factors in the political life of Europe.

Five days previously, on 25th January, 1939, Ribbentrop said in the course of a speech in Warsaw:

> Thus Poland and Germany can look forward to the future with full confidence in the solid basis of their mutual relations.

Following the occupation of Bohemia and Moravia by Germany on 15th March, 1939, which was a flagrant breach of the Munich Agreement, Great Britain gave an assurance to Poland on 31st March, 1939, that in the event of any action which clearly threatened Polish independence, and which the Polish Government accordingly considered it vital to resist with their national forces, Great Britain would feel itself bound at once to lend Poland all the support in its power. The French Government took the same stand. It is interesting to note in this connection, that one of the arguments frequently presented by the defence in the present case is that the defendants were influenced to think that their conduct was not in breach of international law by the acquiescence of other Powers. The declarations of Great Britain and France showed, at least, that this view could be held no longer.

On 3rd April, 1939, a revised OKW directive was issued to the armed forces, which after referring to the question of Danzig made reference to Fall Weiss (the code name for the German invasion of Poland) and stated:

> The Führer had added the following directions to Fall Weiss:
>
> 1. Preparations must be made in such a way that the operation can be carried out at any time from 1st September, 1939, onwards.
>
> 2. The High Command of the Armed Forces has been directed to draw up a precise timetable for Fall Weiss and to arrange by conferences the synchronised timings between the three branches of the Armed Forces.

On 11th April, 1939, a further directive was signed by Hitler and issued to the armed forces, and in one of the annexes to that document the words occur:

> Quarrels with Poland should be avoided. Should Poland, however, adopt a threatening attitude towards Germany, "a final settlement" will be necessary, notwithstanding the pact with Poland. The aim is then to destroy Polish military strength, and to create in the East a situation which satisfies the requirements of defence. The Free State of Danzig will be incorporated into Germany at the outbreak of the conflict at the latest. Policy aims at limiting the war to Poland, and

this is considered possible in view of the internal crisis in France, and British restraint as a result of this.

In spite of the contents of these two directives, Hitler made a speech in the Reichstag on 28th April, 1939, in which, after describing the Polish Government's alleged rejection of an offer he had made with regard to Danzig and the Polish Corridor, he stated:

> I have regretted greatly this incomprehensible attitude of the Polish Government, but that alone is not the decisive fact; the worst is that now Poland like Czechoslovakia a year ago believes, under the pressure of a lying international campaign, that it must call up its troops, although Germany on her part has not called up a single man, and had not thought of proceeding in any way against Poland . . . The intention to attack on the part of Germany . . . was merely invented by the international Press.

It was four weeks after making this speech that Hitler, on 23rd May, 1939, held the important military conference to which reference has already been made. Among the persons present were the defendants Goering, Raeder and Keitel. The adjutant on duty that day was Lieutenant-Colonel Schmundt, and he made a record of what happened, certifying it with his signature as a correct record.

The purpose of the meeting was to enable Hitler to inform the heads of the armed forces and their staffs of his views on the political situation and his future aims. After analysing the political situation and reviewing the course of events since 1933, Hitler announced his decision to attack Poland. He admitted that the quarrel with Poland over Danzig was not the reason for this attack, but the necessity for Germany to enlarge her living space and secure her food supplies. He said:

> The solution of the problem demands courage. The principle by which one evades solving the problem by adapting oneself to circumstances is inadmissible. Circumstances must rather be adapted to. This is impossible without invasion of foreign states or attacks upon foreign property.

Later in his address he added:

> There is therefore no question of sparing Poland, and we are left with the decision to attack Poland at the first suitable opportunity. We cannot expect a repetition of the Czech affair. There will be war. Our task is to isolate Poland. The success of the isolation will be decisive . . . The isolation of Poland is a matter of skilful politics.

Lt.-Col. Schmundt's record of the meeting reveals that Hitler fully realised the possibility of Great Britain and France coming to Poland's assistance. If, therefore, the isolation of Poland could not be achieved, Hitler was of the opinion that Germany should attack Great Britain and France first, or at any rate should concentrate primarily on the war in the West, in order to defeat Great Britain and France quickly, or at least to destroy their effectiveness. Nevertheless, Hitler stressed that war with England and France would be a life and death struggle, which might last a long time, and that preparations must be made accordingly.

During the weeks which followed this conference, other meetings were held and directives were issued in preparation for the war. The defendant Ribbentrop was sent to Moscow to negotiate a non-aggression pact with the Soviet Union.

On 22nd August, 1939, there took place the important meeting of that day, to which reference has already been made. The Prosecution have put in evidence two unsigned captured documents which appear to be records made of this meeting by persons who were present. The first document is headed: "The Führer's speech to the Commanders-in-Chief on the 22nd August, 1939". The purpose of the speech was to announce the decision to make war on Poland at once, and Hitler began by saying:

> It was clear to me that a conflict with Poland had to come sooner or later. I had already made this decision in the Spring, but I thought that I would first turn against the West in a few years, and only afterwards against the East . . . I wanted to establish an acceptable relationship with Poland in order to fight first against the West. But this plan, which was agreeable to me, could not be executed since essential points have changed. It became clear to me that Poland would attack us in case of a conflict with the West.

Hitler then went on to explain why he had decided that the most favourable moment had arrived for starting the war:

> Now Poland is in the position in which I wanted her . . . I am only afraid that at the last moment some Schweinehund will make a proposal for mediation . . . A beginning has been made for the destruction of England's hegemony.

This document closely resembles one of the documents put in evidence on behalf of the defendant Raeder. This latter document consists of a summary of the same speech, compiled on the day it was made, by one Admiral Böhm, from notes he had taken during the meeting. In substance it says that the moment had arrived to settle the dispute with Poland by military invasion; that although a conflict between Germany and the West was unavoidable in the long run, the likelihood of Great Britain and France coming to Poland's assistance was not great; and that even if a war in the West should come about, the first aim should be the crushing of the Polish military strength. It also contains a statement by Hitler that an appropriate propaganda reason for invading Poland would be given, the truth or falsehood of which was unimportant, since "the Right lies in Victory".

The second unsigned document put in evidence by the Prosecution is headed: "Second Speech by the Führer on the 22nd August, 1939", and it is in the form of notes of the main points made by Hitler. Some of these are as follows:

> Everybody shall have to make a point of it that we were determined from the beginning to fight the Western Powers. Struggle for life or death . . . destruction of Poland in the foreground. The aim is elimination of living forces, not the arrival at a certain line. Even if war should break out in the West, the destruction of Poland shall be the primary objective. I shall give a propagandist cause for starting the war – never mind whether it be plausible or not. The victor shall not be asked later on whether we told the truth or not. In starting and making a war, not the Right is what matters, but Victory . . . The start will be ordered probably by Saturday morning. (That is to say, 26th August.)

In spite of it being described as a second speech, there are sufficient points of similarity with the two previously mentioned documents to make it appear very probable that this is an account of the same speech, not as detailed as the other two, but in substance the same.

These three documents establish that the final decision as to the date of Poland's destruction, which had been agreed upon and planned earlier in the year, was reached by Hitler shortly before 22nd August, 1939. They also show that although he hoped to be able to avoid having to fight Great Britain and France as well, he fully realised there was a risk of this happening, but it was a risk which he was determined to take.

The events of the last days of August confirm this determination. On 22nd August, 1939, the same day as the speech just referred to, the British Prime Minister wrote a letter to Hitler, in which he said:

> Having thus made our position perfectly clear, I wish to repeat to you my conviction that war between our two peoples would be the greatest calamity that could occur.

On 23rd August Hitler replied:

> The question of the treatment of European problems on a peaceful basis is not a decision which rests with Germany, but primarily on those who since the crime committed by the Versailles Diktat have stubbornly and consistently opposed any peaceful revision. Only after a change of spirit on the part of the responsible Powers can there be any real change in the relationship between England and Germany.

There followed a number of appeals to Hitler to refrain from forcing the Polish issue to the point of war. These were from President Roosevelt on 24th and 25th August; from His Holiness the Pope on 24th and 31st August; and from M. Daladier, the Prime Minister of France, on 26th August. All these appeals fell on deaf ears.

On 25th August Great Britain signed a pact of mutual assistance with Poland, which reinforced the understanding she had given to Poland earlier in the year. This, coupled with the news of Mussolini's unwillingness to enter the war on Germany's side, made Hitler hesitate for a moment. The invasion of Poland, which was timed to start on 26th August, was postponed until a further attempt had been made to persuade Great Britain not to intervene. Hitler offered to enter into a comprehensive agreement with Great Britain, once the Polish question had been settled. In reply to this, Great Britain made a counter-suggestion for the settlement of the Polish dispute by negotiation. On 29th August Hitler informed the British Ambassador that the German Government, though sceptical as to the result, would be prepared to enter into direct negotiations with a Polish emissary, provided he arrived in Berlin with plenipotentiary powers by midnight for the following day, 30th August. The Polish Government were informed of this, but with the example of Schuschnigg and Hácha before them, they decided not to send such an emissary. At midnight on 30th August the defendant Ribbentrop read to the British Ambassador at top speed a document containing the first precise formulation of the German demands against Poland. He refused, however, to give the Ambassador a copy of this, and stated that in any case it was too late now, since no Polish plenipotentiary had arrived.

In the opinion of the Tribunal, the manner in which these negotiations were conducted by Hitler and Ribbentrop showed that they were not entered into in good faith or with any desire to maintain peace, but solely in the attempt to prevent Great Britain and France from honouring their obligations to Poland.

Parallel with these negotiations were the unsuccessful attempts made by Goering to effect the isolation of Poland by persuading Great Britain not to stand by her pledged word, through the services of one Birger Dahlerus, a Swede. Dahlerus, who was called as a witness by Goering, had a considerable knowledge of England and of things English, and in July, 1939, was anxious to bring about a better understanding between England and Germany, in the hope of preventing a war between the two countries. He got into contact with Goering as well as with official circles in London, and during the latter part of August Goering used him as an unofficial intermediary to try and deter the British Government from their opposition to Germany's intentions towards Poland. Dahlerus, of course, had no knowledge at the time of the decision which Hitler had secretly announced on 22nd August, nor of the German military directives for the attack on Poland which were already in existence. As he admitted in his evidence, it was not until 26th September, after the conquest of Poland was virtually complete, that he first realised that Goering's aim all along had been to get Great Britain's consent to Germany's seizure of Poland.

After all attempts to persuade Germany to agree to a settlement of her dispute with Poland on a reasonable basis had failed, Hitler, on 31st August, issued his final directive, in which he announced that the attack on Poland would start in the early morning hours of 1st September, and gave instructions as to what action would be taken if Great Britain and France should enter the war in defence of Poland.

In the opinion of the Tribunal, the events of the days immediately preceding 1st September, 1939, demonstrate the determination of Hitler and his associates to carry out the declared intention of invading Poland at all costs, despite appeals from every quarter. With the ever increasing evidence before him that this intention would lead to war with Great Britain and France as well, Hitler was resolved not to depart from the course he had set for himself. The Tribunal is fully satisfied by the evidence that the war initiated by Germany against Poland on 1st September, 1939, was most plainly an aggressive war, which was to develop in due course into a war which embraced almost the whole world, and resulted in the commission of countless crimes, both against the laws and customs of war and against humanity.

THE INVASION OF DENMARK AND NORWAY

The aggressive war against Poland was but the beginning. The aggression of Nazi Germany quickly spread from country to country. In point of time the first two countries to suffer were Denmark and Norway.

On 31st May, 1939, a Treaty of Non-Aggression was made between Germany and Denmark, and signed by the defendant Ribbentrop. It was there solemnly stated that the parties to the Treaty were "firmly resolved to maintain peace between Denmark and Germany under all circumstances". Nevertheless, Germany invaded Denmark on 9th April, 1940.

On 2nd September, 1939, after the outbreak of war with Poland, Germany sent a solemn assurance to Norway in these terms:

> The German Reich Government is determined in view of the friendly relations which exist between Norway and Germany, under no circumstance to prejudice the inviolability and integrity of Norway, and to respect the territory of the Norwegian State. In making this declaration the Reich Government naturally expects, on its side, that Norway will observe an unimpeachable neutrality towards the Reich and will not tolerate any breaches of Norwegian neutrality by any third party which might occur. Should the attitude of the Royal Norwegian Government differ from this so that any such breach of neutrality by a third party occurs, the Reich Government would then obviously be compelled to safeguard the interests of the Reich in such a way as the resulting situation might dictate.

On 9th April, 1940, in pursuance of the plan of campaign, Norway was invaded by Germany.

The idea of attacking Norway originated, it appears, with the defendants Raeder and Rosenberg. On 3rd October, 1939, Raeder prepared a memorandum on the subject of "gaining bases in Norway", and among the questions discussed was the question: "Can bases be gained by military force against Norway's will, if it is impossible to carry this out without fighting?" Despite this fact, three days later, further assurances were given to Norway by Germany, which stated:

> Germany has never had any conflicts of interest or even points of controversy with the Northern States, and neither has she any today.

Three days later again, the defendant Doenitz prepared a memorandum on the same subject, namely bases in Norway, and suggested the establishment of a base in Trondheim with an alternative of supplying fuel in Narvik. At the same time the defendant Raeder was in correspondence with Admiral Karls, who pointed out to him the importance of an occupation of the Norwegian coast by Germany. On 10th October Raeder reported to Hitler the disadvantages to Germany which an occupation by the British would have. In the months of October and November Raeder continued to work on the possible occupation of Norway, in conjunction with the "Rosenberg Organisation". The "Rosenberg Organisation" was the Foreign Affairs Bureau of the NSDAP, and Rosenberg as Reichsleiter was in charge of it. Early in December, Quisling, the notorious Norwegian traitor, visited Berlin and was seen by the defendants Rosenberg and Raeder. He put forward a plan for a *coup d'état* in Norway. On 12th December the defendant Raeder and the naval staff, together with the defendants Keitel and Jodl, had a conference with Hitler, when Raeder reported on his interview with Quisling, and set out Quisling's views. On 16th December Hitler himself interviewed Quisling on all these matters. In the report of the activities of the Foreign Affairs Bureau of the NSDAP for the years 1933–1943, under the heading of "Political preparations for the military occupation of Norway", it is stated that at the interview with Quisling Hitler said that he would prefer a neutral attitude on the part of Norway as well as the whole of Scandinavia, as he did not desire to extend the theatre of war, or to draw other nations into the conflict. If the enemy attempted to extend the war he would be compelled to guard himself against that undertaking; however, he promised Quisling financial support, and assigned to a special military staff the examination of the military questions involved.

On 27th January, 1940, a memorandum was prepared by Keitel regarding the plans for the invasion of Norway. On 28th February, 1940, Jodl entered in his diary:

> I proposed first to the Chief of OKW and then to the Führer that "Case Yellow" [that is the operation against the Netherlands] and Weser Exercise [that is the operation against Norway and Denmark] must be prepared in such a way that they will be independent of one another as regard both time and forces employed.

On 1st March Hitler issued a directive regarding the Weser Exercise which contained the words:

The development of the situation in Scandinavia requires the making of all
preparations for the occupation of Denmark and Norway by a part of the German
Armed Forces. This operation should prevent British encroachment on Scandinavia
and the Baltic; further, it should guarantee our ore base in Sweden and give our
Navy and Air Force a wider start line against Britain ... The crossing of the Danish
border and the landings in Norway must take place simultaneously ... It is most
important that the Scandinavian States as well as the Western opponents should be
taken by surprise by our measures.

On 24th March the naval operation orders for the Weser Exercise were
issued, and on 30th March the defendant Doenitz as Commander-in-Chief
of U-boats issued his operational order for the occupation of Denmark and
Norway. On 9th April, 1940, the German forces invaded Norway and
Denmark.

From this narrative it is clear that as early as October, 1939, the question
of invading Norway was under consideration. The defence that has been
made here is that Germany was compelled to attack Norway to forestall an
Allied invasion, and that her action was therefore preventive.

It must be remembered that preventive action in foreign territory is justified only in case of "an instant and overwhelming necessity for self-defence,
leaving no choice of means, and no moment of deliberation" (The Caroline
Case, Moore's *Digest of International Law*, II, 412). How widely the view was
held in influential German circles that the Allies intended to occupy Norway
cannot be determined with exactitude. Quisling asserted that the Allies
would intervene in Norway with the tacit consent of the Norwegian
Government. The German Legation at Oslo disagreed with this view,
although the Naval Attaché at that Legation shared it.

The War Diary of the German Naval Operations Staff for 13th January,
1940, stated that the Chief of the Naval Operations Staff thought that the
most favourable solution would be the maintenance of the neutrality of
Norway, but he harboured the firm conviction that England intended to
occupy Norway in the near future, relying on the tacit agreement of the
Norwegian Government.

The directive of Hitler issued on 1st March, 1940, for the attack on
Denmark and Norway stated that the operation "should prevent British
encroachment on Scandinavia and the Baltic".

It is, however, to be remembered that the defendant Raeder's memorandum of 3rd October, 1939, makes no reference to forestalling the Allies, but
it is based upon "the aim of improving our strategical and operational position". The memorandum itself is headed "Gaining of Bases in Norway". The
same observation applies *mutatis mutandis* to the memorandum of the defendant Doenitz of 9th October, 1939. Furthermore, on 13th March, the
defendant Jodl recorded in his diary:

Führer does not give order yet for 'W' (Weser Exercise). He is still looking for an excuse. [Justification?]

On 14th March, 1940, he again wrote:

Führer has not yet decided what reason to give for "Weser Exercise".

On 21st March, 1940, he recorded the misgivings of Task Force XXI about the long interval between taking up readiness positions and the close of the diplomatic negotiations, and added:

Führer rejects any earlier negotiations, as otherwise calls for help go out to England and America. If resistance is put up it must be ruthlessly broken.

On 2nd April he records that all the preparations are completed; on 4th April the Naval Operation Order was issued; and on 9th April the invasion was begun.

From all this it is clear that when the plans for an attack on Norway were being made, they were not made for the purpose of forestalling an imminent Allied landing, but, at the most, that they might prevent an Allied occupation at some future date.

When the final orders for the German invasion of Norway were given, the diary of the Naval Operations Staff for 23rd March, 1940, records:

A mass encroachment by the English into Norwegian territorial waters . . . is not to be expected at the present time.

And Admiral Assmann's entry for 26th March says:

British landing in Norway not considered serious.

Documents which were subsequently captured by the Germans are relied on to show that the Allied plan to occupy harbours and airports in western Norway was a definite plan, although in all points considerably behind the German plans under which the invasion was actually carried out. These documents indicate that an altered plan had been finally agreed upon on 20th March, 1940, that a convoy should leave England on 5th April, and that mining in Norwegian waters would begin the same day; and that on 5th April the sailing time had been postponed until 8th April. But these plans were not the cause of the German invasion of Norway. Norway was occupied by Germany to afford her bases from which a more effective attack on England and France might be made, pursuant to plans prepared long in advance of the Allied plans which are now relied on to support the argument of self-defence.

It was further argued that Germany alone could decide, in accordance with the reservations made by many of the Signatory Powers at the time of the conclusion of the Kellogg–Briand Pact [see p.444], whether preventive action was a necessity, and that in making her decision her judgment was conclusive. But whether action taken under the claim of self-defence was in fact aggressive or defensive must ultimately be subject to investigation and adjudication if international law is ever to be enforced.

No suggestion is made by the defendants that there was any plan by any belligerent, other than Germany, to occupy Denmark. No excuse for that aggression has ever been offered.

As the German armies entered Norway and Denmark, German memoranda were handed to the Norwegian and Danish Governments which gave the assurance that the German troops did not come as enemies, that they did not intend to make use of the points occupied by German troops as bases for operations against England, as long as they were not forced to do so by measures taken by England and France, and that they had come to protect the North against the proposed occupation of Norwegian strong points by English–French forces.

The memoranda added that Germany had no intention of infringing the territorial integrity and political independence of the Kingdom of Norway then or in the future. Nevertheless, on 3rd June, 1940, a German Naval memorandum discussed the use to be made of Norway and Denmark, and put forward one solution for consideration that the territories of Denmark and Norway acquired during the course of the war should continue to be occupied and organised so that they could in the future be considered as German possessions.

In the light of all the available evidence it is impossible to accept the contention that the invasions of Denmark and Norway were defensive, and in the opinion of the Tribunal they were acts of aggressive war.

THE INVASION OF BELGIUM, THE NETHERLANDS AND LUXEMBURG

The plan to seize Belgium and the Netherlands was considered in August, 1938, when the attack on Czechoslovakia was being formulated, and the possibility of war with France and England was contemplated. The advantage to Germany of being able to use these countries for their own purposes, particularly as air bases in the war against England and France, was emphasised. In May of 1939, when Hitler made his irrevocable decision to attack Poland, and foresaw the possibility at least of a war with England and France in consequence, he told his military commanders:

> Dutch and Belgian air bases must be occupied . . . Declarations of neutrality must be ignored.

On August 22nd in the same year, he told his military commanders that England and France, in his opinion, would not "violate the neutrality of these countries". At the same time he assured Belgium and Holland and

Luxemburg that he would respect their neutrality; and on 6th October, 1939, after the Polish campaign, he repeated this assurance. On 7th October General von Brauchitsch directed Army Group B to prepare "for the immediate invasion of Dutch and Belgian territory, if the political situation so demands". In a series of orders, which were signed by the defendants Keitel and Jodl, the attack was fixed for 10th November, 1939, but it was postponed from time to time until May of 1940 on account of weather conditions and transport problems.

At the conference on 23rd November, 1939, Hitler said:

> We have an Achilles heel: The Ruhr. The progress of the war depends on the possession of the Ruhr. If England and France push through Belgium and Holland into the Ruhr, we shall be in the greatest danger . . . Certainly England and France will assume the offensive against Germany when they are armed. England and France have means of pressure to bring Belgium and Holland to request English and French help. In Belgium and Holland the sympathies are all for France and England . . . If the French Army marches into Belgium in order to attack us, it will be too late for us. We must anticipate them . . . We shall sow the English coast with mines which cannot be cleared. This mine warfare with the Luftwaffe demands a different starting point. England cannot live without its imports. We can feed ourselves. The permanent sowing of mines on the English coasts will bring England to her knees. However, this can only occur if we have occupied Belgium and Holland . . . My decision is unchangeable; I shall attack France and England at the most favourable and quickest moment. Breach of the neutrality of Belgium and Holland is meaningless. No one will question that when we have won. We shall not bring about the breach of neutrality as idiotically as it was in 1914. If we do not break the neutrality, then England and France will. Without attack, the war is not to be ended victoriously.

On 10th May, 1940, the German forces invaded the Netherlands, Belgium and Luxemburg. On the same day the German Ambassadors handed to the Netherlands and Belgian Governments a memorandum alleging that the British and French armies, with the consent of Belgium and Holland, were planning to march through those countries to attack the Ruhr, and justifying the invasion on these grounds. Germany, however, assured the Netherlands and Belgium that their integrity and their possessions would be respected. A similar memorandum was delivered to Luxemburg on the same date.

There is no evidence before the Tribunal to justify the contention that the Netherlands, Belgium and Luxemburg were invaded by Germany because their occupation had been planned by England and France. British and French staffs had been co-operating in making certain plans for military operations in the Low Countries, but the purpose of this planning was to defend these countries in the event of a German attack.

The invasion of Belgium, Holland and Luxemburg was entirely without justification.

It was carried out in pursuance of policies long considered and prepared, and was plainly an act of aggressive war. The resolve to invade was made without any other consideration than the advancement of the aggressive policies of Germany.

THE AGGRESSION AGAINST YUGOSLAVIA AND GREECE

On 12th August, 1939, Hitler had a conversation with Ciano and the defendant Ribbentrop at Obersalzberg. He said then:

> Generally speaking, the best thing to happen would be for the neutrals to be liquidated one after the other. The process could be carried out more easily if on every occasion one partner of the Axis covered the other while it was dealing with the uncertain neutral. Italy might well regard Yugoslavia as a neutral of this kind.

This observation was made only two months after Hitler had given assurances to Yugoslavia that he would regard her frontier as final and inviolable. On the occasion of the visit to Germany of the Prince Regent of Yugoslavia on 1st June, 1939, Hitler had said in a public speech:

> The firmly established reliable relationship of Germany to Yugoslavia, now that owing to historical events we have become neighbours with common boundaries fixed for all time, will not only guarantee lasting peace between our two peoples and countries, but can also represent an element of calm to our nerve-racked continent. This peace is the goal of all who are disposed to perform really constructive work.

On 6th October, 1939, Germany repeated these assurances to Yugoslavia, after Hitler and Ribbentrop had unsuccessfully tried to persuade Italy to enter the war on the side of Germany by attacking Yugoslavia. On 28th October, 1940, Italy invaded Greece, but the military operations met with no success. In November Hitler wrote to Mussolini with regard to the invasion of Greece, and the extension of the war in the Balkans, and pointed out that no military operations could take place in the Balkans before the following March, and therefore Yugoslavia must if at all possible be won over by other means and in other ways. But on 12th November, 1940, Hitler issued a directive for the prosecution of the war, and it included the words:

> The Balkans: The Commander-in-Chief of the Army will make preparations for occupying the Greek mainland north of the Aegean Sea, in case of need entering through Bulgaria.

On 13th December he issued a directive concerning the operation "Marita", the code name for the invasion of Greece, in which he stated:

> 1. The result of the battles in Albania is not yet decisive. Because of a dangerous situation in Albania, it is doubly necessary that the British endeavour be foiled to

create air bases under the protection of a Balkan front, which would be dangerous above all to Italy as to the Romanian oilfields.

2. My plan therefore is (*a*) to form a slowly increasing task force in southern Romania within the next month, (*b*) after the setting in of favourable weather, probably in March, to send a task force for the occupation of the Aegean north coast by way of Bulgaria and if necessary to occupy the entire Greek mainland.

On 20th January, 1941, at a meeting between Hitler and Mussolini, at which the defendants Ribbentrop, Keitel, Jodl and others were present, Hitler stated:

The massing of troops in Romania serves a threefold purpose:

(*a*) An operation against Greece;
(*b*) Protection of Bulgaria against Russia and Turkey;
(*c*) Safeguarding the guarantee to Romania . . .

It is desirable that this deployment be completed without interference from the enemy. Therefore, disclose the game as late as possible. The tendency will be to cross the Danube at the last possible moment, and to line up for attack at the earliest possible moment.

On 19th February, 1941, an OKW directive re the operation "Marita" stated:

On 18th February the Führer made the following decision regarding the carrying out of Operation Marita. The following dates are envisaged: commencement of building bridge, 28th February; crossing of the Danube, 2nd March.

On 3rd March, 1941, British troops landed in Greece to assist the Greeks to resist the Italians; and on 18th March, at a meeting between Hitler and the defendant Raeder, at which the defendants Keitel and Jodl were also present, the defendant Raeder asked for confirmation that the "whole of Greece will have to be occupied, even in the event of a peaceful settlement", to which Hitler replied: "The complete occupation is a prerequisite of any settlement".

On 25th March, on the occasion of the adherence of Yugoslavia to the Tripartite Pact at a meeting in Vienna, the defendant Ribbentrop, on behalf of the German Government, confirmed the determination of Germany to respect the sovereignty and territorial integrity of Yugoslavia at all times. On 26th March the Yugoslav Ministers, who had adhered to the Tripartite Pact, were removed from office by a *coup d'état* in Belgrade on their return from Vienna, and the new Government repudiated the Pact. Thereupon, on 27th March, at a conference in Berlin with the High Command at which the defendants Goering, Keitel and Jodl were present, and the defendant Ribbentrop part of the time, Hitler stated that

Yugoslavia was an uncertain factor in regard to the contemplated attack on Greece, and even more so with regard to the attack upon Russia, which was to be conducted later on. Hitler announced that he was determined, without waiting for possible loyalty declarations of the new Government, to make all preparations in order to destroy Yugoslavia militarily and as a national unit. He stated that he would act with "unmerciful harshness".

On 6th April German forces invaded Greece and Yugoslavia without warning, and Belgrade was bombed by the Luftwaffe. So swift was this particular invasion that there had not been time to establish any "incidents" as a usual preliminary, or to find and publish any adequate "political" explanations. As the attack was starting on 6th April, Hitler proclaimed to the German people that this attack was necessary because the British forces in Greece (who were helping the Greeks to defend themselves against the Italians) represented a British attempt to extend the war to the Balkans.

It is clear from this narrative that aggressive war against Greece and Yugoslavia had long been in contemplation, certainly as early as August of 1939. The fact that Great Britain had come to the assistance of the Greeks, and might thereafter be in a position to inflict great damage upon German interests, was made the occasion for the occupation of both countries.

THE AGGRESSIVE WAR AGAINST THE UNION OF SOVIET SOCIALIST REPUBLICS

On 23rd August, 1939, Germany signed the Non-Aggression Pact with the Union of Soviet Socialist Republics.

The evidence has shown unmistakably that the Soviet Union on their part conformed to the terms of this pact; indeed the German Government itself had been assured of this by the highest German sources. Thus, the German Ambassador in Moscow informed his Government that the Soviet Union would go to war only if attacked by Germany, and this statement is recorded in the German War Diary under the date of 6th June, 1941.

Nevertheless, as early as the late summer of 1940, Germany began to make preparations for an attack on the USSR, in spite of the Non-Aggression Pact. This operation was secretly planned under the code name "Case Barbarossa", and the former Field Marshal Paulus testified that on the 3rd September, 1940, when he joined the German General Staff, he continued developing "Case Barbarossa", which was finally completed at the beginning of November, 1940; and that, even then, the German General Staff had no information that the Soviet Union was preparing for war.

On 18th December, 1940, Hitler issued directive No. 21, initialled by Keitel and Jodl, which called for the completion of all preparations connected with the realisation of "Case Barbarossa" by 15th May, 1941. This directive stated:

The German Armed Forces must be prepared to crush Soviet Russia in a quick
campaign before the end of the war against England ... Great caution has to be
exercised that the intention of an attack will not be recognised.

Before the directive of 18th December had been made, the defendant
Goering had informed General Thomas, Chief of the Office of War
Economy of the OKW, of the plan, and General Thomas made surveys of
the economic possibilities of the USSR, including its raw materials, its
power and transport system and its capacity to produce arms.

In accordance with these surveys, an economic staff for the Eastern territories with many military-economic units (inspectorates, commandos,
groups) was created under the supervision of the defendant Goering. In conjunction with the military command, these units were to achieve the most
complete and efficient economic exploitation of the occupied territories in
the interest of Germany.

The framework of the future political and economic organisation of the
occupied territories was designed by the defendant Rosenberg over a period
of three months, after conferences with and assistance by the defendants
Keitel, Jodl, Raeder, Funk, Goering, Ribbentrop and Frick or their representatives. It was made the subject of a most detailed report immediately
after the invasion.

These plans outlined the destruction of the Soviet Union as an independent State, its partition, the creation of so-called Reich Commissariats,
and the conversion of Estonia, Latvia, Byelorussia and other territories into
German colonies.

At the same time Germany drew Hungary, Romania and Finland into
the war against the USSR. In December, 1940, Hungary agreed to participate on the promise of Germany that she should have certain territories at
the expense of Yugoslavia.

In May, 1941, a final agreement was concluded with Antonescu, the
Prime Minister of Romania, regarding the attack on the USSR, in which
Germany promised to Romania, Bessarabia and Northern Bukovina the
right to occupy Soviet territory up to the Dnieper.

On 22nd June, 1941, without any declaration of war, Germany invaded
Soviet territory in accordance with the plans so long made.

The evidence which has been given before this Tribunal proves that
Germany had the design carefully thought out, to crush the USSR as a
political and military power, so that Germany might expand to the east
according to her own desire. In *Mein Kampf*, Hitler had written:

If new territory were to be acquired in Europe, it must have been mainly at Russia's
cost, and once again the new German Empire should have set out on its march
along the same road as was formerly trodden by the Teutonic Knights, this time to
acquire soil for the German plough by means of the German sword and thus
provide the nation with its daily bread.

But there was a more immediate purpose, and in one of the memoranda of the OKW that immediate purpose was stated to be to feed the German armies from Soviet territory in the third year of the war, even if "as a result many millions of people", as the defendant Rosenberg said, "will be starved to death if we take out of the country the things necessary for us."

The final aims of the attack on the Soviet Union were formulated at a conference with Hitler on 16th July, 1941, in which the defendants Goering, Keitel, Rosenberg and Bormann participated:

> There can be no talk of the creation of a military power west of the Urals, even if we should have to fight 100 years to achieve this ... All the Baltic regions must become part of the Reich. The Crimea and adjoining regions (north of the Crimea) must likewise be incorporated into the Reich. The region of the Volga as well as the Baku district must likewise be incorporated into the Reich. The Finns want eastern Karelia. However, in view of the large deposits of nickel, the Kola peninsula must be ceded to Germany.

It was contended for the defendants that the attack upon the USSR was justified because the Soviet Union was contemplating an attack upon Germany, and making preparations to that end. It is impossible to believe that this view was ever honestly entertained.

The plans for the economic exploitation of the USSR, for the removal of masses of the population, for the murder of commissars and political leaders, were all part of the carefully prepared scheme launched on 22nd June without warning of any kind, and without the shadow of legal excuse. It was plain aggression.

WAR AGAINST THE UNITED STATES

Four days after the attack launched by the Japanese on the United States fleet in Pearl Harbor on 7th December, 1941, Germany declared war on the United States.

The Tripartite Pact between Germany, Italy and Japan, had been signed on 27th September, 1940, and from that date until the attack upon the USSR, the defendant Ribbentrop, with other defendants, was endeavouring to induce Japan to attack British possessions in the Far East. This, it was thought, would hasten England's defeat, and also keep the United States out of the war.

The possibility of a direct attack on the United States was considered and discussed as a matter for the future. Major von Falkenstein, the Luftwaffe Liaison Officer with the Operations Staff of the OKW, summarising military problems which needed discussion in Berlin in October of 1940, spoke of the possibility "of the prosecution of the war against America at a later date". It is clear, too, that the German policy of keeping America out of the war, if possible, did not prevent Germany promising support to Japan even against the United States. On 4th April, 1941, Hitler told Matsuoka, the Japanese Foreign Minister, in the presence of the defendant Ribbentrop, that Germany would "strike without delay" if a Japanese attack on Singapore should lead to war between Japan and the United States. The next day Ribbentrop himself urged Matsuoka to bring Japan into the war.

On 28th November, 1941, ten days before the attack on Pearl Harbor, Ribbentrop encouraged Japan, through her Ambassador in Berlin, to attack Great Britain and the United States, and stated that should Japan become engaged in a war with the United States, Germany would join the war immediately. A few days later, Japanese representatives told Germany and Italy that Japan was preparing to attack the United States, and asked for their support. Germany and Italy agreed to do this, although in the Tripartite Pact, Italy and Germany had undertaken to assist Japan only if she were attacked. When the assault on Pearl Harbor did take place, the defendant Ribbentrop is reported to have been "overjoyed", and later, at a ceremony in Berlin, when a German medal was awarded to Oshima, the Japanese Ambassador, Hitler indicated his approval of the tactics which the Japanese had adopted of negotiating with the United States as long as possible, and then striking hard without any declaration of war.

Although it is true that Hitler and his colleagues originally did not consider that a war with the United States would be beneficial to their interest, it is apparent that in the course of 1941 that view was revised, and Japan was given every encouragement to adopt a policy which would almost certainly bring the United States into the war. And when Japan attacked the United States fleet in Pearl Harbor and thus made aggressive war against the United States, the Nazi Government caused Germany to enter that war at once on the side of Japan by declaring war themselves on the United States.

VIOLATIONS OF INTERNATIONAL TREATIES

The Charter defines as a crime the planning or waging of war that is a war
of aggression or a war in violation of international treaties. The Tribunal has
decided that certain of the defendants planned and waged aggressive wars
against twelve nations, and were, therefore, guilty of this series of crimes. This
makes it unnecessary to discuss the subject in further detail, or even to
consider at any length the extent to which these aggressive wars were also
"wars in violation of international treaties, agreements or assurances". These
treaties are set out in the Indictment. Those of principal importance are the
following.

THE HAGUE CONVENTIONS

In the 1899 Convention the signatory powers agreed:

> before an appeal to arms ... to have recourse, as far as circumstances allow, to the
> good offices or mediation of one or more friendly powers.

A similar clause was inserted in the Convention for Pacific Settlement of
International Disputes of 1907. In the accompanying Convention Relative
to Opening of Hostilities, Article I contains far more specific language:

> The Contracting Powers recognise that hostilities between them must not
> commence without a previous and explicit warning, in the form of either a
> declaration of war, giving reasons, or an ultimatum with a conditional declaration of
> war.

Germany was a party to these conventions.

THE VERSAILLES TREATY

Breaches of certain provisions of the Versailles Treaty are also relied on by the Prosecution: not to fortify the left bank of the Rhine (Art. 42–44); to "respect strictly the independence of Austria" (Art. 80); renunciation of any rights in Memel (Art. 99) and the Free City of Danzig (Art. 100); the recognition of the independence of the Czecho-Slovak State; and the military, naval and air clauses against German rearmament found in Part V. There is no doubt that action was taken by the German Government contrary to all these provisions, the details of which are set out in the Indictment. With regard to the Treaty of Versailles, the matters relied on are:

1. The violation of Articles 42 to 44 in respect of the demilitarised zone of the Rhineland.
2. The annexation of Austria on 13th March, 1938, in violation of Article 80.
3. The incorporation of the district of Memel on 22nd March, 1939, in violation of Article 99.
4. The incorporation of the Free City of Danzig on 1st September, 1939, in violation of Article 100.
5. The incorporation of the provinces of Bohemia and Moravia on 16th March, 1939, in violation of Article 81.
6. The repudiation of the military naval and air clauses of the Treaty, in or about March of 1935.

On 21st May, 1935, Germany announced that, whilst renouncing the disarmament clauses of the Treaty, she would still respect the territorial limitations, and would comply with the Locarno Pact. (With regard to the first five breaches alleged, therefore, the Tribunal finds the allegation proved.)

TREATIES OF MUTUAL GUARANTEE, ARBITRATION AND NON-AGGRESSION

It is unnecessary to discuss in any detail the various treaties entered into by Germany with other powers. Treaties of Mutual Guarantee were signed by Germany, at Locarno in 1925, with Belgium, France, Great Britain and Italy, assuring the maintenance of the territorial status quo. Arbitration treaties were also executed by Germany at Locarno with Czechoslovakia, Belgium and Poland. Article I of the latter treaty is typical, providing:

> All disputes of every kind between Germany and Poland . . . which it may not be possible to settle amicably by the normal methods of diplomacy, shall be submitted for decision to an arbitral tribunal.

Conventions of Arbitration and Conciliation were entered into between Germany, the Netherlands and Denmark in 1926; and between Germany and Luxemburg in 1929. Non-aggression treaties were executed by Germany with Denmark and Russia in 1939.

KELLOGG–BRIAND PACT

The Pact of Paris was signed on 27th August, 1928, by Germany, the United States, Belgium, France, Great Britain, Italy, Japan, Poland and other countries; and subsequently by other powers. The Tribunal has made full reference to the nature of this Pact and its legal effect in another part of this Judgment. It is, therefore, not necessary to discuss the matter further here, save to state that in the opinion of the Tribunal this Pact was violated by Germany in all the cases of aggressive war charged in the Indictment. It is to be noted that on 26th January, 1930, Germany signed a Declaration for the Maintenance of Permanent Peace with Poland, which was explicitly based on the Pact of Paris, and in which the use of force was outlawed for a period of ten years.

The Tribunal does not find it necessary to consider any of the other treaties referred to in the Indictments, or the repeated agreements and assurances of her peaceful intentions entered into by Germany.

THE LAW OF THE CHARTER

The jurisdiction of the Tribunal is defined in the Agreement and Charter, and the crimes coming within the jurisdiction of the Tribunal, for which there shall be individual responsibility, are set out in Article 6. The law of the Charter is decisive, and binding upon the Tribunal.

The making of the Charter was the exercise of the sovereign legislative power by the countries to which the German Reich unconditionally surrendered; and the undoubted right of these countries to legislate for the occupied territories has been recognised by the civilised world. The Charter is not an arbitrary exercise of power on the part of the victorious nations, but in the view of the Tribunal, as will be shown, it is the expression of international law existing at the time of its creation; and to that extent is itself a contribution to international law.

The Signatory Powers created this Tribunal, defined the law it was to administer, and made regulations for the proper conduct of the Trial. In doing so, they have done together what any one of them might have done singly; for it is not to be doubted that any nation has the right thus to set up special courts to administer law. With regard to the constitution of the court, all that the defendants are entitled to ask is to receive a fair trial on the facts and law.

The Charter makes the planning or waging of a war of aggression or a war in violation of international treaties a crime; and it is, therefore, not strictly necessary to consider whether and to what extent aggressive war was a crime before the execution of the London Agreement. But in view of the great importance of the questions of law involved, the Tribunal has heard full argument from the Prosecution and the Defence, and will express its view on the matter.

It was urged on behalf of the defendants that a fundamental principle of all law – international and domestic – is that there can be no punishment of crime without a pre-existing law: "*Nullum crimen sine lege, nulla poena sine lege.*" It was submitted that *ex post facto* punishment is abhorrent to the law of all civilised nations, that no sovereign power had made aggressive war a crime at the time the alleged criminal acts were committed, that no statute had defined aggressive war, that no penalty had been fixed for its commission and no court had been created to try and punish offenders.

In the first place, it is to be observed that the maxim *nullum crimen sine lege* is not a limitation of sovereignty, but is in general a principle of justice. To assert that it is unjust to punish those who in defiance of treaties and assurances have attacked neighbouring states without warning is obviously untrue, for in such circumstances the attacker must know that he is doing wrong, and so far from it being unjust to punish him, it would be unjust if his wrong were allowed to go unpunished. Occupying the positions they did in the Government of Germany, the defendants, or at least some of them, must have known of the treaties signed by Germany outlawing recourse to war for the settlement of international disputes; they must have known that they were acting in defiance of all international law when in complete deliberation they carried out their designs of invasion and aggression. On this view of the case alone, it would appear that the maxim has no application to the present facts.

This view is strongly reinforced by a consideration of the state of international law in 1939, so far as aggressive war is concerned. The General Treaty for the Renunciation of War of 27th August, 1928, more generally known as the Pact of Paris or the Kellogg–Briand Pact, was binding on sixty-three nations, including Germany, Italy and Japan, at the outbreak of war in 1939. In the preamble, the signatories declared that they were:

Deeply sensible of their solemn duty to promote the welfare of mankind; persuaded that the time has come when a frank renunciation of war as an instrument of national policy should be made to the end that the peaceful and friendly relations now existing between their peoples should be perpetuated . . . all changes in their relations with one another should be sought only by pacific means . . . thus uniting civilised nations of the world in a common renunciation of war as an instrument of their national policy.

The first two Articles are as follows:

Article I: The High Contracting Parties solemnly declare in the names of their respective peoples that they condemn recourse to war for the solution of international controversies and renounce it as an instrument of national policy in their relations to one another.

Article II: The High Contracting Parties agree that the settlement or solution of all disputes or conflicts of whatever nature or of whatever origin they may be, which may arise among them, shall never be sought except by pacific means.

The question is: What was the legal effect of this Pact? The nations who signed the Pact or adhered to it unconditionally condemned recourse to war for the future as an instrument of policy, and expressly renounced it. After the signing of the Pact, any nation resorting to war as an instrument of national policy breaks the Pact. In the opinion of the Tribunal, the solemn renunciation of war as an instrument of national policy necessarily involves the proposition that such a war is illegal in international law; and that those who plan and wage such a war, with its inevitable and terrible consequences, are committing a crime in so doing. War for the solution of international controversies undertaken as an instrument of national policy certainly includes a war of aggression, and such a war is therefore outlawed by the Pact. As Mr Henry L. Stimson, then Secretary of State of the United States, said in 1932:

> War between nations was renounced by the signatories of the Kellogg–Briand Treaty. This means that it has become throughout practically the entire world ... an illegal thing. Hereafter, when nations engage in armed conflict, either one or both of them must be termed violators of this general treaty law ... We denounce them as law breakers.

But it is argued that the Pact does not expressly enact that such wars are crimes, or set up courts to try those who make such wars. To that extent the same is true with regard to the laws of war contained in the Hague Convention. The Hague Convention of 1907 prohibited resort to certain methods of waging war. These included the inhumane treatment of prisoners, the employment of poisoned weapons, the improper use of flags of truce and similar matters. Many of these prohibitions had been enforced long before the date of the Convention; but since 1907 they have certainly been crimes, punishable as offences against the laws of war; yet the Hague Convention nowhere designates such practices as criminal, nor is any sentence prescribed, nor any mention made of a court to try and punish offenders. For many years past, however, military tribunals have tried and punished individuals guilty of violating the rules of land warfare laid down by this Convention. In the opinion of the Tribunal, those who wage aggressive war are doing that which is equally illegal, and of much greater moment than a breach of one of the rules of the Hague Convention. In interpreting the words of the Pact, it must be remembered that international law is not the product of an international legislature, and that such international agreements as the Pact of Paris have to deal with general principles of law, and not with administrative matters of procedure. The law of war is to be found not only in treaties, but in the customs and practices of states which gradually obtained universal recognition, and from the general principles of justice applied by jurists and practised by military courts. This law is not static, but by continual adaptation follows the needs of a changing world. Indeed, in many cases treaties do no more than express and define for more accurate reference the principles of law already existing.

The view which the Tribunal takes of the true interpretation of the Pact is supported by the international history which preceded it. In the year 1923 the draft of a Treaty of Mutual Assistance was sponsored by the League of Nations. In Article I the Treaty declared "that aggressive war is an international crime", and that the parties would "undertake that not one of them will be guilty of its commission". The draft treaty was submitted to twenty-nine States, about half of whom were in favour of accepting the text. The principal objection appeared to be in the difficulty of defining the acts which would constitute "aggression", rather than any doubt as to the criminality of aggressive war. The preamble to the League of Nations 1924 Protocol for the Pacific Settlement of International Disputes ("Geneva Protocol"), after "recognising the solidarity of the members of the international community", declared that "a war of aggression constitutes a violation of this solidarity and is an international crime". It went on to declare that the contracting parties were "desirous of facilitating the complete application of the system provided in the Covenant of the League of Nations for the pacific settlement of disputes between the states and of ensuring the repression of international crimes". The Protocol was recommended to the League of Nations by a unanimous resolution of the forty-eight members. These members included Italy and Japan, but Germany was not then a member of the League.

Although the Protocol was never ratified, it was signed by the leading statesmen of the world, representing the vast majority of the civilised states and peoples, and may be regarded as strong evidence of the intention to brand aggressive war as an international crime.

At the meeting of the Assembly of the League of Nations on 24th September, 1927, all the delegations then present (including the German, the Italian and the Japanese) unanimously adopted a declaration concerning wars of aggression. The preamble to the declaration stated:

> The Assembly:
> Recognising the solidarity which unites the community of nations;
> Being inspired by a firm desire for the maintenance of general peace;
> Being convinced that a war of aggression can never serve as a means of settling
> international disputes, and is in consequence an international crime . . .

The unanimous resolution of 18th February, 1928, of twenty-one American Republics of the Sixth (Havana) Pan-American Conference, declared that "war of aggression constitutes an international crime against the human species".

All these expressions of opinion, and others that could be cited, so solemnly made, reinforce the construction which the Tribunal placed upon the Pact of Paris, that resort to a war of aggression is not merely illegal, but is criminal. The prohibition of aggressive war demanded by the conscience of the world finds its expression in the series of pacts and treaties to which the Tribunal has just referred.

It is also important to remember that Article 227 of the Treaty of Versailles provided for the constitution of a special Tribunal, composed of representatives of five of the Allied and Associated Powers which had been belligerents in the First World War opposed to Germany, to try the former German Emperor "for a supreme offence against international morality and the sanctity of treaties". The purpose of this trial was expressed to be "to vindicate the solemn obligations of international undertakings, and the validity of international morality". In Article 228 of the Treaty, the German Government expressly recognised the right of the Allied Powers "to bring before military tribunals persons accused of having committed acts in violation of the laws and customs of war".

It was submitted that international law is concerned with the action of sovereign States, and provides no punishment for individuals; and further, that where the act in question is an act of State, those who carry it out are not personally responsible, but are protected by the doctrine of the sovereignty of the State. In the opinion of the Tribunal, both these submissions must be rejected. That international law imposes duties and liabilities upon individuals as well as upon States has long been recognised. In the recent case of Ex Parte Quirin (1942 317 US 1), before the Supreme Court of the United States, persons were charged during the war with landing in the United States for purposes of spying and sabotage. The late Chief Justice Stone, speaking for the Court, said:

> From the very beginning of its history this Court has applied the law of war as including that part of the law of nations which prescribes for the conduct of war, the status, rights and duties of enemy nations as well as enemy individuals.

He went on to give a list of cases tried by the Courts, where individual offenders were charged with offences against the laws of nations, and particularly the laws of war. Many other authorities could be cited, but enough has been said to show that individuals can be punished for violations of international law. Crimes against international law are committed by men, not by abstract entities, and only by punishing individuals who commit such crimes can the provisions of international law be enforced.

The provisions of Article 228 of the Treaty of Versailles already referred to illustrate and enforce this view of individual responsibility.

The principle of international law, which under certain circumstances, protects the representatives of a state, cannot be applied to acts which are condemned as criminal by international law. The authors of these acts cannot shelter themselves behind their official position in order to be freed from punishment in appropriate proceedings. Article 7 of the Charter expressly declares:

> The official position of defendants, whether as Heads of State, or responsible officials in government departments, shall not be considered as freeing them from responsibility, or mitigating punishment.

On the other hand, the very essence of the Charter is that individuals have international duties which transcend the national obligations of obedience imposed by the individual State. He who violates the laws of war cannot obtain immunity while acting in pursuance of the authority of the State if the State in authorising action moves outside its competence under international law.

It was also submitted on behalf of most of these defendants that in doing what they did they were acting under the orders of Hitler, and therefore cannot be held responsible for the acts committed by them in carrying out these orders. The Charter specifically provides in Article 8:

> The fact that the defendant acted pursuant to order of his Government or of a superior shall not free him from responsibility, but may be considered in mitigation of punishment.

The provisions of this Article are in conformity with the law of all nations. That a soldier was ordered to kill or torture in violation of the international law of war has never been recognised as a defence to such acts of brutality, though, as the Charter here provides, the order may be urged in mitigation of the punishment. The true test, which is found in varying degrees in the criminal law of most nations, is not the existence of the order, but whether moral choice was in fact possible.

THE LAW AS TO THE COMMON PLAN OR CONSPIRACY

In the previous recital of the facts relating to aggressive war, it is clear that planning and preparation had been carried out in the most systematic way at every stage of the history.

Planning and preparation are essential to the making of war. In the opinion of the Tribunal, aggressive war is a crime under international law. The Charter defines this offence as planning, preparation, initiation or waging of a war of aggression "*or* participation in a common plan or conspiracy for the accomplishment . . . of the foregoing". The Indictment follows this distinction. Count One charges the common plan or conspiracy. Count Two charges the planning and waging of war. The same evidence has been introduced to support both counts. We shall, therefore, discuss both counts together, as they are in substance the same. The defendants have been charged under both counts, and their guilt under each count must be determined.

The "common plan or conspiracy" charged in the Indictment covers twenty-five years, from the formation of the Nazi Party in 1919 to the end of the war in 1945. The Party is spoken of as "the instrument of cohesion among the defendants" for carrying out the purposes of the conspiracy – the overthrowing of the Treaty of Versailles, acquiring territory lost by Germany in the last war and *Lebensraum* in Europe, by the use, if necessary, of armed force, of aggressive war. The "seizure of power" by the Nazis, the use of terror, the destruction of trade unions, the attack on Christian teaching and on churches, the persecution of the Jews, the regimentation of youth – all these are said to be steps deliberately taken to carry out the common plan. It found expression, so it is alleged, in secret rearmament, the withdrawal by Germany from the Disarmament Conference and the League of Nations, universal military service and seizure of the Rhineland. Finally, according to the Indictment, aggressive action was planned and carried out against Austria and Czechoslovakia in 1936–1938, followed by the planning and waging of war against Poland; and, successively, against ten other countries.

The Prosecution says, in effect, that any significant participation in the affairs of the Nazi Party or Government is evidence of a participation in a conspiracy that is in itself criminal. Conspiracy is not defined in the Charter. But in the opinion of the Tribunal the conspiracy must be clearly outlined in its criminal purpose. It must not be too far removed from the time of decision and of action. The planning, to be criminal, must not rest merely on the declarations of a party programme, such as are found in the twenty-five points of the Nazi Party, announced in 1920, or the political affirmations expressed in *Mein Kampf* in later years. The Tribunal must examine whether a concrete plan to wage war existed, and determine the participants in that concrete plan.

It is not necessary to decide whether a single master conspiracy between the defendants has been established by the evidence. The seizure of power by the Nazi Party, and the subsequent domination by the Nazi State of all spheres of economic and social life, must of course be remembered when the later plans for waging war are examined. That plans were made to wage wars, as early as 5th November, 1937, and probably before that, is apparent. And thereafter, such preparations continued in many directions, and against the peace of many countries. Indeed the threat of war – and war itself if neces-sary – was an integral part of the Nazi policy. But the evidence establishes with certainty the existence of many separate plans rather than a single con-spiracy embracing them all. That Germany was rapidly moving to complete dictatorship from the moment that the Nazis seized power, and progressively in the direction of war, has been overwhelmingly shown in the ordered sequence of aggressive acts and wars already set out in this Judgment.

In the opinion of the Tribunal, the evidence establishes the common planning to prepare and wage war by certain of the defendants. It is immate-rial to consider whether a single conspiracy to the extent and over the time set out in the Indictment has been conclusively proved. Continued planning, with aggressive war as the objective, has been established beyond doubt. The truth of the situation was well stated by Paul Schmidt, official interpreter of the German Foreign Office, as follows:

> The general objectives of the Nazi leadership were apparent from the start, namely the domination of the European Continent, to be achieved first by the incorporation of all German-speaking groups in the Reich, and secondly, by territorial expansion under the slogan *Lebensraum*. The execution of these basic objectives, however, seemed to be characterised by improvisation. Each succeeding step was apparently carried out as each new situation arose, but all consistent with the ultimate objectives mentioned above.

The argument that such common planning cannot exist where there is com-plete dictatorship is unsound. A plan in the execution of which a number of persons participate is still a plan, even though conceived by only one of them; and those who execute the plan do not avoid responsibility by showing that they acted under the direction of the man who conceived it. Hitler could not make aggressive war by himself. He had to have the co-operation of statesmen, military leaders, diplomats and businessmen. When they, with knowledge of his aims, gave him their co-operation, they made themselves parties to the plan he had initiated. They are not to be deemed innocent because Hitler made use of them, if they knew what they were doing. That they were assigned to their tasks by a dictator does not absolve them from responsibility for their acts. The relation of leader and follower does not preclude responsibility here any more than it does in the comparable tyranny of organised domestic crime.

Count One, however, charges not only the conspiracy to commit aggressive war, but also to commit war crimes and crimes against humanity. But the Charter does not define as a separate crime any conspiracy except the one to commit acts of aggressive war. Article 6 of the Charter provides:

> Leaders, organisers, instigators and accomplices participating in the formulation or execution of a common plan or conspiracy to commit any of the foregoing crimes are responsible for all acts performed by any persons in execution of such plan.

In the opinion of the Tribunal, these words do not add a new and separate crime to those already listed. The words are designed to establish the responsibility of persons participating in a common plan. The Tribunal will, therefore, disregard the charges in Count One that the defendants conspired to commit war crimes and crimes against humanity, and will consider only the common plan to prepare, initiate and wage aggressive war.

WAR CRIMES AND CRIMES AGAINST HUMANITY

The evidence relating to war crimes has been overwhelming, in its volume and its detail. It is impossible for this Judgment adequately to review it, or to record the mass of documentary and oral evidence that has been presented. The truth remains that war crimes were committed on a vast scale, never before seen in the history of war. They were perpetrated in all the countries occupied by Germany, and on the High Seas, and were attended by every conceivable circumstance of cruelty and horror. There can be no doubt that the majority of them arose from the Nazi conception of "total war", with which the aggressive wars were waged. For in this conception of "total war", the moral ideas underlying the conventions which seek to make war more humane are no longer regarded as having force or validity. Everything is made subordinate to the overmastering dictates of war. Rules, regulations, assurances and treaties all alike are of no moment; and so, freed from the restraining influence of international law, the aggressive war is conducted by the Nazi leaders in the most barbaric way. Accordingly, war crimes were committed when and wherever the Führer and his close associates thought them to be advantageous. They were for the most part the result of cold and criminal calculation.

On some occasions, war crimes were deliberately planned long in advance. In the case of the Soviet Union, the plunder of the territories to be occupied, and the ill-treatment of the civilian population, were settled in minute detail before the attack was begun. As early as the autumn of 1940, the invasion of the territories of the Soviet Union was being considered. From that date onwards, the methods to be employed in destroying all possible opposition were continuously under discussion.

Similarly, when planning to exploit the inhabitants of the occupied countries for slave labour on the very greatest scale, the German Government conceived it as an integral part of the war economy, and planned and organised this particular war crime down to the last elaborate detail.

Other war crimes, such as the murder of prisoners of war who had escaped and been recaptured, or the murder of commandos or captured airmen, or the destruction of the Soviet Commissars, were the result of direct orders circulated through the highest official channels.

The Tribunal proposes, therefore, to deal quite generally with the question of war crimes, and to refer to them later when examining the responsibility of the individual defendants in relation to them. Prisoners of war were ill-treated and tortured and murdered, not only in defiance of the well-established rules of international law, but in complete disregard of the elementary dictates of humanity. Civilian populations in occupied territories suffered the same fate. Whole populations were deported to Germany for the purposes of slave labour upon defence works, armament production and similar tasks connected with the war effort. Hostages were taken in very large numbers from the civilian populations in all the occupied countries, and were shot as suited the German purposes. Public and private property was systematically plundered and pillaged in order to enlarge the resources of Germany at the expense of the rest of Europe. Cities and towns and villages were wantonly destroyed without military justification or necessity.

MURDER AND ILL-TREATMENT OF PRISONERS OF WAR

Article 6(*b*) of the Charter defines war crimes in these words:

> War crimes: namely, violations of the laws or customs of war. Such violations shall include, but not be limited to, murder, ill-treatment or deportation to slave labour or for any other purpose of civilian population of or in occupied territory, murder or ill-treatment of prisoners of war or persons on the seas, killing of hostages, plunder of public or private property, wanton destruction of cities, towns or villages, or devastation not justified by military necessity.

In the course of the war, many Allied soldiers who had surrendered to the Germans were shot immediately, often as a matter of deliberate, calculated policy. On 18th October, 1942, the defendant Keitel circulated a directive authorised by Hitler, which ordered that all members of Allied "commando" units, often when in uniform and whether armed or not, were to be "slaughtered to the last man", even if they attempted to surrender. It was further provided that if such Allied troops came into the hands of the military authorities after being first captured by the local police, or in any other way, they should be handed over immediately to the SD. This order was supplemented from time to time, and was effective throughout the remainder of the war, although after the Allied landings in Normandy in 1944 it was made clear that the order did not apply to "commandos" captured within the immediate battle area. Under the provisions of this order, Allied "com-

mando" troops, and other military units operating independently, lost their
lives in Norway, France, Czechoslovakia and Italy. Many of them were killed
on the spot, and in no case were those who were executed later in concentration camps ever given a trial of any kind. For example, an American
military mission which landed behind the German front in the Balkans in
January, 1945, numbering about twelve to fifteen men and wearing uniform,
were taken to Mauthausen under the authority of this order and, according
to the affidavit of Adolf Zutte, the adjutant of the Mauthausen concentration
camp, all of them were shot.

In March, 1944, the OKH issued the "Kugel" or "Bullet" Decree, which
directed that every escaped officer and NCO prisoner of war who had not
been put to work, with the exception of British and American prisoners of
war, should on recapture be handed over to the SIPO and SD. This order was
distributed by the SIPO and SD to their regional offices. These escaped officers and NCOs were to be sent to the concentration camp at Mauthausen,
to be executed upon arrival by means of a bullet shot in the neck.

In March, 1944, fifty officers of the British Royal Air Force, who escaped
from the camp at Sagan where they were confined as prisoners, were shot
on recapture, on the direct orders of Hitler. Their bodies were immediately
cremated, and the urns containing their ashes were returned to the camp. It
was not contended by the defendants that this was other than plain murder,
in complete violation of international law.

When Allied airmen were forced to land in Germany, they were sometimes killed at once by the civilian population. The police were instructed
not to interfere with these killings, and the Ministry of Justice was informed
that no one should be prosecuted for taking part in them.

The treatment of Soviet prisoners of war was characterised by particular
inhumanity. The death of so many of them was not due merely to the action
of individual guards, or to the exigencies of life in the camps. It was the result
of systematic plans to murder. More than a month before the German invasion of the Soviet Union, the OKW were making special plans for dealing
with political representatives serving with the Soviet armed forces who
might be captured. One proposal was that "political Commissars *of the Army*
are not recognised as *Prisoners of War*, and are to be *liquidated* at the latest in
the transient prisoner of war camps". The defendant Keitel gave evidence
that instructions incorporating this proposal were issued to the German
Army.

On 8th September, 1941, regulations for the treatment of Soviet prison-
ers of war in all prisoner of war camps were issued, signed by General
Reinecke, the head of the prisoner of war department of the High
Command. These orders stated:

> The Bolshevist soldier has, therefore, lost all claim to treatment as an honourable
> opponent, in accordance with the Geneva Convention . . . The order for ruthless and
> energetic action must be given at the slightest indication of insubordination,

especially in the case of Bolshevist fanatics. Insubordination, active or passive resistance, must be broken immediately by force of arms (bayonets, butts and firearms) . . . Anyone carrying out the order who does not use his weapons, or does so with insufficient energy, is punishable . . . Prisoners of war attempting escape are to be fired on without previous challenge. No warning shot must ever be fired . . . The use of arms against prisoners of war is as a rule legal.

The Soviet prisoners of war were left without suitable clothing, the wounded without medical care; they were starved, and in many cases left to die.

On 17th July, 1941, the Gestapo issued an order providing for the killing of all Soviet prisoners of war who were or might be dangerous to National Socialism. The order recited:

The mission of the Commanders of the SIPO and SD stationed in Stalags is the political investigation of all camp inmates, the elimination and further "treatment" (a) of all political, criminal or in some other way unbearable elements among them, (b) of those persons who could be used for the reconstruction of the occupied territories . . . Further, the Commanders must make efforts from the beginning to seek out among the prisoners elements which appear reliable, regardless if there are Communists concerned or not, in order to use them for Intelligence purposes inside of the camp, and, if advisable, later in the occupied territories also. By use of such informers, and by use of all other existing possibilities, the discovery of all elements to be eliminated among the prisoners must proceed step by step at once . . .

Above all, the following must be discovered: all important functionaries of State and Party, especially professional revolutionaries . . . all People's Commissars in the Red Army, leading personalities of the State . . . leading personalities of the business world, members of the Soviet Russian Intelligence, all Jews, all persons who are found to be agitators or fanatical Communists. Executions are not to be held in the camp or in the immediate vicinity of the camp . . . The prisoners are to be taken for special treatment, if possible into the former Soviet Russian territory.

The affidavit of Warlimont, Deputy Chief of Staff of the Wehrmacht, and the testimony of Ohlendorf, former Chief of Amt III of the RSHA, and of Lahousen, the head of one of the sections of the Abwehr, the Wehrmacht's Intelligence Service, all indicate the thoroughness with which this order was carried out.

The affidavit of Kurt Lindown, a former Gestapo official, states:

There existed in the prisoner of war camps on the Eastern Front small screening teams (Einsatzkommandos) headed by lower ranking members of the Secret Police (Gestapo). These teams were assigned to the camp commanders and had the job to segregate the prisoners of war who were candidates for execution according to the orders that had been given, and to report them to the office of the Secret Police.

On 23rd October, 1941, the camp commander of the Gross Rosen concentration camp reported to Müller, Chief of the Gestapo, a list of the Soviet prisoners of war who had been executed there on the previous day.

An account of the general conditions and treatment of Soviet prisoners of war during the first eight months after the German attack upon Russia was given in a letter which the defendant Rosenberg sent to the defendant Keitel on 28th February, 1942:

> The fate of the Soviet prisoners of war in Germany is on the contrary a tragedy of the greatest extent ... A large part of them has starved, or died because of the hazards of the weather. Thousands also died from spotted fever.
>
> The camp commanders have forbidden the civilian population to put food at the disposal of the prisoners, and they have rather let them starve to death.
>
> In many cases, when prisoners of war could no longer keep up on the march because of hunger and exhaustion, they were shot before the eyes of the horrified population, and the corpses were left.
>
> In numerous camps, no shelter for the prisoners of war was provided at all. They lay under the open sky during rain or snow. Even tools were not made available to dig holes or caves.

In some cases Soviet prisoners of war were branded with a special permanent mark. There was put in evidence the OKW order dated 20th July, 1942, which laid down that:

> The brand is to take the shape of an acute angle of about 45 degrees, with the long side to be 1 cm in length, pointing upwards and burnt on the left buttock ... This brand is made with the aid of a lancet available in any military unit. The colouring used is Chinese ink.

The carrying out of this order was the responsibility of the military authorities, though it was widely circulated by the Chief of the SIPO and the SD to German police officials for information.

Soviet prisoners of war were also made the subject of medical experiments of the most cruel and inhuman kind. In July, 1943, experimental work was begun in preparation for a campaign of bacteriological warfare; Soviet prisoners of war were used in these medical experiments, which more often than not proved fatal. In connection with this campaign for bacteriological warfare, preparations were also made for the spreading of bacterial emulsions from planes, with the object of producing widespread failures of crops and consequent starvation. These measures were never applied, possibly because of the rapid deterioration of Germany's military position.

The argument in defence of the charge with regard to the murder and ill-treatment of Soviet prisoners of war – that the USSR was not a party to the Geneva Convention – is quite without foundation. On 15th September, 1941, Admiral Canaris protested against the regulations for the treatment of Soviet prisoners of war, signed by General Reinecke on 8th September, 1941. He then stated:

> The Geneva Convention for the treatment of prisoners of war is not binding in the relationship between Germany and the USSR. Therefore, only the principles of general international law on the treatment of prisoners of war apply. Since the 18th century these have gradually been established along the lines that war captivity is neither revenge nor punishment, but solely protective custody, the only purpose of which is to prevent the prisoners of war from further participation in the war. This principle was developed in accordance with the view held by all armies that it is contrary to military tradition to kill or injure helpless people . . . The decrees for the treatment of Soviet prisoners of war enclosed are based on a fundamentally different viewpoint.

This protest, which correctly stated the legal position, was ignored. The defendant Keitel made a note on this memorandum:

> The objections arise from the military concept of chivalrous warfare. This is the destruction of an ideology. Therefore, I approve and back the measures.

MURDER AND ILL-TREATMENT OF CIVILIAN POPULATION

Article 6(*b*) of the Charter provides that "ill-treatment . . . of civilian population of or in occupied territory . . . killing of hostages . . . wanton destruction of cities, towns or villages" shall be a war crime. In the main, these provisions are merely declaratory of the existing laws of war as expressed by the Hague Convention, Article 46:

> Family honour and rights, the lives of persons and private property, as well as religious convictions and practices, must be respected.

The territories occupied by Germany were administered in violation of the laws of war. The evidence is quite overwhelming of a systematic rule of violence, brutality and terror. On the 7th December, 1941, Hitler issued the directive since known as the "Nacht und Nebel Erlass" (Night and Fog Decree), under which persons who committed offences against the Reich or the German forces in occupied territories, except where the death sentence was certain, were to be taken secretly to Germany and handed over to the SIPO and SD for trial or punishment in Germany. This decree was signed by the defendant Keitel. After these civilians arrived in Germany, no word of them was permitted to reach the country from which they came or their relatives; even in cases when they died awaiting trial the families were not informed, the purpose being to create anxiety in the minds of the family of the arrested person. Hitler's purpose in issuing this decree was stated by the defendant Keitel in a covering letter, dated 12th December, 1941, to be as follows:

> Efficient and enduring intimidation can only be achieved either by capital punishment or by measures by which the relatives of the criminal and the population do not know the fate of the criminal. This aim is achieved when the criminal is transferred to Germany.

Even persons who were only suspected of opposing any of the policies of the German occupation authorities were arrested, and on arrest were interrogated by the Gestapo and the SD in the most shameful manner. On 12th June, 1942, the Chief of the SIPO and SD published, through Müller, the Gestapo Chief, an order authorising the use of "third degree" methods of interrogation, where preliminary investigation had indicated that the person could give information on important matters, such as subversive activities, though not for the purpose of extorting confessions of the prisoner's own crimes. This order provided:

> Third degree may, under this supposition, only be employed against Communists, Marxists, Jehovah's Witnesses, saboteurs, terrorists, members of resistance movements, parachute agents, anti-social elements, Polish or Soviet Russian loafers or tramps; in all other cases my permission must first be obtained . . . Third degree can, according to circumstances, consist amongst other methods of very simple diet (bread and water), hard bunk, dark cell, deprivation of sleep, exhaustive drilling, also in flogging (for more than twenty strokes a doctor must be consulted).

The brutal suppression of all opposition to the German occupation was not confined to severe measures against suspected members of resistance movements themselves, but was also extended to their families. On 19th July, 1944, the Commander of the SIPO and SD in Radom, Poland, published an order, transmitted through the Higher SS and Police leaders, to the effect that in all cases of assassination or attempted assassination of Germans, or where saboteurs had destroyed vital installations, not only the guilty person, but also all his or her male relatives should be shot, and female relatives over sixteen years of age put into a concentration camp.

In the summer of 1944, the Einsatzkommando of the SIPO and SD at Luxemburg caused persons to be confined at Sachsenhausen concentration camp because they were relatives of deserters, and were therefore "expected to endanger the interest of the German Reich if allowed to go free".

The practice of keeping hostages to prevent and to punish any form of civil disorder was resorted to by the Germans; an order issued by the defendant Keitel on 16th September, 1941, spoke in terms of fifty or a hundred lives from the occupied areas of the Soviet Union for one German life taken. The order stated that "it should be remembered that a human life in unsettled countries frequently counts for nothing, and a deterrent effect can be obtained only by unusual severity". The exact number of persons killed as a result of this policy is not known, but large numbers were killed in France and the other occupied territories in the West, while in the East the slaughter was on an even more extensive scale. In addition to the killing of hostages, entire towns were destroyed in some cases; such massacres as those of Oradour-sur-Glane in France and Lidice in Czechoslovakia, both of which were described to the Tribunal in detail, are examples of the organised use of terror by the occupying forces to bring down and destroy all opposition to their rule.

One of the most notorious means of terrorising the people in occupied territories was the use of concentration camps. They were first established in Germany at the moment of the seizure of power by the Nazi Government. Their original purpose was to imprison without trial all those persons who were opposed to the Government, or who were in any way obnoxious to German authority. With the aid of a secret police force, this practice was widely extended and in course of time concentration camps became places of organised and systematic murder, where millions of people were destroyed.

In the administration of the occupied territories the concentration camps were used to destroy all opposition groups. The persons arrested by the Gestapo were as a rule sent to concentration camps. They were conveyed to the camps in many cases without any care whatever being taken for them and great numbers died on the way. Those who arrived at the camp were subject to systematic cruelty. They were given hard physical labour, inadequate food, clothes and shelter, and were subject at all times to the rigour of a soulless régime, and the private whims of individual guards. In the report of the War Crimes Branch of the Judge Advocate's Section of the 3rd US Army, under date 21st June, 1945, the conditions at the Flossenburg concentration camp were investigated, and one passage may be quoted:

> Flossenburg concentration camp can be described as a factory dealing in death. Although this camp had in view the primary object of putting to work the mass slave labour, another of its primary objects was the elimination of human lives by the methods employed in handling the prisoners. Hunger and starvation rations, sadism, inadequate clothing, medical neglect, disease, beatings, hangings, freezing, forced suicides, shooting, etc., all played a major rôle in obtaining their object. Prisoners were murdered at random; spite killings against Jews were common, injections of poison and shooting in the neck were everyday occurrences; epidemics of typhus and spotted fever were permitted to run rampant as a means of eliminating prisoners; life in this camp meant nothing. Killing became a common thing, so common that a quick death was welcomed by the unfortunate ones.

A certain number of the concentration camps were equipped with gas chambers for the wholesale destruction of the inmates, and with furnaces for the burning of the bodies. Some of them were in fact used for the extermination of Jews as part of the "final solution" of the Jewish problem. Most of the non-Jewish inmates were used for labour, although the conditions under which they worked made labour and death almost synonymous terms. Those inmates who became ill and were unable to work were either destroyed in the gas chambers or sent to special infirmaries, where they were given entirely inadequate medical treatment, worse food if possible than the working inmates, and left to die.

The murder and ill-treatment of civilian populations reached its height in the treatment of the citizens of the Soviet Union and Poland. Some four weeks before the invasion of Russia began, special task forces of the SIPO and SD, called Einsatz Groups, were formed on the orders of Himmler for the purpose of following the German armies into Russia, combating partisans and members of resistance groups, and exterminating the Jews and Communist leaders and other sections of the population. In the beginning, four such Einsatz Groups were formed, one operating in the Baltic States, one towards Moscow, one towards Kiev, and one operating in the south of Russia. Ohlendorf, former Chief of Amt III of the RSHA, who led the fourth group, stated in his affidavit:

> When the German army invaded Russia, I was leader of Einsatzgruppe D, in the southern sector, and in the course of the year during which I was leader of the Einsatzgruppe D it liquidated approximately 90,000 men, women and children. The majority of those liquidated were Jews, but there were also among them some Communist functionaries.

In an order issued by the defendant Keitel on 23rd July, 1941, and drafted by the defendant Jodl, it was stated that:

> in view of the vast size of the occupied areas in the East, the forces available for establishing security in these areas will be sufficient only if all resistance is punished, not by legal prosecution of the guilty, but by the spreading of such terror by the armed forces as is alone appropriate to eradicate every inclination to resist among the population ... Commanders must find the means of keeping order by applying suitable draconian measures.

The evidence has shown that this order was ruthlessly carried out in the territory of the Soviet Union and in Poland. A significant illustration of the measures actually applied occurs in the document which was sent in 1943 to the defendant Rosenberg by the Reich Commissar for Eastern Territories, who wrote:

> It should be possible to avoid atrocities and to bury those who have been liquidated. To lock men, women and children into barns and set fire to them does not appear to be a suitable method of combating bands, even if it is desired to exterminate the population. This method is not worthy of the German cause, and hurts our reputation severely.

The Tribunal has before it an affidavit of one Hermann Graebe, dated 10th November, 1945, describing the immense mass murders which he witnessed. He was the manager and engineer in charge of the branch of the Solingen firm of Josef Jung in Spolbunow, Ukraine, from September, 1941, to January, 1944. He first of all described the attack upon the Jewish ghetto at Rovno:

> Then the electric floodlights which had been erected all round the ghetto were switched on. SS and militia details of four to six members entered or at least tried to enter the houses. Where the doors and windows were closed, and the inhabitants did not open upon the knocking, the SS men and militia broke the windows, forced the doors with beams and crowbars, and entered the dwelling. The owners were driven on to the street just as they were, regardless of whether they were dressed or whether they had been in bed . . . Car after car was filled. Over it hung the screaming of women and children, the cracking of whips and rifle shots.

Graebe then described how a mass execution at Dubno, which he witnessed on 5th October, 1942, was carried out:

> Now we heard shots in quick succession from behind one of the earth mounds. The people who had got off the trucks, men, women and children of all ages, had to undress upon the orders of an SS man, who carried a riding or dog whip . . . Without screaming or crying, these people undressed, stood around by families, kissed each other, said farewells, and waited for the command of another SS man, who stood near the excavation, also with a whip in his hand . . . At that moment the SS man at the excavation called something to his comrade. The latter counted off about 20 persons, and instructed them to walk behind the earth mound . . . I walked around the mound and stood in front of a tremendous grave; closely pressed together, the people were lying on top of each other so that only their heads were visible. The excavation was already two-thirds full; I estimated that it contained about a thousand people . . . Now already the next group approached, descended into the excavation, lined themselves up against the previous victims and were shot.

The foregoing crimes against the civilian population are sufficiently appalling, and yet the evidence shows that at any rate in the East, the mass murders and cruelties were not committed solely for the purpose of stamping out opposition or resistance to the German occupying forces. In Poland and the Soviet Union these crimes were part of a plan to get rid of whole native populations by expulsion and annihilation, in order that their territory could be used for colonisation by Germans. Hitler had written in *Mein Kampf* on these lines, and the plan was clearly stated by Himmler in July, 1942, when he wrote:

> It is not our task to Germanise the East in the old sense, that is to teach the people there the German language and the German law, but to see to it that only people of purely Germanic blood live in the East.

In August, 1942, the policy for the Eastern Territories as laid down by Bormann was summarised as follows:

> The Slavs are to work for us. In so far as we do not need them, they may die. Therefore, compulsory vaccination and Germanic health services are superfluous. The fertility of the Slavs is undesirable.

It was Himmler again who stated in October, 1943:

> What happens to a Russian, a Czech, does not interest me in the slightest. What the nations can offer in the way of good blood of our type, we will take. If necessary, by kidnapping their children and raising them here with us. Whether nations live in prosperity or starve to death interests me only in so far as we need them as slaves for our *Kultur*, otherwise it is of no interest to me.

In Poland the intelligentsia had been marked down for extermination as early as September, 1939, and in May, 1940, the defendant Frank wrote in his diary of "taking advantage of the focusing of world interest on the Western Front, by wholesale liquidation of thousands of Poles, first leading representatives of the Polish intelligentsia". Earlier, Frank had been directed to reduce the "entire Polish economy to absolute minimum necessary for bare existence. The Poles shall be the slaves of the Greater German World Empire." In January, 1940, he recorded in his diary that "cheap labour must be removed from the General Government by hundreds of thousands. This will hamper the native biological propagation." So successfully did the Germans carry out this policy in Poland that by the end of the war one-third of the population had been killed, and the whole of the country devastated.

It was the same story in the occupied area of the Soviet Union. At the time of the launching of the German attack in June, 1941, Rosenberg told his collaborators:

> The object of feeding the German people stands this year without a doubt at the top of the list of Germany's claims on the East, and there the southern territories and the northern Caucasus will have to serve as a balance for the feeding of the German people ... A very extensive evacuation will be necessary, without any doubt, and it is sure that the future will hold very hard years in store for the Russians.

Three or four weeks later Hitler discussed with Rosenberg, Goering, Keitel and others his plan for the exploitation of the Soviet population and territory, which included among other things the evacuation of the inhabitants of the Crimea and its settlement by Germans.

A somewhat similar fate was planned for Czechoslovakia, by the defendant von Neurath, in August, 1940; the intelligentsia were to be "expelled", but the rest of the population was to be Germanised, since there was a shortage of Germans to replace them.

In the West the population of Alsace were the victims of a German "expulsion action". Between July and December, 1940, 105,000 Alsatians were either deported from their homes or prevented from returning to them. A captured German report dated 7th August, 1942, with regard to Alsace states that:

> The problem of race will be given first consideration, and this in such a manner that persons of racial value will be deported to Germany proper, and racially inferior persons to France.

Article 49 of the Hague Convention provides that an occupying power may levy a contribution of money from the occupied territory to pay for the needs of the army of occupation, and for the administration of the territory in question. Article 52 of the Hague Convention provides that an occupying power may make requisitions in kind only for the needs of the army of occupation, and that these requisitions shall be in proportion to the resources of the country. These Articles, together with Article 48, dealing with the expenditure of money collected in taxes, and Articles 53, 55 and 56, dealing with public property, make it clear that, under the rules of war, the economy of an occupied country can only be required to bear the expenses of the occupation, and these should not be greater than the economy of the country can reasonably be expected to bear. Article 56 reads as follows:

> The property of municipalities, of religious, charitable, educational, artistic and scientific institutions, although belonging to the State, is to be accorded the same standing as private property. All pre-meditated seizure, destruction or damage of such institutions, historical monuments, works of art and science is prohibited and should be prosecuted.

The evidence in this case has established, however, that the territories occupied by Germany were exploited for the German war effort in the most ruthless way, without consideration of the local economy, and in consequence of a deliberate design and policy. There was in truth a systematic "plunder of public or private property", which was criminal under Article 6(*b*) of the Charter. The German occupation policy was clearly stated in a speech made by the defendant Goering on the 6th August, 1942, to the various German authorities in charge of occupied territories:

> God knows, you are not sent out there to work for the welfare of the people in your charge, but to get the utmost out of them, so that the German people can live. That is what I expect of your exertions. This everlasting concern about foreign people must cease now, once and for all. I have here before me reports on what you are expected to deliver. It is nothing at all, when I consider your territories. It makes no difference to me in this connection if you say that your people will starve.

The methods employed to exploit the resources of the occupied territories to the full varied from country to country. In some of the occupied countries in the East and the West, this exploitation was carried out within the framework of the existing economic structure. The local industries were put under German supervision, and the distribution of war materials was rigidly controlled. The industries thought to be of value to the German war effort were compelled to continue, and most of the rest were closed down altogether. Raw materials and the finished products alike were confiscated for the needs of the German industry. As early as 19th October, 1939, the defendant Goering had issued a directive giving detailed instructions for the administration of the occupied territories. It provided:

> The task for the economic treatment of the various administrative regions is different, depending on whether the country which is involved will be incorporated politically into the German Reich, or whether we will deal with the Government-General, which in all probability will not be made a part of Germany. In the first mentioned territories, the ... safeguarding of all their productive facilities and supplies must be aimed at, as well as a complete incorporation into the Greater German economic system, at the earliest possible time. On the other hand, there must be removed from the territories of the Government-General all raw materials, scrap materials, machines, etc., which are of use for the German war economy. Enterprises which are not absolutely necessary for the meagre maintenance of the naked existence of the population must be transferred to Germany, unless such transfer would require an unreasonably long period of time, and would make it more practicable to exploit those enterprises by giving them German orders, to be executed at their present location.

As a consequence of this order, agricultural products, raw materials needed by German factories, machine tools, transportation equipment, other finished products and even foreign securities and holdings of foreign exchange were all requisitioned and sent to Germany. These resources were requisitioned in a manner out of all proportion to the economic resources of those countries, and resulted in famine, inflation and an active black market. At first the German occupation authorities attempted to suppress the black market, because it was a channel of distribution keeping local products out of German hands. When attempts at suppression failed, a German purchasing agency was organised to make purchases for Germany on the black market, thus carrying out the assurance made by the defendant Goering that it was "necessary that all should know that if there is to be famine anywhere, it shall in no case be in Germany".

In many of the occupied countries of the East and the West, the authorities maintained the pretence of paying for all the property which they seized. This elaborate pretence of payment merely disguised the fact that the goods sent to Germany from these occupied countries were paid for by the occupied countries themselves, either by the device of excessive occupation costs or by forced loans in return for a credit balance on a "clearing account", which was an account merely in name.

In most of the occupied countries of the East, even this pretence of legality was not maintained; economic exploitation became deliberate plunder. This policy was first put into effect in the administration of the Government-General in Poland. The main exploitation of the raw materials in the East was centred on agricultural products, and very large amounts of food were shipped from the Government-General to Germany.

The evidence of the widespread starvation among the Polish people in the Government-General indicates the ruthlessness and the severity with which the policy of exploitation was carried out.

The occupation of the territories of the USSR was characterised by premeditated and systematic looting. Before the attack on the USSR, an economic staff – Oldenburg – was organised to ensure the most efficient exploitation of Soviet territories. The German armies were to be fed out of Soviet territory, even if "many millions of people will be starved to death". An OKW directive issued before the attack said:

> To obtain the greatest possible quantity of food and crude oil for Germany – that is the main economic purpose of the campaign.

Similarly, a declaration by the defendant Rosenberg, of 20th June, 1941, had advocated the use of the produce from southern Russia and of the northern Caucasus to feed the German people, saying:

> We see absolutely no reason for any obligation on our part to feed also the Russian people with the products of that surplus territory. We know that this is a harsh necessity, bare of any feelings.

When the Soviet territory was occupied, this policy was put into effect; there was a large-scale confiscation of agricultural supplies, with complete disregard of the needs of the inhabitants of the occupied territory.

In addition to the seizure of raw materials and manufactured articles, a wholesale seizure was made of art treasures, furniture, textiles and similar articles in all the invaded countries.

The defendant Rosenberg was designated by Hitler on 29th January, 1940, Head of the Centre for National Socialist Ideological and Educational Research, and thereafter the organisation, known as the "Einsatzstab Rosenberg", conducted its operations on a very great scale. Originally designed for the establishment of a research library, it developed into a project for the seizure of cultural treasures. On 1st March, 1942, Hitler issued a further decree, authorising Rosenberg to search libraries, lodges and cultural establishments, and to seize material from these establishments, as well as cultural treasures owned by Jews. Similar directions were given where the ownership could not be clearly established. The decree directed the co-operation of the Wehrmacht High Command, and indicated that Rosenberg's activities in the West were to be conducted in his capacity as Reichsleiter, and in the East in his capacity as Reichsminister. Thereafter, Rosenberg's activities were extended to the occupied countries. The report of Robert Scholz, Chief of the Special Staff for Pictorial Art, stated:

> During the period from March, 1941, to July, 1944, the Special Staff for Pictorial Art brought into the Reich 29 large shipments, including 137 freight cars with 4,174 cases of art works.

The report of Scholz refers to twenty-five portfolios of pictures of the most valuable works of the art collection seized in the West, which portfolios were presented to the Führer. Thirty-nine volumes, prepared by the Einsatzstab, contained photographs of paintings, textiles, furniture, candelabra and numerous other objects of art, and illustrated the value and magnitude of the collection which had been made. In many of the occupied countries private collections were robbed, libraries were plundered and private houses were pillaged.

Museums, palaces and libraries in the occupied territories of the USSR were systematically looted. Rosenberg's Einsatzstab, Ribbentrop's special "Battalion", the Reichscommissars and representatives of the Military Command seized objects of cultural and historical value belonging to the people of the Soviet Union, which were sent to Germany. Thus, the Reichscommissar of the Ukraine removed paintings and objects of art from Kiev and Kharkov and sent them to East Prussia. Rare volumes and objects of art from the palaces of Peterhof, Tsarskoye Selo and Pavlovsk were shipped to Germany. In his letter to Rosenberg of 3rd October, 1941, Reichscommissar Kube stated that the value of the objects of art taken from Byelorussia ran into millions of roubles. The scale of this plundering can also be seen in the letter sent from Rosenberg's department to von Milde-Schreden, in which it is stated that during the month of October 1943 alone, about 40 box-cars loaded with objects of cultural value were transported to the Reich.

With regard to the suggestion that the purpose of the seizure of any treasures was protective and meant for their preservation, it is necessary to say a few words. On 1st December, 1939, Himmler, as the Reich Commissioner for the "strengthening of Germanism", issued a decree to the regional officers of the secret police in the annexed Eastern Territories and to the commanders of the security service in Radom, Warsaw and Lublin. This decree contained administrative directions for carrying out the art seizure programme, and in Clause 1 it is stated:

> To strengthen Germanism in the defence of the Reich, all articles mentioned in Section 2 of this decree are hereby confiscated ... They are confiscated for the

benefit of the German Reich, and are at the disposal of the Reich Commissioner for the strengthening of Germanism.

The intention to enrich Germany by the seizures, rather than to protect the seized objects, is indicated in an undated report by Dr Hans Posse, Director of the Dresden State Picture Gallery:

> I was able to gain some knowledge on the public and private collections, as well as clerical property, in Cracow and Warsaw. It is true that we cannot hope too much to enrich ourselves from the acquisition of great art works of paintings and sculptures, with the exception of the Veit-Stoss altar, and the plates of Hans von Kulnback in the Church of Maria in Cracow . . . and several other works from the national museum in Warsaw.

SLAVE LABOUR POLICY

Article 6(*b*) of the Charter provides that the "ill-treatment or deportation to slave labour or for any other purpose of civilian population of or in occupied territory" shall be a war crime. The laws relating to forced labour by the inhabitants of occupied territories are found in Article 52 of the Hague Convention, which provides:

> Requisition in kind and services shall not be demanded from municipalities or inhabitants except for the needs of the army of occupation. They shall be in proportion to the resources of the country, and of such a nature as not to involve the inhabitants in the obligation of taking part in military operations against their own country.

The policy of the German occupation authorities was in flagrant violation of the terms of this Convention. Some idea of this policy may be gathered from the statement made by Hitler in a speech on 9th November, 1941:

> The territory which now works for us contains more than 250,000,000 men, but the territory which works indirectly for us includes now more than 350,000,000. In the measure in which it concerns German territory, the domain which we have taken under our administration, it is not doubtful that we shall succeed in harnessing the very last man to this work.

The actual results achieved were not so complete as this, but the German occupation authorities did succeed in forcing many of the inhabitants of the occupied territories to work for the German war effort, and in deporting at least 5,000,000 persons to Germany to serve German industry and agriculture.

In the early stages of the war, manpower in the occupied territories was under the control of various occupation authorities, and the procedure varied from country to country. In all the occupied territories compulsory labour service was promptly instituted. Inhabitants of the occupied countries were conscripted and compelled to work in local occupations, to assist the German war economy. In many cases they were forced to work on German fortifications and military installations. As local supplies of raw materials and local industrial capacity became inadequate to meet the German require-ments, the system of deporting labourers to Germany was put into force. By the middle of April, 1940, compulsory deportation of labourers to Germany had been ordered in the Government-General; and a similar procedure was followed in other eastern territories as they were occupied. A description of this compulsory deportation from Poland was given by Himmler. In an address to SS officers he recalled how in weather 40 degrees below zero they had to "haul away thousands, tens of thousands, hundreds of thousands". On a later occasion Himmler stated:

> Whether ten thousand Russian females fall down from exhaustion while digging an anti-tank ditch interests me only in so far as the anti-tank ditch for Germany is finished ... We must realise that we have 6–7 million foreigners in Germany ...They are none of them dangerous so long as we take severe measures at the merest trifles.

During the first two years of the German occupation of France, Belgium, Holland and Norway, however, an attempt was made to obtain the neces-sary workers on a voluntary basis. How unsuccessful this was may be seen from the report of the meeting of the Central Planning Board on 1st March, 1944. The representative of the defendant Speer, one Koehrl, speak-ing of the situation in France, said: "During all this time a great number of Frenchmen were recruited, and voluntarily went to Germany." He was interrupted by the defendant Sauckel: "Not only voluntary, some were recruited forcibly." To which Koehrl replied: "The calling up started after the recruitment no longer yielded enough results." To which the defendant Sauckel replied: "Out of the five million workers who arrived in Germany, not even 200,000 came voluntarily." Koehrl rejoined: "Let us forget for the moment whether or not some slight pressure was used. Formally, at least, they were volunteers."

Committees were set up to encourage recruiting, and a vigorous pro-paganda campaign was begun to induce workers to volunteer for service in Germany. This propaganda campaign included, for example, the promise that a prisoner of war would be returned for every labourer who volun-teered to go to Germany. In some cases it was supplemented by withdrawing the ration cards of labourers who refused to go to Germany, or by discharging them from their jobs and denying them unemployment benefit or an opportunity to work elsewhere. In some cases workers and their families were threatened with reprisals by the Police if they refused to go to Germany. It was on 21st March, 1942, that the defendant Sauckel was appointed Plenipotentiary-General for the Utilisation of Labour, with authority over "all available manpower, including that of workers recruited abroad, and of prisoners of war".

The defendant Sauckel was directly under the defendant Goering as Commissioner of the Four Year Plan, and a Goering decree of 27th March, 1942, transferred all his authority over manpower to Sauckel. Sauckel's instructions, too, were that foreign labour should be recruited on a voluntary basis, but also provided that "where, however, in the occupied territories the appeal for volunteers does not suffice, obligatory service and drafting must under all circumstances be resorted to". Rules requiring labour service in Germany were published in all the occupied territories. The number of labourers to be supplied was fixed by Sauckel, and the local authorities were instructed to meet these requirements by conscription if necessary. That conscription was the rule rather than the exception is shown by the statement of Sauckel, already quoted, on 1st March, 1944.

The defendant Sauckel frequently asserted that the workers belonging to foreign nations were treated humanely, and that the conditions in which they lived were good. But whatever the intention of Sauckel may have been, and however much he may have desired that foreign labourers should be treated humanely, the evidence before the Tribunal establishes the fact that the conscription of labour was accomplished in many cases by drastic and violent methods. The "mistakes and blunders" were on a very great scale. Manhunts took place in the streets, at motion picture houses, even at churches and at night in private houses. Houses were sometimes burnt down, and the families taken as hostages, practices which were described by the defendant Rosenberg as having their origin "in the blackest periods of the slave trade". The methods used in obtaining forced labour from the Ukraine appear from an order issued to SD officers, which stated:

> It will not be possible always to refrain from using force ... When searching villages, especially when it has been necessary to burn down a village, the whole population will be put at the disposal of the Commissioner by force ... As a rule no more children will be shot ... If we limit harsh measures through the above orders for the time being, it is only done for the following reason ... The most important thing is the recruitment of workers.

The resources and needs of the occupied countries were completely disregarded in carrying out this policy. The treatment of the labourers was governed by Sauckel's instructions of 20th April, 1942, to the effect that:

> All the men must be fed, sheltered and treated in such a way as to exploit them to the highest possible extent, at the lowest conceivable degree of expenditure.

The evidence showed that workers destined for the Reich were sent under guard to Germany, often packed in trains without adequate heat, food, clothing or sanitary facilities. The evidence further showed that the treatment of the labourers in Germany in many cases was brutal and degrading. The evidence relating to the Krupp Works at Essen showed that punishments of the most cruel kind were inflicted on the workers. Theoretically at least the workers were paid, housed and fed by the DAF, and even permitted to transfer their savings and to send mail and parcels back to their native country; but restrictive regulations took a proportion of the pay; the camps in which they were housed were insanitary; and the food was very often less than the minimum necessary to give the workers strength to do their jobs. In the case of Poles employed on farms in Germany, the employers were given authority to inflict corporal punishment and were ordered, if possible, to house them in stables, not in their own homes. They were subject to constant supervision by the Gestapo and the SS, and if they attempted to leave their jobs they were sent to correction camps or concentration camps.

The concentration camps were also used to increase the supply of labour. Concentration camp commanders were ordered to work their prisoners to the limits of their physical power. During the latter stages of the war the concentration camps were so productive in certain types of work that the Gestapo was actually instructed to arrest certain classes of labourers so that they could be used in this way.

Allied prisoners of war were also regarded as a possible source of labour. Pressure was exercised on non-commissioned officers to force them to consent to work, by transferring to disciplinary camps those who did not consent. Many of the prisoners of war were assigned to work directly related to military operations, in violation of Article 31 of the Geneva Convention. They were put to work in munition factories and even made to load bombers, to carry ammunition and to dig trenches, often under the most hazardous conditions. This condition applied particularly to the Soviet prisoners of war. On 16th February, 1943, at a meeting of the Central Planning Board, at which the defendants Sauckel and Speer were present, Milch said:

> We have made a request for an order that a certain percentage of men in the Ack-Ack artillery must be Russians; 50,000 will be taken altogether, 30,000 are already employed as gunners. This is an amusing thing, that Russians must work the guns.

And on 4th October, 1943, at Posen, Himmler, speaking of the Russian prisoners captured in the early days of the war, said:

> At that time we did not value the mass of humanity as we value it today, as raw material, as labour. What, after all, thinking in terms of generations, is not to be regretted, but is now deplorable by reason of the loss of labour, is that the prisoners died in tens and hundreds of thousands of exhaustion and hunger.

The general policy underlying the mobilisation of slave labour was stated by Sauckel on 20th April, 1942. He said:

> The aim of this new gigantic labour mobilisation is to use all the rich and tremendous sources conquered and secured for us by our fighting armed forces

under the leadership of Adolf Hitler, for the armament of the armed forces, and also for the nutrition of the Homeland. The raw materials, as well as the fertility of the conquered territories and their human labour power, are to be used completely and conscientiously to the profit of Germany and her Allies ... All prisoners of war from the territories of the West, as well as the East, actually in Germany, must be completely incorporated into the German armament and nutrition industries ... Consequently it is an immediate necessity to use the human reserves of the conquered Soviet territory to the fullest extent. Should we not succeed in obtaining the necessary amount of labour on a voluntary basis, we must immediately institute conscription or forced labour ... The complete employment of all prisoners of war, as well as the use of a gigantic number of new foreign civilian workers, men and women, has become an indisputable necessity for the solution of the mobilisation of the labour programme in this war.

Reference should also be made to the policy which was in existence in Germany by the summer of 1940, under which all aged, insane, and incurable people, "useless eaters", were transferred to special institutions where they were killed, and their relatives informed that they had died from natural causes. The victims were not confined to German citizens but included foreign labourers, who were no longer able to work and were therefore useless to the German war machine. It has been estimated that at least some 275,000 people were killed in this manner in nursing homes, hospitals and asylums, which were under the jurisdiction of the defendant Frick, in his capacity as Minister of the Interior. How many foreign workers were included in this total it has been quite impossible to determine.

PERSECUTION OF THE JEWS

The persecution of the Jews at the hands of the Nazi Government has been proved in the greatest detail before the Tribunal. It is a record of consistent and systematic inhumanity on the greatest scale. Ohlendorf, Chief of Amt III in the RSHA from 1939 to 1943, and who was in command of one of the Einsatz groups in the campaign against the Soviet Union, testified as to the methods employed in the extermination of the Jews. He said that he employed firing squads to shoot the victims in order to lessen the sense of individual guilt on the part of his men; and the 90,000 men, women and children who were murdered in one year by his particular group were mostly Jews.

When the witness Bach Zelewski was asked how Ohlendorf could admit the murder of 90,000 people, he replied:

I am of the opinion that when, for years, for decades, the doctrine is preached that the Slav race is an inferior race, and Jews not even human, then such an outcome is inevitable.

But the defendant Frank spoke the final words of this chapter of Nazi history when he testified in this court:

> We have fought against Jewry; we have fought against it for years: and we have
> allowed ourselves to make utterances and my own diary has become a witness
> against me in this connection – utterances which are terrible . . . A thousand years
> will pass and this guilt of Germany will not be erased.

The anti-Jewish policy was formulated in Point 4 of the Party Programme, which declared:

> Only a member of the race can be a citizen. A member of the race can only be
> one who is of German blood, without consideration of creed. Consequently, no
> Jew can be a member of the race.

Other points of the programme declared that Jews should be treated as foreigners; that they should not be permitted to hold public office; that they should be expelled from the Reich if it were impossible to nourish the entire population of the State; that they should be denied any further immigration into Germany; and that they should be prohibited from publishing German newspapers. The Nazi Party preached these doctrines throughout its history. *Der Stürmer* and other publications were allowed to disseminate hatred of the Jews, and in the speeches and public declarations of the Nazi leaders, the Jews were held up to public ridicule and contempt.

With the seizure of power, the persecution of the Jews was intensified. A series of discriminatory laws were passed, which limited the offices and professions permitted to Jews; and restrictions were placed on their family life and their rights of citizenship. By the autumn of 1938, the Nazi policy towards the Jews had reached the stage where it was directed towards the complete exclusion of Jews from German life. Pogroms were organised, which included the burning and demolishing of synagogues, the looting of Jewish businesses, and the arrest of prominent Jewish businessmen. A collective fine of one billion marks was imposed on the Jews, the seizure of Jewish assets was authorised, and the movement of Jews was restricted by regulations to certain specified districts and hours. The creation of ghettos was carried out on an extensive scale, and, by an order of the Security Police, Jews were compelled to wear a yellow star to be worn on the breast and back.

It was contended for the Prosecution that certain aspects of this anti-Semitic policy were connected with the plans for aggressive war. The violent measures taken against the Jews in November, 1938, were nominally in retaliation for the killing of an official of the German Embassy in Paris. But the decision to seize Austria and Czechoslovakia had been made a year before. The imposition of a fine of one billion marks was made, and the confiscation of the financial holdings of the Jews was decreed, at a time when German armament expenditure had put the German Treasury in difficulties, and when the reduction of expenditure on armaments was being considered. These steps were taken, moreover, with the approval of the defendant Goering, who had been given responsibility for economic matters of this kind and who was the strongest advocate of an extensive rearmament programme notwithstanding the financial difficulties.

It was further said that the connection of the anti-Semitic policy with aggressive war was not limited to economic matters. The German Foreign Office circular, in an article of 25th January, 1939, entitled "Jewish question as a factor in German Foreign Policy in the year 1938", described the new phase in the Nazi anti-Semitic policy in these words:

> It is certainly no coincidence that the fateful year 1938 has brought nearer the solution of the Jewish question simultaneously with the realisation of the idea of Greater Germany, since the Jewish policy was both the basis and consequence of the events of the year 1938. The advance made by Jewish influence and the destructive Jewish spirit in politics, economy and culture paralysed the power and the will of the German people to rise again, more perhaps even than the power policy opposition of the former enemy Allied powers of the First World War. The healing of this sickness among the people was, therefore, certainly one of the most important requirements for exerting the force which, in the year 1938, resulted in the joining together of Greater Germany in defiance of the world.

The Nazi persecution of Jews in Germany before the war, severe and repressive as it was, cannot compare, however, with the policy pursued during the war in the occupied territories. Originally the policy was similar to that which had been in force inside Germany. Jews were required to register, were forced to live in ghettos, to wear the yellow star, and were used as slave labourers. In the summer of 1941, however, plans were made for the "final solution" of the Jewish question in all of Europe. This "final solution" meant the extermination of the Jews, which early in 1939 Hitler had threatened would be one of the consequences of an outbreak of war, and a special section in the Gestapo under Adolf Eichmann, as Head of Section B4 of the Gestapo, was formed to carry out the policy.

The plan for exterminating the Jews was developed shortly after the attack on the Soviet Union. Einsatzgruppen of the Security Police and SD, formed for the purpose of breaking the resistance of the population of the areas lying behind the German armies in the East, were given the duty of exterminating the Jews in those areas. The effectiveness of the work of the Einsatzgruppen is shown by the fact that in February, 1942, Heydrich was able to report that Estonia had already been cleared of Jews and that in Riga the number of Jews had been reduced from 29,500 to 2,500. Altogether the Einsatzgruppen operating in the occupied Baltic States had killed over 135,000 Jews in three months.

Nor did these special units operate completely independently of the German Armed Forces. There is clear evidence that leaders of the Einsatzgruppen obtained the co-operation of Army Commanders. In one case the relations between an Einsatzgruppe and the military authorities were described at the time as being "very close, almost cordial"; in another case the smoothness of an Einsatzkommando's operation was attributed to the "understanding for this procedure" shown by the Army authorities.

Units of the Security Police and SD in the occupied territories of the East, which were under civil administration, were given a similar task. The planned and systematic character of the Jewish persecutions is best illustrated by the original report of the SS Brigadier-General Stroop, who was in charge of the destruction of the ghetto in Warsaw, which took place in 1943. The Tribunal received in evidence that report, illustrated with photographs, bearing on its title page: "The Jewish Ghetto in Warsaw no longer exists." The volume records a series of reports sent by Stroop to the Higher SS and Police Führer East. In April and May, 1943, in one report, Stroop wrote:

> The resistance put up by the Jews and bandits could only be suppressed by energetic actions of our troops day and night. The Reichsführer–SS ordered, therefore, on 23rd April, 1943, the cleaning out of the ghetto with utter ruthlessness and merciless tenacity. I therefore decided to destroy and burn down the entire ghetto, without regard to the armament factories. These factories were systematically dismantled and then burnt. Jews usually left their hideouts, but frequently remained in the burning buildings, and jumped out of the windows only when the heat became unbearable. They then tried to crawl with broken bones across the street into buildings which were not afire … Life in the sewers was not pleasant after the first week. Many times we could hear loud voices in the sewers … Tear gas bombs were thrown into the manholes, and the Jews driven out of the sewers and captured. Countless numbers of Jews were liquidated in sewers and bunkers through blasting. The longer the resistance continued, the tougher became the members of the Waffen SS, Police and Wehrmacht, who always discharged their duties in an exemplary manner.

Stroop recorded that his action at Warsaw eliminated "a proved total of 56,065 people. To that we have to add the number of those killed through blasting, fire, etc., which cannot be counted." Grim evidence of mass murders of Jews was also presented to the Tribunal in cinematograph films depicting the communal graves of hundreds of victims which were subsequently discovered by the Allies.

These atrocities were all part and parcel of the policy inaugurated in 1941, and it is not surprising that there should be evidence that one or two German officials entered vain protests against the brutal manner in which the killings were carried out. But the methods employed never conformed to a single pattern. The massacres of Rovno and Dubno, of which the German engineer Graebe spoke, were examples of one method, the systematic extermination of Jews in concentration camps, was another. Part of the "final solution" was the gathering of Jews from all German-occupied Europe in concentration camps. Their physical condition was the test of life or death. All who were fit to work were used as slave labourers in the concentration camps; all who were not fit to work were destroyed in gas chambers and their bodies burnt. Certain concentration camps such as Treblinka and Auschwitz were set aside for this main purpose. With regard to Auschwitz, the Tribunal heard the evidence of Hoess, the Commandant of the camp from 1st May, 1940, to 1st December, 1943. He estimated that in the camp of Auschwitz alone in that time 2,500,000 persons were exterminated, and that a further 500,000 died from disease and starvation. Hoess described the screening for extermination by stating in evidence:

> We had two SS doctors on duty at Auschwitz to examine the incoming transports of prisoners. The prisoners would be marched by one of the doctors who would make spot decisions as they walked by. Those who were fit for work were sent into the camp. Others were sent immediately to the extermination plants. Children of tender years were invariably exterminated since by reason of their youth they were unable to work. Still another improvement we made over Treblinka was that at Treblinka the victims almost always knew that they were to be exterminated and at Auschwitz we endeavoured to fool the victims into thinking that they were to go through a delousing process. Of course, frequently they realised our true intentions and we sometimes had riots and difficulties due to that fact. Very frequently women would hide their children under their clothes, but of course when we found them we would send the children in to be exterminated.

He described the actual killing by stating:

> It took from three to fifteen minutes to kill the people in the death chamber, depending upon climatic conditions. We knew when the people were dead because their screaming stopped. We usually waited about one half-hour before we opened the doors and removed the bodies. After the bodies were removed our special commandos took off the rings and extracted the gold from the teeth of the corpses.

Beating, starvation, torture, and killing were general. The inmates were subjected to cruel experiments. At Dachau in August, 1942, victims were immersed in cold water until their body temperature was reduced to 28° Centigrade, when they died immediately. Other experiments included high altitude experiments in pressure chambers, experiments to determine how long human beings could survive in freezing water, experiments with poison bullets, experiments with contagious diseases, and experiments dealing with sterilisation of men and women by X-rays and other methods.

Evidence was given of the treatment of the inmates before and after their extermination. There was testimony that the hair of women victims was cut off before they were killed, and shipped to Germany, there to be used in the manufacture of mattresses. The clothes, money and valuables of the inmates were also salvaged and sent to the appropriate agencies for disposition. After the extermination the gold teeth and fillings were taken from the heads of the corpses and sent to the Reichsbank.

After cremation the ashes were used for fertilizer, and in some instances attempts were made to utilise the fat from the bodies of the victims in the commercial manufacture of soap. Special groups travelled through Europe to find Jews and subject them to the "final solution". German missions were sent to such satellite countries as Hungary and Bulgaria to arrange for the shipment of Jews to extermination camps, and it is known that, by the end of 1944, 400,000 Jews from Hungary had been murdered at Auschwitz. Evidence has also been given of the evacuation of 110,000 Jews from part of Romania for "liquidation". Adolf Eichmann, who had been put in charge of this programme by Hitler, has estimated that the policy pursued resulted in the killing of 6,000,000 Jews, of which 4,000,000 were killed in the extermination institutions.

THE LAW RELATING TO WAR
CRIMES AND CRIMES AGAINST HUMANITY

Article 6 of the Charter provides:

(*b*) War Crimes: namely, violations of the laws or customs of war. Such violations
shall include, but not be limited to, murder, ill-treatment or deportation to slave
labour or for any other purpose of civilian population of or in occupied territory,
murder or ill-treatment of prisoners of war or persons on the seas, killing of
hostages, plunder of public or private property, wanton destruction of cities, towns or
villages, or devastation not justified by military necessity;

(*c*) Crimes against Humanity: namely, murder, extermination, enslavement,
deportation, and other inhumane acts committed against any civilian population,
before or during the war, or persecutions on political, racial or religious grounds in
execution of or in connection with any crime within the jurisdiction of the
Tribunal, whether or not in violation of the domestic law of the country where
perpetrated.

As heretofore stated, the Charter does not define as a separate crime any conspiracy except the one set out in Article 6(*a*), dealing with crimes against peace.

The Tribunal is of course bound by the Charter, in the definition
which it gives both of war crimes and crimes against humanity. With
respect to war crimes, however, as has already been pointed out, the crimes
defined by Article 6, section (*b*), of the Charter were already recognised as
war crimes under international law. They were covered by Articles 46, 50,
52 and 56 of the Hague Convention of 1907, and Articles 2, 3, 4, 46 and
51 of the Geneva Convention of 1929. That violations of these provisions
constituted crimes for which the guilty individuals were punishable is too
well settled to admit of argument.

But it is argued that the Hague Convention does not apply in this case, because of the "general participation" clause in Article 2 of the Hague Convention of 1907. That clause provided:

> The provisions contained in the regulations (Rules of Land Warfare) referred to in Article 1 as well as in the present Convention do not apply except between contracting powers, and then only if all the belligerents are parties to the Convention.

Several of the belligerents in the recent war were not parties to this Convention.

In the opinion of the Tribunal it is not necessary to decide this question. The rules of land warfare expressed in the Convention undoubtedly represented an advance over existing international law at the time of their adoption. But the Convention expressly stated that it was an attempt "to revise the general laws and customs of war", which it thus recognised to be then existing, but by 1939 these rules laid down in the Convention were recognised by all civilised nations, and were regarded as being declaratory of the laws and customs of war which are referred to in Article 6(*b*) of the Charter.

A further submission was made that Germany was no longer bound by the rules of land warfare in many of the territories occupied during the war, because Germany had completely subjugated those countries and incorporated them into the German Reich, a fact which gave Germany authority to deal with the occupied countries as though they were part of Germany. In the view of the Tribunal, it is unnecessary in this case to decide whether this doctrine of subjugation, dependent as it is upon military conquest, has any application where the subjugation is the result of the crime of aggressive war. The doctrine was never considered to be applicable so long as there was an army in the field attempting to restore the occupied countries to their true owners, and in this case, therefore, the doctrine could not apply to any territories occupied after 1st September, 1939. As to the war crimes committed in Bohemia and Moravia, it is a sufficient answer that these territories were never added to the Reich, but a mere protectorate was established over them.

With regard to crimes against humanity, there is no doubt whatever that political opponents were murdered in Germany before the war, and that many of them were kept in concentration camps in circumstances of great horror and cruelty. The policy of terror was certainly carried out on a vast scale, and in many cases was organised and systematic. The policy of persecution, repression and murder of civilians in Germany before the war of 1939, who were likely to be hostile to the Government, was most ruthlessly carried out. The persecution of Jews during the same period is established beyond all doubt. To constitute crimes against humanity, the acts relied on before the outbreak of war must have been in execution of, or in connection with, any crime within the jurisdiction of the Tribunal. The Tribunal is of the opinion that revolting and horrible as many of these crimes were, it has not been satisfactorily proved that they were done in execution of, or in connection with, any such crime. The Tribunal, therefore, cannot make a general declaration that the acts before 1939 were crimes against humanity within the meaning of the Charter, but from the beginning of the war in 1939 war crimes were committed on a vast scale, which were also crimes against humanity; and insofar as the inhumane acts charged in the Indictment, and committed after the beginning of the war, did not constitute war crimes, they were all committed in execution of, or in connection with, the aggressive war, and therefore constituted crimes against humanity.

THE ACCUSED ORGANISATIONS

Article 9 of the Charter provides:

> At the trial of any individual member of any group or organisation the Tribunal may declare (in connection with any act of which the individual may be convicted) that the group or organisation of which the individual was a member was a criminal organisation.
>
> After receipt of the Indictment the Tribunal shall give such notice as it thinks fit that the Prosecution intends to ask the Tribunal to make such declaration and any member of the organisation will be entitled to apply to the Tribunal for leave to be heard by the Tribunal upon the question of the criminal character of the organisation. The Tribunal shall have power to allow or reject the application. If the application is allowed, the Tribunal may direct in what manner the applicants shall be represented and heard.

Article 10 of the Charter makes clear that the declaration of criminality against an accused organisation is final, and cannot be challenged in any subsequent criminal proceeding against a member of that organisation. Article 10 is as follows:

> In cases where a group or organisation is declared criminal by the Tribunal, the competent national authority of any Signatory shall have the right to bring individuals to trial for membership therein before national, military or occupation courts. In any such case the criminal nature of the group or organisation is considered proved and shall not be questioned.

The effect of the declaration of criminality by the Tribunal is well illustrated by Law Number 10 of the Control Council of Germany, passed on the 20th day of December, 1945, which provides that "each of the following acts is recognised as a crime":

(*d*) Membership in categories of a criminal group or organisation declared criminal by the International Military Tribunal . . .

(3) Any person found guilty of any of the crimes above mentioned may upon conviction be punished as shall be determined by the Tribunal to be just. Such punishment may consist of one or more of the following:

(*a*) Death.

(*b*) Imprisonment for life or a term of years, with or without hard labour.

(*c*) Fine, and imprisonment with or without hard labour, in lieu thereof.

In effect, therefore, a member of an organisation which the Tribunal has declared to be criminal may be subsequently convicted of the crime of membership and be punished for that crime by death. This is not to assume that international or military courts which will try these individuals will not exercise appropriate standards of justice. This is a far-reaching and novel procedure. Its application, unless properly safeguarded, may produce great injustice.

Article 9, it should be noted, uses the words "The Tribunal may declare" so that the Tribunal is vested with discretion as to whether it will declare any organisation criminal. This discretion is a judicial one and does not permit arbitrary action, but should be exercised in accordance with well settled legal principles, one of the most important of which is that criminal guilt is personal, and that mass punishments should be avoided. If satisfied of the criminal guilt of any organisation or group, this Tribunal should not hesitate to declare it to be criminal because the theory of "group criminality" is new, or because it might be unjustly applied by some subsequent tribunals. On the other hand, the Tribunal should make such declaration of criminality so far as possible in a manner to ensure that innocent persons will not be punished.

A criminal organisation is analogous to a criminal conspiracy in that the essence of both is co-operation for criminal purposes. There must be a group bound together and organised for a common purpose. The group must be formed or used in connection with the commission of crimes denounced by the Charter. Since the declaration with respect to the organisations and groups will, as has been pointed out, fix the criminality of its members, that definition should exclude persons who had no knowledge of the criminal purposes or acts of the organisation and those who were drafted by the State for membership, unless they were personally implicated in the commission of acts declared criminal by Article 6 of the Charter as members of the organisation. Membership alone is not enough to come within the scope of these declarations.

Since declarations of criminality which the Tribunal makes will be used by other courts in the trial of persons on account of their membership in the organisations found to be criminal, the Tribunal feels it appropriate to make the following recommendations:

1. That so far as possible throughout the four zones of occupation in Germany the classifications, sanctions and penalties be standardised. Uniformity of treatment so far as practical should be a basic principle. This does not, of course, mean that discretion in sentencing should not be vested in the court; but the discretion should be within fixed limits appropriate to the nature of the crime.

2. Law No. 10, to which reference has already been made, leaves punishment entirely in the discretion of the trial court even to the extent of inflicting the death penalty. The De-Nazification Law of 5th March, 1946, however, passed for Bavaria, Greater-Hesse and Württemberg-Baden, provides definite sentences for punishment in each type of offence. The Tribunal recommends that in no case should punishment imposed under Law No. 10 upon any members of an organisation or group declared by the Tribunal to be criminal exceed the punishment fixed by the De-Nazification Law. No person should be punished under both laws.

3. The Tribunal recommends to the Control Council that Law No. 10 be amended to prescribe limitations on the punishment which may be imposed for membership in a criminal group or organisation so that such punishment shall not exceed the punishment prescribed by the De-Nazification Law.

The Indictment asks that the Tribunal declare to be criminal the following organisations: the Leadership Corps of the Nazi Party; the Gestapo; the SD; the SS; the SA; the Reich Cabinet; and the General Staff and High Command of the German Armed Forces.

LEADERSHIP CORPS OF THE NAZI PARTY

Structure and component parts

The Indictment has named the Leadership Corps of the Nazi Party as a group or organisation which should be declared criminal. The Leadership Corps of the Nazi Party consisted, in effect, of the official organisation of the Nazi Party, with Hitler as Führer at its head. The actual work of running the Leadership Corps was carried out by the Chief of the Party Chancellery (Hess, succeeded by Bormann) assisted by the Party Reich Directorate, or Reichsleitung, which was composed of the Reichsleiters, the heads of the functional organisations of the Party, as well as of the heads of the various main departments and offices which were attached to the Party Reich Directorate. Under the Chief of the Party Chancellery were the Gauleiters, with territorial jurisdiction over the main administrative regions of the Party, the Gaus. The Gauleiters were assisted by a Party Gau Directorate or Gauleitung, similar in composition and in function to the Party Reich

Directorate. Under the Gauleiters in the Party hierarchy were the Kreisleiters, with territorial jurisdiction over a Kreis, usually consisting of a single county, and assisted by a Party of Kreis Directorate, or Kreisleitung. The Kreisleiters were the lowest members of the Party hierarchy who were full-time paid employees. Directly under the Kreisleiters were the Ortsgruppenleiters, then the Zellenleiters and then the Blockleiters. Directives and instructions were received from the Party Reich Directorate. The Gauleiters had the function of interpreting such orders and issuing them to lower formations. The Kreisleiters had a certain discretion in interpreting orders, but the Ortsgruppenleiters had not, but acted under definite instructions. Instructions were only issued in writing down as far as the Ortsgruppenleiters. The Block- and Zellenleiters usually received instructions orally. Membership in the Leadership Corps at all levels was voluntary.

On 28th February, 1946, the Prosecution excluded from the declaration all members of the staffs of the Ortsgruppenleiters and all assistants of the Zellenleiters and Blockleiters. The declaration sought against the Leadership Corps of the Nazi Party thus includes the Führer, the Reichsleitung, the Gauleiters and their staff officers, the Kreisleiters and their staff officers, the Ortsgruppenleiters, the Zellenleiters and the Blockleiters, a group estimated to contain at least 600,000 people.

Aims and activities

The primary purpose of the Leadership Corps from its beginning was to assist the Nazis in obtaining and, after 30th January, 1933, in retaining, control of the German State. The machinery of the Leadership Corps was used for the widespread dissemination of Nazi propaganda and to keep a detailed check on the political attitudes of the German people. In this activity the lower political leaders played a particularly important rôle. The Blockleiters were instructed by the Party Manual to report to the Ortsgruppenleiters all persons circulating damaging rumours or criticism of the régime. The Ortsgruppenleiters, on the basis of information supplied them by the Blockleiters and Zellenleiters, kept a card index of the people within their Ortsgruppe which recorded the factors which would be used in forming a judgment as to their political reliability. The Leadership Corps was particularly active during plebiscites. All members of the Leadership Corps were active in getting out the vote and ensuring the highest possible proportion of "yes" votes. Ortsgruppenleiters and political leaders of higher ranks often collaborated with the Gestapo and SD in taking steps to determine those who refused to vote or who voted "no", and in taking steps against them which went as far as arrest and detention in a concentration camp.

Criminal activity

These steps, which relate merely to the consolidation of control of the Nazi Party, are not criminal under the view of the conspiracy to wage aggressive war, which has previously been set forth. But the Leadership Corps was also used for similar steps in Austria and those parts of Czechoslovakia, Lithuania, Poland, France, Belgium, Luxemburg and Yugoslavia which were incorporated into the Reich and within the Gaus of the Nazi Party. In those territories the machinery of the Leadership Corps was used for their Germanisation through the elimination of local customs and the detection and arrest of persons who opposed German occupation. This was criminal under Article 6(*b*) of the Charter in those areas governed by the Hague Rules of Land Warfare, and criminal under Article 6(*c*) of the Charter as to the remainder.

The Leadership Corps played its part in the persecution of the Jews. It was involved in the economic and political discrimination against the Jews, which was put into effect shortly after the Nazis came into power. The Gestapo and SD were instructed to co-ordinate with the Gauleiters and Kreisleiters the measures taken in the pogroms of 9th and 10th November in the year 1938. The Leadership Corps was also used to prevent German public opinion from reacting against the measures taken against the Jews in the East. On 9th October, 1942, a confidential information bulletin was sent to all Gauleiters and Kreisleiters entitled "Preparatory Measures for the Final Solution of the Jewish Question in Europe: Rumours concerning the Conditions of the Jews in the East". This bulletin stated that rumours were being started by returning soldiers concerning the conditions of Jews in the East which some Germans might not understand, and outlined in detail the official explanation to be given. This bulletin contained no explicit statement that the Jews were being exterminated, but it did indicate they were going to labour camps, and spoke of their complete segregation and elimination and the necessity of ruthless severity. Thus, even at its face value, it indicated the utilisation of the machinery of the Leadership Corps to keep German public opinion from rebelling at a programme which involved condemning the Jews of Europe to a life of slavery. This information continued to be available to the Leadership Corps. The August 1944 edition of *Die Lage*, a publication circulated among the political leaders, described the deportation of 430,000 Jews from Hungary.

The Leadership Corps played an important part in the administration of the Slave Labour Programme. A Sauckel decree dated 6th April, 1942, appointed the Gauleiters as Plenipotentiary for Labour Mobilisation for their Gaus with authority to co-ordinate all agencies dealing with labour questions in their Gaus, with specific authority over the employment of foreign workers, including their conditions of work, feeding and housing. Under this authority the Gauleiters assumed control over the allocation of labour in their Gaus, including the forced labourers from foreign countries. In carrying out this task the Gauleiters used many Party offices within their Gaus, including subordinate political leaders. For example, Sauckel's decree of 8th September, 1942, relating to the allocation for household labour of 400,000 women labourers brought in from the East, established a procedure under which applications filed for such workers should be passed on by the Kreisleiters, whose judgment was final.

Under Sauckel's directive the Leadership Corps was directly concerned with the treatment given foreign workers, and the Gauleiters were specifically instructed to prevent "politically inept factory heads" from giving too much consideration to the care of Eastern workers. The type of question which was considered in their treatment included reports by the Kreisleiters on pregnancies among the female slave labourers, which would result in an abortion if the child's parentage would not meet the racial standards laid down by the SS and usually detention in a concentration camp for the female slave labourer. The evidence has established that under the supervision of the Leadership Corps, the industrial workers were housed in camps under atrocious sanitary conditions, worked long hours and were inadequately fed. Under similar supervision, the agricultural workers, who were somewhat better treated, were prohibited transportation, entertainment and religious worship, and were worked without any time limit on their working hours and under regulations which gave the employer the right to inflict corporal punishment. The political leaders, at least down to the Ortsgruppenleiters, were responsible for this supervision. On 5th May, 1943, a memorandum of Bormann instructing that mistreatment of slave labourers cease was distributed down to the Ortsgruppenleiters. Similarly, on 10th November, 1944, a Speer circular transmitted a Himmler directive which provided that all members of the Nazi Party, in accordance with instructions from the Kreisleiter, would be warned by the Ortsgruppenleiters of their duty to keep foreign workers under careful observation.

The Leadership Corps was directly concerned with the treatment of prisoners of war. On 5th November, 1941, Bormann transmitted a directive down to the level of Kreisleiter instructing them to ensure compliance by the Army with the recent directives of the Department of the Interior ordering that dead Russian prisoners of war should be buried wrapped in tar paper in a remote place without any ceremony or any decorations of their graves. On 25th November, 1943, Bormann sent a circular instructing the Gauleiters to report any lenient treatment of prisoners of war. On 13th September, 1944, Bormann sent a directive down to the level of Kreisleiter ordering that liaison be established between the Kreisleiters and the guards of the prisoners of war in order "to better assimilate the commitment of the prisoners of war to the political and economic demands". On 17th October, 1944, an OKW directive instructed the officer in charge of the prisoners of war to confer with the Kreisleiters on questions of the productivity of labour. The use of prisoners of war, particularly those from the East, was accompanied by a widespread violation of the rules of land warfare. This evidence establishes that the Leadership Corps down to the level of Kreisleiter was a participant in this illegal treatment.

The machinery of the Leadership Corps was also utilised in attempts made to deprive Allied airmen of the protection to which they were entitled under the Geneva Convention. On 13th March, 1940, a directive of Hess transmitted instructions through the Leadership Corps down to the Blockleiter for the guidance of the civilian population in case of the landing of enemy planes or parachutists, which stated that enemy parachutists were to be immediately arrested or "made harmless". On 30th May, 1944, Bormann sent a circular letter to all Gau- and Kreisleiters reporting instances of lynchings of Allied low-level fliers in which no police action was taken. It was requested that Ortsgruppenleiters be informed orally of the contents of this letter. This letter accompanied a propaganda drive which had been instituted by Goebbels to induce such lynchings, and clearly amounted to instructions to induce such lynchings or at least to violate the Geneva Convention by withdrawing any police protection. Some lynchings were carried out pursuant to this programme, but it does not appear that they were carried out throughout all of Germany. Nevertheless, the existence of this circular letter shows that the heads of the Leadership Corps were utilising it for a purpose which was patently illegal and which involved the use of the machinery of the Leadership Corps at least through the Ortsgruppenleiters.

Conclusion

The Leadership Corps was used for purposes which were criminal under the Charter and involved the Germanisation of incorporated territory, the persecution of the Jews, the administration of the slave labour programme and the mistreatment of prisoners of war. The defendants Bormann and Sauckel, who were members of this organisation, were among those who used it for these purposes. The Gauleiters, the Kreisleiters and the Ortsgruppenleiters participated, to one degree or another, in these criminal programmes. The Reichsleitung as the staff organisation of the Party is also responsible for these criminal programmes as well as the heads of the various staff organisations of the Gauleiters and Kreisleiters. The decision of the Tribunal on these staff organisations includes only the Amtsleiters who were heads of offices on the staffs of the Reichsleitung, Gauleitung and Kreisleitung. With respect to other staff officers and party organisations attached to the Leadership Corps other than the Amtsleiters referred to above, the Tribunal will follow the suggestion of the Prosecution in excluding them from the declaration.

The Tribunal declares to be criminal within the meaning of the Charter the group composed of those members of the Leadership Corps holding the positions enumerated in the preceding paragraph who became or remained members of the organisation with knowledge that it was being used for the commission of acts declared criminal by Article 6 of the Charter, or who were personally implicated as members of the organisation in the commission of such crimes. The basis of this finding is the participation of the organisation in war crimes and crimes against humanity connected with the war; the group declared criminal cannot include, therefore, persons who had ceased to hold the positions enumerated in the preceding paragraph prior to 1st September, 1939.

GESTAPO AND SD

Structure and component parts

The Prosecution has named the Geheime Staatspolizei (Gestapo) and Sicherheitsdienst des Reichsführer–SS (SD) as groups or organisations which should be declared criminal. The Prosecution presented the cases against the Gestapo and SD together, stating that this was necessary because of the close working relationship between them. The Tribunal permitted the SD to present its defence separately because of a claim of conflicting interests, but after examining the evidence has decided to consider the case of the Gestapo and SD together.

The Gestapo and the SD were first linked together on 26th June, 1936, by the appointment of Heydrich, who was the Chief of the SD, to the position of Chief of the Security Police, which was defined to include both the Gestapo and the Criminal Police. Prior to that time the SD had been the intelligence agency, first of the SS, and, after 4th June, 1934, of the entire Nazi Party. The Gestapo had been composed of the various political police forces of the several German Federal States which had been unified under the personal leadership of Himmler, with the assistance of Goering. Himmler had been appointed Chief of the German Police in the Ministry of the Interior on 17th June, 1936, and in his capacity as Reichsführer–SS and Chief of the German Police issued his decree of 26th June, 1936, which placed both the Criminal Police, or Kripo, and the Gestapo in the Security Police, and placed both the Security Police and the SD under the command of Heydrich.

This consolidation under the leadership of Heydrich of the Security Police, a State organisation, and the SD, a Party organisation, was formalised by the decree of 27th September, 1939, which united the various state and Party offices which were under Heydrich, as Chief of the Security Police and SD, into one administrative unit, the Reich Security Head Office (RSHA), which was at the same time both one of the principal offices (Hauptämter) of the SS under Himmler, as Reichsführer–SS, and an office in the Ministry of the Interior under Himmler, as Chief of the German Police. The internal structure of the RSHA shows the manner in which it consolidated the offices of the Security Police with those of the SD. The RSHA was divided into seven offices (Ämter), two of which (Amt I and Amt II) dealt with administrative matters. The Security Police were represented by Amt IV, the head office of the Gestapo, and by Amt V, the head office of the Criminal Police. The SD were represented by Amt III, the head office for SD activities inside Germany, by Amt VI, the head office for SD activities outside of Germany, and by Amt VII, the office for ideological research. Shortly after the creation of the RSHA, in November, 1939, the Security Police was "co-ordinated" with the SS by taking all officials of the Gestapo and Criminal Police into the SS at ranks equivalent to their positions.

The creation of the RSHA represented the formalisation, at the top level, of the relationship under which the SD served as the intelligence agency for the Security Police. A similar co-ordination existed in the local offices. Within Germany and areas which were incorporated within the Reich for the purpose of civil administration, local offices of the Gestapo, Criminal Police and SD were formally separate. They were subject to co-ordination by Inspectors of the Security Police and SD on the staffs of the local Higher SS and Police leaders, however, and one of the principal functions of the local SD units was to serve as the intelligence agency for the local Gestapo units. In the occupied territories the formal relationship between local units of the Gestapo, Criminal Police and SD was slightly closer. They were organised into local units of the Security Police and SD and were under the control of both the RSHA and of the Higher SS and Police leader who was appointed by Himmler to serve on the staff of the occupying authority. The offices of the Security Police and SD in occupied territory were composed of departments corresponding to the various Amts of the RSHA. In occupied territories which were still considered to be operational military areas or where German control had not been formally established, the organisation of the Security Police and SD was only slightly changed. Members of the Gestapo, Kripo and SD were joined together into military type organisations known as Einsatzkommandos and Einsatzgruppen, in which the key positions were held by members of the Gestapo, Kripo and SD and in which members of the Order Police, the Waffen SS and even the Wehrmacht were used as auxiliaries. These organisations were under the overall control of the RSHA, but in front line areas were under the operational control of the appropriate Army Commander.

It can thus be seen that from a functional point of view both the Gestapo and the SD were important and closely related groups within the organisation of the Security Police and the SD. The Security Police and SD was under a single command, that of Heydrich and later Kaltenbrunner, as Chief of the Security Police and SD; it had a single headquarters, the RSHA; it had its own command channels and worked as one organisation both in Germany, in occupied territories and in the areas immediately behind the front lines. During the period with which the Tribunal is primarily concerned, applicants for positions in the Security Police and SD received training in all its components, the Gestapo, Criminal Police and SD. Some confusion has been caused by the fact that part of the organisation was technically a formation of the Nazi Party while another part of the organisation was an office in the Government, but this is of no particular significance in view of the law of 1st December, 1933, declaring the unity of the Nazi Party and the German State.

The Security Police and SD was a voluntary organisation. It is true that many civil servants and administrative officials were transferred into the Security Police. The claim that this transfer was compulsory amounts to nothing more than the claim that they had to accept the transfer or resign their positions, with a possibility of having incurred official disfavour. During the war a member of the Security Police and SD did not have a free choice of assignments within that organisation, and the refusal to accept a particular position, especially when serving in occupied territory, might have led to serious punishment. The fact remains, however, that all members of the Security Police and SD joined the organisation voluntarily, under no other sanction than the desire to retain their positions as officials.

The organisation of the Security Police and SD also included three special units which must be dealt with separately. The first of these was the Frontier Police or Grenzpolizei, which came under the control of the Gestapo in 1937. Their duties consisted in the control of passage over the borders of Germany. They arrested persons who crossed the borders illegally. It is also clear from the evidence presented that they received directives from the Gestapo to transfer foreign workers whom they apprehended to concentration camps. They could also request the local office of the Gestapo for permission to commit persons arrested to concentration camps. The Tribunal is of the opinion that the Frontier Police must be included in the charge of criminality against the Gestapo.

The border and customs protection of Zollgrenzschutz became part of the Gestapo in the summer of 1944. The functions of this organisation were similar to the Frontier Police in enforcing border regulations with particular respect to the prevention of smuggling. It does not appear, however, that their transfer was complete, but that about half of their personnel of 54,000 remained under the Reich Finance Administration or the Order Police. A few days before the end of the war the whole organisation was transferred back to the Reich Finance Administration. The transfer of the organisation to the Gestapo was so late, and it participated so little in the overall activities of the organisation, that the Tribunal does not feel that it should be dealt with in considering the criminality of the Gestapo.

The third organisation was the so-called Secret Field Police, which was originally under the Army but which in 1942 was transferred by military order to the Security Police. The Secret Field Police was concerned with security matters within the Army in occupied territory, and also with the prevention of attacks by civilians on military installations or units, and committed war crimes and crimes against humanity on a wide scale. It has not been proved, however, that it was a part of the Gestapo, and the Tribunal does not consider it as coming within the charge of criminality contained in the

Indictment, except such members as may have been transferred to Amt IV of the RSHA or were members of organisations declared criminal by this Judgment.

Criminal activity

Originally, one of the primary functions of the Gestapo was the prevention of any political opposition to the Nazi régime, a function which it performed with the assistance of the SD. The principal weapon used in performing this function was the concentration camp. The Gestapo did not have administrative control over the concentration camps, but, acting through the RSHA, was responsible for the detention of political prisoners in those camps. Gestapo officials were usually responsible for the interrogation of political prisoners at the camps.

The Gestapo and the SD also dealt with charges of treason and with questions relating to the press, the churches and the Jews. As the Nazi programme of anti-Semitic persecution increased in intensity, the role played by these groups became increasingly important. In the early morning of 10th November, 1938, Heydrich sent a telegram to all offices of the Gestapo and SD giving instructions for the organisation of the pogroms of that date and instructing them to arrest as many Jews as the prisons could hold "especially rich ones", but to be careful that those arrested were healthy and not too old. By 11th November, 1938, 20,000 Jews had been arrested and many were sent to concentration camps. On 24th January, 1939, Heydrich, the Chief of the Security Police and SD, was charged with furthering the emigration and evacuation of Jews from Germany, and on 31st July, 1941, with bringing about a complete solution of the Jewish problem in German-dominated Europe. A special section of the Gestapo office of the RSHA under Standartenführer Eichmann was set up with responsibility for Jewish matters; it employed its own agents to investigate the Jewish problem in occupied territory. Local offices of the Gestapo were used first to supervise the emigration of Jews and later to deport them to the East, both from Germany and from the territories occupied during the war. Einsatzgruppen of the Security Police and SD operating behind the lines of the Eastern front engaged in the wholesale massacre of Jews. A special detachment from Gestapo headquarters in the RSHA was used to arrange for the deportation of Jews from Axis satellites to Germany for the "final solution".

Local offices of the Security Police and SD played an important role in the German administration of occupied territories. The nature of their participation is shown by measures taken in the summer of 1938 in preparation for the attack on Czechoslovakia, which was then in contemplation. Einsatzgruppen of the Gestapo and SD were organised to follow the Army into Czechoslovakia to provide for the security of political life in the occupied territories. Plans were made for the infiltration of SD men into the area in advance, and for the building up of a system of files to indicate what inhabitants should be placed under surveillance, deprived of passports or liquidated. These plans were considerably altered due to the cancellation of the attack on Czechoslovakia, but in the military operations which actually occurred, particularly in the war against the USSR, Einsatzgruppen of the Security Police and SD went into operation, and combined brutal measures for the pacification of the civilian population with the wholesale slaughter of Jews. Heydrich gave orders to fabricate incidents on the Polish–German frontier in 1939 which would give Hitler sufficient provocation to attack Poland. Both Gestapo and SD personnel were involved in these operations.

The local units of the Security Police and SD continued their work in the occupied territories after they had ceased to be an area of operations. The Security Police and SD engaged in widespread arrests of the civilian population of these occupied countries, imprisoned many of them under inhumane conditions, subjected them to brutal third degree methods, and sent many of them to concentration camps. Local units of the Security Police and SD were also involved in the shooting of hostages, the imprisonment of relatives, the execution of persons charged as terrorists and saboteurs without a trial, and the enforcement of the "Nacht und Nebel" decrees, under which persons charged with a type of offence believed to endanger the security of the occupying forces were either executed within a week or secretly removed to Germany without being permitted to communicate with their family and friends.

Offices of the Security Police and SD were involved in the administration of the Slave Labour Programme. In some occupied territories they helped local labour authorities to meet the quotas imposed by Sauckel. Gestapo offices inside of Germany were given surveillance over slave labourers and responsibility for apprehending those who were absent from their place of work. The Gestapo also had charge of the so-called work training camps. Although both German and foreign workers could be committed to these camps, they played a significant rôle in forcing foreign labourers to work for the German war effort. In the latter stages of the war, as the SS embarked on a slave labour programme of its own, the Gestapo was used to arrest workers for the purpose of ensuring an adequate supply in the concentration camps.

The local offices of the Security Police and SD were also involved in the commission of war crimes involving the mistreatment and murder of prisoners of war. Soviet prisoners of war in prisoner of war camps in Germany were screened by Einsatzkommandos acting under the directions of the local Gestapo offices. Commissars, Jews, members of the intelligentsia, "fanatical Communists" and even those who were considered incurably sick were classified as "intolerable", and exterminated. The local offices of the Security Police and SD were involved in the enforcement of the "Bullet" decree, put into effect on 4th March, 1944, under which certain categories of prisoners of war, who were recaptured, were not treated as prisoners of war but taken to Mauthausen in secret and shot. Members of the Security Police and the

SD were charged with the enforcement of the decree for the shooting of parachutists and commandos.

Conclusion

The Gestapo and SD were used for purposes which were criminal under the Charter and involved the persecution and extermination of the Jews, brutalities and killings in concentration camps, excesses in the administration of occupied territories, the administration of the Slave Labour Programme and the mistreatment and murder of prisoners of war. The defendant Kaltenbrunner, who was a member of this organisation, was among those who used it for these purposes. In dealing with the Gestapo, the Tribunal includes all executive and administrative officials of Amt IV of the RSHA or concerned with Gestapo administration in other departments of the RSHA and all local Gestapo officials serving both inside and outside of Germany, including the members of the Frontier Police, but not including the members of the Border and Customs Protection or the Secret Field Police, except such members as have been specified above. At the suggestion of the Prosecution, the Tribunal does not include persons employed by the Gestapo for purely clerical, stenographic, janitorial or similar unofficial routine tasks. In dealing with the SD, the Tribunal includes Amts III, VI and VII of the RSHA and all other members of the SD, including all local representatives and agents, honorary or otherwise, whether they were technically members of the SS or not.

The Tribunal declares to be criminal within the meaning of the Charter the group composed of those members of the Gestapo and SD holding the positions enumerated in the preceding paragraph who became or remained members of the organisation with knowledge that it was being used for the commission of acts declared criminal by Article 6 of the Charter, or who were personally implicated as members of the organisation in the commission of such crimes. The basis for this finding is the participation of the organisation in war crimes and crimes against humanity connected with the war; this group declared criminal cannot include, therefore, persons who had ceased to hold the positions enumerated in the preceding paragraph prior to 1st September, 1939.

The PRESIDENT: There is a correction which the Tribunal wishes to make in the Judgment pronounced with reference to the SD.

The Tribunal's attention has been drawn to the fact that the Prosecution expressly excluded honorary informers who were not members of the SS, and members of the Abwehr who were transferred to the SD. In view of that exclusion by the Prosecution, the Tribunal also excludes those persons from the SD, which was declared criminal.

THE SS

Structure and component parts

The Prosecution has named the Schutzstaffel of the Nationalsozialistische Deutsche Arbeiter Partei (commonly known as the SS) as an organisation which should be declared criminal. The portion of the Indictment dealing with the SS also includes the Sicherheitsdienst des Reichsführers–SS (commonly known as the SD). This latter organisation, which was originally an intelligence branch of the SS, later became an important part of the organisation of Security Police and SD and is dealt with in the Tribunal's Judgment on the Gestapo.

The SS was originally established by Hitler in 1925 as an élite section of the SA for political purposes under the pretext of protecting speakers at public meetings of the Nazi Party. After the Nazis had obtained power, the SS was used to maintain order and control audiences at mass demonstrations and was given the additional duty of "internal security" by a decree of the Führer. The SS played an important role at the time of the Röhm purge of 30th June, 1934, and, as a reward for its services, was made an independent unit of the Nazi Party shortly thereafter.

In 1929, when Himmler was first appointed as Reichsführer, the SS consisted of 280 men who were regarded as especially trustworthy. In 1933 it was composed of 52,000 men drawn from all walks of life. The original formation of the SS was the Allgemeine SS, which by 1939 had grown to a corps of 240,000 men, organised on military lines into divisions and regiments. During the war its strength declined to well under 40,000.

The SS originally contained two other formations, the SS Verfügungstruppe, a force consisting of SS members who volunteered for four years' armed service in lieu of compulsory service with the Army, and the SS Totenkopfverbände, special troops employed to guard concentration camps, which came under the control of the SS in 1934. The SS Verfügungstruppe was organised as an armed unit to be employed with the Army in the event of mobilisation. In the summer of 1939, the Verfügungstruppe was equipped as a motorised division to form the nucleus of the forces which came to be known in 1940 as the Waffen SS. In that year the Waffen SS comprised 100,000 men, 56,000 coming from the Verfügungstruppe and the rest from the Allgemeine SS and the Totenkopfverbände. At the end of the war it is estimated to have consisted of about 580,000 men and 40 divisions. The Waffen SS was under the tactical command of the Army, but was equipped and supplied through the administrative branches of the SS and under SS disciplinary control.

The SS Central Organisation had twelve main offices. The most important of these were the RSHA, which has already been discussed; the WVHA or Economic Administration Main Office, which administered concentration camps along with its other duties; a Race and Settlement Office together with auxiliary offices for repatriation of racial Germans (Volksdeutschemittelstelle). The SS Central Organisation also had a legal office and the SS possessed its own legal system; its personnel were under the jurisdiction of special courts. Also attached to the SS main offices was a research foundation known as the Experiments Ahnenerbe. The scientists attached to this organisation are stated to have been mainly honorary members of the SS. During the war an institute for military scientific research became attached to the Ahnenerbe and conducted extensive experiments involving the use of living human beings. An employee of this institute was a certain Dr Rascher, who conducted these experiments with the full knowledge of the Ahnenerbe, which was subsidised and under the patronage of the Reichsführer–SS, who was a trustee of the foundation.

Beginning in 1933 there was a gradual but thorough amalgamation of the Police and SS. In 1936 Himmler, the Reichsführer–SS, became Chief of the German Police with authority over the regular uniformed police as well as the Security Police. Himmler established a system under which Higher SS and Police leaders, appointed for each Wehrkreis, served as his personal representatives in co-ordinating the activities of the Order Police, Security Police and SD and Allgemeine SS within their jurisdictions. In 1939 the SS and Police systems were co-ordinated by taking into the SS all officials of the Security and Order Police, at SS ranks equivalent to their rank in the Police.

Until 1940 the SS was an entirely voluntary organisation. After the formation of the Waffen SS in 1940, there was a gradually increasing number of conscripts into the Waffen SS. It appears that about a third of the total number of people joining the Waffen SS were conscripts, that the proportion of conscripts was higher at the end of the war than at the beginning, but that there continued to be a high proportion of volunteers until the end of the war.

Criminal activities

SS units were active participants in the steps leading up to aggressive war. The Verfügungstruppe was used in the occupation of the Sudetenland, of Bohemia and Moravia and of Memel. The Henlein Free Corps was under the jurisdiction of the Reichsführer–SS for operations in the Sudetenland in 1938 and the Volksdeutschemittelstelle financed fifth column activities there.

The SS was even a more general participant in the commission of war crimes and crimes against humanity. Through its control over the organisation of the Police, particularly the Security Police and SD, the SS was involved in all the crimes which have been outlined in the section of this Judgment dealing with the Gestapo and SD. Other branches of the SS were equally involved in these criminal programmes. There is evidence that the shooting of unarmed prisoners of war was the general practice in some Waffen SS divisions. On 1st October, 1944, the custody of prisoners of war and interned persons was transferred to Himmler, who in turn transferred prisoner of war affairs to SS Obergruppenführer Berger and to SS Obergruppenführer Pohl. The Race and Settlement Office of the SS together with the Volksdeutschemittelstelle were active in carrying out schemes for Germanisation of occupied territories according to the racial principles of the Nazi Party and were involved in the deportation of Jews and other foreign nationals. Units of the Waffen SS and Einsatzgruppen operating directly under the SS main office were used to carry out these plans. These units were also involved in the widespread murder and ill-treatment of the civilian population of occupied territories. Under the guise of combating partisan units, units of the SS exterminated Jews and people deemed politically undesirable by the SS, and their reports record the execution of enormous numbers of persons. Waffen SS divisions were responsible for many massacres and atrocities in occupied territories, such as the massacres at Oradour and Lidice.

From 1934 onwards the SS was responsible for the guarding and administration of concentration camps. The evidence leaves no doubt that the consistently brutal treatment of the inmates of concentration camps was carried out as a result of the general policy of the SS, which was that the inmates were racial inferiors to be treated only with contempt. There is evidence that where manpower considerations permitted, Himmler wanted to rotate guard battalions so that all members of the SS would be instructed as to the proper attitude to take to inferior races. After 1942, when the concentration camps were placed under the control of the WVHA, they were used as a source of slave labour. An agreement made with the Ministry of Justice on 18th September, 1942, provided that anti-social elements who had finished prison sentences were to be delivered to the SS to be worked to death. Steps were continually taken, involving the use of the Security Police and SD and even the Waffen SS, to ensure that the SS had an adequate supply of concentration camp labour for its projects. In connection with the administration of the concentration camps, the SS embarked on a series of experiments on human beings which were performed on prisoners of war or concentration camp inmates. These experiments included freezing to death, and killing by poison bullets. The SS was able to obtain an allocation of Government funds for this kind of research on the grounds that they had access to human material not available to other agencies.

The SS played a particularly significant rôle in the persecution of the Jews. The SS was directly involved in the demonstrations of 10th November, 1938. The evacuation of the Jews from occupied territories was carried out under the directions of the SS with the assistance of SS Police units. The extermination of the Jews was carried out under the direction of the SS central organisation. It was actually put into effect by SS formations. The Einsatzgruppen engaged in wholesale massacres of the Jews. SS police units were also involved. For example, the massacre of Jews in the Warsaw Ghetto was carried out under the directions of the SS Brigadeführer and Major General of the Police, Stroop. A special group from the SS central organisation arranged for the deportation of Jews from various Axis satellites, and their extermination was carried out in the concentration camps run by the WVHA.

It is impossible to single out any one portion of the SS which was not involved in these criminal activities. The Allgemeine SS was an active participant in the persecution of the Jews and was used as a source of concentration camp guards. Units of the Waffen SS were directly involved in the killing of prisoners of war and the atrocities in occupied countries. It supplied personnel for the Einsatzgruppen and had command over the concentration camp guards after its absorption of the Totenkopf SS, which originally controlled the system. Various SS Police units were also widely used in the atrocities in occupied countries and the extermination of the Jews there. The SS central organisation supervised the activities of these various formations and was responsible for such special projects as the human experiments and "final solution" of the Jewish question.

The Tribunal finds that knowledge of these criminal activities was sufficiently general to justify declaring that the SS was a criminal organisation to the extent hereinafter described. It does appear that an attempt was made to keep secret some phases of its activities, but its criminal programmes were so widespread, and involved slaughter on such a gigantic scale, that its criminal activities must have been widely known. It must be recognised, moreover, that the criminal activities of the SS followed quite logically from the principles on which it was organised. Every effort had been made to make the SS a highly disciplined organisation composed of the élite of National Socialism. Himmler had stated that there were people in Germany "who become sick when they see these black coats" and that he did not expect that "they should be loved by too many". Himmler also indicated his view that the SS was concerned with perpetuating the élite racial stock with the object of making Europe a Germanic Continent, and the SS was instructed that it was designed to assist the Nazi Government in the ultimate domination of Europe and the elimination of all inferior races. This mystic and fanatical belief in the superiority of the Nordic German developed into the studied contempt and even hatred of other races which led to criminal activities of the type outlined above being considered as a matter of course if not a matter of pride. The actions of a soldier in the Waffen SS who in September, 1939, acting entirely on his own initiative, killed fifty Jewish labourers whom he had been guarding, were described by the statement that as an SS man he was "particularly sensitive to the sight of Jews", and had acted "quite thoughtlessly in a youthful spirit of adventure", and a sentence of three years' imprisonment imposed on him was dropped under an amnesty. Hess wrote with truth that the Waffen SS were more suitable for the specific tasks to be solved in occupied territory owing to their extensive training in questions of race and nationality. Himmler, in a series of speeches made in 1943, indicated his pride in the ability of the SS to carry out these criminal acts. He encouraged his men to be "tough and ruthless" – he spoke of shooting "thousands of leading Poles" – and thanked them for their co-operation and lack of squeamishness at the sight of hundreds and thousands of corpses of their victims. He extolled ruthlessness in exterminating the Jewish race and later described this process as "delousing". These speeches show the general attitude prevailing; the SS was consistent with these criminal acts.

Conclusions

The SS was utilised for the purposes which were criminal under the Charter and involved the persecution and extermination of the Jews, brutalities and killings in concentration camps, excesses in the administration of occupied territories, the administration of the Slave Labour Programme and the mistreatment and murder of prisoners of war. The defendant Kaltenbrunner was a member of the SS implicated in these activities. In dealing with the SS, the Tribunal includes all persons who had been officially accepted as members of the SS, including the members of the Allgemeine SS, members of the Waffen SS, members of the SS Totenkopfverbände and the members of any of the different police forces who were members of the SS. The Tribunal does not include the so-called SS riding units. The Sicherheitsdienst des Reichsführers–SS (commonly known as the SD) is dealt with in the Tribunal's Judgment on the Gestapo and SD.

The Tribunal declares to be criminal within the meaning of the Charter the group composed of those persons who had been officially accepted as members of the SS as enumerated in the preceding paragraph, who became or remained members of the organisation with knowledge that it was being used for the commission of acts declared criminal by Article 6 of the Charter, or who were personally implicated as members of the organisation in the commission of such crimes, excluding, however, those who were drafted into membership by the State in such a way as to give them no choice in the matter, and who had committed no such crimes. The basis of this finding is the participation of the organisation in war crimes and crimes against humanity connected with the war; this group declared criminal cannot include, therefore, persons who had ceased to belong to the organisations enumerated in the preceding paragraph prior to 1st September, 1939.

THE SA

Structure and component parts

The prosecution has named the Sturmabteilungen of the Nationalsozialistische Deutsche Arbeiter Partei (commonly known as the SA) as an organisation which should be declared criminal. The SA was founded in 1921 for political purposes. It was organised on military lines. Its members wore their own uniforms and had their own discipline and regulations. After the

Nazis had obtained power the SA greatly increased in membership due to the incorporation within it of certain veterans' organisations. In April, 1933, the Stahlheim, an organisation of one and a half million members, was transferred into the SA, with the exception of its members over 45 years of age and some others, pursuant to an agreement between their leader Seldte and Hitler. Another veterans' organisation, the so-called Kyffhauserbund, was transferred in the same manner, together with a number of rural riding organisations.

Until 1933 there is no question but that membership in the SA was voluntary. After 1933 civil servants were under certain political and economic pressure to join the SA. Members of the Stahlheim, the Kyffhauserbund and the rural riding associations were transferred into the SA without their knowledge, but the Tribunal is not satisfied that the members in general endeavoured to protest against this transfer or that there was any evidence, except in isolated cases, of the consequences of refusal. The Tribunal, therefore, finds that membership in the SA was generally voluntary.

By the end of 1933 the SA was composed of four and a half million men. As a result of changes made after 1934, in 1939 the SA numbered one and a half million men.

Activities

In the early days of the Nazi movement the storm troopers of the SA acted as the "strong arm of the Party". They took part in the beer hall feuds and were used for street fighting in battles against political opponents. The SA was also used to disseminate Nazi ideology and propaganda and placed particular emphasis on anti-Semitic propaganda, the doctrine of *Lebensraum*, the revision of the Versailles Treaty and the return of Germany's colonies.

After the Nazi advent to power, and particularly after the elections of 5th March, 1933, the SA played an important role in establishing a Nazi reign of terror over Germany. The SA was involved in outbreaks of violence against the Jews and was used to arrest political opponents and to guard concentration camps, where they subjected their prisoners to brutal mistreatment.

On 30th June and 1st and 2nd July, 1934, a purge of SA leaders occurred. The pretext which was given for this purge, which involved the killing of Röhm, the Chief of Staff of the SA, and many other SA leaders, was the existence of a plot against Hitler. This purge resulted in a great reduction in the influence and power of the SA. After 1934 it rapidly declined in political significance.

After 1934 the SA engaged in certain forms of military or para-military training. The SA continued to engage in the dissemination of Nazi propaganda. Isolated units of the SA were even involved in the steps leading up to aggressive war and in the commission of war crimes and crimes against humanity. SA units were among the first in the occupation of Austria in March, 1938. The SA supplied many of the men and a large part of the equipment which composed the Sudeten Free Corps of Henlein, although

it appears that the corps was under the jurisdiction of the SS during its operation in Czechoslovakia.

After the occupation of Poland, the SA group Sudeten was used for
transporting prisoners of war. Units of the SA were employed in the guarding of prisoners in Danzig, Posen, Silesia and the Baltic States.

Some SA units were used to blow up synagogues in the Jewish pogrom
of 10th and 11th November, 1938. Groups of the SA were concerned in the
ill-treatment of Jews in the ghettos of Vilna and Kaunas.

Conclusion

Up until the purge beginning on 30th June, 1934, the SA was a group composed in large part of ruffians and bullies who participated in the Nazi
outrages of that period. It has not been shown, however, that these atrocities
were part of a specific plan to wage aggressive war, and the Tribunal, therefore, cannot hold that these activities were criminal under the Charter. After
the purge, the SA was reduced to the status of a group of unimportant Nazi
hangers-on. Although in specific instances some units of the SA were used
for the commission of war crimes and crimes against humanity, it cannot be
said that its members generally participated in or even knew of the criminal
acts. For these reasons the Tribunal does not declare the SA to be a criminal
organisation within the meaning of Article 9 of the Charter.

THE REICH CABINET

The Prosecution has named as a criminal organisation the Reich Cabinet
(Reichsregierung), consisting of members of the ordinary cabinet after 30th
January, 1933, members of the Council of Ministers for the defence of the
Reich and members of the Secret Cabinet Council. The Tribunal is of opinion that no declaration of criminality should be made with respect to the
Reich Cabinet for two reasons: (1) because it is not shown that after 1937 it
ever really acted as a group or organisation; (2) because the group of persons
here charged is so small that members could be conveniently tried in proper
cases without resort to a declaration that the Cabinet of which they were
members was criminal.

As to the first reason for our decision, it is to be observed that, from the
time that it can be said that a conspiracy to make aggressive war existed, the
Reich Cabinet did not constitute a governing body, but was merely an
aggregation of administrative officers subject to the absolute control of
Hitler. Not a single meeting of the Reich Cabinet was held after 1937, but
laws were promulgated in the name of one or more of the Cabinet members. The Secret Cabinet Council never met at all. A number of the Cabinet
members were undoubtedly involved in the conspiracy to make aggressive
war; but they were involved as individuals, and there is no evidence that the
Cabinet as a group or organisation took any part in these crimes. It will be

remembered that, when Hitler disclosed his aims of criminal aggression at the Hoszbach Conference, the disclosure was not made before the Cabinet and that the Cabinet was not consulted with regard to it, but, on the contrary, that it was made secretly to a small group upon whom Hitler would necessarily rely in carrying on the war. Likewise no Cabinet order authorised the invasion of Poland. On the contrary, the defendant Schacht testifies that he sought to stop the invasion by a plea to the Commander-in-Chief of the Army that Hitler's order was in violation of the Constitution because it was not authorised by the Cabinet.

It does appear, however, that various laws authorising acts which were criminal under the Charter were circulated among the members of the Reich Cabinet and issued under its authority, signed by the members whose departments were concerned. This does not, however, prove that the Reich Cabinet, after 1937, ever really acted as an organisation.

As to the second reason, it is clear that those members of the Reich Cabinet who have been guilty of crimes should be brought to trial; and a number of them are now on trial before the Tribunal. It is estimated that there are 48 members of the group, that eight of these are dead and 17 are now on trial, leaving only 23 at the most as to whom the declaration could have any importance. Any others who are guilty should also be brought to trial; but nothing would be accomplished to expedite or facilitate their trials by declaring the Reich Cabinet to be a criminal organisation. Where an organisation with a large membership is used for such purposes, a declaration obviates the necessity of inquiring as to its criminal character in the later trial of members who are accused of participating through membership in its criminal purposes, and thus saves much time and trouble. There is no such advantage in the case of a small group like the Reich Cabinet.

GENERAL STAFF AND HIGH COMMAND

The Prosecution has also asked that the General Staff and High Command of the German Armed Forces be declared a criminal organisation. The Tribunal believes that no declaration of criminality should be made with respect to the General Staff and High Command. The number of persons charged, while larger than that of the Reich Cabinet, is still so small that individual trials of these officers would accomplish the purpose here sought better than a declaration such as is requested. But a more compelling reason is that in the opinion of the Tribunal the General Staff and High Command is neither an "organisation" nor a "group" within the meaning of those terms as used in Article 9 of the Charter.

Some comment on the nature of this alleged group is requisite. According to the Indictment and evidence before the Tribunal, it consists of approximately 130 officers, living and dead, who at any time during the period from February, 1938, when Hitler reorganised the Armed Forces, to May, 1945, when Germany surrendered, held certain positions in the military hierarchy. These men were high-ranking officers in the three armed services: OKH – Army, OKM – Navy, and OKL – Air Force. Above them was the overall Armed Forces authority, OKW – High Command of the German Armed Forces, with Hitler as the Supreme Commander. The officers in the OKW, including defendant Keitel as Chief of the High Command, were in a sense Hitler's personal staff. In the larger sense they co-ordinated and directed the three services, with particular emphasis on the functions of planning and operations.

The individual officers in this alleged group were, at one time or another, in one of four categories: (1) Commanders-in-Chief of one of the three services; (2) Chief of Staff of one of the three services; (3) Oberbefehlshabers, the Field Commanders-in-Chief of one of the three services, which of course comprised by far the largest number of these persons; or (4) an OKW officer, of which there were three: defendants Keitel and Jodl and the latter's Deputy Chief, Warlimont. This is the meaning of the Indictment in its use of the term "General Staff and High Command".

The Prosecution has here drawn the line. The Prosecution does not indict the next level of the military hierarchy, consisting of commanders of Army Corps, and equivalent ranks in the Navy and Air Force, nor the level below, the division commanders or their equivalent in the other branches. And the staff officers of the four staff commands of OKW, OKH, OKM and OKL are not included, nor are the trained specialists who were customarily called General Staff Officers.

In effect, then, those indicted as members are military leaders of the Reich of the highest rank. No serious effort was made to assert that they composed an "organisation" in the sense of Article 9. The assertion is rather that they were a "group", which is a wider and more embracing term than "organisation".

The Tribunal does not so find. According to the evidence, their planning at staff level, the constant conferences between staff officers and field commanders, and their operational technique in the field and at headquarters were much the same as that of the armies, navies and air forces of all other countries. The overall effort of OKW at co-ordination and direction could be matched by a similar, though not identical, form of organisation in other military forces, such as the Anglo-American Combined Chiefs of Staff.

To derive from this pattern of their activities the existence of an association or group does not, in the opinion of the Tribunal, logically follow. On such a theory the top commanders of every other nation are just such an association rather than what they actually are – an aggregation of military men, a number of individuals who happen at a given period to hold the high-ranking military positions.

Much of the evidence and the argument has centred around the question of whether membership in these organisations was or was not voluntary; in this case, it seems to the Tribunal to be quite beside the point. For this alleged criminal organisation has one characteristic, a controlling one, which sharply distinguishes it from the other five indicted. When an individual became a member of the SS, for instance, he did so voluntarily or otherwise, but certainly with the knowledge that he was joining something. In the case of the General Staff and High Command, however, he could not know he was joining a group or organisation, for such organisation did not exist except in the charge of the Indictment. He knew only that he had achieved a certain high rank in one of the three services, and could not be conscious of the fact that he was becoming a member of anything so tangible as a "group", as that word is commonly used. His relations with his brother officers in his own branch of the service and his association with those of the other two branches were, in general, like those of other services all over the world.

The Tribunal, therefore, does not declare the General Staff and High Command to be a criminal organisation.

Although the Tribunal is of the opinion that the term "group" in Article 9 must mean something more than this collection of military officers, it has heard much evidence as to the participation of these officers in planning and waging aggressive war, and in committing war crimes and crimes against humanity. This evidence is, as to many of them, clear and convincing.

They have been responsible in large measure for the miseries and suffering that have fallen on millions of men, women and children. They have been a disgrace to the honourable profession of arms. Without their military guidance the aggressive ambitions of Hitler and his fellow Nazis would have been academic and sterile. Although they were not a group falling within the words of the Charter, they were certainly a ruthless military caste. The contemporary German militarism flourished briefly with its recent ally, National Socialism, as well as or better than it had in the generations of the past.

Many of these men have made a mockery of the soldier's oath of obedience to military orders. When it suits their defence they say they had to obey; when confronted with Hitler's brutal crimes, which are shown to have been within their general knowledge, they say they disobeyed. The truth is they actively participated in all these crimes, or sat silent and acquiescent, witnessing the commission of crimes on a scale larger and more shocking than the world has ever had the misfortune to know. This must be said.

Where the facts warrant it, these men should be brought to trial so that those among them who are guilty of these crimes should not escape punishment.

THE DEFENDANTS

Article 26 of the Charter provides that the Judgment of the Tribunal as to the guilt or innocence of any defendant shall give the reasons on which it is based.

The Tribunal will now state those reasons in declaring its Judgment on such guilt or innocence.

GOERING

Goering is indicted on all four counts. The evidence shows that after Hitler he was the most prominent man in the Nazi régime. He was Commander-in-Chief of the Luftwaffe, Plenipotentiary for the Four Year Plan and had tremendous influence with Hitler, at least until 1943 when their relationship deteriorated, ending in his arrest in 1945. He testified that Hitler kept him informed of all important military and political problems.

Crimes against peace

From the moment he joined the Party in 1922 and took command of the street-fighting organisation, the SA, Goering was the adviser, the active agent of Hitler and one of the prime leaders of the Nazi movement. As Hitler's Political Deputy he was largely instrumental in bringing the National Socialists to power in 1933, and was charged with consolidating this power and expanding German armed might. He developed the Gestapo and created the first concentration camps, relinquishing them to Himmler in 1934; conducted the Röhm purge in that year; and engineered the sordid proceedings which resulted in the removal of von Blomberg and von Fritsch from the Army. In 1936 he became Plenipotentiary for the Four Year Plan, and in theory and in practice was the economic dictator of the Reich.

Shortly after the Pact of Munich, he announced that he would embark on a five-fold expansion of the Luftwaffe and speed rearmament with emphasis on offensive weapons.

Goering was one of the five important leaders present at the Hoszbach Conference of 5th November, 1937, and he attended the other important conferences already discussed in this Judgment. In the Austrian Anschluss, he was indeed the central figure, the ringleader. He said in Court:

> I must take 100 per cent responsibility . . . I even overruled objections by the Führer and brought everything to its final development.

In the seizure of the Sudetenland, he played his rôle as Luftwaffe Chief by planning an air offensive which proved unnecessary, and his rôle as a politician by lulling the Czechs with false promises of friendship. The night before the invasion of Czechoslovakia and the absorption of Bohemia and Moravia, at a conference with Hitler and President Hácha, he threatened to bomb Prague if Hácha did not submit. This threat he admitted in his testimony.

Goering attended the Reich Chancellery meeting of 23rd May, 1939, when Hitler told his military leaders "there is, therefore, no question of sparing Poland", and was present at the Obersalzburg briefing of 22nd August, 1939. And the evidence shows he was active in the diplomatic manoeuvres which followed. With Hitler's connivance, he used the Swedish businessman, Dahlerus, as a go-between to the British, as described by Dahlerus to this Tribunal, to try to prevent the British Government from keeping its guarantee to the Poles.

He commanded the Luftwaffe in the attack on Poland and throughout the aggressive wars which followed.

Even if he opposed Hitler's plans against Norway and the Soviet Union, as he alleged, it is clear that he did so only for strategic reasons; once Hitler had decided the issue, he followed him without hesitation. He made it clear in his testimony that these differences were never ideological or legal. He was "in a rage" about the invasion of Norway, but only because he had not received sufficient warning to prepare the Luftwaffe offensive. He admitted he approved of the attack: "My attitude was perfectly positive." He was active in preparing and executing the Yugoslavian and Greek campaigns, and testified that "Plan Marita", the attack on Greece, had been prepared long beforehand. The Soviet Union he regarded as the "most threatening menace to Germany", but said there was no immediate military necessity for the attack. Indeed, his only objection to the war of aggression against the USSR was its timing; he wished for strategic reasons to delay until Britain was conquered. He testified: "My point of view was decided by political and military reasons only."

After his own admissions to this Tribunal, from the positions which he held, the conferences he attended and the public words he uttered, there can remain no doubt that Goering was the moving force for aggressive war second only to Hitler. He was the planner and prime mover in the military and diplomatic preparation for war which Germany pursued.

War crimes and crimes against humanity

The record is filled with Goering's admissions of his complicity in the use of slave labour.

> We did use this labour for security reasons so that they would not be active in their own country and would not work against us. On the other hand, they served to help in the economic war.

And again: "Workers were forced to come to the Reich. That is something I have not denied." The man who spoke these words was Plenipotentiary for the Four Year Plan, charged with the recruitment and allocation of manpower. As Luftwaffe Commander-in-Chief, he demanded from Himmler more slave labourers for his underground aircraft factories:

> That I requested inmates of concentration camps for the armament of the Luftwaffe is correct and it is to be taken as a matter of course.

As Plenipotentiary, Goering signed a directive concerning the treatment of Polish workers in Germany and implemented it by regulations of the SD, including "special treatment". He issued directives to use Soviet and French prisoners of war in the armament industry; he spoke of seizing Poles and Dutch and making them prisoners of war if necessary, and using them for work. He agrees Russian prisoners of war were used to man anti-aircraft batteries.

As Plenipotentiary, Goering was the active authority in the spoliation of conquered territory. He made plans for the spoliation of Soviet territory long before the war on the Soviet Union. Two months prior to the invasion of the Soviet Union, Hitler gave Goering the overall direction for the economic administration in the territory. Goering set up an economic staff for this function. As Reichsmarschal of the Greater German Reich, "the orders of the Reichsmarschal cover all economic fields, including nutrition and agriculture". His so-called "Green" folder, printed by the Wehrmacht, set up an "Economic Executive Staff, East". This directive contemplated plundering and abandonment of all industry in the food deficit regions and, from the food surplus regions, a diversion of food to German needs. Goering claims its purposes have been misunderstood but admits "that as a matter of course and a matter of duty we would have used Russia for our purposes", when conquered.

And he participated in the conference of 16th July, 1941, when Hitler said the National Socialists had no intention of ever leaving the occupied countries, and that "all necessary measures – shooting, desettling, etc." should be taken.

Goering persecuted the Jews, particularly after the November 1938 riots, and not only in Germany where he raised the billion mark fine as stated elsewhere, but in the conquered territories as well. His own utterances then and his testimony now show this interest was primarily economic – how to get their property and how to force them out of the economic life of Europe. As these countries fell before the German Army, he extended the Reich's anti-Jewish laws to them; the *Reichsgesetzblatt* for 1939, 1940 and 1941 contains several anti-Jewish decrees signed by Goering. Although their extermination was in Himmler's hands, Goering was far from disinterested or inactive, despite his protestations in the witness box. By decree of 31st July, 1941, he directed Himmler and Heydrich to bring "about a complete solution of the Jewish question in the German sphere of influence in Europe".

There is nothing to be said in mitigation. For Goering was often, indeed almost always, the moving force, second only to his leader. He was the leading war aggressor, both as political and as military leader; he was the director of the Slave Labour Programme and the creator of the oppressive programme against the Jews and other races, at home and abroad. All of these crimes he has frankly admitted. On some specific cases there may be conflict of testimony, but in terms of the broad outline his own admissions are more than sufficiently wide to be conclusive of his guilt. His guilt is unique in its enormity. The record discloses no excuses for this man.

Conclusion

The Tribunal finds the defendant Goering guilty on all four counts.

HESS

Hess is indicted under all four counts. He joined the Nazi Party in 1920 and participated in the Munich Putsch on 9th November, 1923. He was imprisoned with Hitler in the Landsberg fortress in 1924 and became Hitler's closest personal confidant, a relationship which lasted until Hess's flight to the British Isles. On 21st April, 1933, he was appointed Deputy to the Führer, and on 1st December, 1933, was made Reichsminister without Portfolio. He was appointed Member of the Secret Cabinet Council on 4th February, 1938, and a member of the Ministerial Council for the Defence of the Reich on 30th August, 1939. In September, 1939, Hess was officially announced by Hitler as successor designate to the Führer after Goering. On 10th May, 1941, he flew from Germany to Scotland.

Crimes against peace

As Deputy to the Führer, Hess was the top man in the Nazi Party with responsibility for handling all Party matters, and authority to make decisions in Hitler's name on all questions of Party leadership. As Reichsminister without Portfolio he had the authority to approve all legislation suggested by the different Reichsministers before it could be enacted as law. In these positions, Hess was an active supporter of preparations for war. His signature appears on the law of 16th March, 1935, establishing compulsory military service. Throughout the years he supported Hitler's policy of vigorous rearmament in many speeches. He told the people that they must sacrifice for armaments, repeating the phrase, "Guns instead of butter". It is true that between 1933 and 1937 Hess made speeches in which he expressed a desire for peace and advocated international economic co-operation. But nothing which they contained can alter the fact that of all the defendants none knew better than Hess how determined Hitler was to realise his ambitions, how fanatical and violent a man he was, and how little likely he was to refrain from resort to force, if this was the only way in which he could achieve his aims.

Hess was an informed and willing participant in German aggression against Austria, Czechoslovakia and Poland. He was in touch with the illegal Nazi Party in Austria throughout the entire period between the murder of Dollfuss and the Anschluss, and gave instructions to it during that period. Hess was in Vienna on 12th March, 1938, when the German troops moved in; and on 13th March, 1938, he signed the law for the reunion of Austria within the German Reich. A law of 10th June, 1939, provided for his participation in the administration of Austria. On 24th July, 1938, he made a speech in commemoration of the unsuccessful Putsch by Austrian National Socialists which had been attempted four years before, praising the steps leading up to Anschluss and defending the occupation of Austria by Germany.

In the summer of 1938 Hess was in active touch with Henlein, Chief of the Sudeten German Party in Czechoslovakia. On 27th September, 1938, at the time of the Munich crisis, he arranged with Keitel to carry out the instructions of Hitler to make the machinery of the Nazi Party available for a secret mobilisation. On 14th April, 1939, Hess signed a decree setting up the government of the Sudetenland as an integral part of the Reich; and an ordinance of 10th June, 1939, provided for his participation in the administration of the Sudetenland. On 7th November, 1938, Hess absorbed Henlein's Sudeten German Party into the Nazi Party, and made a speech in which he emphasised that Hitler had been prepared to resort to war if this had been necessary to acquire the Sudetenland.

On 27th August, 1939, when the attack on Poland had been temporarily postponed in an attempt to induce Great Britain to abandon its guarantee to Poland, Hess publicly praised Hitler's "magnanimous offer" to Poland, and attacked Poland for agitating for war and England for being responsible for Poland's attitude. After the invasion of Poland Hess signed decrees incorporating Danzig and certain Polish territories into the Reich, and setting up the General-Government (Poland).

These specific steps which this defendant took in support of Hitler's plans for aggressive action do not indicate the full extent of his responsibility. Until his flight to England, Hess was Hitler's closest personal confidant.

Their relationship was such that Hess must have been informed of Hitler's aggressive plans when they came into existence. And he took action to carry out these plans whenever action was necessary.

With him on his flight to England, Hess carried certain peace proposals which he alleged Hitler was prepared to accept. It is significant to note that this flight took place only ten days after the date which Hitler fixed, 22nd June, 1941, as the time for attacking the Soviet Union. In conversations carried on after his arrival in England, Hess wholeheartedly supported all Germany's aggressive actions up to that time and attempted to justify Germany's action in connection with Austria, Czechoslovakia, Poland, Norway, Denmark, Belgium and the Netherlands. He blamed England and France for the war.

War crimes and crimes against humanity

There is evidence showing the participation of the Party Chancellery, under Hess, in the distribution of orders connected with the commission of war crimes – that Hess may have had knowledge of even if he did not participate in the crimes that were being committed in the East – and proposed laws discriminating against Jews and Poles; and that he signed decrees forcing certain groups of Poles to accept German citizenship. The Tribunal, however, does not find that the evidence sufficiently connects Hess with these crimes to sustain a finding of guilt.

As previously indicated the Tribunal found, after a full medical examination of and report on the condition of this defendant, that he should be tried, without any postponement of his case. Since that time further motions have been made that he should again be examined. These the Tribunal denied, after having had a report from the prison psychologist. That Hess acts in an abnormal manner, suffers from loss of memory and has mentally deteriorated during this trial may be true. But there is nothing to show that he does not realise the nature of the charges against him, or is incapable of defending himself. He was ably represented at the trial by counsel, appointed for that purpose by the Tribunal. There is no suggestion that Hess was not completely sane when the acts charged against him were committed.

Conclusion

The Tribunal finds the defendant Hess guilty on Counts One and Two: and not guilty on Counts Three and Four.

RIBBENTROP

Ribbentrop is indicted under all four counts. He joined the Nazi Party in 1932. By 1933 he had been made Foreign Policy Adviser to Hitler, and in the same year the representative of the Nazi Party on Foreign Policy. In 1934 he was appointed Delegate for Disarmament Questions, and in 1935 Minister Plenipotentiary at Large, a capacity in which he negotiated the Anglo-German Naval Agreement in 1935 and the Anti-Comintern Pact in 1936. On 11th August, 1936, he was appointed Ambassador to England. On 4th February, 1938, he succeeded von Neurath as Reichsminister for Foreign Affairs as part of the general reshuffle which accompanied the dismissal of von Fritsch and von Blomberg.

Crimes against peace

Ribbentrop was not present at the Hoszbach Conference held on 5th November, 1937, but on 2nd January, 1938, while still Ambassador to England, he sent a memorandum to Hitler indicating his opinion that a change in the status quo in the East in the German sense could only be carried out by force, and suggesting methods to prevent England and France from intervening in a European war fought to bring about such a change. When Ribbentrop became Foreign Minister, Hitler told him that Germany still had four problems to solve, Austria, Sudetenland, Memel and Danzig, and mentioned the possibility of "some sort of a showdown" or "military settlement" for their solution.

On 12th February, 1938, Ribbentrop attended the conference between Hitler and Schuschnigg at which Hitler, by threats of invasion, forced Schuschnigg to grant a series of concessions designed to strengthen the Nazis in Austria, including the appointment of Seyss-Inquart as Minister of Security and Interior, with control over the Police. Ribbentrop was in London when the occupation of Austria was actually carried out and, on the basis of information supplied him by Goering, informed the British Government that Germany had not presented Austria with an ultimatum, but had intervened in Austria only to prevent civil war. On 13th March, 1938, Ribbentrop signed the law incorporating Austria into the German Reich.

Ribbentrop participated in the aggressive plans against Czechoslovakia. Beginning in March, 1938, he was in close touch with the Sudeten German Party and gave them instructions which had the effect of keeping the Sudeten German question a live issue which might serve as an excuse for the attack which Germany was planning against Czechoslovakia. In August, 1938, he participated in a conference for the purpose of obtaining Hungarian support in the event of a war with Czechoslovakia. After the Munich Pact he continued to bring diplomatic pressure with the object of occupying the remainder of Czechoslovakia. He was instrumental in inducing the Slovaks to proclaim their independence. He was present at the conference of 14th–15th March, 1939, at which Hitler, by threats of invasion, compelled President Hácha to consent to the German occupation of Czechoslovakia. After the German troops had marched in, Ribbentrop signed the law establishing a Protectorate over Bohemia and Moravia.

Ribbentrop played a particularly significant rôle in the diplomatic activity which led up to the attack on Poland. He participated in a conference held on 12th August, 1939, for the purpose of obtaining Italian support if the attack should lead to a general European war. Ribbentrop discussed the German demands with respect to Danzig and the Polish Corridor with the British Ambassador in the period from 25th August to 30th August, 1939, when he knew that the German plans to attack Poland had merely been temporarily postponed in an attempt to induce the British to abandon their guarantee to the Poles. The way in which he carried out these discussions makes it clear that he did not enter them in good faith in an attempt to reach a settlement of the difficulties between Germany and Poland.

Ribbentrop was advised in advance of the attack on Norway and Denmark and of the attack on the Low Countries, and prepared the official Foreign Office memoranda attempting to justify these aggressive actions.

Ribbentrop attended the conference on 20th January, 1941, at which Hitler and Mussolini discussed the proposed attack on Greece, and the conference in January, 1941, at which Hitler obtained from Antonescu permission for German troops to go through Romania for this attack. On 25th March, 1941, when Yugoslavia adhered to the Axis Tripartite Pact, Ribbentrop had assured Yugoslavia that Germany would respect its sovereignty and territorial integrity. On 27th March, 1941, he attended the meeting, held after the *coup d'état* in Yugoslavia, at which plans were made to carry out Hitler's announced intention to destroy Yugoslavia.

Ribbentrop attended a conference in May, 1941, with Hitler and Antonescu relating to Romanian participation in the attack on the USSR. He also consulted with Rosenberg in the preliminary planning for the political exploitation of Soviet territories and in July, 1941, after the outbreak of war, urged Japan to attack the Soviet Union.

War crimes and crimes against humanity

Ribbentrop participated in a meeting of 6th June, 1944, at which it was agreed to start a programme under which Allied aviators carrying out machine gun attacks on the civilian population should be lynched. In December, 1944, Ribbentrop was informed of the plans to murder one of the French Generals held as a prisoner of war and directed his subordinates to see that the details were worked out in such a way as to prevent its detection by the protecting powers. Ribbentrop is also responsible for war crimes and crimes against humanity because of his activities with respect to occupied countries and Axis satellites. The top German official in both Denmark and Vichy France was a Foreign Office representative, and Ribbentrop is therefore responsible for the general economic and political policies put into effect in the occupation of those countries. He urged the Italians to adopt a ruthless occupation policy in Yugoslavia and Greece.

He played an important part in Hitler's "final solution" of the Jewish question. In September, 1942, he ordered the German diplomatic representatives accredited to various Axis satellites to hasten the deportation of Jews to the East. In June, 1942, the German Ambassador to Vichy requested Laval to turn over 50,000 Jews for deportation to the East. On 25th February, 1943, Ribbentrop protested to Mussolini against Italian slowness in deporting Jews from the Italian occupation zone of France. On 17th April, 1943, he took part in a conference between Hitler and Horthy on the deportation of Jews from Hungary and informed Horthy that the "Jews must either be exterminated or taken to concentration camps". At the same conference Hitler had likened the Jews to "tuberculosis bacilli" and said if they did not work they were to be shot.

Ribbentrop's defence to the charges made against him is that Hitler made all the important decisions and that he was such a great admirer and faithful follower of Hitler that he never questioned Hitler's repeated assertions that he wanted peace, or the truth of the reasons that Hitler gave in explaining aggressive action. The Tribunal does not consider this explanation to be true. Ribbentrop participated in all of the Nazi aggressions from the occupation of Austria to the invasion of the Soviet Union. Although he was personally concerned with the diplomatic rather than the military aspect of these actions, his diplomatic efforts were so closely connected with war that he could not have remained unaware of the aggressive nature of Hitler's actions. In the administration of territories over which Germany acquired control by illegal invasion, Ribbentrop also assisted in carrying out criminal policies, particularly those involving the extermination of the Jews. There is abundant evidence, moreover, that Ribbentrop was in complete sympathy with all the main tenets of the National Socialist creed, and that his collaboration with Hitler and with other defendants in the commission of crimes against peace, war crimes and crimes against humanity was wholehearted. It was because Hitler's policy and plans coincided with his own ideas that Ribbentrop served him so willingly to the end.

Conclusion

The Tribunal finds Ribbentrop guilty on all four counts.

KEITEL

Keitel is indicted on all four counts. He was Chief of Staff to the then Minister of War von Blomberg from 1935 to 4th February, 1938; on that day Hitler took command of the Armed Forces, making Keitel Chief of the High Command of the Armed Forces. Keitel did not have command authority over the three Wehrmacht branches which enjoyed direct access to the Supreme Commander. OKW was in effect Hitler's military staff.

Crimes against peace

Keitel attended the Schuschnigg conference in February, 1938, with two other generals. Their presence, he admitted, was a "military demonstration", but since he had been appointed OKW Chief just one week before, he had not known why he had been summoned. Hitler and Keitel then continued to put pressure on Austria with false rumours, broadcasts and troop manœuvres. Keitel made the military and other arrangements and Jodl's diary noted "the effect is quick and strong". When Schuschnigg called his plebiscite, Keitel that night briefed Hitler and his generals, and Hitler issued "Case Otto", which Keitel initialled.

On 21st April, 1938, Hitler and Keitel considered making use of a possible "incident", such as the assassination of the German Minister at Prague, to preface the attack on Czechoslovakia. Keitel signed many directives and memoranda on "Fall Grün", including the directive of 30th May, containing Hitler's statement: "It is my unalterable decision to smash Czechoslovakia by military action in the near future." After Munich, Keitel initialled Hitler's directive for the attack on Czechoslovakia, and issued two supplements. The second supplement said the attack should appear to the outside world as "merely an act of pacification and not a warlike undertaking". The OKW Chief attended Hitler's negotiations with Hácha when the latter surrendered.

Keitel was present on 23rd May, 1939, when Hitler announced his decision "to attack Poland at the first suitable opportunity". Already he had signed the directive requiring the Wehrmacht to submit its "Fall Weiss" timetable to OKW by 1st May.

The invasion of Norway and Denmark he discussed on 12th December, 1939, with Hitler, Jodl and Raeder. By directive of 27th January, 1940, the Norway plans were placed under Keitel's "direct and personal guidance". Hitler had said on 23rd May, 1939, he would ignore the neutrality of Belgium and the Netherlands, and Keitel signed orders for these attacks on 15th October, 20th November and 28th November, 1939. Orders postponing this attack 17 times until spring, 1940, were all signed by Keitel or Jodl.

Formal planning for attacking Greece and Yugoslavia had begun in November, 1940. On 18th March, 1941, Keitel heard Hitler tell Raeder complete occupation of Greece was a prerequisite to settlement, and also heard Hitler decree on 27th March that the destruction of Yugoslavia should take place with "unmerciful harshness".

Keitel testified that he opposed the invasion of the Soviet Union for military reasons, and also because it would constitute a violation of the Non-Aggression Pact. Nevertheless, he initialled "Case Barbarossa", signed by Hitler on 18th December, 1940, and attended the OKW discussion with Hitler on 3rd February, 1941. Keitel's supplement of 13th March established the relationship between the military and political officers. He issued his timetable for the invasion on 6th June, 1941, and was present at the briefing of 14th June when the generals gave their final reports before attack. He appointed Jodl and Warlimont as OKW representatives to Rosenberg on matters concerning the Eastern Territories. On 16th June he directed all army units to carry out the economic directives issued by Goering in the so-called "Green Folder", for the exploitation of Russian territory, food and raw materials.

War crimes and crimes against humanity

On 4th August, 1942, Keitel issued a directive that paratroopers were to be turned over to the SD. On 18th October Hitler issued the Commando Order which was carried out in several instances. After the landing in Normandy, Keitel reaffirmed the order, and later extended it to Allied missions fighting with partisans. He admits he did not believe the order was legal but claims he could not stop Hitler from decreeing it.

When, on 8th September, 1941, OKW issued its ruthless regulations for the treatment of Soviet POWs, Canaris wrote to Keitel that under international law the SD should have nothing to do with this matter. On this memorandum in Keitel's handwriting, dated 23rd September and initialled by him, is the statement: "The objections arise from the military concept of chivalrous warfare. This is the destruction of an ideology. Therefore I approve and back the measures." Keitel testified that he really agreed with Canaris and argued with Hitler, but lost. The OKW Chief directed the military authorities to co-operate with the Einsatzstab Rosenberg in looting cultural property in occupied territories.

Lahousen testified that Keitel told him on 12th September, 1939, while aboard Hitler's headquarters train, that the Polish intelligentsia, nobility and Jews were to be liquidated. On 20th October Hitler told Keitel the intelligentsia would be prevented from forming a ruling class, the standard of living would remain low and Poland would be used only for labour forces. Keitel does not remember the Lahousen conversation, but admits there was such a policy and that he had protested without effect to Hitler about it.

On 16th September, 1941, Keitel ordered that attacks on soldiers in the East should be met by putting to death 50 to 100 Communists for one German soldier, with the comment that human life was less than nothing in the East. On 1st October he ordered military commanders always to have hostages to execute when German soldiers were attacked. When Terboven, the Reich Commissioner in Norway, wrote to Hitler that Keitel's suggestion that workmen's relatives be held responsible for sabotage could work only if firing squads were authorised, Keitel wrote on this memorandum in the margin: "Yes, that is the best."

On 12th May, 1941, five weeks before the invasion of the Soviet Union, the OKW urged upon Hitler a directive of the OKH that political commissars be liquidated by the Army. Keitel admitted the directive was passed on to field commanders. And on 13th May Keitel signed an order that civilians suspected of offences against troops should be shot without trial, and that prosecution of German soldiers for offences against civilians was unnecessary. On 27th July all copies of this directive were ordered destroyed without affecting its validity. Four days previously he had signed another order that legal punishment was inadequate and troops should use terrorism.

On 7th December, 1941, as already discussed in this opinion, the so-called "Nacht und Nebel" decree, over Keitel's signature, provided that in occupied territories civilians who had been accused of crimes of resistance against the army of occupation would be tried only if a death sentence was likely; otherwise they would be handed to the Gestapo for transportation to Germany.

Keitel directed that Russian POWs be used in German war industry. On 8th September, 1942, he ordered French, Dutch and Belgian citizens to work on the construction of the Atlantic Wall. He was present on 4th January, 1944, when Hitler directed Sauckel to obtain four million new workers from occupied territories.

In the face of these documents Keitel does not deny his connection with these acts. Rather, his defence relies on the fact that he is a soldier, and on the doctrine of "superior orders", prohibited by Article 8 of the Charter as a defence. There is nothing in mitigation. Superior orders, even to a soldier, cannot be considered in mitigation where crimes as shocking and extensive have been committed consciously, ruthlessly and without military excuse or justification.

Conclusion

The Tribunal finds Keitel guilty on all four counts.

KALTENBRUNNER

Kaltenbrunner is indicted under Counts One, Three and Four. He joined the Austrian Nazi Party and the SS in 1932. In 1935 he became leader of the SS in Austria. After the Anschluss he was appointed Austrian State Secretary for Security, and when this position was abolished in 1941 he was made Higher SS and Police Leader. On 30th January, 1943, he was appointed Chief of the Security Police and SD and Head of the Reich Security Head Office (RSHA), a position which had been held by Heydrich until his assassination in June, 1942. He held the rank of Obergruppenführer in the SS.

Crimes against peace

As leader of the SS in Austria, Kaltenbrunner was active in the Nazi intrigue against the Schuschnigg Government. On the night of 11th March, 1938, after Goering had ordered Austrian National Socialists to seize control of the Austrian Government, 500 Austrian SS men under Kaltenbrunner's command surrounded the Federal Chancellery, and a special detachment under the command of his adjutant entered the Federal Chancellery while Seyss-Inquart was negotiating with President Miklas. But there is no evidence connecting Kaltenbrunner with plans to wage aggressive war on any other front. The Anschluss, although it was an aggressive act, is not charged as an aggressive war, and the evidence against Kaltenbrunner under Count One does not in the opinion of the Tribunal, show his direct participation in any plan to wage such a war.

War crimes and crimes against humanity

When he became Chief of the Security Police and SD and Head of the RSHA on 30th January, 1943, Kaltenbrunner took charge of an organisation which included the main offices of the Gestapo, the SD and the Criminal Police. As Chief of the RSHA, Kaltenbrunner had authority to order protective custody to and release from concentration camps. Orders to this effect were normally sent over his signature. Kaltenbrunner was aware of conditions in concentration camps. He had undoubtedly visited Mauthausen, and witnesses testified that he had seen prisoners killed by the various methods of execution, hanging, shooting in the back of the neck and gassing, as part of a demonstration. Kaltenbrunner himself ordered the execution of prisoners in those camps, and his office was used to transmit to the camps execution orders which originated in Himmler's office. At the end of the war Kaltenbrunner participated in the arrangements for the evacuation of inmates of concentration camps, and the liquidation of many of them, to prevent them from being liberated by the Allied armies.

During the period in which Kaltenbrunner was Head of the RSHA, it was engaged in a widespread programme of war crimes and crimes against humanity. These crimes included the mistreatment and murder of prisoners of war. Einsatzkommandos operating under the control of the Gestapo were engaged in the screening of Soviet prisoners of war. Jews, Commissars and others who were thought to be ideologically hostile to the Nazi system were reported to the RSHA, which had them transferred to a concentration camp and murdered. An RSHA order issued during Kaltenbrunner's régime established the "Bullet Decree", under which certain escaped prisoners of war who were recaptured were taken to Mauthausen and shot. The order for the execution of commando troops was extended by the Gestapo to include parachutists while Kaltenbrunner was Chief of the RHSA. An order signed by Kaltenbrunner instructed the Police not to interfere with attacks on bailed out Allied fliers. In December, 1944, Kaltenbrunner participated in the murder of one of the French Generals held as a prisoner of war.

During the period in which Kaltenbrunner was Head of the RHSA, the Gestapo and SD in occupied territories continued the murder and ill-treatment of the population, using methods which included the torture and confinement in concentration camps, usually under orders to which Kaltenbrunner's name was signed.

The Gestapo was responsible for enforcing a rigid labour discipline on the slave labourers, and Kaltenbrunner established a series of labour reformatory camps for this purpose. When the SS embarked on a slave labour programme of its own, the Gestapo was used to obtain the needed workers by sending labourers to concentration camps.

The RSHA played a leading part in the "final solution" of the Jewish question by the extermination of the Jews. A special section under Amt IV of the RSHA was established to supervise this programme. Under its direction approximately six million Jews were murdered, of which two million were killed by Einsatzgruppen and other units of the Security Police. Kaltenbrunner had been informed of the activities of these Einsatzgruppen when he was a Higher SS and Police Leader, and they continued to function after he had become Chief of the RSHA.

The murder of approximately four million Jews in concentration camps has heretofore been described. This part of the programme was also under the supervision of the RSHA when Kaltenbrunner was head of that organisation, and special missions of the RSHA scoured the occupied territories and the various Axis satellites arranging for the deportation of Jews to these extermination institutions. Kaltenbrunner was informed of these activities. A letter which he wrote on 30th June, 1944, described the shipment to Vienna of 12,000 Jews for that purpose, and directed that all who could not work would have to be kept in readiness for "special action", which meant murder. Kaltenbrunner denied his signature to this letter, as he did on a very large number of orders on which his name was stamped or typed, and, in a few instances, written. It is inconceivable that in matters of such importance his signature could have appeared so many times without his authority.

Kaltenbrunner has claimed that when he took office as Chief of the Security Police and SD and as Head of the RSHA he did so pursuant to an understanding with Himmler under which he was to confine his activities to matters involving foreign intelligence, and not to assume overall control over the activities of the RSHA. He claims that the criminal programme had been started before his assumption of office; that he seldom knew what was going on; and that when he was informed he did what he could to stop them. It is true that he showed a special interest in matters involving foreign intelligence. But he exercised control over the activities of the RSHA, was aware of the crimes it was committing and was an active participant in many of them.

Conclusion

The Tribunal finds that Kaltenbrunner is not guilty on Count One. He is guilty under Counts Three and Four.

ROSENBERG

Rosenberg is indicted on all four counts. He joined the Nazi Party in 1919, participated in the Munich Putsch of 9th November, 1923, and tried to keep the illegal Nazi Party together while Hitler was in jail. Recognised as the Party's ideologist, he developed and spread Nazi doctrines in the newspapers *Völkischer Beobachter* and *N S Monatshefte*, which he edited, and in the numerous books he wrote. His book, *Myth of the Twentieth Century*, had a circulation of over a million copies.

In 1930 Rosenberg was elected to the Reichstag and he became the Party's representative for Foreign Affairs. In April, 1933, he was made Reichsleiter and head of the Office of Foreign Affairs of the NSDAP (the APA). Hitler, in January, 1934, appointed Rosenberg his Deputy for the supervision of the entire spiritual and ideological training of the NSDAP. In January, 1940, he was designated to set up the "Hohe Schule", the Centre of National Socialistic Ideological and Educational Research, and he organised the *Einsatzstab Rosenberg* in connection with this task. He was appointed Reich Minister for the Occupied Eastern Territories on 17th July, 1941.

Crimes against peace

As head of the APA, Rosenberg was in charge of an organisation whose agents were active in Nazi intrigue in all parts of the world. His own reports, for example, claim that the APA was largely responsible for Romania's joining the Axis. As head of the APA, he played an important role in the preparation and planning of the attack on Norway.

Rosenberg, together with Raeder, was one of the originators of the plan for attacking Norway. Rosenberg had become interested in Norway as early as June, 1939, when he conferred with Quisling. Quisling had pointed out the importance of the Norwegian coast in the event of a conflict between Germany and Great Britain, and stated his fears that Great Britain might be able to obtain Norwegian assistance. As a result of this conference Rosenberg arranged for Quisling to collaborate closely with the National Socialists and to receive political assistance by the Nazis.

When the war broke out, Quisling began to express fear of British intervention in Norway. Rosenberg supported this view, and transmitted to Raeder a plan to use Quisling for a coup in Norway. Rosenberg was instrumental in arranging the conferences in December, 1939, between Hitler and Quisling which led to the preparation of the attack on Norway, and at which Hitler promised Quisling financial assistance. After these conferences Hitler assigned to Rosenberg the political exploitation of Norway. Two weeks after Norway was occupied, Hitler told Rosenberg that he had based his decision to attack Norway "on the continuous warnings of Quisling as reported to him by Reichsleiter Rosenberg".

Rosenberg bears a major responsibility for the formulation and execution of occupation policies in the Occupied Eastern Territories. He was informed by Hitler on 2nd April, 1941, of the coming attack against the Soviet Union, and he agreed to help in the capacity of a "Political Adviser". On 20th April, 1941, he was appointed Commissioner for the Central Control of Questions connected with the East European Region. In preparing the plans for the occupation, he had numerous conferences with Keitel, Raeder, Goering, Funk, Ribbentrop and other high Reich authorities. In April and May, 1941, he prepared several drafts of instructions concerning the setting up of the administration in the Occupied Eastern Territories. On 20th June, 1941, two days before the attack on the USSR, he made a speech to his assistants about the problems and policies of occupation. Rosenberg attended Hitler's conference of 16th July, 1941, in the course of which policies of administration and occupation were discussed. On 17th July, 1941, Hitler appointed Rosenberg Reich Minister for the Occupied Eastern Territories, and publicly charged him with responsibility for civil administration.

War crimes and crimes against humanity

Rosenberg is responsible for a system of organised plunder of both public and private property throughout the invaded countries of Europe. Acting under Hitler's orders of January, 1940, to set up the "Hohe Schule", he organised and directed the Einsatzstab Rosenberg, which plundered museums and libraries, confiscated art treasures and collections and pillaged private houses. His own reports show the extent of the confiscations. In "Action-M" (Möbel), instituted in December, 1941, at Rosenberg's suggestion, 69,619 Jewish homes were plundered in the West, 38,000 of them in Paris alone, and it took 26,984 railroad cars to transport the confiscated furnishings to Germany. As of 14th July, 1944, more than 21,903 art objects, including famous paintings and museum pieces, had been seized by the Einsatzstab in the West.

With his appointment as Reich Minister for Occupied Eastern Territories on 17th July, 1941, Rosenberg became the supreme authority for those areas. He helped to formulate the policies of Germanisation, exploitation, forced labour, and extermination of Jews and opponents of Nazi rule, and he set up the administration which carried them out. He took part in the conference of 16th July, 1941, in which Hitler stated that they were faced with the task of "cutting up the giant cake according to our needs, in order to be able: first, to dominate it, second, to administer it, and third, to exploit it", and he indicated that ruthless action was contemplated. Rosenberg accepted his appointment on the following day.

Rosenberg had knowledge of the brutal treatment and terror to which the Eastern people were subjected. He directed that the Hague Rules of Land Warfare were not applicable in the Occupied Eastern Territories. He had knowledge of and took an active part in stripping the Eastern Territories of raw materials and foodstuffs, which were all sent to Germany. He stated that feeding the German people was first on the list of claims on the East, and that the Soviet people would suffer thereby. His directives provided for the segregation of Jews, ultimately in ghettos. His subordinates engaged in mass killings of Jews, and his civil administrators in the East considered that cleansing the Eastern Occupied Territories of Jews was necessary. In December, 1941, Rosenberg made the suggestion to Hitler that in a case of shooting 100 hostages, Jews only be used. Rosenberg had knowledge of the deportation of labourers from the East, of the methods of "recruiting" and the transportation horrors, and of the treatment Eastern labourers received in the Reich. He gave his civil administrators quotas of labourers to be sent to the Reich, which had to be met by whatever means necessary. His signature of approval appears on the order of 14th June, 1944, for the "Heu Aktion", the apprehension of 40,000 to 50,000 youths, aged 10–14, for shipment to the Reich.

Upon occasion Rosenberg objected to the excesses and atrocities committed by his subordinates, notably in the case of Koch, but these excesses continued and he stayed in office until the end.

Conclusion

The Tribunal finds that Rosenberg is guilty on all four counts.

FRANK

Frank is indicted under Counts One, Three and Four. Frank joined the Nazi Party in 1927. He became a member of the Reichstag in 1930, the Bavarian State Minister of Justice in March, 1933, and when this position was incorporated into the Reich Government in 1934, Reich Minister without Portfolio. He was made a Reichsleiter of the Nazi Party in charge of Legal Affairs in 1933, and in the same year President of the Academy of German Law. Frank was also given the honorary rank of Obergruppenführer in the SA. In 1942 Frank became involved in a temporary dispute with Himmler as to the type of legal system which should be in effect in Germany. During the same year he was dismissed as Reichsleiter of the Nazi Party and as President of the Academy of German Law.

Crimes against peace

The evidence has not satisfied the Tribunal that Frank was sufficiently connected with the common plan to wage aggressive war to allow the Tribunal to convict him on Count One.

War crimes and crimes against humanity

Frank was appointed Chief Civil Administration Officer for occupied Polish territory and, on 12th October, 1939, was made Governor-General of the occupied Polish territory. On 3rd October, 1939, he described the policy which he intended to put into effect by stating: "Poland shall be treated like a colony; the Poles will become the slaves of the Greater German World Empire." The evidence establishes that this occupation policy was based on the complete destruction of Poland as a national entity, and a ruthless exploitation of its human and economic resources for the German war effort. All opposition was crushed with the utmost harshness. A reign of terror was instituted, backed by summary police courts which ordered such actions as the public shootings of groups of twenty to two hundred Poles, and the widespread shootings of hostages. The concentration camp system was introduced in the General-Government by the establishment of the notorious Treblinka and Maydanek camps. As early as 6th February, 1940, Frank gave an indication of the extent of this reign of terror by his cynical comment to a newspaper reporter on von Neurath's poster announcing the execution of the Czech students: "If I wished to order that one should hang up posters about every seven Poles shot, there would not be enough forests in Poland with which to make the paper for these posters." On 30th May, 1940, Frank told a police conference that he was taking advantage of the offensive in the West, which diverted the attention of the world from Poland, to liquidate thousands of Poles who would be likely to resist German domination of Poland, including "the leading representatives of the Polish intelligentsia". Pursuant to these instructions the brutal AB action was begun under which the Security Police and SD carried out these exterminations which were only partially subjected to the restraints of legal procedure. On 2nd October, 1943, Frank issued a decree under which any non-Germans hindering German construction in the General-Government were to be tried by summary courts of the Security Police and SD and sentenced to death.

The economic demands made on the General-Government were far in excess of the needs of the army of occupation, and were out of all proportion to the resources of the country. The food raised in Poland was shipped to Germany on such a wide scale that the rations of the population of the Occupied Territories were reduced to the starvation level and epidemics were widespread. Some steps were taken to provide for the feeding of the agricultural workers who were used to raise the crops, but the requirements of the rest of the population were disregarded. It is undoubtedly true, as argued by Counsel for the Defence, that some suffering in the General-Government was inevitable as a result of the ravages of war and the economic confusion resulting therefrom. But the suffering was increased by a planned policy of economic exploitation.

Frank introduced the deportation of slave labourers to Germany in the very early stages of his administration. On 25th January, 1940, he indicated his intention of deporting one million labourers to Germany, suggesting on 10th May, 1940, the use of police raids to meet this quota. On 18th August, 1942, Frank reported that he had already supplied 800,000 workers for the

Reich, and expected to be able to supply 140,000 more before the end of the year.

The persecution of the Jews was immediately begun in the General-Government. The area originally contained from 2,500,000 to 3,500,000 Jews. They were forced into ghettos, subjected to discriminatory laws, deprived of the food necessary to avoid starvation and finally systematically and brutally exterminated. On 16th December, 1941, Frank told the Cabinet of the Governor-General: "We must annihilate the Jews wherever we find them and wherever it is possible, in order to maintain there the structure of the Reich as a whole." By 25th January, 1944, Frank estimated that there were only 100,000 Jews left.

At the beginning of his testimony, Frank stated that he had a feeling of "terrible guilt" for the atrocities committed in the Occupied Territories. But his defence was largely devoted to an attempt to prove that he was not in fact responsible; that he ordered only the necessary pacification measures; that the excesses were due to the activities of the Police which were not under his control; and that he never even knew of the activities of the concentration camps. It has also been argued that the starvation was due to the aftermath of the war and policies carried out under the Four Year Plan; that the forced labour programme was under the direction of Sauckel; and that the extermination of the Jews was by the Police and SS under direct orders from Himmler.

It is undoubtedly true that most of the criminal programme charged against Frank was put into effect through the Police; that Frank had jurisdictional difficulties with Himmler over the control of the Police; and that Hitler resolved many of these disputes in favour of Himmler. It therefore may well be true that some of the crimes committed in the General-Government were committed without the knowledge of Frank, and even occasionally despite his opposition. It may also be true that some of the criminal policies put into effect in the General-Government did not originate with Frank but were carried out pursuant to orders from Germany. But it is also true that Frank was a willing and knowing participant in the use of terrorism in Poland; in the economic exploitation of Poland in a way which led to the death by starvation of a large number of people; in the deportation to Germany as slave labourers of over a million Poles; and in a programme involving the murder of at least three million Jews.

Conclusion

The Tribunal finds that Frank is not guilty on Count One but guilty under Counts Three and Four.

FRICK

Frick is indicted on all four counts. Recognised as the chief Nazi administrative specialist and bureaucrat, he was appointed Reichsminister of the

Interior in Hitler's first cabinet. He retained this important position until August, 1943, when he was appointed Reich Protector of Bohemia and Moravia. In connection with his duties at the centre of all internal and domestic administration, he became the Prussian Minister of the Interior, Reich Director of Elections, General Plenipotentiary for the Administration of the Reich, and a member of the Reich Defence Council, the Ministerial Council for Defence of the Reich and the "Three Man College". As the several countries incorporated into the Reich were overrun, he was placed at the head of the Central Offices for their incorporation.

Though Frick did not officially join the Nazi Party until 1925, he had previously allied himself with Hitler and the National Socialist cause during the Munich Putsch, while he was an official in the Munich Police Department. Elected to the Reichstag in 1924, he became a Reichsleiter as leader of the National Socialist faction in that body.

Crimes against peace

An avid Nazi, Frick was largely responsible for bringing the German nation under the complete control of the NSDAP. After Hitler became Reich Chancellor, the new Minister of the Interior immediately began to incorporate local governments under the sovereignty of the Reich. The numerous laws he drafted, signed and administered abolished all opposition parties and prepared the way for the Gestapo and their concentration camps to extinguish all individual opposition. He was largely responsible for the legislation which suppressed the trade unions, the Church and the Jews. He performed this task with ruthless efficiency.

Before the date of the Austrian aggression Frick was concerned only with domestic administration within the Reich. The evidence does not show that he participated in any of the conferences at which Hitler outlined his aggressive intentions. Consequently, the Tribunal takes the view that Frick was not a member of the common plan or conspiracy to wage aggressive war as defined in this Judgment.

Six months after the seizure of Austria, under the provisions of the Reich Defence Law of 4th September, 1938, Frick became General Plenipotentiary for the Administration of the Reich. He was made responsible for war administration, except the military and economic, in the event of Hitler proclaiming a state of defence. The Reich Ministries of Justice, Education, Religion and the Office of Spatial Planning were made subordinate to him. Performing his allotted duties, Frick devised an administrative organisation in accordance with wartime standards. According to his own statement, this was actually put into operation after Germany decided to adopt a policy of war.

Frick signed the law of 13th March, 1938, which united Austria with the Reich, and he was made responsible for its accomplishment. In setting up German administration in Austria, he issued decrees which introduced

German law, the Nürnberg Decrees, the Military Service Law and he provided for police security by Himmler.

He also signed the laws incorporating into the Reich the Sudetenland, Memel, Danzig, the Eastern Territories (West Prussia and Posen) and Eupen, Malmedy and Moresnot. He was placed in charge of the actual incorporation and of the establishment of German administration over these territories. He signed the law establishing the Protectorate of Bohemia and Moravia.

As the head of the Central Offices for Bohemia and Moravia, the Government-General and Norway, he was charged with obtaining close co-operation between the German officials in these occupied countries and the supreme authorities of the Reich. He supplied German civil servants for the administrations in all Occupied Territories, advising Rosenberg as to their assignment in the Occupied Eastern Territories. He signed the laws appointing Terboven as Reich Commissioner to Norway and Seyss-Inquart to Holland.

War crimes and crimes against humanity

Always rabidly anti-Semitic, Frick drafted, signed and administered many laws designed to eliminate Jews from German life and economy. His work formed the basis of the Nürnberg Decrees, and he was active in enforcing them. Responsible for prohibiting Jews from following various professions, and for confiscating their property, he signed a final decree in 1943, after the mass destruction of Jews in the East, which placed them "outside the law" and handed them over to the Gestapo. These laws paved the way for the "final solution", and were extended by Frick to the Incorporated Territories and to certain of the Occupied Territories. While he was Reich Protector of Bohemia and Moravia, thousands of Jews were transferred from the Terezin Ghetto in Czechoslovakia to Auschwitz, where they were killed. He issued a decree providing for special penal laws against Jews and Poles in the Government-General.

The Police officially fell under the jurisdiction of the Reichsminister of the Interior. But Frick actually exercised little control over Himmler and police matters. However, he signed the law appointing Himmler Chief of the German Police, as well as the decrees establishing Gestapo jurisdiction over concentration camps and regulating the execution of orders for protective custody. From the many complaints he received, and from the testimony of witnesses, the Tribunal concludes that he knew of atrocities committed in these camps. With knowledge of Himmler's methods, Frick signed decrees authorising him to take necessary security measures in certain of the Incorporated Territories. What these "security measures" turned out to be has already been dealt with.

As the Supreme Reich Authority in Bohemia and Moravia, Frick bears general responsibility for the acts of oppression in that territory after 20th

August, 1943, such as terrorism of the population, slave labour and the deportation of Jews to the concentration camps for extermination. It is true that Frick's duties as Reich Protector were considerably more limited than those of his predecessor, and that he had no legislative and limited personal executive authority in the Protectorate. Nevertheless, Frick knew full well what the Nazi policies of occupation were in Europe, particularly with respect to Jews, at that time, and by accepting the office of Reich Protector he assumed responsibility for carrying out those policies in Bohemia and Moravia.

German citizenship in the occupied countries as well as in the Reich came under his jurisdiction while he was Minister of the Interior. Having created a racial register of persons of German extraction, Frick conferred German citizenship on certain categories of citizens of foreign countries. He is responsible for Germanisation in Austria, Sudetenland, Memel, Danzig, Eastern Territories (West Prussia and Posen) and in the territories of the Eupen, Malmedy and Moresnot. He forced on the citizens of these territories German law, German courts, German education, German police security and compulsory military service.

During the war nursing homes, hospitals and asylums in which euthanasia was practised as described elsewhere in this Judgment, came under Frick's jurisdiction. He had knowledge that insane, sick and aged people, "useless eaters", were being systematically put to death. Complaints of these murders reached him, but he did nothing to stop them. A report of the Czechoslovak War Crimes Commission estimated that 275,000 mentally deficient and aged people, for whose welfare he was responsible, fell victim to it.

Conclusion

The Tribunal finds that Frick is not guilty on Count One. He is guilty on Counts Two, Three and Four.

STREICHER

Streicher is indicted on Counts One and Four. One of the earliest members of the Nazi Party, joining in 1921, he took part in the Munich Putsch. From 1925 to 1940 he was Gauleiter of Franconia. Elected to the Reichstag in 1933, he was an honorary general in the SA. His persecution of the Jews was notorious. He was the publisher of *Der Stürmer*, an anti-Semitic weekly newspaper, from 1923 to 1945 and was its editor until 1933.

Crimes against peace

Streicher was a staunch Nazi and supporter of Hitler's main policies. There is no evidence to show that he was ever within Hitler's inner circle of advisers; nor during his career was he closely connected with the formulation of the policies which led to war. He was never present, for example, at any of the important conferences when Hitler explained his decisions to his leaders. Although he was a Gauleiter there is no evidence to prove that he had knowledge of those policies. In the opinion of the Tribunal, the evidence fails to establish his connection with the conspiracy or common plan to wage aggressive war as that conspiracy has been elsewhere defined in this Judgment.

Crimes against humanity

For his twenty-five years of speaking, writing and preaching hatred of the Jews, Streicher was widely known as "Jew-Baiter Number One". In his speeches and articles, week after week, month after month, he infected the German mind with the virus of anti-Semitism, and incited the German people to active persecution. Each issue of *Der Stürmer*, which reached a circulation of 600,000 in 1935, was filled with such articles, often lewd and disgusting.

Streicher had charge of the Jewish boycott of 1st April, 1933. He advocated the Nürnberg Decrees of 1935. He was responsible for the demolition on 10th August, 1938, of the Synagogue in Nürnberg. And on 10th November, 1938, he spoke publicly in support of the Jewish pogrom which was taking place at that time.

But it was not only in Germany that this defendant advocated his doctrines. As early as 1938 he began to call for the annihilation of the Jewish race. Twenty-three different articles of *Der Stürmer* between 1938 and 1941 were produced in evidence, in which the extermination "root and branch" was preached. Typical of his teachings was a leading article in September, 1938, which termed the Jew a germ and a pest, not a human being, but "a parasite, an enemy, an evil-doer, a disseminator of diseases who must be destroyed in the interest of mankind". Other articles urged that only when world Jewry had been annihilated would the Jewish problem have been solved, and predicted that fifty years hence the Jewish graves "will proclaim that this people of murderers and criminals has after all met its deserved fate". Streicher, in February, 1940, published a letter from one of *Der Stürmer*'s readers which compared Jews with swarms of locusts which must be exterminated completely. Such was the poison Streicher injected into the minds of thousands of Germans which caused them to follow the National Socialists' policy of Jewish persecution and extermination. A leading article of *Der Stürmer* in May, 1939, shows clearly his aim:

> A punitive expedition must come against the Jews in Russia. A punitive expedition which will provide the same fate for them that every murderer and criminal must expect. Death sentence and execution. The Jews in Russia must be killed. They must be exterminated root and branch.

527

As the war in the early stages proved successful in acquiring more and more territory for the Reich, Streicher even intensified his efforts to incite the Germans against the Jews. In the record are twenty-six articles from *Der Stürmer*, published between August, 1941, and September, 1944, twelve by Streicher's own hand, which demanded annihilation and extermination in unequivocal terms. He wrote and published on 25th December, 1941:

> If the danger of the reproduction of that curse of God in the Jewish blood is to finally come to an end, then there is only one way – the extermination of that people whose father is the devil.

And in February, 1944, his own article stated:

> Whoever does what a Jew does is a scoundrel, a criminal. And he who repeats and wishes to copy him deserves the same fate, annihilation, death.

With knowledge of the extermination of the Jews in the Occupied Eastern Territories, this defendant continued to write and publish his propaganda of death. Testifying in this trial, he vehemently denied any knowledge of mass executions of Jews. But the evidence makes it clear that he continually received current information on the progress of the "final solution". His press photographer was sent to visit the ghettos of the East in the spring of 1943, the time of the destruction of the Warsaw Ghetto. The Jewish newspaper, *Israelitisches Wochenblatt*, which Streicher received and read, carried in each issue accounts of Jewish atrocities in the East, and gave figures on the number of Jews who had been deported and killed. For example, issues appearing in the summer and fall of 1942 reported the death of 72,729 Jews in Warsaw, 17,542 in Lodz, 18,000 in Croatia, 125,000 in Romania, 14,000 in Latvia, 85,000 in Yugoslavia, 700,000 in all of Poland. In November, 1943, Streicher quoted verbatim an article from the *Israelitisches Wochenblatt* which stated that the Jews had virtually disappeared from Europe, and commented: "This is not a Jewish lie." In December, 1942, referring to an article in the *London Times* about the atrocities, aiming at extermination, Streicher said that Hitler had given warning that the Second World War would lead to the destruction of Jewry. In January, 1943, he wrote and published an article which said that Hitler's prophecy was being fulfilled, that world Jewry was being extirpated, and that it was wonderful to know that Hitler was freeing the world of its Jewish tormentors.

In the face of the evidence before the Tribunal it is idle for Streicher to suggest that the solution of the Jewish problem which he favoured was strictly limited to the classification of Jews as aliens and the passing of discriminatory legislation such as the Nürnberg Decrees, supplemented if possible by international agreement on the creation of a Jewish State somewhere in the world, to which all Jews should emigrate.

Streicher's incitement to murder and extermination at the time when

Jews in the East were being killed under the most horrible conditions clearly constitutes persecution on political and racial grounds in connection with war crimes, as defined by the Charter, and constitutes a crime against humanity.

Conclusion

The Tribunal finds that Streicher is not guilty of Count One, but that he is guilty on Count Four.

FUNK

Funk is indicted under all four counts. Funk, who had previously been a financial journalist, joined the Nazi Party in 1931, and shortly thereafter became one of Hitler's personal economic advisers. On 30th January, 1933, Funk was made Press Chief in the Reich Government, and on 11th March, 1933, became Under Secretary in the Ministry of Propaganda and shortly thereafter a leading figure in the various Nazi organisations which were used to control the press, films, music and publishing houses. Funk took office as Minister of Economics and Plenipotentiary General for War Economy in early 1938 and as President of the Reichsbank in January, 1939. He succeeded Schacht in all three of these positions. He was made a member of the Ministerial Council for the Defence of the Reich in August, 1939, and a member of the Central Planning Board in September, 1943.

Crimes against peace

Funk became active in the economic field after the Nazi plans to wage aggressive war had been clearly defined. One of his representatives attended a conference on 14th October, 1938, at which Goering announced a gigantic increase in armaments and instructed the Ministry of Economics to increase exports to obtain the necessary exchange. On 28th January, 1939, one of Funk's subordinates sent a memorandum to the OKW on the use of prisoners of war to make up labour deficiencies which would arise in case of mobilisation. On 30th May, 1939, the Under Secretary of the Ministry of Economics attended a meeting at which detailed plans were made for the financing of the war.

On 25th August, 1939, Funk wrote a letter to Hitler expressing his gratitude that he had been able to participate in such world-shaking events; that his plans for the "financing of the war", for the control of wage and price conditions and for the strengthening of the Reichsbank had been completed; and that he had inconspicuously transferred into gold all foreign exchange resources available to Germany. On 14th October, 1939, after the war had begun, Funk made a speech in which he stated that the economic and financial departments of Germany working under the Four Year Plan had been engaged in the secret economic preparation for war for over a year.

Funk participated in the economic planning which preceded the attack on the USSR. His deputy held daily conferences with Rosenberg on the economic problems which would arise in the occupation of Soviet territory. Funk himself participated in planning for the printing of rouble notes in Germany prior to the attack to serve as occupation currency in the USSR. After the attack he made a speech in which he described plans he had made for the economic exploitation of the "vast territories of the Soviet Union", which were to be used as a source of raw material for Europe.

Funk was not one of the leading figures in originating the Nazi plans for aggressive war. His activity in the economic sphere was under the supervision of Goering as Plenipotentiary General of the Four Year Plan. He did, however, participate in the economic preparation for certain of the aggressive wars, notably those against Poland and the Soviet Union, but his guilt can be adequately dealt with under Count Two of the Indictment.

War crimes and crimes against humanity

In his capacity as Under Secretary in the Ministry of Propaganda and Vice-Chairman of the Reich Chamber of Culture, Funk had participated in the early Nazi programme of economic discrimination against the Jews. On 12th November, 1938, after the pogroms of November, he attended a meeting held under the chairmanship of Goering to discuss the solution of the Jewish problem, and proposed a decree providing for the banning of Jews from all business activities, which Goering issued the same day under the authority of the Four Year Plan. Funk has testified that he was shocked at the outbreaks of 10th November, but on 15th November he made a speech describing these outbreaks as a "violent explosion of the disgust of the German people, because of a criminal Jewish attack against the German people", and saying that the elimination of the Jews from economic life followed logically their elimination from political life.

In 1942 Funk entered into an agreement with Himmler under which the Reichsbank was to receive certain gold and jewels and currency from the SS, and instructed his subordinates, who were to work out the details, not to ask too many questions. As a result of this agreement the SS sent to the Reichsbank the personal belongings taken from the victims who had been exterminated in the concentration camps. The Reichsbank kept the coins and banknotes and sent the jewels, watches and personal belongings to Berlin Municipal Pawn Shops. The gold from the eyeglasses, gold teeth and fillings was stored in the Reichsbank vaults. Funk has protested that he did not know that the Reichsbank was receiving articles of this kind. The Tribunal is of the opinion that Funk either knew what was being received or was deliberately closing his eyes to what was being done.

As Minister of Economics and President of the Reichsbank, Funk participated in the economic exploitation of Occupied Territories. He was President of the Continental Oil Company, which was charged with the exploitation of the oil resources of Occupied Territories in the East. He was responsible for the seizure of the gold reserves of the Czechoslovakian National Bank and for the liquidation of the Yugoslavian National Bank. On 6th June, 1942, Funk's deputy sent a letter to the OKW requesting that funds from the French Occupation Cost Fund be made available for black market purchases. Funk's knowledge of German occupation policies is shown by his presence at the meeting of 8th August, 1942, at which Goering addressed the various German occupation chiefs, told them of the products required from their territories and added: "It makes no difference to me in this connection if you say that your people will starve."

In the fall of 1943 Funk was a member of the Central Planning Board, which determined the total number of labourers needed for German industry and required Sauckel to produce them, usually by deportation from Occupied Territories. Funk did not appear to be particularly interested in this aspect of the forced labour programme, and usually sent a deputy to attend the meetings, often SS General Ohlendorf, the former Chief of the SD inside of Germany and the former Commander of Einsatzgruppe D. But Funk was aware that the Board of which he was a member was demanding the importation of slave labourers and allocating them to the various industries under its control.

As President of the Reichsbank, Funk was also indirectly involved in the utilisation of concentration camp labour. Under his direction the Reichsbank set up a revolving fund of 12,000,000 Reichsmarks to the credit of the SS for the construction of factories to use concentration camp labourers.

In spite of the fact that he occupied important official positions, Funk was never a dominant figure in the various programmes in which he participated. This is a mitigating fact of which the Tribunal takes notice.

Conclusion

The Tribunal finds that Funk is not guilty on Count One but is guilty under Counts Two, Three and Four.

SCHACHT

Schacht is indicted under Counts One and Two of the Indictment. Schacht served as Commissioner of Currency and President of the Reichsbank from 1923 to 1930; was reappointed President of the bank on 17th March, 1933; Minister of Economics in August, 1934; and Plenipotentiary General for War Economy in May, 1935. He resigned from these two positions in November, 1937, and was appointed Minister without Portfolio. He was reappointed as President of the Reichsbank for a one-year term on 16th March, 1937, and for a four-year term on 9th March, 1938, but was dismissed on 20th January, 1939. He was dismissed as Minister without Portfolio on 22nd January, 1943.

Crimes against peace

Schacht was an active supporter of the Nazi Party before its accession to power on 30th January, 1933, and supported the appointment of Hitler to the post of Chancellor. After that date he played an important rôle in the vigorous rearmament programme which was adopted, using the facilities of the Reichsbank to the fullest extent in the German rearmament effort. The Reichsbank, in its traditional capacity as financial agent for the German Government, floated long-term Government loans, the proceeds of which were used for rearmament. He devised a system under which five-year notes, known as MEFO bills, guaranteed by the Reichsbank and backed, in effect, by nothing more than its position as a bank of issue, were used to obtain large sums for rearmament from the short-term money market. As Minister of Economics and as Plenipotentiary General for War Economy he was active in organising the German economy for war. He made detailed plans for industrial mobilisation and the co-ordination of the Army with industry in the event of war. He was particularly concerned with shortages of raw materials and started a scheme of stock-piling, and a system of exchange control designed to prevent Germany's weak foreign exchange position from hindering the acquisition abroad of raw materials needed for rearmament. On 3rd May, 1935, he sent a memorandum to Hitler stating that "the accomplishment of the armament programme with speed and in quantity is the problem of German politics, that everything else, therefore, should be subordinated to this purpose".

Schacht, by April, 1936, began to lose his influence as the central figure in the German rearmament effort when Goering was appointed Co-ordinator for Raw Materials and Foreign Exchange. Goering advocated a greatly expanded programme for the production of synthetic raw materials, which was opposed by Schacht on the ground that the resulting financial strain might involve inflation. The influence of Schacht suffered further when on 16th October, 1936, Goering was appointed Plenipotentiary for the Four Year Plan, with the task of putting "the entire economy in a state of readiness for war" within four years. Schacht had opposed the announcement of this plan and the appointment of Goering to head it, and it is clear that Hitler's action represented a decision that Schacht's economic policies were too conservative for the drastic rearmament policy which Hitler wanted to put into effect.

After Goering's appointment, Schacht and Goering promptly became embroiled in a series of disputes. Although there was an element of personal controversy running through these disputes, Schacht disagreed with Goering on certain basic policy issues. Schacht, on financial grounds, advocated a retrenchment in the rearmament programme; opposed as uneconomical

much of the proposed expansion of production facilities, particularly for syn-
thetics; and urged a drastic tightening on government credit and a cautious
policy in dealing with Germany's foreign exchange reserves. As a result of
this dispute, and of a bitter argument in which Hitler accused Schacht of
upsetting his plans by his financial methods, Schacht went on leave of
absence from the Ministry of Economics on 5th September, 1937, and
resigned as Minister of Economics and as Plenipotentiary General for War
Economy on 16th November, 1937.

As President of the Reichsbank, Schacht was still involved in disputes.
Throughout 1938 the Reichsbank continued to function as the financial
agent for the German Government in floating long-term loans to finance
armaments. But on 31st March, 1938, Schacht discontinued the practice of
floating short-term notes guaranteed by the Reichsbank for armament
expenditures. At the end of 1938, in an attempt to regain control of fiscal
policy through the Reichsbank, Schacht refused an urgent request of the
Reichsminister of Finance for a special credit to pay the salaries of civil servants which were not covered by existing funds. On 2nd January, 1939,
Schacht held a conference with Hitler at which he urged him to reduce
expenditures for armaments. On 7th January, 1939, Schacht submitted to
Hitler a report signed by the Directors of the Reichsbank which urged a
drastic curtailment of armament expenditures and a balanced budget as the
only method of preventing inflation. On 19th January, Hitler dismissed
Schacht as President of the Reichsbank. On 22nd January, 1943, Hitler dismissed Schacht as Reich Minister without Portfolio because of his "whole
attitude during the present fateful fight of the German nation". On 23rd
July, 1944, Schacht was arrested by the Gestapo and confined in a concentration camp until the end of the war.

It is clear that Schacht was a central figure in Germany's rearmament
programme, and the steps which he took, particularly in the early days of the
Nazi régime, were responsible for Nazi Germany's rapid rise as a military
power. But rearmament of itself is not criminal under the Charter. To be a
crime against peace under Article 6 of the Charter it must be shown that
Schacht carried out this rearmament as part of the Nazi plans to wage aggressive wars.

Schacht has contended that he participated in the rearmament programme only because he wanted to build up a strong and independent
Germany which would carry out a foreign policy which would command
respect on an equal basis with other European countries; that when he discovered that the Nazis were rearming for aggressive purposes he attempted
to slow down the speed of rearmament; and that after the dismissal of von
Fritsch and von Blomberg he participated in plans to get rid of Hitler, first
by deposing him and later by assassination.

Schacht, as early as 1936, began to advocate a limitation of the rearmament programme for financial reasons. Had the policies advocated by him
been put into effect, Germany would not have been prepared for a general

European war. Insistence on his policies led to his eventual dismissal from all positions of economic significance in Germany. On the other hand, Schacht, with his intimate knowledge of German finance, was in a peculiarly good position to understand the true significance of Hitler's frantic rearmament, and to realise that the economic policy adopted was consistent only with war as its object.

Moreover, Schacht continued to participate in German economic life and even, in a minor way, in some of the early Nazi aggressions. Prior to the occupation of Austria he set a rate of exchange between the mark and the schilling. After the occupation of Austria he arranged for the incorporation of the Austrian National Bank into the Reichsbank and made a violently pro-Nazi speech in which he stated that the Reichsbank would always be Nazi as long as he was connected with it; praised Hitler; defended the occupation of Austria; scoffed at objections to the way it was carried out; and ended with "to our Führer a triple 'Sieg Heil'". He has not contended that this speech did not represent his state of mind at the time. After the occupation of the Sudetenland, he arranged for currency conversion and for the incorporation into the Reichsbank of local Czech banks of issue. On 29th November, 1938, he made a speech in which he pointed with pride to his economic policy, which had created the high degree of German armament, and added that this armament had made Germany's foreign policy possible.

Schacht was not involved in the planning of any of the specific wars of aggression charged in Count Two. His participation in the occupation of Austria and the Sudetenland (neither of which are charged as aggressive wars) was on such a limited basis that it does not amount to participation in the common plan charged in Count One. He was clearly not one of the inner circle around Hitler which was most closely involved with this common plan. He was regarded by this group with undisguised hostility. The testimony of Speer shows that Schacht's arrest on 23rd July, 1944, was based as much on Hitler's enmity towards Schacht, growing out of his attitude before the war, as it was on suspicion of his complicity in the bomb plot. The case against Schacht therefore depends on the inference that Schacht did in fact know of the Nazi aggressive plans.

On this all important question evidence has been given for the Prosecution, and a considerable volume of evidence for the Defence. The Tribunal has considered the whole of this evidence with great care, and comes to the conclusion that this necessary inference has not been established beyond a reasonable doubt.

Conclusion

The Tribunal finds that Schacht is not guilty on this Indictment, and directs that he shall be discharged by the Marshal, when the Tribunal presently adjourns.

DOENITZ

Doenitz is indicted on Counts One, Two and Three. In 1935 he took command of the first U-boat flotilla commissioned since 1918, became in 1936 commander of the submarine arm, was made Vice-Admiral in 1940, Admiral in 1942 and on 30th January, 1943, Commander-in-Chief of the German Navy. On 1st May, 1945, he became the Head of State, succeeding Hitler.

Crimes against peace

Although Doenitz built and trained the German U-boat arm, the evidence does not show he was privy to the conspiracy to wage aggressive wars or that he prepared and initiated such wars. He was a line officer performing strictly tactical duties. He was not present at the important conferences when plans for aggressive wars were announced, and there is no evidence he was informed about the decisions reached there. Doenitz did, however, wage aggressive war within the meaning of that word as used by the Charter. Submarine warfare which began immediately upon the outbreak of war, was fully co-ordinated with the other branches of the Wehrmacht. It is clear that his U-boats, few in number at the time, were fully prepared to wage war.

It is true that until his appointment in January, 1943, as Commander-in-Chief he was not an "Oberbefehlshaber". But this statement underestimates the importance of Doenitz's position. He was no mere Army or division commander. The U-boat arm was the principal part of the German fleet and Doenitz was its leader. The High Seas fleet made a few minor, if spectacular, raids during the early years of the war, but the real damage to the enemy was done almost exclusively by his submarines as the millions of tons of Allied and neutral shipping sunk will testify. Doenitz was solely in charge of this warfare. The Naval War Command reserved for itself only the decision as to the number of submarines in each area. In the invasion of Norway, for example, Doenitz made recommendations in October, 1939, as to submarine bases, which he claims were no more than a staff study, and in March, 1940, he made out the operational orders for the supporting U-boats, as discussed elsewhere in this Judgment.

That his importance to the German war effort was so regarded is eloquently proved by Raeder's recommendation of Doenitz as his successor and his appointment by Hitler on 30th January, 1943, as Commander-in-Chief of the Navy. Hitler, too, knew that submarine warfare was the essential part of Germany's naval warfare.

From January, 1943, Doenitz was consulted almost continuously by Hitler. The evidence was that they conferred on naval problems about 120 times during the course of the war.

As late as April, 1945, when he admits he knew the struggle was hopeless, Doenitz as its Commander-in-Chief urged the Navy to continue its fight. On 1st May, 1945, he became the Head of State and as such ordered the Wehrmacht to continue its war in the East, until capitulation on 9th May, 1945. Doenitz explained that his reason for these orders was to ensure that the German civilian population might be evacuated and the Army might make an orderly retreat from the East.

In the view of the Tribunal, the evidence shows that Doenitz was active in waging aggressive war.

War crimes

Doenitz is charged with waging unrestricted submarine warfare contrary to the Naval Protocol of 1936, to which Germany acceded, and which reaffirmed the rules of submarine warfare laid down in the London Naval Agreement of 1930.

The Prosecution has submitted that on 3rd September, 1939, the German U-boat arm began to wage unrestricted submarine warfare upon all merchant ships, whether enemy or neutral, cynically disregarding the Protocol; and that a calculated effort was made throughout the war to disguise this practice by making hypocritical references to international law and supposed violations by the Allies.

Doenitz insists that at all times the Navy remained within the confines of international law and of the Protocol. He testified that when the war began, the guide to submarine warfare was the German Prize Ordinance taken almost literally from the Protocol; that, pursuant to the German view, he ordered submarines to attack all merchant ships in convoy; and that all refused to stop or used their radio upon sighting a submarine. When his reports indicated that British merchant ships were being used to give information by wireless, were being armed and were attacking submarines on sight, he ordered his submarines on 17th October, 1939, to attack all enemy merchant ships without warning on the ground that resistance was to be expected. Orders already had been issued on 21st September, 1939, to attack all ships, including neutrals, sailing at night without lights in the English Channel.

On 24th November, 1939, the German Government issued a warning to neutral shipping that, owing to the frequent engagements taking place in the waters around the British Isles and the French coast between U-boats and Allied merchant ships which were armed and had instructions to use those arms as well as to ram U-boats, the safety of neutral ships in those waters could no longer be taken for granted. On 1st January, 1940, the German U-boat Command, acting on the instructions of Hitler, ordered U-boats to attack all Greek merchant ships in the zone surrounding the British Isles, which was banned by the United States to its own ships and also merchant ships of every nationality in the limited area of the Bristol Channel. Five days later a further order was given to U-boats to "make immediately unrestricted use of weapons against all ships" in an area of the North Sea, the limits of which were defined. Finally, on 18th January, 1940, U-boats were authorised to sink, without warning, all ships "in those waters near the enemy coasts in which the use of mines can be pretended". Exceptions were to be made for United States, Italian, Japanese and Soviet ships.

Shortly after the outbreak of war the British Admiralty, in accordance with its Handbook of Instructions of 1938 to the Merchant Navy, armed its merchant vessels, in many cases convoyed them with armed escort and gave orders to send position reports upon sighting submarines, thus integrating merchant vessels into the warning network of naval intelligence. On 1st October, 1939, the British Admiralty announced British merchant ships had been ordered to ram U-boats if possible.

In the actual circumstances of this case, the Tribunal is not prepared to hold Doenitz guilty for his conduct of submarine warfare against British armed merchant ships.

However, the proclamation of operational zones and the sinking of neutral merchant vessels which enter those zones presents a different question. This practice was employed in the War of 1914–18 by Germany and adopted in retaliation by Great Britain. The Washington Conference of 1922, the London Naval Agreement of 1930 and the Protocol of 1936 were entered into with full knowledge that such zones had been employed in the First World War. Yet the Protocol made no exception for operational zones. The order of Doenitz to sink neutral ships without warning when found within these zones was, therefore, in the opinion of the Tribunal, violation of the Protocol.

It is also asserted that the German U-boat arm not only did not carry out the warning and rescue provisions of the Protocol but that Doenitz deliberately ordered the killing of survivors of shipwrecked vessels, whether enemy or neutral. The Prosecution has introduced much evidence surrounding two orders of Doenitz, War Order No. 154, issued in 1939, and the so-called "Laconia" Order of 1942. The Defence argues that these orders and the evidence supporting them do not show such a policy and introduced much evidence to the contrary. The Tribunal is of the opinion that the evidence does not establish with the certainty required that Doenitz deliberately ordered the killing of shipwrecked survivors. The orders were undoubtedly ambiguous, and deserve the strongest censure.

The evidence further shows that the rescue provisions were not carried out and that the defendant ordered that they should not be carried out. The argument of the Defence is that the security of the submarine is, as the first rule of the sea, paramount to rescue and that the development of aircraft made rescue impossible. This may be so, but the Protocol is explicit. If the commander cannot rescue, then under its terms he cannot sink a merchant vessel and should allow it to pass harmless before his periscope. The orders, then, prove Doenitz is guilty of a violation of the Protocol.

In view of all the facts proved and in particular of an order of the British Admiralty announced on the 8th May, 1940, according to which all vessels should be sunk at sight in the Skagerrak, and the answers to interrogatories by Admiral Nimitz stating that unrestricted submarine warfare was carried on in the Pacific Ocean by the United States from the first day that nation entered the war, the sentence of Doenitz is not assessed on the ground of his breaches of the international law of submarine warfare.

Doenitz was also charged with responsibility for Hitler's Commando Order of 18th October, 1942. Doenitz admitted he received and knew of the order when he was Flag Officer of U-boats, but disclaimed responsibility. He points out that the order by its express terms excluded men captured in naval warfare, that the Navy had no territorial commands on land, and that submarine commanders would never encounter commandos.

In one instance, when he was Commander-in-Chief of the Navy, in 1943, the members of an Allied motor torpedo boat were captured by German Naval Forces. They were interrogated for intelligence purposes on behalf of the local admiral, and then turned over by his order to the SD and shot. Doenitz said that if they were captured by the Navy their execution was a violation of the Commando Order, that the execution was not announced in the Wehrmacht communiqué and that he was never informed of the incident. He pointed out that the admiral in question was not in his chain of command, but was subordinate to the army general in command of the Norway occupation. But Doenitz permitted the order to remain in full force when he became Commander-in-Chief, and to that extent he is responsible.

In a conference of 11th December, 1944, Doenitz said: "12,000 concentration camp prisoners will be employed in the shipyards as additional labour". At this time Doenitz had no jurisdiction over shipyard construction, and he claims that this was merely a suggestion at the meeting that the responsible officials do something about the production of ships, that he took no steps to get these workers since it was not a matter for his jurisdiction and that he does not know whether they ever were procured. He admits he knew of concentration camps. A man in his position must necessarily have known that citizens of occupied countries in large numbers were confined in the concentration camps.

In 1945 Hitler requested the opinion of Jodl and Doenitz whether the Geneva Convention should be denounced. The notes of the meeting between the two military leaders on 20th February, 1945, show that Doenitz expressed his view that the disadvantages of such an action outweighed the advantages. The summary of Doenitz's attitude, shown in the notes taken by an officer, included the following sentence:

> It would be better to carry out the measures considered necessary without warning, and at all costs to save face with the outer world.

The Prosecution insisted that "the measures" referred to meant the Convention should not be denounced, but should be broken at will. The Defence explanation is that Hitler wanted to break the Convention for two reasons: to take away from German troops the protection of the Convention, thus preventing them from continuing to surrender in large groups to the British and Americans; and also to permit reprisals against Allied prisoners of war because of Allied bombing raids. Doenitz claims that what he meant by "measures" were disciplinary measures against German troops to prevent them from surrendering, and that his words had no reference to measures against the Allies; moreover, that this was merely a suggestion, and that in any event no such measures were ever taken, either against Allies or Germans. The Tribunal, however, does not believe this explanation. The Geneva Convention was not, however, denounced by Germany. The Defence has introduced several affidavits to prove that British naval prisoners of war in camps under Doenitz's jurisdiction were treated strictly according to the Convention, and the Tribunal takes this fact into consideration, regarding it as a mitigating circumstance.

Conclusion

The Tribunal finds Doenitz is not guilty on Count One of the Indictment and is guilty on Counts Two and Three.

RAEDER

Raeder is indicted on Counts One, Two and Three. In 1928 he became Chief of Naval Command and in 1935 Oberbefehlshaber der Kriegsmarine (OKM); in 1939 Hitler made him Grossadmiral. He was a member of the Reich Defence Council. On 30th January, 1943, Doenitz replaced him at his own request, and he became Admiral Inspector of the Navy, a nominal title.

Crimes against peace

In the fifteen years he commanded it, Raeder built and directed the German Navy; he accepts full responsibility until retirement in 1943. He admits the Navy violated the Versailles Treaty, insisting it was "a matter of honour for every man" to do so, and alleges that the violations were for the most part minor, and Germany built less than her allowable strength. These violations, as well as those of the Anglo-German Naval Agreement of 1935, have already been discussed elsewhere in this Judgment.

Raeder received the directive of 24th June, 1937, from von Blomberg requiring special preparations for war against Austria. He was one of the five leaders present at the Hoszbach Conference of 5th November, 1937. He claims Hitler merely wished by this conference to spur the Army to faster rearmament; insists he believed the questions of Austria and Czechoslovakia would be settled peacefully, as they were; and points to the new naval treaty with England which had just been signed. He received no orders to speed construction of U-boats, indicating that Hitler was not planning war.

Raeder received directives on "Fall Grün" and the directives on "Fall Weiss", beginning with that of 3rd April, 1939; the latter directed the Navy to support the Army by intervention from the sea. He was also one of the few chief leaders present at the meeting of 23rd May, 1939. He attended the Obersalzburg briefing of 22nd August, 1939.

The conception of the invasion of Norway first arose in the mind of Raeder and not that of Hitler. Despite Hitler's desire, as shown by his directive of October, 1939, to keep Scandinavia neutral, the Navy examined the advantages of naval bases there as early as October. Admiral Karls originally suggested to Raeder the desirable aspects of bases in Norway. A questionnaire, dated 3rd October, 1939, which sought comments on the desirability of such bases, was circulated within SKL. On 10th October Raeder discussed the matter with Hitler; his War Diary entry for that day says Hitler intended to give the matter consideration. A few months later Hitler talked to Raeder, Quisling, Keitel and Jodl; OKW began its planning and the Naval War Staff worked with OKW staff officers. Raeder received Keitel's directive for Norway on 27th January, 1940, and the subsequent directive of 1st March, signed by Hitler.

Raeder defends his actions on the ground it was a move to forestall the British. It is not necessary again to discuss this defence, which the Tribunal have heretofore treated in some detail, concluding that Germany's invasion of Norway and Denmark was aggressive war. In a letter to the Navy, Raeder said: "The operations of the Navy in the occupation of Norway will for all time remain the great contribution of the Navy to this war."

Raeder received the directives, including the innumerable postponements, for the attack in the West. In a meeting of 18th March, 1941, with Hitler, he urged the occupation of all Greece. He claims this was only after the British had landed and Hitler had ordered the attack, and points out the Navy had no interest in Greece. He received Hitler's directive on Yugoslavia.

Raeder endeavoured to dissuade Hitler from embarking upon the invasion of the USSR. In September, 1940, he urged on Hitler an aggressive Mediterranean policy as an alternative to an attack on Russia. On 14th November, 1940, he urged the war against England "as our main enemy" and that submarine and naval air force construction be continued. He voiced "serious objections against the Russian campaign before the defeat of England", according to notes of the German Naval War Staff. He claims his objections were based on the violation of the Non-Aggression Pact as well as strategy. But once the decision had been made, he gave permission six days before the invasion of the Soviet Union to attack Russian submarines in the Baltic Sea within a specified warning area, and defends this action because these submarines were "snooping" on German activities.

It is clear from this evidence that Raeder participated in the planning and waging of aggressive war.

War crimes

Raeder is charged with war crimes on the high seas. The "Athenia", an unarmed British passenger liner, was sunk on 3rd September, 1939, while outward bound to America. The Germans two months later charged that Mr Churchill deliberately sank the "Athenia" to encourage American hostility to Germany. In fact, it was sunk by the German U-boat 30. Raeder claims that an inexperienced U-boat commander sank it in mistake for an armed merchant cruiser, that this was not known until the U-30 returned several weeks after the German denial, and that Hitler then directed the Navy and Foreign Office to continue denying it. Raeder denied knowledge of the propaganda campaign attacking Mr Churchill.

The most serious charge against Raeder is that he carried out unrestricted submarine warfare, including sinking of unarmed merchant ships, of neutrals, non-rescue and machine-gunning of survivors, contrary to the London Protocol of 1936. The Tribunal makes the same finding on Raeder on this charge as it did as to Doenitz, which has already been announced, up until 30th January, 1943, when Raeder retired.

The Commando Order of the 18th October, 1942, which expressly did not apply to naval warfare, was transmitted by the Naval War Staff to the lower naval commanders with the direction it should be distributed orally by flotilla leaders and section commanders to their subordinates. Two commandos were put to death by the Navy, and not by the SD, at Bordeaux on the 10th December, 1942. The comment of the Naval War Staff was that this was "in accordance with the Führer's special order, but is nevertheless something new in international law, since the soldiers were in uniform". Raeder admits he passed the order down through the chain of command, and he did not object to Hitler.

Conclusion

The Tribunal finds that Raeder is guilty on Counts One, Two and Three.

VON SCHIRACH

Von Schirach is indicted under Counts One and Four. He joined the Nazi Party and the SA in 1925. In 1929 he became the Leader of the National Socialist Students Union. In 1931 he was made Reich Youth Leader of the Nazi Party with control over all Nazi youth organisations including the Hitler Jugend. In 1933, after the Nazis had obtained control of the Government, von Schirach was made Leader of Youth in the German Reich, originally a position within the Ministry of the Interior, but, after 1st December, 1936, an office in the Reich Cabinet. In 1940 von Schirach resigned as head of the Hitler Jugend and Leader of Youth in the German Reich, but retained his position as Reichsleiter with control over Youth

Education. In 1940 he was appointed Gauleiter of Vienna, Reich Governor of Vienna, and Reich Defence Commissioner for that territory.

Crimes against peace

After the Nazis had come to power, von Schirach, utilising both physical violence and official pressure, either drove out of existence or took over all youth groups which competed with the Hitler Jugend. A Hitler decree of 1st December, 1936, incorporated all German youth within the Hitler Jugend. By the time formal conscription was introduced in 1940, 97 per cent of those eligible were already members.

Von Schirach used the Hitler Jugend to educate German Youth "in the spirit of National Socialism" and subjected them to an intensive programme of Nazi propaganda. He established the Hitler Jugend as a source of replacements for the Nazi Party formations. In October, 1938, he entered into an agreement with Himmler under which members of the Hitler Jugend who met SS standards would be considered as the primary source of replacements for the SS.

Von Schirach also used the Hitler Jugend for pre-military training. Special units were set up whose primary purpose was training specialists for the various branches of the service. On 11th August, 1939, he entered into an agreement with Keitel under which the Hitler Jugend agreed to carry out its pre-military activities under standards laid down by the Wehrmacht, and the Wehrmacht agreed to train 30,000 Hitler Jugend instructors each year. The Hitler Jugend placed particular emphasis on the military spirit, and its training programme stressed the importance of return of the colonies, the necessity for *Lebensraum* and the noble destiny of German youth to die for Hitler.

Despite the warlike nature of the activities of the Hitler Jugend, however, it does not appear that von Schirach was involved in the development of Hitler's plan for territorial expansion by means of aggressive war, or that he participated in the planning or preparation of any of the wars of aggression.

Crimes against humanity

In July, 1940, von Schirach was appointed Gauleiter of Vienna. At the same time he was appointed Reich Governor for Vienna and Reich Defence Commissioner, originally for Military District 17, including the Gaus of Vienna, Upper Danube and Lower Danube and, after 17th November, 1942, for the Gau of Vienna alone. As Reich Defence Commissioner, he had control of the civilian war economy. As Reich Governor, he was head of the municipal administration of the city of Vienna, and, under the supervision of the Minister of the Interior, in charge of the governmental administration of the Reich in Vienna.

Von Schirach is not charged with the commission of war crimes in Vienna, only with the commission of crimes against humanity. As has already been seen, Austria was occupied pursuant to a common plan of aggression. Its occupation is, therefore, a "crime within the jurisdiction of the Tribunal", as that term is used in Article 6(c) of the Charter. As a result, "murder, extermination, enslavement, deportation and other inhumane acts" and "persecutions on political, racial or religious grounds" in connection with this occupation constitute a crime against humanity under that Article.

As Gauleiter of Vienna, von Schirach came under the Sauckel decree dated 6th April, 1942, making the Gauleiters Sauckel's plenipotentiaries for manpower with authority to supervise the utilisation and treatment of manpower within their Gaus. Sauckel's directives provided that the forced labourers were to be fed, sheltered and treated so as to exploit them to the highest possible degree at the lowest possible expense.

When von Schirach became Gauleiter of Vienna the deportation of the Jews had already been begun, and only 60,000 out of Vienna's original 190,000 Jews remained. On 2nd October, 1940, he attended a conference at Hitler's office and told Frank that he had 50,000 Jews in Vienna which the General-Government would have to take over from him. On 3rd December, 1940, von Schirach received a letter from Lammers stating that after the receipt of the reports made by von Schirach, Hitler had decided to deport the 60,000 Jews still remaining in Vienna to the General-Government because of the housing shortage in Vienna. The deportation of the Jews from Vienna was then begun and continued until the early fall of 1942. On 15th September, 1942, von Schirach made a speech in which he defended his action in having driven "tens of thousands upon tens of thousands of Jews into the Ghetto of the East" as "contributing to European culture".

While the Jews were being deported from Vienna, reports, addressed to him in his official capacity, were received in von Schirach's office from the office of the Chief of the Security Police and SD. These contained a description of the activities of Einsatzgruppen in exterminating Jews. Many of these reports were initialled by one of von Schirach's principal deputies. On 30th June, 1944, von Schirach's office also received a letter from Kaltenbrunner informing him that a shipment of 12,000 Jews was on its way to Vienna for essential war work, and that all those who were incapable of work would have to be kept in readiness for "special action".

The Tribunal finds that von Schirach, while he did not originate the policy of deporting Jews from Vienna, participated in this deportation after he had become Gauleiter of Vienna. He knew that the best the Jews could hope for was a miserable existence in the ghettos of the East. Bulletins describing the Jewish extermination were in his office.

While Gauleiter of Vienna, von Schirach continued to function as Reichsleiter for Youth Education, and in this capacity he was informed of the Hitler Jugend's participation in the plan, put into effect in the fall of 1944, under which 50,000 young people between the ages of 10 and 20 were evacuated into Germany from areas recaptured by the Soviet forces and used as apprentices in German industry and as auxiliaries in units of the German Armed Forces. In the summer of 1942 von Schirach telegraphed Bormann urging that a bombing attack on an English cultural town be carried out in retaliation for the assassination of Heydrich, which, he claimed, had been planned by the British.

Conclusion

The Tribunal finds that von Schirach is not guilty on Count One. He is guilty under Count Four.

SAUCKEL

Sauckel is indicted under all four counts. Sauckel joined the Nazi Party in 1923 and became Gauleiter of Thuringia in 1927. He was a member of the Thuringian legislature from 1927 to 1933, was appointed Reichsstatthalter for Thuringia in 1932, and Thuringian Minister of the Interior and Head of the Thuringian State Ministry in May, 1933. He became a member of the Reichstag in 1933. He held the formal rank of Obergruppenführer in both the SA and the SS.

Crimes against peace

The evidence has not satisfied the Tribunal that Sauckel was sufficiently connected with the common plan to wage aggressive war or sufficiently involved in the planning or waging of the aggressive wars to allow the Tribunal to convict him on Counts One and Two.

War crimes and crimes against humanity

On 21st March, 1942, Hitler appointed Sauckel Plenipotentiary General for the Utilisation of Labour, with authority to put under uniform control "the utilisation of all available manpower, including that of workers recruited abroad and of prisoners of war". Sauckel was instructed to operate within the fabric of the Four Year Plan, and on 27th March, 1942, Goering issued a decree as Commissioner for the Four Year Plan transferring his manpower sections to Sauckel. On 30th September, 1942, Hitler gave Sauckel authority to appoint Commissioners in the various occupied territories, and "to take all necessary measures for the enforcement" of the decree of 21st March, 1942.

Under the authority which he obtained by these decrees, Sauckel set up a programme for the mobilisation of the labour resources available to the Reich. One of the important parts of this mobilisation was the systematic exploitation, by force, of the labour resources of the occupied territories. Shortly after Sauckel had taken office, he had the governing authorities in the various occupied territories issue decrees, establishing compulsory labour service in Germany. Under the authority of these decrees Sauckel's Commissioners, backed up by the police authorities of the occupied territories, obtained and sent to Germany the labourers which were necessary to fill the quotas given them by Sauckel. He described so-called "voluntary" recruiting by Janates: "a whole batch of male and female agents just as was done in the olden times for shanghaiing". That real voluntary recruiting was the exception rather than the rule is shown by Sauckel's statement on 1st March, 1944, that "out of five million foreign workers who arrived in Germany not even 200,000 came voluntarily". Although he now claims that the statement is not true, the circumstances under which it was made, as well as the evidence presented before the Tribunal, leave no doubt that it was substantially accurate.

The manner in which the unfortunate slave labourers were collected and transported to Germany, and what happened to them after they arrived, has already been described. Sauckel argues that he is not responsible for these excesses in the administration of the programme. He says that the total number of workers to be obtained was set by the demands from agriculture and from industry; that obtaining the workers was the responsibility of the occupation authorities; transporting them to Germany that of the German railways; and taking care of them in Germany that of the Ministries of Labour and Agriculture, the German Labour Front and the various industries involved. He testifies that insofar as he had any authority he was constantly urging humane treatment.

There is no doubt, however, that Sauckel had overall responsibility for the Slave Labour Programme. At the time of the events in question he did not fail to assert control over the fields which he now claims were the sole responsibility of others. His regulations provided that his Commissioners should have authority for obtaining labour, and he was constantly in the field supervising the steps which were being taken. He was aware of ruthless methods being taken to obtain labourers, and vigorously supported them on the ground that they were necessary to fill the quotas.

Sauckel's regulations also provided that he had responsibility for transporting the labourers to Germany, allocating them to employers and taking care of them, and that the other agencies involved in these processes were subordinate to him. He was informed of the bad conditions which existed. It does not appear that he advocated brutality for its own sake, or was an advocate of any programme such as Himmler's plan for extermination through work. His attitude was thus expressed in a regulation:

> All the men must be fed, sheltered and treated in such a way as to exploit them to the highest possible extent at the lowest conceivable degree of expenditure.

The evidence shows that Sauckel was in charge of a programme which involved deportation for slave labour of more than 5,000,000 human beings, many of them under terrible conditions of cruelty and suffering.

Conclusion

The Tribunal finds that Sauckel is not guilty on Counts One and Two. He is guilty under Counts Three and Four.

JODL

Jodl is indicted on all four counts. From 1935 to 1938 he was Chief of the National Defence Section in the High Command. After a year in command of troops, in August, 1939, he returned to become Chief of the Operations Staff of the High Command of the Armed Forces. Although his immediate superior was defendant Keitel, he reported directly to Hitler on operational matters. In the strict military sense, Jodl was the actual planner of the war and responsible in large measure for the strategy and conduct of operations.

Jodl defends himself on the ground he was a soldier sworn to obedience, and not a politician; and that his staff and planning work left him no time for other matters. He said that when he signed or initialled orders, memoranda and letters, he did so for Hitler and often in the absence of Keitel. Though he claims that as a soldier he had to obey Hitler, he says that he often tried to obstruct certain measures by delay, which occasionally proved successful, as when he resisted Hitler's demand that a directive be issued to lynch Allied "terror fliers".

Crimes against peace

Entries in Jodl's diary of 13th and 14th February, 1938, show Hitler instructed both him and Keitel to keep up military pressure against Austria begun at the Schuschnigg conference by simulating military measures, and that these achieved their purpose. When Hitler decided "not to tolerate" Schuschnigg's plebiscite, Jodl brought to the conference the "old draft", the existing staff plan. His diary for 10th March shows Hitler then ordered the preparation of "Case Otto", and the directive was initialled by Jodl. Jodl issued supplementary instructions on 11th March, and initialled Hitler's order for the invasion on the same date.

In planning the attack on Czechoslovakia, Jodl was very active according to the Schmundt Notes. He initialled items 14, 17, 24, 36 and 37 in the Notes. Jodl admits he agreed with OKH that the "incident" to provide German intervention must occur at the latest by 2 pm on X-1 Day, the day before the attack, and said it must occur at a fixed time in good flying weather. Jodl conferred with the propaganda experts on "imminent common tasks" such as German violations of international law, exploitation of them by the enemy and refutations by the Germans, which "task" Jodl considered "particularly important".

After Munich, Jodl wrote:

Czechoslovakia as a power is out . . . The genius of the Führer and his determination not to shun even a World War have again won the victory without the use of force. The hope remains that the incredulous, the weak and the doubtful people have been converted and will remain that way.

Shortly after the Sudeten occupation, Jodl went to a post command and did not become Chief of the Operations Staff in OKW until the end of August, 1939.

Jodl discussed the Norway invasion with Hitler, Keitel and Raeder on 12th December, 1939; his diary is replete with late entries on his activities in preparing this attack. Jodl explains that his comment that Hitler was still looking for an "excuse" to move meant that he was waiting for reliable intelligence on the British plans, and defends the invasion as a necessary move to forestall them. His testimony shows that from October, 1939, Hitler planned to attack the West through Belgium, but was doubtful about invading Holland until the middle of November. On 8th February, 1940, Jodl, his Deputy Warlimont and Jeschonnek, the air forces planner, discussed among themselves the "new idea" of attacking Norway, Denmark and Holland, but guaranteeing the neutrality of Belgium. Many of the seventeen orders postponing the attack in the West for various reasons, including weather conditions, until May, 1940, were signed by Jodl.

He was active in the planning against Greece and Yugoslavia. The Hitler order of 11th January, 1941, to intervene in Albania, was initialled by Jodl. On 20th January, four months before the attack, Hitler told a conference of German and Italian generals in Jodl's presence that German troop concentrations in Romania were to be used against Greece. Jodl was present on 18th March when Hitler told Raeder all Greece must be occupied before any settlement could be reached. On 27th March when Hitler told the German High Command that the destruction of Yugoslavia should be accomplished with "unmerciful harshness", and the decision was taken to bomb Belgrade without a declaration of war, Jodl was also there.

Jodl testified that Hitler feared an attack by Russia and so attacked first. This preparation began almost a year before the invasion. Jodl told Warlimont as early as 29th July, 1940, to prepare the plans since Hitler had decided to attack; and Hitler later told Warlimont he had planned to attack in August, 1940, but postponed it for military reasons. He initialled Hitler's directive of 12th November, 1940, according to which preparations verbally ordered should be continued and also initialled "Case Barbarossa" on 18th December. On 3rd February, 1941, Hitler, Jodl and Keitel discussed the invasion, and he was present on 14th June when final reports on "Case Barbarossa" were made.

War crimes and crimes against humanity

On 18th October, 1942, Hitler issued the Commando Order, and a day later a supplementary explanation to commanding officers only. The covering memorandum was signed by Jodl. Early drafts of the Order were made by Jodl's staff, with his knowledge. Jodl testified he was strongly opposed on moral and legal grounds, but could not refuse to pass it on. He insists he tried to mitigate its harshness in practice by not informing Hitler when it was not carried out. He initialled the OKW memorandum of 25th June, 1944, reaffirming the Order after the Normandy landings.

A plan to eliminate Soviet Commissars was in the directive for "Case Barbarossa". The decision whether they should be killed without trial was to be made by an officer. A draft contains Jodl's handwriting suggesting this should be handled as retaliation, and he testified this was his attempt to get around it.

When in 1945 Hitler considered denouncing the Geneva Convention, Jodl argued the disadvantages outweighed the advantages. On 21st February he told Hitler adherence would not interfere with the conduct of the war, giving as an example the sinking of a British hospital ship as a reprisal and calling it a mistake. He said he did so because it was the only attitude Hitler would consider, that moral or legal arguments had no effect, and argues he thus prevented Hitler from denouncing the Convention.

There is little evidence that Jodl was actively connected with the Slave Labour Programme, and he must have concentrated on his strategic planning function. But in his speech of 7th November, 1943, to the Gauleiters he said it was necessary to act "with remorseless vigour and resolution" in Denmark, France and the Low Countries to compel work on the Atlantic Wall.

By teletype of 28th October, 1944, Jodl ordered the evacuation of all persons in northern Norway and the burning of their houses so they could not help the Russians. Jodl says he was against this, but Hitler ordered it and it was not fully carried out. A document of the Norwegian Government says such an evacuation did take place in northern Norway and 30,000 houses were damaged. On 7th October, 1941, Jodl signed an order that Hitler would not accept an offer of surrender of Leningrad or Moscow, but on the contrary he insisted that they be completely destroyed. He says this was done because the Germans were afraid those cities would be mined by the Russians, as was Kiev. No surrender was ever offered.

His defence, in brief, is the doctrine of "superior orders", prohibited by Article 8 of the Charter as a defence. There is nothing in mitigation. Participation in such crimes as these has never been required of any soldier, and he cannot now shield himself behind a mythical requirement of soldierly obedience at all costs as his excuse for commission of these crimes.

Conclusion

The Tribunal finds that Jodl is guilty on all four counts.

VON PAPEN

Von Papen is indicted under Counts One and Two. He was appointed Chancellor of the Reich on 1st June, 1932, and was succeeded by von Schleicher on 2nd December, 1932. He was made Vice Chancellor in the Hitler Cabinet on 30th January, 1933, and on 13th November, 1933, Plenipotentiary for the Saar. On 26th July, 1934, he was appointed Minister to Vienna, and was recalled on 4th February, 1938. On 29th April, 1939, he was appointed Ambassador to Turkey. He returned to Germany when Turkey broke off diplomatic relations with Germany in August, 1944.

Crimes against peace

Von Papen was active in 1932 and 1933 in helping Hitler to form the Coalition Cabinet and aided in his appointment as Chancellor on 30th January, 1933. As Vice Chancellor in that Cabinet he participated in the Nazi consolidation of control in 1933. On 16th June, 1934, however, von Papen made a speech at Marburg which contained a denunciation of the Nazi attempts to suppress the free press and the church, of the existence of a reign of terror, and of "150 per cent Nazis" who were mistaking "brutality for vitality". On 30th June, 1934, in the wave of violence which accompanied the so-called Röhm Purge, von Papen was taken into custody by the SS, his office force was arrested, and two of his associates, including the man who had helped him work on the Marburg speech, were murdered. Von Papen was released on 3rd July, 1934.

Notwithstanding the murder of his associates, von Papen accepted the position of Minister to Austria on 26th July, 1934, the day after Dollfuss had been assassinated. His appointment was announced in a letter from Hitler which instructed him to direct relations between the two countries "into normal and friendly channels" and assured him of "Hitler's complete and unlimited confidence". As Minister to Austria, von Papen was active in trying to strengthen the position of the Nazi Party in Austria for the purpose of bringing about Anschluss. In early 1935 he attended a meeting in Berlin at which the policy was laid down to avoid everything which would give the appearance of German intervention in the internal affairs of Austria. Yet he arranged for 200,000 marks a month to be transmitted to "the persecuted National Socialist sufferers in Austria". On 17th May, 1935, he reported to Hitler the results of a conference with Captain Leopold, the Leader of the Austrian Nazis, and urged Hitler to make a statement recognising the national independence of Austria, and predicting that the result might be to help the formation of a coalition between Schuschnigg's Christian Socialists and the Austrian Nazis against Starhemberg. On 27th July, 1935, von Papen reported to Hitler that the union of Austria and Germany could not be brought about by external pressure but only by the strength of the National Socialist Movement. He urged that the Austrian Nazi Party change its character as a centralised Reich German Party and become a rallying point for all National Germans.

Von Papen was involved in occasional Nazi political demonstrations, supported Nazi propaganda activities and submitted detailed reports on the activities of the Nazi Party, and routine reports relating to Austrian military defences. His Austrian policy resulted in the agreement of 11th July, 1936, which nominally restored relations between Germany and Austria to "normal and friendly form", but which had a secret supplement providing for an amnesty for Austrian Nazis, the lifting of censorship on Nazi papers, the resumption of political activities by Nazis and the appointment of men friendly to the Nazis in the Schuschnigg Cabinet.

After the signing of this agreement von Papen offered to resign but his resignation was not accepted. Thereafter he proceeded to bring continued pressure on the Austrian Government to bring Nazis into the Schuschnigg Cabinet and to get them important positions in the Fatherland Front, Austria's single legal party. On 1st September, 1936, von Papen wrote to Hitler advising him that anti-Nazis in the Austrian Ministry of Security were holding up the infiltration of the Nazis into the Austrian Government and recommended bringing "slowly intensified pressure directed at changing the régime".

On 4th February, 1938, von Papen was notified of his recall as Minister to Austria, at the same time that von Fritsch, von Blomberg and von Neurath were removed from their positions. He informed Hitler that he regretted his recall because he had been trying since November, 1937, to induce Schuschnigg to hold a conference with Hitler, and Schuschnigg had indicated his willingness to do so. Acting under Hitler's instructions, von Papen then returned to Austria and arranged the conference which was held at Berchtesgaden on 12th February, 1938. Von Papen accompanied Schuschnigg to that conference, and at its conclusion advised Schuschnigg to comply with Hitler's demands. On 10th March, 1938, Hitler ordered von Papen to return to Berlin. Von Papen was in the Chancellery on 11th March when the occupation of Austria was ordered. No evidence has been offered showing that von Papen was in favour of the decision to occupy Austria by force, and he has testified that he urged Hitler not to take this step.

After the annexation of Austria von Papen retired into private life and there is no evidence that he took any part in politics. He accepted the position of Ambassador to Turkey in April, 1939, but no evidence had been offered concerning his activities in that position implicating him in crimes.

The evidence leaves no doubt that von Papen's primary purpose as Minister to Austria was to undermine the Schuschnigg régime and strengthen the Austrian Nazis for the purpose of bringing about Anschluss.

To carry through this plan he engaged in both intrigue and bullying. But the Charter does not make criminal such offences against political morality, however bad these may be. Under the Charter, von Papen can be held guilty only if he was a party to the planning of aggressive war. There is no showing that he was a party to the plans under which the occupation of Austria was a step in the direction of further aggressive action, or even that he participated in plans to occupy Austria by aggressive war if necessary. But it is not established beyond a reasonable doubt that this was the purpose of his activity, and therefore the Tribunal cannot hold that he was a party to the common plan charged in Count One or participated in the planning of the aggressive wars charged under Count Two.

Conclusion

The Tribunal finds that von Papen is not guilty under this Indictment, and directs that he shall be discharged by the Marshal, when the Tribunal presently adjourns.

SEYSS-INQUART

Seyss-Inquart is indicted under all four counts. Seyss-Inquart, an Austrian attorney, was appointed State Councillor in Austria in May, 1937, as a result of German pressure. He had been associated with the Austrian Nazi Party since 1931, but had often had difficulties with that Party and did not actually join the Nazi Party until 13th March, 1938. He was appointed Austrian Minister of Security and Interior with control over the Police, pursuant to one of the conditions which Hitler had imposed on Schuschnigg in the Berchtesgaden conference of 12th February, 1938.

Activities in Austria

Seyss-Inquart participated in the last stages of the Nazi intrigue which preceded the German occupation of Austria, and was made Chancellor of Austria as a result of German threats of invasion.

On 12th March, 1938, Seyss-Inquart met Hitler at Linz and made a speech welcoming the German forces and advocating the reunion of Germany and Austria. On 13th March he obtained the passage of a law providing that Austria should become a province of Germany and succeeded Miklas as President of Austria when Miklas resigned rather than sign the law. Seyss-Inquart's title was changed to Reich Governor of Austria on 15th March, 1938, and on the same day he was given the title of a General in the SS. He was made a Reichsminister without Portfolio on 1st May, 1939.

On 11th March, 1939, he visited the Slovakian Cabinet in Bratislava and induced them to declare their independence in a way which fitted in closely with Hitler's offensive against the independence of Czechoslovakia.

As Reich Governor of Austria, Seyss-Inquart instituted a programme of confiscating Jewish property. Under his régime, Jews were forced to emigrate, were sent to concentration camps and were subject to pogroms. At the end of his régime he co-operated with the Security Police and SD in the deportation of Jews from Austria to the East. While he was Governor of Austria, political opponents of the Nazis were sent to concentration camps by the Gestapo, mistreated and often killed.

Criminal activities in Poland and the Netherlands

In September, 1939, Seyss-Inquart was appointed Chief of Civil Administration of South Poland. On 12th October, 1939, Seyss-Inquart was made Deputy Governor-General of the General-Government of Poland under Frank. On 18th May, 1940, Seyss-Inquart was appointed Reich Commissioner for occupied Netherlands. In these positions he assumed responsibility for governing territory which had been occupied by aggressive wars and the administration of which was of vital importance in the aggressive war being waged by Germany.

As Deputy Governor-General of the General-Government of Poland, Seyss-Inquart was a supporter of the harsh occupation policies which were put in effect. In November, 1939, while on an inspection tour through the General-Government, Seyss-Inquart stated that Poland was to be so administered as to exploit its economic resources for the benefit of Germany. Seyss-Inquart also advocated the persecution of Jews and was informed of the AB action which involved the murder of many Polish intellectuals.

As Reich Commissioner for Occupied Netherlands, Seyss-Inquart was ruthless in applying terrorism to suppress all opposition to the German occupation, a programme which he described as "annihilating" his opponents. In collaboration with the local Hitler SS and Police Leaders he was involved in the shooting of hostages for offences against the occupation authorities and sending to concentration camps all suspected opponents of occupation policies, including priests and educators. Many of the Dutch police were forced to participate in these programmes by threats of reprisal against their families. Dutch courts were also forced to participate, but when they indicated their reluctance to give sentences of imprisonment because so many prisoners were killed, a greater emphasis was placed on the use of summary police courts.

Seyss-Inquart carried out the economic administration of the Netherlands without regard for rules of the Hague Convention, which he described as obsolete. Instead, a policy was adopted for the maximum utilisation of economic potential of the Netherlands, and executed with small regard for its effect on the inhabitants. There was widespread pillage of public and private property, which was given colour of legality by Seyss-Inquart's regulations, and assisted by manipulations of the financial institutions of the Netherlands under his control.

As Reich Commissioner for the Netherlands, Seyss-Inquart immediately began sending forced labourers to Germany. Up until 1942 labour service in Germany was theoretically voluntary, but was actually coerced by strong economic and governmental pressure. In 1942 Seyss-Inquart formally decreed compulsory labour service, and utilised the services of the Security Police and SD to prevent evasion of his order. During the occupation, over 500,000 people were sent from the Netherlands to the Reich as labourers and only a very small proportion were actually volunteers.

One of Seyss-Inquart's first steps as Reich Commissioner of the Netherlands was to put into effect a series of laws imposing economic discriminations against the Jews. This was followed by decrees requiring their registration, decrees compelling them to reside in ghettos and to wear the Star of David, sporadic arrests and detention in concentration camps, and finally, at the suggestion of Heydrich, the mass deportation of almost 120,000 of Holland's 140,000 Jews to Auschwitz and the "final solution". Seyss-Inquart admits knowing that they were going to Auschwitz but claims that he heard from people who had been to Auschwitz that the Jews were comparatively well off there, and that he thought that they were being held there for resettlement after the war. In light of the evidence and on account of his official position it is impossible to believe this claim.

Seyss-Inquart contends that he was not responsible for many of the crimes committed in the occupation of the Netherlands because they were either ordered from the Reich, committed by the Army, over which he had no control, or by the German Higher SS and Police Leader, who, he claims, reported directly to Himmler. It is true that some of the excesses were the responsibility of the Army, and that the Higher SS and Police Leader, although he was at the disposal of Seyss-Inquart, could always report directly to Himmler. It is also true that in certain cases Seyss-Inquart opposed the extreme measures used by these other agencies, as when he was largely successful in preventing the Army from carrying out a scorched earth policy, and urged the Higher SS and Police Leaders to reduce the number of hostages to be shot. But the fact remains that Seyss-Inquart was a knowing and voluntary participant in war crimes and crimes against humanity which were committed in the occupation of the Netherlands.

Conclusion

The Tribunal finds that Seyss-Inquart is guilty under Counts Two, Three and Four. Seyss-Inquart is not guilty on Count One.

SPEER

Speer is indicted under all four counts. Speer joined the Nazi Party in 1932. In 1934 he was made Hitler's architect and became a close personal confidant. Shortly thereafter he was made a Department Head in the German Labour

Front and the official in charge of Capital Construction on the staff of the Deputy to the Führer, positions which he held through 1941. On 15th February, 1942, after the death of Fritz Todt, Speer was appointed Chief of the Organisation Todt and Reich Minister for Armaments and Munitions (after 2nd September, 1943, for Armaments and War Production). The positions were supplemented by his appointments in March and April, 1942, as General Plenipotentiary for Armaments and as a member of the Central Planning Board, both within the Four Year Plan. Speer was a member of the Reichstag from 1941 until the end of the war.

Crimes against peace

The Tribunal is of opinion that Speer's activities do not amount to initiating, planning or preparing wars of aggression, or of conspiring to that end. He became the head of the armament industry well after all of the wars had been commenced and were under way. His activities in charge of German armament production were in aid of the war effort in the same way that other productive enterprises aid in the waging of war; but the Tribunal is not prepared to find that such activities involve engaging in the common plan to wage aggressive war as charged under Count One or waging aggressive war as charged under Count Two.

War crimes and crimes against humanity

The evidence introduced against Speer under Counts Three and Four relates entirely to his participation in the Slave Labour Programme. Speer himself had no direct administrative responsibility for this programme. Although he had advocated the appointment of a General Plenipotentiary for the Utilisation of Labour because he wanted one central authority with whom he could deal on labour matters, he did not obtain administrative control over Sauckel. Sauckel was appointed directly by Hitler, under the decree of 21st March, 1942, which provided that he should be directly responsible to Goering, as Plenipotentiary of the Four Year Plan.

As Reich Minister for Armaments and Munitions and General Plenipotentiary for Armaments under the Four Year Plan, Speer had extensive authority over production. His original authority was over construction and production of arms for the OKH. This was progressively expanded to include naval armaments, civilian production and finally, on 1st August, 1944, air armament. As the dominant member of the Central Planning Board, which had supreme authority for the scheduling of German production and the allocation and development of raw materials, Speer took the position that the Board had authority to instruct Sauckel to provide labourers for industries under its control and succeeded in sustaining this position over the objection of Sauckel. The practice was developed under which Speer transmitted to Sauckel an estimate of the total number of workers needed. Sauckel obtained the labour and allocated it to the various industries in accordance with instructions supplied by Speer.

Speer knew when he made his demands on Sauckel that they would be supplied by foreign labourers serving under compulsion. He participated in conferences involving the extension of the Slave Labour Programme for the purpose of satisfying his demands. He was present at a conference held during 10th August and 12th August, 1942, with Hitler and Sauckel at which it was agreed that Sauckel should bring labourers by force from Occupied Territories where this was necessary to satisfy the labour needs of the industries under Speer's control. Speer also attended a conference in Hitler's headquarters on 4th January, 1944, at which the decision was made that Sauckel should obtain "at least four million new workers from Occupied Territories" in order to satisfy the demands for labour made by Speer, although Sauckel indicated that he could do this only with help from Himmler.

Sauckel continually informed Speer and his representatives that foreign labourers were being obtained by force. At a meeting on 1st March, 1944, Speer's deputy questioned Sauckel very closely about his failure to live up to the obligation to supply four million workers from Occupied Territories. In some cases Speer demanded labourers from specific foreign countries. Thus, at the conference on 10th–12th August, 1942, Sauckel was instructed to supply Speer with "a further million Russian labourers for the German armament industry up to and including October, 1942". At a meeting of the Central Planning Board on 22nd April, 1943, Speer discussed plans to obtain Russian labourers for use in the coal mines, and flatly vetoed the suggestion that this labour deficit should be made up by German labour.

Speer has argued that he advocated the reorganisation of the labour programme to place a greater emphasis on utilisation of German labour in war production in Germany and on the use of labour in occupied countries in local production of consumer goods formerly produced in Germany. Speer took steps in this direction by establishing the so-called "blocked industries" in the Occupied Territories which were used to produce goods to be shipped to Germany. Employees of these industries were immune from deportation to Germany as slave labourers and any worker who had been ordered to go to Germany could avoid deportation if he went to work for a blocked industry. This system, although somewhat less inhumane than deportation to Germany, was still illegal. The system of blocked industries played only a small part in the overall Slave Labour Programme, knowing the way in which it was actually being administered. In an official sense, he was its principal beneficiary and he constantly urged its extension.

Speer was also directly involved in the utilisation of forced labour as Chief of the Organisation Todt. The Organisation Todt functioned principally in the occupied areas on such projects as the Atlantic Wall and the construction of military highways, and Speer has admitted that he relied on compulsory service to keep it adequately staffed. He also used concentration camp labour in the industries under his control. He originally arranged to tap this source of labour for use in small out of the way factories; and later, fearful of Himmler's jurisdictional ambitions, attempted to use as few concentration camp workers as possible.

Speer was also involved in the use of prisoners of war in armament industries, but contends that he only utilised Soviet prisoners of war in industries covered by the Geneva Convention.

Speer's position was such that he was not directly concerned with the cruelty in the administration of the Slave Labour Programme, although he was aware of its existence. For example, at meetings of the Central Planning Board he was informed that his demands for labour were so large as to necessitate violent methods in recruiting. At a meeting of the Central Planning Board on 30th October, 1942, Speer voiced his opinion that many slave labourers who claimed to be sick were malingerers and stated: "There is nothing to be said against SS and Police taking drastic steps and putting those known as slackers into concentration camps." Speer, however, insisted that the slave labourers be given adequate food and working conditions so that they could work efficiently.

In mitigation it must be recognised that Speer's establishment of blocked industries did keep many labourers in their homes and that in the closing stages of the war he was one of the few men who had the courage to tell Hitler that the war was lost and to take steps to prevent the senseless destruction of production facilities, both in Occupied Territories and in Germany. He carried out his opposition to Hitler's scorched earth programme in some of the Western countries and in Germany by deliberately sabotaging it at considerable personal risk.

Conclusion

The Tribunal finds that Speer is not guilty on Counts One and Two, but is guilty under Counts Three and Four.

VON NEURATH

Von Neurath is indicted under all four counts. He is a professional diplomat who served as German Ambassador to Great Britain from 1930 to 1932. On 2nd June, 1932, he was appointed Minister of Foreign Affairs in the von Papen cabinet, a position which he held under the cabinets of von Schleicher and Hitler. Von Neurath resigned as Minister of Foreign Affairs on 4th February, 1938, and was made Reichsminister without Portfolio, President of the Secret Cabinet Council and a member of the Reich Defence Council. On 18th March, 1939, he was appointed Reich Protector for Bohemia and Moravia, and served in this capacity until 27th September, 1941. He held the formal rank of Obergruppenführer in the SS.

Crimes against peace

As Minister of Foreign Affairs, von Neurath advised Hitler in connection with the withdrawal from the Disarmament Conference and the League of Nations on 14th October, 1933; the institution of rearmament; the passage on 16th March, 1935, of the law for universal military service; and the passage on 21st May, 1935, of the secret Reich Defence Law. He was a key figure in the negotiation of the Naval Accord entered into between Germany and England on 18th June, 1935. Von Neurath played an important part in Hitler's decision to reoccupy the Rhineland on 7th March, 1936, and predicted that the occupation could be carried through without any reprisals from the French. On 18th May, 1936, he told the American Ambassador to France that it was the policy of the German Government to do nothing in foreign affairs until "the Rhineland had been digested" and that as soon as the fortifications in the Rhineland had been constructed, and the countries of Central Europe realised that France could not enter Germany at will, "all those countries will begin to feel very differently about their foreign policies and a new constellation will develop".

Von Neurath took part in the Hoszbach Conference of 5th November, 1937. He has testified that he was so shocked by Hitler's statements that he had a heart attack. Shortly thereafter, he offered to resign, and his resignation was accepted on 4th February, 1938, at the same time that von Fritsch and von Blomberg were dismissed. Yet with knowledge of Hitler's aggressive plans he retained a formal relationship with the Nazi régime as Reichsminister without Portfolio, President of the Secret Cabinet Council and a member of the Reich Defence Council. He took charge of the Foreign Office at the time of the occupation of Austria, assured the British Ambassador that this had not been caused by a German ultimatum, and informed the Czechoslovakian Minister that Germany intended to abide by its arbitration convention with Czechoslovakia. Von Neurath participated in the last phase of the negotiations preceding the Munich Pact but contends that he entered these discussions only to urge Hitler to make every effort to settle the issues by peaceful means.

Criminal activities in Czechoslovakia

Von Neurath was appointed Reich Protector for Bohemia and Moravia on 18th March, 1939. Bohemia and Moravia were occupied by military force. Hácha's consent, obtained as it was by duress, cannot be considered as justifying the occupation. Hitler's decree of 16th March, 1939, establishing the Protectorate, stated that this new territory should "belong henceforth to the territory of the German Reich", an assumption that the Republic of Czechoslovakia no longer existed. But it also went on the theory that Bohemia and Moravia retained their sovereignty subject only to the interests of Germany as expressed by the Protectorate. Therefore, even if the doctrine of subjugation should be considered to be applicable to territory occupied by aggressive action, the Tribunal does not believe that this Proclamation amounted to an incorporation which was sufficient to bring the doctrine into effect. The occupation of Bohemia and Moravia must, therefore, be considered a military occupation covered by the rules of warfare. Although Czechoslovakia was not a party to the Hague Convention of 1907, the rules of land warfare expressed in this Convention are declaratory of existing international law and hence are applicable.

As Reich Protector, von Neurath instituted an administration in Bohemia and Moravia similar to that in effect in Germany. The free press, political parties and trade unions were abolished. All groups which might serve as opposition were outlawed. Czechoslovakian industry was worked into the structure of German war production, and exploited for the German war effort. Nazi anti-Semitic policies and laws were also introduced. Jews were barred from leading positions in Government and business.

In August, 1939, von Neurath issued a proclamation warning against any acts of sabotage and stating that "the responsibility for all acts of sabotage is attributed not only to individual perpetrators but to the entire Czech population". When the war broke out on 1st September, 1939, 8,000 prominent Czechs were arrested by the Security Police in Bohemia and Moravia and put into protective custody. Many of this group died in concentration camps.

In October and November, 1939, Czechoslovakian students held a series of demonstrations. As a result, on Hitler's orders, all universities were closed, 1,200 students imprisoned, and the nine leaders of the demonstration shot by Security Police and SD. Von Neurath testified that he was not informed of this action in advance, but it was announced by proclamation over his signature posted on placards throughout the Protectorate, which he claims, however, was done without his authority.

On 31st August, 1940, von Neurath transmitted to Lammers a memorandum which he had prepared dealing with the future of the Protectorate, and a memorandum with his approval prepared by Carl Herman Frank on the same subject. Both dealt with the question of Germanisation and proposed that the majority of the Czechs might be assimilated racially into the German nation. Both advocated the elimination of the Czechoslovakian intelligentsia and other groups which might resist Germanisation, von Neurath's by expulsion, Frank's by expulsion or "special treatment".

Von Neurath has argued that the actual enforcement of the repressive measures was carried out by the Security Police and SD who were under the control of his State Secretary, Carl Herman Frank, who was appointed at the suggestion of Himmler and who, as a Higher SS and Police Leader, reported directly to Himmler. Von Neurath further argues that anti-Semitic measures and those resulting in economic exploitation were put into effect in the Protectorate as the result of policies decided upon in the Reich. However this may be, he served as the chief German official in the Protectorate when the administration of this territory played an important rôle in the wars of aggression which Germany was waging in the East, knowing that war crimes and crimes against humanity were being committed under his authority.

In mitigation it must be remembered that von Neurath did intervene with the Security Police and SD for the release of many of the Czechoslovaks who were arrested on 1st September, 1939, and for the release of students arrested later in the fall. On 23rd September, 1941, he was summoned before Hitler and told that he was not being harsh enough and that Heydrich was being sent to the Protectorate to combat the Czechoslovakian resistance groups. Von Neurath attempted to dissuade Hitler from sending Heydrich, but in vain, and when he was not successful offered to resign. When his resignation was not accepted he went on leave, on 27th September, 1941, and refused to act as Protector after that date. His resignation was formally accepted in August, 1943.

Conclusion

The Tribunal finds that von Neurath is guilty under all four counts.

FRITZSCHE

Fritzsche is indicted on Counts One, Three and Four. He was best known as a radio commentator, discussing once a week the events of the day on his own programme, "Hans Fritzsche Speaks". He began broadcasting in September, 1932; in the same year he was made the head of the Wireless News Service, a Reich Government agency. When on 1st May, 1933, this agency was incorporated by the National Socialists into their Reich Ministry of Popular Enlightenment and Propaganda, Fritzsche became a member of the Nazi Party and went to that Ministry. In December, 1938, he became head of the Home Press Division of the Ministry; in October, 1942, he was promoted to the rank of Ministerial Director. After serving briefly on the Eastern Front in a propaganda company, he was, in November, 1942, made head of the Radio Division of the Propaganda Ministry and Plenipotentiary for the Political Organisation of the Greater German Radio.

Crimes against peace

As head of the Home Press Division, Fritzsche supervised the German press of 2,300 daily newspapers. In pursuance of this function he held daily press conferences to deliver the directives of the Propaganda Ministry to these papers. He was, however, subordinate to Dietrich, the Reich Press Chief, who was in turn a subordinate of Goebbels. It was Dietrich who received the directives to the press of Goebbels and other Reich Ministers, and prepared them as instructions, which he then handed to Fritzsche for the press.

From time to time, the "Daily Paroles of the Reich Press Chief" as these instructions were labelled, directed the press to present to the people certain themes, such as the leadership principle, the Jewish problem, the problem of living space or other standard Nazi ideas. A vigorous propaganda campaign was carried out before each major act of aggression. While Fritzsche headed the Home Press Division, he instructed the press how the actions or wars against Bohemia and Moravia, Poland, Yugoslavia and the Soviet Union should be dealt with. Fritzsche had no control of the formulation of these propaganda policies. He was merely a conduit to the press of the instructions handed him by Dietrich. In February, 1939, and before the absorption of Bohemia and Moravia, for instance, he received Dietrich's order to bring to the attention of the press Slovakia's efforts for independence and the anti-Germanic policies and politics of the existing Prague Government. This order to Dietrich originated in the Foreign Office.

The Radio Division of which Fritzsche became the head in November, 1942, was one of the twelve divisions of the Propaganda Ministry. In the beginning Dietrich and other heads of divisions exerted influence over the policies to be followed by radio. Towards the end of the war, however, Fritzsche became the sole authority within the Ministry for radio activities. In this capacity he formulated and issued daily radio "paroles" to all Reich Propaganda Offices, according to the general political policies of the Nazi régime, subject to the directives of the Radio-Political Division of the Foreign Office and the personal supervision of Goebbels.

Fritzsche, with other officials of the Propaganda Ministry, was present at Goebbels' daily staff conferences. Here they were instructed in the news and propaganda policies of the day. After 1943 Fritzsche himself occasionally held these conferences, but only when Goebbels and his State Secretaries were absent. And even then his only function was to transmit the Goebbels' directives relayed to him by telephone.

This is the summary of Fritzsche's positions and influence in the Third Reich. Never did he achieve sufficient stature to attend the planning conferences which led to aggressive war; indeed according to his own uncontradicted testimony he never even had a conversation with Hitler. Nor is there any showing that he was informed of the decisions taken at these conferences. His activities cannot be said to be those which fall within the definition of the common plan to wage aggressive war as already set forth in this Judgment.

War crimes and crimes against humanity

The Prosecution has asserted that Fritzsche incited and encouraged the commission of war crimes, by deliberately falsifying news to arouse in the German people those passions which led them to the commission of atrocities under Counts Three and Four. His position and official duties were not sufficiently important, however, to infer that he took part in originating or formulating propaganda campaigns.

Excerpts in evidence from his speeches show definite anti-Semitism on his part. He broadcast, for example, that the war had been caused by Jews and said their fate had turned out "as unpleasant as the Führer predicted". But these speeches did not urge persecution or extermination of Jews. There is no evidence that he was aware of their extermination in the East. The evidence moreover shows that he twice attempted to have publication of the anti-Semitic *Der Stürmer* suppressed, though unsuccessfully.

In these broadcasts Fritzsche sometimes spread false news, but it was not proved he knew it to be false. For example, he reported that no German U-boat was in the vicinity of the "Athenia" when it was sunk. This information was untrue; but Fritzsche, having received it from the German Navy, had no reason to believe it was untrue.

It appears that Fritzsche sometimes made strong statements of a propagandistic nature in his broadcasts. But the Tribunal is not prepared to hold that they were intended to incite the German people to commit atrocities on conquered peoples, and he cannot be held to have been a participant in the crimes charged. His aim was rather to arouse popular sentiment in support of Hitler and the German war effort.

Conclusion

The Tribunal finds that Fritzsche is not guilty under this Indictment, and directs that he shall be discharged by the Marshal when the Tribunal presently adjourns.

BORMANN

Bormann is indicted on Counts One, Three and Four. He joined the National Socialist Party in 1925, was a member of the Staff of the Supreme Command of the SA from 1928 to 1930, was in charge of the Aid Fund of the Party and was Reichsleiter from 1933 to 1945. From 1933 to 1941 he was Chief of Staff in the Office of the Führer's Deputy and, after the flight of Hess to England, became Head of the Party Chancellery on 12th May, 1941. On 12th April, 1943, he became Secretary to the Führer. He was political and organisational head of the Volkssturm and a General in the SS.

Crimes against peace

Bormann, in the beginning a minor Nazi, then steadily rose to a position of power and, particularly in the closing days, was of great influence over Hitler. He was active in the Party's rise to power and even more so in the consolidation of that power. He devoted much of his time to the persecution of the churches and of the Jews within Germany.

The evidence does not show that Bormann knew of Hitler's plans to prepare, initiate or wage aggressive wars. He attended none of the important conferences when Hitler revealed piece by piece these plans for aggression. Nor can knowledge be conclusively inferred from the positions he held. It was only when he became Head of the Party Chancellery in 1941, and later in 1943 Secretary to the Führer, when he attended many of Hitler's conferences, that his positions gave him the necessary access. Under the view stated elsewhere which the Tribunal has taken of the conspiracy to wage aggressive war, there is not sufficient evidence to bring Bormann within the scope of Count One.

War crimes and crimes against humanity

By decree of 29th May, 1941, Bormann took over the offices and powers held by Hess; by the decree of 24th January, 1942, these powers were extended to give him control over all laws and directives issued by Hitler. He was thus responsible for laws and orders issued thereafter. On 1st December, 1942, all Gaus became Reich Defence Districts, and the Party Gauleiters responsible to Bormann were appointed Reich Defence Commissioners. In effect, this made them the administrators of the entire civilian war effort. This was so not only in Germany, but also in those territories which were incorporated into the Reich from the absorbed and conquered territories.

Through this mechanism Bormann controlled the ruthless exploitations of the subjected populace. His order of 12th August, 1942, placed all Party agencies at the disposal of Himmler's programme for forced resettlement and denationalisation of persons in the occupied countries. Three weeks after the invasion of Russia, he attended the conference of 16th July, 1941, at Hitler's field quarters with Goering, Rosenberg and Keitel; Bormann's report shows that there were discussed and developed detailed plans of enslavement and annihilation of the population of these territories. And on 8th May, 1942, he conferred with Hitler and Rosenberg on the forced resettlement of Dutch personnel in Latvia, the extermination programme in Russia and the economic exploitation of the Eastern Territories. He was interested in the confiscation of art and other properties in the East. His letter of 11th January, 1944, called for the creation of a large-scale organisation to withdraw commodities from the occupied territories for the bombed-out German populace.

Bormann was extremely active in the persecution of the Jews, not only in Germany but also in the absorbed and conquered countries. He took part in the discussions which led to the removal of 60,000 Jews from Vienna to Poland in co-operation with the SS and the Gestapo. He signed the decree of 31st May, 1941, extending the Nuremberg Laws to the annexed Eastern Territories. In an order of 9th October, 1942, he declared that the permanent elimination of Jews in Greater German territory could no longer be solved by emigration, but only by applying "ruthless force" in the special camps in the East. On 1st July, 1943, he signed an ordinance withdrawing Jews from the protection of the law courts and placing them under the exclusive jurisdiction of Himmler's Gestapo.

Bormann was prominent in the Slave Labour Programme. The Party Leaders supervised slave labour matters in the respective Gaus, including employment, conditions of work, feeding and housing. By his circular of 5th May, 1943, to the Leadership Corps, distributed down to the level of Ortsgruppenleiters, he issued directions regulating the treatment of foreign workers, pointing out they were subject to SS control on security problems, and ordered the previous mistreatment to cease. A report of 4th September, 1942, relating to the transfer of 500,000 female domestic workers from the East to Germany showed that control was to be exercised by Sauckel, Himmler and Bormann. Sauckel, by decree of 8th September, directed the Kreisleiters to supervise the distribution and assignment of these female labourers.

Bormann also issued a series of orders to the Party Leaders dealing with the treatment of prisoners of war. On 5th November, 1941, he prohibited decent burials for Russian prisoners of war. On 25th November, 1943, he directed Gauleiters to report cases of lenient treatment of prisoners of war. And on 13th September, 1944, he ordered liaison between the Kreisleiters with the camp commandants in determining the use to be made of prisoners of war for forced labour. On 29th January, 1943, he transmitted to his leaders OKW instructions allowing the use of firearms, and corporal punishment on recalcitrant prisoners of war, contrary to the Rules of Land Warfare. On 30th September, 1944, he signed a decree taking from the OKW jurisdiction over prisoners of war and handing them over to Himmler and the SS.

Bormann is responsible for the lynching of Allied airmen. On 30th May, 1944, he prohibited any police action or criminal proceedings against persons who had taken part in the lynching of Allied fliers. This was accompanied by a Goebbels' propaganda campaign inciting the German people to take action of this nature and the conference of 6th June, 1944, where regulations for the application of lynching were discussed.

His counsel, who has laboured under difficulties, was unable to refute this evidence. In the face of these documents which bear Bormann's signature it is difficult to see how he could do so even were the defendant present. Counsel has argued that Bormann is dead and that the Tribunal should not avail itself of Article 12 of the Charter which gives it the right to take proceedings *in absentia*. But the evidence of death is not conclusive, and the Tribunal, as previously stated, determined to try him *in absentia*. If Bormann is not dead and is later apprehended, the Control Council for Germany may, under Article 29 of the Charter, consider any facts in mitigation and alter or reduce his sentence, if deemed proper.

Conclusion

The Tribunal finds that Bormann is not guilty on Count One, but is guilty on Counts Three and Four.

THE SENTENCES

Before pronouncing sentence on any of the defendants, and while all of the defendants are present, the Tribunal takes the occasion to advise them that any applications for clemency of the Control Council must be lodged with the General Secretary of this Tribunal within four days from today.

In accordance with Article 27 of the Charter, the International Military Tribunal will now pronounce the sentences on the defendants convicted on this Indictment.

Defendant Hermann Wilhelm Goering, on the counts of the Indictment on which you have been convicted, the International Military Tribunal sentences you to death by hanging.

Defendant Rudolf Hess, on the counts of the Indictment on which you have been convicted, the Tribunal sentences you to imprisonment for life.

Defendant Joachim von Ribbentrop, on the counts of the Indictment on which you have been convicted, the Tribunal sentences you to death by hanging.

Defendant Wilhelm Keitel, on the counts of the Indictment on which you have been convicted, the Tribunal sentences you to death by hanging.

Defendant Ernst Kaltenbrunner, on the counts of the Indictment on which you have been convicted, the Tribunal sentences you to death by hanging.

Defendant Alfred Rosenberg, on the counts of the Indictment on which you have been convicted, the Tribunal sentences you to death by hanging.

Defendant Hans Frank, on the counts of the Indictment on which you have been convicted, the Tribunal sentences you to death by hanging.

Defendant Wilhelm Frick, on the counts of the Indictment on which you have been convicted, the Tribunal sentences you to death by hanging.

Defendant Julius Streicher, on the count of the Indictment on which you have been convicted, the Tribunal sentences you to death by hanging.

Defendant Walther Funk, on the counts of the Indictment on which you have been convicted, the Tribunal sentences you to imprisonment for life.

Defendant Karl Doenitz, on the counts of the Indictment on which you have been convicted, the Tribunal sentences you to ten years imprisonment.

Defendant Erich Raeder, on the counts of the Indictment on which you have been convicted, the Tribunal sentences you to imprisonment for life.

Defendant Baldur von Schirach, on the counts of the Indictment on which you have been convicted, the Tribunal sentences you to twenty years imprisonment.

Defendant Fritz Sauckel, on the counts of the Indictment on which you have been convicted, the Tribunal sentences you to death by hanging.

Defendant Alfred Jodl, on the counts of the Indictment on which you have been convicted, the Tribunal sentences you to death by hanging.

Defendant Arthur Seyss-Inquart, on the counts of the Indictment on which you have been convicted, the Tribunal sentences you to death by hanging.

Defendant Albert Speer, on the counts of the Indictment on which you have been convicted, the Tribunal sentences you to twenty years imprisonment.

Defendant Konstantin von Neurath, on the counts of the Indictment on which you have been convicted, the Tribunal sentences you to fifteen years imprisonment.

The Tribunal sentences the Defendant Martin Bormann, on the counts of the Indictment on which he has been convicted, to death by hanging.

I have an announcement to make. The Soviet Member of the International Military Tribunal desires to record his dissent from the decisions in the cases of the defendants Schacht, von Papen, and Fritzsche. He is of the opinion that they should have been convicted and not acquitted.

He also dissents from the decisions in respect of the Reich Cabinet, the General Staff and High Command, being of the opinion that they should have been declared to be criminal organisations.

He also dissents from the decision in the case of the sentence on the defendant Hess, and is of the opinion that the sentence should have been death, and not life imprisonment.

This dissenting opinion will be put into writing and annexed to the Judgment and will be published as soon as possible.

DISSENTING OPINION OF THE SOVIET MEMBER OF THE INTERNATIONAL MILITARY TRIBUNAL

Statement made by Major General Jurisprudence IT Nikitchenko on the Judgment concerning defendants Schacht, von Papen, Fritzsche and Hess and the accused organisations Reichscabinet, General Staff and OKW

The Tribunal decided:

(*a*) to acquit the defendants Hjalmar Schacht, Franz von Papen and Hans Fritzsche;

(*b*) to sentence the defendant Rudolf Hess to life imprisonment;

(*c*) not to declare criminal the following organisations: the Reichscabinet, General Staff and OKW.

In this respect I cannot agree with the decision adopted by the Tribunal as it does not correspond to the facts of the case and is based on incorrect conclusions.

THE UNFOUNDED ACQUITTAL OF DEFENDANT SCHACHT

The evidence, submitted to the Tribunal in the case of Schacht, confirms the following facts:

(*a*) Schacht established contact with Goering in December, 1930, and with Hitler at the beginning of 1931. He subsequently established contact between the leadership of the Nazi Party and the foremost representatives of the German industrial and financial circles. This, in particular, is confirmed by the testimony of Witness Severing.

(*b*) In July, 1932, Schacht demanded that Papen resign his post as Reich Chancellor in favour of Hitler. This fact is confirmed by Papen's testimony at the preliminary interrogation and by Schacht's own testimony in Court.

(*c*) In November, 1932, Schacht collected signatures of German industrialists, urging them to come out for Hitler's appointment as Reich Chancellor. On 12th November, 1932, Schacht wrote to Hitler:

> I have no doubt that the way we are directing the course of events can only lead to your appointment as Reich Chancellor. We are trying to secure a large number of signatures among the industrial circles to ensure your appointment to this post.

(*d*) In February, 1933, Schacht organised the financing of the pre-election campaign conducted by the Nazi Party, and demanded at the conference of Hitler and Goering with the industrialists that the latter provide three million marks. Schacht admitted in Court that he had pointed out the necessity for providing the Nazi leaders with this sum, while the defendant Funk and the former member of the management of "I.G. Farbenindustrie" Schnitzler, who were present at this conference, both confirmed that it was Schacht who was the initiator of the financing of the pre-election campaign.

(*e*) Utilising his prestige Schacht also repeatedly admitted in his public statements that he asked for the support in the elections of both the Nazi Party and of Hitler.

On 2nd August, 1932, Schacht wrote to Hitler:

> No matter where my activities lead me in the near future, even if some day you see me imprisoned in a fortress, you can always depend on me as your loyal aide.

Thus, Schacht consciously and deliberately supported the Nazi Party and actively aided in the seizure of power in Germany by the Fascists.

Even prior to his appointment as Plenipotentiary for War Economy, and immediately after the seizure of power by the Nazis, Schacht led in planning and developing the German armaments, as follows:

(*a*) On 17th March, 1933, Schacht was appointed President of the Reichsbank, and as he himself stated in a speech before his Reichsbank colleagues on 21st March, 1938, the Reichsbank under his management was "none other than a National Socialist institution".

(*b*) In August, 1934, Schacht was appointed Reich Minister of Economy. His Ministry "was given the task of carrying out the economic preparation for war". A special decree granted Schacht, in his capacity of Reich Minister of Economy, unlimited authority in the field of economy.

(*c*) Making use of these powers in 1934, Schacht launched upon the execution of the "new programme" developed by him, and, as Schacht himself noted in his speech of 29th November, 1938, this organisation played a tremendous part in the course of Germany's rearmament.

(*d*) For the purpose of the most effective execution of this "new programme" Schacht used the property and means of those political
enemies of the Nazi régime, who either became the victims of terror or
were forced to emigrate (Schacht's note to Hitler of 3rd May, 1939).
Schacht used swindler's tactics and coercion "in an effort to acquire raw
material and foreign currency for armaments".

(*e*) During the very first day of his association with Reichsbank, Schacht
issued a series of decrees, which in the long run helped realise the broad
programme of the financing of armaments, developed by him, and with
the aid of which, as he testified, he "had found the way to finance the
rearmament programme".

In his speech in Leipzig on 1st March, 1935, Schacht, while summing up his
preceding economic and financial activities, announced "everything that I
say and do has the Führer's full agreement and I shall not do or say anything
which is not approved by the Führer".

Having become the Plenipotentiary General for War Economy,
Schacht unified under himself the leadership of the entire Germany economy and through his efforts the establishment of the Hitlerite war machine
was accomplished.

(*a*) The secret law of 21st May, 1935, which appointed Schacht the
Plenipotentiary General for War Economy, states as follows: "The task of
the Plenipotentiary General for War Economy is to place all the eco-
nomic resources in the service of warfare . . . The Plenipotentiary
General for War Economy within the framework of his functions is
given the right to issue legal orders, deviating from the existing laws . . .
He is the responsible head for financing wars through the Reich
Ministry and the Reichsbank."

(*b*) Schacht financed German armaments through the MEFO system of
promissory notes, which was a swindling venture on a national scale that
has no precedent, and the success of which was dependent upon the
realisation of the aggressive plans of the Hitlerites. It was because of this
that Schacht set 1942 as the date when the MEFO notes were to mature,
and he pointed out in his speech of 29th November, 1938, the relation
between "the daring credit policy" of the Reichsbank and the aims of
the Hitlerite foreign policy.

(*c*) Having made full use of his plenary powers, Schacht carefully developed and carried out a broad programme of economic mobilisation
which allowed the Hitlerite leaders to wage war at any time considered
most favourable. In particular, from the report of Schacht's deputy,
Wohltat, "The Preparation for Mobilisation carried out by the
Plenipotentiary for War Economy" shows that Schacht provided to the
last detail for the system of exploitation of the German economy in
war time, all the way from the utilisation of industrial enterprises, of

raw material resources and manpower down to the distribution of 80,000,000 ration cards. It is significant that this report was drawn up a month after Hitler's statement at the conference of 5th November, 1937, at which Hitler set forth his concrete plan of aggression.

Summarising his past activity, Schacht wrote in January, 1937:

> I worked out the preparation for war in accordance with the principle that the plan of our war economy must be built in peace time in such a way that there will be no necessity for any reorganisation in case of war.

Schacht confirmed his statement in Court.

Schacht consciously and deliberately prepared Germany for war.

(d) The former Minister of War, von Blomberg, testified that:

> Schacht was fully cognisant of the plans for development and increase of the German Armed Forces, since he was constantly informed ... of all the financing necessary for the development of the German Armed Forces.

On 31st August, 1936, von Blomberg informed Schacht that: "The establishment of all the Air Force units must be completed by 1st April, 1937, and, therefore, large expenditures must be entailed in 1936."

In the spring of 1937, Schacht participated in the military exercises in Godesberg.

(e) In his memorandum to Hitler on 3rd May, 1935, on the "Financing of Rearmament", Schacht wrote:

> A speedy fulfilment of the programme for rearmament on a mass scale is the basis of German policy, and, therefore, everything else must be subordinate to this task; the completion of this task, the achievement of this purpose must meet no obstacles.

In his speech on 29th November, 1938, Schacht announced that the Reichsbank's policy made possible for Germany to create an "unsurpassed machine, and, in turn, this war machine made possible the realisation of the aims of our policy".

One must exclude the supposition that Schacht was not informed as to what purposes these weapons were to serve since he could not but take into consideration their unprecedented scale and an obvious preference for offensive types of weapons, heavy tanks, bombers and so on. Besides, Schacht knew perfectly well that not a single country intended to wage war on Germany, nor had it any reasons to do so.

(a) Schacht utilised the military might growing under his direction to back Germany's territorial demands which grew in proportion to the increase in armaments.

Schacht testified in court that "at first he confined himself (in his demands) to the colonies which had once belonged to Germany".

In September, 1934, during his talk with the American Ambassador Dodd, Schacht pointed out that he "desired annexation if possible without war, but through war, if the US would stay out of it".

In 1935 Schacht announced to the American Consul Fuller: "Colonies are essential to Germany. If it is possible, we shall acquire them through negotiations; if not, we shall seize them."

Schacht admitted in Court that military pressure put upon Czechoslovakia was "in some measure the result and the fruit of his labour".

(b) Schacht personally participated in the plunder of private and State property of the countries which became victims of Hitlerite aggressions.

The minutes of the conference of the Military-Economic Staff on 11th March, 1938, in which Schacht participated, state that those present were given Hitler's latest directives about the invasion of Austria. Further, the minutes state that: "After this, at the suggestion of Schacht, it was decided that ... all the financial accounting will be made in Reichsmarks at the rate of exchange: 2 shillings for one Reichsmark."

Schacht admitted in court that he personally was in charge of the seizure of the Czechoslovak National Bank after the occupation of Czechoslovakia.

(c) At the beginning of 1940, Schacht offered Hitler his services for negotiations with the United States of America in regard to the discontinuance of aid to England, and he informed Goering of his offer.

(d) Schacht considered it his duty to greet and congratulate Hitler publicly after the signing of armistice with France, although Schacht, better than anyone else, understood the usurpatory nature of the armistice.

(e) In his letter to Funk on 17th October, 1941, Schacht suggested a more effective exploitation of occupied territory. In this case, too, Schacht acted on his own initiative.

Schacht also participated in the persecution of the Jews:

(a) He testified in court that he "continued the policy of the persecution of the Jews as a matter of principle", although, he stated, "to a certain extent" it was a matter of conscience which, however, "was not serious enough to bring about a break" between him and the Nazis.

(b) In his capacity as Minister of Economy, Schacht signed a series of decrees, in accordance with which the property of the Jews in Germany was subject to plunder with impunity. Schacht confirmed in Court the fact that he had signed a series of anti-Semitic decrees.

As to the reasons for Schacht's resignation from the post of the Minister of Economy and the Plenipotentiary General for War Economy in November, 1937, and also from the post of the President of the Reichsbank on 20th November, 1939, and finally from the post of the Minister without Portfolio in January, 1943, the evidence submitted establishes the following:

(*a*) The reason is not Schacht's disagreement with the economic preparation for aggressive wars.

Three weeks before leaving the Ministry of Economy and the post of Plenipotentiary General for War Economy, Schacht wrote to Goering: "I also don't consider that my opinion can differ from yours on economic policy."

In his reply Goering states: "You promised me your support and collaboration . . . You have repeated this promise many times, even after differences of opinion began to creep up between us."

Schacht testified in Court that Goering and he "differed in matters of procedure".

In the preliminary examination Goering testified that Schacht's leaving the Reichsbank "had no relation to the programme of rearmament".

The Vice-President of the Reichsbank, Puhl, confirmed that Schacht's resignation from the Reichsbank can be explained by "his desire to extricate himself from a dangerous situation" which developed as the result of Schacht's own crooked financial operations.

(*b*) The reason is not Schacht's disapproval of mass terror conducted by the Hitlerites.

The witness for the Defence, Gesevius, testified that he constantly informed Schacht of the criminal actions of the Gestapo, created by Goering, and that nevertheless, right up to the end of 1936, Schacht looked for "Goering's support".

In his letter to von Blomberg on 24th December, 1935, Schacht suggested that the Gestapo apply "more cautious methods" since the open terror of the Gestapo "hinders the objectives of rearmament".

On 30th January, 1937, Schacht was awarded a golden Party insignia by Hitler. As stated in an official German publication: "He was able to be of greater help to the Party than if he were actually a member of the Party."

Only in 1943, having understood earlier than many other Germans the inevitability of the failure of the Hitlerite régime, did Schacht establish contact with the opposition circles, however, doing nothing to help depose this régime. Therefore, it was not by chance that having found out these connections of Schacht, Hitler still spared Schacht's life.

It is thus indisputably established that:

1. Schacht actively assisted in the seizure of power by the Nazis.
2. During a period of 12 years Schacht closely collaborated with Hitler.

3. Schacht provided the economic and financial basis for the creation of the Hitlerite military machine.
4. Schacht prepared Germany's economy for the waging of aggressive wars.
5. Schacht participated in the persecution of Jews and in the plunder of territories occupied by the Germans.

Therefore, Schacht's leading part in the preparation and execution of the common criminal plan is proved.

The decision to acquit Schacht is in obvious contradiction with the evidence in possession of the Tribunal.

THE UNFOUNDED ACQUITTAL OF DEFENDANT VON PAPEN

The verdict does not dispute the fact that von Papen prepared the way for Hitler's appointment to the post of the Reichskanzler and that he actively helped Nazis in their seizure of power.

In a speech of the 2nd of November, 1933, von Papen said the following on the subject:

> Then and there, on becoming the Reichskanzler (this was in 1932) I spoke in favour of the young and fighting movement for freedom; just as on the 30th of January I was chosen by Fate to surrender power into the hands of our Kanzler and Führer, so today I must tell the German people and all those who have maintained their trust in me: merciful God blessed Germany by granting her in these days of deep sorrow a Führer like this.

It was von Papen who revoked Brüning's order dissolving the SS and the SA, thus allowing the Nazis to realise their programme of mass terror.

Again it was the defendant who, by the application of brute force, did away with the Social Democrat Government of Braun and Severing.

On 4th January, 1933, Papen had a conference with Hitler, Hess and Himmler.

Papen participated in the purge of the State machinery of all personnel considered unreliable from the Nazi point of view; *on the 21st of March, 1933, he signed a decree creating special political tribunals*; he had also signed an order granting amnesty to criminals whose crimes were committed in the course of the "national revolution"; he participated in drafting the text of the order "ensuring party and state unity"; and so on. Subsequently, Papen faithfully served the Hitler régime.

During the Putsch of 1934, *Papen ordered his subordinate Tschirschky to appear in the Gestapo*, knowing full well what awaited him there. Tschirschky, as is well known, was executed while Papen helped to keep the bloody murder secret from public opinion.

Defendant played a tremendous rôle in helping Nazis to take possession of Austria.

Three weeks after the assassination of Dollfuss, on the 26th of July, 1934, Hitler told Papen that he was being appointed Minister to Vienna, specially noting in a letter: "You have been and continue to be in possession of my full and unlimited trust."

In this connection it is impossible to ignore the testimony of the American Ambassador Messerschmidt, who quoted Papen as saying that "the seizure of Austria is only the first step" and that he, von Papen, is in Austria for the purpose of "further weakening the Austrian Government".

Defendant was Hitler's chief adviser in effecting plans for the seizure of Austria. It was he who proposed several tactical manoeuvres, to quiet the vigilance of world opinion, on the one hand, and allow Germany to conclude her war preparations, on the other.

This follows indisputably from Papen's statement to the Austrian Minister Berger-Waldeneck, from the Report of Gauleiter Reuner of 6th July, 1939, from Papen's Report to Hitler of 26th August, 1936, from Papen's Report to Hitler of 1st September, 1936, and from a series of other documents which had been submitted in evidence.

Papen played this game until the issuance of the order for alerting the German Armed Forces for moving into Austria. He participated in arranging the conference between Hitler and Schuschnigg of 12th February, 1938.

It was Papen who in a letter to Hitler emphatically recommended that financial aid be given to the Nazi organisation in Austria known as the "Freedom Union", specifically for "its fight against the Jewry".

Indisputable appears the fact of the Nazi seizure of Austria and of Papen's participation in this act of aggression. After the occupation of Austria, Hitler rewarded von Papen with the golden insignia of the Nazi Party.

Neither is it possible to ignore von Papen's rôle as *agent provocateur* when in his capacity of diplomat he was the German Ambassador to Turkey – whenever evaluation of his activity there is made.

The post of Ambassador to Turkey was at the time of considerable importance in helping the Nazis realise their aggressive plans.

The official Nazi biographer wrote about von Papen as follows:

Shortly after (the occupation of Austria) the Führer had need of von Papen's services again, and on 18th April, 1939, he therefore appointed him German Ambassador in Ankara.

It should also be noted that, for his Turkish activities, Hitler rewarded von Papen with the Knight's Cross for his "military services".

Thus evidence submitted establishes beyond doubt that:

1. Von Papen actively aided the Nazis in their seizure of power.
2. Von Papen used both his efforts and his connections to solidify and

strengthen the Hitlerian terroristic régime in Germany.

3. Von Papen actively participated in the Nazi aggression against Austria culminating in its occupation.

4. Von Papen faithfully served Hitler up to the very end, aiding the Nazi plans of aggression both with his ability and his diplomatic skill.

It therefore follows that defendant von Papen bears considerable responsibility for the crimes of the Hitlerite régime.

For these reasons I cannot consent to the acquittal of defendant von Papen.

THE UNFOUNDED ACQUITTAL OF DEFENDANT FRITZSCHE

The acquittal of defendant Hans Fritzsche follows from the reasoning that Fritzsche, allegedly, had not reached in Germany the official position making him responsible for the criminal actions of the Hitler régime and that his own personal activity in this respect cannot be considered criminal. The verdict characterises him as a secondary figure carrying out the directives of Goebbels and Ribbentrop, and of the Reich Press Director Dietrich.

The verdict does not take into consideration or mention the fact that it was Fritzsche who until 1942 was the Director de facto of the Reich Press and that, according to himself, subsequent to 1942, he became the "Commander-in-Chief of the German radio".

For the correct definition of the rôle of defendant Hans Fritzsche it is necessary, firstly, to keep clearly in mind the importance attached by Hitler and his closest associates (as Goering, for example) to propaganda in general and to radio propaganda in particular. This was considered one of the most important and essential factors in the success of conducting an aggressive war.

In the Germany of Hitler, propaganda was invariably a factor in preparing and conducting acts of aggression and in training the German populace to accept obediently the criminal enterprises of German Fascism. The aims of these enterprises were served by a huge and well centralised propaganda machinery. With the help of the police controls and of a system of censorship it was possible to do away altogether with the freedom of the press and of speech.

The basic method of the Nazi propagandistic activity lay in the false presentation of facts. This is stated quite frankly in Hitler's *Mein Kampf*:

> With the help of a skilful and continuous application of propaganda it is possible to make the people conceive even of heaven as hell and also make them consider heavenly the most miserly existence.

The dissemination of provocative lies and the systematic deception of public opinion were as necessary to the Hitlerites for the realisation of their plans as were the production of armaments and the drafting of military plans. Without propaganda, founded on the total eclipse of the freedom of press and of speech, it would not have been possible for German Fascism to realise its aggressive intentions, to lay the groundwork and then to put into practice the war crimes and the crimes against humanity. In the propaganda system of the Hitler State it was the daily press and radio that were the most important weapons.

In his court testimony, defendant Goering named three factors as essential in the successful conduct of modern war according to the Nazi concept, namely, (1) the military operations of the armed forces, (2) economic warfare, (3) propaganda. With reference to the latter he said: "*Propaganda has tremendous value, particularly propaganda carried by means of radio* . . . Germany has learned this through experience better than anyone else."

With such concepts in ascendance it is impossible to suppose that the supreme rulers of the Reich would appoint to the post of Director of Radio Propaganda – who supervised radio activity of all the broadcasting companies and directed their propagandistic content – a man they considered a secondary figure.

The point of view of the verdict contradicts both the evidence submitted and the actual state of affairs.

Beginning with 1942, and into 1945, Fritzsche was not only Chief of the Radio Department of the Reich Ministry of Propaganda but also "Plenipotentiary for the Political Organisation of Radio in Greater Germany". This circumstance is fully proven by the sworn affidavit of Fritzsche himself. It thus follows that not at all was Fritzsche merely "one of the twelve departmental chiefs in the Ministry of Propaganda" who acquired responsibility for all radio propaganda only toward the end of the war, as the verdict asserts.

Fritzsche was the Political Director of the German radio up and into 1945, i.e., up to the moment of German defeat and capitulation. For this reason it is Fritzsche who bears responsibility for the false and provocative broadcasts of the German radio during the years of the war.

As chief of the Press Section inside Germany it was also Fritzsche who was responsible for the activity of the German daily press consisting of 2,300 newspapers. It was Fritzsche who created and perfected the Information Section, winning from the Reich Government for the purpose an increase in the subsidy granted the newspapers from 400,000 to 4,000,000 marks. Subsequently, Fritzsche participated energetically in the development of the propaganda campaigns preparatory to the acts of aggression against Czechoslovakia and Poland. A similar active propaganda campaign was conducted by the defendant prior to the attack on Yugoslavia, as he himself admitted in court.

Fritzsche was informed of the plan to attack the Soviet Union and was put "au courant" the military intentions at a conference with Rosenberg. Fritzsche headed the German press campaign falsifying reports of Germany's aggressive war against France, England, Norway, the Soviet Union, the USA, and the other states.

The assertion that Fritzsche was not informed of the war crimes and the crimes against humanity then being perpetrated by the Hitlerities in the occupied regions does not agree with the facts. From Fritzsche's testimony in court it is obvious that already in May, 1942, while in the Propaganda Section of the 6th Army, he was aware of Hitler's decree ordering execution for all Soviet political workers and Soviet intellectuals, the so-called Commissar Order. It is also established that already at the beginning of hostilities Fritzsche was fully aware of the fact that the Nazis were carrying out their decision to do away with all Jews in Europe. For instance, when commenting on Hitler's statement that "among results of the war there will be the annihilation of the Jewish race in Europe", Fritzsche stated that: "As the Führer predicted it will occur in the event of war in Europe, the fate of the European Jewry turned out to be quite sad." It is further established that the defendant systematically preached the anti-social theory of race hatred and characterised peoples inhabiting countries victimised by aggression as "subhumans".

When the fate of Nazi Germany became clear, Fritzsche came out with energetic support of the defendant Martin Bormann and of other fanatical Hitler adherents who organised the undercover Fascist association, the so-called "Werewolf".

On the 7th April, 1945, for example, in his last radio address, Fritzsche agitated for all the civilian population of Germany to take active part in the activities of this terroristic Nazi underground organisation. He said:

> Let no one be surprised to find the civilian population, wearing civilian clothes, still continuing the fight in the regions already occupied and even after occupation has taken place. We shall call this phenomenon "Werewolf" since it will have arisen without any preliminary planning and without a definite organisation, out of the very instinct of life.

In his radio addresses Fritzsche welcomes the German use of the new terror weapons in conducting the war, specifically the use of the "V" rockets. On receiving a plan for the introduction of bacterial warfare he immediately forwarded it to the OKW for acceptance.

I consider Fritzsche's responsibility fully proven. His activity had a most basic relation to the preparation and the conduct of aggressive warfare as well as to the other crimes of the Hitler régime.

CONCERNING THE SENTENCE OF THE DEFENDANT RUDOLF HESS

The Judgment of the Tribunal correctly and adequately portrays the outstanding position which Rudolf Hess occupied in the leadership of the Nazi

Party and State. He was indeed Hitler's closest personal confidant and his authority was exceedingly great. In this connection it is sufficient to quote Hitler's decree appointing Hess as his Deputy: "I hereby appoint Hess as my Deputy and give him full power to make decisions in my name on all questions of Party Leadership."

But the authority of Hess was not only confined to questions of Party leadership. The official NSDAP publication *Party Year Book for 1941*, states that:

> In addition to the duties of Party leadership, the Deputy of the Führer has far-reaching powers in the field of the State. These are: First, participation in national and State legislation, including the preparation of Führer's orders. The Deputy of the Führer in this way validates the conception of the Party ... Second, approval of the Deputy of the Führer of proposed appointments for official and labour service leaders. Three, securing the influence of the Party over the self-government of the municipal units.

Hess was an active supporter of Hitler's aggressive policy. The crimes against peace committed by him are dealt with in sufficient detail in the Judgment. The mission undertaken by Hess in flying to England should be considered as the last of these crimes, as it was undertaken in the hope of facilitating the realisation of aggression against the Soviet Union by temporarily restraining England from fighting. The failure of this mission led to Hess's isolation and he took no direct part in the planning and commission of subsequent crimes of the Hitler régime. There can be no doubt, however, that Hess did everything possible for the preparation of these crimes.

Hess, together with Himmler, occupied the rôle of creator of the SS police organisations of German Fascism, which afterwards committed the most ruthless crimes against humanity. The defendant clearly pointed out the "special tasks" which faced the SS formations on occupied territories.

When the Waffen SS were being formed Hess issued a special order through the Party Chancellery which made aiding the conscription of Party members into these organisations by all means compulsory for Party organs. He outlined the tasks set before the Waffen–SS as follows:

> The units of the Waffen–SS composed of National Socialists are more suitable than other armed units for the specific tasks to be solved in the Occupied Eastern Territories due to the intensive training in regard to questions of race and nationality.

As early as 1934 the defendant initiated a proposal that the so-called SD under the Reichsführer–SS (Security Service) be given extraordinary powers and thus become the leading force in Nazi Germany.

On 9th June, 1934, Hess issued a decree in accordance with which the "Security Service of the Reichsführer–SS" was declared to be the "sole political news and defence service of the Party". Thus the defendant played a direct part in the creation and consolidation of the system of special police organs which were being prepared for the commission of crimes on occupied territories.

We find Hess to have always been an advocate of the man-hating "master race" theory. In a speech made on 16th January, 1937, while speaking of the education of the German nation, Hess pointed out:

> Thus, they are being educated to put Germans above the subjects of a foreign
> nation, regardless of their positions or their origin.

Hess signed the so-called "Law for the Protection of Blood and Honour" on 15th September, 1935. The body of this law states that "the Führer's Deputy is authorised to issue all necessary decrees and directives" for the practical realisation of the "Nuremberg decrees".

On 14th November, 1935, Hess issued an ordinance under the Reich citizenship law in accordance with which the Jews were denied the right to vote at elections or hold public office.

On 20th May, 1938, a decree signed by Hess extended the Nuremberg laws to Austria.

On 12th October, 1939, Hess signed a decree creating the administration of Polish occupied territories. Article 2 of this decree gave the defendant Frank the power of dictator.

There is sufficiently convincing evidence showing that this defendant did not limit himself to this general directive which introduced into the occupied Polish territories a régime of unbridled terror. As is shown in the letter of the Reichsminister of Justice to the Chief of the Reich Chancellery dated 17th April, 1941, Hess was the initiator in the formation of special "penal laws" for Poles and Jews in Occupied Eastern Territories. The rôle of this defendant in the drawing up of these "laws" is characterised by the Minister of Justice in the following words:

> In accordance with the opinion of the Führer's Deputy I started from the point of
> view that the Pole is less susceptible to the infliction of ordinary punishment
> . . . Under these new kinds of punishment, prisoners are to be lodged outside prisons
> in camps and are to be forced to do heavy and heaviest labour . . . The introduction
> of corporal punishment which the Deputy of the Führer has brought up for
> discussion has not been included in the draft. I cannot agree to this type of
> punishment . . . The procedure for enforcing prosecution has been abrogated, for it
> seemed intolerable that Poles or Jews should be able to instigate a public indictment.
> Poles and Jews have also been deprived of the right to prosecute in their own names
> or join the public prosecution in an action . . . From the very beginning it was
> intended to intensify special treatment in case of need: When this necessity became
> actual a supplementary decree was issued to which the Führer's Deputy refers in his
> letter.

Thus, there can be no doubt that Hess together with the other major war criminals is guilty of crimes against humanity.

Taking into consideration that among political leaders of Hitlerite Germany Hess was third in significance and played a decisive rôle in the crimes of the Nazi régime, I consider the only justified sentence in his case can be – death.

INCORRECT JUDGMENT WITH REGARD TO THE REICH CABINET

The Prosecution has posed before the Tribunal the question of declaring the Reich Cabinet a criminal organisation. The verdict rejects the claim of the Prosecution, unfoundedly refusing to declare the Hitler Government a criminal organisation.

With such a decision I cannot agree.

The Tribunal considers it proven that the Hitlerites have committed innumerable and monstrous crimes.

The Tribunal also considers it proven that these crimes were as a rule committed intentionally and on an organised scale, according to previously prepared plans and directives ("Plan Barbarossa", "Night and Fog", "Bullet", etc.).

The Tribunal has declared several of the Nazi mass organisations criminal, the organisations founded for the realisation and putting into practice of the plans of the Hitler Government.

In view of this it appears particularly untenable and rationally incorrect to refuse to declare the Reich Cabinet, the directing organ of the State with a direct and active rôle in the working out of the criminal enterprises, a criminal organisation. The members of this directing staff had great power: each headed an appropriate government agency; each participated in preparing and realising the Nazi programme.

In confirmation it is deemed proper to cite several facts:

Immediately after the Nazi ascent to power – on 24th March, 1933 – there was a law passed entitled "The Law of Defence of the People and the State" whereby the Reich Cabinet, besides the Reichstag, received the right of issuing new legislature.

On 26th May, 1933, the Reich Government issued a decree ordering the confiscation of the property of all Communist organisations and on 14th June, the same year, it also confiscated the property of the Social Democrat organisations. On 1st December, 1933, the Reich Government issued the law "Ensuring Party and State Unity".

Following through its programme of liquidating democratic institutions, in 1934, the Government passed a law of the "Reconstruction of the Reich" whereby democratic elections were abolished for both central and local representative bodies. The Reichstag thereby became an institution without functional meaning.

By the law of 7th April, 1933, and others, all Reich government employees, including judges, ever noted for any anti-Nazi tendencies or ever having belonged to leftish organisations, as well as all Jews, were to be removed from the government service and substituted by Nazis. In accordance with the "Basic Positions of the German Law on Government Employees" of 26th January, 1937, "the inner harmony of the official and the Nazi Party is a necessary presupposition of his appointment to his post . . . government employees must be the executors of the will of the National Socialist State, directed by the NSDAP".

On 1st May, 1934, there was created the Ministry of Education, instructed to train students in the spirit of militarism, of racial hatred, and in terms of reality thoroughly falsified by Nazi ideology.

Free trade unions were abolished, their property confiscated and the majority of the leaders jailed.

To suppress even a semblance of resistance the Government created the Gestapo and the concentration camps. Without any trial or even a concrete charge hundreds of thousands of persons were arrested and then done away with merely on a suspicion of an anti-Nazi tendency.

There were issued the so-called Nuremberg Laws against the Jews. Hess and Frick, both members of the Reich Government, implemented these by additional decrees.

It was the activity of the Reich Cabinet that brought on the war which took millions of human lives and caused inestimable damage in property and in suffering borne by the many nations.

On 4th February, 1938, Hitler organised the Secret Council of Ministers, defining its activity as follows: "To aid me by advice on problems of foreign policies I am creating this Secret Council." The foreign policy of the Hitler Government was the policy of aggression. For this reason the members of the Secret Council should be held responsible for this policy. There were attempts in court to represent the Secret Council as a fictitious organisation, never actually functioning. This, however, is an inadmissible position. It is sufficient to recall Rosenberg's letter to Hitler – where the former insistently tried to be appointed member of the Secret Council of Ministers – to appreciate fully the significance of the Council.

Even more important practically in conducting aggressive warfare was the Reich Defence Council headed by Goering. The following were members of the Defence Council, as is well known: Hess, Frick, Funk, Keitel, Raeder, Lammers.

Goering characterised the function of the Defence Council and its rôle in war preparations as follows, during the Court Session of 23rd June, 1939: "The Defence Council of the Reich *was the deciding Reich organ on all questions concerning preparation for war.*"

At the same time Goering emphasised the fact that "the meetings of the Defence Council always took place for the purpose of making the most important decisions". From the minutes of these meetings, submitted as evidence by the Prosecution, it is quite clear that the Council made very important decisions indeed. The minutes also show that other Cabinet ministers sometimes took part in the meetings of the Council for the Defence alongside the members of the Council when war enterprises and war preparedness were discussed.

For example, the following Cabinet ministers took part in the meeting of 23rd June, 1939: of Labour, of Food and Agriculture, of Finance, of Communications and a number of others, while the minutes of the meeting were sent to all the members of the Cabinet.

The verdict of the Tribunal justly points out certain peculiarities of the Hitler Government as the directing organ of the State, namely: the absence of regular Cabinet meetings, the occasional issuance of laws by the individual ministers having unusual independence of action, the tremendous personal power of Hitler himself. These peculiarities do not refute but on the contrary further confirm the conclusion that the Hitler Government is not an ordinary rank-of-the-file Cabinet but a criminal organisation.

Certainly Hitler had an unusual measure of personal power but this in no way frees of responsibility the members of his Cabinet who were his convinced followers and the actual executors of his programme until and when the day of reckoning arrived.

I consider that there is every reason to declare the Hitler Government a criminal organisation.

INCORRECT JUDGMENT WITH REGARD TO THE GENERAL STAFF AND THE OKW

The verdict incorrectly rejects the accusation of criminal activity directed against the General Staff and the OKW.

The rejection of the accusation of criminal activity of the General Staff and of the OKW contradicts both the actual situation and the evidence submitted in the course of the trial.

It has been established beyond doubt that the leadership corps of the Armed Forces of Nazi Germany, together with the SS-Party machine, represented the most important agency in preparing and realising the Nazi aggressive and man-hating programme. This was constantly and forcefully reiterated by the Hitlerites themselves in their official bulletins meant for the officer personnel of the Armed Forces. In the Nazi Party Bulletin called "Politics and the Officer in the III Reich" it is quite clearly stated that the Nazi régime is founded on "two pillars: the Party and the Armed Forces. Both are forms of expression of the same philosophy of life . . . The tasks before the Party and the Armed Forces are in an organic relationship to each other and each bears the same responsibility . . . both these agencies depend on each other's success or failure."

This organic interrelationship between the Nazi Party and the SS on the one hand and the Nazi Armed Forces on the other hand was particularly evident among the upper circles of military hierarchy which the Indictment groups together under the concept of criminal organisation – that is, among the members of the General Staff and the OKW.

The very selection of members of the Supreme Command of the Army in Nazi Germany was based on the criteria of their loyalty to the régime and their readiness not only to pursue aggressive militaristic policies but also to fulfil such special directives as related to treatment meted out to prisoners of war and to the civilian populations of occupied territories.

The leaders of the German Armed Forces were not merely officers who reached certain levels of the military hierarchy. They represented, first of all, a closely knit group which was entrusted with the most secret plans of the Nazi leadership. Evidence submitted to the Tribunal has fully confirmed the contention that the military leaders of Germany justified this trust completely and that they were the convinced followers and ardent executors of Hitler's plans.

It is not accidental that at the head of the Air Force stood the "second man" of the Nazi Reich, namely Goering; that the Commander-in-Chief of the Navy was Doenitz, subsequently designated by Hitler to be the latter's successor; that the command of the Ground Forces was concentrated in the hands of Keitel, who signed the major part of the decrees concerning the execution of the prisoners of war and the civilians in occupied territories.

Thus the comparisons made with the organisation of the Supreme Commands in Allied countries cannot be considered valid. In a democratic country, not one self-respecting military expert would agree to prepare plans for mass reprisals and merciless killings of prisoners of war side by side with plans of the purely military and strategic character.

Meanwhile it is precisely such matters that occupied the Supreme Command of the General Staff and of the OKW in Nazi Germany. The commission by them of the heaviest crimes against peace, of the war crimes and of the crimes against humanity is not denied but is particularly emphasised in the verdict of the Tribunal. And yet the commission of these crimes has not brought the logical conclusion.

The verdict states:

> They have been a disgrace to the honourable profession of arms. Without their military guidance the aggressive ambitions of Hitler and his fellow Nazis would have been academic and sterile.

And subsequently:

> Many of these men have made a mockery of the soldier's oath of obedience to military orders. When it suits their defence they say they had to obey; when confronted with Hitler's brutal crimes, which are shown to have been within their general knowledge, they say they disobeyed. The truth is they actively participated in all these crimes, or sat silent and acquiescent, witnessing the commission of crimes

on a scale larger and more shocking than the world has ever had the misfortune to know . . . This must be said.

All these assertions in the verdict are correct and are based on numerous and reliable depositions. The only thing that remains incomprehensible is the reasoning which does not recognise as criminal that "hundreds of higher ranking officers" who caused the world and their own country so much sorrow, the reasons backing the decision not to declare the organisation criminal.

The verdict advances the following reasons for the decision, reasons quite contradictory to the facts:

(a) That the crimes were committed by representatives of the General Staff and of the OKW as private individuals and not as members of a criminal conspiracy.

(b) That the General Staff and the OKW were merely weapons in the hands of the conspirators and interpreters or executors of the conspirators' will.

Numerous evidence disputes such conclusions:

1. *The leading representative of the General Staff and of the OKW, along with a small circle of the higher Hitlerite officials, were called upon by the conspirators to participate in the development and the realisation of the plans of aggression, not as passive functionaries, but as active participants in the conspiracy against peace and humanity.*

Without their advice and active co-operation, Hitler could not have solved these problems. In the majority of cases their opinion was decisive. It is impossible to imagine how the aggressive plans of Hitler's Germany could have been realised had it not been for the full support given him by the leading staff members of the Armed Forces.

Least of all did Hitler conceal his criminal plans and motivation from the leaders of the Supreme Command.

For instance, while preparing for the attack on Poland, as early as 29th May, 1939, at a conference with the high military commanders of the new Reich Chancellery, he stated:

> For us the matter consists of the expansion of Lebensraum to the East. Thus the
> question of sparing Poland cannot be considered, and, instead, we have to consider
> the decision to attack Poland at the first opportunity.

Long before the seizure of Czechoslovakia, in a directive of 30th May, 1938, Hitler, addressing the representatives of the Supreme Command, cynically stated:

> From the military and political point of view, the most favourable time is a
> lightning attack on the basis of some incident, by which Germany will have been

strongly provoked and which will morally justify the military measures to at least part of the world opinion.

Prior to the invasion of Yugoslavia, in a directive dated 27th March, 1941, addressing the representatives of the High Command, Hitler wrote:

> Even if Yugoslavia declares its loyalty, it must be considered an enemy and must, therefore, be smashed as soon as possible.

While preparing for the invasion of the USSR, Hitler invited the representatives of the General Staff and the OKW to help him work out the related plans and directives not at all as simply the military experts.

In the instructions to apply propaganda in the region "Barbarossa", issued by the OKW in June, 1941, it is pointed out that:

> For the time we should not have propaganda directed at the dismemberment of the Soviet Union.

As early as 13th May, 1941, OKW ordered the troops to use any terrorist measures against the civilian populations of the temporarily occupied regions of the Soviet Union. Here a special stipulation read: "To confirm only such sentences as are in accordance with the political intentions of the Leadership."

2. OKW and the General Staff issued the most brutal decrees and orders for relentless measures against the unarmed peaceful population and the prisoners of war.

In the "decree of special liability to punishment in the region Barbarossa", while preparing for the attack upon the Soviet Union, the OKW abolished beforehand the jurisdiction of the military courts, granting the right of repressions over the peaceful population to individual officers and soldiers. It is particularly stated there that:

> Crimes of hostile civilians are excluded from the jurisdiction of the courts martial . . . Suspected elements must be immediately delivered to the officer. The latter will decide whether they should be shot . . . it is absolutely forbidden to hold suspects for the purpose of bringing them to trial.

There are also provisions for "the most extreme measures, and, in particular, 'measures for mass violence', if circumstances do not permit the rapid detection of the guilty".

In the same decree of the OKW the guarantee of impunity was assured in advance to the military criminals from the service personnel of the German Army. It states there as follows:

> The bringing of suits of actions, committed by officials of the Army and by the service personnel against hostile civilians, is not obligatory even in the cases where such actions at the same time constitute military crimes or offences.

In the course of the war the High Command consistently followed this policy, increasing its terroristic actions with regard to prisoners of war and the peaceful populations of occupied countries.

The OKW directive of 16th September, 1941, states:

> It is important to realise that human life in the countries to which this refers, means nothing, and that intimidating action is possible only through the application of unusual brutality.

Addressing the commanders of the Army groups on 23rd July, 1941, the OKW simply briefed them as follows:

> It is not in the demand for additional security detachments, but in the application of appropriate draconic measures that the commanding officers must use to keep order in the regions under their jurisdiction.

The OKW directive of 16th December, 1941, states:

> The troops . . . have the right and are obliged to apply . . . any measures whatsoever *also against women and children* if this contributes to success.

Among the most brutal OKW directives concerning the treatment of prisoners of war one must consider the order entitled "Night and Fog". The reasons for resorting to capital punishment for prisoners of war were offences which, according to international conventions, generally should not carry any punishment; for example, escape from the camp.

The order states:

> Penalty for such offences, consisting of loss of freedom and even a life sentence, is a sign of weakness. Only death sentences or measures which entail ignorance of the fate of the guilty by local population will achieve real effectiveness.

In the course of the present trial a great deal of evidence of application of this order has been submitted. One example of this kind of crime is the murder of 50 officer-pilots. The fact that this crime was inspired by the High Command cannot be doubted.

OKW also issued an order for the destruction of the "commando" units. The original order was submitted to the Court. According to this order, officers and soldiers of the "commando" units had to be shot, except in cases when they were to be questioned, after which they were shot in any case.

This order was unswervingly carried out by the commanding officers of Army units. In June, 1944, Rundstedt, the Commander-in-Chief of the German troops in the West, reported that Hitler's order in regard to "the treatment of the commando groups of the enemy is still being carried out".

3. *The High Command, along with the SS and the Police, is guilty of the most brutal police actions in the occupied regions.*

The instructions relating to special regions, issued by OKW on 13th March, 1941, contemplated the necessity of synchronising the activities in occupied territories between the Army Command and the Reichsführer of the SS. As is seen from the testimony of the chief of the 3d Department of RSHA and who was concurrently chief of the Einsatzgruppe "D", Otto Ohlendorf, and of the chief of the VI Department of RSHA, Walter Schellenberg, in accordance with OKW instructions there was an agreement made between the general staff and the RSHA about the organisation of special "operational groups" of the Security Police and SD –"Einsatzgruppen" assigned to the appropriate army detachments.

Crimes committed by the Einsatzgruppen on the territory of the temporarily occupied regions are countless. The Einsatzgruppen were acting in close contact with the commanding officers of the appropriate army groups.

The following excerpt from the report of Einsatzgruppe "A" is extremely characteristic as evidence:

> Among our functions is the establishment of personal liaison with the commanding officer both at the front and in the rear. It must be pointed out that the relations with the army were of the best, in some cases very close, almost hearty, as, for instance, the commander of the tank group, Colonel-General Hoppner.

4. *The representatives of the High Command acted in all the echelons of the army as members of a criminal group.*

In spite of the violation of international law and of the customs of war, the directives of the OKW and of the General Staff and the command of individual army units were applied in life and were augmented by even more brutal orders issued as implementation to these directives.

In this connection it is characteristic to note the directive of Field Marshal von Reichenau, Army group commander, addressed to his soldiers: "The soldier in the eastern territories is not only a warrior skilled in the art of warfare but a bearer of a merciless national ideology." And elsewhere, calling for the extermination of the Jews, Reichenau wrote: "Thus the soldier must be in full cognisance of the necessity for harsh and just revenge on those sub-humans, the Jews."

As another example the order of Field Marshal von Mannstein addressed to his soldiers can be referred to. On the basis of the "political aims of the war" the Field Marshal cynically appealed to his soldiers to wage the war in violation of the "recognised laws of warfare in Europe".

Thus, in the course of the hearing of evidence it has been proved beyond all doubt that the General Staff and the Supreme Command of the Hitlerite Army comprised a highly dangerous criminal organisation.

I consider it my duty as a Judge to draw up my dissenting opinion concerning those important questions in which I disagree with the decision adopted by the members of the Tribunal.

Soviet Member IMT,
Major General Jurisprudence,
I. T. NIKITCHENKO

Ten of the defendants who received sentences of death by hanging were executed on 16 October 1946 at the Palace of Justice in Nuremberg. The exception was Hermann Goering, who objected to hanging as a method of execution. He committed suicide by means of a cyanide pill which was smuggled into his cell the night before.

Not all the Nazi leaders underwent trial and punishment. Adolf Hitler, the most notorious of them all, shot himself in a bunker in Berlin in 30 April 1945, Heinrich Himmler and Joseph Goebbels committed suicide; while Martin Bormann mysteriously disappeared, although it is thought that he was shot by Russian snipers in May 1945. A skeleton uncovered in Berlin in 1972 has been declared as that of Bormann by forensic experts.

INDEX

D Day to VE Day, 1944–45

INDEX

The Judgment of Nuremberg, 1946